MATHEMATICAL THEORY IN SOVIET PLANNING

MATHEMATICAL THEORY IN SOVIET PLANNING

Concepts, Methods, Techniques

ALFRED ZAUBERMAN

London School of Economics

Published for

THE ROYAL INSTITUTE OF
INTERNATIONAL AFFAIRS

by

OXFORD UNIVERSITY PRESS
LONDON   NEW   YORK   TORONTO

1976

Oxford University Press, Ely House, London W. 1

GLASGOW NEW YORK TORONTO MELBOURNE WELLINGTON
CAPE TOWN IBADAN NAIROBI DAR ES SALAAM LUSAKA ADDIS ABABA
DELHI BOMBAY CALCUTTA MADRAS KARACHI LAHORE DACCA
KUALA LUMPUR SINGAPORE HONG KONG TOKYO

ISBN 0 19 218307 9

Text set in 10/12 pt. IBM Press Roman, printed by photolithography,
and bound in Great Britain at The Pitman Press, Bath

To my Wife

PREFACE

About the time of the appearance of a book of mine on Soviet "plano-metrics",[1] Andrew Shonfield, the then Director of Studies and now the Director of Chatham House (the Royal Institute of International Affairs), invited me to carry out a further study in this field with a view to pub-lishing the results under the auspices of the Institute. That invitation I very eagerly accepted and my motives are these.

I felt the need to go on in my research work, as it were, beyond the scope of the *Aspects of Planometrics*, and the response to that book con-firmed me in my conviction that there is a vivid interest among Western scholars in what happens in Soviet mathematized economics. This intel-lectual curiosity is, in my submission, easily explainable if only because anybody in touch with the world of mathematics is well aware of the contribution the Russian-Soviet genius has made to virtually every domain of it. One may recall that a panel of distinguished US mathematicians, formed at the beginning of the 1960s, came to the conclusion that in mathematics the two nations — the United States and the USSR — lead the world; that in fact — algebraic geometry aside — there is no major area of mathematics without a significant Soviet contribution. One can safely say that the finding is still true today; one can do so even without com-mitting oneself, with the wisdom of hindsight, as to whether and where the panel's prediction has actually materialized: the prediction to the effect that in such areas as numerical analysis, ordinary and partial dif-ferential equations, and *control theory* (my emphasis, see below) Soviet scholarship will achieve supremacy. (Parenthetically speaking, this writer shares the panel's relevant observation that one of the factors favouring the remarkable Soviet trend is the high status that applied mathematics enjoys in Soviet scholarship: a Soviet pure mathematician, even of the highest calibre, would not hesitate to engage in applicational pursuits.)[2]

At the time the panel carried out this investigation Soviet mathemat-ical economics was only *in statu nascendi* (emerging as it was from the severe constraint of a quarter-of-a-century ban). And the years which fol-lowed saw its amazingly fast and vigorous progress. One of its pioneers, to whose unique brilliance we owe the first formulation of mathematical programming, Academician Kantorovich, recently remarked[3] that economic intuition plays one of the decisive roles in the solution of economic problems in that domain: Soviet theorists have given proof of being endowed with it when assimilating into economics — (to quote a few instances) the methodology of decomposition in linear programming, the Brown-Robinson method of game theory, the method of penalties in non-linear programming. To continue the point made, while in its initial phase the broad orientation of Soviet mathematical economics was focused on numerical methods of optimization arising in economic planning and operational research, the last few years have concentrated attention on some deeper theoretical aspects of process optimization — demonstrably so in what lends itself to an overall categorization as the theory of convex analysis. But it appears, in a kind of dialectical reasoning, that this tendency is seen by many students as strengthening the foundations of . the mathematics employed in economic planning.

My intention then has been to give here an account of this "dialectical" development in the most recent past. And it is in this sense that the present study was meant to advance beyond my *Aspects of Planometrics.*

This is true in particular of the parts of this study devoted to the absorption by Soviet mathematized planning theory of a great and promising "novelty" — the theory of optimal control — which in fact forms the core of the present volume.

Here we are in a "fashionable" area of inquiry in which Soviet scholarship is, to say the least, a co-pioneer and a most effective contributor (*nota bene,* it was very young at the time of the panel mentioned above). Perhaps a few words regarding its background, in the Soviet context, may not be out of place here.[4]

It was in the early 1950s that various methods were evolved in special fields of technology based on the classical calculus of variations, only gradually to crystallize and take shape as part and parcel of an integrating discipline. The impulse came from the new strong interest in the mathematic of rocket motion — (specifically in the problems of the most economical use of the reactive mass with a view to optimizing the relationship between apogee and range in the configuration of a rocket's "minimum energy trajectory").[5]

As a rule requirements for regulated processes were being given the form of conditions put on the spectrum of the linear differential operators employed in process description. Most of these studies were based on the Euler-Lagrange equation and had the effect of making the student aware of the limitations of the classical apparatus. Attempts in automatic regulation are recognized as a strong element in the gestation of the theory of optimal processes. It is a legitimate claim that the remarkable development in the Soviet Union of the qualitative theory of differential equations as well as methods of non-linear mechanics — specifically the theory of nonlinear oscillations in and stability (asymptotic stability) of motion so crucially resting on Lyapunov's method — had laid a solid foundation for that theory. (There comes into play also that very substantive contributing element: the impact of the theory of Markovian processes.) In this context I would note the induced stimulation of the Soviet student's interest in Bellman's powerful function and equation, the conceptual "cousin" of the Hamilton-Jacobi equation, which is extremely fruitful in so many directions. The link-up with the Lyapunov function had very early come to the fore in Soviet research (Lyetov's work has been eminent in this direction). Now, controlling a feedback system must be — on empirical grounds — congenial to the economist interested in normative theorizing — to the planning economist in particular; our reader will see how this congeniality has worked itself through stages of development. While on the point of congeniality, there is no less of it in the mathematical problem of maximum speed in optimally controlled processes (enough to hint at the subjects of economic growth and development). And it is precisely the optimal-time direction that came to predominate in the search for some consistent new variational apparatus where the classical proved disappointing.

Only very rarely is the moment of birth of a discipline detectable in a precise fashion. But this seems to be actually true for the optimal control theory in the Soviet case. Here the critical date is 1953: a year of a joint seminar of engineers and mathematicians, presided over by Pontryagin, at the Institute of Automation (now Institute of Control) of the Academy of Sciences. There Feldbaum's memorable papers on a controlled system's maximum velocity proved to be *the* creative stimulant: the mathematically beautiful and famous construct of Pontryagin and his associates — crucial as the first-order necessary condition of optimality — had followed. I will not continue now to sketch the sequel beyond the original Maximum Principle: the inquiry initiated by Dubovitskiy and Milyutin as a prelude to the attempts to build up a general theory of extrema, or the present-day work of the Pontryagin school (at the Steklov Institute) on the differential game of pursuit and evasion as a generalization of optimal-control theory. But at least one hint may be added now on a ramification which was bound to be of special importance to the economist — the search for a theory of "large-scale" and/or complex systems so very characteristic of developments in the last few years (size and complexity of real life are the nightmares haunting any planner: hence his appeals to the theorist for help in exorcizing them). (Not that the issue of the size and intricacy of interrelation of processes to be described in ordinary equations — of coping with the vast numbers of degrees of freedom — is really an exclusive headache for the mathematical economist; he is here in good fellowship with the mathematized biologist, to name only one companion; but it is in economics that in the view of quite a few students, the issue would prejudge the very *raison d'être* of mathematical planning theory.)

What has been alluded to so far in this preface seems sufficient to show how the Soviet planning theorist has found himself very much "at home" in optimal-control theory once the "exogenous" restraints were removed from the paths of his search. What has happened as a result the reader will discover for himself in this book.

In writing it I have tried to give as extensive an elaboration of my theme as possible within the limited scope of the study. To be sure, I am only too conscious of its incompleteness — if only because of the extraordinary pace of Soviet progress in the field; indeed, in a task like mine one feels all along overtaken in the race. Further, some technical considerations have made inevitable the elimination of certain elements from the body of the study; this applies primarily to a chapter on the stability-theoretic work (on the intimate relation of this topic with that of control theory I remarked above). A more expanded study of mine on Soviet advances in the domain of differential games was too late to be included here; it appeared in 1975 in a series published by the New York University Press. My special monograph on the mathematical theory of decentralization in the East and West has been completed under the aegis of the Social Science Research Council. (I have made use of some results of the SSRC project in chapters 1 and 2 of the present book; this I wish to acknowledge with thanks.)

But in giving this "inventory" of my maturing contributions which may provide some supplementary reading, I should certainly mention in the first place my twin study, the *Mathematical Revolution in Soviet Economics,* the companion of this study in both substance and timing. It appeared earlier in 1975, also under the auspices of Chatham House (published by the Oxford University Press). It deals with some of the results of this inquiry — and provides their background — in non-formal terms; in particular, it discusses the acceptance of the mathematical method, apparatus, and tools into Soviet economics as a part of a search for ways of improving the traditional economic mechanism and — which is seen as interrelated — for ways of modernizing the supporting economic-theoretic basis; another facet of the developments indicated there is the rapid growth of intellectual East-West interpenetration in a domain where, in pre-mathematical times, the lines of communication were effectively blocked. That study is addressed essentially to the non-mathematically oriented reader. But perhaps some readers of this work might find certain aspects of the story treated there not without interest to themselves as well.

To conclude this preface with acknowledgements where they are due is my great pleasure. They go in the first place to the Director of Chatham House, Andrew Shonfield. I am immensely grateful to him not only for his seminal initiative, but also for his friendly and continuous interest in, and support for this study without which it could never mature. I am also grateful to his successors in the office of the Director of Studies, James Fawcett and Ian Smart: to Ian Smart for his untiring efforts to ensure the appearance of this book (and its "twin") at a time of rather tricky publishing conditions. My warm appreciation goes to Miss Hermia Oliver for offering to this study her unique editorial expertise in a way which makes an editor almost a co-author, and for editorially disciplining me — a very difficult job indeed.

My appreciation goes to the London School of Economics for giving me, as in my previous cases, support and facilities for my research work. My thanks on this account are due also to the universities in which, over the time of writing, I held at various periods, the posts of a research associate, or senior fellow, or a visiting professor: Harvard, University of California, University of Toronto, Columbia, New York University, and Konstanz University.

The reader will find that Professor Tintner has contributed a part to my chapter on the stochastic approach. To have a contribution from this distinguished pen is a very great privilege.

The dedication of this study to my wife is but a slight allusion to what I owe to her moral support, devoted as always, and advice, to say nothing of her technical aid.

London School of Economics   A.Z.
March 1974

Notes

1. *Aspects of planometrics* (London, Athlone Press, 1967).
2. J. P. LaSalle / S. Lefschetz, *Recent Soviet contributions to mathematics* (New York, 1962).
3. *Uspyekhi matematicheskikh nauk,* 5 (1970).
4. In what follows I have relied on the excellent survey by N. N. Krassovskiy and N. N. Moiseyev, in *Tekhnicheskaya kibernetika,* 5 (1967).
5. See D. E. Okhotsimskiy, in *PMM,* 2 (1946); cf. also the same jointly with T. A. Eneyev, in *Uspekhi Fizicheskikh Nauk,* 1a (1957) on variational problems relating to the launching of an earth satellite.

CONTENTS

Principal Abbreviations

Amer. Econ. R.	*American Economic Review*
Ann. Inst. Stat. Math.	*Annals of the Institute of Statistics and Mathematics* (Tokyo)
Archiwun aut. i. tel.	*Archiwun automatyki i telemechaniki*
Avt. i tel.	*Avtomatika i telemekhanika*
B. du CEPREMAP	*Bulletin du Centre d'Etudes Prospectives d'Economie Mathématique Appliquées à la Planification*
Brit. J. Phil. Sci.	*British Journal for the Philosophy of Sciences*
Canad. J. Econ.	*Canadian Journal of Economics*
CR	*Compte rendu*
Doklady	*Doklady Akademii NaukSSSR* (Reports of the USSR Academy of Sciences)
EMM	*Ekonomika i matematicheskiye metody*
IEEE, Trans. Sys. Sci. & Cyb.	Institute of Electrical and Electronic Engineering, *Transactions on Systems, Science and Cybernetics*
Int. Econ. R.	*International Economic Review*
J. Anal. Math.	*Journal of Analytical Mathematics*
Opt. plan.	*Optimalnoye planirovanye*
Plan. khoz.	*Planovoye khozyaistvo*
PMM	*Prikladnaya matematike i mekhanika*
Q. J. Econ.	*Quarterly Journal of Economics*
SIAM J.	*SIAM Journal Control*
Sov. Stud.	*Soviet Studies*
Tekh. kib,	*Tekhnicheskaya kibernetika*
Vopr. ekon.	*Voprosy ekonomiki*
UMN	*Uspekhi matematicheskikh naúk*

Note: Where possible, symbolic notation throughout follows the given sourc

PART I
SOME PROBLEMS OF MATHEMATICAL PLANNING

1

EFFICIENCY PRICING

(1)   This chapter is concerned with the Soviet theory of price as an instrument of planning and steering, serving, that is, the construction and implementation of the plan. The conception of the price as performing such a role of a signal and parameter in decision-making is quite new in Soviet thinking. Its origins go back no further than the mid-1950s — it is owed to the new mathematical school. In the traditional approach in Soviet planning doctrine, price is essentially a "recording" — accountancy — instrument. Planning is fundamentally thought of as an operation in quantity physical terms: price would in some sense "reflect" such "natural"-term relations. We say "fundamentally", since in reality this conception has never been and probably could not be, rigorously stated let alone consistently adhered to.[1]

In the doctrine, as professed over decades, price rests structurally on the principle of the averaged material cost-plus: it is thus essentially not the scarcity-measuring, opportunity-cost instrument. Neither has this principle been adhered to consistently; indeed, pricing has been marked by a considerable degree of arbitrariness. (In actual fact there has been in some spheres a more or less inarticulate groping towards a scarcity price — a demand-supply equilibrium price; this is true specifically of the whole sphere of consumption.)

It seems reasonable to argue that such price — whatever its doctrinal justifications — has corresponded to the very limited technical possibilities of the era. Also that is has corresponded to the methodology of direct-centralist normative (mandatory) — we may term it also "nonparametric" — planning: or, rather, with this methodology its limitations have been mitigated. The idea of a nexus between the methodology of planning and the economic mechanism as operated is also novel in Soviet planning thought: it too has been introduced by the mathematical school.

3

(2)   As it has by now crystallized, the new planning doctrine is still wed-
ded to the principle of centralism. It is less axiomatic with respect to the
"directness" in normative planning and control, that is to its "parametric"
variant. Traditionally, Soviet plan construction has been conceived of as a
multilevel dialogue between the centre and the periphery — again a conception severely circumscribed in practice by technical feasibilities, informational and computational. These restrictive factors are certainly becoming weaker; and this widens the area of manoeuvre.

In so far as the TsEMI is representative of the "new" economics — it is
indeed its principal workshop — one may refer to the planning methodology
with which it has explicitly identified itself since around the mid-1960s.[2]
In this, *firstly*, the planning system organically integrates the all-economy
and local criteria so as to secure coherence, at all levels of the economy,
of the physical-term and money-term plan-indicators; and *secondly*, it
determines for each of these levels the set of prices, with the corresponding
(varying) degree of aggregation — prices obtained from the optimal plan
programme — and it does so in a *centralist* fashion: note the emphasis on
the latter. (More specifically the enterprise would work out a set of alternatives with respect to what, from its angle, is final output. These, plus
data on input requirements, would serve the sector — "branch" — grouping
as the basis for setting the point-of-departure valuations of products and
intermediate materials. In terms of these valuations, enterprises would
then determine their plans by maximizing profit: these would be corrected
by the centre— to conform with its own optimality criterion. The procedure would be repeated till a Pareto-type optimum is reached. The emerging
prices would then be adjusted; and, next, plans of all economic macro-
groupings, vertical and horizontal, would be harmonized, and ultimately
macro-aggregative plan indexes with the corresponding prices would be
promulgated by the central planning agency.[3]

What follows is essentially an analysis of the kind of prices entailed in
the devolutional system which is postulated: its theoretical foundations
and the obstacles in implementation will also, in due course, come into
our discussion.

(3)   It is with regard to the concept of the price — parameter — that the
mathematical school has brought about the most profound change in the
mode of Soviet economic thinking, and specifically in planning thought.
Its origins go back to Kantorovich's paper at the end of the 1930s. As
Koopmans correctly and generously remarked in a preface to its translation,

... the paper stands as a highly original contribution of the mathematical mind to problems which few at that time would have perceived as mathematical in nature – on a par with the earlier work of von Neumann on proportional economic growth in a competitive market economy, and the later work of Dantzig.[4]

It took Soviet planning theory two decades to discover and absorb the concept and its implications. When absorbed, Kantorovich's fundamental theorems revealed the duality nexus between the plan's optimality and pricing. These theorems thus showed the valuations as "shadow" prices, inherent in the plan, a plan thought of as the linear programme with a given objective function and subject to constraints, as a rule to inequality constraints.

The optimal production plan x^s – in Kantorovich's theorem – subject as it is to $\Sigma a^{(s)} x^{(s)} \geqslant b_j$, is characterized by a system of his "valuations" corresponding to all its ingredients, the π_j's – the solutions of the dual are such as to satisfy the conditions:

1. all activities (technological processes) included in the plan are at these prices "just justified" (profitable)

$$\Sigma a_j^{(s)} \pi_j = 0 \quad \text{if} \quad x^{(s)} \neq 0;$$

2. all feasible activities (technological processes) are no more than justified $\Sigma a_j^{(s)} \Pi_j \leqslant 0$, this subject to $\pi_j \geqslant 0$ and $\Sigma_j \pi_j > 0$; the $\pi_j = 0$ for the "ingredient" (j) for which the constraints form a strict inequality. The existence of a system of Kantorovich's "OOOs" satisfying these conditions is necessary and sufficient for the plan's optimality.

(4) Duality of the mathematical programme thus stated both focuses and synthesizes the mathematical penetration of Soviet planning thought. The reasons can be detected in the nature of the concept. It is "capsular" in containing the very substance of extremization. In this it has proved amazingly seminal: even the very circumscribed treatment of the problem of the extremum which our theme permits shows how the advances in many directions in the theory of this problems, during well over a quarter of a century, have evolved from seeds detectable in the concept itself – up to the most "modern" happenings in the theories of control and of systems. On the other hand it is intrinsically related to quantification, thereby also to planning. Moreover, as Kuhn puts it,[5] it has two facets; one is the relevance for computational technique demonstrated in the progress starting from the simplex; then the Hungarian method and Ford-Fulkerson, and so onwards. It is much more than mere accident that accounts for the

elements of the progress observed by Neustadt[6] – the intellectual fitness
of mathematical economic models and the continuous flow of algorithms
from the simplex type on (but developments in computational technology
may appear here as our good luck). The point is – and this too is convincingly stressed by Kuhn – that the duality phenomenon is essentially one
in economics: one of minimum expense of scarce resources in trying to
secure maximum benefit, conditioned as it may be by the circumstances.
Hardly any device of mathematics is so much indebted, for its logical
roots, to economics (and, through the behavioural norms embedded, to
economic planning) as is duality. (It seems justifiable to remark that the
Soviet mathematical economists are aware of it.)

(5)   As noted, the unfamiliar concept of price has inevitably evoked oppo-
sition from the traditionalist school. The idea of determining the price – to
use the prevailing parlance at the level of the "closing" enterprise (Fedorenko) – in more conventional terms, the marginalist approach to price –
is in patent conflict with the traditional "averagist" attitude (on the conflict with Marxian theory see in particular Strumilin).[7] On a more philo-
sophical plane, the critics insist that, as against the "objective" nature
of price derived from the version of the labour theory of value to which
they subscribe, that offered by the mathematical programming theory is
"subjective". The controversy in Soviet economics has come to be described
as one of "marginal utility versus value". Such alignment of the contending
schools in value and price theories – possibly somewhat baffling to the
Western theoretical economist – has its historical roots: the great *divide*
marking – in the accepted view – the departure from the labour theory
of value as inherited from Ricardo and Marx had traditionally been seen –
by Böhm-Bawerk, Menger, and the Austrian school – as the introduction
of the "subjective" element synthesized in the marginal-utility concept.
Indeed, the point with respect to the price of the mathematical school is
not illegitimate: it is "subjective" on an acceptable definition – if understood to mean that the programming-type price postulates a choice by the
policy-maker and explicitness of the optimand; but this point has not
been readily conceded by the mathematical school. (Although its distinguished member, Konyus, is inclined to treat the shift from the neg-
ation of the theory of marginal utility – originating in the labour theory
of value – as progress towards a dialectical synthesis.)[8] The intellectual
inhibition is well reflected in the studiously adopted vocabulary: the
shadow price of the plan-programme's dual was termed in Kantorovich's
original system the "*objectively* determined valuation" – the "OOOs" – and

it has retained this name ever since; there is something more to this than mere terminological convenience.

A middle view has tried to reconcile the two contending viewpoints, by arguing that the value-forming labour content of product implies – as its rationality premise – socially necessary labour to be the minimand.

(6) Such reinterpretation of the labour theory of value and price as is indicated here raises the question of its heuristic productivity. What we may describe as the macro-minimax of labour expenditure and national product that is offered fails to provide insight into the nature of price. Admittedly there is no reason[9] why a specific input – labour input in particular – could not be adopted as the numéraire for a specific purpose (the Leontief inversion facilitating this); but this does not help per se to observe the process of price formation: indeed, it appears from the revised theory that this cannot tell us anything about relative prices: to arrive at them some undefined correcting coefficients have to be inserted. At least one Soviet student of mathematical planning (Volkonskiy)[10] points out that, while for many economists it seems natural to express value of all other resources in terms of labour, and while this may help to clarify some theoretical issues (especially that of the use made of labour resources in the whole sphere of production), yet it is inconvenient artificially to employ labour as the "scale" (mashtab) for the valuation of all other resources if only because labour forms only a part, and indeed sometimes a rather small part, of all resources participating in production. This empirically-oriented and convincing reasoning has, we submit, also a reflex on the theoretical significance of the concepts as well.[11] As time goes on, much of the heated controversy between the traditionalists and the mathematical modernizers in Soviet planning theory (referred to in sections 3 and 4) in terms which must appear rather hermetic to the Western student, is bound to lose significance for the Soviet theorizer and in, fact does so. What emerges as focal for him is the planner's ability (or inability) to "price" factors and products in the adopted numéraire so as to reflect (or to approximate) the optimum in the policy-maker's pursuit of his objectives (constraints permitting); and to provide the decision-makers at all levels with parameters shaping their decisions accordingly.

An expositional remark. While price-type and derived categories as considered in this chapter relate to a money-term numéraire, they do not imply a monetary economy – one where money is a quasi-commodity satisfying specific needs. The planning world as formalized here remains a real-term one also where the duality-optimum parameter is introduced.

While in the latter case the coherence of the real-resource-term and money-numéraire-term expressions of duality must be ensured, the problem of co-ordinating real and monetary phenomena does not arise in the sense that it does so in the theory of a capitalist market economy.[12] As a result, we have a "de-sophistication" of the analysis: for the various complicating aspects related to demand for money "as such" (to mention a few problems: those of liquidity; of preferences in holding money as against real assets and as between money assets; of money-creation as against demand for money; of price levels — inflationary and deflationary phenomena — and the impact on employment of factors, all this in statics and dynamics; and quite a few other well-known analytical *pontes asinorum* have no place in the institutional framework of the world with which we are here concerned. We shall not enter into the question whether this would be true of a socialistic economy when differently institutionalized.)

(7) One point raised in the traditionalist critique of the programming approach has led to the latter's advance. We have in mind the point stressed particularly strongly by Boyarskiy, that the Kantorovich-type price construct was essentially static, so it was argued, which of itself disqualified it as a planning instrument. This has been refuted in a restatement of his construct in the time dimension. More, the programming approach has actually led Soviet economics towards the revelation of the price of the resource-time (a concept which was thought to contradict the philosophy of the traditional economic doctrine).

In Kantorovich's reworking of his famous model of a third of a century ago, what we can describe as the pure impact of time on price is measured by means of the coefficient of the price-scale over time, — lambda = the "index of reduction" of output of year t to that of year 1 (in Lurye it is the "coefficient of proportionality" over time).[13] Assume a normative (standardized) collection of products and factors $y_{11}, \ldots, y_{k,n}$: determine the scale of prices in such a way that the price for the collection remains constant. For this purpose introduce a multiplier λ_t, such that (k, i, t standing for the "ingredient", space, time, respectively)

$$\sum_{k,i} y_{k,i}\pi_{i,k,t} = \lambda_t \sum_{k,i} y_{k,i}\pi_{k,i,1}$$

where π denotes prices. The π may be then seen as reflecting "proportionality" of price-levels over time. In other words, if the price-level does not change over time correspondingly with the shadow prices (Kantorovich's "000s"), that is, if $\lambda_t \neq \lambda_{t+1}$, outputs and inputs at t and $(t+1)$ will be made comparable by multiplying the operating prices at t by the factor ratio λ_{t+1}/λ_t ("operating" at $(t+1)$ — by the reciprocal).

(8)   There is an emphasis in Soviet disquisitions on the tenet that the change of the dynamic shadow prices is per se an "objective" process, unrelated to the weighting for intertemporal preference scales (thus in particular Lurye[14] — cf. above). This matter we relegate to the section discussing the welfare-theoretic issues. Here we shall be concerned with another aspect of the "objective" determination of price behaviour over time — its nexus with the system's growth and efficiency.[15]

In the Kantorovich-Makarov dynamic reasoning the argument is this.

First, consider the system's efficiency rate: in this continue the reasoning on the price change over time — as above. Take z_t $(t = 1, \ldots T)$ as the value of all resources in the initial period t, i.e. of some collection $X(t)$, in prices as operated. Then the vector of the 000s, $\pi = (\pi(1), \ldots, \pi(T))$ determined up to the multiplier, is normalized from the condition

$$(\pi(1), X(1)) = z_1.$$

For all the remaining time-points we substitute for the vector $\pi(t)$ the proportionate vector $\hat{\pi}(t)$ determined from

$$\pi(t) = \lambda_t \, \hat{\pi}(t): (\hat{\pi}(t), X(t)) = z_t$$

whence

$$\lambda_t = (\pi(t), X(t))/Z_t.$$

Thus when the $\pi(t)$'s are employed in calculating technological efficiency of activity, we reduce them to the 000s by means of the λ_t. It follows that when we take the value of the norm σ_t^Z as dependent on the normative vector Z, we have

$$\sigma_t^Z = \lambda_{t+1}/\lambda_t - 1.$$

Secondly, the λ is related to the system's growth-rate, to be more precise to what is defined by Kantorovich-Makarov as the "economic" growth-rate, $\beta(t) = (X(t+1), \pi(t))/(X(t+1), \pi(t+1))$: the rate, that is, of decrease in the value of π's weighted by quantities of plan "ingredients" at $(t+1)$. This patently in substance is a Paasche-type index, as distinct from what is in Kantorovich-Makarov terms the *technological* or *natural* growth-rate defined as rate of growth of the ingredients' stockpile ("accumulation") weighted by "000s". For the collection of goods $X(t)$ at t we have then $\sigma_{t-1}(X) = \beta(t-1)$.[16, 17]

Thus to sum up, via the index numbers of prices at optimum the treble nexus has been established by the Kantorovich school between the system's rates: those of its expansion and its productivity and "time-price".

This links up in Kantorovich-Makarov with the von Neumann propositions (cf. in the context our chapters 3 and 4). We may in the present context then point to the ideas developed on parallel lines in the West, especially the elaboration of the balance and growth problems by Kemeny-Thompson-Morgenstern[18] and by Gale,[19] bringing out the relation between the economy's pace of growth and time discount (also in Karlin's analysis of the dynamic price we are shown how the system's expansion rate and interest rate are equalized).[20] To put this more generally, one can demonstrate − as has been done *i.a.* by Malinvaud[21] − that the plan for optimum outputs, technologies and investment, and the corresponding system of prices and other efficiency indicators form an intrinsically integrated whole and cannot be solved independently of each of these factors. (These connections of ideas have been discussed by me elsewhere; they will not detain us here.)

(9) By shedding new light on the nexus of the time-preferences, productivity, and shadow prices of factors, all embedded in an optimal solution, the programming approach has also brought about a major change in the Soviet theory of capital − radical even if not always fully explicit in Soviet writing. (Once again we give warning. We still remain here in the realm of a capital theory concerned with "real", in this sense non-monetary values: money is still here completely sterilized from any wealth-holding role.

Note, however, that this too has become an area of some convergence in the theoretical modes of thinking in East and West.[22] As a matter of fact, in some special "dialectical" sense certain premises of the classical theory are closer to reality in the Soviet-type socialist than in a capitalist environment. For one thing emphasis on the "real" rather than monetary nature of the rate of interest is congenial to socialist economics. Such time-honoured questions as that of the relationship between the "natural" and money rates of interest troubling modern Western schools, specifically those derived from Wicksell, are of little relevance to the Soviet theorizer (though to be sure, there is not much in common with Hicks's approach either). Under the Soviet-type economic mechanism the capital-efficiency rate, or the interest rate, are purely non-monetary phenomena. Further, to turn to the appraisal of efficiency (which, as we shall see in ch. 4, is the

basis of the rate of interest in Soviet economics in the field), when carried
out for an atomistic economy it comes up against the well-known difficulties of the market's imperfections and the multiplicity of its rates:
and the issue of public as against private criteria and their possible conflict.
All this inhibits the classical concept of the single rate of interest as the
one equating the "saver's" time-preference with the capital's productivity
at the margin. Mutatis mutandis in the Soviet institutional framework –
the saver being essentially the state and its authoritarian time-preference
map being the dominant one and the capital market being absent (though
possibly computationally imitated) – this proposition fits the framework
well: hence so also does the concept of the single social discount rate as
related to the opportunity cost-price. At least one representative (Solow)
of the present-day mathematically oriented theory of capital in the West[23]
– to be more specific, of what is dubbed by him the "technocratic approach" can be identified with the view that it is the investment-efficiency
rate derived from the optimality calculation that must be considered fundamental to this theory, rather than specific forms of income receipt in a
capitalist economy, specifically a market rate of profit on the one hand,
and on the other such aspects of capital efficiency as are due to uncertainty
and limited foresight.[24] One may be almost inclined to accept Solow's
remark – paradoxical as it may appear – to the effect that the best way
of understanding the economics of capital may be to think about a
socialist economy. (We indicate *passim* that this reveals itself as true in
other contexts as well.)

(10) A further important novum which Soviet economics owes to the
Kantorovich school is the clarification of the meaning of profit and – on
the theoretical plane – the paving of the way for the idea of profit maximization as an optimality criterion, abstracting that is from any income-
distributional effect.

The Kantorovich-Makarov argument starts from the technological facet.
Suppose technology is employed at optimum as $[a, b]$ with intensity
(activity level) x, where the a and b are input and output vectors respect-
ively. Profit obtained over t appears in operated prices π, as $[(b, \pi(t+1) - a, \pi(t))] \times (t)$ and the rate of profit is then $(b, \pi(t+1)/(a, \pi(t)) - 1$; it is then
identical with the efficiency norm σ_t. This in fact follows its logic since in
substance it is at optimum the rate of "reward" on incremental unit of
resources – the rate of interest. (In Lurye's reformulation, the efficiency
norm of the system is the lower limit of "relative profitability" of marginal
"small measure" still included in the optimal plan; it is also the upper limit

of relative profitability of such "measures" feasible with respect to the plan and thus analytically corresponds to the maxmin principle.)

Methodologically the treatment of intertemporal technology, price, and profit may be usefully compared with that by Gale of what on his definition is a competitive price system;[25] there an optimal T-period programme is determined by the price variable as well as the technological (input-output) variables: the maximand is derived from the choice of the latter such as to secure for each t the maximum profit difference between t the cost of input today and of output tomorrow.[26]

(11) As hinted, the Kantorovich-type construct which has opened new vistas for planning in the real world is valid for a specifically "idealized" one, and ideal in the context means — in the first place — linear. An indication of the consequence is by now if anything overdue in our story.

It may be useful to start by defining the "idealizing" property (the term "linear" is used in planning theory very often in rather confusingly diverse senses). On an acceptable definition, the plan-programme is linear if it extremizes a linear function subject to linear constraints. Where it does not satisfy this definition (where, that is, the function maximized or minimized as well as constraints are not all linear), we are confronted with nonlinearity in a wider sense. As often as not theory and application adopt definitional frames which are narrower to an extent that varies so as to accommodate classes of problems with properties ensuring a relatively greater tractability. As a problem in economic planning the nonlinearity issues are faced first and foremost with respect to economies of scale and externalities.

The first concessions to tractability in theorizing is the adoption of the convexity (concavity) assumption.[27] In this the student is often inclined to forget what Koopmans so pertinently stressed: that this assumption does not really reflect judgement as to the sufficient degree of realism: rather it reflects the state of our knowledge.[28]

(12) Virtually all explorations in the area with which we are now concerned — that of nonlinear extremization — are rooted in the fundamental Kuhn-Tucker theorem (of two decades ago)[29] establishing the existence and optimality conditions for the solution of a problem with a continuously differentiable function. In the accepted formulation it is stated that if we let $f(x)$ and $g_i(x)$ be concave functions defined in n-dimensional Euclidean space and a point x^0 at which g is positive: then $\bar{x}$ maximizes

$f(x)$, subject to $g(x)$ and x being non-negative if and only if there exists a vector $u \geqslant 0$ such that (x, u) is the saddle-point of the $F(x, u)$.

It will be noted then that, as in the generalized Lagrangean system, there is no assumption of linearity: at the same time there is no requirement of either equality of restraints or nonnegativity for variables – as in linear programming. We have then here a generalization of the simplex and of the Lagrangean multipliers.

In this line of approach the Soviet theory finds itself on the ground investigated by Kantorovich as early as 1940, the restatement of this important – and often forgotten – contribution the reader will find in Appendix 2.

(13)   In a way of an excursus we propose to say something more on the importance of the developments in what amounts to a new discipline – the theory of convexity. This is a field where the inquiry rests on a combination of the methods of the duality theory of vectoral spaces, as related to the separation theorems, and of Kantorovich's theory of semi-ordered spaces.[30] Decisive in these developments has been Minkowski's concept of the support function of a convex set; also along the line – of Fenchel's establishing the isomorphism of the cone of convex homogenous functions and of convex compact subsets of Euclidean space.[31]

Fundamental in the field is the contribution by R. T. Rockafellar,[32] pioneering and embracing various aspects. (It is so in convex generalizations of linear algebra; therein what is termed convex bifunctions as a generalization of multivalued mappings parallels linear transformation; and the inner product of convex sets and functions has a definition as extremal values of the duality theorem in Fenchel.)

Also Soviet scholarship must be credited with seminal contributions, in particular in areas of relevance for application in economics, specifically – superlinear point-set mapping (which are in substance "convex" operators with values in the space of convex sets) first introduced, for the finite-dimensional case, by Rockafellar and Rubinov;[33] Rubinov has evolved the general theory of these mappings in random linear-convex programmes.

Rubinov, jointly with Kutateladze,[34] has developed the theory of the H-convex functions, functions that is which form the upper envelope of some families of linear functions; they have of late elaborated a theory of structural duality of functions and sets, specifically the H-class functions. In substance this is an attempt to identify the *"structural"* part of what by now forms the classical duality scheme;[35] and to show that most of the known results of the theory of conjugate functions and sets are of a structural nature. [The formulation rests on these definitions. An ordered set S is termed semi-structure if any two of its elements x and y have the upper edge x v y. Let H be a subset of the semi-structure S; element $p \in S$ is H-convex if there is a set U of H such that p = sup U. The subset U of the set H is H-convex if there exists sup $U = p$.] It is shown by Kutatel-adze-Rubinov that the Minkowski-Fenchel theorem of convex analysis lends itself to formulation and proof in the language of semilineal spaces which are semi-structures ("K-semilineals").

The declared purpose of the Rubinov-Kutateladze exercise is *i.a.* the clarification of the role and of the place of the separation theorems in duality systems of functions and sets. Rubinshtein is credited with being the first to resort to these ideas when he formulated his "abstract" prin-ciple of duality in extremal problems. (As a matter of history, note that the significance of convexity, as well the link between the saddle-points and Lagrangeans, was first pointed out in the classical work of Kuhn-Tucker and, while leaning on the differential calculus, it did conjecture that, in the case of convex functions, some construction not involving differentiability might be substituted for the gradient conditions.)

(14) Rubinshtein has established the sufficient as well as necessary conditions of the existence of additive and homogeneous functionals separating a family of convex polyhedrons starting from a conceptual basis which, as it would appear was first formulated by Dubovitskiy and Milyutin.[36] [Following them the definition in Rubinshtein is this.[37] We have given $r \geqslant 2$ sets $M_1, \ldots, M_r$ in real vectoral space E. The additive and homogeneous functionals $f_1, \ldots, f_r$ — some of them non-trivial — separate the given sets if the conditions $\Sigma_{i=1}^r f_i = 0$, $\Sigma_{i=1}^r s(f_i, M_i) \leqslant 0$ are met, the $s(.)$ denoting the supremum of the functional f on M.]

From our angle a noteworthy development is the elaboration of effect-ive methods of numerical solution of convex programmes. These are largely related to the classical techniques of fastest descent (with the original problem replaced by that of saddle-point of the Lagrange function). Some techniques rest on the proposition that in convex programmes it is suf-ficient to find an admissible vector which is the best from among the neighbouring ones. In the build-up of sequences of vectors monotonically minimizing the criterial function, in choosing the direction of motion, at each step an auxiliary convex-programme problem is being solved that is easier than that of the preceding step. In Soviet writing important contri-butions are owed i.a. to Rubinshtein and to Kaplan.[38]

Note. A very general theory – the "abstract schema" – of duality is stated in Rubinshtein[39] in the following terms.

Consider a system: in an arbitrary set E there are non-empty subsets P, Q, $t \in (\alpha, \beta)$, $-\alpha \leqslant \alpha < \beta \leqslant + \alpha$ where $Q_{t''} \subset Q_{t'}$. There is also some family E^* of sets $F \subset E$. Denote

$$Q = \cup Q_t, \qquad Q_{t+0} = \cup_{t' \subset (t,\beta)} Q_{t'}, \qquad Q_{t-0} = \cap Q_{t'}, \qquad P_0 = P \cap Q,$$
$$t \in (\alpha,\beta) \qquad\qquad\qquad\qquad\qquad\qquad t' \in (\alpha,t)$$

$$P^* = \{F \in E^* : P \subset F\}, \qquad Q_t^* = \{F \subset E^* : Q_{t+0} \cap F = \emptyset\}; \qquad Q^* = \cup Q_t^*;$$
$$P_0^* = P^* \cap Q^* \qquad\qquad\qquad\qquad\qquad\qquad\qquad\qquad\qquad\qquad t \in (\alpha,\beta)$$

and consider the functions:

$$\mu(a) = \sup \{t : a \in Q_t\} \ (!), \quad \nu(F) = \inf \{t : F \in Q_t^*\} \ (!!) \text{ defined on } P_0 \text{ and } P_0^*.$$

The primal "problem" (1) is then defined as determining the element $a \in P_0$ on which the function (!) reaches its maximum. The dual "problem" (2) is defined as determining the element $F \in P_0^*$ on which the (!!) reaches its maximum.

Hence if $a \in P_0$ and $F \in P_0^*$ then $\alpha \leqslant \mu(a) \leqslant \nu(F) < \beta$ and therefore

$$\alpha < \sup_{a \in P_0} \mu(a) \leqslant \inf_{F \in P_0^*} \nu(F) \leqslant \beta \ (!!!)$$

where the sup and inf of the empty set mean respectively the values α and β.

For optimality of the admissible element in one of the two problems considered it is necessary and sufficient that there exists in problem (2) an element such that the corresponding values of (!) and (!!) are identical (the optimality symptom).

The symptom relates to the theorem : Except for the trivial case (when there is no admissible element, i.e. $P_0 = \emptyset$ and $P_0^* = \emptyset$) equality is achievable in the middle-term of (!!!); if there exist admissible elements in both problems then there exist in them also optimal elements; if there are no admissible elements in one of the problems, i.e. if $P_0 = 0$ or $P_0^* = \emptyset$, then neither of the two problems has an optimal element.

(15) The scope for applying the duality conception – in the form of Fenchel's conjugacy correspondence for convex function – to optimal pricing is excellently demonstrated in Rockafellar.[40] He has shown how and why all the problems of existence and of meaning of the Lagrange multipliers in the ordinary convex programme correspond to those on the subgradients of a convex function on R^n, the space of all n-tuples of real numbers. The interpretation of the Lagrangeans is carried out in terms of perturbation: we treat the Lagrangean multiplier as the equilibrium price and relate it to the minimum cost. (We consider the question whether the cost could be lowered by some "perturbing" of the programme constraints. If we take a "perturbation" as one which can be "bought" at the price of λ_i per unit of variable x, the minimum cost in the perturbed programme added to that of the perturbation appears as $p(x) + \lambda x_1 + \ldots + \lambda x_n$ thus where the perturbation $(u_1, \ldots u_n)$ is not "worth buying", the Lagrange multiplier is exactly the price. Fenchel's conjugacy correspondence is taken as the generalization of the Legendre transformation and Rockafellar draws very important conclusions for the Hamiltonian dynamics and thus the dynamization of the optimum price; we revert to this in the context of the Pontryagin principle in our Part II. (Rockafellar's latest research indicates new ways for determining saddle-points by a generalized method of steepest descent. The results of the Arrow-Hurwicz differential equation method are extended by means of a new theory of nonlinear monotonic operators: developments of a class of operators appear related to subdifferentials of convex and concave-convex functions.)[41]

(In anticipation of problems discussed in Part II, we note the important Soviet contribution to the extension of the conceptual framework of convexity. In particular, Gamkrelidze has introduced the concept of quasiconvex sets.[42] (This concept of quasi-convexity is intimately related in his system to that of "chattering" controls. The quasi-convex function has been employed by Gamkrelidze for reformulation of the proof of necessary condition for optimal control (see Part II)).

Further Rubinshtein and his associates have on the one hand generalized the concept of convex, specifically of strictly convex functions; on the other they have systematized the extremization methodology for quasiconvex functions on a convex polyhedron.[43]

The claim is well justified that the area of convex programming is at present nearest to definitive elaboration within the discipline of mathematical programming.

(16) The implications of the convex-programming theory for the theory of optimal pricing have been studied by several writers.[44] Afriat's recent paper[45] commends itself to us on several counts: in the first place because it pinpoints the properties of the convex system against that of general

and also of linear programming; and, last but not least, because in addition to an important original contribution it offers an up-to-date bird's-eye view over the field over the past twenty years, starting from Slater.[46]

Rather than the "purely formal" saddle concept, it is that of the limit function of the programme that is central in Afriat. Mathematical considerations apart, the explicit reason is the significance i.a. in economics: its support gradients heuristically suggest themselves as expressing, in economics, price or marginal value. Implications are deduced from Afriat's general theorem on the maximum solution of the programming problem.[47] Firstly they imply the identity of $\bar{u}$ (standard symbolism) in any saddle solution – the multiplier solution – with the support gradients $\bar{u}$ of the limit function at $\bar{y}$; in other words, with the "support solution";[48] this is to assume the existence of the solution to the programme problem. Thus we have a generalized interpretation of the multiplier solutions as derivatives; but since, differentiability is *not* postulated here, the analogy to the Langrangean multiplier method of the differential calculus is here generalized.

Thus, as against the linearity case, under convexity the saddle solution calls for qualification implying the existence of a support solution of the limit function. Again, it is of relevance for our theme that the issue of the support's existence at any operation point $\bar{y}$ is put into the framework of economics. In this way the reasoning turns on the proposition that any constraint is relaxable "at a cost" rather, that is, than on the prior formal assumptions with respect to the functions $f(x)$ and $f(g)$: a cost would be non-decreasing in the case of convexity (and obviously so in the particular one of linearity). The next consequence is, in Afriat, the presentation of the diminishing-return principle as economic rather than technological in its nature.[49]

(17) The realism of the situation in which the prevailing price relations differ drastically from those of the equilibrium prices (or when indeed the latter do not exist) has turned Soviet research to the problems of "the equilibrium system with disequilibrium prices".[50] The implication is the existence of "deficitary" and "non-deficitary" products and "quotas" in both inputs and outputs. The approach entailed is well illustrated in Braverman's model, in which the plans of operating units are co-ordinated by maximizing – in some special sense – the profit of each under the disequilibrium type of pricing.

This is the substance of the system; it is formed of N elements, P_i's each producing one item; its state is determined by the $(N + 1)$-dimensional vector

$\{y_i, \xi_{1i}, \ldots, \xi_{Ni}\} = \{y_i, x_i\} \geqslant 0$, where the components of $\{y_i, x_i\}$ are interpreted: y_i as quantity of product P_i produced by P_i and ξ_{ki} as quantity of product P_k used up by P_i. With each element we have an associated region G_i of admissible values $\{y_i, x_i\}$, belonging to the non-negative ortant of the $(N+1)$-dimensional space.

For any situation within the system, the required balance for each product entails, $y_i = \Sigma_{k=0}^{N} \xi_{ik}$, (1). Further, for each P_i a price c_i is fixed (non-negative), their totality forming a vector c. A demand function is assumed $F_i(c, \xi_{1o}, \ldots, \xi(i-1)_o, \ldots, \xi_{No})$, $\xi_{io} \leqslant F_i(.)$. In brief notation $\xi_{io} \leqslant F_i(c$, (2). Where the latter turns into equality all the ξ_{io} are expressible as functions of prices, c, only; otherwise — where any products are deficitary — we have a strict inequality affecting the system as a whole. These then, the (1) and (2), are global conditions; and they have to be completed with a hypothesis as to "local" behaviour.

The system's state $\{\tilde{y}_i, \tilde{x}_i\}$, $\tilde{x}_i = (\xi_{1i}, \ldots, \xi_{Ni})$ is defined as that of equilibrium where *firstly*, the (1) and (2) are met, *secondly*, there exists a subset I of the elements' indexing numbers such that for all $i \in I$ the $\{\tilde{y}_i, \tilde{x}_i\}$ is the solution of the problem $\pi_i = c_i y_i - \Sigma_{k=1}^{N} c_k \xi_{ki} = \max$ (3); $\{y_i, k_i\} \in G_i$ (4) and $\xi_{ki} \leqslant \tilde{\xi}_{ki}$ for all $k \in I$ (5). For all $i \notin I$ the (2) is satisfied as equality; here $y_i \leqslant \tilde{y}_i$ (6) (the $\sim$ denotes throughout "local" solution and implied quotas). We add a definition: the element P_i is said to have a "normal technological characteristic" where any set of deficitary products I and any collection of constraints $\tilde{\xi}_{ki}$, $k \in I$ has a solution $\tilde{y}$ of the problem (3)–(5) as a non-decreasing function of the constraints $\tilde{\xi}_{ki}$, $k \in I$ (and for the case of $i \notin I$ the solution $\tilde{\xi}_{ki}$ of the problem subject also to (6) is a non-decreasing function of y_i). (The functional dependence of solutions on constraints entails in all those cases a uniqueness of solution.) We denote the solution $\tilde{y}$ of the problem (3), (4) in the absence of constraints (5), (6), as $y_{i, \max}$. Braverman proves the theorem: Let all elements have the normal technological characteristic and for any i positive c_i and $y_{i, \max}$, and G_i is a convex bounded set containing the origin of co-ordinates; further, the region determined by the (2), contains a continuous curve $x_o(s)$, $0 \leqslant s \leqslant S$, $x(0) = 0$, $\xi_{io}(s)$-monotonically non-decreasing functions of the s parameter; further, the system contains no "resource" elements; then the $\bar{s}$, $0 \leqslant \bar{s} \leqslant S$ will be found such that for any s, $0 \leqslant s \leqslant \bar{s}$ there exists a state of equilibrium with $\tilde{x}_o = x_o(s)$ [a "resource" element is one for which there exist admissible situations with $y_i \neq 0$ even if the corresponding vector $x_i = 0$].

This system is completed with the concept of the "limiting" equilibrium. This term is accorded to the equilibrium $\{(x_i^*, y_i^*)\}$ with a set of

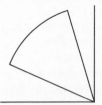

deficitary products I^* when there exists no other equilibrium state $(\{y_i^{**},$
$x_i^{**}\})$ such that $\xi_{ik}^{**} \geqslant \xi_{ik}^*$ for all $i \in I^*$ and at least for one $i \in I^*$ and one $k, \xi_{ik}^{**} >$
ξ_{ik}^* . The existence of this state of limiting equilibrium is proved by Braverman
for the situation where the first two conditions of the theorem above are met
as also in addition at least one of the two further conditions, i.e. that for any
i either the demand function $F_i(c, x_o)$ is a non-decreasing function of the variables
ξ_{ko}, or this function equals the component ξ_i of the solution of the problem
$\Sigma_{k=1}^N a_k \xi_k = \max \Sigma c_k \xi_k = d; \xi_k \leqslant \xi_{ko}$ for all $k \neq 1$.

To sum up, then, this theorem is identifying the situation of possible
maximum output flows under the assumed price disequilibrium. A further
theorem – on the "core" of the equilibrium – formulates a sufficient
condition for a state of equilibrium to be limiting. That means that its
checking does not entail a detailed knowledge of individual elements'
characteristics and inter-element flows of product: the knowledge of the
set I of deficitary products' indexes and a list of products used by every
element would suffice.

(18) Once the convexity assumption is abandoned, the mathematician is
essentially confined to the search for local minima (in this he is usually)
helped by techniques devised for the search for global optima under
convexity.[51,52] Why he has to content himself with the local optimum has
been put excellently by Beale:[53] the obvious cases where the non-convexities are known to be small (or where intuition suggests accepting the local
optimum) apart, the reason is that the only practicable alternative to a
local minimum is a completely arbitrary solution (recall Koopmans – on
p. 12). On the other hand contenting oneself with local optima leaves the
planner with uncertainty as to the distance from anything approximating
an overall optimum.

One more point about approximations. It is usual when faced with
troublesome nonlinearities – to try to linearize the function involved.[54]
How dependable are these short-cuts to handiness? The best study on the
subject – that by Baumol and Bushnell[55] – is anything but encouraging,
at least where strictly linear form (as distinct from piece-wise linear and
integer-linear) is adopted. From Baumol-Bushnell we know now that only

where the criterion function is monotone may one be certain of a gain from
a linear approximation. Otherwise linearization cannot be relied upon to
secure a better answer than a randomly adopted initial solution, let alone a
true maximum. Not only are there types of reduction in curvature which
may fail to ensure improvement, but the linear-programming calculation
can indeed produce a solution poorer than the one serving as the initial
point of calculation. Perhaps the most striking point which emerges from
Baumol-Bushnell is the refutation of the intuitively acceptable proposition
that insignificance of deviation from linearity guarantees by itself an
adequate quality of linearization.

(19) Having duly cautioned the reader as to the near-helplessness of the
present-day programming theory as such in the direct treatment of non-
convex systems, we may make two qualifications.

One of these concerns the handling of discrete systems. From the point
of view of planning, integer programming merits particular attention
here. It is discussed in the next section — within the framework of the
subject-matter of the present chapter.

The other qualification relates to control theory. But it is our repeated
point that control theory is developing as a vast discipline in its own right —
with a great potential for the advance of planning theory: we have devoted
a separate part of our study (Part II) to it and suggest turning to that
Part for a wider background.

(20) As pointed out, continuity versus discreteness is yet another problem
in the idealization in the models as originally offered by programming to
the planning theory. As far as the Soviet theory is concerned, it is legitimate to think that on this count the Kantorovich school was originally
inclined rather to underestimate the difficulty. What little empirical evidence
has been gained since has corrected this impression. (It is only fair to say
that Kantorovich himself has helped such correctives.)

As it appears in the light of Soviet experience,[56] strategic-macroplanning
does provide sufficient scope for models with continuous variables, resting
on heavily aggregated input-output balances: the heavy averaging of index-
numbers of processes and prices over sufficiently long periods and sufficiently aggregated classes of resources appears to ensure a sufficient degree of
stability for initial data and solutions. This is so in spite of the fact that
dynamic situations do entail indivisibilities and "non-compromise" decision
making which by their very nature cannot be accommodated in a contin-

uous-variables model: indeed, where the gestation process of identified capacities is observed in sufficient detail, specifically in the case of sectoral perspective plans, integer variables have to be dealt with.

On the other hand, also in the light of these experiments more surprisingly, models with continuous variables, specifically convex-programming models, have proved intractable in current planning too, although essentially here discrete capacity variables could be expected to be a datum: shadow prices of resource constraints — with variants of construction and reconstruction of capacities derived from some optimality calculus — would seem to be acceptable as optimal. Yet in fact the strong "jerkiness" of capacity constraints over short plan intervals has been found to cause instability of the solving-multiplier type of prices in the course of the implementation of the plan, and as often as not in the course of its construction.[57]

Conscious of this difficulty too, Soviet planning theory has become actively interested in the search for a remedy. One or two remedial procedures suggested in literature are discussed in the next paragraph. But before this, we may point out that the classical Gomory-type algorithm for handling integrality is very slow in convergence and that the assumptions which underlie it very often defeat its purpose. As far as the dual-price system to be obtained from an integer-programme solution goes, its peculiar drawback has been clarified in that i.a. it fails to measure, with any degree of exactness, the marginal revenue of inputs and may impute zero prices to scarce resources (Gomory-Baumol).[58]

(21) Note also some interesting modifications of, and approximations to the known algorithms. Among the former in particular that by Lyubovitskiy.[59] Among the latter — that by Khokhlyuk and associates,[60] which handles the problem stated in these terms: Find linear function

$$I(Y) = C_o + \sum_{j=1}^{n} c_j y_j,$$

subject to

$$\sum_{j=1}^{n} d_{ij} y_j \leqslant d_i; \quad \sum_{j=1}^{n} d_{ij} = d_i$$

where respectively i belongs to I_1 and I_2; $y_j \geqslant 0$; $y_j \equiv 0 \pmod 1$ which is the condition of integrality where I_1, I_2 are mutually complementary subsets; $I = \{1, \ldots, m\}$; m is the number of constraints (equations and inequalities). All parameters, i.e. c_j, d_j and d_i, are integers and the poly-hedral set, constrained as above is bounded. [This applies Martin's algor-ithm; Khokhlyuk has given a finite-form modification. To recall, in the 1960 modification of his original method, Gomory evolved an "all-integer" algorithm. This was remarked by Martin in a build-up of an "accelerated euclidean" algorithm.

The Khokhlyuk et al. algorithm employs Martin's variant of the "cutting planes" method and it carries this out in a finite number of iterations (transformation of the simplex table). These are shown to lead either to an optimal integer solution of the original problem or to the demonstration that such solution is infeasible. Proof of sufficient condi-tions guaranteeing finiteness is offered.] [61]

(22) Among methods of handling integrality, that suggested by Alcaly and Klevorick[62] stands out for the cautiousness of its conclusions.

In this model the all-economy planner would promulgate a system of prices ensuring equality of the total imputed cost of capacity inputs with the total value of outputs, yielded by the optimal integer value of the profit-objective function-plus a flat-sum subsidy: the subsidy-penalty system would bring about zero profits (all free goods being imputed zero profits). It is the adjusted "general-dual prices" that would form the point of departure for allocating — with the use of the Dantzig-Wolfe decompo-sition principle (see below p. 57) — to individual units the production of final goods. In fact Alcaly-Klevorick are defensibly rather sceptical with regard to the effectiveness of the generalized duality system they offer. This scepticism is shared by Balas, the author of yet another attempt to develop one generalized shadow-price theory for discrete systems.

Balas's recent work[63] — as indeed the work of several other students — is inspired by Benders's important contribution[64] to the solution of the mixed variables programme problem of the form

$$\max \left\{ c^T x + f(y) \mid Ax + F(y) \leqslant C, \quad x \in R_p, \quad y \in s \right\}.$$

(*Notation*: $x \in R_p$; $y \in R_q$ and S-arbitrary subset of R_q. A is an (C, p) matri f and F are, respectively, scalar and an m-component vector functions defin on S: b and c are fixed vectors in R_m and R_p.)

The central idea is to partition the problem into two sub-problems; of these one is linear and the other can be either linear or nonlinear, or discrete, and so on, defined respectively on R_p and S. Two procedures as designed lead to a set of constraints which determine the solution of the original problem – in a finite number of steps, each of which entails the solution of a general programming problem. Eventually conditions are identified for application of effective procedures in handling the two problems: (1) where $S = R_q$ or a convex polyhedron in R_q, $F(y) = By$ (B being some (m, q) matrix), $f(y) = r^T y$, $r = R_q$; the key problem is a linear programme; a suggested procedure is that of the dual simplex; (2) where $S = R_q$, $f(y)$ and components of $F(y)$ are convex and differentiable functions defined on S- this problem becomes a convex programming one; finally, (3) where S is the set of all vectors in R_q with non-negative integral-valued components, $F(y) = By$, $f(y) = r^T y$, $r = R_q$ the key problem becomes one of a special class of integer programming.

Several attempts have been made to generalize the Benders models. The Balas algorithm[65] gives a solution of a mixed-integer linear programme in integer-constrained variables: the dual is demonstrated to be equivalent to a pure integer-linear problem with constraints generated by solving a convex programming problem in continuous variables.

As can be seen, generally speaking, the solutions offered (a) are confined to systems reducible to convexity, and (b) depend on effective decomposition.[66]

(23) Originally the plan-programming school gave rise to what came to be described in Soviet writing as the "monistic" approach – the view that price being directly related to the optimal plan can and should be determined by a direct, as contrasted with any component-wise, methods. The recognition that, at least in the current, sufficiently disaggregated, planning, the former are not available, has provided the first impulse to what we may call the school of the second-best. The gradually discovered difficulties with which this chapter has been concerned have strengthened this school. Various shades are by now discernible in it. Some would give prominence in their reasoning first and foremost to the computational barriers on the road to optimal pricing. With others the emphasis is rather on the conceptual obstacles. Both converge in proposing some less-than-consistent approach to the optimality of the price: various hybrid constructs combining the traditionalist "production-price" concept with elements of the programming price have been suggested as corresponding to the "art of

the possible". (One, relatively the most interesting, is presented in
Appendix 4.)

(24) The reservations with respect to the obtainable optimization price
are also being fed by the results of Western inquiries into its effectiveness
as the steering instrument. As a rule these are concerned with micro-
systems (intra-enterprise decentralization), but strict analogy would seem
to permit the application of their results to normatively planning macro-
systems as well. We may direct the reader in particular to the results obtained by Charnes, Clower, and Kortanek,[67] whose purpose is to show that
steering by means of decentralization can be effected where additional
information — additional to price, that is — is transmitted to "divisional
units" in what are termed the "pre-emptive goals". (Under this system no
uniqueness of the divisional optima is required. And it is shown that the
procedure is robust in the sense that even approximate fulfilment of the
pre-emptive goals — i.e. close to optimal divisional solutions — suffices
for practical purposes.) The relevant point is then that in this type of a
hybrid system the determining of these goals and/or their ordering —
whether in the constraints or the criterion function — creates in turn the
problem of its optimization. For our analogy, the Charnes-Clower-Korta-
nek exploration is in any case of considerable value where it synthesizes
the consensus of students of the subject as to the difficulties of devolution
by price alone. As they indicate, (1) difficulties arise in situations where
due to the overall coupling — or externalities — between divisions, optimal-
divisional solutions are non-extreme points of divisional sets; they arise
also in the presence of alternate divisional optima; and (2) the usual nature
of the interdivisional couplings precludes a unique optimum whereby the
possibility of strict convexity of the minimand in the mathematical image
is affected. Mutatis mutandis all this holds for a macro-system. In fact
by now the list of students who agree on the failure of price alone as the
steering parameter is quite large. For particularly pronounced scepticism
we may refer to the Baumol-Fabian findings:[68] it is demonstrated that it is
not only in the nonlinear cases that there might be situations where no set
of prices would induce the executive echelon to adopt choices optimal
for the economy as a whole (cf. what has been said above on the Baumol-
Bushnell findings, p. 19): and even in the case of most tractable nonlinearity, the all-economy constraints could not eliminate the possibility of the
profit function being maximized at some interior point.[69]

[In this section — because of some expositional "indivisibilities" — we
have broached an aspect of pricing related to the problem of decomposi-

tion. Its wider aspects are treated in the next sub-chapter at the cost of some tedious overlapping.]

Note

These and other diagnoses of the troubles with a price-based devolution fail to explain how it is that the private-enterprise economies of real life, affected as they are by crucial non-convexities, operate with a reasonable — indeed, under normal circumstances, a remarkable degree of efficiency; and whether these is a method, and what method, of imitating them. At least the question has been rigorously stated by Vietorisz, who also provides us with a glimpse of some elements of an answer.[70] The crux of the matter is persuasively shown to be the problem of fixed costs generating non-convexities, and the principal points in the Vietorisz findings, if we understand them correctly are these: (a) generally decisions involving incurrence of such costs do not lend themselves to devolution by price; (b) if such decisions are taken out of the devolution system, other sectoral decisions can rest on marginal-cost pricing; (c) to the extent that their devolution is of practical concern, average-cost pricing of the connecting resources — for all intents and purposes, capital and labour in the first place — is preferable to marginal-cost pricing. Back to the first part of our question, it is suggested that the conditions for the reasonably effective work of a predominantly private enterprise economy are that (a) highly indivisible decisions be subject to some kind of "rational centralized deliberation" outside the market, and (b) lesser "lumpinesses" be handled by pricing relying on the average cost in the vicinity of the "highest efficient scale of operation".

If this is the full "secret" one is left with the puzzle as to the actual device — built into the private-enterprise market mechanism — which ensures the automatic meeting of the conditions. Still less clear is the question whether the "visible hand" could effectively simulate its invisible counterpart in its working towards some similarly tolerable suboptimum.

The proposition that a plan-programming — specifically linear plan-programming — model sufficiently closely approximates the working of a competitive mechanism not too far from perfection has had little empirical testing. The only "laboratory" test known to me has been carried out for the Greek economy by Nugent.[71] The "optimal-actual ratios" and the regression results would suggest a not unsatisfactory accountability of departures from the optimum by detectable market imperfections and government intervention. The dependability of results, and still more

their general validity, lends itself to questioning on both methodological
and statistical grounds, as the author fairly concedes. (The exercise seems
however, to have served its declared purpose of demonstrating the feasibility of a testing procedure of this kind.)

(25) The difficulties the theorist on optimal planning discovers in formalizing the price parameter are now influencing the new theory of plan
modelling: a group calls for greater constructional flexibility.

This theory originated as a by-product of the theory of extremization
(to which, it hardly needs to be emphasized at this stage, the Soviet theorist on planning owes the revelation of the nature of the price at optimum).
In this way modelling theory had started from the mathematical concept
of price as a partial derivative of the optimality criterion, constrained as it
may be and made sufficiently stable. What has been said so far hints at the
qualifications to the basic proposition: qualifications called for by the non-
convexity, discountinuity, non-differentiability of the relevant functions,
and so on. The aspect of non-uniqueness of the optimal prices is given
particular attention in the context of decentralization.[72]

This is the background of the second-thought school. Katsenelinboygen — the author of illuminating ideas — advocates a kind of "syn-
cretist" approach to pricing:[73] handling it from the angle of the price's
"function" in the economy's organization as well as that of properties
specific to the type of the model (what is meant in particular are the
vectoral and the scalar models of optimization;[74] the former embracing
in particular the Gale-type equilibrium and game-theoretic constructs).
Organizationally the focus is on the role of price in a system of "autonomy"
for "local elements" which — so it is argued — permits determining the
price invariant with respect to the way the system is designed and not
rigidly connected with specific properties, including stability.

Along this line of thinking the merits of descriptive[75] modelling are
rediscovered — in the process of a synthesis.[76] The idea is that the descriptive model *firstly* provides scope for greater generality with respect to the
ruling preference systems, and *secondly* helps analytically to unravel some
organic properties of the money-physical-term relationship in the system:
viz. of price as the parameter of the system's functioning in its relation to
social cost. (N.B. One consideration is to counter the argument of critics
who oppose the theory of the optimal functioning of the socialist economy
on the ground that while centring on utility it looses the sight of the cost
element.) Last but not least, this school would stress the methodological
gain from modelling a system simultaneously from different angles — the

methodological gain from changing the role of propositions as axioms and as theorems (to exemplify, the existence of individual objective functions is axiomatic in some models and theorematic in others; and so also is the existence of the price parameter. On the other hand some axioms — such as those of feasibility balancing — are invariant in transforming one model into another.) Constructing a descriptive model would demonstrate how, in order to bring in the axiom of individual (specifically Paretian) valuation and price, one has to resort to necessary conditions for the problem's extremum.

To combine in the analytical apparatus instruments operating from different angles may deepen with insight. What seems to require probing is that a descriptive model would necessarily be free from limitations of the extremizing construct.

(26) This and the following sections are intended to form a bridge between the themes of the present and the next chapters: the themes which can hardly be disentangled in a way fully satisfying a systematic build-up of our study.

As an introductory remark, we note that clarification — by the Kantorovich school — of the concept of profit maximization at shadow prices has helped Soviet planning theory to formalize the problem of devolution in decision-making. The issue of its feasibility or otherwise in collectivist systems has had a long history of three-quarters of a century in Western economics — starting with Barone, via Pareto, Lerner, and particularly Oskar Lange. But strikingly this had for decades no echoes in Soviet economics. One may suggest that, in the given institutional environment and with given strategy, it could potentially have but little relevance: and indeed it has *had* hardly any relevance under the adopted system of planning and steering economic processes. But logically it could be expected to gain theoretical significance if, when, and to the extent that an adjustment of this originally evolved mechanism towards devolution in decision-making on effective resource allocation would come under consideration.

The Kantorovich school had offered to planning theory the behavioural precept corresponding to devolution at optimum. For the operative echelon the rule of the game would be — in Kantorovich-Makarov — the same as in Koopmans: with the use of the saddle-point prices, refrain from operations resulting in negative profits: expand those yielding positive profit till the zero-point is reached: then carry on at this level.

What follows will try to elucidate the limits of legitimacy of the micro-rule, related as it is to particular "idealization" of the macro-models.

Notes

1. Leif Johansen has designed a system of pricing for planning in a dynamic setting.[77] His apparatus is that of continuous functions and classical calculus, but results of the exercise are claimed to parallel those of Kantorovich: marginalist accounting prices are of the Lagrangean-multiplier type and the dynamics of the system are organized by a vintage – "choice-of-technique" – production function: on this the pricing over time is built up in a straightforward fashion up to the plan horizon.

In Johansen's reading the kinship with Kantorovich's system will be also found in the latter's allusion to future price trends being derived from a simplified all-economy model (indicating specifically the discounting of the labour input). Strong emphasis is placed on the mechanism for working out future price trends, not only under direct centralization of investment decision but also under decentralization and profit-maximization. While admittedly the logic of the latter would seem not to postulate this, it is argued that practical considerations make necessary consistent and correct expectations about future prices to fulfil optimality requirements. Strictly, we would say, this is so with the respect of the *centre*'s requirements. In Johansen's argument, however, the ability in general an unguided competitive system optimally to shape factor proportions is questioned. (Note the relatedness of the proposition with that of Hahn – on the absence of infinity of future markets as necessitating the visible hand's guidance; also our hint at the parallelism of the dilemma with that brought out in the Kantorovich-Makarov disquisition for the very-long-run tracing of the economy's course under centralism.)[78]

2. Since this comment was written I have been able to acquaint myself with Malinvaud's paper[79] on an aspect of decentralized planning procedures with some implications for our topic: the search for an optimal programme for public consumption – entailing in fact optimization of the programme for private as well as public consumption, and determining the related taxation. One of the methods designed is that of a progressive improvement (by iteration) – through revision of individual taxes by mutual concessions. In the other variant of the method we have progressive improvement of a quantitative, physically feasible programme: "consumers" repeat their marginal willingness to pay for an additionally available good – public or private: eventually the optimal programme is supported by prices for both classes of goods (for the former they are in substance tax rates used for calculating an individual's contribution).

There is no reason why the regime of utility maximization through what we could term "auctioneering" should not be acceptable to a socialist

society. The difficulty may arise rather from the extension of the public
good domain if it is taken to embrace the whole of the dynamics, inasmuch
as the society would reserve for itself the shaping of the economy's future.
(See also the next chapter.)

Moreover the technical design would commend itself to a socialist planning system to the extent that it might permit escaping from some of the
pitfalls indicated here which the price-based devolution comes up against.
The novum in the Malinvaud approach is the stated conception of substituting a different approach for the by now classical treatment of the subject,
i.e. of focusing on the information exchanges within the decision-making
process with a view to getting from this a quantity-term programme —
rather than concentrating attention on the functioning of the price system.
This conception extends the line of the original (1963) Malinvaud model.[80]
(It may be recalled that the construct elicited in its time Koopmans'
comment on the key question — "prices or quantities as the principal
indices".)[81] The emphasis on prices as such indices, he had argued, then
arose through the impact on Lerner, Lange, and their contemporaries
of the smooth U-shaped average-cost textbook curve; his inclination would
be rather to use the quantity indices and obtain price responses — in the
hope of faster convergence. But in spite of the theoretical attractiveness of
proceeding in resource allocation from quantity to price rather than the
other way round, practicability may prove the difficulty owing to the
size of the exercise and difficulties in aggregation.

3. Although we refer *passim* to some of its major works, it would go
far beyond the scope of the present book to provide any analytical survey
of Western literature on price-based devolutional planning procedures.
Malinvaud's paper quoted here and its original versions constitutes in this
literature one of the basic formalizations. Chronologically its foundations
were laid by the contributions of Arrow and Hurwicz ("Decentralization
and computation in resource allocation", in R. Pfouts, ed., *Essays in economics and econometrics,* 1960; cf. also L. Hurwicz, "Conditions for economic efficiency of centralized and decentralized structures", in Grossman,
Value and plan) resting on the concept of Walrasian tâtonnement; in this
it was supplemented by H. Uzawa's "Iterative methods for concave programming", in Arrow et al., *Studies in linear and non-linear programming*
(Stanford, 1958).

To Malinvaud is owed in particular the formulation of properties which
a "decentralized" system, as defined in his model, is expected to possess:
specifically, for the procedure examined, those of feasibility, monotonicity,
and convergence (the work quoted contains a test of the Arrow-Hurwicz

construct with respect to these criteria). Of obvious interest from our angle is Malinvaud's probing into procedures for the Leontief-Samuelson technology and those implying mathematical programming at central level.

Malinvaud's construct has provided the point of departure for numerous studies — published in recent years — of devolutional and also of antithetical systems. Some of these studies have expanded the Malinvaud system, in particular have attempted to dynamize it and/or to build up a "mixed" system.

(27) A few concluding remarks. What explorations in the field treated in this chapter have given to Soviet planning thought first and foremost is an insight into fundamentals. The cognitively and heuristically-invaluable breakthrough caused by the, now classical, Kantorovich construct may at least in part account for the underestimation of obstacles on the road towards a price dependable for the optimal steering of the economy. We have tried in this chapter to identify the obstacles. We have also given some analytical account of Soviet effort — against a wider background of developments in the thinking on these matters — to overcome such obstacles: effort in coping with dimensions, including the time dimension, and with the complexity of economic relationships. We have discussed in particular the limite realism of the formalized regime of a linear, monotonic continuity; we have stressed again and again the link between all these restrictive facets: and we have tried to sketch the progress made in these efforts during the past decade or so.

It seems reasonable to think that — as far as employability of the apparatus goes — these efforts have by now provided the planner with instruments of broad strategic optimization which, all else apart, may be expected to help improve the quality of techniques to hand. On the other hand, one must be less confident that they have equipped him with a price to be fully relied upon for operational planning and plan implementation. The actual degree of reliability can be only a matter of speculation, from which we refrain at this stage.

What has been elucidated must inevitably influence the thinking on the alternatives open with respect to the economic mechanism as well. Again, the assimilation of the programming approach has inspired optimism as to the immediate feasibility of indirect normative centralism:[82] centralism that rests on guidance of the system by means of a centrally-set price parameters *alone* and the micro-rules of behaviour, possibly with the use of a competitive market. We assume that — in any consideration — on the

ground of philosophy adopted alone, devolution with market-formed
prices comes up against some inhibitions a priori because of the implication
with regard to the dominant system of preferences (see our discussion of
the objective function):[83] and a rigorous analysis fails conclusively to
support the proposition of workability of a "mixed" market system
("market socialism"). For the clarification of the stand of a wing within
the Soviet mathematical school the view of Rumyantsev[84] may be rather
significant:

. . . it is fallacious [he argues] to think, as some economists (who
forget about the decisive advantages of a socialist economy) naively do,
that the planned control of economic processes can be assured by only
indirect techniques of planned regulation. If one accepts this, one is not
far from accepting the possibility of controlling the development of a
socialist economy by means of a market mechanism

(a strong accent in the reasoning is placed on the implications for the
society's perspective requirements — the dynamics of the planned system
entailing centralist choice-making).

A recent study of an economy's parametric framework by S. M.
Vishnyev[85] well summarizes the present state of the debate. It starts
with the proposition that, assuming it is possible to find a price system in
the solution of the optimal plan-price "complex", this system is the "best"
by definition. However (Vishnyev remarks) some economists maintain
that the solution of the system of equations which determines optimal
price is fundamentally impossible; others, while considering the problem
theoretically solvable, think it is insoluble in practice — for lack of
sufficient information and owing to the mathematical-computational
difficulties; there are, finally, "optimists" (Vishnyev considers himself to
be one of them) who believe the problem to be theoretically correct,
solvable in the practice of a planned socialist economy, useful and therefore indispensable — but "naturally one can only talk of an approximation
sufficiently exact for the purposes of the practice".[86]

Thus the acceptable degree of a feasible approximation is patently the
major qualification (we have dealt with it on earlier pages). A no less
important one stems from Vishnyev's tenet that the central planner has
to rely in any case on a system of operators, the price-type tools belonging
to one of its classes — that termed in Vishnyev "orientation" operators
(considered in addition to this are the classes of "activators", "disactiva-
tors", and "stabilizers", the last including inventories and reserves of
capacities). This view, pointing to the relevance of a wider organizational-

parametric framework of a system's functioning, has rapidly been gaining acceptance in Soviet mathematical planning theory in recent years: we shall meet this and related views in diverse contexts. (They are discussed in the last section of this Part and in Part II; wider issues are treated in my separate study of a system-theoretic approach.) We may note here that as formulated by Vishnyev, the stand raises the crucial issue of harmonizing the systems of operators in general. It raises in fact the mathematical-technical point as to what extent some operators – and which operators – have to be kept outside the formalism of the optimizing system of equations; and whether they can be left outside without adversely affecting the metric and guiding functions of optimal prices.

On this line of reasoning, where the normative character of the planning system is *posited*, and to the extent that doubts as to dependability of the mechanism of parameters and operators could prove justified, the case for direct normative centralism would be established, at least at the present stage.[87] We disregard in this argument the question of comparative efficiency of alternative mechanisms.

Additional Note

The employment of the dual as price-parameters in normative planning has been the subject of various semi-empirical investigations.

An inhibitive factor stressed in some of these inquiries is the problem of bridging the discrepancy between the actual and the programme-derived price relations. As a matter of fact, analyses carried out for market-formed prices show this discrepancy to be surprisingly small: thus the Nataf inquiry[88] for France would suggest that it is about 5 per cent in four-fifths of the branches; it is of a similar order in Werin's exercise for Sweden.[89] While – quite possibly – to some extent this may be due to heavy aggregation, it seems legitimate to think that the much wider discrepancies observed in non-market economies are largely attributable to their mode of pricing.

One and one almost inevitable source of trouble is the pricing of labour. To be sure disparities on this point are by no means confined to a normatively planned system. They are entailed by specific social-political and welfare factors. Some students would in fact argue (cf. Werin) that there is indeterminacy: that no unique accounting price of labour is derivable from a programme; but this may be due to treating labour as *the* ultimate prime-factor numéraire. (cf. above, sect. 6). Others, Qayum[90] in particular, suggest abandoning the marginality principle in the pricing of labour. As a matter of rationality, however, his stand appears to be related to the special type of environment − in a structural disequilibrium − considered, where manpower, at least unskilled labour when treated as a heterogeneous magnitude, is in surplus, its programming price being thus zero (indeed in such an environment it may be negative). This may also be due to what we see as an a priori proposition: a proposition that optimal utilization of factors is achievable only through the adoption of technologies maximizing output − for the given bill of goods − with "as full as possible" utilization of resources. The problem is shared by planned and unplanned economies alike up to some level of development. And discrepancies between the programme-derived and adopted price of labour, when large, may undermine the rationale of the shadow-price system as a whole.

A major headache in the practice of centralized pricing is the zero-profit type of solution yielded by the programme. As against the market economy, where the reward for factor entrepreneurship is shaped by market prices, there is no dependable principle under normative pricing. More or less arbitrary rules have to be resorted to.

Last but not least, dynamizing the dual creates serious difficulties of its own. Some of them have been brought out incisively in the Czechoslovak quasi-dynamic plan-programming experiment; in particular those entailed in the regime of constant levels and/or price relations over time (and have been analysed in illuminating comments).[91] On the theoretical plane a rigorous solution to the problem is given in Kantorovich-Makarov (cf. p. 406).

This links up the with question of fixing the dual value of time "as such". Virtually all applications of plan-programming techniques in normative planning take it to be a strictly endogeneous parameter − cf. above, sect. 7; more on this will be found in our chapter 4 on investment efficiency. Here we only point to a detected property of the plan-programme as designed: it is the virtual insensitivity of the system with respect to changes in the rate of interest over a strikingly long stretch, followed − at some point − by a drastic response. (With the obvious impact on the number of simplex steps around the critical points.) The behaviour of the magnitude is related to the structural properties of a linear programme (and the algorithm): as a matter of fact the model has revealed in general the strong bias for concentrating resources on investment, and within it, on strikingly few sectors.[92]

What has been said lays stress on the difficulties in adequately "weighting" the planners' objective function and in constraining it in a way which would mitigate the handicaps of linearity. The conclusions of Czechoslovak experimenters appear to be doubly pessimistic: *firstly* they acknowledge the potentialities of the linear-programming instrument for the analysis of problems of macro-economic policies and for designing tools of their implementation, but doubt its micro-economic dependability; and *secondly* they see no unequivocal solution for the system's dual. The second conclusion in our view, however, must be qualified: the ambiguity stems from the way in which the exercise in the profit problem is handled. [93]

As against the cautious Czechoslovak appraisal one finds more optimum in the conclusions derived from a Hungarian ex post examination (in the mid-1960s) of shadow prices.[94] In its light it has been maintained, i.e., that the valuation systems related to the optimality criteria, adopted as broadly realistic, reveal themselves to be only very moderately different from each other in basic proportions; also that already the first approximative calculations permitted the establishment of realistic results for a set of parameters. Hence the expressed conviction that the system of valuations — together with the optimal plan-programmes belonging to it — simulated stage-wise over time do promise an entirely novel approach to the problems of administering the national economy. However, Kornai's experiments in Hungary and their analysis (see ch. 2, pp. 75 f.) would not seem fully to be out this degree of optimism, as yet.

APPENDICES

Appendix 1: Golshtein's Schema of Duality in Functional Spaces

An analytically generalized schema of duality in functional spaces has been conveniently formulated — in Soviet writing — by Golshtein,[95] in the following terms:

Let G be a non-empty set of arbitrary structure, $f(x)$ real functional on G: $\phi(x)$ an operator defined on G, operating from G into the real Banach space E_1; G_1 is a non-empty subset of E_1. Assume

$$R = \{x: \phi(x) \in G_i, x \in G\}.$$

Then the extremal problem considered is to find the supremum of $f(x)$ over the set R, of the form

$$\left. \begin{aligned} f(x) &\to \sup \\ \text{subject to} \quad \phi(x) &\in G_i, \\ x &\in G. \end{aligned} \right\} \quad (!)$$

— a functional analogue of the general mathematical programming problem.

The plan of (!) is defined as the sequence $X = \{x^{(k)}\}$ of points $x^{(k)}$ such that there exists $\lim_{k \to \infty} f(x^{(k)}) = f(x)$. This plan is the solution of the problem if

$$f(x) = \lim_{k \to \infty} f(x^{(k)}) = \sup_{x \in R} f(x) = \nu.$$

Now the dual of the problem is being formed — first for the case where G is a convex cone, i.e. a set such that for any $y', y'' \in G_1$, the $\lambda' \geqslant 0$; $\lambda'' \geqslant 0$ we have

$$\lambda' y' + \lambda'' y'' \in G_1.$$

The G is taken to be a positive cone and the E_1 is taken to be a partly ordered set. For this we introduce for elements E_1 a relationship $\ll \gg$ of the kind

$$y' \leqslant y'' \ (G_1) \underset{(y', y'' \in E_1)}{\Longleftrightarrow} y'' - y' \in G_1$$

The constraint in (!) is restated equivalently as

$$\phi(x) \geqslant 0(G_1).$$

Take $E_1{}^*$ to be the space conjugate of E_1. The positive cone $G_1 \in E_1$ defined on the conjugate space $E_1{}^*$, the convex cone

$$G_1{}^* = \{\lambda: \lambda(y) \geqslant 0, \ \text{if} \ y \geqslant 0(G_1); \lambda \in E_1{}^*\},$$

taken to the positive cone of this space (it is conjugated with G_1). For any arbitrary $x \in G$ and $\lambda \in E_1$

$$F(x, \lambda) = f(x) + \lambda(\phi(x)).$$

Let

$$\psi(\lambda) = \sup_{x \in G} F(x, \lambda).$$

The problem dual to (1) – (3) is then defined as finding

$$\tilde{\nu} = \inf \psi(\lambda)$$

subject to

$$\lambda \geqslant 0(G_1{}^*).$$

This statement is made more specific for special classes of extremal problems by a process of elimination of constraints 'cutting out' the set of the λ-points for which $\psi(\lambda) > \infty$. (This is illustrated in the case where G is a convex cone of a B-space E; A is a finite linear operator from E into E_1, $\phi(x) = -A(x) + b$ where $b \in E_1$: $f(x) = c(x)$ where $c \in E^x$, making the functional analogue of the familiar statement of the linear programme.)

A generalized theorem of duality is then established, to read that for the convex set $\overline{K}$ and the generalized set of plans $\overline{R}$, $\overline{v} = \tilde{v}$, i.e. the value of the upper bound of generalized primal problem (!) equals that of the lower bound of the dual.

A further restatement is this. Let T be a measurable finite subset of metric space M with a measure a, $a(T) < \infty$. Let further for any $t \in T$ be a given set $G(t)$, real functional $f_i(x)$ defined on $G(t)$, operator $\psi_t(x)$, operating from $G(t)$ into a separable Banach space E_1. The problem is then

$$\left. \begin{array}{c} \displaystyle\int\limits_{t \in T} f_t(x_t)d\alpha \to \sup, \\[2ex] \displaystyle\int\limits_{t \in T} \Phi_t(x_t)d\alpha \in G_1, \\[2ex] x_t \in G(t), t \in T, \end{array} \right\} \quad (!!)$$

where G_1 is a convex subset of E_1. The E is defined as a set of functions $f_t(x_t)$ and $\Phi_t(x_t)$ summable over T. Then this problem (!!) reduces to one of the type (!) where G is the subset of elements E satisfying

$$f(x) = \int\limits_{t \in T} f_t(x_t)d\alpha, \qquad \Phi(x) = \int\limits_{t \in T} \Phi_t(x_t)d\alpha,$$

where $x \in G \subset E$. Then the problem dual to the stated one is the minimization of the function $\Psi(\lambda) = \Psi'(\lambda) - \Psi''(\lambda)$ subject to $\lambda \geqslant 0$ $(G_1{}^*)$ where

$$\Psi'(\lambda) = \sup_{x \in G} \int\limits_{t \in T} [f_t(x_t) + \lambda(\Phi_t(x_t))]\,d\alpha, \qquad \Psi''(\lambda) = \inf_{y \in G_1} \lambda(y).$$

It is then shown that the closing set $\overline{K}$ is convex.

Appendix 2: Kantorovich's (1940) Theorems relating to Kuhn-Tucker Theorems

Kantorovich's relevant theorems are:[96]

I.   Let E be a linear normalized space, $\Phi(x)$ a functional in E, $A \in E -$ a convex and locally compact set. If (1) weak convergence $x_n \to x$ entails $\overline{\lim}\ \Phi(x_n) \leqslant \Phi(x)$ and (2) $\Phi(x)$ does not reach even a local maximum within A, then there exists a point $\overline{x}$ on the boundary of A, where $\Phi(x)$ reaches maximum, and a non-zero linear functional $\phi(x)$ reaches maximum and a non-zero linear functional $\phi(x)$ reaches maximum $\overline{x}$ on A also at $\overline{x}$.

II.   Let conditions in I be satisfied and in addition the set $x_c = \{x: \Phi(x) \geqslant C\}$ be convex for any arbitrary C. If there is $\overline{x}$ and a linear functional $\phi(x)$ such that (1) for $x \in A$, $\phi(x) \leqslant \phi(\overline{x})$; (2) either $\phi(x) \geqslant \phi(\overline{x})$ holds on the surface $\Phi(x) = \Phi(\overline{x})$, or $\Phi(x) \leqslant \Phi(\overline{x})$ holds on the plane $\phi(x) = \phi(\overline{x})$; (3) there exists a point $x^* \in A$ for which, with $\phi(x^*) > \phi(\overline{x})$, $\Phi(x^*) > \phi(\overline{x})$, then $\Phi(x)$ reaches its maximum on A at $\overline{x}$.

Kaplan observes that if all the Kuhn-Tucker conditions are met for differentiable $f(x)$ and $g_i(x)$, then for $\Phi(x) \equiv f(x)$ and $A' = \{x: g(x) \geqslant 0, x \geqslant 0\}$ all conditions of Kantorovich's first theorem too are satisfied and the set $X_c = \{x: f(x) \leqslant C\}$ is convex for any C. He next proves the existence of a linear functional $\phi(x)$ such that $\phi(x)$ and $\overline{x}$ satisfy the conditions of Kantorovich's second theorem.

Appendix 3: Some TsEMI Experiments with Iterative Solutions for Discrete Integer Systems

This appendix draws attention to the work on discrete systems at the TsEMI. As we understand, two algorithms have been designed and experimented with.

One – the 'B' integer programme by Golshtein[97] – rests on the cutting-plane method with a novel rule for the build-up of an additional linear constraint. The solution is obtained for a number of canonical problems derived from the original problem rather than directly from the latter itself. The algorithm yields an exact solution for objective function, with non-zero rational coefficients, and with integer variables only; otherwise – a solution with a postulated degree of exactness. While more efficient than the classical cyclical algorithms, it has proved unmanageable even for medium-size problems.

At this stage more hope appears to be staked on an algorithm – based on the random-search method – constructed by Pyatnitskiy–Shapiro and others[98] and experimented with at the TsEMI.

The problem is of the form

$$f(x) = (c, x) \to \max; \quad Ax \leqslant b; \quad 0 \leqslant x \leqslant q : x_j = 0 \text{ or } 1.$$

As in the 'B' algorithm, here too solution is sought for a sequence of "t-problems", $f(x) \geqslant t$, rather then the original one. For the initial plan x^0, some arbitrary sequence of 0 and 1 is adopted. Suppose at the kth step some vector $x^{(k)}$ has been formed; then

$$\Delta_0 = \max \left[(t - (c, x^{(k)}))/\mathcal{C}_0, 0\right], \quad \Delta_i = \max \left[((a_i, x^{(k)}) - b_i)/b_i, 0\right]$$

$$i = 1, \ldots, m$$

are calculated and the probability $p = \min (\lambda \cdot \Delta_i, i = 0, 1, \ldots, M)$ is determined with λ chosen over the $(0, 1)$ interval (in the TsEMI experiments $\lambda = 0.5$). To construct the plan $x^{(k + 1)}$ for all j it is assumed

$$x_j^{(k + 1)} = \begin{cases} x_j^{(k)} \text{ with probability } 1 - p \\ \\ \left. \begin{array}{l} 0, \text{ if } x_j^{(k)} = 1 \\ \\ 1, \text{ if } x_j^{(k)} = 0 \end{array} \right\} \text{with probability } p. \end{cases}$$

The process is concluded by constructing the plan of the t-problem after a fixed number of iterations.

The derived algorithm for the price-profit mechanism (see text p. 12) has this form. Let $p = (p_1, \ldots, p_n)$ be a vector with p_j describing the probability of event $x_j = 1$ and $\pi = (\pi_1, \ldots, \pi_m)$ be the vector of valuation of the $Ax \leqslant b$ constraints. Let further p^t and π^t be vectors p and π as yielded by the tth iteration. By using the random-search mechanism we find the vector x^t assuming its components x_j^t to be independent and equal to unity with probability p_j^t. Next according to some adopted principle the π^t valuations are corrected in conformity with the $Ax^t - b^t$ discrepancy, for instance by increasing the valuations corresponding to positive discrepancy and reducing all the rest. The vector obtained we denote π^{t+1} and use for correcting probabilities $p_{j\bullet}^t$ so as to accord with the profits $(\pi^{t+1} A)_j$ and then total value of loss Ψ^t: we obtain a new vector p^{t+1}, and a new iteration starts, and so on.

Appendix 4: Volkonskiy's Simplified Model of Pricing

A simplified model of pricing designed by Volkonskiy[99] — with the principles borrowed from the classical dynamic input-output system — has the form

$$(I - a^t)x^t \geqslant y^t + \sum_{\tau \geqslant 1} b(t)\Delta x^{t+\tau};$$

further $(1^t, x^t) \leqslant L^t$ where I is unit matrix; a^t is a matrix of direct imputs, including replacement and renovation of capital stock per output per unit; $b(\tau)$ is matrix of capital inputs per incremental unit of capacities over t years up to their maturation; x^t is vector of global output, y^t if final product (consumption and non-productive capital formation), 1^t is vector of labour input coefficients, L^t is manpower resources. It is assumed that $y^t = g^t + h^t e^{\lambda t}$, where g^t and h^t are some known vectors, and λ is the growth rate of consumption — the maximand.

When the respective shadow valuations of the constraints are taken as p and w — in substance, vectors of prices and wage rates — the dual is written

$$p^t(I - a^t) \leqslant w^t L^t - \Delta \left[\sum_{\tau \geqslant 1} p^{t-\tau-1} b(t) \right]$$

with $\Sigma_{t=0}^{\infty} p^t h^t e^{\lambda t} = 1$ (normalized), and the maximand $\Sigma_{t=0}(p^t g^t - w^t L^t)$.

The crucial postulate is that total output forms a geometric series $x_j^t = x_j^0 e^{\alpha j t}$; the exponents α and λ are then the unknowns of the system. Analogously, the assumption of exponential change, i.e. the decline at the rates β and ω, respectively, is adopted for price and wage-rates in the dual: $p_j^t = p_j^T e^{\beta j(T-t)}$ and $w^t = w^0 e^{-\omega t}$, where $t \in T$, and some hypothesis is also adopted with regard to the post-plan behaviour of g, say that $g_j^t =$ const. The problem is then one of finding values for p^t and β^t which, subject to constraint of the dual (above), maximize

$$\psi = \sum_j \sum_{t=0} p_j^T e^{\beta j(T-t)} g_j^t.$$

The original model TsEMI experimented with in the build-up of the 1965-70 plan has been analysed in my *Aspects of Planometrics*. The substance of the nonlinear, n-sector Volkonskiy version[100] can be summarized as follows:

Maximize λ subject to

$$x^t \leqslant M^t$$

$$\Delta S_i^t = \sum_{j=1} b_{ij}^t \sum_{\tau-1} \phi_j(\tau) \Delta N_j^{t+\tau}$$

$$\Delta S^t = B^t \sum_{\tau \geqslant 1} \phi(\tau)\Delta N^{t+\tau};$$

$$\Delta M_i^t = \sum_{\tau \geqslant 1} \psi_i(\tau)\Delta N_i^{t+\tau}$$

$$\Delta M^t = \sum_{\tau \geqslant 1} \psi(\tau)\Delta N^{t+\tau},$$

$$(I - A^t)x^t \geqslant y^t + \Delta S^t + \gamma^t M^t,$$

$$(l^t, x^t) \leqslant L^t.$$

The crux of the construct is formed of money-term, index-number vectors: x^t of global output, M^t of capacities assimilated, N^t of completed construction of fixed capital assets, S^t of fixed capital stock, y^t of final product.

Further: $\phi_i(\tau)$ and $\psi_j(\tau)$ are coefficients of intertemporal structure of, respectively, investment in, and maturation of new capacities; $A^t = ||a_i{}^t{}_j||$, $B^t = ||b_{ii}^t||$, $\gamma^t = ||\gamma_{ii}^t||$ are matrices respectively of current input coefficients, inverse capital coefficients, capital intensities and of replacement (renovation) of capacities, L^t and l^t, respectively total manpower and vector of labour inputs. All these are assumed to be known. It is further assumed that net output (consumption) is subject to a regime $y^t = a + be^{\lambda t}$, where a and b are known vectors and λ is a parameter describing the growth of consumption.

Central in the model is the postulate of exponential growth of the vectors M and N, that is $M_i{}^t = M_j{}^0 e^{\alpha_j t}$ and $N_j{}^t = N_j{}^0 e^{\alpha_j t}$ where the growthrates α_i are to be determined.

Or – what is more convenient – take the epsilon as the diagonal matrix

$$\epsilon^t = \begin{pmatrix} \epsilon_1{}^t & & & & \\ & \epsilon_2{}^t & & & \\ & & \cdot & & \\ & & & \cdot & \\ & & & & \cdot \\ & & & & & \epsilon_n{}^t \end{pmatrix}$$

Then we can assume

$$\epsilon_j^0 = \sim, \ \epsilon_j^t = \frac{1}{tM_j^0} e^{-\beta_j t}, \ t = 1, 2, \ldots, T,$$

and our problem now takes the form

$$\left.\begin{array}{l} \alpha \geqslant F_\lambda^t(\alpha), \ (l^t M^t(\alpha)) \leqslant L^t, \\ \max \lambda, \ \alpha \geqslant 0, \ t = 0, 1, 2, \ldots, T, \end{array}\right\}^*$$

Where F^t — an abbreviation for the right-hand side of (*) is a non-decreasing function of α and λ; M^t is also a non-decreasing.

Then the theorem is proved to the effect that for the problem $x \geqslant f^t(x)$, $x \geqslant 0$, with $t = 0, 1, \ldots, T$, to be solvable it is necessary and sufficient that the sequence of vectors

$$\{z^{(k)}\}; \ z^{(0)} = 0, \ z^{(k+1)} = \langle z^{(k)}, \ f^0(z^{(k)}), \ f^1(z^{(k)}), \ldots, f^T(z^{(k)})\rangle$$

be convergent: then the limiting vector z of the sequence will be the feasible minimum. [Here the $\lozenge$ denotes the set of the component-wise formed maximum of enumerated vectors and the $f^t(x)$ is taken to be non-decreasing.]

The theorem permits to apply, in solving the plan-problem, an algorithm of motion along the lambda parameter (such as to cause the magnitudes to increase monotonically with the change of λ). To find $\nu = \lambda_{\max}$ one may proceed from the initial value λ_1, by some step h, testing the sequence $\{z^{\lambda(k)}\}$, for convergence at each step.

In the II variant an alternative, more realistic but mathematically somewhat more complicated $x^t \lneqq M^t$ is considered. The procedure starts now from rewriting (*)

$$x^t = R^t(y^t + \Delta S^t + \gamma^t M^t), \ \text{where} \ R^t = (I - A^t)^{-1} \geqslant 0$$

and then arithmetically from constraint $M^t \geqslant R^t(y^t + \Delta S^t + \gamma^t M^t)$.

We then again apply the Tkhaitsukov device and write this as $(\alpha - e^t M^t) + e^t R^t(y^t + \Delta S^t + \gamma^t M^t)$.

From this it follows that

$$N_j^0 = \frac{1}{\displaystyle\sum_{\tau \geqslant 1} \psi_j(\tau) e^{\alpha_j \tau}} M_j^0$$

$$\Delta S_j^t = \sum_{i=1}^n b_{ji}^t M_i^0 e^{\alpha_i t}(e^{\alpha_i} - 1) \left(\sum_{\tau \geqslant 1} \phi_i(\tau) e^{\alpha_i \tau} \ \Big| \ \sum_{\tau \geqslant 1} \psi_i(\tau) e^{\alpha_i \tau} \right) \equiv \Phi_j^t(\alpha)$$

the $\phi_j(\tau)$ and $\psi_j(\tau)$ are thus such as to make $\Phi_j{}^t(\alpha)$ non-decreasing. Two variants of possible mathematical formulation are considered.

First, Variant I where $x^t \equiv M^t$ is postulated: the plan problem is then formulated, with unknown $\alpha = (\alpha_1, \ldots, \alpha_n)$ and λ as

$$\left. \begin{array}{c} (I - (A^t + \gamma^t))M^t \geqslant a + be^{\lambda t} + \Delta S^t, \, (*) \\ (l^t, M^t) \leqslant L^t \end{array} \right\}$$

where

$$M_i{}^t = M_i{}^0 e^{\alpha_i t}, \, \Delta S_i{}^t = \Phi_i{}^t(\alpha), \, i = 1, 2, \ldots, n,$$

$$\alpha \geqslant 0, \, \lambda \geqslant 0, \, t = 0, 1, \ldots, T.$$

To bring the problem to a canonical form the (*) is rewritten

$$\alpha \geqslant \alpha + \epsilon^t \left\{ a + be^{\lambda t} + \Delta S^t - [I - (A^t + \gamma^t)]M^t \right\} =$$

$$= (\alpha - \epsilon^t M^t) + \epsilon^t [a + be^{\lambda t} + \Delta S^t + (A^t + \gamma^t)M^t]_1 \equiv F_\lambda{}^{(\alpha)}(**)$$

where the ϵ^t coefficient is chosen such as to make the right-hand side of the inequality non-decreasing function of α. Since the term in square brackets is non-decreasing it is necessary and sufficient that $(\alpha - \epsilon^t M^t)$ too be non-decreasing implying

$$\frac{\partial}{\partial \alpha_j} (\alpha_j - \epsilon^t M_j{}^0 e^{\alpha_i t}) = 1 - \epsilon^t t M_j{}^0 e^{\alpha_j t} \geqslant 0.$$

If it is known from an a priori solution that $\alpha \leqslant \beta$, it suffices to choose for each plan time-interval the epsilon coefficient such that

$$1 - \epsilon^t \cdot t M_j{}^0 e^{\beta_j t} \geqslant 0, \, j = 1, 2, \ldots, n,$$

be satisfied entailing

$$\epsilon^0 = \sim, \, \epsilon^t = \min_j \frac{1}{t M_j{}^0} e^{-\beta_j t}, \, t = 1, 2, \ldots, T.$$

In this variant too we have, with respect to α, a constraint of the form $\alpha \geqslant F^t(\alpha)$, for $t = 0, 1, \ldots, T$ the F being a non-decreasing function of α and λ. And we have also — by analogy — the constraint of the form $H_\lambda{}^t(\alpha) \leqslant L^t$ where the H is a non-decreasing function of α and λ.

Eventually the problem in this variant has the shape

$$\left. \begin{array}{c} \alpha \geqslant F_\lambda{}^t(\alpha), \, \alpha \geqslant 0, \, \lambda \geqslant 0 \\ H_\lambda{}^t(\alpha) \leqslant L^t, t = 0, 1, \ldots, T \end{array} \right\}$$

and here too the motion is along the λ parameter which is the maximand.

Appendix 5

As the stochastic approach acclimatizes itself in Soviet planning theory, considerable work is done on generalizations of stochastically constrained plan programmes. Usually the employment of a stochastic mechanism implicitly assumes independence of "future materialization" random elements as the problem's conditions. Take Zhulenyev's[101] stochastic programme with probabilistic constraints of the form: max $f h (x)$

$$P\left\{ \sum_{j=1}^{n} a_{ij}x_j \leqslant b_i \right\} \geqslant \beta_i, \; i = 1, \ldots, m,$$

$$x \in H$$

In the approach indicated to each random plan x we have assigned a point in the Euclidean space R_e of parameters $(\zeta_1, \ldots \zeta_e)$ of the joint distribution of the components $x_1, \ldots, x_n$. Thus, since for instance, the objective functional, $h(x)$, probability of the constraints and the elements of conditions determining the set H are functions of the R_e, we have an immediately determined equivalent – in this case of the form

$$\max f \, \bar{h} \, (\zeta),$$

$$\zeta \in \bar{H} \cap \bigcap_{i=1}^{m} L_i \subset R_e,$$

$\zeta = \zeta_i, \ldots, \zeta_e; L_i = \left\{ \zeta | G_i(\zeta) \geqslant \beta_i \right\}, \; G_i(\zeta) = P\left\{ \Sigma a_{ij}x_j \leqslant b_i \right\}; \bar{H}$ is a certain subset of R_e, The practical usefulness of the above statement would depend on the ability to detect a practicable variant; from this point of view it is important, indeed decisive, to properly handle the uni-type sets L (i); both from the theoretical and the practical point of view is the case of normal distribution of x one of particular relevance. The argument is that in most cases of practice the number of plan components is very large; hence for an approximate appraisal of the probability of G the central limiting theorem can be applied; from its generalizations it would follow that, within a range of assumptions with regard to x_j, a_{ij} the distribution function of the sum $a_{ij}x_j$ tends towards normality; consequently with a large m, the G is "essentially" determined by the first two moments of the values of x_j and is "almost" independent of their distribution. We write then[102]

$$P\{x_j < t\} = G(t) = \frac{1}{\sqrt{2\pi}} \int_{-\infty}^{t} e^{-z^2/2} \, dz.$$

The applicability would be certainly justified in a simplified case — as in Zhulenyev — where the components x_j are normally distributed independent random magnitudes; the coefficients a_{ij} are constant; and the b_j is arbitrarily set independent of x_j, $P\{b_i < t\} = F(t)$; and finally $\frac{1}{2} < \beta_i < 1$. In the case the L is written down with the use of the form

$$G_i(u, v) = \int \Phi\left(\frac{t-u}{v}\right) dF_i(t) \geqslant \beta_i,$$

where

$$\Phi(t) = \frac{1}{\sqrt{2\pi}} \int\limits_{-\infty}^{t} e^{-z^2/2} dz,$$

$$u = \sum_{j=1}^{n} a_{ij}m_j, \quad v = \sqrt{\sum a_{ij}^2 \sigma_j^2}$$

(In the examination of the set $\overline{L}_i$ the properties of its image

$$L = \{u, v | G_i(u, v) \geqslant \beta_i\}$$

on the plane u, v are explored by Zhulenyev, thus the general theory of the probability set L is built up. Results obtained on conditions for the L's convexity are in particular of interest from the point of view of applicability.)

2. For stochastic pricing Yefimov's[103] attempts deserve to be noted. Assuming that the (sectoral) criterion is the minimum mathematical expectation of cost, the problem for the "plan", $x = (x_i, \ldots, x_n)$ has the form

$$E \sum_{j=1}^{N} (c_j, x_j) + E\{\min [(q^1, y^1) + (q^2, y^2)]\} \to \min,$$

subject to

$$\left.\begin{array}{c} y^1 - y^2 = b - \sum\limits_{j=1}^{N} A_j x_j, \\[2mm] y^1 \geqslant 0;\ y^2 \geqslant 0, \\[2mm] x_j \in X_j,\ j = 1, \ldots, N. \end{array}\right\} \quad (!)$$

Notation: A_j (dimensions $m \times r_j$) is technology matrix for the sector j; x_j is an r_j-dimensional vector of use-intensities of technologies; X_j is a set of admissible technology intensities, convex and closed (it is so in particular due to capacity limitations); b is an m-dimensional vector of demand for the jth sector's output; c_j is an r_j-dimensional vector of technology unit-cost; y^1, y^2, respectively, output surplus and deficit (related to demand), q^1, q^2, respectively, the resulting loss. A_j, b, c are subject to fluctuations.

The term $E\{.\}$ in the minimand above (!) is the optimal value of the objective function for the deterministic version with A_j, b, x_j fixed, and the dual has the form

$$\pi(x, A, b)\left(b - \sum_{j=1}^{N} A_j x_j\right).$$

The equivalence problem will be stated as

$$E \sum_{j=1}^{N} (c_j, x_j) + E\left[\pi(x, A, b)\left(b - \sum_{j=1}^{N} A_j x_j\right)\right] \to \min,$$

$$x_j \in X_j, \ j = 1, \ldots, N.$$

We thus have a convex-programming problem. Assuming absolute continuity of the probability measure the functional continuously differentiable with respect to x and its gradient at point x will have the form

$$(E(c_1 - \pi(x, A, b)A_1), \ldots, E(c_n - \pi(x, A, b)A_N)).$$

The convex functional is replaced by a linear one whose directional vector coincides with the former's gradient at point of optimum. We will write for the dual

$$\sum_{j=1}^{N} [((E\pi(x^*, A, b)A_j - b_j), x_j)] \to \max.$$

This problem is broken up into N independent subproblems

$$(E(\pi(x^*, A, b)A_j - c_j), x_j) \to \max,$$

$$x_j \in X_j, \ j = 1, \ldots, N.$$

and the equilibrium theorem is stated for the sectoral system (!): if the enterprise's objective function is maximization of profit, then there exist prices $\pi(x^*, A, b)$ of output such that a plan optimal for enterprises is also optimal for the sector.

From this theorem the proposition is deduced that, in principle, under stochastic conditions described, decentralization is possible at prices, vector-components of the $\pi(x^*, A, b)$, forming, that is, the solution of $x = x^*$. Where the x^* and the statistical characteristics of the stochastic elements (components) are known, the directing vector of the linear functional for the subproblem would be approximately calculated by the Monte Carlo method.

It seems to us tenable that the method lends itself for all-economy stochastic pricing — by analogy (in the reasoning the economy and its sectors will be substituted for the sector and its enterprises).

Notes

1. The subject has a considerable literature in Western writing; thus see G. Grossman, ed., *Value and plan* (Berkeley, 1960), espec. contributions by Grossman, Zauberman, Montias, Campbell, Ward, Hurwicz, Wiles, Kaser.
2. cf. discussion of the Moscow 1966 session of the scientific council of the Academy of Sciences, and in particular N. P. Fedorenko's contribution as reported in *EMM* 2 (1967); cf. also *Vopr. ekon.,* 5 (1966).
3. cf. Fedorenko's report ibid.
4. T. C. Koopmans, "A note about Kantorovich's paper", *Management Science.* 6/4 (1960).
5. H. W. Kuhn, "Duality in mathematical programming", in H. W. Kuhn / G. P. Szegö, eds., *Mathematical systems theory and economics,* (New York, 1969). The lectures forming this paper stand out for the simplicity and elegance in presentation of various facets of the concept, its development and exemplification.
6. Referred to ibid., p.68.
7. S. Strumilin, in *Vopr. ekon.,* 4 (1968).
8. A. A. Konyus, in *On political economy and econometrics — essays in honour of Oscar Lange* (Warsaw. 1965).
9. Our reader may be usefully directed to M. Barkai ("The empirical assumptions of Ricardo's 93 per cent labour theory of value", *Economica,* Nov. 1967) for a well-defended tenet that any single-input hypothesis, the labour theory of value in particular, fails to provide a sound empirical proposition on relative prices.
10. V. A. Volkonskiy, *Model optimalnogo planirovanya i vazimosvyazi ekonomicheskikh pokazateley* (Moscow, 1967), p. 122.
11. Note the resurgence of attempts in the Gosplan to get an *"objectively"*-based system of price relations by "translating" full-order input coefficients (obtained by matrix inversion) into money terms on a formula of the kind $Z = 100P/Q.Y_{soc}$, where Z stands for the price "level" of output in per cent of the labour "norm", P for price, Y for the "average money equivalent of a labour unit", Q_{soc} for the *"labour-term measure"* of output. cf. I. Doroshin, in *Plan. khoz.,* 10 (1971). One would be inclined to think that difficulties in obtaining a "subjectivist" price system stimulate this kind of thinking: the author indeed expresses the hope that a "fruitful harmonization of prices with *objective* economic laws will permit solution of the pricing problem" (our italics).

12. cf. for instance F. Modigliani, "The monetary mechanism and its interaction
     with real phenomena", *R. Econ. Stud.*, Feb. 1963.
         To take a related point, the absence of a share market is yet another element
     of "de-sophistication" in a socialist planning system (cf. here Radner's paper on
     the existence of equilibrium of plans, prices, and price expectations and also on
     the concept of pseudo-equilibrium in *Econometrica*, 2 (1972)). We leave this
     aspect undiscussed for a socialistic system of "one enterprise", although this
     impoverishes the generalized optimality testing formalism.
13. A. L. Lurye, in *EMM*, 2 (1967).
14. Lurye, *EMM*, 2 (1967).
15. L. V. Kantorovich / V. A. Makarov, in V. S. Nemchinov, *Primenenye matematiki
     v ekonomicheskikh issledovanyakh* (Moscow, 1965).
16. In the Soviet mathematical school Vishnyev raises and answers in the negative,
     the question as to whether the problem of intertemporal "co-measuring" of
     economic magnitudes is definitively answered in the Kantorovich system. It is
     conceded that the Kantorovich conception of dynamic valuations (the "OOOs")
     does answer "objectively" the question of time-weighting: by implication it
     indicates that zero-valued time discount is incompatible with optimality require-
     ment as formulated. But Vishnyev expresses his reservations on at least three
     counts: (a) that the adoption of a horizon does affect the time-weights implicitly,
     (b) that so also does the taking of technological coefficients over time as deter-
     mined since the determination entails a probabilistic treatment and thus assumes
     at least some known distribution law; and first of all (c) that the weighting
     function is implicitly dependent on the objective function, thus the problem
     of social time preference is shifted to that of the criterion. cf. S. M. Vishmyev,
     Ekonomicheskiye parametry, pp. 145 ff (Moscow, 1968). This we discuss also in
     Pt. II.
         The point (a) is expanded upon by V. I. Livshits in his discussion of the
     general question of weighting functions in the context of the time factor in
     optimization; he argues persuasively that the "classical" way of "co-measuring"
     asynchronic cost with reference to one time-point ignores the proposition
     that the form of such functions may change depending on what time-point
     t_0 would be adopted as the basic one. The function would be, for the contin-
     uous case of the form $\int_0^\infty u(X(t)Q(t, t\delta)dt$. From this, under the assumption of
     stationary prices, proportionate to those of the optimal plan, the relative value
     of one rouble would change over $(t, t + dt)$ by $(-E_t dt)$ where E_t is the corres-
     ponding normative rate of efficiency of investment. (The general case of non-
     stationary prices is treated in V. F. Pugachev, *Optimizatsya planirovanya*
     (Moscow, 1968).) cf. Livshits, "Uchet faktora vremeni v zadachakh lokalnoy optimi-
     zatsyi s pomoschyu vzvyeshivayushchikh funktsyi". *EMM*, 6 (1971). cf. also
     discussion in Pt. II.
17. For the critique of the Kantorovich-Makarov by the traditionalist school, that
     by A. I. Kats, *Dinamicheskiy ekonomicheskiy optimum* (Moscow, 1971) is
     typical. Its substance is that the dynamic treatment of the normative rate of
     efficiency should rely on the "basic *objective* causal laws" rather than a prob-
     abilistic approach entailed logically in Kantorovich-Makarov. The argument of
     the traditionalist school on "objective laws" is not unfamiliar; the question,
     however, how to detect them is left unanswered.
18. J. G. Kemeny et al., "A generalization of the von Neumann model of an expanding
     economy", *Econometrica*, 2 (1956).
19. D. Gale, "A closed linear model of production", in H. W. Kuhn / A. W. Tucker,
     eds, *Linear inequalities and related systems* (Princeton Univ., 1965).

20. S. Karlin, *Mathematical methods and theory in games, programming and economics* (London, 1959).

21. E. M. Malinvaud, "Programme d'expansion et taux d'interêt", *Econometrica*, 2 (1959). cf. also M. Morishima, "Economic expansion and the interest rate in generalized von Neumann model", ibid 2 (1960).

22. cf. Zauberman, *Manchester School*, Mar. 1969.

23. R. M. Solow, *Capital theory and the rate of return* (Amsterdam, 1963). For a more recent restatement of his stand see, "The interest rate and transition between techniques" in C. H. Feinstein, ed., *Socialism, capitalism and economic growth*. (Cambridge, 1967); in the later study the stress is on the rate of interest as "the accurate measure of the social return to saving" (under the assumption of full employment and competitive pricing)

24. More on this and on the rate's "pure" and uncertainty-compensating components in Soviet treatment (by Mikhalevskiy) in Part II, pp. 207 ff.

    The uncertainty element in the composite charge on capital has a substantial literature in the West: in most cases some indirect ways of coping are resorted to by its authors; see in particular D. Levhari / D. Patinkin, "The role of money in a simple growth model", *Amer. Econ. R.*, Sept. 1968; also P.A. Samuelson, "What classical and neoclassical monetary theory really was", *Canad. J. Econ.*, Feb. 1968.

25. D. Gale, "On optimal development in a multi-sector economy", *R. Econ. Stud.*, Jan. 1967, and "A geometric duality theorem with economic applications", ibid.

    Because of the influence Gale has exercised on Soviet planning theory in recent years it is rewarding to turn to him when studying the sources of its inspiration.

    With this in mind we may additionally refer the reader to Gale's – joint with W. R. Sutherland – "Analysis of a one good model of economic development" (in G. B. Dantzig / A. F. Veinott, eds., *Mathematics of the decision sciences*, pt. 2 (Providence, Rhode Island, 1968)); therein a "competitive market interpretation" is given to the paths along which producers are maximizing profits and consumers are maximizing utility subject to their budgetary limitations. Under this assumption, proof is offered for the theorem that any optimal programme is "competitive"; and infinite-time analogues are produced for the formal statement linking optimal and competitive programmes, again of patent relevance for the theory of planning.

26. In his analysis of the "Illyrian" market socialism formally modelling a Yugoslav-type of mechanism, B. Ward (*The socialist economy*, New York, 1967, pp. 182ff.) discusses the results of the regime of the wage-maximizing as against that of profit-maximizing behaviour.

    The maximand for the Illyrian manager is the difference between the two averages – of receipts and of cost per worker:

$$py/x - (w + (R/x)) = \max.$$

[*Notation*: p price of product, y output, x labour, w wages per worker, R non-wage cost. Wage cost per worker is assumed to be fixed by the state; product prices – to be formed in a competitive market]. But at the same time the manager would seem to be expected to maximize the workers' (the workers' council's) criterion, which is $S = w + J/R$ where J is profit. (ibid., p. 191, n. 12).

27. The formal definition of a convex function: A real function $y + (f(x)$, defined in the interval $\mathcal{F}$, $a < x < b$ is convex in $\mathcal{F}$ if for x_1, x_2 with $a < x_1 \leqslant x \leqslant x_2 \leqslant b$ we have $f(x) \leqslant 1(x)$ where $1(x)$ is linear function coinciding with $f(x)$ at x_1 and

x_2. (Diagrammatically: $f(x)$ is convex in $\mathcal{F}$ if in each subinterval of the graph of the function $y = f(x)$ lies nowhere above its secant line). A convex function is necessarily continuous (though not when defined in the sense of Jensen). The problem of convex programming is usually formulated as that of finding $x = (x_1, \ldots, x_n)$ satisfying $x_j \geqslant 0$; $g_i \geqslant 0$ and yielding $f(x)$ min, the f and g are some given convex functions defined on n-dimensional vectors x with non-negative elements. Their Lagrangean functions have the form $L(x, u) = f(x) + \sum_i^m u_i g_i(x)$; assuming the existence of an admissible vector x such that $g_i(x)$ is negative for $i = 1, \ldots, m$, the Kuhn-Tucker theorem holds for the problems of convex programming, i.e. that the necessary and sufficient condition for the optimality of the nonnegative vector x^0 is the existence of the vector u^0 such that the pair x^0, u^0 will be the saddle for the corresponding Lagrangean function, that is for all non-negative x and u, we have $L(x, u^0) \geqslant L(x^0, u^0) \geqslant L(x^0, u)$.

cf. G. Sh. Rubinshtein / A. A. Kaplan, in *Matematika i kibernetika v economike*, (Moscow, 1971).

28. T. C. Koopmans, *Three essays on the state of economic science* (New York, 1957), p. 25.
29. H. W. Kuhn / A. W. Tucker, "Non-linear programming", in J. Neyman, ed., *Second Berkeley symposium on mathematical statistics and probability*, 1951. The differential form of the Kuhn-Tucker theorem in complete statement is given by B. N. Pshenichnyi in *Kibernetika*, 5 (1965) and in "Linear optimal control problems", *SIAM J.*, 4 (1966).

For constraint qualifications introduced to prove the necessity of the Kuhn-Tucker conditions, cf. Arrow *et al.*, "Constraint qualifications in maximization problems", *Naval Res. Logist. Q.*, 8 (1961); J. M. Abadie, *Problèmes d'optimisation* (Paris, 1965); Monique Guignard, "Generalized Kuhn-Tucker conditions for mathematical programming problems in Banach space", *SIAM J.*, May 1969. The latter generalization embraces as particular cases the two afore-mentioned: pseudo-convexity is required in this generalization rather than convexity of constraints.

An excellent interpretation of the dual — via the Kuhn-Tucker theorems — as price variables is offered by D. Gale ("A geometric duality theorem with economic applications", *R. Econ. Stud.*, 1967, p. 19). As it is pointed out, for realistic technologies the equality of the classical cases turns in the general case into duality, meaning that the maximum of the growth-rate of input per capital unit is the minimum of all Kuhn-Tucker price vectors.

30. L. V. Kantorovich *et al.*, *Functional analysis in normed spaces* (1965).
31. W. Fenchel, "On conjugate convex functions", *Canad. J. Maths.*, 1 (1949). This is an area which has by now a large and creative Soviet contribution. Some contributing work will be referred to in the related contexts.

We may at this point supplement references to inquiries on properties of sets of supporting functionals by mentioning Pshenichnyi's article in *Kibernetika*, 3 (1965) — a systematic presentation of their properties and connection with directional derivatives; also E. G. Golshtein's article in *Doklady*, 173/5 (1967): it discusses the problem of best approximation with convex sets' elements and certain properties of supporting functionals; among them some not treated in Pshenichnyi.

Of considerable importance is Golshtein's generalizing work: his generalized schema of duality in functional spaces — for this cf. in particular his paper in *EMM*, 4 (1968), restated in the Appendix I, p. 34.

32. See his major work, *Convex analysis* (New Jersey, 1970).
33. A. M. Rubinov, in *Opt. plan.*, 16 (1970).
34. The same, jointly with S. S. Kutateladze, ibid., 17 (1970).

35. The concept is effective theoretically and applicationally. A hyperplane is defined as separating two nonempty sets in R^n if each of them is contained respectively in each of the closed — opposite to each other — halfspaces associated with that hyperplane.

36. cf. A. Ya. Dubovitskiy / A. A. Milyutin, in *Doklady*, 149 (1963), pp. 759 ff.

37. G. M. Rubinshtein, in *Opt. plan.*, 14 (1969). Of his earlier work in the field cf. in particular *Doklady*, 58/2 (1951); ibid. 152 (1963), pp. 288 ff.; "Neskolko primerov dvoystvennykh ekstremalnykh zadach", in *Matematicheskoye programirovany* (Moscow, 1966).

38. For a well systematized survey of numerical methods of solution in convex programming, cf. A. A. Kaplan, in *Opt. plan.*, 17 (1972).

39. G. Sh. Rubinshtein, in *Uspekhi matematicheskikh nauk*, 5 (1970).

In the context we may draw the reader's attention to an important series of articles on the dual method of extremal problems, in *Kibernetika*, nos. 3-5 (1965), in particular to the last of the three dealing with convex programming in a normalized space.

40. R. Rockafellar, "Convex functions and duality in optimization problems and dynamics", in Kuhn / Szegö, (op. cit.); of his earlier writing see, "A general correspondence between dual minimax problems and convex programs", *Pacific J. Mathematics*, 3 (1968), also his lectures at the NATO 1969 Summer School. cf. also R. M. van Slyke and R. J. B. Wets, "A duality theory for abstract mathematical programmes with applications to optimal control theory", *J. Math. Analysis & Applications*, 22 (1968), pp. 679 ff. Their results obtained are essentially the same as those obtained by Rockafellar. The difference rests in the formal framework. Van Slyke / Wets work with the concepts of convex sets, separating and supporting hyperplanes while Rockafellar with those of conjugate convex functions.

41. R. T. Rockafellar, "Saddle points and convex analysis", in H. W. Kuhn / G. P. Szegö, eds., *Differential games and related topics* (Amsterdam, 1971).

42. R.V. Gamkrelidze in *Doklady*, 161/1 (1965); cf. also ibid., 143 (1962), pp. 1243 ff., also the same, *SIAM J.*, ser A., 3/1 (1965).

The definition is loosely this. The family of functions F is quasi-convex if for every (1) compact $X \subset G$, (2) finite $f_1, \ldots, f_r$ elements of F, and (3) $\epsilon > 0$, there exists $f_\alpha \in F$ for every $\alpha \in P^r$ such that the functions $g(x, t, \alpha) = a$

$= \sum_i^r \alpha_i f_i(x, t) - f_\alpha(x, t)$ satisfy:

(1) $|g(x, t; \alpha)| < \bar{m}(t)$; $|g_x(x, t; \alpha)| < \bar{m}(t)$ for $x \in X$, $i \in I$, $\alpha \in P^r$

(2) $|\int_{r_1}^{r_2} g(x, t; \alpha)| dt < \epsilon$ for $x \in X$, $\alpha \in P^r$, $r_1 \in I$, $r_2 \in I$

(3) for sequence $\{a^i\}$, $\alpha^i \in P^r$ converging to some $\bar{\alpha} \in P^r$ the $g(x, t; \alpha^i)$ converges in measure to $g(x, t; \bar{\alpha})$ for $x \in X$.

While thus constrained the "quasi" widens the concept sufficiently to be of considerable help in the theory of control.

43. G. Sh. Rubinshtein / V. I. Shvyryev, in *Optimizatsya*, 1/18 (1972); V. A. Bulavskiy / G. Sh. Rubinshtein, in *Opt. plan.*, 14 (1969).

44. An attempt at "pairing" problems of nonlinear programming under concavity-convexity assumptions with the better known ones of linear problems — and economic interpretation of argument and findings — is contained in a recent paper by M. Balinski/W. J. Baumol ("The dual in nonlinear programming and its economic interpretation", *R. Econ. Stud.*, 1968, pp. 257 ff.). An economic interpretation of the content of the Kuhn-Tucker propositions is offered, these propositions being concerned with the extension of the Lagrange multiplier approach to optimization over equality constraints to that of optimization

over inequality constraints. As shown the linearity-nonlinearity analogue for the dual is quite close, the main difference being that nonlinearity requires the use of the marginality concepts as against linearity, for which the marginal and average values are the same.

An interesting point made is also that because dualization adds to the number of variables in the nonlinear case, the primal is no longer the dual of the dual!

45. S. N. Afriat, "The output limit function in general and convex programming and the theory of production", *Econometrica*, Mar. 1971.

46. M. Slater, "Lagrange multipliers revisited: a contribution to nonlinear programming", Cowles Commissions Discussion Paper, Maths 403, 1950.

47. The general theorem is the same as in Slater, op. cit., as against the classical Kuhn-Tucker theorem which postulates differentiability. The results are also the same in Karlin and Uzawa (resp. Karlin, op. cit., and H. Uzawa, "Duality principles in the theory of cost and production", *Int. Econ. R.*, May 1964), but the Afriat path of argument based on the limit function is different.

48. The point is also made by R. T. Rockafellar, "Duality in nonlinear programming", at the Princeton Symposium, 1967, and D. Gale in *R. Econ. Stud.*, 1967.

49. The reader's attention is also directed to O.L. Mangasarian's work on duality relations under relaxed convexity conditions in his "Pseudo-convex functions", *SIAM J.* 3 (1965), pp. 281 ff. For a most valuable presentation of development in , and up-to-date state of the theory of duality under nonlinearity (methodologies based on the conjugate-function concept, on the minimax theorems, on the symmetric dual nonlinear system), also for the author's own analytical results see Mangasarian's *Nonlinear programming* (New York, 1969).

50. E. M. Braverman, in *EMM*, 2 (1972).

51. For a good Soviet up-to-date review of results obtained in studies of nonlinear minimax problems see V. F. Demyanov / V. N. Maloziemov, in *Uspekhi matematicheskikh nauk.*, May-June 1971. Areas surveyed are in particular: differentiability of directional maximum functions, necessary conditions of the minimax, methods of sequential approximations in the search of stationary points of the minimax functions.

Demyanov himself has made a noteworthy contribution to the methodology of sequential approximation in the search for saddle points (cf. his study, jointly with A. M. Rubinov, *Priblizhennyie metody reshenya ekstremalnykh zadach*, Leningrad, 1968).

While, as indicated here, Volkonskiy has employed the gradient method − in applying a generalized Brown-Robinson technique to convex programming as a two-persons zero-sum game, Demyanov uses the method in the search for a saddle-point of a convex-concave function.

Of earlier Soviet surveys we may draw the reader's attention to an article by Ermolyev in *Kibernetika*, 2/4 (1966), in particular to its section on modified gradient methods (treatment of convex non-differentiable functions by Shor's procedure); and also to its section on the random-search methodology where the non-differentiable payoff function is not formulated in its analytic statement. In the latter the Rastrigin procedure offered is for the simplest case as follows. In a random uniformly distributed direction ξ, we proceed from some arbitrary point x^0, at a step p obeying the equations $x^{s+1} = x^s + \sigma \xi^s$ and $x^{s+1} = x^s$ if $F(x^{s+1})$, respectively, is or is not smaller than $F(x^s)$, the ξ^s being the materialization of the vector ξ at time s.

S. I. Zukhovitskiy *et al.*, *EMM*, 6 (1971) have examined the problems of determining the state of equilibrium, in the Nash approach, in a concave multi-person game wherein some methods of convex programming could be resorted to. The exercise expands Rosen's well-known study ("Existence and uniqueness of equilibrium points for concave N-person games", *Econometrica*, 3 (1965)) and builds up several algorithmic procedures by methods of fastest descent, of Chebyshev's centres (for a system of linear inequalities) and of gradients.

52. An important investigation into the problems of "not necessarily convex" nonlinear programmes in an infinite dimensional space is contained in H. Halkin's paper "Nonlinear nonconcave programme in an infinite dimensional space", in A. V. Balakrishnan / L. W. Neustadt, eds., *Mathematical theory of control* (New York, 1967). (The theory of mathematical programming over infinite dimensional spaces owes its origins to Hurwicz's work. Halkin's devotes attention to aspects specifically related to the theory of control).

53. E. M. L. Beale, "Numerical methods", in J. Abadie, *Nonlinear programming* (Amsterdam, 1967), p. 135.

    The reader's attention may be drawn in the context also to W. I. Zangwill's extensive treatment of algorithmic procedures in nonlinear programming (*Nonlinear programming: a unified approach,* 1969). Steepest ascent, Newton, cyclic co-ordinate ascent, Fibonacci, Bolzano, conjugate gradient, manifold sub-optimization, method of centres, a feasible directions, ϵ-perturbation are among algorithms considered in this study.

54. One of the virtues of convex and concave functions is that they are among the exceptional ones for which sufficient optimality criteria are formalizable; also that they are the only ones for which necessary conditions of optimality can be stated without resorting to linearization, cf. Mangasarian, op. cit. p. 54.

55. W. J. Baumol / R. C. Bushnell, "Error produced by linearization in mathematical programming", *Econometrica*, July-Oct. 1967.

56. Volkonskiy, in *EMM*, 4 (1967).

57. Ibid.

58. R. E. Gomory / W. J. Baumol, "Integer programming and pricing", *Econometrica*, July 1960.

59. L. V. Lyubovitskiy, in *Opt. plan.,* 13 (1969).

60. S. M. Anitsiz / V. I. Khokhlyuk, ibid.

61. V. I. Khoklyuk, ibid.; reference to G. T. Martin, "An accelerated euclidean algorithm for integer linear programs", in R. L. Graves / P. H. Wolfe, eds., *Recent advances in mathematical programming* (1963), pp. 311 ff.

62. R. Alcaly / A. Klevorick, "A note on the dual prices of integer programs", *Econometrica*, Feb. 1966.

63. Egon Balas, *Duality in discrete programming,* Technical Report no. 67-5, 1967, revis. Aug. 1967, Stanford Univ., Calif., mimeo.

64. J. F. Benders, "Partitioning procedures for solving mixed variables programming problems", in *Numerische mathematik*, 3/4 (1962).

65. cf. Egon Balas, *Duality in discrete programming: IV Applications* (mimeo.), Management Sciences Research Report no. 145, Oct. 1968 and literature quoted therein.

66. A methodology of solution developed for convex programming is of importance in our further context, i.e. devolution (and decentralization). Thus Varaiya, starting from a slightly modified usual convex-programme problem, shows how its different specifications yield different classes of problems amenable to solutions by decomposition. In each case considered he demonstrates the existence of a sequence of derived problems simpler than the original one such that solution to this sequence of problems yields a solution to the original problem. (Varaiya, "Decomposition of large-scale systems", in L. A. Zadeh/E. Polak, *Syste*

theory (1969); cf. also the same, "Decomposition of large-scale systems" in *International Conference on Programming and Control* (Colorado Springs, 1965).

67. A. Charnes *et al.*, "Effective control through coherent decentralization with pre-emptive goals", *Econometrica*, Apr. 1967.

68. W. J. Baumol / R. Fabian, "Decomposition, pricing for decentralization and external economics", *Management Science*, 1 (Sept. 1964).

69. A regime of direct, non-price corrective is treated essentially as a help in manageability by C. Almon in ch. 23 of G. B. Dantzig, *Linear programming and extensions* (Princeton, 1963).

70. Thomas Vietorisz, *Decentralization in non-convex systems* (1967, mimeo).

71. J. B. Nugent, "Linear programming models for national planning: demonstration of a testing procedure", *Econometrica*, Nov. 1970.

72. The issue has been recently considered in Soviet literature by V.M. Polterovich in a paper "Nyeyedinstvennost optimalnykh otsenok i problema detsentralizatsyi". Theses of 1st conference on optimal planning and control of national economy, Moscow, 1971.

73. A. I. Katsenelinboygen, in *Voprosy ekonomiko-matematicheskogo modelirovanya* (Moscow, 1971), and the same, in *EMM*, 3 (1972).

In the case of Katsenelinboygen the new stand does reflect the "second thoughts" – it revises the approach of his previous writings.

74. The model of vectoral optimization postulates "given" prices; that of scalar optimization "implies" Lagrangean-type prices. Denote for the k-th "participant": x^k-vector of products used, b^k-vector of resources available; y^k-scale of output, a_{ij}-input-output matrix. The "participant" of the socialist economy solves his problem (in canonical form – inequalities replaced by equations)

(1) under vectoral optimization – as

$$f^k(x_1^k,\ldots,x_n^k) \to \text{extr.}; \ \sum_{i=1}^{n} a_{ij}^k y_i^k = b_j^k; \ \sum_{i=1}^{n} p_i x_i^k = \sum_{i=1}^{n} p_i y_i^k; \ \sum_{k=1}^{l} x_i^k = \sum_{k=1}^{l} y_i^k$$

(2) under scalar optimization – as

$$F = \sum_{k=1}^{l} f^k(x_1^k,\ldots,x_n^k)\lambda^k \to \text{extr}; \ \sum_{j=1}^{m} a_{ij}^k y_i^k = b_j^k; \ \sum_{k=1}^{l} x_i^k = \sum_{k=1}^{l} y_i^k.$$

75. In passing I would indicate a noteworthy tendency to economic theory of East and West. What I am saying here points to the appreciation of the descriptive construct in the theory of the normatively planned system. Elsewhere I have pointed to the growing significance of the normative model in the theory of the competitive system.

76. The term "descriptive" identifies here a class of models – as contrasted with those built up on an explicit variational principle; the models have fully written down their equilibrium conditions; they have no explicit objective functions for individual participants or a system's criterion. Here the equilibrium model has the form

$$p_i^k = \phi_i^k(x_1^k,\ldots,x_n^k); \ \sum_{i=1}^{n} a_{ij}^k y_i^k = b_j^k; \ p_i^k = \sum_{j=1}^{m} a_{ij}^k q_j^k; \ \sum_{i=1}^{n} p_i x_i^k = \sum_{i=1}^{n} p_i y_i^k$$

$$\sum_{k=1}^{l} x_i^k = \sum_{k=1}^{l} y_i^k; \ p_i = p_i^k \lambda^k \text{ (the } q \text{ denotes the } k\text{th participant's "valuation"}$$

of the product).

77. "Some problems of pricing and optimal choice of factor proportions in a dynamic setting", *Economica*, May 1967.
78. cf. F. H. Hahn, "A stable adjustment process for a competitive economy", *R. Econ. Stud.*, 1962. This and Negishi's paper ("A theorem on non-tâtonnement stability", *Econometrica*, July 1962) pioneering the exploration of conditions to a non-tâtonnement quasi-stability of a pure exchange economy under certain behavioural rules. (For a comment postulating restrictions upon market participants' preference structures of services of an "umpire" with an authority for enforcing the desired transactions see E. C. H. Veendorf, "A theorem on non-tâtonnement stability – a comment", ibid., Jan. 1969.) cf. also Zauberman, in *Manchester School*, Mar. 1969.
79. E. Malinvaud, "Procédures pour la détermination d'un programme de consommation collective", presented at the Eur. Econometric Conf., Brussels, 1969.
80. Malinvaud, "Decentralized procedures for planning", in E. Malinvaud/M. O. L. Bacharach, eds., *Activity analysis in the theory of growth and planning* (London 1967). c.f. also *Canad. J. Econ.*, 1 (1968).
81. Malinvaud, op.cit., p.313.
82. Soviet economics has been introduced to the conception of price as "an instrument of indirect regulation" by V. V. Novozhilov, in *EMM*, 5 (1965), p. 647.
83. Zauberman, "The objective function revisited", *Jahrbuch der Wirtschaft Osteuropa*, Bd. 1, 1969, i: *Theorie der Plannung* (Munich Univ., 1970).
84. Rumyantsev, in *EMM*, 5 (1968).
85. Vishnyev, op. cit.
86. Ibid., p. 179.
87. The reader of Vishnyev will be cautioned on this terminology. What in my terminology is direct and indirect normative planning is in Vishnyev, respectively imperative (administrative) and normative planning.
88. A. Nataf, "Variante marginale d'un plan" in C. Parenti, ed., *Modelli econometrici per la programmazione* (Florence, 1965).
89. Lara Werin, *A study of production, trade & allocation of resources* (Stockholm, 1965), p. 137.
90. A. Qayum, *Theory and practice of accounting prices* (Amsterdam, 1960), p. 43.
91. M. Cerny / R. Ocenasek, *Some experience of experimental computations with the macroeconomic decision model for optimal medium-term planning*, and J. Skolka / M. Cerny, *Reflections on the economic interpretation of the solution of a dynamic macro-economic linear programming model* – both papers presented at the European Meeting of the Econometric Society, Brussels, 1969.
92. Cerny / Ocenasek, op. cit., p. 19.
93. There is an illuminating examination of the scope for devolution – in time and space – in the study of the French CERMAP model for the 1962-1991 Plan, by J. Bénard, "Modèle de croissance a long terme linéarisé pour l'économie française", *B. du CEPREMAP*, July 1968).

In the model, as designed, constraints limit the convex domain of production possibilities (it is because the constraints which express – for each branch and period – the limitation of production by prime factors are nonlinear that the model is conceived as nonlinear: some procedures of linearization are in fact applied). The convex domain is projected into the space of consumption and scarce resources.

For the model as designed the existence has been proved of equilibrium prices derivable from the plan programme's dual. But the examination has also shown that even for the relatively well-behaved model they do not form a system of signals permitting devolution in decision-making.

Owing to the assumption of constant returns to scale the fixing of the scale of output would be required. Also where the function $f(K^t/L^t, 1)$ is not strictly concave – the fixing of the techniques of production [K and L stand respectively for capital and labour]. The degeneration is shown to affect even more strongly the choice-making in consumption. The consumer would not be effectively instructed in patterning his consumption corresponding to the model's solution. (Under the assumption of the classical Cobb-Douglas function, decentralized decisions could be effectively made only with respect to the techniques of production, whatever the price system.)

Limitations of dual prices obtained from a plan programme are also discussed – in literature related to French experiments – in A. Moustacchi's comment, "The interpretation of shadow prices in a parametric linear programme" (P. E. Hart et al., eds., *Econometric analysis for national economic planning*, 1965). Some of the observations apply particularly to the specific model of resource allocation for the French 5th Plan. (Here one should probably place observations that the consumers are confronted with intertemporal choice between "bundles" rather than individual commodities; also on the nature of the equilibrium over time; also on the limitations of the dual price system due to insufficient explicitness of the model with respect to financial behaviour.) But some of the comments have a more general validity – among them are those which attribute discrepancy between price relations obtained from the dual and "true" optimal prices i.a. to aggregation.

94. Gyorgy Simon, "Ex-post examination of macro-economic shadow prices", *Economics of Planning*, 3 (1965).

95. E. G. Golshtein, in *EMM*, 4 (1968); cf. also the same, in *Doklady*, 5/172 (1967).

96. cf. L. V. Kantorovich, in *Doklady*, 28/3 (1940), and A. A. Kaplan, in L. V. Kantorovich, ed., *Matematicheskiye modeli i metody optimalnogo planirovanya* (Novosibirsk, 1966).

97. E. G. Golshtein / S. M. Movshovich (in *EMM*, 5 (1967)).

98. I. I. Pyatnitskiy-Shapiro et al., in *Doklady* (1968).

99. cf. Volkonskiy, in *EMM*, 4 (1967). A method of solution is offered in V. Z. Belenkiy, ibid.

100. Presented in Belenkiy, *EMM*, 4 (1967).

101. S. V. Zhulenyev, *EMM*, 5 (1970).

102. The alternatives considered are the distributions Cauchy, Poisson, and Gamma, respectively

$$G(t) = \frac{c}{\pi} \int_{-\infty}^{t} \frac{dz}{c^2 + (z - b)^2}, \, c > 0;$$

$$P\{b_i = k\} = e^{-\lambda} \frac{\lambda^k}{k!}, \, k = 0, 1, \ldots;$$

$$G(t) = \frac{c\gamma}{\Gamma(\gamma)} \int_{0}^{1} z^{\upsilon-1} e^{cz} \, dz, \, c > 0, \, \gamma > 0, \, \Gamma \text{ is the gamma } f.$$

103. V. M. Yefimov, in *EMM*, 3 (1970).

2

DECOMPOSITION THEORY

Foundations of the Theory of Devolution in Decision-Making

(1) What has so far emerged from our discussion of relating the "idealized" price parameter to a planned and controlled reality points to one remarkable fact. It is that of the intrinsic interdependence of what may be broadly termed "the correctives for unrealism" of the ideal construct — on various counts. What has also become clear is that the techniques for such correctives are intimately related to those for "breaking up" the system into some component parts, designed though these techniques are essentially for coping with the otherwise unmanageable size of a plan programme. In turn, reliance for such "breaking up" on price under optimization adds to our interest from the angle of the present discussion. (Clopper Almon very perceptively remarks that one of the most useful roles of the Lagrangean multiplier is that of decomposer or decentralizer[1].) Thus the connection between availability or the "realistic" optimal price and devolution comes into a sharp focus.

It is only right to make it clear that the problem of breaking up the economic system into subsystems with a sufficient degree of independence is per se a valid issue in the theory of its functioning. Hence decomposability — or lack of it — has been a question with which the contemporary economic "modeller" has found himself confronted; he is forced, that is, either to assume it away for the sake of simplicity, or to introduce it — with analytical implications; this is true in particular in dynamics As it would seem, Kemeny-Morgenstern-Thompson[2] were the first directly to attack the decomposability question for the case of the von Neumann-type dynamic system (since then others have made important contributions, in particular Morishima[3] and Weil[4]).[5]

To be sure the break-up of a matrix-formulated system into "primary" non-decomposable components has a much longer history — and its theory has naturally been assimilated by the planning theory and technique, together with matrix algebra, in the treatment of the plan's feasibility.

But the method of a systematic solution of large-scale plan programmes owes its foundations to Dantzig's and Wolfe's brilliant inventiveness. As originally designed the technique carries out the decomposition by means of an alternate solution of linear sub-programmes and one co-ordinating programme obtained from the component parts by linear transformation. (Conceptually it is thought of as a generalized programming problem, wherein columns are drawn from a given convex set; it thus leads to a generalization of the duality theorem: the decomposition procedure generalizes the simplex algorithm.) Note that already the original Dantzig-Wolfe[6] work explicitly alluded to the rationale of decentralization: indeed, the procedure was presented by them as a simulated decentralized iterative decision-making process wherein each independent part would offer a possible bill of goods — a vector of outputs with supporting inputs — to the central agency: the co-ordinator would work out a system of prices for paying each component of the vector (plus a "subsidy" to balance the cost) and elicit new offers from the parts; by using improved overall solutions he would generate a revised set of prices and subsidies, elicit new offers, and so on. In the original construct, the problem obtains a bloc-diagonal structure, thus helping the solution. (More recently a stochastic handling of the decomposition problem has been suggested by Dantzig and Madansky[7].) Its principal features are that: (1) it works with a central memory-retaining proposals; (2) it smoothes out oscillations in the quasi-tâtonnement process of information exchange, and (3) it calls for a quasi-complete central programme at each stage.[8] In practice the heavy burden of computation entailed by the last feature tends to outweigh the signal advantages of the others. Moreover, a difficulty in the Dantzig-Wolfe decomposition as a planning instrument is that of circular linkage. It presupposes for the operating unit, in the course of the operative procedure, the knowledge of values which it can gain only at the end of the cycle. Various ways of escaping from this have been attempted.

Note

In his more recent writings Dantzig[9] has admirably generalized the methodology for handling large-scale programmes and has indicated the place of decomposition technique proper within it. This methodology is ordered under three headings, i.e. those of (1) decomposition principle resting on sub-optimization along interior paths, (2) compact inverse, using a simplex variant, and (3) parametric variation by sub-optimization using simplex method. In particular, the dynamic structure would come under the second heading, including the dynamic Leontief economic model

and staircase system and Markov processes with alternative policies: also
bloc angular systems: we would include here the Kantorovich-Makarov
structure (see p. 406). In this attempt at systematization on the field
parametric methods appear as a variant of the standard simplex process.
Thus in one conceptual class a place is found for methods discussed elsewhere in this part of the book, i.a. for Rosen's partition programming,
Balas's infeasibility pricing, Beale's pseudo-basic variables; also for Gass's
dualplex method (related to Rosen's partition) with its block-pivoting.

(2) Before proceeding any further it may be advisable to relate our discussion, at least very loosely, to the operational function of devolution.
This in turn would require defining the concept involved – of decentralization.

Recent theoretical gropings while clarifying a good deal of its elements
have created a sense of definitional insecurity.

For analytical scaffolding one may easily borrow some elements from
statistical decision theory, and specifically from the J. Marschak-Radner
theory of teams.[10] We may postulate then a world with two sets of variables: decision variables which are controllable by economic agents, and
environmental variables which are not. Agents obtain information about
each other and about the environment thereby characterized by a relationship which is conceived of as a kind of "extremality". The system could be
then defined as completely or partly decentralized (the latter partitioned
by actions and time intervals) according to the structure and intensity of
informational (statistical) interdependence.

Hurwicz's[11] formalizations have greatly helped to discern some of the
definitional elements. To recapitulate, in his system the basis for classifying
allocative mechanisms as centralized, decentralized, and "in between" is
the prevailing type of inter-economy communication; where it is made up
of bids and prices we have decentralization; and centralization where it
consists of complete descriptions of technologies or (and?) preferences
or (and?) resource holdings (as it would appear, the degree of mixture
would determine the place of the "in betweens").

To continue, in Hurwicz, processes are "like competitive" where message
consist of vectors whose dimensionality is the same as that of the commodity space: in the case of central-planning-board processes the criterial
point would be whether or not a message consisting of as many real numbers as there are goods would effectively transfer a complete description
of the production function. As a matter of fact Hurwicz does see situations
where the reasonable communicational characterizing decentralization
fails to screen out processes par excellence centralized (but this is not
relevant for the purpose of his analysis).

The matter has been taken up by T. Marschak[12] with an eye to meeting "common discourse". His is essentially a dichotomy of centralized and "all the rest" of the "*non*-centralized" systems. For the former an agent "totally outside" the economy is introduced and he observes the signals between the agents (not from environment): if the process is centralized with information thus obtained he is able to reproduce the action sequence generated by the process.

Definitions presented here specify the conditions of potential decentralization — feasibility of decentralization (as it has been put, "decentralizability") in an optimally operating system. Our interest is rather in the characteristics of a system working under the principle. We also move farther in the direction of the "common discourse" by extending "informational decentralization" so as to embrace the processing of signals into decisions. With this in view we proceed from the other end, taking as decentralized a system where the "outsider"-agent ("centre" in the parlance of the real world) is either absent or confined to "pure" harmonization of other agents' solutions, that is to securing equilibrium without adjustment for his preferences. All other mechanisms are then "centralized". Positive "intensities", say some $0 < c < 1$ of the "outsider" agents' adjustments, would measure the degree of their centralization. Moving conceptually on a different, in a sense "technical" plane, one could definitionally discern "direct" and "indirect" ("parameteric") centralism, of the normative (mandatory) species depending on the technical nature of ("vertical") signals from the centre to other agents. Where these signals specify technologies, preferences or tasks in flows or stocks, it would be "direct"; it would be "indirect" when they are confined to providing parametric information; pricing would be here a particular case.

All Soviet models of planning decomposability presented in this chapter would appear on such definitions centralized, though to a varying degree, on one plane, and either "direct" or "indirect" — "parametric" — on the other. As the reader will see shortly the least intensive centralism (and the most indirect kind of it) is exemplified in the Volkonskiy model: and its characteristic is that the "centralizing" activities are partitioned between a number of agents, the $(J + 1)$ players. Under all the variants of the Pervozvanskaya-Pervozvanskiy model — whether with "individual" or "matched" prices — centralization is secured by matching them to the overall, that is the centre's objective function. In the Fayerman system the guiding idea is to simplify the setting of sectoral optimal problems — constraints and criterial parameters, to economize information by confining its vertical flows to signals on "global" resources; but the correctives in the process of harmonization reveal a centralized mechanism.

(3) The earliest design for devolutional processes in Soviet literature was suggested as early as a decade ago by Pugachev. The model[13] rests on approximating a production unit's output possibilities by some $\phi(x) \leqslant 0$. — a function bounded in the space x — or, over time, by some parametric system $\phi(x, t) \leqslant 0$. Convexity is postulated so that there would be an approximation by a hyperplane described as $hx \leqslant 1$, the h being the vector of its normalized coefficients understood as the coefficients of the production unit's (the firm's, the sector's) product substitution. The key problem is then how to determine the point-of-departure plan — the approximation point — by means of some "local" optimality criterion and of subsequent exploration of the $\phi(x)$ in the neighbourhood of that plan — by means of its shadow prices. In the general case the criterion would be of some form $W = pdx$ (on Pugachev's refutation of maximum profit as local criterion see p. 102). The procedure would follow the institutional ladder — to the top — and result in the solution of the overall programme under the overall optimality criterion. (A fuller investigation of the structure of the $\phi(x)$ in the neighbourhood of the optimal plan would possibly entail building up a set of optimal plans with varying output structures or varying values of parameters of the W, and then getting the approximating hyperplane through the points thus obtained.)

Pugachev has also initiated[14] in Soviet writing the conceptual elaboration of the relationship between the central and the local objective functions. Consider — so he has argued — a small dx in the kth element's functioning, the assumption being that it is the optimal prices that link the partial changes with the overall criteria. Over a time unit take the impact of the dx on the overall criterion U (whatever this may be, say utility) as some Pdx; or over the period $t_0 - t_k$ (the subscripts denoting the start of observation and the winding up of a unit),

$$dU = \int_{t_0}^{t_k} P(t)\,dxdt = \left[\int_{t_0}^{t_k} P(t)\,dt \right] dx,$$

$P(t)$ standing for optimal prices "reduced" — time-discounted — on the adopted principle. In the context the concept of integral prices of all resources is considered — for the k at t_0 — described by the vector

$$\bar{P}^k(t_0) = \int_{t_0}^{t_k} P(t)\,dt,$$

which is determined by two factors, the life-span of k and the nature of change of prices at optimum. Assume further that both determinants are supported by a forecast of their behaviour: then for each element's group some "proportionality coefficients" are computable between "non-reduced" optimal prices p at t_0 and the corresponding "integral" valuations (prices) — as above; denoting the diagonal matrix of these coefficients H^k, we have $P^k = H^k p$. Then to demonstrate the full impact of the improvement dx with respect the overall criterion U, we can re-write $dU = H^k p dx$, showing the integral of dx impact on k as proportional to $p dx$; in other words the "co-measuring", with reference to optimal prices, of components of any small dx would serve as all-economy valuation: a proposition exact in the last formula up to the multipliers H^k. This provides the valuation principle for social utility of small current changes in the operation of economic units. Over a longer period of life-span we have by integration

$$W = \int_{-\infty}^{t} dx(t_0) \int_{t_0}^{t_k} P(\tau)d\tau = \int_{-\infty}^{t} H^k p dx(t_0),$$

which is then taken as *the* local criterion that corresponds best to overall national-economic optimality. It is then claimed that by employing a criterion of this type we secure the maximum possible co-ordination of the overall social and the individual units' interests; ultimately the conclusion is drawn that W as the local optimality criterion permits resorting to the minimum of "directive" — mandatory — functions in a multilevel system of economic management. What in our submission qualifies the tenet is that this effect is secured under rather drastic simplifying assumptions in the formalization of the interdependence of the "local" activities and the overall objective.

By the early 1970s Pugachev and his associates[15] had made a notable attempt to relate his formulation of the local-versus-central criteria to the "state of art": to the possibilities — conceptual, mathematical, and computational — of multi-level optimization. Directly, as it is now admitted, the basic Pugachev formula for the local criterion,

$$W = \int_{(x)} p(x)dx,$$

(or, in dynamic restatement,

$$W = \iint p(t,a)\frac{\partial x(t,a)}{\partial a}\,da\,dt,)$$

fails to "concretize" the solution of the multi-level problem; indeed, the theoretical solution has not been found, as yet: many algorithms have been suggested — so far, however, attempts to prove convergence and provide a dependable method for appraising its pace have not been successful. Hence the present attempt to build up an empirically-oriented model: the focus is on the tolerable number of iterations in approximating optimum. The basic considerations in this are (1) the effectiveness of the adopted method for *inversible* condensation of information; (2) delimitation of an adequate *neighbourhood* of the "local-optimal" plan.

The experimental model when translated from the original matrix-vectoral into a scalar statement reads: max $U(y)$, possibly interpreted as a consumption-maximand, subject to

$$x_i^k + \sum_{s\neq k} x_i^s = y_i \geqslant 0, \quad i \in \underset{k}{\cup} I_p^k, \quad -\sum_k x_i^k \leqslant R_i, \quad i \in I_R, \quad -x_i^k \leqslant r_i^k,$$

$$i \in I_r^k, \quad x_i^k \geqslant 0, \quad i \in I_o^k, \quad x_i^k = \sum_l \sum_j a_{ij}^{kl}\xi_j^{kl}, \quad \sum_j \xi_j^{kl} \leqslant 1, \quad \xi_j^{kl} \geqslant 0.$$

(*Notation*: i is index of resources; k, s are indexes of branches, l is numbers of branches, j numbers of hyper-plans (vertices of approximating polyhedrons), I_k^p set of i-indexes related to output of kth branch, I_R set of indexes i for limited resources of kth branch, I_0^k set of indexes i for intermediate products of kth branch, y_i final-product components, x_i^k components of the input-output vector of the kth branch, r_i^k available volumes of limited branch resources, R_i same for the economy as a whole, a_{ij}^{kl} components of enterprises' hyper-plans, ξ_j^{kl} scales of hyper-plans.) The existence of a unitary system of resource valuation is postulated for the optimum:

$$\dot{p}_i = \dot{p}_i^k = \frac{\partial W_k(\dot{x}^k)}{\partial x_i^k} = \text{const } (k).(!).$$

In its ultimate aggregative statement the model has the shape:

$$\max \overline{U}_t(Y^t); (I - \overline{A}^t)X^t = Y^t \geqslant \overline{0}_t, \quad \overline{B}^t X^t \leqslant R_t, \quad \overline{0} \leqslant X^t \leqslant \epsilon_t$$

where ϵ is a vector of X^t dimentionally with all 1- components.

The crux of the matter now is the disaggregation of the all-economy indexes and re-calculation of the local-criterial parameters, and this is conceived of as some procedures of vertical and of horizontal "correctives":

Suppose that rather than *the* desirable branch plans $\bar{x}^{kt} = \hat{X}_k{}^t \dot{x}^{kt}$, the branches would obtain plans x^{kt} differing from $\bar{x}^{kt}$ by some Δ in outputs and coinciding with $\bar{\bar{x}}^{kt}$ in inputs

$$\bar{\bar{x}}_i{}^{kt} = \begin{cases} \bar{x}_i{}^{kt} - \Delta_i, & i \in I_p{}^k, \\ \bar{x}_i{}^{kt}, \end{cases}$$

then the task of disaggregation would be taken as completed for the (physical-term) primal of the plan. As to the dual, the plan for the kth branch should satisfy

$$\frac{\partial W_k{}^{t+1}}{\partial x_i{}^k}\bigg|_{x^k = x^{kt}} = \bar{p}_i{}^{kt}, (!!),$$

which appears as the necessary condition of the proper "correction" of parameters of the local criteria. Between them the (!) and (!!) give the number of equations corresponding to the dimensions of the branch plan x^k (note: the ratio between the number of parameters and plan dimension would, obviously, differ for different variants of the local criterion: would be 1 for the linear, 2 for the quadratic in canonical form, $(n + 1)$ for the quadratic in general form; what is relevant from the angle of workability is the number of variable, rather than that of all, parameters).

Such then is the "climb-down" in the ambitions of the plan-modelling architecture. Plans are seen as but "points of gravitation" in the process of multi-level optimization. Its adequacy becomes an empirical problem.

Note
The exercise has family affinity with that of Geoffrion's work on large-scale mechanisms[16] – in Western literature. Essentially he sticks, as far as general structure goes, to the Dantzig-Wolfe classic (except, that is, for the permitted (convex) nonlinearities).[17] The focus here is on computation . The system is taken as decomposable where optimization is of the form

$$\sum_{i=1}^{i=k} f_i(x_i) \to \max; \ x_i \in X_i; \ \sum_{i=1}^{i=k} g_i(x_i) \geqslant b \ (!)$$

(*Notation*: x_i an n_i-dimensional vector associated with ith subsystem, X_i permissible region of R^{ni}; f_i real-valued pay-off function; g_i real-valued function specifying the role of x_i in the m overall "system" constraints; b an m-dimensional real vector; the constraints relate to resource scarcities, to tasks and to interconnections (couplings) between subsystems; the f_i and g_i are concave on convex X_i; (!) is postulated to be solvable.) The (!) are linearly separable in the subsystems' variables; hence the postulated hierarchical or multilevel optimization. The types of co-ordination considered are those of "resource-direction" and "price-direction", a distinction which in substance amounts to that between the primal and the dual. Geoffrion's striking observation of patent relevance for planning techniques relates to the preference for "primalization" because *firstly*, a good feasible solution is usually known as initial, and *secondly*, it is available at some iteration step. The importance of the contribution lies in systematizing, and the novelty of some procedures in both solutional strategy and tactics, the algorithmic techniques resting on the three approaches, viz. the tangential approximation, the "large-step" subgradient (close to Lagrangean decomposition), and the piecewise approach.

(4) Another contemporary Soviet-designed model – that by Volkonskiy[18] takes up a more tractable task of optimality approximation as a process of improving the accuracy of a tolerably good solution available at the start. Here the maximand is some $\phi(u)$, a function of the number of "bundles" of the final product with its linear approximation written

$$\phi(u) = \sum_k z^k u^k .$$

The proportions, sector-("branch")-wise, of final output are given as the vector $\beta^1, \ldots, \beta^k$. We then write for the final product

$$y^k \geqslant \alpha^k + \beta^k u^k; \quad (k = 1, \ldots, K, \text{ indexing the sectors})$$

where α^k, β^k are some given vectors. The $u = (u^1, \ldots, u^K)$ is the vector sought. Denote further [a], [b], and [c] respectively the matrices of outputs (inputs) of external resources; of outputs (inputs) of intermediate products; of inputs of primary factors (labour and capacity-time), limited by some vector $m = (m_1, \ldots, m_K)$. Let now $x(t)$ and $p(t)$ be respectively the plan and price vectors obtained in the tth iteration. Then along the line analogous to the one-step cyclic process (the method of Seidel), or by the dynamic programming method, we successively solve the problem for each sector ("branch"); that of the last sector K will have the form:

$$\left[\sum_{k=1}^{K=1} p^k(t+1)a^{kK} \right] x^K + Z_K u^K = \max,$$

$$a^{KK}x^K - \beta^K u^K \geqslant \alpha^K,$$

$$b^K x^K \geqslant 0;$$

$$c^K x^K \geqslant m^K,$$

$$x^K \geqslant 0.$$

Then the solution sequence of the same problems is reversed (from K to 1); in each, right-hand sides of the first set of constraints are corrected to allow for values of the $x^k(t+1)$ obtained in solving the problems of the preceding "branches". Follows the second cycle, and so on. The economy is supposed to be organised in a bloc-triangular form, as it were a hierarchy based on the stages in processing primary material. In the procedure indicated here, the information flow from branch 1 to K — that is, from extracting to more and more sophisticated processing — is seen to secure increasing precision to coefficients of the objective function or shadow-prices of inputs for the branches that follow in the sequence; the flow in the opposite direction is seen to give greater precision to outputs. A word of warning as to the alternative suggested: Seidel's process may in actual fact converge more slowly than the usual process of successive approximations. Indeed it may diverge where the latter would converge.[19]

(5) In their original (1960) paper, Dantzig and Wolfe indicated the conceptual link-up of their construct with a game-theoretic formulation. This indication has been subsequently followed up by several students of normatively planned systems in Soviet literature — first of all by Volkonskiy. In another context we discuss the strong influence that modern general-equilibrium theory has exercised in recent times on Soviet planning theory — starting from Arrow-Debreu[20] theorems for perfectly competitive systems (the validity of which, as we note, has been rigorously established — under a set of strong assumptions — also for centrally planned economies by Gottinger):[21,22] this again would quite naturally direct those concerned

with decomposition of plan programmes to an equivalent game-theoretic formulation. There has been in fact expectation of its practical possibilities as well as appreciation of its cognitive importance. On the practical side the known virtue of an iterative game-theoretic procedure relates to the storing and transforming of initial data in a compact form — since what is fixed are the non-zero elements of the matrix and information as to their location: by itself this is of help in handling problems of large dimension with sparsely filled matrices.

Volkonskiy,[23] who applies some propositions of Fenchel's[24] theory of conjugate functions with respect to convex optimization, is working with the Arrow-Debreu type of competitive equilibrium for a convex planned system. This he restates as an iterative decomposition procedure in terms of a convex multi-person, non-coalitional zero-sum game of strategy portraying devolution, wherein the unique equilibrium point (Nash point)[25] coincides with the optimum (he establishes for this system the "homeostatic" — we would say Pareto-type — principle: divergence from the optimum would make at least one operational unit strive for a change, while equilibrium would be the unique state which none of the participants would tend to disturb[26]).

Of the n, the first K players are producer-units whose strategies are input-output vectors $y \in Y^k$; the next J players are the controlling agencies each in charge of sectoral supply and demand; the jth player's strategy $(j = K + 1, \ldots, K + J)$ are prices p_j (for the sake of mathematical simplicity, the domain of prices is taken to be bounded, $0 \leqslant p_j \leqslant P$). Finally, the $(K + J + 1)$st player, with the vectors x as his strategies, is responsible for "rational" planning of consumption not exceeding some S. He then tries to maximize his criterion $u(x)$ subject to $(p,x) \leqslant S$. In this a penalty system is operated: with penalty denoted R, the consumer's function is written

$$\phi_0(x, p) = u(x) - R[(p, x) - S]^+ \qquad [a]^+ = \begin{cases} 0 \text{ if } a \leqslant 0 \\ a \text{ if } a > 0. \end{cases}$$

The producer units $(k = 1, \ldots, K)$ are profit maximizers: their pay-off is then

$$\phi_k(y^k; p) = (p, y^k)$$

and for the controlling agencies

$$\phi_j(p_j, x_j, y_j,) = (p_j, x_j - y_j); \qquad j = K + 1, \ldots, K + J.$$

If the production-possibility sets, Y^k, are non-empty and convex and $u(x)$ — are continuous and convex upwards, the game is convex and has an equilibrium point. Each equilibrium point is one of optimum and vice versa; the $(\bar{x}, \bar{y}, \bar{p})$ is the saddle-point of the Lagrange function and the price is of the Lagrange-multiplier type.[27]

Patently the Volkonskiy game system is easily reducible to the Arrow-Debreu model. (Note that in his original fundamental paper Kakutani has proved that his generalization of the fixed-point theorem implies the von Neumann minimax; Brouwer's theorem is employed by von Neumann in establishing general equilibrium of the system.)

The conclusion reached by Volkonskiy[28] for the economic architecture is that inasmuch as optimality is related to general equilibrium, an equilibrium-restoring mechanism must be built in to secure workability and that this would be more effectively achieved by a sufficient dose of decentralization; very broadly, in Volkonskiy it would depend on the volume of information to be processed in plan construction and pricing.

The argument is pursued to its final consequence in contemporary Soviet writing by Makarov — in his model of what he terms the "mixed-planned system".[29] In his most recent construct such a system is steered, as it would appear, towards the centre's goals exclusively by means of "indirect" instruments such as quasi-taxation, profit-transfer parameters, and generally analogues of an Arrow-Debreu allocative mechanism (technically close to the Arrow-Kurz and recent Malinvaud ideas). It is shown that under a set of assumptions with regard to the functioning and organization of the economy the central agency can implement, with the use of such a box of tools, any from a rather wide range of criteria.

In a sense the Makarov results are stronger than those in some recent Western inquiries, in particular by Diamond and Mirrlees: Diamond-Mirrlees, to remind the reader, are employing taxes *and* public production in pursuance of the policy goal — the welfare maximand (they demonstrate the desirability of aggregate production efficiency *provided* that taxes are set at the optimal level; the results are akin to those of Marcel Boiteux working with lump-sum redistributions of income and optimal tax structure. (See references in n 29.)

Notes.

1. The present Note forms a link and in a sense anticipates the subject of the following chapter. For the construct Makarov presents to the reader is concerned with the optimized trajectories, which are very much in the centre of our discussion in chapter 3, but on the other hand it deals with the problem of equilibria (treated in both chapters) and moreover introduces a dichotomic structure of the equilibrium wherein its "local" and the overall facets co-ordinate themselves: and thus it investigates an

important property of a system's decomposition in optimal dynamics. This is the crux of its formalism. The model is given as that of a convex closed cone Z of production processes and a set of the population's preference functions, u; thus as some $M(Z,u)$ (its detailed formation by processes we omit for brevity). The trajectory's optimality is determined by a sequence of nonnegative ℓ-dimensional vectors $\lambda = \left\{ (\lambda_1(t), \ldots \lambda_\ell(t)) \right\}_{t=0}^\infty$. An admissible sequence is (u, λ)-optimal if, whatever the initial state, x, and some number $\epsilon > 0$, a time-point t_ϵ will be found such that

$$\sum_{\tau=0}^{t} \sum_{k=1}^{\ell} \lambda_k(\tau) u_k(\bar{c}^k(\tau)) + \epsilon \geqslant \sum_{\tau=0}^{t} \sum_{\kappa=1}^{\ell} \lambda_k(\tau) u_k(c^k(\tau)); \; t \geqslant t_e$$

(c denoting consumption).

The state of the economy $x = (\phi, \omega)$ determines the problem of equilibrium in the Arrow-Debreu sense (the bracketed terms are respectively capacities and manpower). Let there be, as given, the sequence of income-distribution matrices $\Theta = \left\{ \| \Theta_{ij}(t) \| \right\}_{t=0}^\infty$. The "local-equilibrium" trajectory corresponding to Θ is that sequence $\left\{ \langle \bar{\bar{x}}(t), \bar{\bar{c}}(t), \ldots, \bar{\bar{c}}^\ell(t) \rangle \right\}_{t=0}^\infty$ for which the bracketed vectors are determined by the Arrow-Debreu competitive equilibrium built up with the use of the vector $\bar{x}(t-1)$ and the matrix $\| \Theta_{ij}(t-1) \|$. With some additional assumptions with respect to the $M(Z,u)$, two theorems are formulated. *First*, for any sequence

$$\sum_{\tau=0}^{\infty} \sum_{k=l}^{\ell} \lambda_k(t) u_k(c^k(t) \geqslant K, \text{ for all admissible trajectories starting}$$

from $x(o)$, there exists a (u,λ)-optimal trajectory, and a sequence $\Theta = \left\{ \| \Theta_{ij}(t) \| \right\}_{t=0}^\infty$ can be found such that the corresponding local-equilibrium trajectory coincides with the (u,λ) optimal. *Second*, if the

$$\Theta = \| \Theta_{ij}(t) \| \right\}_{t=0}^\infty \text{ is such that } \sum_{j=1}^{\ell+1} \Theta_{ij}(t) \geqslant \epsilon > 0 \text{ for all } t > 0, \text{ then}$$

a sequence λ can be found such that the (u,λ)-optimal trajectory coincides with the local-equilibrium trajectory corresponding to Θ.

Naturally, the model shares the relation to reality with the Arrow-Debreu idealization on which it leans.

(The idea of the "mixed planned system", shunned in the past, is rapidly finding acceptance in present-day Soviet literature. It has been generalized i.a. by Primak[30] and his associates. He has related it to "general equilibrium optimality" (and his "equilibrium-optimal vector" for his system: for which the proof is based on the Kakutani theorem). Also a nonlinear exchange model of the Gale type is shown to be reducible to the equilibrium-optimal (the equivalence to the Arrow-Debreu model is also clear for some of the "equilibrium-optimal" designs as defined.))

2. Game-theoretic formulation has become a widely accepted method in modelling devolution, in particular in the case of an indicatively planned system. An attractive exercise in the latter category is a model designed by Albin based on "contract-bridge" bidding[31]; it is the more interesting as it tries to deal with the computational, as well as the consistency, convergence, and efficiency aspects. The conclusions are noteworthy also for their organizational implications pointing to the degree of operational freedom that is imminent in the approach. For the working of the model controls appear necessary such as to ensure the right starting-point in bidding within the feasibility space; also the setting of the "contract" formulae for penalties and rewards: counter-incentives and incentives; the last category is tricky in particular in respect of the necessary information flows. The intensity of controls required may justify some doubts (in our submission) as to whether the mechanism is compatible with a non-mandatory type of planning. But the exercise is of value for a theory of planning in general: in particular in demonstrating the limitations of the "formats" based on a two-party information exchange.

A more general "format" of a game-theoretic treatment of the devolutional control problem is adopted in Chidambaram's paper. It is concerned with co-ordination where the controller's task is to maximize overall utility and competition arises from constraints on strategies: the controller's authority to accept or reject strategies is argued to be sufficient to achieve the goal. (The postulated code of behaviour rests on conceptions of rationality in game situations.)

3. Attention may be drawn in the present context to avenues opened up by new methods provided by the complementary pivot theory (conceptions of pivoting method, whose origins are connected with the Gauss-Jordan elimination, and in the more recent past with Dantzig's simplex method, are thus moving one step forward). Lemke and Howson in particular have designed an iterative procedure for finding equilibrium points

of bimatrix games.[32] Here too the existence of the equilibrium point rests
on Nash's proof[33] employing the Brouwer fixed-point theorem (itself a
theoretical antecedent of the Kakutani theorem[34]).

(6) The present acclimatization in Soviet theory of the idea of a "mixed-
planned system" — as well as the Hungarian experiments — make us resume
the issue broached in the previous chapter: of the scope, if any, for combining the work of a formalized decomposition algorithm with that of a
market — as an integrated allocational-pricing mechanism for a planned
system. The kinship in logic — which is that of equilibrating the system by
supply-demand "proposals" or "bids" and the corresponding prices — has
made the idea attractive to more than one student. Thus, on the theoretical
plane, Kronsjö[35],[36] convincingly acknowledges the compatibility of his co-
ordination model for a large convex system with the Arrow-Hurwicz-Uzawa
type of a market mechanism. (The characteristic feature of such a mechanism, to recapitulate, is the penalty functions which tend towards infinity
at the approaches to the feasibility frontier and thereby keep the solution
within it; the main difference, as compared to the Kronsjö system, lies in
that, rather than basing the decisions on the economy's current position, it
elicits proposals of, and "memorizes", proposed activity and price levels.)

More immediately concerned with the applicational problems of a
socialist economy, Kantorovich and Gorstko broach the issue in a recently
published essay and accord superiority to a (Dantzig-Wolfe derived) formalized decomposition as the one that is faster and freer from loss entailed in
regulating the economy by means of the market mechanism. They do concede, however, the possibility of combining effectively — "within certain
limits" — the two mechanisms for a Soviet-type economy. The limits and
technique of their workable combination are not clarified and they are
crucial: for this too the Hungarian experience would seem to us enlightening. (The redeeming point in Kantorovich-Gorstko[38] is the remark that in
any case the mathematical "modelling" approach, combined with the
generalization of practical experience, traces the path for a scientific posing and analysing of the problems.)

(7) A variant of the game-theoretic type of a decomposition algorithm
has been constructed by Fayerman[39] — such as to save on the iteration
burden by concentrating — in the optimization process — on "universal"
resources and capacities. One of its chief features is a cyclical — termed
"oscillatory", in fact shuttle-motion — regime which organizes this process.

Its participants — the producers and controllers respectively of such re-sources and capacities — form a closed system with a postulated sequence logically following their role in the economy. Here is its substance.

Designate the outputs and inputs of each of the participating sectors w, as E_w and I_w respectively, the vectors of parameters of the respective pro-duction processes over a time-period as $x_w^E(t)$ and $x_w^I(t)$, and the system of feasibility conditions as W — possibly an operator or a functional of basic variables. And consider the shuttle-type iteration: having run a full cycle, the iteration is repeated in the opposite direction: a sector which was gen-erating the flows to others now absorbs them from other sectors; we start with the phase one of the cycle, with the optimal task for any sector, of the form

$$U_w = \int_0^T \rho_{j'}^{E'} w(t) E'_w [x_w(t)]\, dt = \max$$

$$E''_w [x_w(t)] \geqslant x_j^{E''} W(t),$$

$$I_w [x_w(t)] \leqslant x_j^I w(t),$$

$$W[x_w(t)] \leqslant 0.$$

The results will permit the calculation of the x's and the shadow prices, the p's. The first group of constraints appears in the form it has because its out-put is supplied not only to sectors w', through which the iteration has al-ready passed in its given phase, but also to all the rest w''. The operator of supplies for the latter, E'', does not participate in the sector's optimization since we have not as yet their evaluation — for the respective "buyers" of their production (from the all-economy point of view). In the general case such supplies are being fixed at the level of the preceding cycle: this limita-tion is being dropped in the reversed run — in the second phase.

Each cycle starts from the sector labour: it is when this sector has been reached that the course of iteration is reversed. The output and input of this sector is von Neumann-wise understood as differentiated man-hours and consumables respectively. In phases one and two it appears as, respect-ively, their "seller" and "buyer". The shadow price of labour appears as

$p_{j+1}^E = p_j^{E'} - p_j^{E''}$, the first and second terms of the right-hand side of this equation are the utility and disutility of the given kind of labour.

The problem (sectoral) in the second phase of a cycle has the shape

$$U_w = \int_0^{T'} (p_{j+1}^{E'} \, w \, E_w' \, [x_w(t)] + p_j^{E''} \, w \, E_w'' \, [E_w''(t)]) \, dt = \max$$

$$I_w' \, [x_w(t)] \leqslant x_j^{I'} \, w(t)$$

$$I_w'' \, [x_w(t)] \leqslant x_{j+1}^{I''} \, w(t)$$

$$W \, [x_w(t)] \leqslant 0.$$

The first group of constraints now pertains to supplies for the given sector from those which follow in the given phase — these correspond to the limits found in the first phase; the second pertains to the preceding sectors and contains limitations found already in the second phase. The functional contains parameters for the whole production: the shadow prices are derived from the second and first phases respectively for the sectors, predecessors and successors in iteration.

The algorithm is thought of as strongly devolutional. One of the virtues of the schema would lie in dispensing with much of the vertical "dialogue" characteristic of other multi-level algorithms: the central co-ordinating function would be carried out by planning the activities of a "branch" responsible for production and distribution of "universal" outputs and for the use of such capacities (resources termed universal — such as metals, fuels, labour, the engineering and building capacities — are those on which the pace and pattern of the system's development crucially depend). The open questions are: *firstly*, how far focusing on such sectors is sufficient to secure consistency; *secondly*, will the degree of control suffice for the purpose of normative planning; *thirdly*, will there be any net saving of time (costs) in iteration when the doubling of the cycle is taken into account?

(8)   The modelling of economic large-scale systems and effective devolution within them looks also for help to "physical" constructs: in Soviet writing Razumikhin's search for approaches is noteworthy for taking this direction.[40] The idea — incidentally, reflecting also the "interdisciplinary" drive — is to widen the scope for analogy by borrowing the apparatus from mechanics and thermodynamics. It is by starting from the physical properties of the system — operated with "ideal gas" as the "working body" — that a general methodology for the construction of algorithms for the solution and decomposition of the extremization problem, the "method of superfluous links", has been designed. The focus is on processes of transi-

tion from state to state, specifically — transition to equilibrium. An approximative solution can be made arbitrarily differing from the exact — since, patently, the physical properties of the ideal gas, in the regions of heavy pressure, may come ideally close to those of a non-compressible fluid. (By sequentially adjusting the character of the "superfluous links" the progress to equilibrium is realized by a sequence of intermediate states.) One of the attractions of the Razumikhin methodology[40] is the handling of the penalty-function tool derived from mechanics, where it is treated as a method for relaxing (discarding) the assumption of ideal relations rather than as that of an approximate solution of problems of the system's motion and equilibrium, under "ideal relations" (note, equality and inequality type of constraints in analytical mechanics are an expression of the concept of such relations). In a word the method is being employed for shifting the *idealized* solutions as close as desired to reality (rather than shifting the obtained solution as close as possible to the "ideal").

This method too has proved itself helpful in trying "rationally" to coordinate centralist control with peripheral autonomy.

Along these lines a "physical" model of decomposition of a large-scale problem and of iterative decomposition procedure has been constructed. (Algorithmically an equilibrium solution for an economy formed of branches with own objectives and budgets has apparently been obtained; the numerical solution algorithm of equilibrium exchange has been evolved,[41]

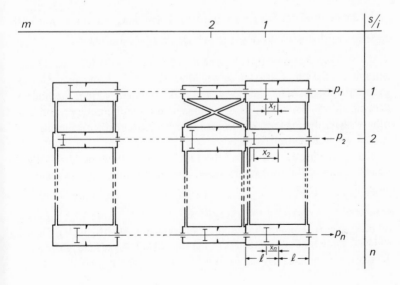

so has the equilibrium price vector for resources corresponding to equilibrium allocation and optimal sectoral plans.)[42]

Some Soviet experimenting with the formalism for the large-scale systems merits attention, in particular where random magnitudes are involved. In most cases one has to deal with a nondifferentiable function such as the extremized function in the system treated by Mikhalevich-Yermolev[43]:

$f^0(x,y) \to$ min, subject to $f^i(x,y) \leqslant$; $x \in X$, $y \in Y$; $i = 1, \ldots, m$ (!).

From Mikhalevich-Yermolev we can acquaint ourselves with a generalized method of gradient descent developed for the minimization of the non-differentiable function as above. [In the problem (!) the vector of generalized gradient for $F(x)$ is of the form $f_x^0(x,y(x)) + \Sigma_{i=1}^m u_i(x)f_x^i(x,y(x))$ where – when the x is fixed – $y(x)$ is the solution of the problem (!) and $u_i(x)$ the corresponding Lagrangean multiplier.]

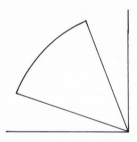

In the method considered a point x^s is being observed as it moves in the direction of the interior normal to $\{x : F(x) \leqslant F(x^s)\}$ that is

$x^{s+1} = x^s + p_s F_x(\dot{x}^s)$; $s = 0, 1 \ldots$ The experiments have confirmed that a suitable regulation of the step p_s would accelerate the convergence up to geometric progression. And this would make tractable various methods of decomposition, parametric programming, and game-theoretic procedures otherwise hardly manageable. In turn this is of patent significance for the formalism of decentralization.

Then a stochastic element is introduced: usually the functions of the objective and of the constraints would depend on some random event,

$f^\nu = \eta^\nu(x,w)$, $\nu = 0,1, \ldots, m$; and the probability is taken here to be expressed by $F^\nu(x) = P\{\eta^\nu(x,w) \leqslant b^\nu\}$; $\nu = 0,1, \ldots m$ (!!). In the method evolved it is assumed that some $F(x)$ is given implicitly in (!!). Then we will find some random vector $\xi(x)$ such that $E\xi(x) \approx \text{grad}F(x)$; therefore the stochastic process has the form $x^{s+1} = x^s - p_s\xi(x^s)$; $s = 0, 1 \ldots$ (!!!).

What appears to have been definitively established in experiments is convergence with probability 1 of the sequence at the minimum point $F(x)$ when the function is nondifferentiable and where there are additional constraints.

The experiments are also noteworthy for optimization in simulation models where we would have to minimize $F^0(x) = E\eta^0(x,\omega)$. Then tractable for minimizing related to (!!!) is the procedure where

$$\xi(x^s) = \sum_{k=1}^{v} \left\{ [\eta^0(x^s + \Delta_s \Theta^k) - \eta^0(x^s)]/\Delta_s \right\}; r \geqslant 1$$

(the Θ^k denotes the vector with components normally distributed over the $[-1, 1]$ interval and Δ_s is the shift operator over this vector).

(9) On the empirical plane, as it would seem, it is the Hungarians who have had relatively the richest experience in the numerical-algorithmic application of the game-theoretic algorithms in planning practice.

As the authors of the outstanding Hungarian construct have noted,[44] the matrix game is stated only in an implicit form since the pay-off matrix is not directly known: apart from computational difficulties, for this reason alone direct computing procedures would not be workable. Hence the idea of employing the "fictitious play" — on Brown's principle,[45] with Julia Robinson's iterative convergence method[46] — wherein against each central strategy of the regular polyhedral game it would be possible to find an optimal counter-strategy. The relative merits and demerits of the two alternative decomposition procedures — viz. that of Dantzig and Wolfe and of Brown and Robinson — were discovered in testing both: and the conclusion is broadly this. As expected, the advantage of the Brown-Robinson-based method proved to be that the plan dimensions are not restricted by the store capacity of the computers. Against this the classical Dantzig-Wolfe procedure shows itself advantageous on several counts: it is finite, faster in convergence, and monotonic; as against the rather erratic course under the Brown-Robinson-based procedure the objective function improves, under the Dantzig-Wolfe, at each step of the iteration. It is largely on the latter count that the Hungarian experimenters have given the verdict in favour of the Dantzig-Wolfe procedure, originally rejected as impracticable.

Eventually experience with the sophisticated algorithms has induced the Hungarian experimenters to content themselves with a far more modest technical apparatus.[47] The approximation method for which they settled is a naïve version of the original Dantzig-Wolfe algorithm. Specifically, as

against the latter, it fails to ensure reaching an exact optimum within a
finite number of iterative steps. The guiding idea is to make as wide as possible a use of non-optimal solutions at hand. What is stressed is that in any
case, if only because of the uncertainty of initial data, the exact optimality
– exact in the mathematical sense of the term – is of limited significance
in planning. This view, realistic though it is, still leaves open the question of
the distance between the solution obtained and the optimum, as well as the
question of practicability. However, in spite of the failures with more ambitious tools, the experiment does take at least an interesting step in the
development of techniques for multi-block plan-programming. One finding
of the experimenters deserves a particular emphasis in our view. It is that
whatever the organizational framework of the planning – be it centralistic
or decentralistic (indirect-centralistic) – plan-programming must embrace
all the basic regulation variables including those at the command of the
plan's addressees. (In the institutional framework of the Hungarian econom
these were taken to be, i.a., the branch-wise allocation of investment credits, or investment proposals relating to major projects, and export obliga-
tions; as against these the national income's growth-rate is taken as a
"prognostic" rather than regulation variable.) The argument in support of
the proposition rests convincingly on the intricacy of interrelationships. It
effectively militates against the widely represented idea that a sufficient degree of decentralization permits dispensing with the highly detailed (disaggregated) approach to the build-up of the central plan.

(10)   The fact that the solution of large programmes adequate for the
central economic plan has never been achieved as yet by any of the known
methods of exact iterative procedure has avowedly inspired yet another
endeavour – by Glowacki and Mycielski[48] in Poland – to secure tractability
of decomposition at the price of a degree of deformalization. Its theoretical foundation is eclectic, trying as it is to "mix" the Dantzig-Wolfe and
the Kornai-Liptak methods while mitigating their weaknesses. (The substance of the first is correctly seen by the authors in the application of the
central programme's dual as the criterial parameters in sectoral programmes;
and that of the second in the adoption by the centre as the criterion – for
direct task-distribution – of the dual variables of the sectoral programmes.
More questionable is the appraisal of the merits and demerits – with
respect to exactness in balancing, convergence and its speed.) Because of
the pessimistic view of the practicability of the "pure" version of the
methods, both on account of data collection and computation techniques,
they are "married" in the Mycielski-Glowacki system with the traditional

direct task-setting. What is obtained is the parallel use of parametric-type directives and direct commands (and in fact the duplicating of their roles). Consequently we have, in the sectoral models' solutions, a specific kind of dual variables — specific in the sense of evaluing the degree of consistency between the two elements of the combination. The advantage of "having it both ways" would be that on the one hand a feasible solution could be secured at each step of the plan construction before, that is, reaching the *optimum optimorum*; on the other the number of iteration steps could be fixed and the optimization process could be suitably fitted in in time.

While this method is quite likely to evade certain troubles known from the application of those which have served as its theoretical basis, its effectiveness must very much depend on the extent to which the direct-task element can, and indeed — to achieve its aim — must, be inserted into it. (The authors' idea is that the centre would resort to direct task-setting where the importance of a given balance and/or of a given operative unit concerned would be considered to warrant this.) The degree of arbitrariness might prove such as to undermine the principle of the adopted combination.

(11) When at the first Soviet conference on optimal planning and control (December 1971) a retrospective look was given to the history of the Soviet mathematical-economic school, three periods were discerned: (1) its emergence in the second half of the 1950s at the tangency plane of the several disciplines involved — mathematics, economics, and "cybernetics"; (2) the "assailing" of some fundamental problems of theory and application during the 1960s; and (3) the opening of the new phase of advance at the beginning of the 1970s — a phase whose main characteristic would be a *systemic* approach[48a]. I deal elsewhere at greater length with the "discovery" of that approach in the Soviet theory of economic planning,[49] but here at least some implications for the subject of this chapter will be indicated.

There are several facets which account for the attraction that the newly "discovered" discipline has found in the field of our present interest. Among them I would single out the coping with dimensionality — temporal and spatial — and providing the efficient informational support. It is these aspects which have of late led Soviet planning thought towards the investigation of the large-scale (or 'complex') system and its formalism originally understood as an extension of its programme-theoretic and control theoretic (see Part II) foundations. While retaining the tools from these two fruitful disciplines, it has been hoped that the systems theory would give

greater suppleness to the apparatus and thus help in handling such phenomena and processes as are not easily formalizable, of which the theorizer
in planning has been increasingly conscious.

There are, let us observe, certain "dialectics" in systems theory. On the
one hand, the system-theoretic approach is the outgrowth of the contemporary inclination towards a philosophy of treating "the whole" rather
than "bits and pieces" (on this cf. White and Tauber;[50] also one of Oskar
Lange's last works).[51] On the other hand, as noted, struggling with dimensionality entails in a "natural" way decomposition of the system – in
time and space, thereby – multi-tier (multi-echelon) hierarchical structures.
That has been indeed *the* principal concern of the Soviet theoretician of
large systems. What we can define as the direct and indirect (parametric)
variants of the centralist-normative system is by students referred to as
"*hierarchically* centralized" (on the other hand in the prevalent parlance
of Western writers, that would be a decentralized system). The "hierarchically centralized" control would be implemented in "open" or "closed"
schemas, depending on whether it materializes "from top to bottom" of
the system or also through some iterative inter-level co-ordination procedures. Decomposition raises the issue of preserving the regime of subordination within the hierarchy. Now, as conceived, the systemic organization
does face conflicts (this is indeed one of the principal subjects of its
theory); but it deals with them in specific co-ordination processes: by analytical processes – either, that is, by problem-solving, or by persuasion processes – or by "bargaining". It does so in the classical Simon[52] system, and
also in the present-day writings of the Mesarovic school (note that the co-
ordination procedure by means of "persuasion" has a tacit underlying
assumption: the reducibility of the family of goals to some common denominator.[53] We shall not probe at this stage into the validity of this
assumption.) What this means can be well observed in the Mesarovic-Macko-
Takahara decomposition performance.[54] (In this we have a conceptual
structure encompassing the postulates of the "infimal" decision-units' problems of co-ordinability as well as consistency of the subsystems' goals.
Logically, this covers the handling of conflicts due to sub-process-inter-
actions, specifically where these decision-units are mutually ignorant of
them. The co-ordinator's strategies ("structure of co-ordination") with respect to interactions can be (1) prediction, (2) decoupling, and (3) estimation
relating to "interface inputs" (or their combination). Respectively, they
mean that the latter are being predicted by a control-input, or treated by
each "infimal" decision unit as either an additional arbitrary variable and/
or as a part of decision x obtained from mapping $\pi_v : X \rightarrow Y$; and/or specified

by the co-ordinator only by their range, his co-ordination inputs γ in determining the set being $U\gamma \subseteq U$; the ith unit treats then the U_i^γ as the estimated range of disturbance. The decomposition problem – the finding of the "infimal" and "supremal" decision solution – is seen then as reducible to co-ordination synthesis, unification, and co-ordination procedure.)

The Mesarovic exercise in decomposition is of particular value in beautifully exemplifying the role of the system-theoretic mode of approach, its strengths and limitations. For decomposition is treated in a sense vastly broader than in mathematical programming:[55] it covers also "on-line" situations with "satisfactoriness" rather than optimum as the performance criterion (recall that generally Mesarovic borrows from Simon the conception of the "satisficing" rather than the classical "optimizing" man; which would mean an "administrative" rather than an economic man).

(12) For the Soviet case *the* issue confronted is how to devise an algorithm providing for the solution of a large-scale hierarchically organized plan-problem via that of a set of small-scale ones, blurred as the macro- and micro-scales are. The theoretician's job is thus to establish the existence of a sequence, be it finite or infinite, of computationally simpler problems whose solution leads to the solution or the original problem.

In other words, along with the exploratory objectives – call it, for short, the analytical penetration of the black-boxes – the direct impulse for the Soviet planning theoretician to study hierarchic decomposition systems has been first and foremost a computational one: the impulse specifically, that is, for coping with the size of the problem the plan programmer has to handle. At the root there is the observed fact of growth of the computational burden being disproportionate – in terms of computer time and/or computer storage-space – to that of the system's size.

Yet once you engage in breaking up the system into components – for basically computational reasons – the problem of behavioural centre-periphery co-ordination has to be treated explicitly. Bringing in an element of devolution becomes a matter of rational modelling. [As a student of systemic modelling Smirnov[56] put it: " . . . treating the system's structure as either fully centralized or fully decentralized leads – even if in a different fashion – to inferior quality of regulation: leads to ignoring the specific characteristics in the functioning of the economic system's components at different levels of the hierarchy".] In turn this raises the issue of motivation in behaviour.

(13) For a long time Soviet optimization theory was working with a homogeneous criterion. (It is essentially with this kind objective function that I have been concerned in my writing on the subject, to which the reader may be referred.)[57] One impact of the systemic approach on Soviet theory of planning has been to arouse greater interest in *multicriteriality*,[58] specifically with respect to *multilevel* systems. The idea is that, as often as not, it is necessary to replace the concept of some absolute optimum by that arising from a "compromise" solution. In Soviet system-theoretic treatment, the broadest outline of the focal issue of "concessions" entailed in such compromise will be found in Maiminas, in particular in his formulation jointly with Vilkas.[59] Take as the maximand, a vector function $F(x)=[(f_1(x_1),\ldots,f_n(x_n)]$ on $x \in M$; the conventional path is that of "concessions" or counter-concessions, "penalties". In the former we may start from some objective $f_1(x_1)$ and "yield" fixed "concessions" on all $i \neq j$, say some Δ_i, thus turning the problem into one of a programme $f_1(x) \to$ max subject to $x \in M$ and $f_i(x) \geqslant$ max $f_i - \Delta_i$. In the penalty-type formulation the problem is stated as $(f_1(x)+\phi_2(x)+\ldots+\phi_n(x)), x \in M$ where the penalty function, monotonically dependent on Δ_i, is the ϕ_i. Under a devolutional regime, the solution aimed at would be one corresponding to the Nash-Volkonskiy equilibrium. Otherwise the planner could work with some Pareto-weighted maximum: for the case of $f_i(x)$ convex on $X \in M$ for each Pareto optimum $\bar{x}$ there would be some non-negative $\lambda_i's$, adding up to unity, such that we would have

$$\sum_{x \in M} \lambda_i f_i(x) = \sum_{i=1} \lambda_i f_i(\bar{x}).$$

Next one of the co-authors has moved to a more specified statement of the problem in terms of a synthesis of partially aggregated orderings.[60] A system's goal-oriented behaviour is describable by the quadruple of parameters $\langle A, N, \mathscr{K}, \{\succ k\} x \in K \rangle$, the first three symbols denoting respectively the sets of alternatives in selection, of quality characteristics and of aggregation characteristics or "coalitions" $(K \subset N)$, and $\succ \mathscr{K}$ the relation of ordering on A. It is assumed that from individual orderings, under some regime, for each $K \in \mathscr{K}$, some aggregated ordering $\succ k$ has been formed; the problem is then one of extending the regime of aggregation over the whole set of characteristics N (the relative significance of the various groups of the latter is taken as deducible from the aggregations) the $\mathscr{N}$ subsets of N are ordered on this principle. Let a set of pairs $\mathcal{N}$ of all subsets of N, ordered according to the $\succ k$, be denoted R_k: the binary relation R_k, $k \in \mathcal{K}$ over A is assumed to be transitive and, for simplicity's sake anti-symmetric and complete (under certain assumptions).

The system $\mathcal{P}$ of coalitions $K \in \mathcal{K}$ is termed a "coverage" of the coalition C if for any $K, K' \in \mathcal{P}$ we have $K \cap K' = \phi$, $K \cap C \neq \phi$; $\underset{K \in \mathcal{P}}{\cup K \supset C}$. Further assume

$R_C(\mathcal{P}) = \underset{K \in \mathcal{P}}{\cap R_K}$; let $R_C^*(\mathcal{P})$ denote the set of all extensions of partial ordering $R_C(\mathcal{P})$ up to complete ordering. Suppose $\{R_N\}$ is the solution of the problem. Then $R_C^*(\mathcal{P}) \subset \{R_N\}$ if (1) C is not dominated with respect to the binary relation $\succ$; and (2) there is no $C' \subset C$ such that $C' \succ C \backslash C'$ and $C \backslash C' \succ C$. The system of orderings is "co-ordinated" $\{\succ k\}_{k \in \mathcal{K}}$ if R_N is non-empty; and it is complete if adding any coalitional ordering changes the $\succ$ relationship between, or within some non-dominated coalitions (proved to be transitive) results in non-co-ordinateness of the extended system. And it is proved that for a system's ordering having a unique solution it is necessary and sufficient that it be co-ordinated and complete.

And lastly, in our methodological sample, a large-systemic multi-criterial exercise relatively closest to the numerically oriented formalism is that by Lerner and Burkov:[61] an exercise in what is termed "open", multi-level planning. It is so inasmuch as it does correspond to the mechanism of planning and counter-planning familiar from Soviet experience. The system is one of three levels. Denote I the "centre", II the intermediate "active subsystem", III the active "element". Each "II" collects the preferences of the "III's", $s = (s_1 \ldots, s_N)$: in the process it builds up its own vector of preferences and submits them to "I". Then, for some project j the "I" solves the problem $\sum_{ij} s_{ij} x_{ij} \to \max$, $\sum_j x_{ij} = a$; $\sum_i j x_{ij} = 1$; $i = 1, \ldots, k$; $j = 1, \ldots, N$.

The "I" determines the "valuations" λ; the x_{ij} equals 1 or 0 where, respectively, the i-th "II" does or does not receive the project. Then the co-ordination conditions have the form $[\max_q (s_{iq} + \lambda_q) - (s_{ij} + \lambda_j)] x_{ij} = 0$; they are patently satisfied where λ is a Lagrangean multiplier under optimum. At the implementation stage the objective function of "III" takes the form $\mu_j + r_j$ where the first term denotes the "valuation" of the j-th project, fixed by "II", and r_j the yield from the realization of the j. Analogously, for the "I" (under assumption of proportionality) the objective function is built up as $\sum (r_{ij} + \sigma_j)$.

The "worst" distribution of valuations for "III" is then $\mu_j = 1/N.(S + M)$

$- s_j$, $M = \sum_1^N \mu_j$; the "guaranteed" value of the objective function is

min $[1/N.(S+M) - s_j + r_j]$, its maximum value being reached with N^j

$s_j = r_j + 1/N.(S-R)$ with $R = \sum_1^{N^j} r_j$.

The centre's system of preferences would be determined by the procedure of ascent. Take the intermediate level's behavioural rule. Denote π co-ordination from N projects on a, and τ the set of all co-ordinations, $F(\pi)$ the value of $\sum s_{ij} x_{ij}$ in the optimal solution, assuming the "II" has received the projects. The distribution of valuations that is the worst for the "I" would be

$o_j = (S+M)/N - s_j; S = \sum_1^N s_j, M = \sum_1^N o_j$. Here the guaranteed value of the objective function is $F(\pi) = 1/N.a.(S+M) - \sum_{j \in k} s_j$. The problem, treated as a linear programme, is then one of determining s_j which maximizes the min $\left[F(\pi) - \sum_{j \in \pi} s_j \right]$ — mathematically in an elementary fashion.

From here Burkov-Lerner[62] have moved to the exploration of workability of a co-ordination regime which could be defensible on the ground of the system's philosophy. By this we mean their formulation of the Principle of Fair Play for a large-scale machine-man system whose operational problem has the shape $\eta^i(\hat{Z}^i, \lambda) = \max_{Z^i \in A^i} \eta^i(A^i, \lambda)$.

(A is a set of feasible plans, Z a plan (the ^ denoting its version sent down from the centre), η the active element's objective function, λ the control vector). What is sought then is "*the plan*", $\hat{Z} \in \mathcal{Z}$, $Z^i \in A^i$, so that the maximum of the system's overall criterial function, $\Phi(\hat{Z}, \lambda)$, is reached. The issue is to cope with the centre's insufficient information on local potentials and information. Now under the "Fair Play Principle", each of the elements reports "upwards" a set of feasible plan versions B^i plus its own preference function $S^i(Z^i, \lambda)$ defined on B^i; it is this function that is used by the centre in setting the objective function. Suppose now $S^i(Z^i, \lambda) = \sim$ for $Z^i \notin B^i$, amounting to each element's having reported only the preference function on A^i; then the condition for planning what is "mutually beneficial" turns into one for what is termed "matched" planning of the form $S^i(\hat{Z}^i, \lambda) = \max_{Z^i \in A^i} S^i(Z^i, \lambda)$. Critically, but rather freely, it is assumed that a class H^i of *feasible* preference functions can be "identified" (although it is admitted that the preference function may not necessarily contain the objective function $\eta^i(Z^i,\lambda)$). The idea is then that since the "active element" can select reasonably its scale of preferences only from H^i, it is likely to adapt to the conditions of the system's functioning. One of the obvious handicaps is the system's instability where H^i does not adequately contain a preference function reflecting an element's aim.

This is one construct where the awareness of limitations of the apparatus has induced attempts — patently not lending themselves easily to effective algorithmization — to content oneself with some localized "quasi-optima". (Others have tried to formalize a quasi-optimality of the large-scale system, in particular Neimark.)[63]

Notes

1. In Neimark the large system's states, the s's, are subject to the regime $x(s + 1) = F(x(s),u(s) \, \xi \, (s),s)$ where $u(s)$ are control actions and $\xi \, (s)$ exogenous, uncontrolled, ones. The control problem consists in optimizing some adopted value measure R by means of the strategy $u(s) = f(x(s), \, \xi \, (s),s)$. The break-up into subsystems has as its corollary decomposition of both x and u into groups $[(x_1,u_1), \ldots, (x_m,u_m)]$. Denote variables x, except for x_i, as η_i and re-write the two equations $x_i(s + 1) = F_i(x_i(s),u_i(s), \xi \, (s) \, \eta_i(s),s)$ and $u_i(s) = f(x_i(s), \, \xi \, (s),\eta_i(s),s)$ (!). If the $(\eta_1, \ldots ,\eta_m)$ jointly with the ξ are considered as exogenous uncontrolled, then the equations (!) are treated as one "independent" description of subsystems. Further take as the strategy with forecasting of the form $u_i(s) = \widetilde{f_i}(x_i(s) \, \xi \, (s),\eta_i(s), \ldots , \eta_i(s+k),s)$, (!!) and assume that the admissible values of $\xi \, (s)$, $\eta_i(s)$, $\xi \, (s+1)$, are those among some set $\sum_i$ (the narrower it is the larger the information stock and possibility of forecasting). With these assumptions we have the intuitively understandable theorem to the effect that the large-scale system admits localized *quasi-optimal* control if the valuation of its performance R is a monotonic function of $R_1, \ldots ,R_m$ of the work of its subsystems, and if there is for none of the subsystems over the set $\sum_i$ a substantial difference in terms of optimal value of that function between the strategies (!) and (!!).

2. Problems of optimal allocation of scarce resources — on different levels of controls in a hierarchic multi-criterial system — are the particular subject of an enquiry by I. N. Kuznetsov (*Tekhnicheskaya kibernetika*, 4 (1970)). Operationally and computationally the most important finding is that where the objective functions on the different levels are mutually "compatible", the multi-dimensional allocation problem is reduced to a

hierarchy of problems of lower dimensionality. As a by-product of the inquiry the necessary and sufficient information volumes on the different hierarchy levels are determined. (An algorithm designed offers the way of finding optimal allocation in a particular case of the hierarchy with objective functions depending on the sum or the product of such functions of the lower-ranking level.) [Similar issues — allocation of resources and the setting of local tasks in hierarchic systems — are treated by V. Dokuchayev in his contribution to the volume *Matematicheskiye voprosy formirovanya ekonomicheskikh modeley*, Novosibirsk, 1970.]

3. Dealing with conflicting criteria comes up against serious difficulties when the attempt is made to quantify them. We may draw attention to procedures designed by Aleksandrov, Petrova, and Tsaturyan[64] for numeric comparison of alternative strategies in multi-criterial systems. Its substance is this. Consider a table of positive numbers

	w_i	...	w_i	...	w_n
v_i	w_{ij}	...	w_{ij}	...	w_{in}
...	...	...	...	...	...
v_i	w_{ij}	...	w_{ij}	...	w_{in}
...	...	...	...	...	...
v_m	w_{mi}	...	w_{mi}	...	w_{mn}

(*Notation*: v_i is variant of strategy; w_j and w_{ij} are respectively the criterion of appraisal and computed value of j-th criterion — understood as cost-benefit of the j-th objective — for the i-th strategy.)

The procedure is of a minimax type: we have in each column the minimal and maximal elements, i.e. $\min_i w_{ij}$ and $\max_j w_{ij}$. A matrix of "losses" $A=(a_{ij})$ is built up respectively with

$$a_{ij} = \frac{\max_i w_{ij} - w_{ij}}{\max_i w_{ij} - \min_i w_{ij}} \qquad a_{ij} = \frac{w_{ij} - \min_i w_{ij}}{\max_i w_{ij} - \min_i w_{ij}}$$

when the criterion w_j is to be maximized or minimized. The matrix of "gains", $B=(b_{ij})$ where $a_{ij}=1-b_j$ is built up correspondingly. Preference will be accorded to a variant for which the sum of losses for the set of criteria $P = \sum a_{ij}$ and the set of gains of criteria $Q = \sum b_{ij}$ are respectively minimum and maximum. For the respective indexes of the rows we will have sign$\left\{ \min_i \sum a_{ij} \right\}$ = sign $\left\{ \max_j \sum b_{ij} \right\}$. By summing up elements of the matrix A or B we obtain additional information on the relative degree to which the respective max w_{ij} or min w_{ij} are achievable on the respective j-th criterion for the set of variants under consideration.

(14)   The progress of the Lerner school well illuminates what we may call the modeller's dilemma: advancing in depth in the inquiry — gaining better insight into the working of the system — has to be paid for moving away from algorithmization. Hence what one can describe as a dichotomic line of advance in present-day Soviet exercises in multilevel optimization and system-decomposition. While some seek clarification of the potentialities of decomposition (and thereby of decentralization) with the use of what is by now the established systemic apparatus, others — "algorithmically" oriented — rely on the apparatus offering sufficient scope for numerical treatment.

We see then some inquiries aspiring to a systemic approach where the systemic specificity consists mainly in benefiting from the conceptual framework of topological and network structures within which the devolutional system's behaviour is observed and analysed; in some it is confined largely to investigating such a system's parametrization — its properties of "parametrizability".

An outstandingly important share in this class of Soviet theoretical writing must be accorded to the work of Pervozvanskiy and Pervozvanskaya and of Polterovich, which is acquiring something of a near-classical status. (Not least among their merits is the attempt to organize analytically the subject-matter of resource allocation in large-scale, complex systems.) For technical reasons I have had to transfer the presentation of their major models to the appendices; the reader is invited to acquaint himself with them. But here we would wish at least in a few words to note certain sobering observations by the writers of this school in their most recent publications (of the 1970s).

Pervozvanskiy's[65] worry now is the staticness of his celebrated construct. In the latest version the stress is on the decisive role — for decomposing the feedback-control problem of the economy into a set of lower-dimension ones — of its dynamics. Especially so with regard to the changing and more-

over usually incompletely known technological characteristics. The basic
element in the new construct is the effect of inventories; we have then in
actual fact only a semi- or quasi-dynamic system: and even then the conclusions of Pervozvanskiy are rather pessimistic as to the possibility of a
practicable rigorous solution for an overall problem with *mutual heterogenous deliveries*. Indeed, it is his view that only the "architecture" of his
model, viz, confining his exercise in approximate optimization to a
"localized" approach, has permitted him to secure whatever meaningful
results have been gained: has permitted him to shift what may be an insoluble problem to a set of independent problems of control, "in the small",
of inventories in "individualized" products; and the solution of the static
problems for a system as a whole — to give an "objective" estimate of
fluctuations in mutual deliveries. The conclusion reached, by itself not
implausible, then stresses the dependence of the system's efficiency on the
level of intermediate-product stocks through such deliveries: that is seen to
provide scope for allowing the basic plan programme for a supplies-inputs
imbalance as possibly feeding the inventories (this is formalized by means
of the familiar Charnes-Cooper and Kataoka techniques).

Polterovich's[66] is an algorithmically-oriented exercise technically relying
on a convex-bloc programming method and the related exercise in optimal
decomposition of a "productive system" into shortest networks. The algorithms designed for the "perspective" allocation of resources differ from
each other with respect to both the local criteria and the exchange of information flows. But generally speaking, the method, as Polterovich is
clearly aware, is a rather rough mechanism: he is no less conscious of his
algorithms failing to secure motion along optimal trajectory (at best yielding an approximation to the optimum). Indeed some handicaps and weaknesses are clearly evident; very major among them is the fact that no
allowance is made on the one hand for time-lags, including those in information exchanges, on the other for the speed of computers. Essentially
Polterovich's intention has been to build some apparatus corresponding to
a "universal" methodology of systemic control, to help a realistic "trial-
and-error" approach in decompositional procedures: in trying to localize
consequences of errors under such conditions rather than eliminating them
"once and for all". This is, quite possibly, as far as algorithmization of
decompositional planning in this field has advanced up to now: Polterovich
sees it in fact as but a "formalized illustration" of his propositions, the
algorithms reflecting each only this or that element of real economic processes; first of all, no claim is put forward for a formalism dependable in
co-measuring the alternatives' efficiency. (As far as computational

"realism" is concerned, note that no allowance is made for the computer's speed!)

The Soviet experience with the system-theoretic treatment of the plan problem might perhaps encourage some second thoughts; as to an apparent non sequitur in the mathematical planner's call for the application of the systemic approach to what does not easily lend itself to a full numerical treatment; for one would argue that only what is "numerable" and quantifiable, at least with some degree of approximation, may be taught to be plannable; and is there a way of planning the unplannable? But when pondering on this we have once again to meditate on the imminent limitations of any modelling of the real world. This is so if only because any formalization of it is condemned to select only some of the variables and functions which ideally should all come into its mathematical image.

(15) An observable shift of the gravity centre in contemporary investigation of devolution is informational. Significantly, the pioneering classic in the field, Hurwicz's concept of the late 1950s was redefined by him by the late 1960s as that of *informational "decentralization"*. Thus in particular the core of the devolutional theory as developed by the Berkeley team-theoretic school of thought — Radner, Jacob, and Thomas Marschak, and their associates — is informational par excellence. The trend in study and cognition has been well indicated by a member of this school (Groves):[67] in its postwar phase the devolutional inquiry had shifted from its initial narrower Lange-Lerner theme — of an economy's workability within some specific socialist organizational frame — to probing into decision-making processes compatible, in informational, incentive, and computational terms, with a wider range of organizational (not necessary socialistic) variants. (Note that in this approach an ideally competitive system may be contemplated as ideally decentralized, or indeed as a particular case of a centralist system with controls reduced to zero.)

Most of the probing has continued under the original premiss of a tâtonnement solution, viz. fixed environment, no uncertainty. This applies in particular to the celebrated construct of Arrow-Hurwicz and (largely also, inspite of the author's efforts,) to that of Debreu; the general equilibrium constructs which, as the reader of Part II of this book must become aware, have had such a powerful impact on Soviet thinking, specifically on Volkonskiy and on Makarov; and through him on the Kantorovich school in general.

However, in the present-day writing many of the "classical" premises are being abandoned or circumscribed. In its analysis of what is termed the "adjustment" mechanism — first and foremost the tâtonnement and decom position processes — the Berkeley school too links up with the Lange-Lerner theoretic framework, but its correctives for realism, which are very crucial ones, bring in the assumption of limited information, cumulative uncertainty, i.a. also through incomplete exchange of information among decision-makers (Radner).[68] Thus in Radner's construction the typical decision function, in particular the production function, has a random element; and his concept of information structure introduces the idea of the incompleteness of the knowledge of the state of environment (focal is the "η^{LL}" — the One-Stage Lange-Lerner information structure η.)

In the Radner-J. Marschak abstract framework the information processes shaping this structure would in the general case be affected by uncertainty. Hence they entail probability orderings.

Within this framework we have in Radner-Marschak two extremal situations:[69] one with no inter-communication (where the i-th unit's information function is $\eta_i(x) = \xi(x)$); the other that of complete communication; possibly where the system's information structure would be generated by all units reporting observations to a central agency which in turn computes the best actions and communicates them to those concerned (realism would postulate bringing in errors in communications to and from the central agency). Thence important conclusions for the appraisal of real-life devolutional systems: all but the simplest organizations are decentralized in this sense "to some extent"; this is so if only because, realistically, processes necessary to bring about a complete identity of information functions are expensive; still more capacities for handling and storing information. (Incidentally, as Radner points out in the context of decentralization, it is also an oversimplification to see a "market" as a homogenous category: different types generate different information structures.)[70,71]

The relativistic stand of this school is also decisive in the matter's of a system's "goodness". Thomas Marschak's[72] acknowledged influence on Soviet thinking is attributable to the fact that he submitted his proposition on the relative superiority of devolutional decision-making to rigorous scrutiny. As early as the late 1950s he formalized the basis of preference appraisal: obtained criteria for ranking alternative schemes and applied them to simple organizations; and he found that a general preference cannot be defended without severely restrictive adjustments of his model; again, as pointed out, all preferences indicated by the criteria adopted would be balanced against the cost of facilities in the systems compared. Marschak's discussion has shown that "to accept without further thought the superiority of decentralized systems over classes of systems, because of their informational autonomy or other properties, is to evade the issues involved in such comparisons".[73] This approach — call it the "non-generality" approach — has been further elaborated in Thomas Marschak's more recent examination of the problem of comparative "goodness" (as now defined, one scheme is better than another — in T. Marschak — if, very roughly speaking, it reaches appropriate new actions more quickly when the information-handling capacity at the disposal of the participants is equal). The relativistic stand has now reached the point at which it is argued that study of the general problem of optimal design of "teams" is unlikely to be fruitful, even for the comparison of specific adjustment processes such as the price mechanism.[74] The abstract-theoretic "non-generality" approach has found strong expression in empirical considerations.[75]

Thus, as it were, the Western and the Soviet inquiries met on the new "platform" of relativism, starting from opposite points of departure. The Western investigation has moved from, and abandoned what amounted to, an axiom of superiority of devolutional decision-making; and the Soviet one has moved from the extreme antithetic stand. The problem as treated in both is that of "degree" of devolution rather than devolution as such.

(16) Contemporary Soviet inquiry while, as has been pointed out, sharing the classical general-equilibrium foundations, is focusing too, and increasingly so, on the informational aspect. In adopting it, it has, nevertheless, some specificities stemming from the economic system's postulated organizational and institutional characteristics. Some of them tend to simplify the treatment of the modus operandi of the informational mechanism. Broadly speaking, under a normatively-planned system the interaction between information-gathering and decision-making (and the corresponding feedback) has a more circumscribed form, thus easing the task of the theoretical modeller as compared with a competitive organization (including, conceptually, a Langovian type of market socialism).[76] Or, to take another trait, the task of the modeller is also eased where the information flows are not constrained by private ownership and secrecy of information data produced or acquired: a constraint for which Western theorizing must allow when bringing abstract constructs closer to reality.

Further, while to the Western theorist the decisional autonomy of the operational level is a *positum*, it is not so to Soviet theory. The degree of autonomy is not a matter of principle; relating this degree to the informational mechanism (seen as "cofunctionally" dependent) is essentially a matter of architectural convenience. The substance of the issue is one of effective economic — informational organization and computation (incidentally the aspect of the propelling mechanism — mechanism of incentives — is not considered in this context either). In other words, what the Soviet student is concerned with is constructing most economically a model for gestating, processing and operating a volume and pattern of information as related to the system's interrelationships and its dimensions in space and time, such as to ensure maximum efficiency. Thus the modelling of the system's informational structure is seen as a part of the theory of its scale and complexity. The build-up of this structure presents itself as one of many trade-offs; the cost of generating, processing, and operating the volume of information is one of them. (However its quantification in Soviet-type mandatory planning is more difficult than in a system where the pricing of information and its elements is carried out by the market.)

Note

We feel, it should be made clear that the notion "informational", as it appears in the last two sections with reference to theories and approaches, has a rather wide sense. It embraces the information-theoretic discipline and approaches in the strict sense; it covers also the Radner-Marschak team-theoretic disciplines and approaches. (Problems of the former and its application are treated at greater length in my paper 'Notes on systemic approach to large-scale decentralization and related matters', *Jahrbuch der Wirtschaft Osteuropas* 1973, Munich University).

Our concern is with information "economics" characterizing an informationally optimal system (defined as their subject in Radner and J. Marschak).[77] In so far as systems theory, specifically general-systems theory, is concerned with optimal information-processing as well as decision making, the overlapping is clear *ex definitione*. This remains true of the "large-scale" systemic approach, the one with which we are specifically dealing here, and which boils down to mathematically "distilling" basic properties of information processing and decision-making structures (the nexus between the approach through abstraction and the multilevel or hierarchic approach — i.e. that resting on system-decomposition and solving subproblems independently — is easily demonstrable, both with respect to motivation and handling the substance, even though from various points of departure.)[78]

(17) What has been said points to a novelty in Soviet theory: viewing system-decomposition as fundamental in the theory of planning (decompos

tion understood in the context as substituting simpler, informationally connected, subproblems for the more complex overall problem). To be sure, its rough lines have been inductively developed over the half-century of Soviet planning. But the economy's growing complexity and the need for translating the co-ordination rules of the system into such algorithms as could lend themselves to the use on a computer have encouraged replacing these rough lines by rigorous, inductively arrived at methods of decomposition; the aspiration for an all-economy automated system of planning and control has been a stimulant in this direction (Ennuste).[79] Thus the problem of the economy's effective co-ordination presents itself as one of decomposing the flows of information in accordance with the adopted hierarchic structure of the system: its point of departure are the values of co-ordinating indices – the plan of the means of co-ordination forming the "instrumental information" to be employed in the solution of the sub-problems (which in turn feeds the co-ordinating centre with "indicative" information). Here too thinking in terms of information flows (and memory) has moved the plan-theoretic analyst and modeller away from a deterministic stand; the planner's goal becoming – in the Radner-Marschak language – his *expected* utility.

Thus a good schematic design of a "bi-co-ordinational" information-oriented decomposition, drawn up by Ennuste,[80] makes a system with all its parameters – coefficients – being random magnitudes described by mean values and dispersions. Its balance relationships have the form

$$E\left[\sum_j g_{ij}(x_j) - b_i\right] \geqslant 0; D\left[\sum_j g_{ij}(x_j) - b_i\right] \leqslant \bar{d}_i; \ i = 1, \ldots, m$$

(the plan of the j-th operational unit is described by the vector $x_j \in X_j$, the X_j forming the constraints on the control of the system which possesses resources – material and informational: the volume (state) of input or output of each, the i-th, resource is constrained by b_i; the operational unit's technologies are described by the g_{ij} function). Of the two inequalities the first states the conditions to be met by expectations; the second limits, by its $\bar{d}$, the deviations from the balance. The alternatives faced by the central planner appear then as some trade-offs. The problem may be of such a trade-off between an activity's cost entailing informational content and risk: the planner's choice could be that of less exacting informational requirements, say requirements in technological information, and greater dispersion of expected results, and vice versa; in this way the resource information has its dual (marginal value) which can be found from the solution of the programme. The impact of random factors causing dispersion — both "subjective" resulting from the planner's incomplete information or "objective", due the environment's uncertainties — could appear in a trade-off against some "insurance", in particular from reserves neutralizing this impact. Here the central planning agency would promulgate prices on dispersions as well as material resources; the price of the former would be the insurance premium payable in the operational unit's work with a given randomness. Thus, assuming stochastic independence, the "local" problem would have the form

$$f_j(x_j) - \sum_i \lambda_i E[g_{ij}(x_j)] - \sum_i \eta_i D[g_{ij}(x_j)]$$

where η_i is the price of risk for the i-th resource. The central agency would promulgate limits for both mean values and dispersion.[81]

(18) The relatively most complete formalization of an "organizational" hierarchical economic system in information-theoretic terms — in Soviet literature — is that owed to Babunashvili, Berman, and Russman:[82] it is conceived in Trapeznikov's[83] fascinating study of control as a "struggle to escape entropy" (the latter is defined).

Some of its constructional assumptions and postulates are: (a) the notion of information quantity is that of Shannon, (b) the relation full information produced/unit value is linear or piecewise-linear.

The system is such as idealized in a graph where X is the sets of "objects" x and y, for the controllers and controlled respectively, Γ is some non-unique transformation: when $y \in \Gamma x$, there exists in G an arc (x,y) — meant to form a communication channel; we have also $G = (X,U)$ where U is tee set of arcs. Let I_1 be the quantity of information supplied to the controlled q_1 — a unit value to user including transmission costs; thus $I_1 q_1$ is full value. Now the loss due to information deficit; the required information quantity and its deficit are respectively I_2 and $I_2 - I_1$, $(I_2 \geqslant I_1)$. When the value of deficient unit is q_2, we have as the condition of optimal control (with respect to information) a minimand:

$$Q = \begin{cases} I_1 q_1 + (I_2 - I_1)q_2, & I_1 \leqslant I_2, \\[2mm] I_1 q_1, & I_1 > I_2. \end{cases}$$

If, realistically, constraints are assumed on volume of produced information and on the transmission capacity, the I_1 minimizing q will be $0 \langle I_1 \langle I_2$.

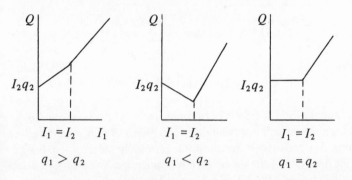

The next stage is the formalization of the overall problem of optimizing the economy's information flows. We have as before $G = (X, U)$ such that the arc of the graph $(x, y) \in U$ agrees with the arc's capacity $c(x, y) > 0$ in terms of the flow's velocity in bits/t, the t denoting the time horizon. For each vertex $x \in X$ there is $[a(x), b(x)]$, the two arguments standing for required and produced information respectively. Over the arcs G the flow function $f(x, y)$ is sought such that

$$0 \leqslant f(x, y) \leqslant c(x, y),$$

$$\sum_{y \in x} f(y, x) \leqslant a(x),$$

$$\sum_{y \in x} f(x, y) \leqslant b(x),$$

the three constraints meaning respectively that the information flow would be nonnegative and would not exceed the information channel's capacity; that supply would not exceed demand for information; that emission would not exceed output of information. Confining now the unit values $q_1(x)$ and $q_2(x)$ to information used only, and denoting the corresponding $q_3(x)$ and

$q_4(x)$ as information produced by x, the cost and loss entailed in producing and obtaining information for x will have the form (the optimand being $\sum\limits_{x \in X} Q(x) \to \min$):

$$Q(x) = q_1(x) \sum_{y \in x} f(y,x) + q_2(x) \left[a(x) - \sum_{y \in x} f(y,x) \right]$$

$$+ q_3(x) b(x) + q_4(x) \left[b(x) - \sum_{y \in x} f(x,y) \right]$$

The assumptions — of information being always of the necessary kind, being always correct and free from disinformation and thus noise-free — are very strong. The construct's significance is essentially didactic — in bringing out the handicap of the modeller in fundamentals. The analogies drawn by the author from mathematical biology ("Dankov's principle") are but common sense: "buy" more time at the cost of looking for more information or try to operate more effectively with a lesser volume of it. The validity is confined to situations where the economic optimand is reducible to time and only to time.

(19) The matter of decomposition of a large-scale system touches upon certain technical problems which, though related to control and information-theoretic aspects (and thus belonging to our Part II), may be usefully treated here.

1.   One concerns the "control by aggregation". Aoki's contribution stands out for its importance and influence on Soviet thinking.[84] It offers a method for approximate treatment — analysis and synthesis, both deterministic and stochastic — of a large-scale system through generalization of the aggregation concept as evolved in mathematical economics; this is dynamized by using for the subsystems the technique of weighted averaging of the state vectors. What Aoki handles by means of the state vector partition is not merely the size problem. Several other matters gain as by-products of the inquiry (such as, in particular, those of regulators with incomplete state feedback, characteristic-value computation, and bounds on the solution of the matrix Riccati differential equation).

2.   The second issue concerns the "information loss" resulting from aggregation — a matter which has had some noteworthy contributions over the last few years. Orcutt-Watts-Edwards[85] (employing the Monte Carlo method) started their inquiry from the premiss that the consequences of aggregation are not affected, qualitatively, by the relative numbers of the

cross-sectional units. This premiss has found support from the Bayes-based Kelejian inquiry (extending Chetty's results).[86] However, in analysing the nature of the information lost in aggregating he has found that the conditions which have to be postulated to keep the built-up variance-covariance matrix unaffected (even asymptotically by the use of cross-sectional data), are quite strong.

Note in the context the findings of Moeseke and Ghellinck[87] on decentralization of systems formulated as separable programming, as defined. The problem is defined as additively separable (relative to domains X_k)

when of the form: $\max \sum f_k(x_k); h_k(x_k) \leqslant b; x_k \in X_k$ where $f_k : R^{nk} \to R$,

$h_k : R^{nk} \to R^m; b \in R^m, X_k \subset R^{nk}$. Here the feasibility constraints are partitioned, and for a large class of cases it is shown that given a set of nonnegative prices for competitively allocated resources (the redundant being "free"), maximization of individual profits, within capacity limits, maximizes overall returns. The generality implies embracing non-differentiability of functions (findings are particularized for the case of convex separable programming).

(20) Time and again have we tried to convey the view that because of the particular Soviet angle — the angle of a theory of *mandatory* planning — the interest of Soviet theorizing lies first and foremost in the *algorithmic* aspect of the devolutional modelling. That is why, we submit, it is illuminating to see how its constructs appear to be, and are, systematized by the Soviet inquiry into algorithmization in our field. For this we turn to the Martines-Soler[88] work, although its classificatory framework does not always effectively delimit the overlapping characteristics.

This framework is formed of three classes — labelled the "centralized", the "games-type", and the "iterative-aggregative". In turn in the first class — depending on the way the set of the subsystems' admissible plans are approximated — two subgroups of the centralized algorithms, which we denote respectively as "1" and "2", are discerned; these are typified respectively by the classical Dantzig-Wolfe, and by Polterovich's "block-method"[89] construct. Their information-exchange mechanisms work respectively on the "price-plan" and "plan-plan" schemas. In "1" we have a sequential stage-by-stage improvement of the overall criterion which monotonically tends towards the optimum; in "2" the centre's and the subsystems' plans tend, in their motion, to the optimum, towards some point of "encounter". Put in other terms, that means that "1" corresponds to the case where the sets of admissible plans of subsystems Q_k are being approximated in the central model, as it were, endogenously: the Q_k, that is, is "mapped" into that model by a convex combination of subsystems' admissible plans from among some finite collection. Against this, in "2" the Q_k are exogenously approximated by collections of the subsystems' draft plans which, at each iteration, are determined from the solution of the subsystems' problems: like those in "1", they serve the purpose of adding precision to the representation of the Q_k in the central problem. In other words the solution of the centre's problem yields a draft plan which generally may fail to meet the subsystems' constraints: the subsystems' problem is then to select a plan variant which, while satisfying all the local constraints, would least possibly differ from the centre's solution.

In the game-type class the subsystems' models contain, in addition to local constraints, supplementary constraints with respect to the build-up of the subsystems' mutual relationship. Again we have here two subgroups ("1", "2") represented respectively by the Pervozvanskaya-Pervozvanskiy[90] and by the Kornai-Liptak[91] and the Volkonskiy (1965)[92] constructs. In "1" all that the centre promulgates are the "limits" (the values of exogenou given parameters related to the overall constraints); in "2" the centre in addition promulgates the parameters of local criteria. Hence in "1" the subsystems, starting from the overall criteria, determine their optimal plans and the dual valuations of the "limits"; these serve the centre for the purpose of forming the central model's local criteria: with reference to them the centre redistributes the "limits" in favour of those subsystems where the dual valuations are the highest: the rule of the game is equalization of valuations at optimum. Under "2" the centre carries out the "averaging" of the plans: of their characteristics, in particular the dual valuations.

Finally, the class of iterative aggregations. In substance their objective is to determine the coefficients of substitution of products and resources: their values, that is, which correspond to the plan's optimum. One subgroup ("1") typified by the Volkonskiy (1966)[93] and the Gavrilyets (1963)[94] models, consists in aggregating, by means of the corresponding dual prices, stage by stage, the subsystems' constraints with respect to output, to input of resources, and to capacities; and at the same time in aggregating the admissible plans, in accordance with the proportions obtained (i.e. in accordance with the coefficients of substitution) in the solution of the subsystems' problems. The coefficients are employed in forming the central aggregated model while the valuation and proportions (substitution) coefficients obtained by subsystems in the recursive iterations add precision to the aggregated indices; in turn the solution of the aggregated problem, and the parameters thereby evaluated, are used by subsystems for making their solutions more exact.

In ("2") the approach, first formalized by Pugachev,[95] consists in approximating the subsystems' production possibilities when "mapping" them into the centre's algorithms. As a result of the centre's solution, each subsystem is given draft plans and dual valuations of resources in the aggregated "nomenclature". These data are adhered to by the subsystems in their mutual transactions and in formulating detailed plans and valuations starting from some local criterion. The emphasis, in the Martines-Soler reasoning lies in the fact that in this class, unlike the previous one, local criteria must serve as evaluators of the system's optimal functioning as well as planning: the local criterion in the algorithm of multilevel planning is conceived of as an instrument for appraising the plan version as such – its technical aspect of harmonizing the solutions – rather than for assessing economic activity. The logic of this distinction is, however, not clear.

We may now return to the classifying properties and ask what is it that brings the diverse constructs into one family – the class. It is the way the point of departure is decomposed. Thus from this point of view the difference between the aggregative iterative class and the rest – the "block algorithms" in Soviet terminology – would be this: while the former too carries out decomposition into submodels, its terminal model is structurally of the same general shape as the starting-point frame although stated in the aggregated parameters. We would say that a system's property of decomposability into components, each of which contains controlled parameters related exclusively to the given subsystem (with the system's corresponding ability of allocating and reallocating the "limits" as between the systems), is in Martines-Soler too restrictively attributed to the game-type class.

The overall assessment of the stock of formalized algorithms broadly agrees with ours. It is that (a) while well reflecting substantive features of real economic processes the available constructs are still rather rough models of multilevel planning, (b) they suffer from some patent technical weaknesses, such as inadequate coping with integer-type and stochastic processes; (c) the convergence conditions of iterative aggregation in particular are not established completely and with full rigour.

POSTSCRIPT

(21) In his recent writing Kornai and his associates[96] appear to have abandoned the idea of price as the principal efficiency indicator and instru-

ment of decentralization (see also Part II). As it is now seen, in both roles it would be replaced by a rather vaguely indicated set of instruments; the main one, to which most of the formalized thinking is devoted, would be the indicator of the state of stocks, specifically of inventories.[97] (In a somewhat more general fashion that is related to the dichotomic characteristic of the state of the market: the "pressure-suction" situation; on a very broad definition there prevails a *"general pressure"* over the entire economy if pressure exists on a large number of important products of the market and suction appears only sporadically; the state of *general suction* can be defined analogously.)[98]

As it would appear, Kornai's motivation in disowning the theoretical position with which he was largely identified in the literature of the subject has to some extent empirical roots. The Hungarian economy, like all other socialist economies, is permanently a "suction" economy on Kornai's definition. Secondly, as he tells the reader, since the late 1960s, when central directive control was drastically reduced in Hungary, at least in the sphere of short-term decisions, only a relatively small part of the economy has been guided by a "pure" price-mechanism adapting itself to the market equilibrium.

First and foremost, Kornai's present stand[99] is related to his fundamental disequilibrium approach to the planning problem. In its negative aspect the rejection of the Walras-derived general equilibrium theory, as transplanted into the theory of socialist economics by Oskar Lange in his famous papers of the 1930s, rests on not unfamiliar lines of reasoning as to the unrealism of its usual assumptions. This pertains in particular to the type of optimization postulated for the firm, specifically the extremization of the behaviour-summarizing index, profit, or a synthesizing plan-fulfilment index rather than some complex response function (the independent variables being "impulses" received, orders from trade-partners, prices, "social effects", and the dependent ones being production activities, output, techniques employed). Further points concern the assumed convexity of the relevant relationships, also the information structure – the implied perfect certainty; above all the staticness of the system with which the general-equilibrium theory traditionally works. This theory, empirically "empty", so Kornai insists, should be replaced by one focused on deviations from equilibrium; in its normative orientation it should deal in particular with specific characteristics of a "surplus" economy – existence of idle resources – and a "shortage" economy with maximum use of capacities. The points made are that firstly, "pedantic" investigation of conditions of the static equilibrium is sterile, and, secondly, it is not the static equilibrium that is desirable but "deviation and momentary realization of aspiration and success".[100]

(A certain kinship is discoverable in Soviet literature with ideas represented by Mikhalevskiy. It is well arguable, in our submission, that while the study of deviations from equilibrium as characteristic of the real-world situations — indeed the adoption of a suitably defined and qualified "disequilibrium approach" — is a legitimate subject of inquiry in the theory of normative planning, general equilibrium is still a helpful construct as a broad theoretical framework and a starting point of the analytical inquiry.)

To continue the Kornai-type argument. It concerns the point that it is the general-equilibrium theory that supplies the standard proof for the economy's capability to operate under the most simple of control and signal systems — the price-control system; this again then appears as related to the highly restrictive and unrealistic assumptions of that theory; in particular the proposition that price is information-saving is related to the assumption of perfect certainty. To sum up, because of the common assumptional basis, the conception of price as the sole and effective control signal and decision-parameter for a planned system stands and falls with that of general equilibrium in dynamics. (The Kornai school questions i.a. the proposition that Schumpeter's doubts as to the efficiency of the competitive system in dynamics would be resolved in the theory of a centralist system.)[101,102,103]

There again operating a system, and in particular a dynamized system, does create a dilemma and calls for devising some correcting mechanisms. (Cf. in particular in the context footnote 106 on the Hahn Enigma. Nor can one question the technical limitations of the optimal price as determinable under the present "state of the art". But parting with the price as an essential steering instrument leaves the devolution in decision-making in large systems without a quantifiable steering tool, one obeying if only sub-optimally a social criterion of goodness. This would seem to be the consideration which has stopped the Soviet protagonists of the systemic approach from drawing the kind of conclusions for the issue of the signal-parameter mechanism that Kornai has arrived at; this seems to be true even of that branch of the Soviet school which subscribes to the general-disequilibrium theory.

It may, however, be noted that the line of the "Eastern" mathematical reasoning has, as it would appear, an independent corollary in Western theorizing on socialist planning. I have in mind in particular Bliss's contribution to the subject,[104] the main points of which are that: there is no necessary nexus between a price system (implying profit as the maximand)

and efficient resource allocation; the dichotomic Barone-Lange conception of the physical-term decisions and pricing formed respectively by the market and by the planner has no "inherent" reason; the growing interest of the economists in planning under the conditions of scale economies underlines the last point. Thence the conclusion that a price-market system is "very unsuitable" for solving the problem of efficiency, which anyway is far from a solution even on an abstract level. The conclusion, as we can see, is much closer to the Hungarian than to the Soviet stand (but it shares with the latter an emphasis − even if admittedly of different strength − on the "organizational" aspect; see below). We may also recall what has been said on Pervozvanskiy's present-day stand as to the possibility of a feasible, rigorous solution of the overall problem for even only a *quasi*-dynamic system with mutual heterogenous deliveries; and on the architectural "tricks" he resorts to by shifting his "insoluble" problem to the set of independent problems of control, "in the small", of inventories (see above).[105]

Notes

1.   The problem of dynamic equilibrium and stability has gained a new focus in the Western writing of recent years − around what we may term the "Hahn Enigma".[106] It has been shown by him from several angles that a uniquely determined momentary competitive equilibrium in output composition presupposes some restrictive assumptions, yet these have evaded casual interpretation; the reaching by the system of any golden-age equilibrium, as in the celebrated simple Solow construct, would fall thereby under some question mark. On the normative plane the question of constraints to be imposed on the production function would arise.

The issue of the Hahn Enigma has been taken up by several writers. Samuelson[107] has argued that most of designed accumulation corresponding to perfect foresight deviates in any case from any golden-age turnpike; but heuristically adjustments should reasonably be expected to be secured by trial and error and speculative correctives. Specific correctives in the institutional environment are postulated too in K. Shell/J. Stiglitz[108] and in Burmeister-Dobell-Kuga[109] (starting from the proposition that the Hahn indeterminacy in a system's development is crucially influenced by anticipated capital gains rather than by heterogeneity of the capital stock as such: hence the concentration on the question of the type of the saving function − as in the original Solow system).

It is in such a framework that the debate in Western literature has led to the problem of the design for a workable mechanism. It has passed completely unnoticed in Soviet literature. However, we may note Samuelson's convincing obiter dictum[110] in the debate to the effect that in a Soviet-type economy the indeterminacy has to be resolved by the planner's aiming and re-aiming at each plan-interval to reach a given goal, naturally assuming ing his awareness of the goal.[111]

We have opened this chapter with the presentation of Kantorovich's pioneering idea – of some decades ago – of the parametric coefficients immanent in the "real" optimum solution of the plan problem. It may be apposite, then, to end it with his present-day view of the search for parameters dependable enough to *regulate* the system.[112] First, we may turn to the search under an approach increasingly attractive to the student: that of a numerical method of national-economic plan solution. Here the weakness lies (in the view of Kantorovich and Makarov) in focusing on algorithmic convergence for extremely idealized structures: the advice is to give more scope to numerical experimentation and adjustments in testing the convergence speed and the latter's dependence on the parameters' values (in this possibly reversing the overall procedure): instead, as is habitual, beginning with a formal statement of the extremization problem and next seeking the solution, starting rather from formalization of the (observed) behaviour and then trying to detect the substance of the problem thereby solved. The precept is, in a word, to be more empirical in what is by its very nature empirically oriented. (Does not difficulty lie precisely in the scope for *conclusive* experimentation?) One's surprise is greater at the diagnosis and therapeutic suggestions for what purports to be an inductive analysis of a "mixed economy": models, that is, postulating decomposition of the set of parameters to be controlled by the system's diverse components, the class which in Kantorovich-Makarov comprises Debreu's and Morishima's[113] constructs, as well as those of Makarov himself (including his latest equilibrium-type model with the planner's box of steering tools reduced to transferring operational profits – via the central agency – as between the basic operational units – see above p. 67). The Kantorovich-Makarov conclusion is that for the construct, as designed, a central agency can – by means of a sufficiently small number of parameters – impose any from among a sufficiently large set of "reasonable" criteria. But then – here lies the emphasis – the system's general equilibrium rests on a set of hypotheses as to the economy's *functioning* – (including, among others, those on the regime of profit maximization and securing that none of the units can materially influence its own prices). For the moral of the present Kantorovich-Makarov stand is that operational indices of an economic system cannot be considered by abstracting from its *"organization"* — which is understood to mean in particular the structure and the component inter-links — the stimulation system and administrative and legal "norms". Such, then, is consequently the framework which, in this view, conditions first and foremost the problem of pricing: indeed its analysis is argued to be incomplete without relating it explicitly to the prices work in a specific *organizational* framework.

What has been said in this section indicates both the length and the direction of the path along which the Soviet optimization thought has travelled over the years. Thus, firstly, it has remained faithful to, and, indeed, if anything fortified in, its general-equilibrium approach as basic to its theorizing in abstracto. But *secondly*, the new stress on the "organizational" aspect points to the extension of theoretical scaffolding beyond that of original programming formalism; this leads directly to the control-theoretic approach and beyond it to an orientation towards the "organizational"-systemic (system-theoretic, information-theoretic) inquiry. The former is the subject of Part II of this book; the latter is the theme of my separate study.

2. The Pugachev school's probing, on a theoretical plane, into the working of a shadow-price mechanism in a hierarchical system has been paralled, over a decade or so, by systematic empirical testing. The results of the latter, as formulated in the 1970s — of crucial relevance for planning theory and practice — are very roughly these:[114] (1) from the angle of convergence a *quadratic* objective function is relatively the most helpful one; (2) bringing in a central co-ordinator speeds up the process: hence the need for some tradeoff between degree of decentralization on this and on other counts; (3) employing, in steering the system, prices *as well as* quantities is more dependable than using either prices *or* physical quantities alone (note a remarkable coincidence with results of Malinvaud's conjectures and reasoning;[115] conceptions of "planning without prices" (e.g. G. Heal)[116] do not seem to find support).

Note also the findings of A. G. Aganbegyan, K. A. Bagrinovskiy, and A. G. Granberg[117] to the effect that merely introducing prices from the overall optimal plan does *not* ensure optimum of local plans.

APPENDICES AND ADDITIONAL NOTE

Appendix 1
Pugachev,[118] evolving his "local criterion", has taken as a positum that all-economy minimax pricing does secure optimality in decentralization. In

conventional notation the criteria are, respectively in statics and dynamics,

$$W = \int\limits_{(a)} P(a)\frac{\partial x^k(a)}{\partial a}\, da = \int\limits_{(a)} P(a)dx^k(a); \text{ and } W = \int\limits_{(a)} \bar{P}(a)dy^k(a), \text{ where } W$$

$x^k(t) = \overset{0}{x}{}^k(t) + y^k$, the y^k being an arbitrary vector independent of t.

Optimal prices are thus expressed as a function of the parameter "a" along some interpretative curve of integration in the space x^k. In the case of $\bar{P}$ we have "summation" of prices over time yielding the "integral price" (the difference is then that the integration is carried out in the space y^k); we have now

$$\frac{\partial \bar{P}_i}{\partial y_j{}^k} = \frac{\partial \bar{P}_j}{\partial y_i{}^k}, \quad i \neq j, \quad \nabla W(y^k) = \bar{P}(y^k), \quad W = \int\limits_{(y^k)} \bar{P}(y^k)dy^k.$$

Take the uni-parametric family of realization

$$y^k(l, t_0) = \begin{cases} y^k(t) \\ y^k(t_0) \end{cases} \text{ with } \begin{cases} t < t_0, \\ t \geq t_0. \end{cases}$$

For this family we have

$$\frac{\partial x^k(t,a)}{\partial a} = \frac{\partial y^k(t,t_0)}{\partial t_0} = \begin{cases} 0 \\ \dfrac{\partial y^k(t_0)}{\partial t_0} \end{cases} \text{ with } \begin{cases} t < t_0, \\ t \geq t_0. \end{cases}$$

$$P(t, a) = P(t, t_0).$$

Hence the transformation

$$W = \iint\limits_{(t, t_0)} P(t, t_0)\frac{\partial y^k(t, t_0)}{\partial t_0}\, dt_0 dt = \int\limits_0^\infty \frac{\partial y^k(t_0)}{\partial t_0}\, dt_0 \int\limits_{t_0}^\infty P(t, t_0)dt =$$

$$= \int\limits_{(t_0)} dy^k(t_0) \int\limits_{(t \geq t_0)} P(t, t_0)dt,$$

where the internal integral $\bar{P}(t_0) = \int\limits_{(t \geq t_0)} P(t, t_0)dt.$

Appendix 2

1.   While Hungarian experiments with the Robinson algorithms had
proved a failure, those undertaken in the meantime in the Soviet Academy
of Sciences have been claimed to pave the way for a successful application
of the Brown Principle in iterative methods of optimal planning.[119]

The formulae determining the solution process under the Brown method
can be written

$$x_k = \lambda_k \widetilde{x}_k + (1 - \lambda_k)x_{k-1}; y_k = \mu_k \widetilde{y}_k + (1 - \mu_k)y_{k-1}$$

with $\lambda_k = \mu_k = 1/k$.

(*Notation*: k is the number of iteration; x and y are pure strategies of each
of the two players, respectively, and $\widetilde{x}$ and $\widetilde{y}$ their respective mixed
strategies.)

The slow convergence of the iterative process has been found[120] to be
related to the non-variability of the λ_k and μ_k which are fixed in advance.
Hence attempts to overcome this disadvantage by computing their values
at each iterative step rather than fixing their sequence in advance. (It has
been shown that under some additional assumptions it is sufficient for the
convergence of the Brown-type processes that the numbers λ_k, μ_k satisfy
the conditions:

$$\lambda_k \to 0, \mu_k \to 0 \text{ when } k \to \infty; \sum_{k=1}^{N} \lambda_k \to \infty, \sum_{k=1}^{N} \mu \to \infty \text{ with } N \to \infty.)$$

The variants experimented with lead, just as does the original Brown
method, to a change — at each step — of only one component of the current mixed strategy. But it is maintained that a choice of the players' mixed
strategies, related to the analysis of the game generated by some submatrix
of tolerable dimensions, can substantially accelerate the iterative procedure.
Further interesting suggestions are made by Golshtein and Movshovich[121],
who advocate a symbiosis of solution methods of games and "noncongruent"
systems of linear equations. Insofar as most of the components of current
mixed strategies, corresponding to the zero components of optimal strategies, tend rapidly to decline in value, it is suggested that, as soon as this
point is reached, they should be put equal to zero and the remaining components determined by solving a system of linear — in the general case noncongruent — equations by some iterative procedure.

2.   Good results have been reported in Soviet experiments with an
algorithm produced by Amvrosyenko.[122] In the usual Brown-type iteration

process each player applies several times one and the same strategy, and the number of repetitions tends to grow with the number of iterations. Amvrosyenko's idea is to replace repetitive moves by a single iteration. With the simultaneous choice of strategies after iterations, the number of successive repetitions is determined by the smaller of the ℓ's where

$$\ell'_j = \left\{1 + \left[\frac{s(AW^{(s)})k'' - s(AW^{(s)})i}{a_{ik'} - a_{k''k'}}\right]\right.$$

$$\ell''_1 = \left\{1 + \left[\frac{s(U^{(s)}A)j - s(U^{(s)}A)k'}{a_{k''k'} - a_{k''j}}\right]\right. \quad \text{where} \quad \begin{cases} a_{ik'} > a_{k''k'}, \\ a_{ik'} \leqslant a_{k''k'}, \\ a_{k''j} < a_{k''k'}, \\ a_{k''j} \geqslant a_{k''k'}, \end{cases}$$

$$i = 1, 2, \ldots, m, \quad j = 1, 2, \ldots, n$$

(where k'' is the number of the maximum element of the column $AW^{(s)}$, k' is the number of minimum element of the row $U^{(s)}A$, a_{ij} are elements of the A matrix). The precision of the solution of the matrix game is usually measured (under the Brown method) by $\epsilon = c/\sqrt{N^{n+m+2}}$, where m, n are the dimensions of the matrix, c is a constant depending on these and the form of the matrix, and N is the number of iterations. For a matrix with elements distributed uniformly over $[0, 1]$, Amvrosyenko obtained $c' = 0.003(n)^2$.[26]

3.   In Soviet literature the game-theoretic approach to the solution of the plan-programming problem is seen, as far as techniques go, as an alternative i.a. to that of penalty-function methods. One such method, designed by Bulavskiy, is akin to that of Uzawa (the iterative process takes into its optimand a "small" non-linearity: the solution is reached with the help of some auxiliary quadratic-programming procedures). Apparently the Computation Centre of the USSR Academy of Sciences has had particularly good results with the method elaborated in Poland by Tomasz Pietrzykowski.[123]

Take the plan programme problem as

$$L = (C, X) \rightarrow \max,$$

$$\varphi_i(X) = (A^{(i)}, X) - b_i \geqslant 0, \quad i = 1, 2, \ldots, m,$$

$$\varphi_{m+j}(X) = x_j = (e_j, X) \geqslant 0, \quad j = 1, 2, \ldots, n_1., n,$$

where $A^{(i)}$ is the i-th vector row of the matrix of constraints and e_j an n-dimensional identity vector. Assuming $A^{(m+1)} = e_j$, $b_{m+1} = 0$; $i = 1, \ldots, n$, the constraints are restated as

$$\varphi_i(X) = (A^{(i)}, X) - b_i \geqslant 0, \quad i = 1, 2, \ldots, m + n_1.$$

Then the following functional (assuming $C = 0$) is built up

$$G_\mu(X) = (C, X) + \frac{\mu}{2} \sum_{i=1}^{m+n_1} \delta_i \left[\varphi_i(X)\right] \left[\varphi_i(X)\right]^2,$$

where

$$\delta_i \left[\varphi_i(X)\right] = \delta_i(X) = \begin{cases} 0, \text{ if point } X \text{ satisfies the } i\text{-th constraint} \\ -1 \text{ otherwise.} \end{cases}$$

In the Pietrzykowski model the penalty is made dependent on deviation represented by the function

$$\Phi(\varphi) = \sum_{i=1}^{m+n_1} \Phi_i(\varphi_i) = \frac{\mu}{2} \sum_{i=1}^{m+n_1} \delta_i(\varphi_i) \left[\varphi_i(X)\right]^2.$$

As has been pointed out, the convergence of the method will not be affected if the penalty function is replaced by any smooth function which decreases monotonically with the growth of φ and turns into zero when the constraints of the plan problem are met.

Appendix 3

The Pervozvanskaya and Pervozvanskiy[127] basis problem is stated in these terms: find for each component — sector — of the system ϵ_i the "use intensities" of means of production and intersectoral deliveries such as to

maximize the value of the final product $f = \sum\limits_{i \in J_1 \, (n+1)} z_i P_{i,n+1}$, subject to constraints on, respectively, overall output, intersectoral deliveries, external deliveries, and "own" resources

$$B_i u_i = \sum_{j \in J_1(i)} P_{ij}; \quad C_i u_i = \sum_{j \in J_1(i)} D_{ij} P_{ji}; \quad \sum_{j \in J_1(0)} P_{0,j} = b;$$

$$u_i \in U_i'', \ (i = 1, 2, \ldots, n).$$

Notation reflects the specific constructional approach. For each sector ϵ_i we have a column matrix P_{ij} of output supplied to other sectors ϵ_j; the total output of the i-th sector is thus

$$P_i = \sum_{j \in J_1(i)} P_{ij}.$$

Further, the final output is treated as "sector", ϵ_{n+1}; thus the final bill of goods — production delivered to the ϵ_{n+1} — is

$$\sum_{i \in J_1(n+1)} P_{i,n+1}.$$

We have further matrices: z_i of fixed prices of final production, B_i of output; C_i of cost; D_{ij} of the "use of supplies". In the adopted interpretation u_i is a set of control parameters.

Two alternatives of the generalized structure are formalized in Pervozvanskaya-Pervozvanskiy according to the mode of price formation: one of them is the case of prices formed "individually", the other that of "adjusted" prices.

To start with the former, there the Lagrangeans λ', λ'' are treated for each component as the sellers' and buyers' prices respectively. The problem for the ϵ_i — that of price adjustment — then has the form

$$f_i(\lambda_i', \lambda_i'') = \max_{u_i \in U_i''} (\lambda_i' B_i - \lambda_i'' C_i) u_i,$$

while the centre's problem is to minimize

$$\{ f(\Lambda) = \lambda_0 b + \sum_{i=1}^{n} f_i(\lambda_i', \lambda_i'') - \lambda_i' + \lambda_j'' D_{ij} = 0, \text{s.t.}$$

$$j \in J_1(i), z_j - \lambda_j' = 0, j \in J_1(n+1); \lambda_j'' D_{j0} - \lambda_0 = 0, j \in J(0) \ .$$

Under the second alternative we have a redesignation of symbols so as to differentiate as between the inflows and outflows; prices adjusted as between sellers and buyers are denoted μ_{ij}. The Lagrange function is then written

$$\Psi = \sum_{i \in J_1 (n+1)} z_i P_{i,n+1} + \sum_{i=1}^{n} \sum_{j=1}^{n} \mu_{ij}(P_{ij}'' - P_{ij}') + \mu_0 (b - \sum_{j \in J_2 (0)} P_{0j}').$$

Now the centre's problem is

$$f(M) = \mu_0 b + \sum_{i=1}^{n} f_i [\mu_{ij}, i \in J_1 (i), j \in J_2 (i)] = \min$$

subject to

$$B_i u_i = \sum_{i \in J_2 (i)} P_{ij}''; C_i u_i = \sum_{j \in J_1 (i)} D_{ij} P_{ij}'; u_i \in U_i''.$$

Note that the f_i are a datum being implicit in the solution of the n partial-parametric problems

$$f_i = \max \left[z_i P_{i,n+1} + \sum_{j \in J_1 (i)} \mu_{ij} P_{ij}'' - \sum_{j \in J_1 (i)} \mu_{ji} P_{ji}' - \mu_0 P_{0i}' \right].$$

Thence, with prices given, the values for intersectoral deliveries corresponding to the optimum are found $P_{ij,0}''; j \in J_2 (i); P_{ij,0}'; j \in J_1 (i)$.

Assuming that the solution yields unique plans, the direction of price-variation is found, *by-passing the centre*, from

$$\mu_{ij}(\theta) = \mu_{ij}^0 - \theta \left[P_{ij}'' - P_{ji}' \right].$$

The parameter θ determines the "absolute level of change" — it is in fact the only parameter issued from the centre after the lower-echelon elements have notified the parameters of the piecewise-linear function of the form

$$f_i(0) = \max_r (\beta_{ri} + \alpha_{ri} 0)$$

with α and β constant. (The procedure of solution of the parametric plan-programming involved had been suggested by Pervozyanskaya-Pervozvanskiy in their paper of 1966.)[125]

When the assumption of the uniqueness of the plans is abandoned the iterative procedure adopted is that of gradient descent in the space of the "matched" prices, the μ's. Its substance is the "averaging" of the gradient resting on the average partial derivatives of the functions $f_i(\mu_i \mu_{i-1})$ with respect to the μ_{ik} at the point μ_i, μ_{i-1}^{ℓ}

$$\left(\overline{\frac{\partial f_i}{\partial \mu_{ik}}}\right)_{\ell} = \lim_{\substack{\epsilon \to 0 \\ \epsilon > 0}} \frac{1}{2\epsilon}\left[f_i(\mu_i{\ell} + \epsilon e_k, \mu_{i-1}^{\ell-i}) - f_i(\mu_i^{\ell} - \epsilon e_k, \mu_{i-1}^{\ell-i})\right],$$

and

$$\left(\overline{\frac{\partial f_i}{\partial \mu_{i-1,k}}}\right)_{\ell} = \lim_{\substack{\epsilon \to 0 \\ \epsilon > 0}} \frac{1}{2\epsilon}\left[f_i(\mu_i^{\ell}, \mu_{i-1}^{\ell} + \epsilon e_k) - f_i(\mu_i^{\ell}, \mu_{i-1}^{\ell} - \epsilon e_k)\right],$$

the $e_k = (0, \ldots, 0, 1, 0, \ldots, 0)$.

Thence the formulae

$$\left(\overline{\frac{\partial f_i}{\partial \mu_{ik}}}\right)_{\ell} = \frac{1}{2}\left[\min_{s \in S_i^{\ell}} p''_{ik,s} + \max_{s \in S_1^{\ell}} p''_{ik,s}\right],$$

$$\left(\overline{\frac{\partial f_i}{\partial \mu_{i-1,k}}}\right)_{\ell} = -\frac{1}{2}\left[\min_{s_{\ell} \in S_i^{\ell}} p'_{ik,e} + \max_{s \in S_1^{\ell}} p'_{ik,s}\right].$$

The regime of search for the descent direction is defined as

$$\mu_{ik}(\theta) = \mu_{ik}^{\ell} - \theta\left[\left(\overline{\frac{\partial f_i}{\partial \mu_{ik}}}\right)_{\ell} + \left(\overline{\frac{\partial f_{i+1}}{\partial \mu_{ik}}}\right)\right]; \theta > 0; k = 1, \ldots, k_i;$$

$$i = 1, \ldots, n-1.$$

To return to the claim put forward for the procedure — termed that of "descent by the average antigradient". The argument on the intensity of "decentralization" in the decomposition construct is based on *firstly*, the small amount of information moving "upwards", and *secondly*, on the value of θ. This may be correct but the matter hinges on two points: *firstly* how manageable is the single θ? *Secondly*, does it ensure the implementation of the centre's strategy objectives? Whatever the answer to these questions may be, the Pervozvanskaya-Pervozvanskiy exercise advances the technical experimentation by a noteworthy step.

Note

Recent years have seen in Soviet planning economics the recognition of the gradient method as such as an effective decentralization instrument — in its own right helping optimal distribution of resources. Soviet writers are now crediting Samuelson with pioneering in this field as early as 1949 (reference to his *Market Mechanism and Maximizations*. Cf. V. N. Varshavskiy, in *EMM*, 3 (1971)).[126]

Appendix 4

Polterovich[127] examines in his 1970 paper the efficiency of the allocation of resources where each participant has at each step information only about the state of a fixed number of others. The argument is broadly this.

The system consists of m participants each characterized by a concave $f_k(x_k), x_k \in R^n, k = 1, \ldots, m$. The $n \times m$ vectors $x = (x_1 \ldots x_k ., x_m)$ with nonnegative components are the system's states. Assume

$$f(x) = \sum_{k=1}^{m} f(x_k).$$ For each subset of participants $a \subset M = \{1, 2, \ldots m\}$,

with nonnegative x, we have the image

$$\xi_a(x) = \left\{ z \mid z \in G_a(x), f(z) = \max_{y \in G_a(x)} f(y) \right.$$

where

$$G_a(x) = \left\{ y \mid y = (y_i, \ldots, y_k, \ldots y_m), y_k \in R^n, y \geq 0, \right.$$

$$\sum_{k \in a} y_k = \sum_{k \in a} x_k; y_k = x_k \text{ for } k \in a \right\}.$$

Let A be a system of subsets of the set M, $A = \{a\}$, $a \subset M$, $a = \xi$. The image

$\xi_a(x)$ is an admissible transformation, or admissible transaction, if $a \in A$. A nonnegative point x is optimal if it solves

$$f(y) = \sum_{k=1}^{m} f_k(y_k) \to \max, \quad \sum_{k=1}^{m} y_k = \sum_{k=1}^{m} x_k, y_k \geq 0, k=1, \ldots m.$$

In the economic interpretation of $f_k(x_k)$ is that of the utility of x_k. It is shown that to guarantee the existence of the optimizing sequence, the participation of some number of participants is required at each step; and that this number depends on the number of resources, n, and on the differentiability properties of the utility function. In handling the latter aspect some results of Pshenichnyi are made use of, and a concept of a quasi-summatory function[128] is introduced.

Next the concept of a "collection" of resources is defined, $v \in N$ in x^0. With respect to the $f(x), x_k \in R^n$, if (1) all $f_k(x_k)$ are quasi-summatory on $\{x_{jk} \in v\}$ at x_k^0, and (2) the property (1) is not owned by any subset of the N set. Thence follows the proposition that at any point the totality of collections forms the decomposition of the set N.

On the adopted definitions an admissible transformation $\xi_a(x)$ is efficient at the nonnegative point x if $f(\xi_a(x)) > f(x)$; if $a \in A$ and $f(\xi_a(x)) = \max_{\beta \in A} f(\xi_\beta(x))$, the transformation is called "most efficient" at point x; the point $x \geq 0$ is termed a "limiting" point if at this point no transformation admissible is efficient.

It is then proved that

1.   Where $f_k(x_k)$ are concave, $\tilde{x}$ is a limiting point and θ the maximum number of resources forming at it a collection, $\theta < m$, if transactions between any $\theta + 1$ participants are admissable, then x is optimal.

2.   Where $x^s \in \xi_a^s(x^{s-1})$, $s = 1, 2, \ldots, a_s \in A$, if (a) the set of admissible transactions is chosen so as to ensure that any limiting point is optimal, and (b) the sequence ξ_n contains an infinite subsequence of most efficient transactions, then $f(x^s) \to f(x^0)$ for $s \to \infty$.

3.   Where for any $y \geq 0$, $\sum_{k=1}^{m} y_k = \sum_{k=1}^{m} x_k^0$, with $x^0 \geq 0$, the maximum number of resources in a collection does not exceed some number θ, if all transactions between $\theta + 1$ participants are admissible then there exists an optimizing sequence of states originating from x^0.

From (2) it is deduced that absence of non-optimal points indicates also the absence of 'isolating' points (the nonnegative x is defined as "isolated" if it does not contain any optimizing sequences of states). From (1) it is deduced that the set of non-optimal limiting points belongs to the set of non-differentiability points of $f(x)$ — (assuming that transactions are only pair-wise admissible) — and therefore have a zero (Lebesgue) measure. (However, by exemplification it is shown that the measure of the set of isolated points need not necessarily equal zero; thence the conclusion that "local" changes in $f_k(x_k)$ can bring about "global" effects.)

It is because, in accordance with (2), finding the optimizing sequence requires that the most efficient transactions materialized on the infinite subsequence of steps, the question is raised whether this condition can be met without assuming for the system a centralized information. The answer is sought under the assumption that the participants enter into transactions under some random mechanism. In the general case no proof is produced as to the meeting of conditions with probability 1 for differentiable concave, if not strictly concave, $f_k(x_k)$, but some approximations are proved for schemes with relatively weak conditions.

We should stress that in the interpretation of the $f_x(x_k)$ the concept of utility (as above) is understood to mean utility to the participants. To the extent then to which optimality or near-optimality of the Polterovich system is realizable, it is so under elimination of centralist utility as distinct from that of participants. It is this that in our appraisal is crucial.

Additional Note

1.   When turning to the systemic approach Soviet planning thought has sought support in information theory: for any theorizing in the field is bound to come up against the vexed question of quantifying information. Very broadly, Soviet systemic thinking has tried, as it were, to negotiate the theoretical middle-ground between the realms of Wiener-Shannon[129] and Bar-Hillel-Carnap: between the statistical, communication-theoretic, and the semantic formulations of the information-transmission problems. In this, in most recent years, the emphasis seems to have shifted more in the direction of the latter type of formulation. It may be convincingly argued that the very nature of economic communication does involve the *content* of symbols: the Carnap-Bar-Hillel construct resting on inductive probability is more congenial to economic-planning theory in that it relates to the linguistic *and* logical forms (and inasmuch as it is concerned with the reduction of uncertainty it has been validly classified

as "non-subjective"; as a matter of fact, Shannon himself has tried to remove the misunderstanding as to his fundamental concepts by making it clear that the measure of "surprise" does *not* define information[130] as such).

The attraction links up with the realization by the Soviet information-theoretic school in planning theory that an adequate formulation of an informational system — its structure and regime-calls for making explicit the parameter of language. (The constructor of a planning system must reckon with something analogous to what MacKay describes as the epistemological Principle of Relativity in human sciences.[131] As a matter of fact, the impulse to Soviet theorizing in the field seems to have come from practice, concerned as it is today with harmonizing the universal computer languages with the language of economic planning.)

To be sure, the probes along the purely semantic-information-theoretic path have not been immediately fruitful either. This is patently due, in the first place, to the very disparities in complexity that separate the real-life planning language from the Bar-Hillel-Carnap system, their $L_n\pi$,[132] and the inevitably rudimentary nature of the instrument for measuring the information-content conveyed in this language by the message, their *cont* $(i) = m(\sim i)$. It has been realized that, while in areas of deductive reasoning the Bar-Hillel-Carnap functions *cont*, *inf*, and *m* can be handled adequately with their simple $m\ ^+$, this is not true of areas which by their nature call for inductive reasoning as well. Again, it is only fair to remark that Bar-Hillel-Carnap themselves did warn the "impatient" student that the tools offered by them do not constitute a solution of the task confronting those with contents or designata of symbols, or, in a pragmatic sense, the use of symbols.

In so far as the syntactic aspect of the semiotics is confined to the quantification of symbols it fails to come to grips with what is the economic planner's central criterion, that is, the value criterion. So does in fact the semantic approach, closer though it is to that criterion — inasmuch as it at least is concerned with the signals' contents, in the general sense.

The limitations of the classical approaches to quantifying information have inspired Kolmogorov in his attempt of the mid-1960s to shift the issue to yet another plane.[133] In that plane, as alternative to the two approaches — the combinatorial and the probabilistic — he introduces the third, the "algorithmic", technically resting on the mathematical-logical theory of recursive functions. In this, the central concept is a "qualitative" one — of the "complexity" of information; the relative complexity of object y with a given x is the minimal length $l(p)$ of the "programme" p

for obtaining y from x, the "programme" being a partly recursive $\phi(p,x)$ $= y$; for each function of this kind it is assumed

$$K(y/x) = \begin{cases} \min l(p) \\ \phi(p,x) = y \\ \\ \infty, \text{ if there is no } p \text{ such that } \phi(p,x) = y. \end{cases}$$

The existence is proved of a partly recursive $A(p,x)$, such that for any other recursive $\phi(p,x)$ we have $K_A(y/x) \leqslant K_\phi(y/x) + C$ where the constant C does not depend on x and y. Then $K_A(y) = K_A(y/x)$ is the "complexity of object y'' and the "quantity of information in x with respect to $y*$ is determined from $I_A(x:y) = K_A(y) - K_A(y/x)$; the $I_A(x:y)$ being not smaller than some negative C which depends on adopted method of "programming".

2.   Issues of devolution (decentralization) are among those of great complexity which seem to lend themselves eminently to digital-computer modelling and simulation or gaming. There are several reasons for this. In the light of results of our probing, one is confronted here with problems, essentially mathematizable, yet such in which "established" approaches fail to yield a conclusive answer (non-convex nonlinearities, large dimensions, conflict and stochastic elements are among the most obvious snags). To the extent indications for such an answer can be secured heuristically, laboratory imitation of the real life behaviour of systems may carry considerable promise; indeed this would seem to be an area of promise for an algorithmic-heuristic combination. Some specific features add to this quality. Thus, sequential processing does agree with the multilevel, multistage hierarchic (state-to-state change) nature of problems involved. An effective programme can be then coded and processed at high speed and with good control of the problem's logic. Moreover, this "logic-control" may be reasonably expected to elucidate causality links otherwise hidden from the student; possibly to penetrate what the mathematical modeller would normally treat as a black box and what obscures our theoretical perception. More generally, there appears to be considerable scope for deepening his insights into the issues to be examined, to some extent by what we would term feedback-suggestions for adjusting the model itself. Last but not least, inasmuch as the devolution (decentralization) problem leads to the question of the system's "goodness", there again, machine-"mimicking" may prove of help. Our programme-theoretic inquiry has indicated that this issue evades the "best" solution. And simulation is

operated without a criterion for optimal outcome; as Siegel-Wolf[134] put it
'... the simulation technique does not purport to find the "best" solution
to any problem, rather it demonstrates the consequences of a particular
set of input conditions and applied to a process'. Thus the system-architect
is offered scope for a trade-off.[135]

Notes

1. C. Almon, Jr., *Matrix methods in economics* (Reading, Mass., 1967), p. 92.
2. J. G. Kemeny, *et al.*, "A generalization of the von Neumann model of an
   expanding economy", *Econometrica*, Apr. 1956.
3. M. Morishima, *Equilibrium, stability and growth* (Oxford, 1964).
4. R. L. Weil, "The decomposition of economic production systems",
   Econometrica, Apr. 1968. This paper is of considerable technical interest. It
   investigates various types of decomposability for systems both linear and nonlinear; also-precedence relationships as between the sub-economies. Graph-
   theoretic techniques are employed not only for square-matrix systems but also
   to rectangular production systems. Of interest is Weil's investigation of the
   process of putting the input-output system into the canonical form presented.
5. Problems of decomposition (and decentralization) occupy an important place
   in the economic system-theoretic analysis. A noteworthy contribution in that
   field is contained in S. S. Sengupta/R. L. Ackoff, "Systems theory from an
   operational point of view", *General systems* (1965). Some discussion of it will
   be found in the control-theoretic context (Part II, pp. 427 ff.).
6. Dantzig, Wolfe, in *Operations Research*, 8/1 (1960).
7. G. B. Dantzig A. Madansky, "On the solution of two-stage linear program
   under uncertainty", Proc. 4th Berkeley Symposium on Math. Statistics,Berkeley,
   Calif. 1960.
8. R. Dorfman's contribution to discussion in Malinvaud/Bacharach, op. cit., p. 313.
9. G. B. Dantzig, "Large scale linear programming", in Dantzig/Veinott, op. cit.,
   and literature cited therein.
10. cf. Roy Radner, "Team decision problems", *Ann. Math. Statist.*, Sept. 1962; the
    same, "Competitive equilibrium under uncertainty", *Econometrica*, Jan. 1968;
    J. Marschak, in C. P. Bonini *et al.*, eds, *Management controls* (1964).
11. L. Hurwicz, in *Amer. Econ. R.*, May 1969. cf. his contribution to Grossman,
    op. cit., – a pioneering work in the field.
12. T. Marschak, "On the comparison of centralized and decentralized economic
    systems", *Amer. Econ. R.*, May 1969.
13. V. F. Pugachev, in A. L. Vainshtein, ed., *Narodnokhozyaistvennyie modeli*
    (Moscow, 1963).
14. V. F. Pugachev, *Optimisatsya planirovanya;* this has been further elaborated
    by him in articles in *EMM*, 1969 & 1970, see Appendix .
15. V. F. Pugachev *et al.*, in *EMM*, 5 (1972).
16. A. A. Geoffrion, "Primal resource-directive approaches for optimizing nonlineaɪ
    decomposable systems", *Operations Research*, 18/3 (1970); cf. also his *Elements of
    large-scale mathematical programming* (Management Science Inst., Univ. of California,
    Los Angeles, Dec. 1968).
17. Decomposition for systems with stronger nonlinearities is treated in W. Zangwill's
    paper "A decomposable non-linear programming approach", *Operations
    Research*, 15/6 (1967). The system with which he works is $f(x) \to \max$, $g_i(x) \geqslant 0$, $l_i(x) = 0$
    where the f is pseudo-concave, and of the constraints g_i – quasi-concave, l – linear.

On definition a function f is pseudo-concave when differentiable and if $\Delta f(x^1)'$ $(x^2 - x^1) \leqslant 0$ implies $f(x^2) < f(x^1)$. (Δ stands for the gradient of f evaluated at x ' denotes transpose). The g is termed "quasi-concave" if the set $x|g(x) \geqslant \alpha$ is convex for any scalar α. The pseudo-concave function's principal property is that having started decreasing in some direction it continues to do so.

The maximization is carried out by large-step algorithms recursively handling the sequences of points x^k and of directions s^k; alternative procedures for selecti the latter are presented, some of which recommend themselves for large-scale sys (The exercise studies also some suboptimization procedures in the treatment of "jamming" in convergence; it generalizes the Dantzig quadratic algorithm.)

18.   Volkonskiy, *Model optimalnogo planirovanya* . . . .
19.   cf. D. K. Faddeev/V. H. Faddeeva, *Computational methods of linear algebra*, (San Francisco, 1963).
20.   K. J. Arrow/G. Debreu, "Existence of an equilibrium for a competitive economy", *Econometrica*, 1954; G. Debreu, *Theory of value* (New York, 1959).
21.   Hans-Werner Gottinger, "Die Existenz eines planökonomischen Gleichgewichts", *Zeitschr. für die gesamte Staatswissenschaft*, Aug. 1968.
22.   cf. also Zauberman, *Reforms formalized (a comment)* submitted to the Eur. Econometric Conf., Brussels, Oct. 1969 (summary in *Econometrica*, July 1971).
23.   V. A. Volkonskiy, *Optimum planning schemes and methods of their conjugation* (mimeo), presented at the Warsaw Sept. 1966 meeting of the Econometric Society and the Inst. of Management Sciences.
24.   W. Fenchel, in *Canad. J. Maths.* (1949); also T. Bonessen/W. Fenchell, "Theorie der konvexen Koerper", in *Ergebnisse der Mathematik*, 3(1934).
25.   J. F. Nash, "Equilibrium points in N-person games", *Proc. Nat. Acad. Sci. USA*, 1950.
26.   Volkonskiy, *Model optimalnogo planirovanya* . . . .
27.   Choose a constant C —in the problem of maximizing the function $Cu(x) = $ max subject to $(p,x) \leqslant S$, such that the Lagrange multiplier $\equiv 1$. Then (over $x \in X, y \in Y$, $0 \leqslant p \leqslant P$) the point $(\bar{x}, \bar{y}, \bar{p})$ is the saddle-point of the Lagrange function

$$L(x,y,p) = Cu(x) + (p, \sum_k yk - x).$$

28.   cf. Volkonskiy, in *EMM*, 2(1965). His reasoning is that if the "society" as a whole is treated as *the* consumer with a given objective function, then it can be proved that the state of equilibrium coincides − in the problem of plan optimizing − with the optimum.
29.   See Makarov's papers: on the optimal "mixed" model of an economy in *EMM*, 6(1970); on conditions of competitive economic equilibrium in *Kibernetika*, 1(1968); and on the optimal "local-equilibrium" trajectories of economic dynamics, *Opt. plan.*, 10(1968). The construct in the latter appears to me to complete that presented in the Note to ch. 3, p. 137.
      The papers by A. Diamond and J. Mirrlees mentioned in sect. 5 were published in *Amer. Econ. R.*, Mar. & June 1971.
30.   M. E. Primak, in *Doklady*, 200/3(1971).
31.   P. S. Albin, "Uncertainty; information exchange and the theory of indicative planning", *Econ. J.*, Mar. 1971.
      In the model the planner is supposed to be only sure of the "capsule" form of the function $q_i = q_i(q_i, Y, r, y_j^i) + u_j$; the sign of some partial derivatives of the function, specifically $\partial q_i / \partial Y$ and $\partial q_i / \partial r$. (Notation: q and $p = $ quantity and

price, Y is disposable income r is measure of "credit ease", y_j^i is vector of variables of "peculiar interest" to the firm). The firm is maximizing $u_i = u_i(x_i, \pi_i, z_j^i)$ also known to the planner as well the signs of partial derivatives (the last two terms in the bracket stand for profits and "unspecified variables").

For Chidambaram's design see *Management Science*, 16/9(1970); for Harsanyi's "code" see *Econometrica*, 3(1966).

32. cf. C. E. Lemke/J. T. Howson, Jr., "Equilibrium points of bimatrix games", *J. Soc. Ind. & Applied Maths.*, 2(1964) and C. E. Lemke, "Bimatrix equilibrium points and mathematical programming", *Management Science*, 11(1965). For an interesting extension in determining the equilibrium point by the method see T. O. M. Kronsjö, *Two-person nonzero-sum game* (Birmingham, 1969, mimeo).

33. cf. J. F. Nash, "Noncooperative games", *Ann. Maths*, 1951.

34. Shizuo Kakutani, "A generalization of Brouwer's fixed point theorem", *Duke Math. J.*, 8(1941).

35. T. O. M. Kronsjö, *Optimal co-ordination of a large convex economic system*, paper no. 16, Birmingham Univ., 1968.

36. Since this chapter was written, Kronsjö has further elaborated his imaginative and elegant construct in a contribution to the Planning Seminar at the London School of Economics (subsequently published in *Jahrbücher für Nationaloekonomie und Statistik*, 183/5 (1969).

The decomposition regime of the system – a non-linear, convex, separable system – is conceived as one of a *"trilogue"* between (1) the primal master, (2) the dual master, and (3) the common sub-problem or sub-problems. In this the ϵ-optimum solution is sought for the problem stated as minimization of the form

$$f^1(x_1) + f^2(x_2) + f^3(x_3)$$
$$x_1, x_2, x_3$$

subject to

$$g_1{}^1(x_1) + g_1{}^2(x_2) + g_1{}^3(x_3) \leqslant 0; g_2{}^1(x_1) + g_2{}^2(x_2) \leqslant 0;$$

$$g_3{}^1(x_1) \leqslant 0.$$

(*Notation*: the x's – indexed 1,2,3 – are column vectors of activity levels; the $f^j(x_j)$'s are convex scalar functions and the $g_1{}^j(x_j)$'s convex column vector functions: the row vectors of the dual variables, u's, measure marginal costs of the respective resource requirements – and they correspond to the three groups of constraints.)

The common sub-problem obtains from the primal master proposals for prices u_k^1 for the first group of resources and the activity levels x_3^k; from the dual master problems it obtains proposals with respect to activity levels x_1^1. It then minimizes total cost (including the cost of the first group of resources $f^2(x_2) + u_k^1 g_1^2(x_2)$, it meets at the same time the net demand for the second group of resources $g_2(x_1^1) + g_1^2(x_2) \leqslant 0$. The common sub-problem determines the optimal activity levels, $x_2^1 = x_2^k$ and optimal marginal costs u_k^2 of the second type of resources.

The dual master obtains from the primal marginal cost and activity proposals u_k^1, x_2^k and from the common sub-problem u_k^2, x_2^k, and the primal master from the dual master proposals for activity levels x_1^1 and from the common sub-problem x_2^1.

It has the form

$$f = \underset{\substack{x_1,x_2,x_3 \\ u^1,u^2,u^3}}{\text{Max}} \quad \{ f^1(x_1) + f^2(x_2) + f^3(x_3)$$

$$+ u^1(g_1{}^1(x_1) + g_1{}^2(x_2) + g_1{}^3(x_3))$$

$$+ u^2(g_2{}^1(x_1) + g_2{}^2(x_2))$$

$$+ u^3 g_3{}^1(x_1)$$

$$\frac{df^1}{dx_1} + u^1 \frac{dg_1{}^1}{dx_1} + u^2 \frac{dg_2{}^1}{dx_1} + u^3 \frac{dg_3{}^1}{dx_1} = 0$$

$$\frac{df^2}{dx_2} + u^1 \frac{dg_1{}^2}{dx_2} + u^2 \frac{dg_2{}^2}{dx_2} = 0$$

$$\frac{df^3}{dx_3} + u^1 \frac{dg_1{}^3}{dx_3} = 0$$

$$u^1 \geqslant 0 \quad u^2 \geqslant 0 \quad u^3 \geqslant 0 \}$$

37. Arrow *et al.*, *Studies in linear and non-linear programming* (Stanford, 1958).
38. Kantorovich/Gorstko, op.cit.
39. E. Yu. Fayerman, (in *EMM*, 5 (1969)).
40. B. S. Razumikhin, "Fizicheskiye modeli i algoritmy reshenya nekotorykh zadach matematicheskogo programmirovanya i matematicheskoy ekonomiki". in V. A. Trapeznikov ed., *Vsesovuznoye sovyeshchanye po problemam upravlenya* (Moscow, 1971); also the same, in *Avt. i tel.*, 4(1972).
41. This has the form

$$\max \left\{ \sum_{i=1}^{n} C_1{}^{(s)} X_1{}^{(s)} \,\middle|\, \sum_{i=1}^{m} p_1 X_1{}^{(s)} \leqslant P_s, \; \sum_{s=1}^{m} X_1{}^{(s)} = X_i \; s = \overline{1,m}, i = \overline{1,} \right.$$

$$X_i{}^{(s)K+1} = \frac{X_i P_s C_i{}^{(s)} X_i{}^{(s)K}}{\left(\sum\limits_{j=1}^{n} C_j{}^{(s)} X_j{}^{(s)} \right) \sum\limits_{\sigma=1}^{m} \dfrac{P_s C_i{}^{(s)} X_i{}^{(s)K}}{\sum\limits_{j=1}^{n} C_j{}^{(s)} X_j{}^{(s)K}}}$$

42. The Razumikhin box of tools for optimization has a recurrence algorithm for a numerical solution of a quadratic-programme problems with the minimand

$$\min \left\{ \sum_{i=1}^{n} r_{ui} x_i + \frac{1}{2} \sum_{i,j=1}^{n} r_{ij} x_i x_j \,\middle|\, \sum_{i=1}^{n} a_s, x_i = b_j, \, x_i \geqslant u \right\}$$

$$X_\alpha{}^{(\nu+1)} = \Phi_\alpha{}^{(N)} \, 1 \, \left[\Phi_\alpha{}^{(N)} \right], \; \begin{matrix} N=y \, . \, n+\alpha \\ 0 \leqslant \alpha < n \end{matrix}$$

$$\Phi_\alpha{}^{(N)} = X_\alpha{}^{(v)} - \frac{P_\alpha(x^{(N)}) + q^0 \sum\limits_{s=1}^{m} \dfrac{a_{s\alpha}}{a_s} y_s{}^{(N)}}{r_{\alpha\alpha} + q^0 \sum\limits_{s=1}^{m} \dfrac{a_s{}^2}{a_s}},$$

$$P_\alpha(x^{(N)}) = r_{0\alpha} + \sum_{j=1}^{\alpha-1} r_{\alpha j} x_j{}^{(v+1)} + \sum_{j=\alpha}^{n} r_{\alpha j} x_j{}^{(v)},$$

$$a_s = \sum_{t=1}^{n} |a_{si}| \quad y_s{}^{(N)} = \sum_{i=1}^{\alpha-1} a_{si} x_i{}^{(v+1)} + \sum_{i=1}^{n} a_{s_1} x_i{}^{(v)} - b_s.$$

43. V. S. Mikhalevich/Yu. M. Yermolev, "O nekotorykh matematicheskikh voprosakh analiza i sinteza slozhnykh sistem", in B. V. Gnedenko, ed., *Bolshiye sistemy-teoriya, metodologya, modelirovanye* (Moscow, 1971). cf. also in the context Yermolev's paper — jointly with N. Z. Shor — in *Kibernetika*, 1 (1968).
44. cf. J. Kornai, *Mathematical planning of structural decisions* (Amsterdam, 1967).
45. G. W. Brown, "Iterative solution of games by fictitious play", in T. C. Koopmans *Activity analysis of production and allocation* (New York, 1951).
46. J. Robinson, "An iterative method of solving a game", *Ann. Maths*, 1951.
47. cf. J. Kornai, *Multi-level programming* (Budapest, July 1968).
48. J. Glowacki/J. Mycielski, *Two-level planning in foreign trade*, presented at Eur. Econometric Conf., Brussels, 1969.
48a. See reference to the address by E. Z. Maiminas (in *EMM*, 3 (1972), p. 458).
49. cf. my paper 'Notes on systemic approach to large-scale, decentralization', *Jahrbuch der Wirtschaft Osteuropas*, 1973.
50. H. J. White/S. Tauber, *Systems analysis* (Philadelphia, 1969).
51. O. Lange, "Whole and parts in the light of cybernetics" (Oxford, 1965) and the same, *Introduction to cybernetics* (1970) (both Engl. trans.).
52. cf. H. Simon, *The new science of management decision* (1960); also the same, "Architecture of complexity", in L. von Bertalanffy/A. Rapoport, *General systems*, X (1965).
53. In Soviet literature the Simon ideas were developed, with an eye to planning, in the mid-1960s by P. A. Vatnik ("O primenenyi metodov teorii avtomaticheskogo regulirovanya i statisticheskoy dinamiki dla reshenya ekonomicheskikh zadach", in V. V. Novozhilov *et al.*, eds, *Matematiko-ekonomicheskiye problemy* (Leningrad, 1966)). The formalization rests on the Laplace transform

$\bar{x}(p) = \int_0 x(t) e^{-pt} dt$ where $x(t)$ is some function of time, $\bar{x}(p)$ its image — a function of some complex argument p. For systems with discretely changing time the z-transform would be used $\bar{x}(z) = \Sigma_{n=0} x(n) z^n$, n being discrete time interval, $x(n)$ and $\bar{x}(z)$ respectively a discrete time function and its image. The working of the system and its mechanism is based on the rule: in the domain of images the operation of the linear stationary operator is equivalent to the product of the image of the signal by some function of the complex argument:

$\bar{x}(p)=K(p)\bar{y}(p)$, $\bar{x}(z)=K(z)\bar{y}(z)$, where $\bar{y}(p)$, $\bar{y}(z)$ describe input activities, $\bar{x}(p)$, $\bar{x}(z)$ output activities, $K(p)$, $K(z)$ are functions describing the element observed (transfer functions).

The operation of the system is exemplified, in Vatnik too, on the case of stocks control.

54. M. D. Mesarovic *et al.*, *Theory of hierarchical multilevel systems* (New York, 197)

55. It is instructive to compare the yield from the Mesarovic *et al.* approach and that of the prototype programming-decomposition procedure. In Dantzig-Wolfe, the sub-problems do not provide directly the overall solution, formed as it is by convex combination of the sub-problems' solution optima. The essential point stressed by Mesarovic *et al* is that in Dantzig-Wolfe there exists *notionally* no optimal co-ordination input or parameter; nor is there in that method any decomposition of constraints: whereas the Mesarovic method does yield "balance constraints" which is a decomposition of the system's overall constraint-coefficients' matrix.

56. A. D. Smirnov, *Modelirovanye i prognozirovanye sotsyalisticheskogo vosproiz-vodstva* (Moscow, 1970), p.131. For a further discussion of this work see Part II, p. 424.

57. cf. Zauberman, "The objective function for Soviet economy", *Economica*, Aug. 1965; also the same, "The objective function revisited", *Jahrbuch der Wirtschaft Osteuropas* (Munich-Vienna), 1 (1970).

58. The point of departure in the treatment of this problem in Soviet literature has been inquiries into that of determining a vectorally-optimal plan, as in M. E. Salukvadze, in *Avt.i tel.*, 5 (1972). The problem is then seen as one reducible to convex programming: say, we have a given convex function $R(X)$ defined on a set of points $X \in \Omega$; we have to find a point $X^* \in \Omega$ which satisfies the condition $R(X^*) = \min_{X \in \Omega} R(X)$. For the convex problem the local minimum coincides with the absolute, minimizing, that is, the function within the Ω region. Technically then all the practicable methods of solution are here employable, in particular those of gradient descent.

There has been also considerable interest in the multicriterial case of minimization of a convex (upwards) function over a convex polyhedral set. The problem is multicriterial in the sense that it has local minima, though patently only at the polyhedron's extremal points. It has been suggested that the case can be coped with effectively by means of a general algorithm for convex programming designed by Huang Tui (*Doklady*, 159/1 (1964)). Doubts have been expressed, however, as to the relief it offers as compared with the complete "look-through" of the extremal point.

Handling the problem of multicriteriality in general has been classified in three categories: (1) integrating and weighting component criteria, (2) adopting one as the leading criterion and subjecting it to others as constraints, and (3) seeking a "compromise" solution such as to minimize the distances from it to individual optima within the criterial space. Thus in a generalized formulation by Avdeyev-Lazarev, we minimize the sum of squares of these distances $(q_i(X))$, i.e. $\sum_i^n [q_i(X)]^2 \to \min$, and we look in the space for a point such that the point in the normalized space of criteria which corresponds to it is the one least remote from the origin of coordinates. Where not all $F_i(X)$ are smooth the operation is kept within convexity by this procedure: Normalize the space X and take the distance of the solution for component x_j from the overall optimal solution as $p_i(x_j) = x_j/y_{j,i} - 1$ here $y_{j,i}$ stand for the value of this component of vector Y_i i.e. vector of solutions which extremize the individual functions).

Then we extremize the sum $\sum^{n}_{i=1} \sum^{m}_{j=1} [P_i(x_j)]^2 \to \min$, (V. I. Avdeyev/G. B. Lazarev, in *EMM*, 2 (1972)).

59. E. I. Vilkas/Ye. Z. Maiminas, in *Kibernetika* (1968); E. Z. Maiminas, *Protsesy planirovanya v ekonomike – informatsionnyi aspect* (Vilna, 1967).
60. E. I. Vilkas, in Trapeznikov, *V vsesoyuznoye sovyeschanye* . . .
61. V. N. Burkov/A. Ya. Lerner, "Printsip otkrytogo upravlenya v mnogourovne-vykh sistemakh", ibid.
62. V. N. Burkov/A. Ya. Lerner, "Fair play in control of active system", in Kuhn/ Szegő, *Differential games*. . . .
63. Yu. I. Neimark, "Lokalizovannyie kvazioptimalnyie upravlenya bolshoy sistemy", in Trapeznikov, ed., *V vsesoyuznoye sovyeshchanye*. . . .
64. A. D. Aleksandrov *et al.*, ibid.
65. A. A. Pervozvanskiy, *Avt. i tel.*, 8 (1971).
66. V. M. Polterovich, *EMM*, 4 (1970).
67. T. F. Groves, *The allocation of resources under uncertainty; the informational and incentive roles of prices and demands in a team*, Technical report no. 1,. Univ. of California, Aug. 1969.
68. cf. (i.a.) R. Radner, *Allocation of resources in a team*, Technical report no. 7, Univ. of California, Dec. 1970.
   The object of the quoted inquiry by Radner was to prove that – for the case considered – i.e. quadratic case – a *single* exchange of price-demand information between the "resource manager" and enterprise managers produces as good results as rules based on complete information for the "resource manager" and on information about supplies of resources on the part of the enterprise managers. (Groves, op.cit., generalized the analysis to the case of many resources and offered approximation theorem for the non-quadratic case.)
69. J. Marschak/R. Radner, *Economic theory of teams* (New Haven, 1972), *passim*, esp. pp. 187 ff.
70. cf. i.a. R. Radner, *Decision and organization*, Working paper no. 255, Center for Research in Management Science, Univ. of California, June 1968.
   Also starting from the Radner-Marschak conceptual framework of their "team", the informational aspect of a competitive equilibrium has been elaborated by Radner in several monographs – with immediate implications for devolutional decision-making; see in particular his "Competitive equilibrium under uncertainty", *Econometrica*, 1 (1968); as he puts it, "the Arrow-Debreu world is strained to the limit by the problem of choice of information. It breaks down completely in the face of limits on the ability of agents to *compute* optimal strategies" (ibid. p.35; our italics).
71. Note that of relevance for the study of decentralization, with complete information assumed away, are the explorations of "co-operative" decision-making under uncertainty. Thus the necessary and sufficient conditions for the "sharing" rule to be optimal (Pareto optimal) are formulated in Borch and in Wilson. Reasoning along these lines has been extended by Rosing by applying the game-theoretic approach of Nash and Harsanyi. These studies deepen the insight into problems of decentralization by starting as it were from the other end – the forming of groups for co-operative decision-making (See K. Borch, "Economic equilibrium under uncertainty", *Int. Econ. R.*, 3 (1968); R. Wilson, *"The theory of syndicates"*, *Econometrica*, 1 (1968); J. Rosing, "The formation of groups for co-operative decision making under uncertainty", ibid, 3 (1970); J. Nash, "The two-person co-operative game", ibid., 1 (1953); J. C. Harsanyi, "Approaches to the bargaining problem before and after the theory of games", ibid., 2 (1956)).

72. T. A. Marschak, "Centralization and decentralization in economic organization", *Econometrica*, 1959.
73. Ibid., p. 429.
74. cf. T. A. Marschak, "Computation in organizations' comparison of price mechan isms and other adjustment processes", in K. Borch/J. Mossin, eds., *Risk and uncertainty* (New York, 1958).
75. T. Marschak, *Decentralizing the command economy: the study of a pragmatic strategy for reformers,* Center for Research in Management Science, Univ. of California, Tech. report no. 8, Nov. 1970.

The generalized problem of informational co-ordination of complex economi systems, extending beyond the parametric function of the price signal as the "decentralizer", has been intensively investigated by a Czechoslovak school as a "semantic" one: "language", as defined, is seen as the efficiency-limiting factor. Representative for this school of thought is P. Pelikan's "Language as a limiting factor for centralization", *Amer. Econ. R.,* Sept. 1969; also O. Kyn's paper in *Czechoslovak Econ. Papers,* 11 (1969).
76. One can think here in terms of decision and feedback operators as modelled in R. Day/P. E. Kennedy, "Recursive decision systems", *Econometrica,* 5 (1970).
77. Thus e.g. in Jacob Marschak's "Problems in information economics", in Bonini *et al.,* op.cit.
78. Thus in Michajlo Mesarovic's writing. See in particular his (*et al.*) *Theory of hierarchical multi-level systems*; also a good résumé in Mesarovic's "Mathematica theory of general systems", in P. C. Hammer, ed., *Advances in mathematical systems theory* (London, 1969).

Mesarovic's general theory of multi-level systems rests on his principles of co-ordinability (intuitively arrived at criteria), specifically on those of "inter-action prediction" and of "balance". Their applicability conditions are ex-pressible in terms of adopted goal properties: thus the two principles imply respectively the conditions of the system's local "harmony" and of global har-mony and monotonicity, respectively; the principles, the harmony properties, and the relations between them form the basis for *decentralization* of the system. (The sophistication of the latter is moved, in the writings, from an ele-mentary construct up to a linear dynamic system with a quadratic performance criterion and an arbitrary number of subsystems on the operational level; further to nonlinear systems – some types of convex performance functions.)

The structuring of the problem – its co-ordinability principles – make for their close kinship with the feedback principle (controls based on observing the output and minimizing the difference between it and the postulated course); thereby also to the optimality principle (controls under the assumption that at the next stage of decision-making too the control enforced will be on the opti-mal basis; see our discussion of dynamic programming in Part II). Generally the foundations of the symbolic apparatus in strict logic insure for the abstractions, worked out, their role as generalizers of results obtainable by numerically-oriented methods.
79. Yu. A. Ennuste, in *EMM,* 4 (1972).
80. Ibid., pp. 541 ff.
81. The Ennuste methodology attracts attention also by formalizing the inverse approach, i.e. the build-up of a *decompositional* system via *composition* of the objective. Thus assume p partial problems

$$\max_{x} a_k y_k \left. \right\} g(x) \geqslant b; y_e(x) \geqslant y_{ek}^{\varrho}; e = 1, \ldots, p; e \neq k; x \in X$$

where y_{ek}^{ϱ} for each of the k objectives, at each step 1, is given by the co-ordinating centre. Solutions of the dual problem y_{ek} corresponding to the second constraint of the problem k are brought into the dual problem for finding the $y_{ek}^{\varrho+1}$.

Usually in the treatment of the primal problem the valuation of the coefficients a_k makes a serious difficulty (in handling, that is, the objective functions of the form $\Sigma^p_{k=1} a_k y_k(x)$); hence in planning/practice direct co-ordination of the sub-problems is being evaded; in solving each of them, others' objectives are taken as constraints based on "tradition", or-intuitively. By harmonizing the constraints on such a basis the "effective" point is taken as the suboptimal plan. Let such a "good" point correspond to $\max\limits_{x} y_k(x)\}$, $g(x) \geqslant b$; $g_{ek}(x) \geqslant y_{ek}^*$; $e = 1, \ldots, p$; $e \neq k$; $x \in X$. Then on some assumptions this problem is equivalent to that of the form $\max\{[y_k(x) + \Sigma_e\xi^*{}_{ek}g_{ek}(x)]\}$, $g(x) \geqslant b$; $g_{ek}(x) \geqslant y_{ek}^*$; valuation a_k appears expressed by ξ_k. From such an analytical examination we obtain the valuation which helps in composition of the objective function.

The ideas on stability in aggregation-disaggregation appear to have been borrowed from Lasdon's work on decomposition in mathematical programming, cf. IEEE, *Trans.Sys.Sci. & Cyb.* (SSC-4)2, 1968. In turn this relies on the important Fisher-Fuller findings on matrix stability crucial in decomposable systems (viz. that if a real square matrix P fulfils certain general conditions, then there exists a real diagonal matrix D such that the characteristic equation of DP is stable and aperiodic; this equation is termed stable if the real parts of its roots are negative; if the latter are all real and simple it is termed aperiodic). cf. M. E. Fisher/ A. T. Fuller, *Proc. Camb. Philos. Soc.*, 53(1957), p.878.

82. Babunashvili *et al.*, *EMM*, 2 (1969); cf. also Russman, in Fedorenko, *Issledovanye potokov informatsyi* (Moscow, 1968).
83. Trapeznikov, *Avt. i tel.*, 1 (1966); cf. also reference in Maiminas, *Sistemy ekonomicheskoy informatsyi* (1967).
84. M. Aoki, "Control of large-scale dynamic systems by aggregation", IEEE *Trans. on Automatic Control*, AC-13/3 (1968).
85. G. Orcutt *et al.*, "Data aggregation and information loss", *Amer. Econ. R.*, 1968.
86. H. H. Kelejian, "Information lost in aggregation: a Bayesian approach", *Econometrica*, 1 (1972) (reference to V. Chetty, "Pooling of time series and cross section data", *Econometrica*, 1968).
87. P. V. Moeseke/Guy de Ghellinck, "Decentralization in separable programming", ibid., 1 (1969).
88. F. Martines-Soler, in *Vestnik moskovskogo Univ. – Ekonomika*, 2 (1971).
89. V. M. Polterovich, *EMM*, 6 (1970).
90. T. N. Pervozvanskaya/A. A. Pervozvanskiy, in *EMM*, 5(1966).
91. J. Kornai/Th. Liptak, "Two-level planning", *Econometrica*, Jan.1965. A "decentralization" model of the Dantzig-Wolfe family (Russian version reprinted in Nemchinov, ed., *Primenenye matematiki* (iii), exercised considerable influence, in its time, on Soviet theoretical thinking on the subject. See for discussion Zauberman, *Aspects of planometrics* (1967), p. 96 and *passim*).
92. Printsipy optimalnogo planirovanya (Moscow, 1973).
93. Volkonskiy, *EMM*, 2 (1966).
94. Yu. N. Gavrilyets, "Problema agregirovanya v uslovyakh bolshoy razmernosti", in *Optimalnoye planirovanye v uslovayakh bolshoy razmernosti* (Moscow, 1963).
95. V. F. Pugachev, *Optimalnoye planirovanye-teoreticheskiye problemy* (Moscow, 1968).

96. See J. Kornai/B. Martos, *Autonomous control of the economic system* (1970) and *Econometrica*, 3 (1973).

For the impact of this line of thinking on the modelling of economic mechanism of Hungary cf. M. Tardos, "A model of the behaviour of Central Agencies and enterprises", *Acta oeconomica Academiae Scientiarum Hungaricae*, 4/1 (1969).

On the other hand Kornai's new scepticism is clearly influenced by the disappointments acknowledged in the "man-model" dialogue in practice. Thus, for instance, in the light of experience emphasis is placed on difficulties in the transformation in model systems. As it appears, the well known experiment in Hungary, with linear transformation between input-output tables in value terms and a two-level plan model with physical-term magnitudes – on which empiricists staked considerable hopes – has not proved a success (cf. *Wirtschaftswissenschaft*, 4 (1968). It seems that it is this and similar disappointments that have led Kornai to the view that "in reality there are unreliable models . . . ; there are only relatively good, and – one can say – relatively bad ones" (ibid, p.551; our translation).

97. On this some affinity is acknowledged with Arrow *et al.*, *Studies in mathematical theory of inventory and production* (Stanford, 1960). We could also add for reference in the context Hoth *et al.*, *Planning production, inventories and work force*. However the meaningfulness of the analogy is somewhat weakened by the essentially *micro*-economic orientation of these works and the assumption of a strictly competitive market framework.

(In Kornai/Martos the profit motive is somewhat vaguely replaced by "identifying oneself with, and living on and of the firm with smooth running".)

98. This conception is expanded upon in J. Kornai, *Pressure and suction of the market* (Indiana Univ. Working Papers, no.7, Dec. 1971).

99. Kornai, in *Acta oeconomica*, 6/4 (1971).

100. Ibid., p.314.

101. cf. Sukhamoy Chakravarty, *Capital and development planning* (Cambridge, Mass., 1969), p.264.

102. The present "anti-equilibrium" tendency in some of the control-oriented schools in socialist planning economics is the more interesting as it comes at a time when the new results in equilibrium analysis are noteworthy i.a. for the community of mathematical apparatus with the control theory. This is true of the work with the ideally competitive systems with atomless measure space of economic agents, specifically the theorem of measurable selections, as well as the classical Lyapunov theorems cf. Werner Hildenbrand. "The core of competitive equilibrium" and G. Debreu, "Economic equilibrium", in Kuhn/Szegö, *Math. systems theory . . .*, respectively vols. 2 & 1 – both point to the community of formalisms. (cf. also on the subject Szegö's "The core of an economy with a measure space of economic agents", *R. Econ. Stud.*, Oct. 1968). See also Addendum.

103. It may be of interest to note that a change of the traditionalist stand is also advocated *within* the equilibrium theory "camp". Thus in his critique of the Debreu framework Allais argues that it is paradoxical that the majority of present-day theorists in the field rely on hypotheses refuted by both introspection and observation specifically those of general convexity and stability. In Allais's contention the "exaltation of the formal rigour" intensifies the non-realism. He rejects what he describes as the monistic in favour of pluralistic theory. In the latter, in putting emphasis on the "realization of surpluses", the "markets' model" of the economy – so he argues – becomes essentially dynamic for, as it is postulated, this both implements the casuality links and the interdependence with the neighbourhood of an equilibrium situation which results (Maurice Allais,

"Les théories de l'équilibre économique général et de l'efficacité maximale – impasses récentes et nouvelles perspectives", *R. d'écon. pol.*, May-June 1971).

The problem of staticness of the traditionalist constructs is clearly focal in the search for new more realistic approaches.

104. C. J. Bliss, "Prices, markets and planning", *Econ. J.*, Mar. 1972.

105. cf. also Vishnyev's discussion of the parametric system ("operators" in planning), including the index of the state of inventories, above, p. 32.

106. See F. Hahn, "Equilibrium dynamics with heterogenous capital goods", *Q.J. Econ.*, Nov. 1966. Wider contexts are treated in his "On warranted growth path", *R. Econ. Stud.*, 1968 and "Some adjustment problems", *Econometrica*, 1 (1970). Cf. also K. J. Arrow/F. H. Hahn, *General competitive analysis* (San Francisco, 1971).

107. P. Samuelson, 'Indeterminacy of development in a heterogeneous capital model with constant saving propensities', in K. Shell, ed., *Essays on the theory of optimal economic growth* (1967).

108. K. Shell/J. Stiglitz, 'Investment allocation in a dynamic economy', *Q. J. Econ.*, Nov. 1967.

109. E. Burmeister *et al.,* 'A note on the global stability of a simple model with many capital goods', ibid., Nov.1968.

110. op. cit., p. 228.

111. The question of the conflict between 'current' devolutional decision-making and the centralist dynamic decision-making has been brought out by me in the critique of Lange's model of the 1960s (see Zauberman, "Statica e dinamica; mercato e piano", in *Programmazione e progresso economico* (Milan, 1969).

In Polish writing the conflict was perceptibly hinted at by W. Trzeciakowski, *Systems of indirect management in a planned economy* (1971 – Cowles Foundation Discussion Paper, no. 312).

112. L. V. Kantorovich/L. V. Makarov, in Trapeznikov, ed., *V vsesoyuznoye sovyeshchanye . . .*

113. G. Debreu, *Theory of value* and Morishima, *Equilibrium, stability and growth.*

114. V. F. Pugachev/G. V. Martynov, *EMM*, 2 (1973); V. F. Pugachev/A. K. Pitelin, *EMM*, 6 (1974).

115. *Canad. J. Econ.*, 1, 1968.

116. *R. Econ. Stud.*, 1969 & 1971.

117. *Sistema modeley narodnokhoziaystvennogo planirovanya*, (1972).

118. V. F. Pugachev, in *EMM*, 2 (1970).

119. As has been pointed by Danilov-Danilyan ("Iterativnyie metody optimalnogo planirovanya", *Matematika i kibernetika v ekonomike*) the term "iterative methods" of optimal planning is in Soviet tradition applied to the class of approximate (asymptotic) methods of optimization "coming up to" Brown's solution of matrix games and the iterative gradient method of concave plan-programming. And the imprecision has been stressed since on the one hand it leaves out the finite methods of linear and quadratic programming; on the other hand patently not all approximate methods belong to iterative class.

120. E. N. Borisov/I. V. Magarik, in *EMM*, 5(1966).

121. Golshtein/Movshovich, in *EMM*, 5 (1967).

122. cf. V. V. Amvrosyenko (ibid., 4 (1965) and restatement of his method and comment in D. B. Yudin/E. G. Golshtein, *Lineynoye programirovanye – teorii, metody, i prilozhenya* (Moscow, 1969), p. 407.

123. Restated by Yudin/Golshtein, ibid., from a paper by the Zaklad Aparatow Matematycznych PAN, Warsaw, 1961, p. 409.

124. Pervozvanskaya/Pervozvanskiy, in *Avt. i tel.*, 7 (1968), pp. 60ff.; cf. also the same, in *EMM*, 5 (1966).

125. *EMM*, 5 (1966).
126. cf. also M. V. Rybashov, in *Avt. i tel.*, 11 (1970) and S. M. Movshovich, in *Tekh. kib.*, 6 (1966).
127. V. M. Polterovich, *EMM*, 4 (1970).
128. The function $\varphi(y)$ is defined as quasi-summatory for $y_i, i \in V$ at y^0 if $\varphi'(y^0, h)$ exists and for all $h \in R^n$ the $\varphi'(y^0, h) = \varphi'(y^0, Pr_v h)$. The $\varphi'(y, h)$ $h \in R^n$ denotes the interval

$$\varphi'(y, h) = \lim_{t \to +0} \frac{\varphi(y + th) - \varphi(y)}{t}.$$

129. While aware of differences in some fundamentals, I am bracketing them here together because of the common nature of the probabilistic approach.
130. C. E. Shannon, in S. Dock/P. Bernanys, eds., *Information and prediction in sciences* (1965); and in H. V. Foerster, ed., *Cybernetics* (1951), p.219.
131. D. M. MacKay, in C. Cherry, ed., *Information theory* (1961).
132. R. Carnap/Y. Bar-Hillel, *An outline of the theory of semantic information*, Technical report 247, MIT, Research Laboratory in Electronics, 1953; and the same in *Brit. J. Phil. Sci.*, 4/14 (1953-4).
133. A. N. Kolmogorov, in *Problemy peredachi informatsyi*, 1 (1965); for his pioneering work in the field cf. his paper (jointly with I. M. Gelfand and A. M. Yaglom) in *Doklady*, 111/4 (1956).
134. A. Siegel/J. J. Wolf, *Man-machine simulation models* (1969).
135. In Soviet literature problems of simulation in the treatment of complex systems are discussed, i.a., by N. P. Buslenko, *Modelirovanye slozhnykh sistem* (1968).

3

THE NEW THEORY OF ECONOMIC GROWTH

(1) A student is tempted to preface a discussion of the contemporary Soviet theory of growth by reference to Marx. There are some good reasons for this. Marx, and through him Ricardo, provided the Soviet economists with certain conventions in conceptualizing economic phenomena. Moreover, in our present particular context it may be acknowledged that Marx, the designer of the first formalized — even if formalized in a very elementary way — dynamic system has imparted to Soviet economics the intellectual climate of decisive dynamic orientation. We will have an opportunity to indicate the degree of persistence of the Marxian legacy and the elements of its continuity. Having said this, it must be qualified in the sense that what persists in the theory of growth is still the general mode of Marxian thinking. For by now Marx's analytical apparatus, belonging to the history of economic ideas, is being rapidly displaced in the Soviet economist's more modern apparatus. To be sure, it is still de rigeur in investigations into some specific properties of the capitalist mechanism, such as Marx's theory of income distribution and capital formation. In the first place, Marx's model of growth is employed to discover the resolution of the famous controversy as to the indefinite viability or otherwise of the theory of the collapse of capitalism. This controversy, initiated by Tugan-Baranovskiy,[1] Rosa Luxemburg,[2] and Bukharin, continued to preoccupy a fair number of theoreticians in the earlier decades of this century and continues to remain one of the standard themes of Soviet writing. Conveniently, however, the increasing compartmentalization of Soviet economics has virtually insulated such political-economic themes from analytical work and the economics of planning: they are of hardly any significance for the development of the latter. There is no need to concern ourselves with them in the present study.

For reasons hinted at in the preceding paragraphs Marxian dynamics helped to articulate the Soviet attitudes towards the issues of growth in the

phase of breakthrough. It seems to me well tenable that the crucial fact in
the history of the Soviet theory of growth is that in the "heroic" period of
the country's industrialization its conditions – the "environment" in the
broadest sense – were in agreement, or at least were not in conflict with,
the basic hypotheses and premises of Marx's model (such as are explicit as
well as those which are not spelt out in the design, including those of which
its author himself seems to have not been quite aware). Hence the congeniality of the model to Soviet strategists. As this period has been drawing to
its conclusion and the "environment" – in the sense indicated – has been
undergoing a drastic change, the strategy precepts rationalized in the
Marxian model have appeared to be obsolescent and have tended to be
de facto abandoned.

It is at this stage that the tenet of universal validity of the strategy
precepts derived from Marx's model has become *the* critical issue in
traditional Soviet doctrine. That permitted joining in attempts to unravel
the inexplicit assumptions of the model and investigating the qualifying
effect of its characteristics and its assumptional framework, explicit or inexplicit, on its "realism" and on its applicational potential in time and
space. (The heart-searching is still continuing in Soviet traditionalist
growth-theoretic literature.) Among characteristics thus brought into the
foreground is the type of aggregation; and crucial among inexplicit
assumptions is the constancy of technology. By that time the issues treated
traditionally as axiomatic have at last been recognized as open to investigation, as pointed out by Khachaturov.[3]

The Soviet theoretical investigation is helped by contemporary studies
carried out elsewhere. Morishima's work is in this respect of exceptional
significance: for it is most penetrating and definitive in analytically taking
Marx's construct "to bits": it is also unsurpassed in synthesis: in indicating
the ways by which that construct lends itself to adjustment and reformulation which can give it a place in the modern growth theory; the
analytical part helps to appraise what for nearly half a century Soviet
doctrine was considering as the necessary and sufficient condition for
growth and for which it was invoking Marx's authority – the principle of
the prioritarian growth of the "Department I" as derived from his model.
What we owe to Morishima[4] is his demonstration that the relationship
between the two "departments" rests on a deus ex machina manipulation
in Marx's arithmetical example-model; and that it is the artificial assumption that secures a perfect dynamic equilibrium, stronger than in the
neo-classics.

These developments offer a new scope for Soviet writing aimed at reconciling Marx with the contemporary mathematical economic mode of thinking: Nemchinov, Novozhilov, and Konyus did devote a good deal of effort to this purpose.[5] However, the matter, as we have suggested, has essentially historic-theoretical significance, even if one agrees with Morishima's plausible tenet that Marx's model can be regarded as the prototype of the systems of Leontief and von Neumann — both so decisive, as it is argued in the present book, for contemporary Soviet theory of planning growth; and even if one would accept Leontief's own paradoxical observation that while, on the one hand, mathematical methodology has gained ground in the economics of socialist countries, Western constructors of theoretical growth models have become "conscious of the fact that the approach has more in common with Ricardo, Marx, and other classical economists than with Marshall or with Keynes".[6]

Notes

1.   The re-working of Marx's model in a way which relates its system of "expanded reproduction" to the present-day's luggage of the theoretical economist has proceeded for quite a time and in several directions. Certain tendencies in the theory of production factors — particularly the reconsideration of the traditional dichotomy of prime factors, the widening of the concept of capital — have helped the process.[7]

The modernization of the apparatus in Marx's model began with reformulation in terms of a production function. In the West Samuelson's[8] restatement in these terms threw some new light on Marx's conclusions. As we shall see, there have been several restatements in these terms in Soviet literature: at least in one of its production-function growth constructs, the Kantorovich school has adopted Marx's basic framework, i.e. a two-sector, two-product system (however, as it will appear from sect. 10 of this chapter, it has done so *not* for Marx's fundamental purpose of determining the laws of differential sectoral advance).

There have also been attempts to apply contemporary formalism for consistency.and optimization to Marx's system. Oskar Lange was the first in the literature of socialist countries to re-work Marx's model in Leontief's — to be more precise in Leontief's *static* terms (Lange's exercise has been discussed by me elsewhere).[9]

Marx's basic framework has been used by some Soviet students for rigorous testing of the path towards the optimum.[10] But, we will see in a while, the optimand is not necessarily that of Marx.

2.   Some experiments with numerical (empirical) modelling, carried out at the TsEMI point to the relevance for the issue of the break-up of

the "Department I" into "subdepartments" feeding capital formation in respectively producer-goods and consumer-goods sectors. Logically then the question arises as to why the break-up of the system should not be carried out throughout the matrix. This has been attempted by Mayevskiy,[11] whose model has the form of a system of linear homogeneous differential equations $FD(y) = y$ where F is the capital/output matrix for the [in application 14] capacity forming sectors, y is the vector of their capacities, $D(y)$ is the vector of final product, D being a differentiation operator. The solution shows the expansion of these sectors as $Y(t) = che^{\lambda t}$ (c being an arbitrary constant permitting the determination of the capacities' initial values, h a vector describing the structure of capacities in the capacity-forming system). The final product's dynamics coincides with that of the capacities, $D(y) = che^t$. A noteworthy point is that the λ is *not* exogenously given: it is conceived as computable — dependent on the matrix of capital coefficients F: mathematically it appears as the eigenvalue of the matrix.

Taking the share of the first subgroups in the total output of the capital-producing industry [empirically, in the Soviet case apparently no more than 18 per cent] as some η, we have $\lambda = (1 - \alpha)\eta\lambda$ where α denotes the share of the capital-replacement-producing branches. Considering the capacities of the second subgroup of Department I as the constraining re-source and taking some adopted variant of the objective function with respect to the structure of consumption as known, the problem would be solved as one of programming.

3.   Dadayan's model of a very-long-term plan[12] is symptomatic of the new relativistic interpretation of the principle of faster advance in "Department I" derived from Marx's "schema" (a new approach certainly not unrelated intellectually to the change in traditional Soviet planning practice). Its optimand is

$$\sum_{t=1}^{T} (1 + \lambda)^{t-1} \Pi_t \to \max,$$

i.e. living standard, constrained by

$$\left\{ \begin{array}{l} b_1/\rho_1 . K_1 \qquad\qquad\qquad\qquad\qquad + b_1/\rho_1 \Pi_1 = F_1{}^* \\ \dotfill \\ - K_1 - K_2 - K_3 - \dots . - K_{T-1} + b_T/\rho_T K_T + \; + b_T/\rho_T \Pi_T = F_1{}^* \\ \min \Pi_t = \Pi_{\min}^{*(t)}; \qquad \min K_t = K_{\min}^{*(t)}; \qquad K_t \geqslant 0 \qquad \Pi_t \geqslant 0 \end{array} \right.$$

The solution is then shaped as follows

t	$1, 2, \ldots \ldots t$	$t + 1, \ldots \ldots, T$
K	Max $= \rho_t / b_t F_t - \Pi_{\min}^{*(t)}$	Min $= K_{\min}^{*(t)}$
Π	Min $= \Pi_{\min}^{*(t)}$	Max $= \rho_\theta / b_\theta F_\theta.$

(*Notation*: F is stock of productive capacities ("funds"), P social product, K productive investment, Π consumption, b capital-intensity coefficient, λ rate of time discount, t, θ, t time indexes; ρ share of productive investment in national product.)

The idea of strategy is to pursue the objective over two phases: phase 1, up to some year t, of faster growth-rates in accumulation of capacities than in consumption; and phase 2, from $t+1$ onwards, of a switch of the "accumulation potential" toward raising consumption. Patently then the crux of the matter is determining the breakthrough year t. The way for fixing the value of a "regulator", r, for determining t is not indicated with any degree of rigour; as Dadayan puts it, "formulation of any exact and rigorous proposition as to the limits for the regulator 'r' must be left to technical-economic expertise". The model is interesting in posing the issue rather than answering it.

(2) When concerned with Soviet theory of growth and its relation to Marx's modelling heritage one is likely to find of interest the family of models originated in Uzawa's[13] basic two-sector construct (itself rooted in Meade's[14] neo-classical model), reworked as a Pontryagin programme by Shell.[15] There, illuminatingly from our angle, the nature of the Pontryagin-Hamiltonian multiplier (cf. Part II p. 302) appears as that of the dynamic social demand price, at optimum, of the capital good in terms of the consumer-good numéraire. The vexed issue of the Soviet theory of growth over decades, to be sure, is not treated explicitly, but some clear indications for it evolve from the analysis, even under the conventionally stringent assumptions (starting with that of linearity throughout). This applies in particular to the demonstration that the bi-sectorally (capital-goods/consumer-goods sectors) differentiated capital-labour ratio, when "efficient", is an increasing function of the wage-rental ratio. There follows the related

point on bi-sectorally differentiated production functions – differentiated
with respect to relative primary-factor intensities: patently relevant for the
stationary solution to the capital-formation equations indicating the maximum "sustainable" capital-labour ratio under optimum.

The analysis helps also to discern the implications of certain elements
in the choice and sectoral differentiation of technology which evade
"modelling" but have been strongly represented in Soviet doctrine; here
belong considerations for promotion of technical progress; also for full
employment of factors, while in the models discussed this corresponds to
optimum.

The point of relevance for our theme that emerges from such analysis
is this. With the two ratios, those of capital/labour and wage/rental, as a
datum, not only the sectoral factor allocation and sectoral prices of
products – mutually in terms of each other – but also the efficient
relative sectoral scales of output are uniquely determined.

Srinivasan[16] had established a tenet as to the critical value of the capital-
labour ratio that is maximally sustainable in the two-sector system: to the
effect that if the initial ratio is smaller (resp. larger) than this value, we have
specialization, under optimum, in investment (resp. consumption) until
this value is reached, and the Golden Age is approached in a non-
specialization process. (In fact Uzawa tried to establish this theorem without a capital-intensity assumption which has been further elaborated by
Haque.)[17]

A bridge between Marx and itself has been found by the Soviet mathematical school in the rediscovered Feldman[18] system: it tries to establish
the link with him in its recent writing. Apart from Feldman being its
precursor in using some elements of the mathematical apparatus, the
common ground is the inquiry into the nature of dynamic equilibrium and
the trajectories of growth that lead to it: the behaviour and interactions of
key elements in growth: factor relations and their efficiency. The pace of
growth is determined in Feldman by the growth-rate of capacities and the
efficiency of their use, and by changes in the input of labour and its
productivity. (In the last analysis, under conditions of a labour surplus, the
expansion and efficiency of capacities are decisive; with a labour deficit, it
is the growth of labour efficiency that is the determinant.)

(The reader "conditioned" by the theory of growth of the capitalistic
economy will have to bear in mind as a positum that in that of growth of a
Soviet-type economy monetary factors are perfectly neutral in determining
the pace, path, and structural characteristics of the growth processes and
of capital formation; and thereby also of factor employment. Feldman's

was the pioneering formalization of Soviet growth processes from this angle as well.)

As in Marx, in Feldman too there is no explicitly formalized optimization procedure. But he has an explicit maximand. Consumption is treated as the objective of the growing system: Feldman's declared purpose is the exploration of its behaviour as a function of the economy's structural conditions. Consumption is indeed focal in Feldman's analysis. (This incidentally accounts for his departure — the first in Soviet writing — from Marx's fundamental dichotomy. Unlike Marx, Feldman includes in his first sector the production of means of production for securing the output of consumer goods at the postulated level; in the second sector he includes securing the replacement of, and expansion of, capacities. In this respect the Feldman system is closer to that of Mahalanobis,[19] where the intermediate-good industries are split between the two sectors, so that each can yield its net output independently of another. There is also an analogy with Kalecki's new model of growth.)[20] It is from the point of view of the stated objective that the system's strategic interrelations are observed: the planner is offered a "menu" with respect to this objective — a constant consumption level, or its growth accompanying the system's growth at either a constant or increasing rate (steady and accelerated growth respectively). The implications of the choice are clarified — the saving rate being exogenously determined in Feldman. (The treatment of this rate as such a parameter corresponds to the traditional stand of the theory of normative planning; on the whole it persists in contemporary writing, e.g. in the new Kalecki model. However, at least as its earlier stage the Soviet mathematical school tended to turn it into an endogenous variable and sought a methodology for optimizing it — the tangency on contemporary Western inquiries is indicated in my discussion of the objective function. The more recent attitude is marked by some scepticism as to possibilities of such approach: this is true of the Kantorovich school.)

What in general distinguishes Feldman from his precursors in modelling growth — from Marx in the first place — is the standpoint from which the process is observed. It is essentially a normative-planning angle: the purpose, as we have seen, is to offer the planner aid in decision-making: to put into his hand key parameters and show their use in pursuing the objectives. To this extent it clearly anticipates the plan-programming approach. A crucial element is that the planner's choice includes — in Feldman — also the alternatives of the type of growth, *balanced or unbalanced*: we will show in the sequel also the revival of this proposition by the programming school.

(3)   A more easily discernible influence on Soviet thinking on growth is that of von Neumann.[21] This is treated in my separate study, to which the reader is referred.[22]

What is it that accounts for the strong attraction the von Neumann system has had for the Soviet theory of growth during the last decade? The elements of its "unrealism" are well known and have been stressed in Soviet literature. To begin with, this is so with respect to the assumption of the optimality of the initial state of the system: and indeed with respect to its fundamental characteristic as one that is closed and completely describable in terms of linear technologies.

But the von Neumann construct has proved valuable in adjusting Soviet thinking to the modern approach. In this respect its merits have been those which Koopmans[23] brought into strong relief in his brilliant aperçu of its career in contemporary economics, viz. as the first explicit statement of the relations between prices and input-output coefficients characterizing the system's efficiency and competitive equilibrium (here linking up with Wold) — all this as well as the rigour and explicitness first offered to a non-aggregative theory of capital.

To continue along the Koopmans line, there are also crucial implications for the strategy for growth. The substitution by Dorfman, Samuelson, and Solow[24] of the objective of a maximal capital stock of postulated structure at a sufficiently distant time-point for the original one — maximal growth "*as such*" — is stressed by Koopmans as the decisive step towards realism. But as far as Soviet strategy for growth is concerned, *both* approaches are in a special sense "realistic". The two fit in well with Soviet experience.

Both the build-up of a maximum capacity of a given composition for a distant horizon and what on the face of it — because of the horizon's remoteness — has the appearance of "growth for growth sake", have been supplementing each other in the Soviet strategic approach.

Moreover Koopmans's strongest objection on the count of unrealism — on the ground that in von Neumann's system, consumption is not the ultimate aim, consumer goods being treated as input into the output of the labour-time producing sector — is in historical perspective not necessarily a conceptual obstacle to the Soviet student. To be sure present-day Soviet doctrine would no longer formalize the problem in this way. But taking the supply of labour and consumption as its "real cost", and in this sense logically a minimand or a fixed-level constraint, is not intellectually unacceptable as a point of departure for theorizing on growth.[25]

To put the matter in a somewhat different way, the congeniality of the von Neumann construct to the Soviet traditionalist planning theory's treatment of the problems lies in the nature of intertemporal extremization. In the sense familiar to the reader from Western literature of economic growth, its criterion is "efficiency";[26] appraising, that is, a plan version by the terminal capacity stock, its size and structure: a variant's efficiency is understood to mean its target for the capacity-stock vector: the vector non-dominated by any alternative. As our story progresses, we will indicate the contemporary shift in the Soviet mode of thinking and formalization in terms of utility, specifically in terms of consumption utility as the objective function.[27]

The acclimatization of the Neumannian ideas in Soviet theory may legitimately be identified first and foremost with the writing of Kantorovich and his associates. This alone adds to our interest in his views on the merits and demerits of the von Neumann system.

Note

These writings have appeared in print since this chapter was written — and they may help to see the adjustments in the line of the dominant school of thought.

The criterial proposition in Kantorovich's[28] present-day reasoning is that to be adequate the dynamic model must "reflect" the characteristics of "socialist production", specifically: optimality; technological variability and product substitution; labour's role as the unique source of value; presence of non-reproducible primary factors; continuity of technical advance. Kantorovich's point is that while the first two elements are to a certain extent allowed for in von Neumann's system, it fails to allow for all the rest of them. In particular it does so with respect to the special role of labour: in that system — and in Leontief's model — labour is assumed to be always available in any amount required. Two consequences are drawn: (1) a complete unsuitability of the von Neumann model for deriving even the first approximation to the normative rate of return from investment (a focal issue in Soviet theory of growth — see the following chapter); (2) the faulty appraisal in both von Neumann's and Leontief's models of the dynamically generated requirements of capital, allowing as they do only for those entailed in the expanding scale of output but not those resulting from technical progress and replacement of assets becoming technologically obsolescent.

It will be granted that the implicit assumption of unconstrained availability of labour affects the scarcity value of capital (in Kantorovich it is one of the scarce resources). For realism relative factor scarcities have to be

allowed for: this does not detract, however, from the basic validity of the
Neumannian concept of capital price. Indeed, in Kantorovich's modelling
it is the point of departure for valuation of the marginal return on capital
under optimum.

(4)   Several elements contribute to the reception of the von Neumann
ideas. The strongest and most immediate is quite probably their kinship
with Leontief, his fundamental ideas and technical constructs. To start with
the latter. It was the adoption of his classical method of inter-industry
analysis — itself a brilliant rigorous idealization of the method of balances
pioneered in Soviet planning — that had opened the era of mathematics in
Soviet economics. Within a few years Nemchinov[29] was arguing that it is
the Leontievian construct that has permitted solving the von Neumann problem. (We see here the link-up with Western writing of the period: Gale's
work on Leontief's irreducible systems,[30] Morishima's on the "no joint
production" system,[31] McKenzie's on a generalized Leontief system with a
period structure,[32] Tsukui's contributions already mentioned,[33] the
Kemeny-Morgenstern-Thompson[34] tenet on the Leontief dynamic system
as a particular case of that of von Neumann.)
     In the fundamental idea there is the approach to the Neumannian gen-
eral equilibrium via what we may validly term the Walras-Dmitriev-Leontief
concept.[35]
     The immediate relevance of the Neumann-type modelling for Soviet
planning theory had become clear when the celebrated Dorfman-Samuelson-
Solow turnpike conjecture[36] was formally proved — in Radner,[37]
Morishima,[38] McKenzie,[39] Nikaido[40] and, for an infinite continuum, by
Furuya and Inada. And patently also when Morishima had shown that,
and why, the Dorfman-Samuelson-Solow trajectory has a planning nature
in the sense of postulating the determination by a planner of the terminal[41]
ray. Thus the normative character of the Neumannian system had been
established in the Dorfman-Samuelson-Solow restatement, and its follow-
up: by itself a point of congeniality with Soviet planning theory.
     The restatement itself with the turnpike theory and its implications
were introduced almost immediately to the Soviet student by Mikhalevskiy[42]
— in the context of the issue of balanced versus unbalanced planned growth
(he has been ever since associated with the conception of their combination, see p. 213). The Mikhalevskiy contribution owes an acknowledged inspiration both to Morishima's analysis of the stability of equilibrium in the
Leontief dynamized system[43] with a spectrum of techniques and to

Jorgenson's theory of disequilibrium. The choice confronting the plan modeller was thus presented there as that between the two approaches, i.e. those of (a) the strictly causally determined dynamic input-output system at full employment of capacities with the associated dual solution, and (b) the dynamic programme. The (a) in its "pure" form would suffer from reduced number of degrees of freedom; moreover the (b) would offer a wider scope for the policy-maker's manoeuvring, specifically on account of time-lags and variants in the use of resources. Generally speaking in (b) investment policy would be the economic system's *"controller"*. In Mikhalevskiy's reasoning, then, the (b) would commend itself by its offering greater scope for disequilibrium solutions a la Jorgenson: the faster tempo of disproportionate advance would outweigh the handicaps of its disproportionality. On balance a sequential solution combining the (a) and (b), with sufficient scope for the latter, is the precept for the modeller.

Note

Throughout this chapter we focus on the problem of growth equilibrium. It has been remarked that equilibrium models are essentially descriptive rather than normative. Patently the Soviet theory of growth is interested in the normative approach (Karlin).[44]

The origins of a formalized conception of equilibrium in Russian writing are traceable back to the beginning of its mathematical school — to Dmitriev's work[45] at the turn of the century (he is the Russian protagonist of the Cournot-Walras concepts). It was revived in the framework of inter-industry analysis in the pioneering of plan construction (one can indeed validly talk of the Walras-Dmitriev-Leontief concept of equilibrium).[46] It was disowned by official doctrine by the end of the decade — at the threshold of the plan era — as inhibiting growth; however, in this doctrine it has been axiomatically assumed that planned growth is tautologically interpretable as balanced or "proportionate" growth. This stand would be inconsistent on the definition of the balanced and equilibrium growth path implying outputs growing at the same proportionate rate, or — on stronger definition — at a constant rate (cf. e.g. Bliss on "putty-clay" growth).[47] However, Soviet doctrine has been evading a definition: in actual fact the strategy pursued has been based on unbalanced growth, on what has rightly been described as the "bottleneck effect" (Wiles).[43]

As noted, the equilibrium concept reappeared — in its modern rigorous form, as implied in the theory of optimization. We have indicated the explicit assimilation in Soviet planning theory of the Arrow-Debreu concepts.

Here we will point out that in Soviet writing too the emphasis is on the "myopia" as the disequilibrating factor. Mikhalevskiy deserves a particular mention in the present context since he stands for the thesis that it is under conditions of limited foresight and strictly constrained variation ranges of key variables that the growth of a planned economy becomes a process of a continual interaction between a tendency towards a stationary equilibrium and disturbances. Hence the conception of a strategy precept – a combination of the equilibrium and disequilibrium (balanced and unbalanced, proportionate and disproportionate) types of non-stationary growth. At the price of affecting the balance, the latter would accelerate the pace by adding to the plan's realism and adaptability; the former would ensure greater smoothness of the growth processes but would handicap them by accentuating the impact of scarcities, thereby decelerating the potential pace. In choosing the combination an optimum would have to be aimed at, at some point equalizing marginal gain and loss from the two (note the return in Soviet theoretical thinking on growth – within the new formalized scaffolding – to the idea of the choice put forward thirty years earlier by Feldman – see p. 132). The implication of this concept of such a non-stationary regime is a correspondingly disequilibrated system of shadow pricing (Gavrilyets-Mikhalevskiy-Leibkind).[49]

(5)   The Neumann-Leontief type of mechanism has found application in some numerically oriented Soviet models. Among this Movshovich's[50] design, akin to those of McKenzie and Tsukui,[51] deserves attention. As it appears, a construct of his design has been employed (jointly with Yefimov) in determining maximum growth-rates, sectoral proportions and prices, and the impact of the consumption and investment ratios on these magnitudes.

Balance relations between parameters of the system's states, sequentially in time, are given by

$$(A' - I)x'_t + cy_t + \Gamma z_t + B \sum_{\tau=0}^{\tau_0} \Psi(\tau)x_t^\tau \leqslant 0,$$

$$lx_t' - y_t \leqslant 0,$$
$$x_t' - z_t \leqslant 0,$$

$$z_t - \sum_{\tau=0}^{\tau_0} \Phi(\tau)x_t^\tau \leqslant z_{t-1}, \tag{1}$$

$$x_t^\tau \leqslant x_{t-1,}^{\tau+1} \quad \tau = 0, 1, \ldots, \tau_0 - 1,$$

$$x_t', y_t, z_t, x_t^\tau \geqslant 0, i = 1, \ldots, T.$$

(*Notation*: Matrices denote: A intermediate inputs, B capital/output, Γ-replacement inputs, $\Psi(t)$ and $\Phi(t)$ distribution over time of investment and capacity maturation, respectively; I identity; vectors: c represents structure of consumption, x_t the scale of sectoral capacities, z_t capacity stocks; x_t^τ capacity volume initiated in year t to mature in year τ, y_t employed labour.)

As can be seen, the statement is akin to McKenzie's and Tsukui's[52] turnpike models of a Leontief dynamic system (partly more and partly less general than theirs). Presented in a compact form it simply reads $L_1 x_t \leqslant L_2 x_{t-1}$, (2), x being nonnegative, the L's square matrices of the n-th order, x_t an n-dimensional vector describing the economy's state. Its dual has the form $p_{t-1} L_1 \geqslant p_t L_2$ (3), p_t being nonnegative. The von Neumann primal and dual corresponding to the (2) and (3) are: $\alpha \to \max$ with $\alpha L_1 x \leqslant L_2 x$, (4), and $\beta \to \min$ with $\beta p L_1 \geqslant p L_2$, (5). The solution of (4) $(\alpha_0 x)$ exists — with growth-rate $\alpha_0 \geqslant 1$ and the vector of proportions x, unique and positive — where the system (1) is solvable and nondecomposable and the diagonal matrices $\Phi(t)$ and $\Psi(t)$ strictly consistent; the duality theorem holds $(\alpha_0 = \beta_0)$ where $\alpha_0 > 1$; the Neumannian price vector p is also unique and positive.

The Movshovich system (2) is taken to meet four conditions, i.e. (1) the L's are square matrices with L_2 nonnegative; (2) from $L_1 x$ nonpositive and x nonnegative it follows that $x = 0$; (3) the Neumannian vectors $\bar{x}$ and $\bar{p}$ exist, are unique, and positive; (4) of the roots of the characteristic equation $|\lambda L_1 - L_2| = 0$ only the simple root $\lambda = \alpha_0$ is found on the circle of the radius α_0.

Among theorems proved by Movshovich we single out here those for the primal-dual of the problem (2) and adopted social-utility maximand $U(X_0^T) = c x_T, c \geqslant 0$ subject to the additional conditions ((1)) – ((4)) of of the preceding paragraph.[52] The turnpike theorem for the optimal trajectory $\tilde{X}_0^T$ establishes that for any positive ϵ an M, common to all optimal trajectories and independent of T, will be found such that $p(x_t, \bar{x}) < \epsilon$ with $M \leqslant t \leqslant T - M$; and the dual for $\tilde{P}^{T-1}$ to the effect that for a given positive ϵ an M, common to all optimal trajectories and independent of T will be found such that $p(\bar{p}_t, \bar{p}) < \epsilon$ for $t \in M, \ldots, T - M$ (the ρ denoting angular distance).

(6)   Mikhalevskiy's ideas on the reception of the Neumannian conceptions into the body of Soviet planning theory agree at least with one point of the observed tendency: from the very start dynamic programming has been its main methodological vehicle. Thus this reception is — in the context — part and parcel of the assimilation of the *optimal-control* theory. That is true first and foremost of the fundamental construct in the field, the model of perspective planning, designed by Kantorovich and Makarov with its acknowledged kinship with the systems of *both* von Neumann and Bellman. That is why we discuss the contribution of the Kantorovich school essentially — and present its formalism — in Part II of this book. However, for the sake of continuity in our treatment of the Soviet theory of growth a very concise restatement is given at the present stage, with elaboration of some points of special growth-theoretic importance.

The reader will find in Part II what we describe as the "theoretical infrastructure" of that model formed largely by a set of theorems which are owed to two members of the Kantorovich school, Makarov and Romanovskiy. These theorems rigorously establish the inherent linkage of the system's motion under the rule of Bellman's Optimality Principle and von Neumann's regime. In Romanovskiy, in particular, we have the proof that the structure of production processes along the dynamic-programme path approaches the optimal one of the von Neumann system, the sum of deviations not exceeding some constant the existence of which is proved too; and that the growth-rate of the system is independent of the vector of terminal product-values and asymptotically approaches the maximum rate of the von Neumann system's growth.

(7)   The description of the Kantorovich-Makarov model itself, built up on this "infrastructure", is also given in our Part II. Its core is formed by a system of sequentially paired matrices, paired that is as those of output and input, the A's and B's, a feature of this no-primary-factor system being something like a double decomposition, of activities and of time (see ch. 7 p. 406). Thus multi-period capital formation is reduced to a sequence of neighbouring periods: over this sequence multi-periodicity is reflected in the degree of maturity of capacities — positive and, analogously, negative (that is, wear and tear and/or obsolescence). Activity to be employed as from period $(t+1)$ has a special ingredient in the matrix: with regard to it, for all plan intervals at $t \leqslant 0$ the entries are zero. The pace of growth — technological ("natural") and economic — thus generated is discussed on p. 409. We may, however, in the present context recall the Kantorovich-

Makarov formulation of dynamic efficiency as the quadruplet of the inter-related rates — of growth, technological (natural) and economic, of time discount, of return on (or normative efficiency rate of) investment, and of profit.

For the system the uniqueness of the limiting plan is derived from the Makarov-Romanovskiy's set of theorems. Moreover it is established that for this path the limit of directing cosines is formed of those of von Neumann's optimal path. From such a theoretical basis — as we shall see — Kantorovich-Makarov proceed to a pragmatic rule.

Because — so they argue — the finding of the terminal plan is a matter not yet theoretically explored with any degree of adequacy, and in any case it is tricky in numerical solution, the precept is to treat the plan prob-lem in a way of tolerable approximation with linear programming techniques.[53] The idea is then that the plan thus obtained would be aban-doned at some point of the path. The point has been restated and developed in Kantorovich's writing in more recent years.[54] As restated it is this: the choice of a criterion does affect substantially the plan as *a whole* but has little effect on the decisions in, and indices for *initial* phases of the long-run plan. And it is precisely its nearer phases that are of interest to the planner. Moreover, it must be realistically assumed that in any case the later phases of "perspective" plan would normally call for adjustments in the light of both new data and new objectives.

It is only fair to say that the Kantorovich-Makarov "architectural pre-cept" for plan-modelling found corroboration in other empirical as well as theoretical inquiries. (Of great interest in this respect is the work of Tsukui and his associates: in so far as all efficient paths at some time approach the von Neumann ray and spend most of the planning period in its neighbour-hood, whatever the target, the Tsukui recommendation for the planner too is to put aside value judgements and to lead the economy to, and then to keep it growing along that ray. On this too there is for the Tsukui construct a strong claim to empirical validation.)[55]

It seems to us that the Kantorovich-Makarov plan construction precept has a weaker intuitive justification for a developed than for a developing economy — if only because the latter's dominating objective must be, over a long horizon, to build up some basic infrastructure, whatever the farther remote goals.[56] Not surprisingly the Kantorovich-Makarov plan-construction rule has become a subject of controversy in Soviet mathematical-economic literature. It centres on the questions of the length of the plan horizon and of the provision for the beyond-the-horizon "tail" of the plan. It is granted by critics that the longer the plan period the less relevant is the tail prob-

lem and that in any case technological progress may be expected to force
the planner to abandon the plan at some time-point. The open question is,
however, how to determine the point of the switch-over from one plan to
another, and to determine it in such a way as to neutralize the handicap-
ping impact – from the technological angle – of the "old plan".[57]

In this controversy the middle-of-the-road school of thought, while con-
ceding the advantages of the flexible terminal point of the plan, argues that
this would entail – as the plan programme minimand – time: the time for
achieving posited targets; but in this we are back to "square one" – the
need to specify the output and consumption goals.

A satisfactory solution to these problems has not been arrived at in
planning literature.[58,59]

To recapitulate, from this point of view, it is precisely the non-commital
policy with respect to the eventual shape of the segment-by-segment fastest
proportionate advance that characterizes the heuristic Kantorovich-
Makarov approach. This approach – call it the flexible capacity "targeting"
approach – appears related to the nature of efficiency extremization we
have defined above; it is only right to indicate, however, that with different,
specifically welfare-oriented "targeting", the idea of segmentary turnpikes
unrelated to terminal conditions of very-long-distance plans has in the
meantime gained recognition in Western writing too.[60]

(8)   In addition to the plan-construction precept, the Kantorovich-
Makarov inquiry is also of considerable interest in its analysis of the basic
parameter's behaviour in a system growing under the strategic plan.[61] In
what follows we will discuss some of the findings under varying assumptions with respect to the number of available technologies. The conclusions
for the case where the latter are finite are relatively trivial: whatever the
initial state and the growth-rate of labour resources, if the final use of output per unit of labour is taken to be an unlimitedly increasing function,
then there exists some time-point such that the system fails to meet final
demand – as postulated. Of greater interest is the case where the number
of technologies is infinite – assuming the system's growth to be capital-
intensive: the growth-rate of investment exceeds that of labour resources
(if it does not do so, the case boils down to that with a limited number of
technologies). The implication is that labour productivity can also grow
unlimitedly. Formally, the model is then stated in this form.

All "enterprises" – current technologies – produce the same quantity
of product P but differ as to inputs of P per their capacity unit: these are
the smaller the lower the productivity of labour. Assume, for the sake of

simplicity, that labour resources are unlimited, they are then disregarded as the technology component in the canonical matrix for a given type of enterprise:

P	A	P	A
-1	0	0	Q
0	-1	1	1

where Q denotes numbers of "enterprises" A obtained from a unit of P. In the system's von-Neumann-type growth its technological growth-rate is the greatest modulo eigenvector of the output matrix $\left[\begin{smallmatrix} 0 & Q \\ 1 & 1 \end{smallmatrix}\right]$, that is $\alpha = (1 + \sqrt{4Q + 1})/2$ which increases with increasing Q. Thus we have a non-sequitur: the assumption of unlimited growth of labour productivity results in the growth-rate of product becoming, as from some time-point, arbitrarily small, smaller that is than that of labour resources. It follows that the infinite range of technologies cannot materialize. The overall conclusion is, then, that a system as described cannot work over an arbitrarily long time — with labour resources increasing exponentially when final use per labour unit is permitted to grow unlimitedly. One can now compare the results with those for the Golden Rule type of growth obtained by Grebennikov (see below) with respect to factor-augmenting growth.

[The discussion of the Kantorovich paradox bears some logical relationship with that in Western literature on the switch and re-switch of technology. For the fundamentals of the theory the reader may be referred to the Dorfman-Samuelson-Solow classic.] [62]

(9)   Also mainly for continuity's sake we mention here another Soviet growth-theoretic model belonging to the class of optimally controlled, to be more specific in substance resting, technically, on the Pontryagin principle — the Smirnov model.[63]

Here we confine ourselves to pointing to its Leontievian system of constraints

$$x(t) = a(t)x(t) + k(t)dx/dt + y(t)$$
$$x(t_0) = x_0; \ 0 < \bar{y} \leqslant y(t) \leqslant x(t)$$

a classical Leontief-type dynamic input-output system with the usual economic interpretation: gross output, growing over time, is formed of intermediate inputs, $a(t)x(t)$, of increments in capital stock supporting this growth $k(t)dx/dt$, and of the economy's "load": $y(t)$ describes consumption and accumulation "infertile" in material production over the horizon. (In the alternative, the "cybernetical" interpretation, the system is fed a control signal $y(t)$ while the output is the vector function $x(t)$ characterizing the state of the system.)

The building into an optimally-controlled system — in his specific way — a production function with one factor and two technologies being explicit (for the intermediate and the stock-forming inputs) is Smirnov's noteworthy experiment. Simpler, more conventional, production functions have been employed for growth models by other authors. To them we presently turn.

Before departing from the present context of the Leontievian-Neumannian, we may point here to Brody's[64] thought-provoking observation (in the Hungarian contribution to the subject), in his attempt to relate an approach à la Pontryagin, or to be more precise, its discrete Katz-type version,[65] with that of the inter-industry-analytic approach to growth problems à la Leontief, as in Smirnov.

Central in Brody's findings is the proposition that, however control variables are constrained, when the system is at optimum their values are extremal of the range. (The path alternatives considered are maximization of output over some horizon possibly tending to infinity, and minimization of time for reaching the goal set.) Since in the control-theoretic analysis this is also characteristic of some non-linear systems, Brody offers an interesting hypothesis of some nexus between optimality and "swinging to extremes". But what is its nature? The conjecture expressed is that there is in this yet another appearance of the phenomenon characteristic of "overstrained" systems in general. However, the analogy pointed out with the "flutter" (known to designers of engineering systems) does not answer the problem of the economic system and its possible spectrum of "flutter frequencies". Nor is the extremizing "flutter" explained by the hinted link with the von Neumann path and its dual, seen by Brody as a production-price vector of Smith-Ricardo-Marx yielding an averaged profit rate. Quite possibly one may suspect that the clue should be sought in the mathematics of the statement of Brody's problem, which are intriguing and worth further investigation.[66]

At this interim stage we may just as well say this. By the time we reach the end of the present chapter we shall see the various ramifications of the contemporary Soviet theory of growth. None the less it is legitimate to say that the von Neumann-derived class of systems has become *the* principal scaffolding of contemporary Soviet theorizing on growth. And that in using the scaffolding, it shares the interests of Western von Neumann-based disquisitions. We can well identify some of the principal ones in a glance at Jorgenson's list:[67] the conceptualization of efficiency (possibly à la Malinvaud,[68] present value of consumption minus labour input being the maximand); the stability of the closed model of accumulation, the problem of efficient path of open systems — patently wider than the class resting on the classical turnpike in the stricter sense (and last but not least, algorithmization of the von Neumann class of systems).

(In his magnificent *Theory of Economic Growth*[69] Morishima talks of the Neumannian "revolution — bloodless but still violent": a revolution which by dramatically changing the mode of thinking is a parallel in dynamics to the Keynesian in statics. The impact of the Neumann ideas pre-eminently deserves this label with regard to Soviet economics.)

A variation on the Kantorovich-Makarov theme is the Volkonskiy[70] model: it brings the former to its logical conclusion as a formalization of planning growth, with a rolling horizon. (We discuss this too in different contexts.)

(10)   Until not long ago Soviet doctrine shunned the production-function formulation of the process of growth. True, as early as forty years ago, in Soviet literature Goldberg[71] drew attention to the possibilities of the Cobb-Douglas construct. Thereafter it was ignored for decades, the principal objection being its link with the production-factors concept of J. B. Clark (Paul H. Douglas has stood explicitly committed to Clark's concept).

We have noted before the attempts to restate Marx's own "expanded reproduction" model in production-function form, in particular by Samuelson.[72] And in fact Samuelson has shown that thus translated Marx's system does share some of the usual premises of the activity-analysis constructs — with production functions of the two "departments" of the fixed-coefficient type. True, to anticipate a further context, the same analysis brings into relief the impact of the Marxian emphasis on labour rather than market-exchange values. This does not embarrass the mathematical-economic school. (As to the issue of the productivity of capital, this is being evaded by simply adopting the hypothesis that capital has the role of a catalyser whose presence influences the process of production. See on this the elegant formalism of Konyus in Nemchinov's *Festschrift* (1974).)

First to use the instrument have been Kantorovich and his school.[73]

Parallel to fully-fledged optimization, or supplementing it, the production-function apparatus has been employed for a broad analysis, ex ante as well as ex post, of planned growth processes and related matters (especially the calculation of the normative investment-efficiency parameter — see on this chapter 4, also survey — B. Mityagin, *UMN*, 1972).

The applications of the construct go back to the late 1950s when Kantorovich and Gorkov[74] published a set of models, framed in different-ial, integer-differential, and other functional equations, some assuming instantaneous convertibility of capital, others making explicit the processes of wear and tear and obsolescence of its physical shapes.

A distinctive feature of these explorations of this school is that they are not concerned with the allocation of product as between consumption and capital accumulation — this is postulated to have been carried out somehow in an optimal way.

Take the recent Kantorovich-Globenko (1967) exercise which, as we shall see, has become the starting point for the Kantorovich-Vainshtein method of calculation of the investment-"norm".[75] The production function $U(K(t)T(t))$ is positively homogeneous. Under the assumption of additivity of effects and feasibility of a convex-linear combination of technologies, the necessary and sufficient condition for this is that with $0 \leqslant x < \infty$, the $U(x, 1)$ is concave downward.

The volume of consumption is exogenously fixed; but it could be determined implicity by the model's parametric system. For this two hypo-theses are typically considered. One is that it is proportional to net output $P(t)$, i.e. that some share, γ, of national product is saved, and another that consumption is proportional to manpower $V(t) = aL(t)$. The economy's growth is then described by a differential equation of the function of fixed and working capital $K(t)$:

$$dk/dt = P(t) - V(t) = U(K(t), L(t) - V[t, K(t), 1(t), P(t)];$$

for the two hypotheses we would have respectively

$$dK/dt = \gamma U K, L$$

and

$$dK/kL = U[K(t), L(t)] - aL(t).$$

Here too the focus is on the asymptotic behaviour of key variables. In particular the following theorems are established for the equation assuming $\lim_{t \to \infty} L'/L = \lambda$:

let c be the root of the equation

$$\lambda x = \gamma U(x, 1) \text{ with } 0 < x < \infty$$

and K be the solution of the equation, then $\lim K/T = c$. If $\gamma U(x,1) > \lambda x$, then $\lim_{t \to \infty} \ln K/L = a\gamma$, where $a = \lim U(x, 1)$.

Further, a simple case of technological progress is considered with output $P(t) = e^{\rho t} U(K,L)$, whence $K' = e^{\rho t}(K,L) - v(t)$. Assume that in the neighbourhood of the zero point $t^{\alpha-1} U(1,t) = [c_0 + 0(t)]$ and bounds exist for $x U_x'(x,1)/U(x,1)$ with $x \to$. Then

$$\lim_{t \to \infty} K/e^{\frac{P}{1 - \alpha^t}} \qquad T = \left[\frac{(1 - \alpha)c_0\,\gamma}{\rho + (1 - 1)\lambda} \right]^{1/(1 - \alpha)}$$

(These results have been given further refinement by bringing in wear and tear and obsolescence: this we leave out of account.) What is worth noting is the use of the technique for a strategic analysis of four key elements in the economy's development, specifically for probing the behaviour of its capital intensity, also with given expectations with regard to technological progress when obeying some simple law. The perspective picture has been obtained thanks to a set of assumptions, some of them rather strong: in particular that of ideal instantaneous convertibility of capital from one of its "embodiments" into another to follow the behind-the-scene optimization of technology choices.

A later version of the Kantorovich-Globenko construct adopts Marx's framework: two products and two sectors ("departments"). For the producer-goods and consumer-goods sectors, respectively, the production functions are $P_1 = U_1[K_1,L_1]\,P_2 = U_2[K_2,L_2]$. The instantaneous convertibility of capital is now assumed to be only intra-sectoral: there is none inter-sectorally. The differential optimization would require then an inter-sectoral allocation of capital and labour such as to bring about equality of yield, viz.

$$\frac{\partial U_1}{\partial K_1} \frac{\partial U_2}{\partial L_2} = \frac{\partial U_1}{\partial L_1} \frac{\partial U_2}{\partial K_2}.$$

The limits assumed are $\lim_{t \to \infty} L_1/L = a \neq 0$; $\lim_{t \to \infty} L'/L = \lambda$; $\lim_{t \to \infty} V(t)/L(t) = b$. For the case where the straight line $y = \lambda x$ and the curve $y = U_1(x - c_2, a)$ intersect in two points $c_0 < c_1$ (the c_2 being the root of the equation $b = U_2(x, 1 - a)$, $c_2 \leqslant x < +\infty$), we have for the limiting sectoral capital intensities

$$\lim_{t \to \infty} K_2/L = c_2 \,; \lim_{t \to \infty} \frac{K_1}{L} = \begin{cases} \text{a) } c_0 - c_2. \\ \text{b) } c_1 - c_2. \end{cases} ;$$

if there exists a constant $c > c_0$ such that values of t, no matter how distant, can be found for which $s(t) \geq c$, then the alternative "a)" applies; otherwise "b)" applies.

(11)   A further and major contribution to the production-function type of modelling growth with an eye to numerical exercises has been made by Mikhalevskiy.[76] It is in fact more ambitious in scope, for its purpose is not merely analytical. Mikhalevskiy has identified himself with the view that the tool can be relied upon in actual planning — at least for planning with a not too distant horizon, so that parameters could be taken as subject to relatively moderate change only.[77]

Structural parameters would help — Mikhalevskiy contends — to determine the final product. And they would help in determining the prime factors — capital stock and labour force — entailed in securing the growth target. Such claims for the possibilities of the tool in planning have met with criticism in Soviet writing. It has been pointed out (by Shlyapentokh) that for a dependable prognosis of final product the planner must know his factor availabilities: the reproach of circularity in reasoning seems legitimate.

Gradually extending his function, Mikhalevskiy has evolved by now an expanded system of equations meant to trace the economy's advance under the plan. It describes, that is, the principal macro-economic interdependencies characterizing planned growth: the dynamic conditions of availability of resources under exogenously-given fixed coefficients of their employment and the system of income distribution. The mechanism of capital formation, renovation, and replacement provides the link with the structure of the uses of the final product and distribution of income. The growth process itself is a non-stationary one, under non-neutral technical progress.

Rather than reproduce the original system, formed of complicated non-linear differential and difference equations, we give here a simplified synthesis. It is based on yearly averages (rather than continuous index number series); another class of simplification concerns the gross savings rate: it is assumed partly — with respect to replacement investment — to depend on renovation policy (the $S^\gamma \gtrless 0$) and the expected dynamics of capital intensity, i.e. the type of technical progress $(K/Y')/(K/T) \gtrless 0$. Mathematically symbolized the growth process is:

$$\frac{q_1'}{q} = a_2 \, \frac{(K/L)'}{K/L} + a_3 \, \frac{(N/L)'}{N/L} + \hat{g} \left[1 - \frac{q + \lambda^*}{\lambda \chi \left(1 + \dfrac{\Psi^{**}}{c}\right)} \right]$$

$$g = \frac{\lambda^* \chi^* \left(1 + \frac{\Psi^{**}}{c}\right)}{g + \lambda^*} \left[(a_1 + a_3)\left(\hat{g} - \frac{q_1'}{q_1}\right) \right] + a_3 \frac{(N/L)'}{N/L} + $$

$$+ \pi + \frac{a_2(s_1 + s\gamma)(1 + \hat{g}) Y}{K + (s_1 + s\gamma)(1 + \hat{g}) Y} \right]$$

(*Symbols*: Y is final product used, const. prices; K capital assets, constant prices, with amortization allowed for; L man-hours employed; N land used (in hectares); s and $s\gamma$ respectively rates of net investment and of replacement investment (shares in national product); c household consumption; $\hat{g}$ growth-rate of final product, with lags allowed for; a_h share of resources in national income, const. prices; resp. capital, labour, land $h = 1,2,3$; χ employment coefficient of resources; Ψ^{**} parameter of returns to scale; λ^* average "normative" of reaction (lag); π rate of autonomous (non-embodied) technical progress; q output per hour per operative.)

One of the weakest structural facets of the Mikhalevskiy model — in so far as it appears to be intended also for medium-term (five-year) planning — is the handling of technical advance. As has been incisively remarked, its treatment as an exogenous factor is "a confession of our ignorance" (Bergstrom).[79]

The aspirations of the model go beyond "physical-term" planning. It is intended to portray the connection of the "physical-term" motion of the economy, with its money-term system of income distribution, with the mechanism of capital formation, of the formation of the profit rate in the wholesale price, and also of the investment-efficiency rate and the long-term-interest rate (this being in Mikhalevskiy the lower limit of the former — see below). This, then, is what is offered as the "instruments of indirect control".

How dependable is it? This question is broached in the next section.

(12)   This may be a suitable context for a few more general remarks on the question of valuation of factors and products in the production-function type of planned-growth models. A strictly technological, "engineering" system of relationships is possible in micro-application under homogeneity of elements, such as e.g. reducing the estimates to labour-time and plant-time.

Once, however, we move to the macro-level, once the heterogeneity of elements and/or time come into play, there is no escape from "accountancy" — price valuation: the problem of factor price is crucial in technological decision-making.

The matter of factor valuation has been investigated by several students Arrow-Chenery-Minhas-Solow[80] (in their work on the CES family of functions) have made explicit the competitive-market assumption (to be more specific, they have adopted the observed logarithmic relationship between value added per factor unit under perfect competition). Paroush[81] has shown that the assumption is not necessary: what has appeared, how-ever, from his examination of it is that once it is dropped there still remains the crucial question as to how to estimate the parameters. In Soviet literature (i.e. in a Russian journal) the problem has been raised by the Hungarian writers Stahl and Szakolczai.[82] The meaning of the proposi-tion from which they start, that in normatively planned economies the allocation of resources rests on material balances, is not clear in the contex But they are certainly right in saying that the assumption (underlying the production-function system) of equality or proportionality of marginal product, wages, and the investment efficiency "norm" is for the type of economies considered a priori even less tenable than it is for a capitalist economy: and that the difficulties are intensified where — as is the case in a socialist economy — disguised unemployment or short-term oscillations in it conform with some socio-economic principles. It is mainly to allow for this element that a remedy is suggested. Whatever its worth otherwise, the inquiry is important inasmuch as it bears out the negative applicational point: for the weakness of the production-function model does reside largely in the shaky valuation basis. This specifically is true of the Mikhale-vskiy quasi-dual with respect to its optimality (see also our remarks on the Kantorovich-Vainshtein model, below).

Notes

1.   Having overcome its fundamentalist reservation with respect to the production function, Soviet planning theory is still sensitive to the Western analyses of its weaknesses (see e.g. *Plan. khoz.*, 7 (1972). The res-ponse to the discussions of the late 1960s is characteristic. This is true in particular of Arrow's observations (*AER*, May 1969) on the causal co-determinacy of advance in technical knowledge and economic processes; hence also of his confession of helplessness: the point that while the production function is helpful descriptively, there is its failure in detecting the principal properties of the processes of formation and dissemination technical knowledge. This applies also to Domar's proposition (ibid.) on the essentially *micro*-scale nature of the technical advances, and the suppo-sition that rather than a production function of, say Cobb-Douglas type, it

is the Leontief methodology, of twenty years ago, for deriving the index of structural change, that would appear promising.

It seems legitimate to observe that Soviet economic theory shares with Western economic thought its perplexity: the awareness of instrument's both conceptual and technical poverty and at the same time the feeling that "somehow" it proves workable.

2. Mikhalevskiy[83] continues to represent in Soviet growth theory the "unbalanced-growth" school and has been responsible for the elaboration of, and, as it appears, also experimentation at the TsEMI — with the one-sector dynamic model with a structural disequilibrium (it forms the "top-level" component of a five-levels' system — see Appendix 2). The model is designed under the acknowledged impact of Bruno's ideas:[84] his conception of disequilibrium is extended in Mikhalevskiy to several spheres in particular those of

(1) resources, including the impact of non-neutral technological progress;
(2) final demand, including the disequilibrium in the use of final product — in particular because of the national defence and the balance-of-payments elements;
(3) physical versus financial aspects of final demand,
(4) marginal price versus marginal factor productivity and final-product increment,
(5) relationship of the rates of return, of efficiency of investment and of interest.

The technical apparatus is based on a CES type production function

$$Y_t = \delta \, (L_t^{a_1} \, K_t^{a_2} \, N_t^{a_3} \, e^{\pi t})^{\Psi}, \, a_1 + a_2 + a_3 = 1$$

[*Notation:* Y_t is final product; L_t, K_t, N_t are manpower, capital stock (with technical progress embodied), land-respectively; π "autonomous" technical progress: Ψ parameter of return to scale; $\hat{\epsilon}/\epsilon, \dot{\epsilon}/\epsilon^*$ rate of technical progress with and without structural inbalance respectively; w_t, r_t wage and rent rates respectively; $\hat{g}$ rate of growth of final product; ρ_t rate of return; q, q^* parameters of disequilibrium; μ_i rate of depreciation; i^* rate of investment.]

Formal conditions of structural disequilibrium in resources are written:

$$\frac{Y_t}{L_t} = c_1 w_t + d_1; c_1 > 0, d_1 = \frac{q + m_1 \, {}^*(a_2 + a_3) \, \Psi}{(1 - a_2 - a_3) \, \Psi} \, ,$$

$$\frac{\partial Y_t}{\partial L_t} = pw_t + q, \quad c_1{}^* = \frac{p^*}{(1 - a_1 - a_2)\,\Psi} \quad ,$$

$$\frac{Y_t}{N_t} = c_1{}^* r_t{}^* + d_1{}^*; \, c_1{}^* > 0, d^* = \frac{q^* + m_2{}^*(a_1 + a_2)\,\Psi}{(1 - a_1 - a_2)\,\Psi} \quad ,$$

$$\frac{\partial Y_t}{\partial N_t} = p^* r_t{}^* + q^*, \quad \frac{\partial Y_t}{\partial K_t} = \rho_t = \frac{L_t}{K_t}\left(\frac{\partial Y_t}{\partial L_t} - w_t\right) - \frac{N_t}{K_t}\left(\frac{\partial Y_t}{\partial N_t} - r_t{}^*\right)$$

$$c_1 = \frac{p}{(1 - a_2 - a_3)\,\Psi}$$

The reader will find the meaning of these formulations clear in Bruno's type of interpretation. To start with the first equation, its substance is a wage-productivity adjustment (the implication is constancy of marginal factor shares): the two parameters, the positive c and the d, indicate the impact of the environmental and technological situation; the sign of $d(\pm)$ and its 0 value indicate rising, falling, or constant labour's average share wL/Y. The second equation relates labour's marginal product to its real wage: the p and q can be seen as institutional and/or behavioural parameters. The sense of the Ψ in adjustment for scale economies has been already indicated: finally the m in the transformation for c and d are some technological parameters. The formulations for natural resources (factor "land") are analogous. Finally we have the rate of return on capital related to its marginal productivity, allowance made for the disequilibrium correctives with regard to the two other factors.

From the disequilibrium formulations for labour a partial differential equation is obtained:

$$\frac{\partial Y_t}{\partial L_t} - \Psi (1 - a_2 - a_3) + \frac{Y_t}{L_t} + m_1{}^* (a_2 - a_3) = 0,$$

and re-written:

$$L_t \frac{\partial(Y_t/L_t)}{\partial L_t} + \Psi (a_2 + a_3) \cdot \frac{Y_t}{L_t} + m_1{}^*(a_2 + a_3) = 0.$$

This has the uni-parametric family of solutions with respect to labour and analogously we have a solution with respect to natural resources

$$Y_t = A(K_t,t)L_t{}^{(1 - a_2 - a_3)\,\Psi} - m_1{}^*L_t{}^*; \; Y_t$$

$$= A^*(K_t,t)N_t{}^{(1 - a_2 - a_1)\,\Psi} \, m_2{}^*N_t{}^\Psi.$$

Here in the constant of integration A and A^* appear as a function of arguments whose operation is not explicitly introduced: with regard to K_t, this would be nonnegativity and diminishing marginal factor productivity and the presence of Ψ; with regard to t, the exponential type of technological progress

$$A(K_t, t) = A^*(K_t, t) = \delta \, (K_t^{a_2} e^{\pi t})\Psi.$$

Allowing for additivity of disequilibrium effects and complementarity of autonomous technological progress, Mikhalevskiy writes:

$$Y_t = \delta \left(L_t^{a_1} K_t^{a_2} N_t^{a_3} e^{\pi t} \right)^{\Psi} - \left(m_1 {}^* L_t^{\Psi} + m_2 {}^* N_t^{\Psi} \right), \sum a_h = 1.$$

Where the m's are zero this becomes the Cobb-Douglas function: where they are positive the elasticities of factor substitution are less than unity; the reverse is true for negative m's; in both cases the m's tend to unity; thus a high degree of industrialization will tend to a Cobb-Douglas form.[85]

Mikhalevskiy's fundamental equation of the economy's dynamics under structural disequilibrium in resources employed (and their differentiated age composition) is

$$\hat{g} \, \Psi^{-1} (1 - e^{-\mu T})^{-1} = t^* \left\{ \frac{Y}{K} \left(a_1 \Psi - \frac{p-1}{c_1} - \frac{p^*-1}{c_1{}^*} \right) + \right.$$

$$+ \frac{L}{K} \left(\frac{d_1 (p-1)}{c_1{}^*} - q \right) + \frac{N}{K} \left. \left(\frac{d_1{}^*(p^*-1)}{c_1{}^{*2}} - q^* \right) \right\} +$$

$$+ \pi - a_2 \mu + (1 - m_1{}^*) \left[\frac{p}{c_1} \, \frac{\dot{L}}{L} + \left(q - \frac{p d_1}{c_1} \right) \frac{L}{Y} \right] +$$

$$+ (1 - m_2{}^*) \left[\frac{p^*}{c_1{}^*} \, \frac{\dot{N}}{N} + \left(q^* - \frac{p^* d_1{}^*}{c_1{}^*} \right) \frac{N}{Y} \right].^{86}$$

We discussed in a previous context Mikhalevskiy's ideas on unbalanced growth. We shall not expand on his conclusion from this exercise, that structural disequilibrium may tend to speed up economic expansion; except for a few remarks on points raised here.

It is tenable that structural disequilibria qualify the postulate of profit maximization rather than invalidate it, as Mikhalevskiy maintains. What they call for on this argument is an adaptive criterion, being a compromise between requirements with respect to growth-rate, employment, invest-

ment rate, private and public consumption, foreign trade, income
distribution, type and pace of technological progress, and stability of
prices and monetary circulation. But while the construct commends itself
as an analytical tool, all these decision elements do not come explicitly into an objective function permitting a plan-programming treatment.

(13) To return in the present context of the production function as the
tool for the purposes of the grand strategy for growth, a point deserves to be
made: the noticeable deepening of interest, in the Soviet theory of growth,
in the nature of the relation between capital formation and growth. In the
axiomatic tenet, as in the received doctrine, the link is direct and automatic
This accords with the Marxian tradition: in Marx's system, given the initial
stock, the advance engendered is ruled exclusively by the rate of accumulation (in turn determined – under capitalism – by the mechanism for
keeping wages at a subsistence level), and this is decisive for the level of
techniques under the given state of technological knowledge.[87]

As it would be legitimate to suppose, a school of thought now stresses
the consequences of the metamorphosis in the economic environment. Its
key hypothesis is that the initial industrialization phase is intrinsically
one of a capital-deepening fast growth of capital intensity – *fondovoorush-
ennost* – of the capital-labour coefficient: and this is the leading element
in the economy's growth. But as maturity is approached, the lead is changed: labour's productivity tends to catch up with and outpace the rate of
growth of capital: the economy's growth process is characterized by the
growing rate of return on capital (*fondootdacha*). These views, ascribed to
Golanskiy,[88] have been taken up in particular by Volkonskiy in his hypothesis on the production-consumption feedback.[89] Non-productive
consumption (so he argues) assumes to a large extent the role of investment
in the society's "technological resources". Disturbing – in one direction
or another – the necessary relationship between this and investment in
material resources may be expected to bring about a lowering of the pace
of growth. Volkonskiy, moreover, is inclined to accept as an empirically
established tendency a relatively high degree of stability for the growth of
the consumption levels: this in fact is one of the adopted premises of his
growth model.

In passing we may point to a certain kinship of this Soviet school and
ideas identified with Srinivasan[90] and Uzawa.[91] In Srinivasan the savings-
income ratio asymptotically approaches a constant derived for the adopted
maximand (the stream of consumption per operative discounted at some
positive rate). In expanding the argument, Uzawa has demonstrated that –

within his framework — in an environment with a relatively low capital-labour ratio, the consumer-good output tends to be close to the minimum-requirement level of consumption until a certain critical point is reached: thereafter it rises towards some balanced growth level.[92] The similarity with the ideas of Srinivasan and Uzawa is explicitly acknowledged: in fact equally close or possibly closer are points of resemblance (in Soviet writing) with some other post-Ramseyan writings. To quote only one, in Cass[93] we have a path optimal with respect to consumption over a finite planning period: in following it the system's advance is of a nearly Golden Rule balanced type for the whole period except for the turnpike-type switches in the starting and the terminating phases: we shall meet certain elements of this kind of balanced advance presently in the Grebennikov construct.[94]

(14) Grebennikov's is a fuller — and on some points a stricter — formalization of ideas touched upon in Volkonskiy. His prime concern is the interaction of the rate of return and the rates of accumulation and of growth of national product; the central tenet in his proposition is that the latter tends towards stability with regard to certain parameters. We propose to lend somewhat more attention to this inquiry, for in many respects it is a landmark in the emerging Soviet contemporary theory of growth. (We shall meet the ideas — at a further stage — when, in our Part II we come to Soviet control-theoretic oriented work.)

The model starts from a Kaldor-type technological-progress function relating the growth-rates of labour and of capital productivity: a function, in other words, which relates the pace of capital accumulation — the new vintage capital being the prime carrier of progress — and of demographic development. In this, full employment of factors is postulated — a realistic assumption (but see the Stahl-Szakolczai qualifications on p. 150).

When linearized, the function describes the growth of labour productivity ($g_t = Y_t/L_t$) (capital intensity being $F_t = K_t/L_t$) as

$$\dot{g}_t/g_t = \alpha \dot{F}_t/F_t + \gamma; \, 0 < \alpha < 1; \gamma > 0 \qquad (1)$$

whence for the growth of the rate of return ($Q_t = Y_t/K_t$) we have

$$\dot{Q}_t/Q_t = -(1-\alpha)\dot{F}_t/F_t + \gamma.$$

It is then shown how the position changes at the phase of maturity both with respect to $\dot{F}_t/F_t$ and to γ (cf. the argument above: in this way the "watershed" is indicated).

The system is shifted next from the Kaldor-type to the Cobb-Douglas framework. The function is generalized for the case $\alpha + \beta = 1$, say $\alpha + \beta = 1 + \mu$ (the $\beta \equiv$ elasticity of product with respect to labour). With the labour force growing proportionately to employable population at some almost constant exponential rate

$$\pi, (L_t = L_0 e^t) \tag{2}$$

$$Y_t = K_t L_t^{1-\alpha} L_t^\mu e^{\gamma t} \quad \text{thus} \quad Y_t = K_t^a L_t^{1-\alpha} e^{(\mu\pi+\gamma)} L_0^\mu$$

whence

$$\dot{g}_t/g_t = \alpha \dot{F}_t/F_t + \gamma' \quad \text{where} \quad \gamma' = \mu\pi + \gamma.$$

In other words, the same growth-rate for capital-labour ratio is accompanied by a greater or smaller growth-rate of labour productivity depending on how fast employment and consequently also capacities grow. The growth of γ — measuring the "efficiency" of social production — is thus related to that of capacities. We leave out of consideration Grebennikov's treatment of the gestation process of capacities. Suffice it to note for the dynamics of the capital stock that

$$dK/dt = m_s^s Y_t \tag{3}$$

where m is a coefficient related to lags and s stands for the net investment rate. Thus the proposition is arrived at that the growth-rate of the national product is stable with respect to a certain value of $\dot{Y}_t/Y_t = \pi + \gamma'/(1 - a)$.[95]

The central tenet, to rephrase it, is that whatever the initial state of the system and the accumulation rate, its growth-rate of national product will in time come arbitrarily close to a magnitude determined by the growth-rate of employment and the parameters α and γ, but not the accumulation rate. In yet other words, in Grebennikov, there is a balance growth-rate that reflects a tendency corresponding to a certain level of technological-economic development: forming the "fundamental axis" of advance. (This tenet is shown to hold also when the formalization is shunted to a Solovian function with embodied technological progress for which the Cobb-Douglas system would be the limiting case, and also for further modification of the latter — we shall not rework this argument.) The explanation offered rests on the dynamics of the rate of return on investment and the nature of its relationship with the accumulation rate: raising the latter is shown to "freeze" the former at a certain level.[96]

The results link up with the Phelps (1962) system.[97] To summarize, in that system the elasticity of the limiting exponential growth with respect to investment rate appears to depend solely on the capital-elasticity of output: in turn the latter is not dependent on the type of technological progress. For the Phelps configuration, permanent finite modernization of the capacity stock is not achievable by increased thrift. (We have already noted the confluence of Soviet thinking with the "Golden Rule" conceptions – in our reference to Cass (Part II, sect. 26); further reference for similarity of the order of ideas could include in particular Sato's elaboration on the Phelps theme;[98] also Gale's[99] on his "good programme" as asymptotically approaching an optimal-stationary, or a balanced or a Golden Rule growth.) In so far as in Grebennikov the analogy of his system with Phelps's world is pointed out, it may be worth noting here one of the implications of relevance for the type of growth and strategy involved: it is shown by Phelps[100] that when "Golden Age" consumption is maximal with respect to the technical-advance effort, the rate of growth becomes equal to the rate of return to investment in technology (as distinct from investment in "tangibles").[101]

We have pointed to the abandonment by the mathematical school – at some stage of its progress – of its search for a rigorous answer to the question of the optimal saving rate. We can now see how the issue crops up again – how the school comes back to it in a roundabout way, by trying to locate the point beyond which, from the growth-promotion angle, raising of the investment rate may prove ineffective or even counterproductive. This, to recapitulate, is a distinct point of divorce from the traditional Soviet doctrine of growth. It has a direct bearing upon Soviet realities: and the implied sermon addressed to the Soviet economic strategist is unmistakable (one of the morals concerns the role of technological progress in shifting upwards the economy's production curve). [For further developments see Appendices, and Part II.]

Notes

1. The connection between the type of technical progress and the choice of capital intensity as it confronts the normative planner is analysed in Kalecki's theory of growth under socialism[102] (some of its other elements are discussed in other contexts). In Kalecki, for such a system the strategy rule is to choose the degree of the technique's capital intensity, correlated with the investment rate, according to its effect – ceteris paribus – on labour productivity. Take the overall production function $Y = f(K, Z; t)$, the two bracketed capital letters denoting capital and employment; labour productivity is then $w = Y/Z$ and capital-intensity coefficient $m = K/Z$. We have thus $\alpha^0(m,t) = 1/w.\partial w/\partial t$. According to the α^0's dependence on m, i.e. whether the $\partial \alpha^0/\partial m = \alpha^0_m$ is positive, negative, or zero, the technologi-

cal progress is P^+, P^-, P^0 — the Kalecki capital-intensity promoting, discouraging and neutral, respectively.

In the Kalecki school Chilosi and Gomulka have convincingly demonstrated the basic equivalence of the Kalecki and the Harrod classifications of technical advance. They have also analysed[103] the asymptotic growth paths of income and capital under the (differently defined) types of technical progress plus the substitution-elasticity parameter of the production curve; also their different Golden Age behaviour. It is striking to find (as shown by Chilosi-Gomulka) that while in Phelps, and also in Arrow, technical advance is an endogenous variable, Kalecki takes it to be exogenous (time-dependent) even for a normatively planned system.

2. The proposition of the optimality of stationary growth as such has by now met with criticism in Soviet literature: thus e.g. Liberman.[104] His *argumento a contrario* rest on two points

(a) the construct is artificial inasmuch as the concepts of intensity of accumulation (and discount rate) would become meaningless: the question of the length of time in the estimates of cost-benefit (consumption versus future benefits) would become unanswerable.

On the other hand, in so far as all feasible variants of the growth and accumulation rates would share the property of stationarity, the question would have to be answered as to the preference of one stationarity system over another;

(b) even within the framework of a stationarity hypothesis it is unlikely that every increase in the accumulation rate would have an adequate reflection in a growth-rate: it should be then assumed that there exists a point beyond which a switch to a stationary regime with higher parameters is unfeasible. If this is so there must be also a limit for the preservation of the stationarity regime itself: and it is suggested that the limit is determined by socio-economic conditions.

The tenet is, then, that optimality of the growth regime implies non-stationarity (a theorem is formulated that under conditions of a constantly increasing capital-intensity coefficient, a constant accumulation rate is non-optimal). It is further contended that a continuous and stationary growth as the optimality criterion requires supplementing the "traditionalist" exponential formulation of growth in the equations of national product and consumption curves with a term $\pm k \sin 2\pi t/T$ where k describes the oscillations of the two variables with respect to the trend and T stands for the plan period over which the growth parameters pass through a full oscillation cycle.

Whether the label of "artificiality" is justified or not (and in whatever

sense it could be justified), the argument (a) does not affect the logic of
the theoretical construct. Nor is the theoretical abstraction affected by
argument (b) which rests on extra-economic considerations.

(15)   The progress of analytical work on growth-propulsion and the clarification of theoretical obstacles in the path of fixing "objective" rules for
the selection of the most desirable rate of investment (consumption) have
induced, by the early 1970s, an intensive Soviet search for a heuristic methodology. Empirically rooted and oriented, all the attempts accept some
finite plan horizon — one corresponding to what in Soviet practice is termed
perspective planning (longer-term planning with a period of more than five
years — the traditional length of the basic, medium-run plan; usually around
fifteen years); they all adopt a set of strong assumptions such as to simplify
the formalization while keeping it sufficiently close to reality; they aim at
numerical solutions within value ranges suggested by practice; and they
aspire at approximation to what is defined as theoretical optimum — with an
eye to the needs of the economic-strategy maker. Two such attempts will
be now presented. One, by Valtukh, is concerned with "experimental"
determination of the optimum rate of capital formation, the other, by
Anchishkin, theoretically more ambitious, is concerned with the optimal
distribution of the final product as well.

The Valtukh[105] model explicitly adopts maximum consumption as the
policy objective (an alternative which takes instead the working day as a
minimand will not be considered here). It rests on two functions, those
weighting welfare and strain, over the perspective t, respectively $p(t)$,
$(dp/dt < 0)$ and $s(I_p)$, $(ds/dI_p > 0)$ where I_p is the volume of incremental
saving. It is assumed that in each direction of incremental saving, i, the
negative impact on consumption in the initial period and the positive impact
on the subsequent periods are known; with the use of the $p(t)$ function the
positive and negative effects are appraised so that each direction receives
its efficiency index ϵ_i. The s and the ϵ are equi-dimensional. The strategy
rule is then to include in the plan — the optimal plan — such "directions"
in accumulation as to satisfy the requirements of sufficient efficiency
$\epsilon_i \geqslant s(I_p^0)$. The model then has the form:

$$I \rightarrow \max; I_\pi \leqslant I(s) \ (dI_\pi < 0) \ ; I \leqslant I_p(s) \ (dI_p/ds > 0),$$

the optimum being characterized by $I^0 = I^0_\pi = I^0_p$, where I and I_π stand,
respectively, for the "real" volume of accumulation and the volume of
requirements in accumulation satisfying the postulated condition.

In its empirical use the model relies on the information obtained by means of a dynamic input-output model. The computational procedure starts from the proposition that since maximum consumption is the ultimate aim, minimum investment as such is "absolutely" efficient; the problem thus appears as one of determining the efficiency and taking into the plan increments of accumulation over the minimum year by year; in this for the sake of comparability the effects are reduced to one and the same period by means of the weighting function $p(t) = 1 - \alpha(t - n)$, where the α is a coefficient of a yearly decline in value of a unit of increment in the consumption "fund" as compared with the initial year of the plan period, and t and n are, respectively, numbers denoting the year for which the coefficient is being computed and the plan year. (It has been empirically established that the effect of accumulation can be taken as zero as from the ninth year, then the $\alpha = 0, 125$.) The α serves for appraising the economic effect of the postponement of consumption resulting from increasing accumulation, in a given plan year.

The empirically striking fact is the near-invariance of the optimal plan: its low dependence on even a substantial variation of both p and s (in particular for the former the alternatives considered are assumed to be linear and exponential growth). The matter still calls for an investigation (recall the findings of Pugachev elsewhere discussed by the present writer).[106] A point of justified suspicion should be in any case as to the way the p and s are arrived at.

(16) . The other of the two inquiries, that by Anchishkin,[107] starts from a simple formulation of inter-dependence between the dynamics of consumption and final product, and the use-distribution of the latter

$$C_t = Y_0 (1 + \epsilon x)^t (1 - xb).$$

(*Notation*: C is consumption, including non-productive capital formation and replacement, Y final social product, x the share of productive investment in final product, ϵ efficiency of investment $[\epsilon \equiv y/x$ where y is the averaged annual growth rate of the product] , b the ratio of non-consumption components to total product.) What is sought is the value of x such as to maximize consumption allocation between the 6-th and the 15-th plan years; or when we turn from a discrete to a continuous statement

$$\int_0^t e^{ct} dt = \int_0^t e^{cxt} dt \; \frac{1 - xb}{1 - x_0 b_0} \; \rightarrow \max$$

– here the left and the right-hand functionals describe the totals over the
plan period, respectively: of consumption, in relative numbers, under equal
average yearly consumption growth-rate c, and of final-product average
growth-rate ($\epsilon x \equiv y$); the $(1 - xb)$ measures the average consumption share
in final product. For the more complicated case of variable x and c the
functional becomes

$$\int_0^t e^{\int_0^t c(t)\,dt}\,dt = \int_0^t e^{\epsilon.\int_0^t x(t)\,dt}\,dt - \frac{[1 - x(t)b]}{1 - x_0 b_0} \quad \text{max.}$$

Two existence theorems are easily offered: where ϵ and b or the law of
their change are given, there exists in the positivity region of x a value
maximizing the first functional and thereby the c; and analogously there
exists a value of $\triangle x$ maximizing the second functional and thereby the c
when $x(t) = x_0 + \triangle xt$. Central in the system is the law of change of the
parameters, ϵ and b: first of all of the ϵ, the rate of marginal return on
capital (investment efficiency) which, with a given technology, depends on
the scale and combination with other resources. In the simplest form we
have the relationship $\epsilon(x,t)$: in its analysis use is made of the inverse
logistic function of x with its parallel shift in time:

$$\epsilon_t = a_1 + \frac{a_4}{1 + a_2 e^{a_3 (x - x_0)}} + a_5 t,$$

the a_1, a_2, a_3, a_4 (the last two negative) being parameters of the logistic
function, x_0 being the shift of the function with respect to the abscissae
axis, and a_5 the coefficient of the shift over time which, when zero, positive and negative, indicates respectively, unchanged economic and technological conditions and, under changed conditions, a changed – increased
and decreased – investment efficiency. The general economic interpretation
is related to the investment "saturation" under a given technology; it is
that an expanded scale of investment, being a "burden" on the system,
tends to reduce its efficiency but at the same time the change in economic
and technical conditions tends to raise the return on investment, thus shifting the logistic function over time. Of the four parameters of the function,
two indicate the upper and the lower asymptote, the other two the point

of the shift and the angle coefficient at this point. With given x_0, known a_3 and a_5 as described below, the a_1, a_2, a_4 are obtained from

$$\lim \epsilon(x,t) = \epsilon_{max} = a_1 + \frac{a_4}{1 + a_2 e^{a_3(-x_0)}},$$

$$x \to 0, \, t = 0,$$

$$\epsilon(x,t) = \epsilon_0 = a_1 + \frac{a_4}{1 + a_2},$$

$$x = x_0, \, t = 0,$$

$$\lim \epsilon(x,t) = \epsilon_{min} = a_1 + \frac{a_4}{1 + a_2 e^{a_3(0.5x_0)}},$$

$$x \to 0.5, \, t = 0.$$

As to the $b(x)$, it too is expressed as an inverse logistic function, but unlike the ϵ_t is not shiftable over time: $b = a_6 + \dfrac{a_9}{1 + a_7 e^{a_3(x - y_0)}}$; yet the parametric framework carries a close analogy. Ultimately the basic functional takes the form

$$\int_0^t e^{\epsilon t} \, dt = \int_0^t e^{\epsilon(x,t)xt} dt \, \frac{1 - xb(x)}{1 - x_0 b_0}.$$

To return to the ϵ_t, the decisive role is that of a_5 — and it is taken as normatively given. It is indeed controlling what can be thought of as the trade-off in the ϵ: the latter results from the depressing and enhancing effects of capital formation on productivity.

The conclusions of the theoretical investigations of the trade-off and their numerical application lead the author to some significant diagnostic indications *pro domo sua*; the principal among them is that, at the present state of capital formation and its technical level, the share of accumulation in the Soviet final product would seem to have gone beyond the economically justified norm and that possibly the level and pace in the growth of accumulation are by now "one of the causes for the declining efficiency of investment and of a certain retardation in growth of resources for consumption".[108] On them we shall not expand here. We will only note that in substance the Anchishkin conclusions tend to supplement those of Valtukh.[109]

Note

The growing consciousness of the need for, and the underdevelopment of, a stochastic methodology has inspired more attempts at a probabilistic approximation in longer-run planning. Among more imaginative ones an attempt at delimiting, in a practicable fashion, a "zone of indeterminacy" in near-optimal growth, made by Makarov, Makarova, and Zeyliger,[110] in our view deserves to be singled out. The procedure begins with selecting intuitively some basic alternatives in development and then moves to forming a considerable number of random combinations of the initial data by means of the Monte Carlo method, allowance made for multi-causality of the relationships, for synchronic variations in some random factors which condition the correlational links between components of initial data stocks; for individual "dispersion" — variation coefficients and the possible shape of the distribution law — for each of the operating factors. That would result in the build-up of thousands of random combinations of non-inconsistent sets of initial data. Next the combinations are "sorted out" into N groups by the method of image recognition, the N made dependent on the computer's capacity. For each of the sums optimal solution is sought in a linear model, with a possible averaging of data. These solutions are given interpretation as points in an m-dimensional space with co-ordinates determined from the values of the m substantive variables or parameters; then from points fixed in the m-dimensional space some series of "condensation" are detected. We are further offered a special three-variant procedure for allowing for the economic risk, λ_r^n. Which of the three formulas is to be employed depends on whether under the combination of initial data P^n, for a variant r the random magnitudes are the system's economic indices (coefficients of the system's functional Φ) only, or its "natural indices" (constraints) only, or both, respectively

$$\lambda_r^n = \begin{cases} P^n X_r - P^n X_n = \Phi_r{}^n - \Phi_{0pt}^n \\[2mm] \varphi_r B^n - \varphi_n B^n = \Phi_r{}^n - \Phi_{0pt}^n \\[2mm] P^n U_r B^n - P^n U_n B^n = \Phi_r{}^n - \Phi_{0pt}^n . \end{cases}$$

(*Notation*: X_r, X_n are variants of the system's development (pattern and productivity of capacities optimal under the P^n); φ_r, φ_n are prices of the optimal plan under the postulated and realized $B^{\bar{n}}$ i.e. requirements in the system's products and constraints on resources; U_r, U the inverse matrix of the optimal base under the postulated and the realized values of initial data; Φ – total cost). The value-matrix of risk is:

Random combination of conditions

Optimal development variants

	P_1	P_2	...	P_N
X_1	$\lambda_1{}^1$	$\lambda_1{}^2$	...	$\lambda_1{}^N$
X_2	$\lambda_2{}^1$	$\lambda_2{}^2$	...	$\lambda_2{}^N$
⋮	⋮	⋮	⋮	⋮
X_R	$\lambda_R{}^1$	$\lambda_R{}^2$	...	$\lambda_R{}^N$

The traditional criterion of minimum cost would as a rule make it possible to delimitate the "zone of indeterminancy" of the system's optimal development. In comparing variants within this zone this is modified as the "criterion of minimum economic risk". Since, however, a variant is characterized not by a single, but by a set N of values of the latter – the problem faced is, then, which parameter of the curve of distribution of the values of economic risk should be adopted as the criterion for the comparison of alternative variants?

As a rule (that is except for specifically conditioned sectors of the economy) the variant chosen would be that with a minimum mean value of economic risk; in the exceptional cases the minimax value of economic risk; viz. respectively

$$\lambda = \min_r \lambda_r = \min_r \frac{\sum_{n=1}^{N} \lambda_r^n}{N}\,; \bar{\lambda} = \min_r \bar{\lambda} = \min_r \max_n \lambda_r^n .$$

As against the latter favourable outcomes are given a more fair chance when the matrix is interpreted as a two-person zero-sum game and solved as a linear programme

$$\min \left\{ \sum_{n=1}^{N} y_n \mid \sum_{n=1}^{N} \lambda_r{}^n y_n \geqslant 1; y_n \geqslant 0 \right\}.$$

In that case a new variant of the economy's development is formed with the value of the mean risk $(\bar{\lambda})$ higher than in the first alternative; but it also guarantees a smaller loss (ν) than under the minimax criterion

$$\left(\tilde{\lambda} = \sum_{r=1}^{R} \gamma_r \lambda_r \right) > (\lambda = \min_r \lambda_r); \quad \nu < (\bar{\lambda} = \min_r \lambda_r).$$

(17) Our last remarks will give a hint of some tendencies of the contemporary Soviet theory of growth. For this we return to Grebennikov, to note his observation, which may perhaps be treated as symptomatic: the observation of a tangency of his results on Keynesian economics. Patently some elements usually identified with Keynes's world appear to lose relevance in the Soviet-type growth system. Very generally the mode of operation specific to the automaticity of a private-enterprise competitive-market enterprise, its processes of determination of savings and consumption, factor relations and choice of techniques, and the levels of factor employment and cyclical oscillations of the activity levels — all these disappear from the Soviet focus. Keynes's crucially active money and credit have no place in the Soviet theory: for this reason alone his type of multiplier cannot be fitted into it.[111]

The more remarkable is the tracing of the common ground with Keynes in a very generalized idea of what for lack of a better term we may describe as the active consumption function in growth propulsion. For once common ground on this point is established, the way is opened for the search of a "very general" theory of growth, accommodating as special cases those of specific mechanisms in control of its element: indeed perhaps it is opened for "distilling" initially from Keynes's general theory. This new-found generality of problems is certainly worth noting.

Notes

1. The problems of "effective" equilibrium growth with *infinite* horizon

— as conceptually closer to those of the centrally planning socialist society, including those of the Golden Age state — are Makarov's area of exploration in his 1969 paper.[112] It starts where his original inquiry stopped (see above). Now the growth process is qualified: optimality is defined as utility maximization and the questions investigated are those of the existence of the u-optimal trajectory,[113] its uniqueness, the state-to-state transition, the properties of equilibrium in balanced growth-Golden Age growth, the asymptotic characteristics of the u-optimal trajectories (do they and how do they tend to the Golden Age style?), and the kind of dependence of all these questions on the values of the time-discount coefficient of the utility function. (The state of equilibrium (balanced) growth as such is defined by analogy to von Neumann-Gale.)

As in the previous models, the production possibilities are given by the technology set Z. If we have at time-point t products of quantity x, it is technologically possible to have them at $(t + 1)$ in quantity $y = (y_1, \ldots, y_r$ where $y \in a(x)$; the two-dimensional vector $(x,y) \in Z$ if and only if $y \in a(x)$. Consumption is described by a numerical utility function $u(x)$. The Z is a convex open cone. There is only one kind of labour resources measured by the nth "product"; they grow at a positive rate ρ: if $(x,y) \in Z$ and x_n is positive, then $y_n/x_n = \rho$. The utility function is normalized w.r.t. labour; replace the cone Z by $Z' = \{(\rho x, y): (x,y) \in Z\}$: the labour resources in the Z' grow at a rate equal to 1.

When the vector of output allocated to final consumption is $c = (c_1, \ldots, c_{n-1}, 0)$, the problem is to find $u(c) = \max$ subject to

$$(1) \quad y - c \geq x; \quad (2) \quad (x,y) \in Z'; \quad (3) \quad x_n = 1.$$

The focus is on variants $M(\overline{Z})$ and $M(\overline{Z}(\lambda))$. For the former the cone $\overline{Z}$ is defined this way. Let the quantity of an additional $(n+1)$th "product" characterize the deviation of the utility function from $\bar{u}$. This cone is determined by the processes: by

$[(x, \bar{u} - u(c); (y - c, 0)]$ if $\bar{u} - u(c) \geq 0$ and $[(x, 0); (y - c, u(c) - \bar{u})]$ if $u(c) - \bar{u} \geq 0$.

Here $(x,y) \in Z'$, $x_n = 1$, $y \geq c$. The latter process implements the "stocking" of the $(n + 1)$th product. The processes $[(\bar{x}, \gamma); (y - c, \gamma)] \in Z$ (where γ is an arbitrary positive number), $(\bar{x}, \bar{y})$ and $\bar{c}$ determine the state of equilibrium (balanced growth).

Now the variant $M(Z(\lambda))$, which differs from the $M(Z)$ only by its way of "stocking" the $(n + 1)$th product. The technology $\overline{Z}(\lambda)$ is determined analogously by $[(x,0); (y - c, u(c)]$ where $(x,y) \in Z'$ with the "stocking" process of the form $[(0, \ldots, 0, 1): (0, \ldots, 0, \lambda)], \lambda > 1$.

In a previous paper Makarov had established the duality theorem for the problem of finding the trajectory $\{x(t), \gamma(t)\}_{t=0}^{t=T}$ where $\bar{\gamma}(T)$ is the greatest from among all $\gamma(T)$ determined by the technologically feasible trajectories. This is now extended to the case of $t = \infty$: that is, the infinite optimal – "effective" – trajectory is examined. The trajectory $\{(\bar{x}(t), \gamma(t)\}_{t=0}^{t=\infty}$ of the model $M(\bar{Z}(\lambda))$, $\lambda \geqslant 1$ – admissible with (x_0, γ_0) – is defined as infinitely optimal if there exists no trajectory such that $(x(t), \gamma(t)) = \mu(\bar{x}(t), \bar{\gamma}(t))$, $\mu \geqslant 1$ for any t. It follows then, from the theorem established in Makarov's previous paper quoted, that each infinite optimal trajectory $\{(\bar{x}(t), \bar{\gamma}(t)\}_{t=0}^{t=\infty}$ can be identified with some equilibrium state of the model $[(\widetilde{x,y} - c), \widetilde{p,a}]$ such that

$$[\bar{x}(t + 1)\widetilde{p} + \gamma(t + 1)\widetilde{p}_{n+1}]/[\bar{x}(t)\widetilde{p} + \gamma(t)p_{n+1}] \to \bar{a} \text{ for } t \to \infty.$$

The focus is then on such infinite optimal trajectories for which this relation holds, where the equilibrium prices are $\bar{p}' = (\bar{p}, 1)$ of the balanced equilibrium growth and $\widetilde{a} = \lambda$.

It is proved then that in the model $M(\bar{Z}(\lambda))$, $\lambda \geqslant 1$, for the trajectory $\{\bar{x}(t), \bar{\gamma}(t)\}_{t=0}^{t=\infty}$, admissible with (x_0, γ_0) to be infinitely optimal, it is necessary and sufficient that there exists a sequence of nonnegative vectors of prices $\{\bar{p}(t)\}_{t=0}^{t=\infty}$ such that *firstly*, for all $t = 0, 1, \ldots$ and all processes $(z, z') \in Z(\lambda)$, $\bar{p}(t)z \geqslant p(t+1)z'$, and *secondly*, for all t, $\bar{p}(0)(x_0, \gamma_0) = \bar{p}(t)(x(t), \bar{\gamma}(t)) > 0$.

The existence of the u-optimal trajectory is established for the model $M(\bar{Z}(\lambda))$, $\lambda > 1$ with the initial conditions (x_0, γ_0) under the propositions stated. Here the conceptual framework is extended beyond that of Gale so as to handle the case with $\lambda = 1$: the admissible trajectory is defined as weakly u-optimal wherever a sub-sequence $\{t_k\}$ is found such that for any trajectory $\{x(t), \gamma(t)\}_{t=0}^{t=\infty}$; $\bar{\gamma}(t_k) \geqslant \gamma(t_k)$ and there exists no admissible trajectory $\{x(t), \gamma(t)\}_{t=0}^{t=\infty}$ such that $\gamma(t) \geqslant \bar{\gamma}(t)$ for all t, whereby the inequality is strict for at least one time-point.

The Makarov reasoning is carried out essentially under the assumption of discrete time. Eventually the Koopmans and Inagaki continuous-time approach[114] is borrowed and extended: admissibility and u-optimality (and strong optimality) of the trajectory in $M(\bar{Z}(\lambda))$, $\lambda \geqslant 1$ for continuous time is defined.[115] It is suggested, though without proof, that the results obtained (in particular those with respect to duality) are transferable to t⁺ continuous-time systems.

The economic justification for a planned system is significant. The key point is that the modelling of the kind offered would help in clarifying the state-to-state transition and offer a practical precept for capital formation. In particular, under given conditions, when the continuous-time model is applied, only *differential properties* of the Z technology and the u function at points $x(t)$, $c(t)$ are required for determining (when at $x(t)$) how much output and of what kind is required at $y(t)$, what of it to allocate for $c(t)$ and what for further production $y(t)-c(t)$; and patently differential properties are easier to measure than the Z and the u themselves. The stress on the technical advantages of the u-modelling for planning practice and the plea for the concept of utility deserve note in the context of the controversy — in Soviet economics — concerning this concept.

One more remark: the "realistic" adjustments of the von Neumann-derived turnpike-type construct have rapidly built up voluminous literature in the West. This applies in particular to models of utility and consumption turnpikes; indeed, the impact of alternatives in criterial functions has been investigated.[116] For reasons suggested before the original von Neumann approach, treating that is consumption as an input and thereby a minimand had not been uncongenial to the Soviet theory of planning. In other words, the intertemporal efficiency criterion congenial to that theory has been traditionally related to terminal capacities, viz, to reach a pledged stock, volume, and composition, along the most economical among feasible paths (not dominated by any alternative): the Kantorovich-Makarov construct of the early 1960s typifies the approach. (To be sure, the concept of utility is just as well employable with respect to the productive-capital stock; this has not been familiar, however, in Soviet traditional conceptual usage.) The consumption-based utility functional attracted the attention of Soviet theoreticians of planning when adopted in modelling the turnpike-type catenary motion under the Modified Golden Rule: in a system no longer closed, with welfare as the maximand and labour now turned into an exogenous resource postulated to expand in some statistically extrapolated way (starting from a given initial value and pledged to attain some terminal value of the capacity stocks); it may be made clear that this has not affected the stand on the substance and the measuring of social welfare and its institutional framework. Makarov has been one of the first Soviet students to assimilate the utility optimand thus conceived.

2. For an incisive comparative analysis of alternative conceptual equilibrium-growth trajectories — specifically of the Cassel-von Neumann balanced-growth path, the Hicks-Malinvaud perfect equilibrium over time, the Lindahl-Hicks sequence of temporary equilibrium — the reader should

turn to Morishima's latest work.[117] This is related in Morishima to the "limited" Ramsey problem – the choice of the saving rate such as to secure the "best" from among the family of balanced growths: in fact the solution for the latter problem appears in Morishima to be that of general equilibrium – wherever the system is given sufficient time (optimality is in the context appraised by the Pareto criterion). The best from among the balanced paths turns out to be that generated by the Golden Rule of Accumulation. Turnpike theorems – in Morishima's reasoning – validate the "classical" saving programme: that of the Marx-von Neumann-Joan Robinson type.

I would like to draw attention – in my context – to Morishima's inquiry into the stability of the Golden Equilibrium path. The central question treated here is that as to whether the competitive regime per se does or does not permit attaining the Golden Age (specifically what is examined is whether starting from some historically reached state the Hicks-Malinvaud equilibrium trajectory can bring about a successive approximation of the Golden Equilibrium). This convergence is compared with the turnpike type. The point made by Morishima – of special interest here – is that the application of this may only occur in "more or less" planned economies, but not in "purely" competitive ones.[118]

* * *

To sum up, the last few sections have made it clear, we hope, how far and fast Soviet doctrine is moving away from its rigid faith in simple causality assumptions that had rationalized the economic strategist's principles in a simple environment, in the heroic period of growth (see sect. 1). It is safe to say that at the time of writing, the doctrine is passing through a phase of acute theoretical heart-searching. The feedback effect of the strategy on the theoretical thinking may be well illustrated by these words in a paper on the trends in capital formation published in a recent issue of the principal Soviet mathematical-economic journal.[119] It says broadly this. Two tendencies are observable in socialist economies with respect to the rate of productive accumulation. One, which is towards maximum growth of efficiency, leads to the lowering of that rate; then the dynamics of the economy is characterized by a smooth, stationary growth. The second is determined by the drive towards retaining "at any cost" the high growth-rates; the raising of the accumulation rate entailed in this policy leads to fluctuating growth-rates, to a chronic overstrain, and to a cyclical type of growth ("jumps" in the accumulation ratios, capital-output ratios, and growth-rates).

The very presentation of the strategy alternatives is a reflection of current developments in theoretical thought.

APPENDICES

Appendix 1: Makarov's System of Input-Output Information-Supporting Growth

An interesting elaboration of the dynamic model discussed here, based on the information of an input-output system, is due to Makarov,[120] one of its co-authors. Its substance is this.

We have n "branches", m kinds of labour. In each branch, i, there are k identified types of capacities: $\sum_i k_i = K$. Thus the s-th activity yielding output i during t appears as

$$(\ldots - f_{n+m+k}^{s,t} \ldots - a_1^{s,t} \ldots 1 - a_i^{s,t} \ldots - a_n^{s,t} - \ldots$$
$$- W_{n+1}^{s,t} \ldots - W_{n+m}^{s,t} \ldots + f_{n+m+k}^{s,t+1}).$$

(*Symbols:* $a_i^{s,t}$ are inputs of i' per output-unit of i; $W_{n+j}^{s,t}$ labour input; $f_{n+m+k}^{s,t}$ input of k-th capacity-time ($k = 1, 2, \ldots, K$). Then the s-th capacity-forming activity, over t, is written

$$(\ldots - b_1^{s,t-\tau} \ldots - b_n^{s,t-\tau} \ldots - b_1^{s,t-\tau+1} \ldots - b_n^{s,t-\tau+1} \ldots$$
$$- b_1^{s,t-1} \ldots - b_n^{s,t-1} \ldots 1).$$

The overall activity-matrix (technology row) has the form

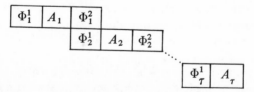

The A's relate to "current" inputs, those of the Φ_t^1 and Φ_t^2 to capacities and natural resources. On the Kantorovich-Makarov "chain" principle, the $\boxed{\Phi_t^1 \mid A_t \mid \Phi_t^2}$ describe multi-period production: current activities employing the same kind of capacities over neighbouring time intervals are combined into one. Thus a current activity will have the form

$$(\ldots - f_{n+m+k}^{s,\tau} \ldots - a_1^{s,\tau} \ldots 1 - a_1^{s,\tau} \ldots - a_n^{s,\tau} - W_{n+1}^{s,\tau} \ldots W_{n+m}^{s,\tau} -$$

$$- a_1^{s,\tau+1} \ldots - W_{n+m}^{s,\tau+1} \ldots - a_1^{s,\tau+\theta} \ldots - a_n^{s,\tau+\theta} - W_{n+1}^{s,\tau+\theta} \ldots$$

$$\ldots - W_{n+m}^{s,\tau+\theta} \ldots + f_{n+m+k}^{s,\tau+\theta+1} \ldots).$$

The vector is formed so that those relating to columns of Φ_1^1 describe initial capacities of each kind in each branch; relating to columns of A_t, the volume of final use of products over t; and relating to W_t, the labour availabilities. Some vector $\xi^t = (\xi_1^t, \ldots, \xi^t{}_K)$ is adopted for weights of various types of capacities $[n+m+1] \ldots [m+n+K]$, by means of which their sum is maximized. The base $(t = 0)$ plan is obtained from the solution of the programme with the matrix $\boxed{\;\Phi_1^1\;|\;A_1\;}$ and coefficients of the linear $\Phi_1^2\ \xi^1$. For decomposition of activity, assume that its coefficients are $\lambda = (\lambda^1, \ldots, \lambda^T); \lambda^t = (\lambda_1^t, \ldots, \lambda^t{}_{m+n+K})$. For activity included over t we have $\lambda^1, \ldots, \lambda^{t=1} = 0$ and (1) $\lambda^t = (f_t^{s_0}, a^{s_0})B_t{}^{-1}(0)$;

(2) $\lambda^{t+1} = \Phi_t^2(0)\lambda^t B_{t+1}^{-1}(0)$; and so on up to λ^T. (The $B_t(0)$ is the matrix of all activities included into the base-year plan.) The lambdas are found in an iterative procedure.

Appendix 2: Mikhalevskiy's Sketch of a Production-Function "Complex"

Naturally the use of the production function as a planning tool, as distinct from its general strategy task, brings in the troublesome problem of aggregation. It is the one ever-present problem in our subject-matter and we touch upon it in almost every context. But relating a heroically condensed macro-production-function growth model to an operational system poses a problem in itself.

An answer to it has been at least outlined by Mikhalevskiy[121] in a broad graph-theoretic fashion (the exacting informational and computational requirement apart, he is sceptical of the operational workability in macro-planning of the more classical methods of decomposition, if only because the latter is usually understood as one of only vertical subordination in the production-technology sphere). The structural outline of the Mikhalevskiy system of models combined with a one-product production

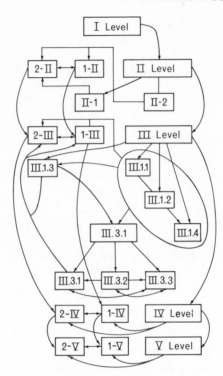

Legend: *I Level*: one-sector dynamic model; *2-II* – output and material-financial resources for civilian sector; *1-II* – the same for military sector. *II Level*: decomposition of all-economy indices at one-sector level; *II-1* – material structure of final
product in constant and current prices. Total availability of resources and volume of
gross product; *II-2* – financial structure of final product in constant and current
prices; its distribution by financial sectors; income and expenditure of financial
sectors. *2-III* – output and material-financial resources for the civilian sector; *1-III* –
the same for the military sector. *III Level*: transfer to the 15-20 sectors models of
final demand, production, resources, finance, and organizational structure; *III.1.1* –
final demand; *III.1.2* – output and capacity volume; *III.1.3* – availability of
resources and gross investment by sectors; *III-2* – efficiency norms for resources and
formation of accounting prices; *III.1.4* – aggregated distribution of net product by
incomes; *III.3.1* – formation of resources and gross investment by financial sectors;
III.3.2 – formation of final and overall production by financial sectors; *III.3.3* –
formation – from net product – of incomes and expenditures of financial sectors.
IV Level: transfer to disaggregated plan with 80-100 branches; *2.IV* – output and
material-financial resources for the civilian sector; *1.IV* – the same for military
sector. *V Level*: formation of the investment specification ("list"); *2-V* – investment
project for civilian sector; *1.V* – the same for military sector.

function for medium run (10-year period) with 15-20 sectors is reproduced on this page. It is, we think, self-explanatory as far as it goes. The system is designed for a multi-stage decomposable "complex" with both horizontal and vertical recursive links. Co-ordination is supposed to be iterative — along them. As is usual in tree-like structures with sequentially organized blocks, vertical co-ordination is secured by means of control-units' results along the hierarchy lines and special procedures of aggregation and harmonization of multi-component forecasts (regression with variable coefficients subject to constraints and allowance made for errors in independent variables, for autocorrelation and for heteroscedasticities of some variances; some matrix models are built in). A feature of the Mikhalevskiy complex is that horizontal co-ordination between parallel sub-items is obtained by producing "artificial autonomy": the horizontal couplings are disconnected and linking constraints (=0 or =const.) substituted for variables of parallel levels.

Only parts of the Mikhalevskiy "complex" have been formalized. The very substance of decomposability is not adequately explored. The path of such explorations is indicated i.a. in Weil's work.[122] It shows, with the use of much more rigorous graph-theoretic techniques, the way to ascertain decompositions of a production system: it evolves a canonical form of a decomposable system and demonstrates the constructing of a precedence graph from this form.

Appendix 3: Movshovich's System of Generalized Turnpike Equilibrium

Following Makarov's inquiries into the non-uniqueness of the turnpike as defined under the assumption of equilibrium,[123] Movshovich has generalized the concept of the von Neumann equilibrium[124] and introduced that of turnpike "generalized equilibrium". This is employed in the analysis of the trajectories' properties.

The point of departure is the von Neumann-Gale system of the familiar form. It operates in discrete time $t = 0, \ldots, T, \ldots$: at t it is described by the nonnegative n-dimensional vector $y_t = (y_t^1, \ldots, y_t^n)$; its i-th component indicates the presence of the i-th product. Transition from state y_t into y_{t+1} is carried out by means of the technological process (y_t, y_{t+1}) where y_t and y_{t+1} are conceived of, respectively, as the input at the start of the cycle $(t, t+1)$ and output at its end. For the set of technological processes K it is assumed that

(I) the K is a convex cone belonging to the positive orthant of the $2n$-dimensional Euclidean space R^{2n}; (II) if $(0,y) \in K$, then $y = 0$; (III) there exists a process $(x,y) \in K$ such that y is positive.

The von Neumann equilibrium of balanced growth is defined so that the following inequalities are satisfied: (1) $ax_0 < y_0$; (2) $ap_0 x > p_0 y$ for all $(x,y) \in K$; (3) $p_0 y_0 > 0$. The vector $p_0 = (p_0^1 \ldots, p_0^n) \geq 0$ $\Sigma_1^n = p_0^i = 1$; pz is a scalar product of p and z. Where y_p is the initial state, the sequence $Y = (y_0, \ldots y_t, y_{t+1})$ is the trajectory if $(y_t, y_{t+1}) \in K$ for all t. In addition to notation above the P_0 stands here for the price vector, a for rate of balanced growth.

It is taken from Kemeny-Morgenstern-Thompson[125] that where K is a polyhedral cone, the equilibrium (1)-(3) always exists and the number of equilibria with different a is not greater than min (m,n) where m denotes the number of the cone's facets; thence the conclusion that for an arbitrary von Neumann-Gale system with different a's there too are no more than n equilibria. The feasible number of the equilibrium a's has been found by Makarov.[126] Now Movshovich shows that the existence of the equilibrium is not guaranteed. And he proves the following theorems.

1. There exist positive numbers c and ϵ_0 such that for any $0 < \epsilon < \epsilon_0$ and any $k = 1, \ldots, n$ a price vector $p_k(\epsilon)$ will be found such that

$$p_k(\epsilon) y \leq (a_k + \epsilon) p_k(\epsilon) x \text{ for all } (x,y) \in K$$

$$p_k^i(\epsilon) \geq c\epsilon \text{ for all } i \in A^k$$

$$p_k^i(\epsilon) \geq 0; i = 1, \ldots, n; \Sigma^n_{i=1} p_k^i(\epsilon) = 1$$

the $A^k = \{ i: a_i \leq a_k \}$ being the set of indices of products with n_k elements whose maximum rate of balanced growth does not exceed a_k.

2. Let the cone K satisfy (I)-(III), let a_k be the constant growth-rate of social utility u for given y_0, $B_k = \{ i: a_i = a_k \}$ $F_k \cap F(p)$ the von Neumann facet. If $(p_k^*)^i > 0$ for all $i \in B^k \cap \{ i: u^i > 0 \}$ then for any positive δ, M_0 will be found such that for an arbitrary T and any u-optimal trajectory the number of cycles, where $(y_t, y_{t+1}) \in F_k^\delta$ does not exceed M_0.

3. Let the cone K satisfy (I)–(III), and a_k be a strongly stationary rate of growth of social utility with a given y_0. Then for any positive δ an M_0 will be found such that for any T and u-optimal trajectory the number of cycles where $(y_t, y_{t+1}) \in F^\delta$ does not exceed $m_0 \log T$.

4. Let the cone K satisfy (I)–(III) and let a_k be a stationary rate of growth of social utility with given y_0. Then for any positive δ and any u-optimal trajectory Y_T the ratio of the number of periods M (when $(y_t, y_{t+1}) \in F_k^\delta$) to the length of the trajectory T tends towards zero whenever $T \to \infty$.

The maximum growth-rate of the k-th product over the Y sequence is here $\theta_k = \lim\limits_{t \to \infty} T\sqrt{y^k(T)}$, where the $y^k(T)$ is the greatest value of the k-th component of the vector y_T over the set of trajectories $Y_T = (y_0, \ldots, y_T)$. For the three classes of growth considered in the theorems the Movshovich definitions are

(1) $\vartheta\phi_k = \lim\limits_{t \to \infty} \sqrt{y^h(T)}$, where it exists, is the *stationary rate of growth* of the k-th product. Hence for an arbitrary T an $\epsilon(T)$ can be found such that for all $t \geq T$, we have $y^k(t) \geq (a_k - \epsilon(T))^t = a_k{}^t(1 - (\epsilon(T)/a_k))^t$

(2) the a_k is a *strongly stationary growth-rate* of product k if for some positive c the statement $(1 - (\epsilon(T)/a_k))^T = 0(1/T^c)$ holds

(3) the δ_k is a *constant growth-rate* of product k if δ_k is stationary and there exists a positive d such that for all T, from k onwards some value,

$$y^k(T) \geq d\theta^T_k$$

For a given technology set K the growth-rate may be either stationary or non-stationary depending on the initial state y_0.

Where a_k is either a constant, or a stationary or a strongly stationary growth-rate of $u(t)$ and the $u(y)$ satisfies the Lipschitz condition $u(y_1) - u(y_2) \leq L \, |y_1 - y_2|$ for any nonnegative y_1 and y_2, the turnpike theorems 2,3, and 4 are analogously valid.

In the general case, however, once the requirement of stationarity is abandoned, the turnpike theorem will not hold even where, in the case of the multi-facet cone K, the equilibrium (1)-(3) does hold.

As indicated in the opening paragraph, the declared intention of Movshovich is to move beyond the system of Radner,[127] McKenzie,[128] Tsukui,[129] and Dradnakis.[130] Note that, as Dradnakis points out, the classical Radner proof of the turnpike theorem makes the model essentially applicable to a centrally, we would say directly-mandatory planned economy: in a word, it does not permit decentralization of the system. This would be true of Movshovich's last construct.

Appendix 4: Modelling of Regional Development

Under Soviet conditions the problems of interregional location and development strategy have a particular significance. However, the first experimental plan programming was started only in the late 1960s. Below we reproduce the substance of basic formalization of the model developed in the Economics Institute of USSR Academy's Siberian branch:[131] $z \to \max$

s.t.
$$\sum (\delta_{ij} - a_{ij}{}^r - b_{ij}{}^r) V_j r - \sum (\delta_{ij} - a_{ij}{}^r) W_j^r$$

$$- \sum_q a_{iq}{}^r x_q^r - \alpha_i{}^r z - \sum_{s \neq r} x_i^{rs} + \sum_{s \neq r} x_i^{sr} = \bar{y}_i{}^r;$$

$$i = 1, \ldots, n; \quad r = 1, \ldots, m,$$

where $\delta_{ij} \begin{cases} = 1, i = j, \\ = 0, i \neq j; \end{cases}$

$$- \sum_j a_{qj}{}^{rr} V_j^r + \sum_j a_{qj}^{rr} W_j^r + x_q^r -$$

$$- \sum_{s,j} (a_{qj}{}^{rs} - a_{qj}^{rr}) x_j^{rs} - \sum_{s,j} a_{qj}{}^{rr} x_j^{sr} = \bar{y}_q{}^r; \quad q = 1, \ldots, p;$$

$$r = 1, \ldots, m;$$

$$\sum_j \ell_j r V_j r - \sum_j \ell_j r W_j r + \sum_q \ell_q{}^r x_q r \leqslant \bar{L}^r, \quad r = 1, \ldots, m;$$

$$\sum_{r,j} h_{kj} r V_j r \leqslant H_k, \quad k = 1, 2, \ldots;$$

$$0 \leqslant V_j r \leqslant d_j r,$$

$$0 \leqslant W_j r \leqslant N_j r;$$

$$x_q{}^r \geqslant 0;$$

$$x_j^{rs} \geqslant 0.$$

In this

$$\bar{y}_i{}^r = - \sum_j (\delta_{ij} - a_{ij} r) N_j{}^r, \quad y_q{}^r = \sum a_{qj}{}^{rr} N_j{}^r, \quad \bar{L}^r = L^r - \sum \ell_j{}^r N_j{}^r.$$

[*Notation*: n sectors (transport excluded) — $(i,j = 1, \ldots, n)$ and m regions $(r,s = 1, \ldots, m)$. Variables relating to the plan's last year: x_i^r is output volume; x_q^r volume of transport services, q, in r-th region; x_i^{rs} — delivery of i-th product from r to the neighbouring s region; z — total non-productive consumption. Parameters: N_i^r — volume of output obtainable in last year from capacities installed at the start of the plan. H_K — limit of k-th net investment over the plan period for the country: L^r — limit of labour for "productive" sphere in r; d^r — "ceiling" on permissible increment of j-th output in r; a_{ij}^r — input-output coefficients in r; h_{kj}^r — share of k-th invest-ment for production of j-th sector in r; b_{ij}^r capital coefficients for incre-mental i-th output in r; ℓ — labour–input coefficients in r; a_{iq}^r — mater-ial input coefficients on q-th transport in r; ℓ_q^r — ditto labour coefficients a_{qj}^{rr} — input coefficients of intra-regional transport q in output of j in r; a_{qj}^{rs} — ditto for inter-regional transport; α_i^r — share of r in the country's non-productive consumption of i. The V and W, respectively, are interpreted as increment and decrease in output over the plan period resulting from investment and withdrawal of capacities; thus $x_j^r = N_j^r + V_j^r - W_j^r$].

Some simplifying assumptions have been adopted for the model (com-puted for 16 sectors over 10 years); among them the following. The model is essentially static in the sense that the solution is sought for the terminal plan year: in this, investment in that year is taken to have a fixed share in the plan-period total. One technology is adopted for each region. Invest-ments in transport are taken to be known: the H_k are adjusted accordingly. Labour is in principle allocated region-wise. Essentially transport expendi-ture is calculated pair-wise as between two neighbouring regions: they are debited to the region-exporter and assumed to move along one path.

The numerical solution yielded also regional shadow prices of the form

$$v_j^r = \sum_i (a_{ij}r + b_{ij}r)\, v_i^r + \sum_q a_{qj} v_q{}^r + \ell_j^r\, w_i^r$$

$$+ \sum_k h_{kj}^r w_k + w_j^r; \quad \sum_{i,r} a_i^r v_i^r = 1$$

[Shadow prices respectively of: j-th output in $r - v_j^r$; q-th transport in $r - v_q{}^r$; labour in $r - w_1{}^r$; k-th investment w_k.]

In Soviet literature several *nonlinear* inter-regional models have been worked upon. The simplest would have the form

$$\sum_{i=1}^m \varphi_i(x_i) x_i + \sum_{i=1}^m \sum_{j=1}^n \ell_{ij} x_{ij} = \min, \text{ subject to}$$

$$\sum_{j=1}^{m} x_{ij} = b_j; \quad \sum_{j=1}^{n} x_{ij} = x_i; c_i \leqslant x_i \leqslant d_i x_{ij} \geqslant 0 \quad \begin{cases} i = 1, m \\ j = 1, n. \end{cases}$$

[*Notation*: b_{ij} requirement of product in j; c_{ij} expenditure on production and delivery of output unit from i to j; x_{ij} delivery volume from i to j; x capacity at i: $\varphi_i(x_i)$ — function describing dependence of costs on volume of output at i; t_{ij} unit cost of transport from i to j].

The $f_i(x_i) = \varphi_i(x_i) x_i$ when approximated by piece-wise linear functions becomes (by Langrange formula)

$$f_i(x_i) = f_i(c_i) + f'_i(x_i)(x_i - c_i)$$

$$f_i(x_i) = [f_i(d_i) - f_i(c_i)] / (d_i - c_i).$$

Notes

1. M. I. Tugan-Baranovskiy, *Theoretische Grundlagen des Marxismus* (Leipzig, 1905).
2. Rosa Luxemburg, *The accumulation of capital* (London, 1951).
3. T. Khachaturov, in *Vopr. ekon., 8* (1971) and also A. Dorovskikh, in *Plan. khoz.,* 9 (1971); also F. N. Klotsvog *et al.*, in *EMM,* 5 (1971).
4. The deus ex machina, on Moroshima's showing, is that the rate of accumulation in "Department II" is adjusted — in the institutional frame considered — by capitalists of that "department"— to the exogenously-determined rate in "Department I" (Moroshima, *Equilibrium, stability and growth*).
    The reader is strongly advised to acquaint himself with Morishima's splendid revisiting of the matter in his *Marx's economics; A dual theory of value and growth* (Cambridge, 1973).
5. V. S. Nemchinov, *Ekonomiko-matematicheskiye metody i modeli* (Moscow, 1966); A. A. Konyus, in *On political economy and econometrics, Essays in honour of Oskar Lange.*
    Similar in purpose is Andras Brody's *Proportions, prices and planning* (Londo 1970). As stated by himself, this purpose is to translate Marx's approach into mathematical terms and to show the path from it to modern quantitative economic reasoning. Then an attempt is made to demonstrate the mathematical equivalence of a variety of theories and models, such as labour theory of value, game theory, Leontief systems — open and closed, static and dynamic — linear programming, the theory of optimal processes and general equilibrium models. (The results obtained are plausible when the generalization levels are pushed up sufficiently: in this sense cognitive gains are being made.) What is then obtained as the common basis is applied to the practical tasks: analysis, forecasting, planning, control of economic systems.
6. W. Leontief, "Preface" to Brody's *Proportions . . . ,* p. 7.
7. See illuminating observations made on this point by H. G. Johnson, "The state of theory in relation to empirical analysis" (mimeo, 1970(?)).

8. P. A. Samuelson, "Wages and interest: a modern dissection of Marxian economics", *Amer. Econ. R.*, Dec. 1964.

9. O. Lange, "Some observations on input-output analysis", *Sankhya*, Feb. 1957: also his *Introduction to econometrics*. For a discussion of Lange's *Sankhya* paper see Zauberman, *Sov. Stud.*, 4 (1959).

10. Of interest also is V. S. Dadayan's work in this field, cf. his *Ekonomicheskiye raschety po modeli rasshirennogo vosproizvodstva* (Moscow, 1966). Also his article in *EMM*, 5 (1967). In the last-named work he restates Marx's schema of "expanded reproduction" in the form of a Leontief input-output matrix and suggests the way for its employment in multi-variant choice-making (this exemplified with Soviet statistical data).

   Cf. M. Boselt, in *EMM*, 4 (1968). In Boselt the optimal value of the objective function of Marx's "Department I" equals labour inputs entailed in the programme: in Marxian symbols: min $z' = v_1 + m_{iv}$. It is further shown that min $z' + m_i = $ max $z'' = c_2 + m_{2c}$, which is the objective function of the problem of "Department II".

11. cf. Mayevskiy, in *Vopr. ekon.*, 11 (1971).

12. V. Dadayan, in *Vopr. ekon.*, 9 (1971). The somewhat confused state of the official doctrine on the subject is reflected in contemporary writing.

   The principle of faster growth of "Department I" is not disowned, but it is recognized that at the present stage the group of light industries ("B") has to be planned to grow faster than the group of heavy industries ("A").

   It is strongly conjectured that the validity of faster advance in "Department I" depends decisively on the type of technological progress; cf. Khachaturov, ibid. 8 (1971).

13. H. Uzawa, "On a two-sector model of economic growth", *R. Econ. Stud.*, Oct. 1961 and part II, June 1963; and his "Optimal growth in a two-sector model of capital accumulation", ibid., Jan. 1964.

14. J. E. Meade, *A neoclassical theory of economic growth* (New York, 1961).

15. K. Shell, "Application of Pontryagin's maximum principle to economics", "Lecture II", in Kuhn/Szegö, *Mathematical systems theory*.

16. T. N. Srinivasan, "Optimal savings in a two-sector model of growth", *Econometrica*, July 1964.

17. W. Haque, "Sceptical notes on Uzawa's 'optimal growth in a two-sector model of capital accumulation', and a precise characterization of optimal path", *R. Econ. Stud.*, July 1970.

   It has been argued by Cass and Yaari that in a stylized neo-classical economy the ultimately decisive consumer choices would be not sufficient to guarantee dynamic efficiency. From another angle Shesinski argues that the competitive economy tends to settle to a steady state with investment below what is social optimum: the reason, according to him, would be that under competitive conditions those responsible for technical progress are not rewarded with full marginal product.

   Cass-Yaari postulate as a corrective that to secure efficiency investment should be ultimately controlled by the firm as such and not by stock-holders. The consideration (whatever its realism for capitalism) brings into analysis the institutional element with some implications for a socialist economy. Contrary to the author's view, the issue is not related to Marx's theory of growth. (David Cass/M. E. Yaari, "Individual saving, capital accumulation and efficient growth", in Shell, *Essays on the theory of optimal economic growth*.)

18. G. A. Feldman, in *Plan. khoz.*, 11 & 12 (1928); cf. also comment in Kantorovich/Vainshtein, in *EMM*, 5(1967), p.698.

19. P. C. Mahalanobis, "Some observations on the process of growth of national income", *Sankhya*, 12 (1953); cf. also the same with M. Mukherjee, "Operational research models used for planning in India", 2nd Conf. on Operational Research, 1960.
20. M. Kalecki, *Zarys teorii wzrostu gospodarki socjalistycznej* (Warsaw, 1968). To the same school of thought belongs Laski's work on the theory of growth of a socialist system. It is strongly influenced by Kalecki but develops some of the latter's ideas in an independent and interesting way. cf. K. Laski, *Zarys tehorii reprodukcji socjalistycznej* (Warsaw, 1965): the reader's attention is drawn in particular to Parts II and III analysing the growth process and equilibrium.
      For a comment on Kalecki's theories of growth see Zauberman, "A few remarks on Kalecki's theory of economic growth under socialism", *Kyklos*, 3(1966)
21. J. von Neumann, "Über ein okonomisches Gleichungs-System und eine Verallgemeinerung des Brouwerschen Fixpunktsatzes", publ. 1937, trans. as "A model of general economic equilibrium", *R. Econ. Stud.*, 1945-6.
22. Zauberman, in G. Bruckman/W. Weber, eds., *Contributions to the von Neumann growth model* (Vienna, 1971).
23. T. C. Koopmans, "Economic growth at maximal rate", *Q. J. Econ.*, Aug. 1964.
24. R. Dorfman *et al.*, *Linear programming and economic analysis* (London, 1958).
25. Note the theoretical argument – a relevant and empirical investigation based on Japanese experience – by Jinkichi Tsuku. In his exercise an objective function is formulated and brought into a Leontief dynamic system such as to ensure maximum terminal value of capital stocks, with the turnpike configuration (N.B. the movement is found to be catenary even over short periods). In this exercise labour is taken to be a non-scarce factor: the effect of technological progress is the cutting down of the labour coefficient (with input-output and stock-flow matrices constant). Thus under disguised unemployment the per capita output grows, under invariant technology, by continuous accumulation of capital. Validation by the Japanese data is claimed. cf. J. Tsukui, "Application of a turnpike theorem to planning for efficient accumulation: the example of Japan", *Econometrica*, Jan.1968; also his "A turnpike theorem under exogenous labour growth", ibid. suppl. issue, 1966, p.17.
26. cf. S. J. Turnovsky, "Turnpike theorem and efficient economic growth", in E. Burmeister/A. R. Dobell, *Mathematical theories of economic growth* (London, 1970).
27. For reference see in particular P. A. Samuelson's writing on "catenary turnpike", in particular his "A catenary turnpike theorem involving consumption and the golden rule", *Amer. Econ. R.*, June 1965, which initiated a considerable literature.
28. L. V. Kantorovich, in *Opt. plan.*, 8 (1967).
29. *Ekonomiko-matematicheskiye metody* . . .
30. D. Gale, in *R. Econ. Stud.*, 1967, pt. 2.
31. M. Morishima, "Proof on a turnpike theorem: the 'no joint production case'", ibid., 1961.
32. L. W. McKenzie, "Turnpike theorem for a generalized Leontief model", *Econometrica*, Jan.-Apr. 1963.
33. In n. 25 above.
34. Kemeny *et al.*, in *Econometrica*, 1956.
35. Zauberman, "Presentation", in V. K. Dmitriev, *Essais économiques* (Paris, 1968).
36. Dorfman *et al.*, *Linear programming*.
37. R. Radner, "Paths of economic growth that are optimal with regard only to final states: a turnpike theorem", *R. Econ. Stud.*, 1961.
38. Morishima, in *R. Econ. Stud.*, 1961.

39. L. W. McKenzie, in *Econometrica*, 1/2 (1963).
40. H. Nikaido, "Persistence of continual growth near the von Neumann ray: a strong version of the Radner turnpike theorem", *Econometrica*, 1964.
41. Morishima (as n. 31 above); cf. also for his subsequent elaboration, *The theory of economic growth*.
42. B. N. Mikhalevskiy in V. S. Nemchinov, ed., *Matematicheskiy analiz rasshirennogo vosproizvodstva* (Moscow, 1962).
43. Dynamization of the Leontief system has been given a good deal of attention by Soviet students – on both the theoretical and empirical planes. The matter is discussed in Zauberman, in *Economia internazionale*, May 1968.
44. Karlin, *Mathematical methods and theory* . . . .
45. V. K. Dmitriev, *Ekonomicheskiye ocherki* (Moscow, 1904).
46. A. Zauberman, "A few remarks on a discovery in Soviet economics", *Oxford Univ. Inst. Statist. Bull.*, Nov. 1962; also the same, "Presentation" to V. K. Dmitriev, *Essais économiques (Ricardo, Cournot, Walras)*.
47. C. J. Bliss, "On putty-clay", *R. Econ. Stud.*, 1968.
48. P. J. D. Wiles, *Communist international economics* (London, 1968).
49. Gavrilyets *et al.*, in Nemchinov, *Primenenye matematiki . . .* iii; cf. also Zauberman, *Aspects of planometrics*.
      There is a striking kinship between ideas evolved in the 1960s by the Mikhalevskiy school of thought and those represented in the late 1950s in the West by P. Streeten (cf. *Oxford Econom. Pap*, 2 (1959)). Two points are emphasized in his reasoning. Firstly, that in order to get growth one may have to sacrifice balance since unbalance can be a condition of, and a stimulus to, growth. Secondly, that the relevant division is not so much between adherents of the market economy and planners as between those of balanced and unbalanced growth, since either is compatible with both types of economic system.
50. S. M. Movshovich, in *EMM*, 2 (1972); the same and M. N. Yefimov, in 1st Conf. on Optimal Planning, Moscow, 1971. The experimental computation was carried for a model of 15 sectors with information based on 1965.
51. McKenzie (as n.32 above) and I. Tsukui, in *Econometrica*, suppl. 1966; cf. also Zauberman, "Soviet work related to the von Neumann and turnpike theories", in G. Bruckmann/W. Weber, eds., *Contributions to the von Neumann growth model*, suppl. 1, 1971.
52. Along with the objective function $U = \left\{X_0^T | x_0^T(x_0, \ldots, x_T)\right\} = cx_T c \geqslant 0$, that of $U(X_0^T) = \Sigma_{t=1}^{T} \lambda^t u(x_t)$ is considered where $u(x)$ is smooth, convex monotonic.

    Moreover $U(X_0^T)$ satisfies $\alpha\lambda \geqslant 1$ where α is the Neumannian growth rate, $\lim_{\alpha \to \infty} \bar{u}'(\alpha)\alpha^{1-n} \log \alpha > 0; u(\alpha) = \bar{u}(\alpha\bar{x}), \eta = -\log \lambda/\log \alpha_0$.
53. Kantorovich/Makarov, in Nemchinov, *Primenenye matematiki ...*
54. Kantorovich, in *Opt. plan.*, 8(1967).
55. For this see in particular T. Murakami *et al.*, *Various turnpike models of the Japanese economy*, submitted to 2nd World Congress of Econometric Society, 1970. This study offering a numerical confirmation for the Japan case is also of considerable general significance showing the flexibility of the von Neumann-derived model in planning. The Murakami-Tokoyama-Tsukui study indicates that it permits the building into it of consumption as a target function with a discount rate; also of technological progress.
56. The problems of "rolling planning"; and in particular the issues which arise when it commits the country to investments over some short- or medium-length phase of development; and the issues of setting the terminal conditions for a finite horizon so as not to influence the optimal initial policy by the arbitrarily chosen

length of the horizon have been raised by several writers in the West.

We would like to draw attention in particular in the context to a paper by A. S. Manne ("Sufficient conditions for optimality in an infinite horizon development plan", *Econometrica*, Jan. 1970). It establishes a set of sufficient conditions such as to ensure that optimality for a finite horizon plan coincides with that for an infinite horizon plan. The restrictive conditions include: a gradualist consumption path, no primary factors which cannot be produced within the economy, a Leontief technology, and the positiveness of terminal investment and output levels in the optimal finite-horizon solution.

The paper gives a bibliography of the subject, in particular reference to writings of Bruno-Fraenkel-Dougherty, Chakravarty-Lefeber, Eckhaus-Parikh, Manne-Weiskopf.

57. A. L. Lurye, *O matematicheskikh metodakh reshenya zadach na optimum pri planirovanyi sotsyalisticheskogo khozyaistva* (Moscow, 1964).
58. Katsenelenboygen *et al.*, *Metodologicheskiye voprosy . . .*
59. A hint for a switch of a turnpike due to a change in final demand (by means of a nonlinear programme) is contained in the paper of Murakami *et al.* (n. 55 above).
60. The properties have been related to the question of "multiple turnpike"; see in particular in the context N. Liviatan/P. A. Samuelson, "Notes on turnpikes: stable and unstable", *J. Economics*, 1970.
61. Kantorovich/Makarov, in Nemchinov, *Primenenye matematiki . . .*, pp. 66 ff. It is not surprising that the originator of the programming methodology has turned to the production-function modelling. The logical link has been demonstrated by A. A. Walters in his excellent econometric survey of production and cost functions (*Econometrica*, 1–2 (1963). As he argued, the activity analysis result differs from the classical production function analysis in that the transformation curve consists of a series of flat segments instead of a smooth surface.
62. cf. also in the context a Soviet contribution on optimal planning in complex systems – with variable matrices: cf. L. G. Pluskin/A. I. Tupikhin, "Optimalnoye planirovanye v slozhnykh sistemakh pri peremannykh matritsakh", in Trapeznikov, *Vsesoyuznoye sovyeshchanye . . . .*
63. A. D. Smirnov, *Problems of construction of an optimal inter-branch model of socialist reproduction* (paper presented to 4th Int. Conf. on Input-Output Techniques, Geneva, 1968) and its subsequent variant are discussed in Part II, pp. 424 ff.
64. A. Brody, *Optimal and time-optimal paths of the economy*, paper submitted to 4th Int. Conf. on Input-Output Techniques, Geneva, 1968. See also Pt. II, p. pp. 452 ff.
65. S. Katz, "A discrete version of Pontryagin's maximum principle", *J. Electronics & Control*, 13/179 (1962).
66. Since these pages were written the ideas have been further developed by Brody in his *Proportions, prices and planning*. The conjecture on the "flutter" phenomenon as a companion of optimization is expanded and the question posed as to the effectiveness of expressing the primal-dual oscillations around the balanced-growth path and equilibrium prices by means of a control-theoretic statement of the system's dynamics. Now hopes for the interpretation of the analysed relationships are staked on empirical inquiries: relating the spectra of flutter frequencies, computed from the flow and stock matrices to the spectral analysis of time series.
67. D. W. Jorgenson, "Linear models of economic growth", *Int. Econ. R.*, Feb. 1968.
68. E. Malinvaud, "Capital accumulation and efficient allocation of resources", *Econometrica*, Apr. 1953.
69. Oxford, 1969, p. 91.

70. Volkonskiy, *Model optimalnogo planirovanya* . . . , p. 27.
71. R. Goldberg, in *Put industrializatsyi*, 11 (1929).
72. P. A. Samuelson, *Amer. Econ. R.*, Dec. 1964.
73. Interesting remarks on the uses of the production-function apparatus in contemporary plan modelling can be found in L. Spaventa/E. Volpe di Prignano, "Economic structure and uses of medium-term models", in Parenti, *Modeli econometrici*, pp.334 ff.; also in Jean Paelinck's contribution to the discussion, ibid., p. 403.
74. Kantorovich/L. I. Gorkov, in *Doklady*, 129/4 (1959).
75. Kantorovich/I. G. Globenko, (ibid., 174/3 (1967)); reference for the "Marxian" version of the Kantorovich-Globenko model discussed in sect. 10 is *Doklady*, 176/5, 1967.
76. B. N. Mikhalevskiy, *Perspektivnyie raschety na osnovye prostykh dinamicheskikh modeley* (Moscow, 1965) and the same, in *EMM*, 1 (1968); cf. also the same, ibid., 2 (1967).
77. Empirical inquiries into the stability of macro-production-function parameters carried out in the 1960s in the Soviet Union are reported in A. I. Gladyshevskiy, in *EMM*, 2 (1968).
78. V. E. Shlyapentokh, *Ekonometrika i problemy ekonomicheskogo rosta* (Moscow, 1966), p. 172.
79. A. R. Bergstrom, *The construction and use of economic models* (London, 1967), p. 92.
80. Arrow, *et al.*, "Capital-labour substitution and economic efficiency", *R. Econ. Stud.*, Aug. 1961.
81. J. Paroush, "A note on the CES production function", *Econometrica*, Jan.-Apr. 1964.
82. J. Stahl/G. Szakolczai, in *EMM*, 4 (1967).
83. B. N. Mikhalevskiy, in *EMM*, 4 (1970).
84. Michael Bruno, "Estimation of factor contribution to growth under structural disequilibrium", *Int. Econ. R.*, Feb. 1968.
85. The reader will find of great interest the comparison of this with Wiles's Cobb-Douglas-based inquiry into Soviet factor productivities (in agriculture). Cf. his "Is the Soviet agricultural plan for 1966-70 reasonable?" in P. J. D. Wiles, ed., *The prediction of communist economic performance* (Cambridge, 1971).
86. As it appears in the system of models experimented with at the TsEMI, at the lower levels — each elementary process is described by means of regression equations describing non-stationary processes with subsequent iterative co-ordination — within the level's "block" between same level's "blocks" and within neighbouring levels. The computation in "iterative procedure of decompositional planning" at the first three levels required 5-6 machine days of 5 computers with 10^5 power. On the level III the "material aspect" of a medium-term plan with 15 sectors was checked; on the levels IV and V requirements in basic products and selection of investment projects were respectively tested (report in *EMM*, 4 (1970), p. 63).
87. For this interpretation see Irma Adelman, *Theories of economic growth and development* (Stanford, 1962). As is shown by her, the rate of investment is expressible as $dK'/dt = F(K', dK'/dt, d^2 K'/dt^2, \ldots, t)$. The functional form, in addition to the initial stock, fully determines the system's path.
88. M. M. Golanskiy, *Ekonomicheskoye razvitye i modelirovanye*, doctoral thesis as quoted by C. G. Grebennikov, in *EMM*, 4 (1968).
89. Volkonskiy, *Model optimalnogo planirovanya*, p. 48.
90. T. N. Srinivasan, in *Econometrica*, July 1964.
91. H. Uzawa, in *R. Econ. Stud.*, Jan. 1964.

92. See on this development the illuminating comment by T. C. Koopmans, "Objectives, constraints and outcomes in optimal growth models", *Econometrica*, Jan. 1967, p. 6.
93. D. Cass, "Optimum growth in an aggregative model of capital accumulation: a turnpike theorem", ibid., Oct. 1966.
94. Grebennikov, in *EMM*, 4 (1968).
95. The proof follows the line that from (1), (2) and (3) an equation is obtained describing the dynamics of Y_t for some initial Y_0 and Q_0.

$$Y_t = \frac{Y_0}{B^{\alpha/(1-\alpha)}} \left[m(1-\alpha)s'Q_0(e^{Bt} - 1) + B \right]^{\alpha/(1-\alpha)} e^{Bt},$$

where $B = (1-\alpha)\pi + \gamma'$. Whence

$$\frac{\dot{Y}_t}{Y_t} = \frac{aB}{1-\alpha} \left[\frac{m(1-\alpha)s'Q_0 e^{Bt}}{m(1-\alpha)s'Q_0(e^{Bt} - 1) + B} \right]$$

$$\text{and} \lim_{t \to \infty} \frac{\dot{Y}_t}{Y_t} = \frac{B}{1-\alpha} = \pi + \frac{\gamma'}{1-\alpha},$$

since for $t \to \infty$ the expression in square brackets tends towards unity.

96. This reveals itself mathematically from the growth-rate of return on capital

$$\frac{\dot{Q}_t}{Q_t} = B - \frac{Be^{Bt}}{e^{Bt} + \dfrac{B}{Q_0 ms'(1-\alpha)} - 1}.$$

which is obtained from the dynamics of return on capital as related to the accumulation rate

$$Q_t = \frac{B}{m(1-\alpha)s'} \left[\frac{1}{1 + (\dfrac{B}{Q_0 ms'(1-\alpha)} - 1)e^{-Bt}} \right],$$

tending towards

$$\lim_{t \to \infty} Q_0 = \frac{B}{m(1-\alpha)s'}.$$

97. E. S. Phelps, "The new view of investment: a neoclassical analysis", *Q. J. Econ.*, Nov. 1962. In Phelps's argument it is the concept of the Golden Rule path which is the consumption-maximizing Golden Age path: the policy of maintaining the economy on this path by continuously relating tangible investment to the competitive earnings of capital is termed the Golden Rule of Accumulation. The Golden Rule path is one on which every variable changes at a constant proportionate rate.

98. K. Sato, "On the adjustment time in neoclassical growth models", *R. Econ. Stud.*, July 1966.

99. David Gale, "Optimal programs for a multi-sector economy with an infinite time horizon", *Econometrica*, Suppl. issue 1967, p. 17.

100. E. S. Phelps, *Golden rules of economic growth* (New York, 1966), espec. pt. 3. For an imaginative presentation of the Golden Rule principle of a central planner's *Gedankenexperiment* aiming at maximum consumption per worker and in this choosing the capital intensity he would maintain "ever after" see Shell, in Kuhn/Szegö, *Mathematical systems theory*.

101. Estimates by Mikhalevskiy, unique of their kind, show the following percentage contribution of technological progress to the growth of the Soviet economy (rounded):

Accounted for by	1951-63	of this 1959-63	1964-70 (planned)
technological progress			
embodied	14.2	–	3.2
"autonomous"	7.4	–	2.5
returns to scale	10.2	–	13.1
total	31.8	5.6	18.8

(cf. Mikhalevskiy, in *EMM*, 2 (1957)).
        According to Brown, three-quarters of the US growth of output is accounted for by factor growth over 1890-1921, which also agrees with Tinbergen's results; and over 1921-40 only one-half. Thus the share of technological progress during the later period was double that in the first period and was almost entirely of the neutral type. This also accords with Solow's findings (cf. M. Brown, *On the theory and measurement of technological change*, Cambridge, 1966 and review by C. G. F. Simkin, *Econometrica*, Jan. 1968). Mikhalevskiy's methodological frame is perhaps closest to that of Denison: hence the results might be relatively the most comparable. According to the latter the economic growth of the USA in the first half of the 20th century is accounted for by up to as much as 85 per cent by the increase in the education of labour force, and the increase per unit of output is due to the spread of technical knowledge and to economies of scale. (cf. E. F. Denison, *The sources of economic growth in the United States and the alternatives before us*, 1962).
        See also Zauberman, "Pushing the technological frontier through trade", in S. Wasowski, ed., *East-West trade and the technology gap* (New York, 1970). Cf. illuminating findings of S. Gomulka, *Inventive activity, diffusion and stages of economic growth* (1971).

102. Kalecki, *Zarys teorii* . . . .

103. A. Chilosi/S. Gomulka, in *Ekonomista*, 1 (1969).

104. Ya. G. Liberman, in *EMM*, 1 (1970).

105. K. K. Valtukh, "Problemy optimizatsyi nakoplenya" in *Problemy narodno-khozyaistvennogo optimuma* (Moscow, 1969) and *EMM*, 3 (1971).

106. Zauberman, in *Economica*, Aug. 1965.

107. A. I. Anchishkin, in *EMM*, 5 (1970); cf. also the same jointly with Yu. V. Yaremenko, *Tempy i proportsyi ekonomicheskogo razvitya* (Moscow, 1967).

108. op.cit., p. 668.

109. The overall view is this: Two broad tendencies are observable in socialist econo- mies with respect to the rate of productive accumulation. One oriented towards

maximum growth of efficiency leads to the lowering of that rate; then the dynamics of the economy is characterized by a smooth, stationary growth. The second tendency is determined by the drive towards retaining "at any cost" the high growth-rates; the raising of the accumulation rate entailed in this policy leads to fluctuating growth-rates, chronic overstrain, declining efficiency rates, and cyclical development ("jumps" of the accumulation rate, growth-rates, and capital-output ratios).

110. A. A. Makarov *et al.*, in *EMM*, 6 (1970).

111. Cf. Wiles, *Communist international economics*, ch. 4.

112. Makarov, in *EMM*, 4 (1969).

113. In familiar notation Makarov classifies the trajectories in three groups:

(1) $\left\{\bar{x}(t)\bar{c}(t)\lambda\right\}_{t=0}^{\infty}$ as "(u,λ) optimal" if $\Sigma_{t=1}^{\infty} u(\bar{c}(t))\lambda_t \geqslant \Sigma_{t=1}^{\infty} \lambda_t u(c(t))$

(2) $\left\{\bar{x}(t)\right\}_{t=0}^{T}$ as (c,T) optimal if $\bar{c}x(T)$ for all admissible trajectories

(here $c \in E_n^+$); (3) $\left\{x(t)\right\}_{t=0}^{\infty}$ as "effective" or "∞-optimal" if there is no trajectory $\left\{x(t)\right\}$ starting from x_0 such as $x(t) = \mu x(t)$, $\mu > 1$ for any t). cf.
V. L. Makarov, "Matematicheskiye modeli ekonomicheskoy dinamiki", *Matematika i kibernetika v ekonomike*.

114. T. C. Koopmans, "On the concept of optimal economic growth", *Pontificiae academiae scientiarum scripta varia*, 28 (1965) and M. Inagaki, *The theorem of existence under utility maximization*, Neth. Econ. Inst. Publ., no. 36/1966.

115. These are definitions:

i.   A trajectory $\left\{x(t),\gamma(t)\right\}_{t=0}^{t=\infty}$ of the model $M(\bar{Z}(\lambda))$, $\lambda \geqslant 1, t \in [0,\infty]$ is technologically admissible with the initial (x_0,γ_0) if there exists an $(n + 1)$ dimensional vector-function z, which is summable over any $[0,t]$ interval, such that over $t \in [0,\infty]$

$(x(t),\gamma(t)) = (x_0,\gamma_0) + \int_0^t z(t)\, dt$ and

$z(t) = ((y(t),\gamma'(t)) - (x(t),\gamma(t))$

$[x(t),\gamma(t)); (y(t),\gamma'(t)] \in \bar{Z}(\lambda)$ – for every $t \in [0,t]$

ii.   A trajectory $\left\{\bar{x}(t),\bar{\gamma}(t)\right\}_{t=0}^{t=\infty}$ of the model $M(\bar{Z}(\lambda))$, $\lambda \geqslant 1$, admissible with (x_0,γ_0) is "strongly optimal" (u-optimal) if for any admissible – under (x_0,γ_0) – trajectory $\left\{(x(t),\gamma(t))\right\}_{t=0}^{t=\infty}$ a time point t_0 can be found such that for all $t \geqslant t_e$, $\bar{\gamma}(t) + \epsilon e^{(\lambda - 1)t} \geqslant \gamma(t)$ the ϵ being positive.

116. Thus e.g. cf. R. Radner, "Optimal growth in a linear logarithmic economy", *Int. Econ. R.*, Jan. 1966.

117. *Theory of economic growth* (Oxford, 1969).

118. Cf. my discussion of Morishima's book in *J. Royal Statist. Soc.*, 1971.

119. Yu. L. Selivanov, in *EMM*, 5 (1970).

120. Makarov, in Kantorovich, *Matematicheskoye planirovanye* (Moscow, 1966).

121. B. N. Mikhalevskiy, in *EMM*, 5 (1967).

122. R. L. Weil, jr., "The decomposition of economic production systems", *Econometrica*, Apr.1968. The paper indicates the way the graph-theoretic techniques for decomposition of a square matrix can be extended for purposes of the build-up of operatively independent subeconomies in the case of rectangular production systems.

See also a reference to a paper by Roman and Kettler on transformation of matrices for the use of a decomposition algorithm for linear programmes (ibid., p. 278).

123. cf. Makarov, in *EMM*, 1 (1965).
124. Movshovich, ibid., 6 (1969).
125. Kemeny, *et al.*, in *Econometrica*, 2 (1956).
126. Makarov, in *Sibirskiy Mat. Zhurnal*, 4/7 (1966).
127. Radner, in *R. Econ. Stud.*, 2 (1961).
128. McKenzie, in *Econometrica*, 1/2 (1963).
129. Ibid., 2 (1966).
130. E. M. Dradnakis, op. cit. The same is held for the H. Furuya-K. Inada model, *Int. Econ. R.*, 3 (1963) for efficient paths of infinite duration. Dradnakis himself has introduced this into type of model decentralization explicitly (ibid., pp. 335 ff).

131. cf. A. G. Granberg, in *EMM*, 3 (1970).

4

APPRAISING THE EFFICIENCY OF INVESTMENT

(1) The half-century of economic history of the Soviet Union is one of a textbook case of normatively planned growth supported by a massive investment effort. Logically the appraisal of its efficiency has thus been *the* central issue of economic theory and practice, but the formulation of the principles of such an appraisal has encountered a host of difficulties.[1]

The problem has two related aspects. One concerns the methodology for setting the normative criterion (the "norm"). The second concerns the method of its employment in the patterning of investment, reducible to selection of projects: assessing, with reference to the "norm", the given project's worth — its acceptability and comparative advantage as against feasible alternatives.

The first aspect patently confronts a capitalist economy with less difficulty than a socialist economy. In the former the price of capital emerges within the framework of a capital market. It would be idle to revert in this context to vexed questions as to how far this market deviates from perfect competition, whether it is or is not affected by myopia, and so on. One may repeat that here too a certain approximation to equilibrium pricing is carried out by an "invisible" process of adjustments within a broadly competitive framework. Nor has the question of compatibility with, or the workability under socialism of, such a capital market immediate relevance for Soviet economic thinking, which rejects it outright. Parenthetically one may note the rather hesitant and not adequately articulated attempts in this direction in the Yugoslav experience; also the similarly vague ideas in the pre-1969 thinking of Czechoslovak reformers (the matter of compatibility of the quasi-competitive solution relates to the issue as to whether surrendering the capital-formation processes to market forces is acceptable for, and a still broader issue of workability of a market mechanism in, a socialist society).[2]

Here one is on sufficiently safe ground in saying that the market-formed long-term rate of interest provides at least a point of departure for a calculation of the minimal required efficiency of invested capital — and time-discount, as is in particular the case in public investment under capitalism. And that the normative planner is deprived of this benefit.

(While there is a logical kinship between the problems of optimal investment in a system of mandatory planning and — with respect to *public* investment — in a competitive economy (and consequently between the instruments employed respectively in these two spheres) it is worth bearing in mind the differences. Arrow and Kurz[3] ascribe the differences and difficulties for the latter sphere to: possible divergence of private and public objectives; the political framework for setting the public instruments; the impact of the market mechanism. We would stress in particular the consequences of exposing the investment policy to the influence of market forces.)

(2)   On the approaches to the era of planned industrialization, one or two attempts have been made in Soviet literature to deal with the problem. The most outstanding for its theoretical elaboration is that by Feldman.[4] We have mentioned his contribution to the theory of growth propulsion; its byproduct is the Feldman concept of "efficiency of capital employment", $C = ND/K$ (where ND denotes the sum total of "newly created values" and K the "sum total of capital"). Thence the marginal-type rate is derived as

$$T = dND/dt \cdot 1/ND = d(CK)/dt \cdot 1/ND$$

However, the quest for an efficiency norm was stopped by the ruling doctrine at the threshold of a great investment expansion. (Perhaps the attitude can be rationalized by relating it to the motives of rejection of the concept of equilibrium — see above.) It was then resumed under different guises, stimulated by the acute need of some gauge in investment practice.

Theoretical inquiry suffered from certain inhibitions with respect to the return on capital as such, and in this sense, the productivity of capital (see section 14). We have discussed — in the context of the economy's objective function — the difficulties experienced by Soviet doctrine in finding the rationale of the time-discount. We have indicated there also the answer to the problem offered in Soviet economics within the labour-theoretic framework — in the 1940s — in Strumilin's fundamental paper.[5] This paper had also opened in Soviet theoretical disquisition the question of optimal levels of technology — of overall and sectoral relative factor intensity: the relative factor productivities were not made explicit.

(3)   Parallel to the Strumilin-type theoretical elaboration Soviet doctrine has pioneered in empirically evolving — since the 1940s — a rough instrument of investment appraisal (codified in 1960 as the *"Typical Methodology"*)[6]: one based on the concept of the recoupment period — the asset's useful lifetime needed for recovering the investment resources. In other words, the tool measures marginal efficiency, marginal in the sense of forming the threshold of acceptability for the commitment of these resources. Thus the minimum recoupment period is the criterion of comparative advantage for the choice from among alternatives.

(To be more precise, the traditional typical methodology works with two concepts of efficiency: in addition to "comparative" efficiency there is that of "overall" efficiency.)

The index of "overall" efficiency is meant to reflect the level of profitability (rentabelnost') of new projects throughout the economy. (The underlying conception has been interpreted to be that — taking, computationally, the wage level as constant — "profitability" measures the national-product increment due to fixed-capital formation.)[7]

In practice the operational criterion on the *micro*-level is the comparative-efficiency "norm". Its important characteristic is that it is sectorally ("branch"-) differentiated. No articulate concept of *macro*-equilibrium underlies it. (Indeed, some recent inquiries have demonstrated — by both deduction and induction — that the two indices, the comparative and overall profitability indices, will as a rule conflict with each other.)[8]

Broadly speaking the concept of the normative comparative efficiency is static rather than dynamic; it is seen in a "technological" rather than economic framework. The methodology for determining the criterial marginal values has not been defined with any adequate precision; as broadly indicated, it should correspond to "advanced technology", actually prevailing or expected. In actual practice the determining of the normative rate has rested on some rules of thumb: the values and their sectoral differentiation have been largely arbitrary. More will be said on the instrument in the section discussing it in the light of the latest conceptual adjustments.[9]

Notes
    1. Matters related to our theme — broadly speaking those of effective patterning of investment — and thereby of the choice of technology —

have had a noteworthy literature, in the West, initiated by Joan Robinson's important contribution in her *Exercises in economic analysis* (1960).

The matter was subsequently taken up, using her assumptions, by Nobuo Okishio, who derived a criterion for the choice of techniques for a planned socialist economy under full employment ("Technical choice under full employment in a socialist economy", *Econ. J.*, Sept. 1966). The criterion was shown to depend mainly on investment policy, knowledge of alternative techniques, the time horizon in planning, and time preference.

More recently the Robinson-Okishio solution was critically examined by Joseph E. Stiglitz ("A note on technical choice under full employment in a socialist economy", ibid., Sept. 1968). Having discarded one of their crucial assumptions (on constancy of the proportion of labour devoted to the consumer-goods sector), Stiglitz arrived at the conclusion that an optimal solution entails the choice of equipment which minimizes labour costs quite independently of the "menu" of techniques available or initial endowment of the economy. The minimand as formulated embraces indirect as well as direct labour input, which makes the conclusion intuitively obvious. The equipment is shown to be the one for which the steady-state consumption per man is at its maximum.

2. The rule-of-thumb efficiency "norm" for a normatively planned system has been criticized by several students, in particular by I. M. D. Little and J. A. Mirrlees (*Manual of industrial project analysis in developing countries,* Paris, 1969). The points made are that the "norm" gives too little weight to what happens beyond the pay-off period and also sectoral diversification of the rates; preference is given by these authors to investment-project selection based on profit discounting. (Their own cost-benefit approach leads to a present social-value formula for a project — designed with an eye to the special conditions of an underdeveloped economy: the rule is roughly speaking devised so as to ensure the choice of long-lived, slow-yielding projects with a low rate of the gross investment aggregate or a high rate of the latter with the reverse characteristics of projects.)

It is very much the adopted definitional contents of the two instruments — the rates of normative efficiency investment and of interest — that determine their mutual relationship and their usefulness from the angle of the theory of normative planning. (Mikhalevskiy's assumed task is to clarify the contents and relationship and to synthesize their function in this kind of planning; on this see a later context.)

The functions of the two instruments entailed are ultimately those discussed in Western writing under the heading of "technique switching". Of

the vast corpus of this writing we may refer only to a few examples:
P. Sraffa, *Production of commodities by means of commodities*
(Cambridge, 1960); Morishima's *Theory of economic growth*; D. Levhari,
"A nonsubstitution theorem and switching of techniques", *Q. J. Econ.*,
Feb. 1965; L. Pasinetti, "Changes in the rate of profit and switches of
technique", ibid., Nov. 1966; R. M. Solow, in Feinstcin, *Socialism . . .*,
G. C. Harcourt ("Investment-decision criteria, capital-intensity and the
choice of techniques", in J. T. Dunlop/N. P. Fedorenko, eds, *Planning and
the markets: modern trends in various economic systems,* New York,
1970) has attempted a comparison of the economic effect in application
of the prevailing "capitalist" and "socialist" investment criteria, and of
their "biases" with respect to factor intensities.[10] On his showing the
"capitalist" criterion of the "pay-off period" would often result in the
adoption of a more capital-intensive technique than any of the remaining
"capitalist" criteria (i.e. those of the present value, of internal rate of
return, of rate of profit), or the "socialist" criterion of the recoupment
period in either of its two variants (choosing the technique for which the
sum of average operating and investment outlay averaged over the standard
period — or in the second variant-also per year — is the least). The findings
are weakened however, by the ceteris paribus assumption with respect to
pricing.

According to the same source, the theoretically more discussed "discounted cash flow" criteria (i.e. those of present value, of internal rate of
return, and of pay-off period) are rather uncommon in "capitalist" practice. More prevalent appears to be the simpler criterion resting on the
highest average accounting rate of profit ("the rate of profit criterion").

Soviet pioneering in the field has had an immediate response in both
the theory and practice of other socialist countries. In turn, subsequent
advances in the theory of the latter have been not without effect on Soviet
thinking.

(4)   Outstanding in this respect is the impact of the Polish school, in particular that of Lange's, and even more so of Kalecki's elaboration of the
theme (in the last revisions of his theory of economic growth under socialism).[11] This may justify our devoting some space to the presentation of
his stand.

Logically, in Kalecki the process of fixing the normative rate is related
to that of fixing the investment rate: parenthetically speaking, he belongs
to the sceptics with regard to an "objective" determination of the latter.
He starts then from positing some a priori $\omega(i)$, a function describing the

society's "disinclination" — negative propensity — to reduce its consumption levels. The condition determining the investment rate would then be

$$\Delta r/\Delta i = \omega(i)/(1 - i)$$

appraising its incremental Δr in terms of raising the growth-rate of national income by some incremental Δi. Once the rate of investment has been determined, normative investment efficiency is obtained from a (convex) production curve. Taking g as the wage-rate for "simple" labour, the total cost of an income increment, in terms of labour expenditure, is $A = C/g$.

Next in a simple diagrammatic argument it is shown that the gradient of the tangent to the production curve at any point A,B (the latter describing investment) equals $1/gT$: thence the T is determined for the given combi-

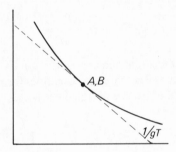

nation of investment and "simple" labour (or total cost in its terms). The curve is a set of equilibrium points each uniquely determining the "recoupment" period as related to the co-ordinates. The higher the T the more capital-intensive and the less labour-intensive-variants of production are being admitted in the process of choice-making.

A final reformulation of Kalecki's system is contained in his paper first published posthumously (in 1970) in the Soviet Union.[12] At the first step the investment-efficiency index is taken as a linear function of investment and labour cost per incremental output unit, $rP_t dt$ as

$$E_t = \epsilon . i_t \; \frac{r+a}{a} + \left(c_t \; \frac{r+a}{a} \; - x_t \; \frac{a}{r} \; \right) \rightarrow \min.$$

(*Notation*: P is output, r growth rate, i_t, c_t are respectively marginal capital and labour intensity of production, a rate of obsolescence (scrapping),

ϵ positive parameter (uniform for the economy), x_t maximal labour intensity of output with given equipment.) Where the i value is the same for investment variants the choice criterion is $\epsilon i_t + c_t = \min$. Adjusting the ϵ parameter would regulate the capital intensity of investment variants. Graphically it corresponds to the slope of the polyhedral-convex curve such that (with W and I denoting respectively investment variants and the entailed addition to the wage bill) we have

$$\frac{\dot{W}_{t,k} - \dot{W}_{t,k-1}}{\dot{I}_{t,k-1} - \dot{I}_{t,k}} = \epsilon_k.$$

Assuming replacement for $aP_t i_t dt$, its purpose would be to economize labour: $aP_t(x_t - c_t)dt$. Related to investment, which is the "price" to be paid for this, it is $(x_t - c_t)/i_t$. Thus the increment in the labour cost for a given variant allowance made for modernization is

$$\rho_t = rc_t - af_t \frac{(x_t - c_t)}{i_t},$$

the f_t being a decreasing function and $f_t(x_t - c_t)/i_t \geqslant x_t - c_t$ with equality corresponding to the absence of possibilities for purposeful modernization. The investment-efficiency index now becomes

$$E_t = i_t \cdot \frac{r+a}{r} + c_t - \frac{a}{r} f_t \left(\frac{x_t - c_t}{i_t} \right) \to \min.$$

A further adjustment pertains to import substitution. Denoting δ_t the foreign-exchange "deflection" of direct intermediate (material) inputs from the "norm", the "reduced" cost per unit of output will be $\epsilon i_t + c_t + \delta_t(\epsilon j_t + k_t)$; with given ϵ, equipment to be scrapped is that for which $x_t + \lambda_t(\epsilon j_t + k_t)$ attains the maximum (here j stands for investment and k for labour cost per unit of foreign-exchange cost of import substitutes; and the two symbols x_t and λ_t stand, respectively for the labour intensity of output with investment to be scrapped and the foreign-exchange deflection from the input "norm"). Now the norm of investment efficiency becomes

$$E_t = \epsilon \left[i_t \cdot \frac{r+a}{r} + j_t \left(\delta_t \frac{r+a}{r} - \lambda_t \frac{a}{r} \right) \right]$$

$$- \left[(c_t + \delta_t k_t) \cdot \frac{r+a}{r} - (x_t + \lambda_t k_t) \frac{a}{r} \right] \to \min$$

and with r, a, j, k, λ uniform for all variants (with respect to λ — this is true for a given ϵ) the criterion for the choice of the most efficient investment variants comes down to

$$\epsilon(i_t + \delta_t j_t) + (c_t + \delta_t k_t) = \min.$$

As can be seen, the present formulation reflects in a more elaborate shape Kalecki's fundamental approach. It is the minimization of capital outlay compatible with the increment in labour to be employed (exogenously determined): or, to put this in other words, the maximization of output with maximal labour intensity of output producible with the given equipment and the given wear-and-tear rate. The changes in technology are implied in both the relative capital-labour intensities and the obsolescence (scrapping) rates.

The basic conception is tenable in so far as the choice-making in investment rests on the strategy for expansion, related to resource availability and the state of technology. Where it is inadequate is in the reliance in comparisons of efficiency on the first order rather than the full-order magnitudes of the prime-factor uses involved; the shortcoming is the greater as intermediate inputs entailed are not explicit; they are taken as ultimately implied in the prime-factor expenditure. (Technically the formulation would gain therefore from matrix-algebraic statement. Also the several disjointed maximizations and minimizations of the respective magnitudes, in particular outputs and factors inputs (uses) would gain from bringing them together into a programme or control-theoretic form.)

(5)   In this digression into Polish economics one may refer here also to Oskar Lange's stand on the subject.[13] The point of departure is the obvious proposition: the rate of growth of GNP is the product of the investment rate multiplied by the latter's efficiency, $R = \alpha\beta$. The planner's task, as persuasively argued, is one of selecting either λ_j or μ_i, the sectoral pattern of investment or its physical composition. Where B_{ij} is the inverse of the technology-of-investment matrix, Lange has the system of n balance equations of the form

$$\sum_{i=1}^{n} \mu_i B_{ji} = \lambda_{ji}\beta_i.$$

Thus the plan designed to maximize the economy's growth is rigourized by Lange as one of finding the values of the λ_j's such as to maximize

$$\sum_{j=1}^{n} \lambda_j \beta_j,$$

subject to the constraint of desired minimum consumption levels. There is also in Lange a dynamic version of this programme, for finding the optimum allocation of investment over time and of output lags. The exercise is useful methodologically as far as it goes; its weakness, however, is that it has no value-termed explicit rate of time-preference. As it appears, Lange's intention was to establish the primarily technological aspect of choices facing the macro-planner of investment (and, as a footnote suggests, to refute the conception of productivity of waiting). Whatever the motivation, the planner's intertemporal preferences are tucked away in the lagging of outputs. As a result, the crucial element of the investment efficiency rate as a part and parcel of the dual of the optimal plan programme has dropped out. We shall see that in the meantime Soviet doctrine, under the influence of the programming school, has abandoned its inhibition against such a treatment of this rate.

(6)   Further, experience with the tool, and analysis and experiments in other socialist countries — again in the first place in Poland,[14] thanks to the Kalecki school[15] — have posed several methodological issues. They concern in particular certain assumptions with regard to technology. The traditional stand is to assume its constancy — and the constancy of the efficiency "norm" over time, viz. over the lifetime of assets. This links up with an assumption as to the length of the gestation period and useful life-span in calculating efficiency. In turn this raises the problem of the treatment of depreciation, which was ignored in the original Soviet investment-efficiency instruments.

The answers given to the problem appear from the following precept-formulae, the central formula being that for total cost: the yearly, constant weighted average per unit of output

$$Z_i = \left[\sum_{t=1}^{T_{p,i}} (K_{ti} + C_{ti}) B_t \right] : \sum_{t=1}^{T_{p,i}} X_{ti} B_t,$$

where K_{ti} denotes investment cost during t on the subsystem operational unit i, C_{ti} current cost, X_{ti} output, B_t discount coefficient.

The T_p is the "calculation period". Where the life-span of the project is difficult to assess, the T will be taken as the proposed life-span or the period of dependable expectation for the project's technical-economic indices, whichever of the two is shorter.

Where the technical-economic indices can be taken as constant and investment is completed before the start of operation, the total cost formula is calculated as

$$Z_i = C_i + EK_{\text{tot},i},$$

where C denotes current cost of exploitation of the ith operational unit. In the general case, the investment, possibly continuing during the operational phase, is calculated as

$$K_{\text{tot},i} = K_i \sum_{t=1}^{T_{\text{con},i} + T_{\text{ex},i}} \delta_{\tau i}(1 + E)^{T_{\text{con},i} - \tau}.$$

Here the T_{con} and T_{ex} mean respectively periods of construction (preceding the start of operations) and of exploitation over which investment is required: τ denotes the year of construction of the ith unit and $\delta_{,i}$ the share of total of investment (fraction of 1) in year of construction. In the case considered, yearly amortization charges for renovation — constant over the period — are added to total cost and calculated from

$$C = (K_{\text{tot},i} - K_{\pi,i}) \frac{E}{(1 + E) T_{\text{sp},i} - 1},$$

($K_{,i}$ is the "liquidation" (scrapping) value of the object at the end of service time, $T_{\text{sp},i}$ service-time proposed.)

(7)   Somewhere in between — between the Kalecki and the programming-school treatment — we find several Soviet studies of the subject. Among them we may single out, for its rigour, Sukhotin's[16] investigation of investment efficiency in equilibrium — within the system of "inter-industry relations".

Sukhotin starts with fixed capacity $p_i = \text{const.}$, $(i = 1, .. ,n)$, a spectrum of combinations of capital (k_i) and current cost (c_i) per output unit, and some functional relations $c_i = f_i(k_i)$ and $k_i = \varphi_i(c_i)$: the functions are taken to be continuously differentiable and have a negative first derivative. The problem, when set as one of minimizing current cost with given capital resources K_0, is written

$$F(k_1 \ldots, k_n) = \sum_{i=1}^{n} c_i p_i = \sum_{i=1}^{n} f_i(k_i)p_i = \min.,$$

subject to

$$\sum_{i=1}^{n} k_i p_i = K_0.$$

This minimum is found from the Lagrangean function

$$F(k_1, \ldots, k_n) = \sum_{i=1}^{n} f_i(k_i)p_i + \lambda \left(\sum_{i=1}^{n} k_i p_i - K_0 \right),$$

whence

$$\partial F / \partial k_i = f_i{}'(k_i)p_i + \lambda p_i = 0 .$$

From this system of $n + 1$ equations all the values for k_i° and for the coefficient λ are found. The "norm" of comparative efficiency, E, appears then as the first derivative, $f_i{}' = -\lambda$. An analogously formulated problem for the minimization of investment yields

$$\phi_i' = 1/f(k_i)$$

the normative pay-off period obtained via the Lagrangean is then

$$\mu = 1/\lambda = 1/E ,$$

the inverse of the comparative efficiency norm.

The point often missed in Soviet traditionalist literature on the subject is that the theory of comparative efficiency is concerned with the minimization of actual expenditure on the result, i.e. the plan of the production processes, these being results fixed a priori as distinct from the method of maximizing the overall result with given resources. This point is not missed in Sukhotin: in continuing the Lagrange-based argument he traces the path for dealing with the problem. The diagram (A) is self-explanatory. Points on the curves linked by straight lines with the co-ordinates and their origin represent the selected variants of the production units. The tangents of the gradient angles to the C axes of the curve-segments (convex to the origin) give the numerical values of K_i/C_i for each production unit and the K_0/C_0 their total. Clearly the values may differ as between individual units and also between them and the overall volume. The question arises of harmonizing this with the requirement that $f_i'(k) = -E$, $\varphi_i'(c_i) = -1/E_i$, the requirement, that is, of equality of all differential efficiencies and the efficiency norm. Rather than trying to equate the local k_i/c_i to overall k_0/c_0, the optimal local-capital intensities and current-cost intensities are determined by adjusting the values of the E, as in the diagram (B). While his treatment too is essentially static, Sukhotin does at least out-

(A)

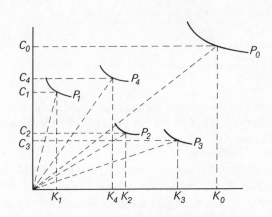

(B)

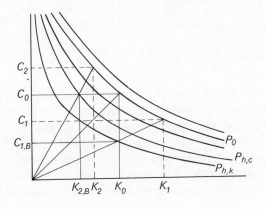

line the problems involved in its dynamization: he determines the inter-
connection between the volume of resources over time, the dynamics
of their efficiency, and the growth of national product — broadly reflected
in the following system of index equations (where respectively K and P
denote investment and the net national product, L and Φ labour expenditure and capital, and the subscripts 0 and 1 the base and current plan
periods):

$$I_K \frac{I \Delta P}{K} = \frac{K_1 \Delta P_1 K_0}{K_0 K_1 \Delta P_0} = \frac{\Delta P_1}{\Delta P_0} = I_{\Delta P}, \qquad (1)$$

$$I_L \frac{I_P}{K} = \frac{L_1 P_1 L_0}{L_0 L_1 P_0} = \frac{P_1}{P_0} = I_P, \qquad (2)$$

$$I \frac{I_P}{\Phi} = \frac{\Phi_1 P_1 \Phi_0}{\Phi_0 \Phi_1 P_0} = \frac{P_1}{P_0} = I_P. \qquad (3)$$

The product of the index of the volume of investment, I_K, multiplied by
that of its efficiency, $I_{P/K}$, determines the index of national income increments. The $I_{\Delta K}$ in turn is expressed as $\eta_1 P_1 / \eta_0 P_0$, the η's denoting normative investment coefficients.

The index of return on capital, σ, is found as a function of the pace of
growth of capital stock, $\Delta\Phi/\Phi_0$ (where $\Delta\Phi \equiv K$) and of the ν; the latter
relates the investment efficiency of the given plan period to that of the
base period, i.e. $\Delta P/\Delta\Phi = \nu . P_0/\Phi_0$. We then have

$$\sigma = (1 + \Delta\Phi/\Phi_0 . \nu)/(1 + \Delta\Phi/\Phi_0).$$

In turn

$$\Delta\Phi/\Phi_0 = \eta . P_0/\Phi_0 ;$$

it is independent of ν.

Secondly, in Sukhotin — as against Kalecki — there is (and rightly so) a
strong emphasis on the point that the offered method of solution for the
problem of the "absolute" efficiency presupposes a "ready" capacity plan;
it does not shed any light on the patterning of capacities itself. In conced-
ing this Sukhotin points to the lack of workable methodology of co-
ordination of outputs with the volume and structure of social requirements. This is but one of the elements of the optimization of the E which

escapes under the procedure adopted. The full answer to the problem can be given only by a fully-fledged programming-type method articulating the objective function as well as constraints.

(8) Before turning to this matter we shall pick up the thread of our narrative from section (7). Under the impact of the theoretical developments — first of all under the influence of a quarter of a century's experience — the methodology for the appraisal of investment came under a theoretical reconsideration when the new principles[17] of "optimal planning for the development and location of production" were adopted (they will be referred to hereafter as the "1968 Principles").

The first point on which a new stand is taken is the issue of the single versus multiple rate of investment efficiency. Under the influence of ideas initiated elsewhere (in particular in Polish literature — introduced by the Kalecki school)[18] and the programming school which had challenged the traditional doctrine, the controversy has been settled — at least in principle (see below) — in favour of the unique rate throughout the system. The 1968 Principles prescribe the application of the "discount coefficient",

$$B_t = (1 + E)^{\tau - t}$$

(for the case of discounting to some given year, the E standing for the investment efficiency norm: for the case of discount to the base year it becomes the "coefficient of time remoteness", written $1/(1 + E)^{t - 1}$). They do not commit the official doctrine with regard to the way the E is to be found (all they have to say about it is that at present its value "can be taken to equal 0.15"). This crucial matter is left open.

The next methodological issue resolved by the 1968 Principles concerns the two approaches in efficiency calculation: of cost minimization versus profit maximization.

The point is made that adopting return as the maximand permits comparison of variants differing with respect to inputs and/or outputs. Under the minimum-cost approach, demand is taken as a datum, subject, that is, to compulsory satisfaction of the quota (allowance made for possible substitution of products). Whatever the optimand, the latter condition would be included into the constraints along with the system's initial state, interrelations between the sequential states, and so on.

It is the cost-minimization approach that is favoured by Soviet practice. The advice given now is to resort to it as a rule only where price elasticity of demand (subject, that is, to "compulsory satisfaction of the quota") is negligible, and constraints with respect to the availability of resources are relatively less certain than demand. On the other hand "under the prevailing conditions" the profit-maximization approach is recommended where the volume of demand is substantially price-elastic, and first of all where price expectation or relative efficiency indices of products may be taken to be sufficiently dependable (more dependable than expectations of demand). The ceteris paribus − "prevailing conditions" − clause may be interpreted to refer to accessible methods of efficiency-type price computations as well as forecasting.

It is indeed the emphasis on the kind of price available for efficiency calculation that we believe to be the decisive innovation. As indicated here, it is the framework of "non-efficiency" prices for products as well as factors that has been vitiating the traditional methodology. The 1968 Principles at least state the minimum requirement: whatever the optimand, the resources should be calculated at prices that as far as possible correspond to the all-economy optimum: and the same applies to prices of products under the maximum-profit optimand. The programming school must then be given credit for casting light on the fundamentals. Whether and how far the sine qua non condition can be met the reader can deduce from the discussion in the present chapter.[19]

While non-committal, as we have seen, with respect to the problem of determining the "norm", the Principles do commend the application of formal programming techniques in the choice-making process, a signal symptom of the degree of their acclimatization.

(9)   As it appears, the publication of the 1968 Principles was not meant to abrogate what is usually referred to as the traditional "typical methodology". But the relationship of the two has been left unspecified: apparently the 1968 Principles have been intended to rationalize the application of the old "methodology". However, the last few years' experience does not seem to have satisfied the critique from the mathematical school. Thus Fedorenko[20] makes it clear that the clause permitting the differentiation of the investment-efficiency "norm" sectorally ("branch-" wise) in exceptional, justified cases has long since turned into a widespread practice.

In turn this tendency accounts in Fedorenko's opinion for another significant fact observed: the failure of the profitability index to justify itself as one of the primary "normative" indices of the plan. In fact (as it appears from the argument) in Soviet investment experience, premia for exceeding the targets tend to reduce the economic efficiency of scientific-technological progress. Prima facie, sectoral differentiation of the "norm" is the chief cause of the distorting effect. However, other factors also contribute to a considerable degree: among them — the structure of the price system (see our remarks above and the way gestation of investment is allowed for in the appraisal of operational return over time).

Whatever else can be said about the 1968 Principles, their very major contribution to the problems of measuring the efficiency of investment and comparing alternatives is that they had articulated the sanction — by official doctrine — for the programming approach. Here again we stress the decisive role of Kantorovich's work.

We have simply to recall in this connection what has been said in this Part, in chapters 1 and 3, which links up with what will be said in Part II, chapter 7, sect. 15; in particular — the findings to which Kantorovich's modelling of dynamics has led him and his associates. To restate, these findings relate in the first place to the rate of return from investment (thereby the rate of "efficiency of investment"), thereby also to the dynamically viewed system of shadow prices, corresponding to whatever is the extremized optimand and reflecting the intensity of its constraints. Thus also the basis for "rentals" on durable capital assets has revealed itself. In the second place, the findings have shown the nature of the relationship between the return from investment and the price of the resource "time" as such, thus also the time-discount. (A point is worth mentioning here: it is the programming approach that has also contributed to the clarification of the issue which has long baffled Soviet economics: the fundamental justification — and nature — of the principle of discounting the future.) Thirdly, these findings have thrown light on the relationship between rate of return from investment and profit; thereby also on the substance of profit maximization under optimum. Finally, and this is of particular analytical and didactic importance, from these findings the rates have emerged logically integrated. On integration procedure see V. Pugachev and A. K. Pitelin, EMM, 6, 1974.

Notes

1. The Kantorovich school has not taken an explicit stand on the issue of the "objective" versus "subjective" rate of time-discount which has for some time been intensively discussed in Soviet literature. In particular, Pugachev and Volkonskiy represent the subjective school of thought; this links up with modelling the very-long-term plan: Pugachev's view agrees with that of Western students who maintain that in continuous, infinite-horizon planning, an exponential discount function is required to secure convergence of a welfare criterion functional; cf. Pugachev's *Optimizatsya*

planirovanya; also T. C. Koopmans, *Econometrica,* 1960 and Koopmans *et al.* ibid., 1964; also Zauberman, "The objective function for Soviet economy", *Economica,* 1967. (The matter is discussed in an interesting way in Polish literature by O. Gedymin, in *Studia ekonomiczne,* 1971.)

2. A system of assumptions which in a "natural" way generate some parameters $\lambda - 1, \lambda > 1$, serving *at the same time* as the normative rates of (a) return on capital (efficiency of capital accumulation), (b) rent on fixed productive assets, and (c) interest on credit, has been rigorously examined by Katsenelinboygen *et al.,* in *EMM,* 5 (1970).

On the time-weighting see also my discussion in *Jahrbuch der Wirtschaft Osteuropas* (Bd. 1, 1969).

Katsenelinboygen *et al.* refer the reader to Vishnyev (*Ekonomicheskiye parametry*). Vishnyev's general stand can be summed up as follows: (1) The theoretical "norm" of time-discount for each plan ingredient is determined from a multi-product dynamic plan programme; (2) the optimization approach as such does not prejudge the rational elements in various conceptions of time-weighting, i.e. the model's conditions (criterion, horizon, constraints, "norms") would be expected to contain the basic "objective" moments which permit the calculation of the optimal "norm" of time-discount; (3) the economic appraisal of time factor expresses only the nexus between the economic (active) and the astronomic (passive) time; the faster the "pulse" of economic life the higher the valuation of the time factor; (4) the theoretically most adequate, criterial conception of time is not directly applicable in practice; the "real" discount rate has to be established more or less empirically and would be expected to approximate the optimal as planning improved technically.

The stress in Vishnyev is throughout on the "non-subjective" nature of measuring the impact of time. Thus ". . . there is no mystique in the economic appraisal of the time factor . . ."; "on the co-measuring of economic magnitudes there is an objective fact stemming in the last instance from the scarcities of resources as against the society's rising needs; the subjective-psychological interpretation of this objective fact should be rejected; and the co-measuring over time amounts to the appraisal of the economic significance of inputs and yields depending on their location in the time scale — in accordance with the social priority of needs" (op. cit., pp. 150 ff).

What is quoted here may invalidate, or at least circumscribe the tenet. Relating to the needs and placing their satisfaction on the time scale is by itself "subjective": so is, technically, the formulation of the criterial function in dynamics.

3. I am aware of the controversy, in contemporary theory of capital, on the relationship of the rates of return, of marginal product and of profit; a controversy which itself arose from the discussion on switches of technique (cf. L. L. Pasinetti, "Switches of techniques and the 'rate of return' in capital theory", *Econ. J.*, Sept. 1969, and the exchange of views, in "Notes and memoranda", ibid., June 1970, between the author and R. M. Solow). One obvious conclusion from this controversy points to the risks of discussing the relationship without agreement as to the definition of the concepts used.

It seems to me that for the purposes of the present book our definitional reference — reference, that is, to the definitional framework emerging from the theory of extremization as applied — sufficiently clarifies the meaning attributed to the concepts.

(10) Volkonskiy's [21] construct — a part of his analysis of the interrelation between the "indices" of an optimal plan and the place which the investment-efficiency index takes among them — well typifies the use of a mathematical programme for the purpose. It has both a discrete and a continuous version. Under the latter a feasible spectrum or variation area of parameters is expected to be programmed: the technical-economic indices of variants are formed on the assumptions of some behavioural laws, say some nonlinear "law" for returns to scale. In the discrete case a finite number of variants for bringing capacities to maturity and "specialization" is to be formed. In either case each variant is to be handled en bloc — on the "yes-no" basis.

A good example of such handling (1 or 0 basis) of the project alternatives is a Volkonskiy-designed linear-integer programme of the form

$$\sum_{j,k} Z_j^k \, \delta_j^k = \min; \sum_{j,k} a_{ij}^k \, \delta_j^k \geqslant m_i; \cdot \sum_j \delta_j^k = 1, \delta_j^k = 0 \text{ or } 1.$$

(*Notation:* k, j, i are numbers, respectively, of the enterprise, of its development variant, and type of output; a_{ij}^k are production possibilities of the ith output in terminal year in the kth unit under jth variant; m_i is the economy's requirements in the ith product in that year; ΣZ_j^k discounted sum-total of investment at current cost in the kth unit under the jth variant.)

Next denote expenditure on the ith resource of the kth unit in the tth year of construction as $v_i^k(t)$; further denote output dependent on the construction period as $a_i^k(t)$, the price in the plan year t of the capital resource i as $P^k(+)$, the output target of the jth product as $y(t)$, and expected profit in the year after the start of construction as $P^k(\cdot)$, then the problem is written

$$\sum_{i=1}^{\infty} \left[\sum_k P^k(t-\theta_k) - \sum_{i,k} Z_i(t)v_i^k(t-\theta_k) \right] = \max$$

$$\sum_k a_j^k(t-\theta_k) \geqslant y_j(t).$$

The θ_k denote the start of construction with some possible upper bound corresponding to output capacities of engineering and so on. In a perspective model the $Z(t)$ would be replaced by "prices of prognosis", $\hat{Z}(t)$, obtained from $\hat{Z}_i(t) = e^{\rho t}Z_i(t)$; if the coefficient is not expected substantially to change over time, it would be assumed that $e^{\rho} \equiv 1 + E$ where the parameter E is analogous to the single efficiency norm (it corresponds to the B of the new Principles).[22]

(11) Once the capital cost is introduced in its two forms – depreciation and discount – as the use-cost, the theoretical issue arises as to the basis of this break-up into two components. It is generally tacitly adopted as one, as it were, of obvious validity. Far from this, it is arguable that the break-up is arbitrary.

However Arrow,[23] who brings up this point in his analysis of optimal capital policy (and argues that planning investment requires *total* capital cost and not any particular decomposition), shows that the decomposition is legitimate if the depreciation element is itself made dependent on the future interest rate: such policy postulates the equality

$$\partial P/\partial K = \rho(t) + \bar{r}(t)$$

where the $\bar{r}(t)$ is a certain weighted average of replacements over time, the weights themselves depending on the behaviour of the rate of interest. (The $P(K,t)$ is the operating profit from capital stock K.) In turn the weighted average of replacements has the form

$$\bar{r}(t) = \int_0^{\sigma} r(t)\rho(t+\tau) \cdot \alpha(t+\tau)/(t) \cdot dt$$

(where the α is the rate at which cash flows are discounted back to time 0) and it is being shown that in this the expression following $r(t)$ is essentially a probability density.

(12) In a sense in Soviet literature Mikhalevskiy[24] takes up the matter where Arrow concludes: he isolates the risk element by breaking up the efficiency "norm".

On his definition Mikhalevskiy distinguishes the current and long-run "norms" of investment efficiency, respectively ρ_t and $\bar\rho$; the current and long-run rate of interest, respectively r_t and $\bar r$; and the rate of risk i.

Then the long-run efficiency norm is obtained when the present-day value of the investment "effect" (discounted over the period of its operation, T) plus present-day value of the residuum of the capital assets H will exactly equal their initial value

$$R_O = \int_0^T Q_0(Y_t)e^{-(\bar\rho + \bar r)t}dt + e^{-\bar r T} \cdot H$$

where Q is the "effect function" and Y final product. It is shown further that approximately

$$\bar\rho = e^{\bar r}\rho_0{}^{-\bar r},$$

i.e. that the maximum long-term norm of efficiency approximates the difference between the maximum discounted efficiency "norm" in the initial time-interval and the maximum long-term interest-rate. Next a convex function

$$Q(\rho) = 1 - e^{-i\rho}$$

is maximized. This characterizes the nexus between the effect and the risk-affected decision-making, where

$$i = - Q_0''(Y_0)/Q'_0(Y_0) \ e^{\bar r T}.$$

Here the i describes the allowance for risk, rising over time and expressed in terms of the relative negative acceleration of the function of effect. With normal distribution of ρ, the mean and dispersion being almost independent of the normality assumption, we have

$$\max \int_{-\infty}^{\infty} (1 - e^{-i\rho})e^{-(i-\pi)^2/2\sigma^2}di,$$

where the π and σ^2 are the mean and dispersion of ρ_t over T years of the expected remaining working lifetime of capital goods of a given vintage.

From this it is shown that the efficiency norm yielding max $Q(p)$ will be

$$\rho = \pi - i\sigma^2/2.$$

In this way[25] the existence is proved of a maximum long-run rate of interest such as to bring to equality the maximum "current" efficiency norm of the base period and the norm of profit averaged over the whole period — the norm forming a premium for the employment of highly efficient "round-about" methods. This identification of the risk element brings one step further the Kalecki-type analysis with which one detects points of affinity with regard to the capital-intensity element. (We will not pursue further the description of the Mikhalevskiy procedure: it leads from the evaluation of the parameter $Q_t(Y_t)$ over the whole of T through finding the maximum variable growth-rate of the final product over T, through finding the ρ_t and consequently π and σ^2, through first approximation to $\bar{r}$, to the finding of ρ.)

Note

Since this section was written, Arrow's argument appears to have come still closer to that of Mikhalevskiy. As Arrow-Kurz argue[26] in their recent book, the issue of investment-decision as related to the rate of interest appears "banal" only at the first glance — when one sticks to the definition by which the rate is the marginal productivity of capital. Qualifications come when one takes into account, as one should, the several parameters involved, in particular, the subjective rate of discount. It is the discrepancy between the rate of interest and the subjective rate that is decisive for the direction of capital change; and the subjective rate is the long-run steady-state interest rate. (In the long run there is no ground for expecting asymptotic convergence of the rate of interest and marginal productivity of capital.) Hence the endorsing by Arrow-Kurz of Haavelmo's point on the meaninglessness of the prevalence in post-Keynesian models scheduling investment as related to the rate.[27]

(13) Soviet planning theory has been made aware only by the mathematical school of the kind of nexus relating the efficiency norm (and rate of interest) with the amortization charge and strategy for renovation. (As a matter of fact the concept of amortization is relatively young in that theory.) The Kantorovich school was first to stress that an analysis of the

charge must rely on a dynamic dual-price system derived from the optimal "perspective" plan. It has also to be credited with the indication of certain implications of technological advance – the patterning of coexistence of the old with the new techniques and the discarding of the former – on the treatment of amortization. It has also shown that the allowance for the "first facet" of this advance – the reduction of cost of equipment – leads to a redistribution of charges with heavier load on the earlier stages of the service; and the same applies broadly to the second – i.e. the appearance of equipment with better performance-indices – provided, of course, that they are foreseeable.

(14) What constitutes the subject of this chapter is an area intrinsically afflicted by uncertainty. But we have had quite a few opportunities to stress in our story that a probabilistic approach was alien to Soviet planning theory: it was for decades deterministic also in its approach to problems of efficiency of investment.

Deterministic treatment was also long characteristic of the closely related matters of the optimal replacement policy as patently dependent on the economically useful lifetime of assets. That indeed can be related to the strategy of physical rather than technological "survival" of capacities under the acute shortage of capital in the "heroic" phase of investment and growth.

(In fairness, it may be noted that a deterministic approach to the theory of replacement has an established tradition, going back to the pioneering works of Wicksell and Hotelling.[28] The contemporary study of these matters in the West is stochastically oriented though it still has in the main to content itself with simplified analytical – and quintessentially so – operational devices.) For acquaintance with the present state of such oriented study the reader will most usefully address himself to the excellent work by Jorgenson, McCall, and Radner: he will also find there designs for some fundamental policy models; for simple and preventive maintenance policy in a Markovian environment, as well as for the case of a constant failure in a random equipment; also a discussion of the Bayesian approach to the case of the failure mechanism under uncertainty.[29]

(15) Recent years have marked a change of the basic attitude in this field – as also in other areas of Soviet planning theory. Mikhalevskiy[30] can be credited with gradually introducing a stochastic treatment of the investment-efficiency problem to the Soviet theoretician. We could see his first attempt in the handling the risk component of the efficiency rate.

A fuller stochastic version is offered in his model — of the end of the 1960s — for project selection with a basic formula familiar to Western students from cost-benefit analysis.[31] Of this he has been conscious in his latest work when striving to obtain some synthesis of the two criteria:

$$(A) \qquad \max V^* - \int_0^T Q(t)e^{-k^*t}dt + C(O) + R(T)e^{-k^*T} > 0$$

and

$$(B) \qquad C(O) = \int_0^T Q(t)e^{-\rho t}dt + R(T)e^{-\rho T}.$$

(*Notation*: $C(O)$ is initial investment; $Q(t)$ net profit from investment; T life-span of the project; R residual value of the project; V present value of the project; respectively the ρ, $\hat{\rho}_0$, $\hat{\rho}^*$, $\hat{\rho}_0^*$ deterministic and stochastic "internal" efficiency rates of the project and the stochastic all-economy and sectoral rates of efficiency; τ_k constants of time-lags; $k = 1, .., r$ the rate of normative efficiency; L Laplace transform; σ^2 variance.)

The (A) is the present-value maximand. In Mikhalevskiy's interpretation, the k^* forms the link with economy's overall investment efficiency norm. Two antithetic propositions would then be considered. *First*, the k^* acts as the long-run interest rate ($k^* = r$); and *second*, it is the economy's investment-efficiency norm proper ($k^* = \hat{\rho}_0^*$). In the first case the criterion has a built-in "bias" of a smaller number of capital-intensive variants implying a lower capital-formation rate and slower rates of replacement and technological progress; the reverse is true of the second alternative.

The (B) is the "internal" rate-of-return maximand combined with the solution rule: the selection of the successive project by the decreasing ρ max — up to the exhaustion of sectoral investment quotas. With $T = \infty$, $\rho = R = O$, we have the particular case — the minimum-recoupment period criterion. (The rate is internal in the sense that it is endogenously determined — not dependent on k.) This criterion favours lesser capital intensity and shorter service-spans but tends to secure higher rates of accumulation and growth-rates, with full reinvestment of operational profit and faster technical progress.

The deterministic formulation is turned into a stochastic one by a successive introduction of (1) the risk element stemming from subjective uncertainty, and the space of indeterminacy, (2) the random element in the dynamics based on "objective" probability, (3) randomness of the service-span, (4) randomness in lags, and (5) errors in initial appraisal of investment (which incidentally — in the light of Soviet experience — are taken to make up usually no less than 25-30 per cent).

The procedure leads to maximization of the mathematical expectation of the continuous "effect function"

$$\bar{F}(Q) = \int_{-\infty}^{\infty} F(Q)f(Q)dQ,$$

or as a Taylor series

$$F(Q) = F(\bar{Q}) + (Q - \bar{Q})\dot{F}(Q) + \tfrac{1}{2}(Q - Q)^2\ddot{F}(\bar{Q}) + \ldots$$

The risk coefficient is taken as a constant:

$$\tfrac{1}{2}\ddot{F}(\bar{Q}) = -k^* = \text{const},$$

whence

$$F(\bar{Q}) = F[C(O)] + k^*\sigma^2(Q).$$

Considering that

$$F\left(\frac{\Delta Q(O)}{C(O)}\right) \equiv \rho_0,$$

mathematical expectation of the ρ is obtained as

$$E(\rho^*) = \rho_0 + k\sigma^2.$$

Along this line the risk element is obtained as

$$k^* = \tfrac{1}{2}\left(1 + \frac{\rho^{*2}}{V_{\rho^*}{}^2\,\rho_0^{*2}}\right),$$

leading to

$$\rho_0^* = \rho^* + \tfrac{1}{2}(\rho^{*2} + \sigma_{\rho^*}{}^2).$$

Eventually — by expressing the mean-square error by the coefficient of variation and applying the three-sigmas rule — the confidence interval for the value of the project's efficiency norm appears as

$$\rho_0^* = \rho^* \left(1 - \frac{1 - V_\rho^{*2}}{2} \rho^*\right) \pm 3V_\rho^* \rho^*.$$

In trying to synthesize the (A) and (B) Mikhalevskiy intends to avoid the indeterminacy which — as it appears from the argument — is particularly strong in the former. It affects, however, also the (B): it results there formally from the possible multiplicity of the positive roots of the equation. While "leaning" in this synthesis towards the (B), Mikhalevskiy tries to avoid the difficulty by greater specificity with respect to economic characteristics of the project.

His compromise criterion is formed by introducing into (B) a distributed time-lag

$$C(O) = \int_0^T \int_0^\infty f(\tau)[Q(t-\tau)e^{-\rho t}dt + R(T)e^{-\rho T}]d\tau; \int_0^\infty f(\tau)d\tau = 1.$$

Then, by means of a Laplace transform, this becomes

$$C(O) = L\left\{f(\tau) * \left\{L(Q(t)[U(t) - U(t-T)]) + R(T).e^{-\rho T}.\right.\right.$$

$$. [U(t) - (U(t-\tau)]\right\}; U(t) = \begin{cases} 1, & t > 0, \\ 0, & t < 0. \end{cases}$$

When abbreviated

$$C(O) = L\, f(\tau) * \bar{Q}\, [U(t) - U(t-\tau)] ,$$

where

$$\bar{Q} = L\left\{Q(t)\, [U(t) - U(t-T)] + R(T)e^{-\rho T}\right\} .$$

Further, a cascade is introduced of independent distributed lags, its physical components being the average "freeze" period of the invested resources: these are the lags in construction, in reaching the potential operational capacity and some postulated technical-economic indices. Since

$$\int_0^\infty f(\tau)d\tau = 1$$

is considered as a probability, the sum of the lags is written

$$f(\tau^*) = f(\tau_k) * [U(t) - U(t-\tau_k)] ; k = 1, \dots, r.$$

By substitution we then have

$$C(O) = L \left\{ f(\tau_k) * f \left[U(t) - U(t - \tau_k) \right] * \bar{Q} \right\}.$$

Thus the cascade from a sum of independent lags in the Laplace plane is turned into a product.

Further specifying the overall lag as due, respectively, to those in completion of construction, in maturation of capacities, and in reaching the required performance (technical and economic) indices with respective coefficients λ_1, λ_2, λ_3, we will have

$$C(O) = e^{-\rho\tau_1} \frac{\lambda_1 \lambda_2 \lambda_3}{(\rho + \lambda_1)(\rho + \lambda_2)(\rho + \lambda_3)} \bar{Q}(\rho).$$

Technical interest apart, the 1969 Mikhalevskiy contribution is significant for its rejection of the principle of a single "norm" as an instrument of project selection — in this it is a novum in the Soviet mathematical school of planning; Mikhalevskiy's critique extends also to the employment of such a rate in price formation. In this among others Lurye and Novozhilov no less than Khachaturov — and Western students, among others Marglin and Eckaus — do likewise.

Two points stand out in this critical analysis. One centres on the use of the money-term indices as the unique criterion. The incidence of error would be accentuated by the presence of projects which, owing to their size and role in the economy, must heavily affect the overall "norm" of those with intrinsically unquantifiable characteristics. The other objection raised by Mikhalevskiy concerns the exaggerated emphasis — in project selection and still more so in locational decision-making — on the general equilibrium. Here the main reproach is that the mechanism of variant selection is taken — in modelling — to imitate the competitive principle, whereas this is a domain where the postulates of divisibility and additivity are particularly unrealistic in planning practice. The matter links up, on a more fundamental plane, in Mikhalevskiy, with his reservation with respect to the equilibrium-growth strategy and advocacy of a mixed equilibrium-disequilibrium strategy (this has found its expression in the model of perspective planning, experimented with by the TsEMI of which he was co-author)[32]. Some of the handicaps indicated in the Mikhalevskiy critique are conceded to be mitigated by the suggested compromise method (the solution that is based on the ranging — by a decreasing maximum — of the stochastically-determined "normative") but not eliminated.

We would argue that — at least conceptually — the points raised could be coped with by a complex, nonlinear programme formulation of the criterion, sufficiently constrained: but practical obstacles stand in its way.

(16) From our presentation it is patent that the conceptual advance in the field has been rooted, over the past decade or so, in Kantorovich's fundamentals. Whatever sophistication there has been added in a collection of the constructs demonstrated — it has been built upon them; and, as noted, it is these fundamentals that have been incorporated into official doctrine by the 1968 Principles. But, to recall, the Principles are silent as to the way the investment-efficiency "norm" is to be obtained; and it is to the modelling of a practicable procedure for a numerical solution to the problem that the writing of the Kantorovich school has to a considerable extent been devoted. A series of preliminary designs, published over the years, led — by the end of the 1960s — to more complete versions — by Kantorovich and Vainshtein.[33] A basic and stated consideration with them is still manageability — hence the drastic simplifications. The construct rests on the Cobb-Douglas function — the apparatus is borrowed from the Kantorovich-Gorkov model of growth.

The point-of-departure function is written

$$Y(t) = U[K(t), L(t)] ,$$

L is taken to be determinable from the dynamics of the labour force, in turn derivable from demographic trends. The $K(t)$ describes the economy's productive resources, its initial value $K(O)$ is given. The U is postulated to be positively homogenous.

Capital stocks — and capacities — are assumed to be perfectly malleable. No matter what their actual physical shape, they are taken to lend themselves to instantaneous ideal transformation. Labour is homogeneous.

Overall consumption is a datum. It is taken as either exogenously given at each time-point, or, alternatively, as determined by some parameters of the function: say, a fixed consumption rate or a parameter relating it to the labour input.

The most important of all postulates: it is assumed that the available resources which the U embodies have been somehow organized in the best possible way: best in the sense of yielding maximum output per time-unit. With the conditions met, the $U(x,1)$ is assumed to be concave (downwards)

As defined, the efficiency norm measures the net product yielded by the marginal unit of capital when "purposefully" employed — over a time-unit, $\eta = \partial U(K,L)/\partial K$. When capital intensity — capital/labour ratio is denoted $S = K/L$, we have $\eta = U_S'(S,1)$ and the equation of the national income increment takes the form

$$dP/dt = d/dt. \ [LU(S,1)] = L'U(S,1) + LU_S'(S,1)S'$$

(the prime denotes time sequence).

Arrived at in this way the "norm" does not give the statement of the production function in an explicit way. Rather it is indirectly expressed through some key indicators of the economy's growth. When various correctives have been brought in, it takes the form

$$\eta = [1/Y \cdot dY/dt - (L'/L + \rho)] \ (1 + \beta)^\mu /$$
$$[1 - C/Y - \delta\bar{K}/Y - L'/L \cdot \bar{K}/Y \cdot (1 + \beta)^\mu].$$

The meaning will be clear when the formula is considered term by term.

Numerator:

1. $1/Y. dY/dt$ is the growth-rate of national product.

2. L'/L is the growth of labour input; it measures, that is, the contribution of the incremental labour unit to the growth-rate of national product.

3. ρ is the coefficient of technical progress: when allowed for, the production function takes the form $Y(t) = e^{\rho t}(K,L)$; thence the ρ is obtained.

4. β is the gestation-lag of investment. It is taken to correspond to $\beta = 1/Y. dY/dt$; when obsolescence of capacities is allowed for (see below), it is written $\beta = 1/y. dY/dt + \delta$. When μ is the capacities' mean period of gestation corrected for "assimilation" over time, the multiplier $(1 + \beta)^\mu$ allows for the time-lag between saving and their maturation.

Denominator:

1. C/Y is the consumption ratio (to national product): thus the investment (saving) rate is $1 - C/Y$.

2. δ is the coefficient of depreciation — of loss of "production value" of capital stock due to disparity between its structure and that of demand. Loss on other counts, including obsolescence due to other causes and wear and tear, is allowed for in the difference $(K - \bar{K})$, the difference between "nominal" and "actual" value of capital assets. The $\bar{K}/Y$ is thus the "actual" capital intensity — capital/output — ratio and the δ adjusts it for the loss in the "production value" as described.

3. Multiplying the actual capital/output ratio by L'/L allows for the effect of growth of the labour force, and the multiplier $(1 + \beta)^\mu$ for bringing investment to full potential capacity.

Thus the formula relates the "pure" growth-rate of national product — pure in the sense of the contribution of growth in factor inputs — to the "pure" growth-rate of capacity resulting from transforming the saved unit of product into capital.

On the authors' recognition, the purpose of the exercise is primarily to offer the planning practice an "objective" method for the calculation of the parameter needed in pricing as well as in decision-making for investment.

The Kantorovich-Vainshtein design has become the subject of a noteworthy controversy in Soviet literature: Lurye[34] has argued that it is the marginal ratio of density increments — of the useful effect and investment — that should form the basis of the efficiency "norm". The emphasis in the argument is on that over a given finite time interval, the efficiencies of individual projects inevitably differ: hence over any Δt the useful effect/ investment ratio, $\Delta P/\Delta K$ presents itself as some relative average: the normative efficiency — its lower limit for individual projects — should then equal the incremental ratio; as we move from the small time interval Δt to the time moment, t, it is the respective densities rather than the useful effect and the investment volume that must be considered; then in order to preserve the role of the efficiency norm as the (lower) limiting value of the relative efficiency of raising capital expenditure on the individual enterprise, it should form the marginal ratio of the increment in the density of the useful effect to that in the density of investment. In turn the density of the useful effect, $dP(t)/dt$, is functionally dependent on the density of investment, $dK(t)/dt$, and the form of this dependence would be determined by the structure of capital — characterizing the factor relation, thereby the adopted technique — as well as its volume. Hence the density of the useful effect, $dP(t)/dt$, is taken as the functional of the functions $dK(t)/dt$ and $L(t)$ over the interval from some past date up to the moment t

$$\frac{dP(t)}{dt} = F\left(\frac{\partial K(\tau)}{d(\tau)}, L(\tau), \tau \leqslant t\right)$$

and the efficiency norm would be determined as

$$\eta_\theta = \lim_{s \to t} \lim_{\Delta \to o} \frac{F(\varphi_s(\tau), L(\tau); \tau \leqslant t) - F(\varphi(\tau), L(\tau); \tau \leqslant t)}{\Delta},$$

where $\varphi(\tau) = dK(\tau)/d\tau$, the φ_s differing from the φ only over the interval (s,t), i.e. $\varphi_s(\tau) = \varphi(\tau) + \Delta : s < \tau < t$. (For the sake of simplicity, Lurye would be prepared, however, to assume that the values of $K(t)$ and $L(t)$ determine the relative relationship for each time-point and to write the dependence of the density of incremental output on the growth-rate of capital stock as

$$\frac{dP(t)}{dt} = f\left[\frac{dK(t)}{dt}, \; K(t), L(t)\right].$$

The partial derivative of f with respect to $dK(t)/dt$ would then be the normative rate of efficiency

$$\eta_\theta = \frac{\partial f(x,y,z)}{dx},$$

where $x = dK(t)/dt; y = K(t); z = L(t)$ or

$$\eta_\theta = \partial \; \frac{dP(t)}{dt} \Big/ \partial \; \frac{dK(t)}{dt} \; .)$$

The reasoning is convincing as a theoretical proposition (with the patent implication for planning practice that relying on the absolute minimal rather than marginal density value tends to overstate the normative value of investment efficiency). So too is Lurye's relating the root of the technical deficiency in the Kantorovich-Vainshtein construct to the assumption with respect to the impact of technological progress: merely introducing the exponential multiplier does not do full justice to it since this ignores the change in capital intensity usually accompanying the change in the production method. More immediately related to the difficulty is the postulate of the positive homogeneity of the function U and the hypothesis of instantaneous convertibility of capital.

When this point of the criticism is conceded, it is right to point to the fact that Kantorovich-Vainshtein are well aware of the strength of their assumption. This is particularly true of the hypothesis of instantaneous convertibility: one may note parenthetically — strong as it is — it would appear rather innocuous since in real life the need for such a conversion is a rather rare occurrence: hence what seems to be the strongest abstraction from reality in the model is almost inoperative;[35] and anything weaker would give little gain in realism at the price of mounting complexity.

It is precisely the price in terms of manageability that defensibly dictates the Kantorovich-Vainshtein compromise between the requirements of realism and technical build-up of their model. And it is fair to judge the results also in these terms. It is enlightening to see what, having offered the critique of the Kantorovich-Vainshtein construct, Lurye can offer as a manageable alternative: it is no more than a rough procedure which is based on some empirically adopted, "more or less" probable, limiting rate of efficiency, a rate adjusted in trial-and-error way for consistency with the proposed volume of investment and with the expected changes in manpower and sectoral structure of the economy. Surely, granted the points of criticism, the Kantorovich-Vainshtein procedure remains more promising than that!

Their professed aim is the build up of a passable bridge between theory and the reality of planning, and on this count it can be given the benefit of the doubt. As far as it goes, the exercise has moreover a didactic virtue which is enhanced by the painstaking explicitness of the assumptions. We would stress the "differential optimization" as the key one: by this is meant choosing at each time-point a policy which secures the fastest growth of the capacity stock subject to restraints for the consumption levels, the stock being adjusted to the needs of output of the required structure, and corresponding to the most efficient technology. This is postulated to be carried out invisibly.

The model carries, then, an illuminating indication as to what the originator of the plan-programming conception finds to be the workable second-best treatment of the matter.[36]

Note

Since we completed this chapter, Kantorovich and his associates[37] have reworked the formalism of the theoretical fundamentals in appraising the "absolute" effect of investment with hints at the incompatibility of the "Typical Methodology".

This is handled within a general presentation of the optimality characteristics for a convex system. To recall the Kantorovich principle for a convex plan problem $\{X,b\}$, where the negative ortant of R^n belongs to X and either there exists η such that (b,η) is interior point of the set X, or X is a polyhedral set, and there exists η' such that $(b,\eta') \epsilon X$. For $\bar{x}$ to be optimal solution it is necessary and sufficient that there exists a system of prices $\pi = (\pi_1, \ldots, \pi_n)$ such that $\pi \geqslant 0$; $\pi_n = 1$; $\pi x \leqslant 0$ for all $x \in X$; $\pi\bar{x} = 0$.

In this framework the concepts of direct, supplementary (indirect) and full effects are given interpretation of scalar products, respectively $\tilde{x}\pi$,

$\tilde{x}'\pi$, and $(\tilde{x} + \tilde{x}')\pi$ where the $\tilde{x}$ is the vector of investment defined as technological "novelty".

Hence the rule on inclusion of the "novelty" $\tilde{x} \in X$ – discovery, invention, project – into the plan x; its substance is the comparison of the scalar product $\pi\tilde{x}$ with zero; the positiveness and negativeness of this product mean respectively that the "novelty" is acceptable and that it cannot improve optimal solution $\bar{\eta}$. (A general formula stated for appraising is thus based on the "comparison principle" $\pi x \lessgtr 0$, where prices, π, are "optimal at least approximately for the initial point of the dynamic plan" and the dynamics of the optimal system of prices "are sufficiently well approximated by the average yearly rate of their decrease, viz. $(1 + E)^{-1}$".)

The volume and optimal pricing of the new capacities are determined in this reasoning: their build-up and implementation are described correspondingly by the vectors $(x(h),h)$ and $(y(h), - h)$, where h is an arbitrary positive number which characterizes the volume of production of the new equipment, $x(h)$ an n-dimensional vector describing the process of producing h units of this equipment, and $y(h)$ an n-dimensional vector of employing these h units. Then when creation and exploitation of the new product are appraised, the optimal volumes are determined from

$$(y(\bar{h}) + x(\bar{h}))\pi = \max (y(h) + x(h))\pi ,$$

with h being nonnegative. The optimum price for the new "technology" will be then $\pi_{n+1} = -x(h)\pi/h$ and the full effect of its build-up and "implementation" will be $(y(\bar{h}) + x(\bar{h}))\pi$ or – which is the same – $y(\bar{h})\pi - \pi\bar{h}$. (Expanded by Kantorovich, EMM, 4, 1974);
$\phantom{y(\bar{h})\pi -}_{n+1}$

The paper concludes with a counter-argument with respect to what (as the reader must have noticed) is our central point – the problem of prices. From this important section we quote:

Strictly speaking, the appraisal methods for the efficiency of investment presented here as well as the recommended simplifications . . . are applicable only to "small" investments, whose materialization does not bring about a basic change in the plan and in the system of prices which characterizes it. . . . "Large" investments definitionally do not lend themselves to characterization by local information which differs from that contained in the description of the plan as a whole, *hence for the "large" investment the problem of efficiency as defined . . . does not exist.* The purposefulness as well as the efficiency of such investment can be tested

only by optimization of the plan as a whole — by setting against each
other plans which do and which do not contain a given (*investment*) solution [our italics].

The point thus spelt out reduces the claim to scope in applicability of
methodologies offered — and to the same extent our reservations. Note
that our reservations — and the Kantorovich-Bogachev-Makarov clarification, as we understand it — applies also, mutatis mutandis, to instability of
prices over time as well.

This chapter has outlined what is a fascinating case of a planning instrument which, arising from intuitive groping of Soviet practice, has become
over the decade a central issue of planning theory. We have seen how,
following reluctantly in its wake, the theory has gradually raised the conceptual status of the "normative" rate: in the first place when realizing
that the very rationality of the investment-selection index postulates its
generality-equalization throughout the system. And once the optimization
approach has been adopted in quantifying it, the "norm" has revealed itself
as something more: as the efficiency index of the system *as such*. The
question has been posed for discussion as to the legitimacy of the focus on
the particular prime factor. In answering it Kantorovich and his associates
pertinently make two points:[38] (a) although the patterning of the allotted
quantum of investment is but a part of the overall issue of a rational employment of scarce resources, problems of optimality constrained by investment have a special significance — a significance due to the *economic
content* of the duality appraisal of investment; and (b) the special place the
"norm" takes in the system — of Kantorovich's "000's" — of "objectively
conditioned valuations"[39] — is justified since, by determining the general
economic significance of incremental productive stocks, it thereby determines the economic valuation of time as an economic "good". The points
are valid but the answer may perhaps be somewhat strengthened. The
"norm" — when derived from an adequately idealized optimization — presents itself as a *synthesizing* index: a synthesizing index in the sense of
appraising the increment in productive stocks of productive capital when
combined with all other factors under optimum. It is the suitability —
non-absolute as it may be — for this role that gives the "norm" a special
significance as a universal instrument in the hand of a normative planner;
and this emphasizes the handicaps in attempts to quantify it with a
sufficient degree of precision, which have been indicated in the present
chapter.

APPENDICES

Appendix 1

We may draw attention in particular to Kantorovich's two contributions:

1. A paper written jointly with I. V. Romanovskiy in *Doklady* (1965, vol. 162, no. 5) devoted to the analysis of the optimal build-up of the equipment stock.

The broad line of argument for the simplest – basic – case is this: postulate over the time interval $[t, t + \tau]$ the unit "load" requiring one machine's work ϑ_1 and ϑ_2 the double load for two machines; $\vartheta_1 + \vartheta_2 \leqslant 1$. The new machine has initial "work resource" of $\bar{R}$.

Let at $t = 0$ the resource "residue" be R_1 and R_2 for the two machines respectively ($\bar{R} \geqslant R_1 \geqslant R_2 \geqslant 0$). The problem is defined as one of determining the time points $t_3, t_4, \ldots$ ($t_1 = t_2 = 0$, $t_{k+1} \geqslant t_k$, $t_n \to \infty$) for the purchase of new machines such as to ensure the carrying of the "load" and to make the discounted cost of acquisition of new machines over the whole time period $[0, \infty]$.

$$c \sum_{k=1}^{\infty} e^{-\sqrt{} t_k} = \min,$$

the $\sqrt{}$ being the "efficiency norm".

Denote

$$\vartheta_1 + \vartheta_2 = \theta, \quad \vartheta_2/\theta = \beta, \quad \exp(\overset{\approx}{R}/\vartheta_2) = \alpha.$$

The strategy, $\bar{q}$, is established by means of the Bellman Principle of Optimality.

The substance of the theorem is that where $\alpha \geqslant \beta$ the behaviour is optimal when the relations

$$q(R_1, R_2) = \begin{cases} Q \\ q_{R_2/\theta_2} \\ q_{\bar{i}'} \end{cases} \text{ where } \begin{cases} R_1 + R_2 \leqslant \bar{R} \text{ or } R_2 = 0, \\ R_2 \leqslant \vartheta_2(R_1 - \bar{R}) \text{ and } R_2 > 0, \\ \text{otherwise} \end{cases}$$

$$\bar{t} = \min\left\{\frac{1}{\vartheta_1(\vartheta_1 + 2\vartheta_2)}\left[\vartheta_2(\bar{R} - R_1) + \theta R_2\right] , \frac{1}{\vartheta_2 + 2\vartheta_2}[R_1 + R_2 + \bar{R}]\right\}$$

hold.

Over a sufficiently long period the q process will be found only in the states of the form $(\bar{R} + x/\beta, x)$ where $0 \leqslant x \leqslant R$. The graph to the left indicates the "zones" of the strategies and the trajectories over time. The discontinuous lines give the trajectory of the process started at the point S with the purchase of the new machine up to the reaching of stationary state described by the continuous line.

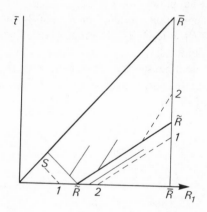

2. The paper published subsequently on the amortization charges and the evaluation of new technique — under optimal planning. ("Amortizatsyonnyie otchislenya i otsenka effektivnosti novoy tekhniki v sisteme optimalnogo planirovanya", in V. V. Novozhilov *et al.*, eds., *Matematiko-ekonomicheskiye problemy.*)

What Kantorovich offers planning practice is a very simplified formula abstracting from the dynamic optimality calculus and disregarding obsolescence. Its feature is the allowance for two factors determining the wear and tear, i.e. calendar time (number of service years — n) and actual employment time (t). When scale multipliers, respectively α and β, are adopted, the use-up of the equipment is expressed as $J = \alpha n + \beta t$. The equipment is workable so long as $J > 1$.

Under the assumed, averaged regime of the employment and service time of equipment, the amortization charge appears as

$$a = \alpha K \; \frac{(1 + \alpha)^{n_0}}{(1 + \alpha)^{n_0} - 1} = \alpha K \; \frac{(1 + \alpha)^{\frac{1}{\gamma + \beta\tau}}}{(1 + \alpha)^{\frac{1}{\gamma + \beta\tau}} - 1}.$$

Where the employment time deviates in a given year from the τ by some $\Delta\tau$, the a is corrected by means of an addend

$$\frac{da}{d\tau} \Delta\tau = \frac{da}{dn_0} \cdot \frac{dn_0}{d\tau} \Delta\tau = \frac{\beta n_0^2 \; 1n(1 + \alpha)}{(1 + \alpha)^{n_0} - 1} \; a\Delta\tau.$$

Thus an hour's increment (positive or negative) in the employment time will increase (reduce) the charge by

$$\frac{\Delta a}{\Delta\tau} = \frac{\beta n_0^2 \; 1n(1 + \alpha)}{(1 + \alpha)^{n_0} - 1} \; a.$$

Appendix 2

1. The Sadokhin-Sedelev[40] model is one of the capacities' average useful service-span under limited availability of information.

The probabilistic element relates to the average service life of capacity increments $V(t)$'s forming the capacity stock, $Q(i)$. In the general case it is determined by the mathematical expectation composed of the average service period of fully surviving increments, T, and some g characterizing the average service period of every, still active, part of increments with respect to the interval centre of extinction $W(t)$ of a given year's increment; by definition, the mathematical expectation

$$g = \int_{a-j}^{a} ty(t)\,dt \Big/ \int_{a-j}^{a} y(t)\,dt,$$

where $y(t)$ describes the capacities' "law of extinction". For the first fully surviving capacity increment $j = 2a$; hence integration is carried out over the interval $(-a) - (+a)$. In the general case the location of the average service period of t years' capacity increments is determined by $(t + T + g)$. Insofar as they all have survived until the beginning of the current year, i, the average period of the future service of each of them diminishes by the $(i-1)$ year and for the totality of partly extinct increments equals

$$(i - T - a - 1 + j) + (T + g) - (i - 1) = g - (a - j)$$

where $1 \leqslant j \leqslant (2a - 1)$, and for the totality of the fully preserved ones

$$(i - T + a - 1 + j) + T - (i - 1) = (a + j)$$

where $0 \leqslant j \leqslant T - a$.

Now, each of these service periods is being weighted by the volume of the corresponding increments: thus the average future service period for all increments forming the capacity stock of the i-th year, the $\Phi(i)$, becomes

$$Q(i) = 1 \cdot 1/\Phi(i) \cdot \left\{ \sum_{j=1}^{2a=1} [g - (a - j)] \cdot V (i - T - a - 1 + j) \right.$$

$$\int_{a-j}^{a} y(t) \mathrm{d}t + \sum_{j=0}^{T-a} (a + j) V (i - T + a - 1 + j).$$

Homogeneity of the capacity stock is assumed but ways of relaxing it are being indicated.

The principal distinctive feature of the Sadokhin-Sedelev construct, as against the classical methods of prognosis, lies in that here the prognosis is, as it were, automatic: if the plan horizon does not exceed the lag interval, $(T - a + 1)$, there is no need for prediction of the originating dynamic series, in particular that of capacity extinctions.

Under the traditional methods, such as those employing a regression analysis, confidence intervals for $W(i)$ tend to widen and the indeterminateness of the prediction tends to rise with the remoteness of the horizon. By contrast, a constancy of the measure of indeterminateness of the predicted value for $W(i)$ is claimed for the Sadokhin-Sedelev construct (the common assumption being that of constant dispersion of deviations of the basic (initial) magnitudes from the trend over time).

Where the horizon exceeds the lag interval, one has to resort to forecasts of the generating dynamic series for capacity increments — outside the models. The $W(i)$ will include various components of the $V(t)$ values; their indeterminateness will tend to grow with i, and so will the confidence intervals for $W(t)$: however, in this case an indeterminateness less than under the regression prognosis is claimed too — whatever the length of the plan horizon.

2. An integrated flow-stock analysis of the capacity-formation process in its positive and negative aspects — gestation and depreciation — has been produced by Zhdanko for a stationary regime.[41] The processes are investigated with respect to two variables — the positive incremental rate of capacity formation λ and useful life-span T. In a previous study Zhdanko took the latter as a stochastic variable with some law of distribution:[42] it is taken to be deterministic in the present exercise, expressing the technically reasonable and the optimal on some economic-criterion exploitation period of a capacity unit. Both λ and T are taken constant over time and are unique.

The structural indices in the analysis are divided into two classes, one describes the relation between flows and the capacity stocks; the other between the gross formation and its two components from the point of view of economic purpose, i.e. replacement and addition to stocks; the indices of the two classes are termed respectively "norms" and "coefficients". We have thus the "norms" k and r — of gross formation and replacement, and the coefficients c and ρ — of incremental and replacement formation (the $k = \lambda + r$).

The point of departure in the analysis is the "motion" of the physical-terms volume of stocks as expressed by the dynamics of the flows $K(t)$ and $R(T)$ (respectively gestation and depreciation) and of stocks, $\Phi(t)$ including their increments $C(t) = \Phi(t)/dt$, the first three being differentials and the last one an integral magnitude. The magnitudes are written

$$K(t) = K_0 e^{\lambda t}; R(t) = K(t - T) = K(t)e^{-\lambda T};$$

$$C(t) = K(t) - R(t) = K(t)[1 - e^{-\lambda T}];$$

$$\Phi(t) = \int_{-\infty}^{t_1} C(u)\mathrm{d}u = \int_{t=T}^{t} K(s)\mathrm{d}s = \int_0^T K(t-\tau)\mathrm{d}\tau = K(\tau)\,\frac{1 - e^{-\lambda T}}{\lambda}.$$

Analogous equations are written for money-term values.

In addition to the two pairs mentioned — k and r, and c and ρ several more parameters are then observed. Of them we shall mention these magnitudes: the averages of age and of "survival" — the remaining life-span of capacities, $\bar{t}$ and $\bar{\theta}$ respectively and their age distribution, $\varphi(\tau)$. In money terms $\bar{s}$, $\bar{u}$ — are coefficients of fixed capacities; finally ϑ, is the share of amortization in financing gross formation.

What follows summarizes the parameters of capacity growth as functions of incremental rates of installation and life span, as noted — in a stationary regime.

Function	Limit with $\lambda \to \infty$	$T \to \infty$
1. $k = \dfrac{\lambda}{1-e^{-\lambda T}}$	$\dfrac{1}{T}$	λ
2. $r = \dfrac{\lambda e^{-\lambda T}}{1-e^{-\lambda T}}$	$\dfrac{1}{T}$	0
3. $\rho = e^{-\lambda T}$	1	0
4. $c = 1-e^{-\lambda T}$	0	1
5. $\sigma = \dfrac{\lambda T - (1-e^{-\lambda T})}{\lambda T}$	0	1
6. $\bar{u} = \bar{\tau} = \dfrac{1-e^{-\lambda T}-\lambda T e^{-\lambda T}}{\lambda T (1-e^{-\lambda T})}$	$\dfrac{1}{2}$	0
7. $\bar{s} = \bar{v} = \dfrac{\lambda T - (1-e^{-\lambda T})}{\lambda T (1-e^{-\lambda T})}$	$\dfrac{1}{2}$	1
8. $\bar{\tau} = \dfrac{1-e^{-\lambda T}-\lambda T \cdot e^{-\lambda T}}{\lambda (1-e^{-\lambda T})}$	$\dfrac{1}{2}T$	$\dfrac{1}{\lambda}$
9. $\bar{\theta} = \dfrac{\lambda T - (1-e^{-\lambda T})}{\lambda (1-e^{-\lambda T})}$	$\dfrac{1}{2}T$	∞
10. $\varphi(\lambda, T, \tau) = \dfrac{\lambda e^{-\lambda \tau}}{1-e^{-\lambda T}}$	$\dfrac{1}{T}$	$\lambda e^{-\lambda \tau}$

3. Of late Zhdanko added to the realism of his constructs by synthesizing the two in a new stochastic model.[43] It borrows from the deterministic version the exponential type of growth for the "flow" and from the original stochastic one the assumption of randomness of the life-span. We have then τ, a positive random variable describing the age of the "dropping-out" units, $f(\tau)$ the probability densities of the life-span. Then the surviving collection will be expressed by an additional function of the distribution of service periods $G(\tau) = 1 - F(t) = \int_{\tau}^{\infty} f(\xi)d\xi$, the expected total number of stock-time ("fund-time") which remains to be worked by the unit collection in the future — by means of the index $H(\tau) = \int_{\tau}^{\infty} G(\xi) \, d\xi,$

and the average remaining service period of the surviving unit by the index $\vartheta(\tau) = H(\tau)/G(\tau)$.

These two indices between them are meant to express the changes in the residual unit age-group and the average surviving unit (under the adopted assumption) by means of time coefficients

$$h(\tau) = H(\tau)/T_a \vartheta(\tau) = \theta(\tau)/T_a$$

where

$$T_a = \int_0^\infty \tau f(\tau)\,\mathrm{d}\tau = \int_0^\infty G(\tau)\,\mathrm{d}\tau$$

is a new capital-stock unit's average value for the service period. The coefficients serve also for expressing the total share of the "drop-out" and the survival and the depreciation of the collection and the average surviving unit as the, respective, differences. The rate of depreciation growth of an age-group, and of its amortization fund appears as

$$f_h(t) = -h'(\tau) = G(\tau)/T_a.$$

The method of estimating the T_a — the average service period — stems from a critique of the Sadokhin-Sedelev original schema for the computation of the distribution density of the service spans (it concerned the problem of the uniqueness of solution of the problem of optimal choice of probability density of the service period). In Zhdanko's approach (admittedly, rougher but more promising in practice) one starts from the formula $T = (\log k - \log r)/\lambda$ (as above) which we have in both models. Taking $m = \Phi(t)/K(t)$ from the statistical series for $K(t)$ and $\Phi(t)$, and admitting the two interpretations — deterministic and probabilistic — with respect to the service period (and thereby the motion of the fixed-capital stock), Zhdanko works with the formulae:[44]

$$m_\Phi = m_\Phi^*, \text{ or}$$

$$\int_0^\infty e^{-\lambda\tau}\mathrm{d}\tau = \int_0^\infty e^{-\lambda\tau}G(\tau)\mathrm{d}\tau; e^{-\lambda T_e} = \int_0^\infty e^{-\lambda\tau} f(\tau)\mathrm{d}\tau.$$

Notes

1. cf. Zauberman, "Economic thought in the Soviet Union—economic law and the theory of value", *Econ. Stud.*, 16/39 (1948–9); the same, "The Soviet and Polish quest for a criterion of investment efficiency", *Economica*, Aug. 1962; the same, *Aspects of planometrics*, pt IIC.

2. The operation of a quasi-capital market under socialism seems to be implied in Lerner's comments on Lange models of the mid-1930s. See A. P. Lerner, "A note on socialist economics", *R. Econ. Stud.,* Oct. 1936 and Oskar Lange, "Mr Lerner's note on socialist economics", ibid. Jan. 1937.

3. K. Arrow/M. Kurz, *Public investment, the rate of return and optimal fiscal policy* (Baltimore, 1970).

4. *Plan. khoz.,*1928.

5. S. G. Strumilin, in the *Bulletin* of the USSR Academy of Sciences, 1946; for a comment see Zauberman, "Economic Thought in the Soviet Union", *R. Econ. Stud.,* 16/2 (1949–50).

6. *Tipovaya metodika opredelenya ekonomicheskoy effektivnosti novoy tekhniki v narodnom khozyaistve SSSR.* Akad Nauk., (Moscow, 1960).

7. cf. L. A. Vaag/S. N. Zakharov, *Metody ekonomicheskoy otenski v energetike* (Moscow, 1966).

8. cf. V. A. Drozdovskiy, in *EMM,* 2 (1972); also B. N. Bogachev, *Strok okupayemost* (Moscow, 1966).

9. Within the framework of the traditional "typical methodology" a team of authors has elaborated a tool for appraising the three-dimensional efficiency (intertemporal, intersectoral, interregional) in planning economic development. The "reduced" cost is appraised by the formula

$$F = \sum_j \sum_f \sum_r \sum_{t=1}^{t=m} (K_{jfrt} + S_{jfrt})(1 + E)^{T-t^*} + (\sum_j \sum_f \sum_r S_{jfmr})/E$$

(*Notation: K* is respective cost of building up the "production base" over the time interval *t; S* is the "exploitation" (current) expenditure in the last time interval to secure output of the *j*-th product by the *f*-th technology; *E* normative rate of efficiency of investment; *T* time horizon; *t** computational co-ordinate of the interval.) cf. Yu. P. Syrov *et al.,* in *Optimizatsya,* 2/19 (1971).

10. Some kinship can be discovered between the Soviet "norm" of the efficiency of investment, as it historically developed, and instruments evolved by the engineering practice in the West which defenders of the Soviet traditional tool find comforting. Cf. in particular the NAA Research Report New York, 1959 on the formula for the recoupment period, i.e. $k = s/c$. $[1 - (1 + k^n)]$ where *s, c,* and *k* stand respectively for yearly return, cost, and the "internal" rate of return. Also C. C. Pegels, "A comparison of decision criteria for capital investment", *Engineering Economist,* 4/13 (1968).

11. Kalecki, *Zarys teorii iii*; cf. the "Annex" added to the 2nd ed. (Warsaw, 1968).

   Kalecki's ideas are further developed in the Dobb Festschrift ("The curve of production and the evaluation of the efficiency of investment", in Feinstein, *Socialism,* (. . .)) with special consideration of the question of differential "norms"; his tenet is as follows. Given the level of the recoupment period, the investment outlay (*I*) and labour force (*R*) the "curve of production" represents a downward-sloping curve. When a uniform "norm" of recoupment is adopted the curve has these three properties: (1) with given manpower, the least capital outlay, (2) the curve is concave, (3) the slope of tangent in points *I, R* corresponds to the recoupment period i/g. *T* (notation, p. 193). Sectoral differentiation of recoupment periods deprives the curve of the last two characteristics.

12. (Kalecki, in *EMM,* 5 (1970).

13. *Intro. to econometrics,* App. II, "The economic and technological foundations of the efficiency of investment".

14. The Polish investment efficiency formula, as it eventually evolved, has the shape

$$[1/T . I(1 + q_z n_z) + K_{st} Y_n]/P_{st} Z_n + O_s q_s/P.$$

The symbols denote: $1/T$ the "norm" (inverse of recoupment period); I investment outlay; q_z freeze-coefficient for fixed capital; n_z period of construction; K_{st} constant overhead minus depreciation plus maintenance; Y_n coefficient of conversion of cost to those for a project with standard lifespan; O working capital; q_s freeze-coefficient for the latter; Z_t conversion coefficient analogous to Y_{st}; P_{st} and P are output, respectively the capacity and actual output.

In actual Polish practice the coefficients in general and those of Y and Z, with the implied discount rates, are being rather arbitrarily determined.

15. The Polish doctrine is extensively discussed in M. Rakowski, ed., *Efficiency of investment in a socialist economy*, with a preface by M. Kalecki (London, 1966); see also Zauberman, *Aspects of planometrics*.

The Kalecki methodology has been examined and generalized in Western writing by A. Bhaduri, "An aspect of project-selection: durability versus construction-period", *Econ. J.*, June 1968. It is shown that where projects 1 and 2 have respectively durability n_1 and n_2 and the gestation lags θ_1 and θ_2, with the same capital/output ratio, the output flows will display the relationship

$$(1 - 1/e^{rn_1}) \cdot e^{r\theta_2}/(1 - 1/e^{rn_2}) \cdot e^{r\theta_1},$$

the r denoting the continuous rate of increase in aggregate investment in plant.

$$F = \frac{1 - \dfrac{1}{e^{rn_1}}}{1 - \dfrac{1}{e^{rn_2}}} \cdot \frac{e^{r\theta_2}}{e^{r\theta_1}} \cdot \frac{X_1}{X_2} \gtrless 1.$$

16. Yu. V. Sukhotin, *Effektivnost' kapitalnykh vlozheniy i mezhotraslevyie svyazi* (Moscow, 1966).

17. *Osnovnyie polozhenya optimalnogo planirovanya razvitya i razmeshchenya proizvodstva* (Moscow, 1968). A new version of the "Typical Methodology" was published subsequently to co-ordinate it with the 1968 Principles – under the title "Tipovaya metodika opredelenya ekonomicheskoy effektivnosti kapitalnykh vlozheniy", in *Ekonomicheskaya gazeta*, 39 (1969).

18. See above, sect. 6.

19. Since this chapter was written D. A. Arzamatsyev (in *EMM*, 6 (1969)) has spelt out our fundamental point: it is that for its validity the Kantorovich–Makarov formula of the investment-efficiency "norm" presupposes a system of *optimality prices* (in fairness, it would seem implied in Kantorovich–Makarov in some general assumption of optimization behind the scenes).

In Arzamatsyev's reasoning where – as in Soviet reality – the assumption is illegitimate, correctives would have to be brought in – in each branch – for deviation from optimal prices. For a project j of branch i he writes

$$C' = \sigma_i C_j; \quad K'_j = \pi_i K'_j; \quad -\partial C'_j/\partial K'_j = \theta_i^n; \quad \theta_i = \sigma_i/\pi_i,$$

the θ being the corrective coefficient. Thence the conclusion that under non-optimal pricing, investment efficiency "norms" must be branch-differentiated. We would stress, however, that optimal prices do not lend themselves to determining prices for a branch in isolation from those of the system as a whole: hence there is no way of quantifying the deviation from optimal prices.

We are here taking optimality prices to be identical with those corresponding to the dual. The problem of calculation of the repayment period of investment where "optimal" prices are obtained by some manipulation of the dual is interestingly discussed in Skolka/Cerny, *Reflections on the economic interpreta-*

tion of the solution of a dynamic macro-economic linear programming model,
p. 23.
20. Fedorenko, in *EMM*, 2 (1971).
21. *Model optimalnogo planirovanya.*
22. The Volkonskiy methodology is related to his model of capacity generation of considerable interest also for its technical organization. It has the form

$$ax(t) = v(t) + \Delta z_k(t) + \Lambda(t)$$

$$bx(t) \geqslant \Delta z_n(t)$$

$$cx(t) \leqslant m(t).$$

The a, b, c are technological matrices: the first two describe inputs–outputs, respectively, of "external" resources and intermediate products; the third describes work–time inputs of both capacities and labour. The x is the vector of activity levels, and $\Delta z_n(t)$, $\Delta z_k(t)$ denote increments in stock of intermediate and of final products and $\Lambda(t)$ non-productive consumption – all non-negative (foreign trade being assumed away). Total cost of the j-th variant of capacity to be generated over a period t after the θ_j time-point is

$$v(t) = \sum_j v_j(t - \theta_j)\delta_j$$

and the "balance" vector of capacities at the time-point t is written

$$m(t) = m(o) + \sum_j m_j(t - \theta_j)\delta_j.$$

A similar equation would be built up for labour, with a (demographic) constraint $l(t) \leqslant L(t)$, and analogously for non-man-made resources. The system with unknowns δ_j, θ_j, $x(t)$, $Z(t)$, $\Lambda(t)$ and a criterion formed as a functional from vectors $\Lambda(t)$; $t = 0, 1, \ldots, T$ would be then conceivable for any T.

(As in Kantorovich–Makarov, it is assumed that with a sufficiently large T its extension would have little significance for plan indices of the nearer-time planperiods. (In the absence of indication to the contrary from the trend, terminal capital stock for each sector is based on the assumption of constant growth-rate [averaged for the period observed]. The length of the plan period is chosen as one of "compromise", allowance being made for the average gestation period of capacities and the greater degree of the indeterminateness of the system rising over time.)

23. K. J. Arrow, "Optimal capital policy, the cost of capital and myopic decision rules", in *Ann. Inst. Statist. Math.*, part I,(Tokyo, 1964). Cf. also in the context Arrow's discussion of optimization of capital formation in his "Optimal capital adjustment" in Arrow et al., eds. *Studies in applied probability and management science* (Stanford, 1962). Take the capital stock K yielding a flow of operating profits $\pi(K)$ and the net surplus of receipts over expenditure at any time t as $\pi[K(t)] - I(t)$: then the present value of the capital "policy" $K(t)$ is

$$VK(t) = \int_0^{+\infty} e^{-\alpha t} \left\{ \pi[K(t)] - I(t) \right\} dt.$$

The related function of net profits has the form $P(K) = (K) - (\alpha + \beta)K$. The α and β are the rates of interest and depreciation charges.
24. In *EMM*, 2 (1965).
25. The "reduction" of return on capital in Mikhalevskiy is related to past capital expenditure; it is excluded only if the present sacrifices and future benefits are

uniformly distributed as between generations. In this there is affinity with Tinbergen, Malinvaud, Marglin. Cf. Vishnyev, *Ekonomicheskiye parametry*, p. 141.

26. *Public investment*, pp. 73 ff.
27. Reference to his *A study in the theory of investment* (Chicago, 1960).
28. K. Wicksell, "Dr Gustaf Akerman's Real Kapital und Kapitalzins", *Ekonomisk tidskrift*, 1923; H. Hotelling, "A general mathematical theory of depreciation", *J. Amer. Statist. Ass.*, 1925.
29. D. W. Jorgenson *et al.*, *Optimal replacement policy* (Amsterdam, 1967).
30. Mikhalevskiy, in *EMM*, 4 (1969).
31. Sakari T. Jutila, "A note on the evaluation of the marginal efficiency of capital", *Econometrica*, Apr. 1962. H. Peuman, *Theorie et pratique de calculs d'investisse-ment* (Paris, 1965) and in particular the illuminating survey A. R. Prest/R. Turvey, "Cost benefit analysis: a survey", *Econ. J.*, Dec. 1965, p. 699.
32. See my *Aspects of planometrics*; also Mikhalevskiy's contribution to planning seminars in *EMM*, 3 (1965), p. 466 and his *Perspektivnyie raschety . . .*, pp. 261, 279. Cf. also Gavrilyets et al., in Nemchinov, *Primenenye matematiki*, iii. 152.
33. Kantorovich/Vainshtein, in *EMM*, 5 (1967).
34. In *EMM*, 3 (1969). In sect. 16 on p. 216 above we present the reasoning by Lurye on the weightime function in measuring the impact of the time factor in problems of "local" optimization. In following the reasoning he arrives at a normative rate of efficiency of investment

$$E_t = -[(Q(t + dt, t\sigma) - Q(t, t\sigma)]/Q(t + dt, t\sigma)dt =$$
$$= -d/dt \cdot \log \phi(t), \quad \text{where } \phi(t) = e^{-\int_0^t E_k dk}$$

(notation as in section referred to). The "norm" of efficiency appears thus as the logarithmic derivative of the weighting function and is independent of the reduction base.

The rentals for the service period of a fixed capital asset would be of the form

$$\sum_{t=\tau+1}^{t=\tau+t} \text{ser } \delta(t, \tau)Q(t, \tau) = K^\tau - K_{serv}^\tau Q(t + \tau_{serv}, \tau)$$

where K_{serv} is the scarp value. The renovation "norm" assuming constancy would be $K_{ren} = [(1 - K_{serv}/K)\phi(t_{serv})]/\sum_{t=1}^{t=\tau} \text{ser } \phi(t)$. Further assuming $\phi = (1 + E)^{-t}$ and $K_{serv} = 0$ we arrive at Lurye's formula for renovation $K_{ren} = E/(1 + E)^t \text{serv} - 1)$. Allowance made for renovation, the rental would then be
$\delta(t + \tau) = E_t K^t + K_{ren}(t + \tau)K^t$ where the K^t is the asset's price.

35. For a good discussion of implication of rigidity of installed capital see e.g. M. Brown, *Theory and measurement of technological change*, p. 70.
36. Since these pages were written the controversy has gained further clarification in an exchange of views.

To the Lurye point that the Kantorovich–Vainshtein efficiency norm rests on some value averaged over a time interval rather than marginal magnitudes, the answer offered is that it inevitably must bridge some time-segment if only because of the deviations – in practice – from the theoretical formulation: in particular those due to integrality and nonlinearity of the magnitudes concerned and the continuity of technical progress; but (they maintain) in real life the differences prove acceptably small.

On the "density of capital accumulation" issue raised by Lurye (in his argument, to recall the relevant formula would be $dK/dt = \varphi(P(t) - V(t)t)$, Kantorovich–Vainshtein point to the acceptance in literature (Stone, Houthakker,

Taylor) – for reasons of simplicity – of their identity saving-capital accumulation ≡ net output-consumption. The emphasis is on the virtual impossibility of determining statistically Lurye's φ. (We would note that the identity holds for a normative system to a higher degree than for a competitive market economy).

The criticism of the hypothesis on the positive first-order homogeneity of the national-income production function is met by the contention that for the purposes of real life one can take $U(K, L, t) \approx e^{\rho(t-t_0)}U(K, L)$ as a tolerable approximation. Lurye has clarified his stand in rejecting Kantorovich's and Vainshtein's adoption of the $e^{\rho t}$ multiplier and of the Cobb–Douglas function for the numerical estimation of their ρ. (The introduction of a multiplier invariantly rising over time is – in Lurye's reasoning – invalid since the shape and the very nature of the function varies over time.) There again the stress in the Kantorovich–Vainshtein reply is that replacing the function adopted by $U(K(t), L(t), t)$ – as suggested by Lurye without consideration of the form and nature of the relationship between U and t – would deprive the planner of any possibility of numerical estimation. A very similar answer is given to Lurye's point on the turning by Kantorovich–Vainshtein of their three-factor function (borrowed from Mikhalevskiy, see sect. 15) into a two-factor function by simply alloting the share of "natural" resources to those of capital and labour – proportionally.

The manner in which the debate on what Kantorovich–Vainshtein describe as one of the most important issues in the planning of a socialist economy has proceeded, if anything, has strengthened our pointer to the length they feel they have to go in concessions to empirical practicability of their construct. (Kantorovich/Vainshtein, *EMM,* 3 (1970); Lurye. ibid.).

37. In *EMM,* 6 (1970).
38. Ibid.
39. We may note – with interest – how the programming approach has by now taken strong root in the Soviet doctrine.

   A critical point made in a recent review by A. V. Zhdanko of P. Massé's classic (*Le choix des investissements,* Paris 1964, 2nd ed.) in *EMM,* 3 (1969) is that he had failed to offer a general answer to the fundamental question on the intrinsic nature of investment efficiency and time-discount. (Parenthetically speaking, this reproach is undeserved; the reviewer himself, in fact, refers to Massé's indication of the relationship between the rate of discount and the von Neumann growth-rate) The reviewer's stress is on that ". . . the answer to the question can be obtained only from the theory of optimal programming, which proves that discounting expresses the weighting over time of a certain weight-function that reflects the decrease of the objective-function increment generated by an additional input unit as the plan horizon is approached, the assumption in the simpler formulae being that this decrease has a relative constant rate and it is the value of its rate that the constant discount norm measures."
40. cf. Yu. N. Sadokhin/V. V. Sedelev, in *EMM,* 1 (1969).
41. A. V. Zhdanko, in *EMM,* 2 (1970).
42. The same, ibid., 5 (1969).
43. Zhdanko, in *EMM,* 1 (1971).
44. In a further contribution in *EMM,* 5 (1971), Zhdanko has moved one step further towards realism by discarding the assumption of homogeneity with respect to useful lifetime of assets. That entails the explicit determination of the aggregation methods of the respective values.

5

THE STOCHASTIC APPROACH TO PLANNING

As my discussion of advances in the formalization of some of the key planning problems proceeded over the time this book was written, I found it necessary to present, in various contexts, the rapidly expanding attempts at their probabilistic treatment, specifically the expanding Soviet attempts in this direction. Then a look back had suggested that it might be useful to supplement this presentation (a presentation as it were *a casu ad casum*) with some more integrated remarks. This chapter was thus conceived. Intended as one of supplementary notes, it should be read in conjunction with our discussions – in the chapters concerned – of probabilistic approaches and methods in handling particular aspects of plan-programming. The origin and nature of this chapter being what they are, some overlapping was unavoidable.

Moreover, because the subject of stochastic aspects in planning – mandatory planning in particular – is still a comparatively underdeveloped domain, it has seemed to me advisable to precede my presentation of Soviet progress in the field by some more general introduction, indeed general enough to offer, as a background for the theme, a broad discussion of stochastic elements in economics. This purpose is served by section 1 in the present chapter, by Gerhard Tintner (in which I have preserved his system of references).

I SOME STOCHASTIC ASPECTS OF PLANNING

by Gerhard Tintner

1. Stochastic elements in economics

Whereas there is a very lively dispute about the meaning of probability, (see Tintner 1968) there is general agreement among mathematicians and statisticians about the validity of the laws of probability. For an excellent introduction into modern probability theory see Feller (1968, 1966).

Probability theory as traditionally presented in statistics texts (see e.g. Mood and Graybill 1963) is essentially static. We assume a given probability distribution and investigate its properties. Probability distributions may be discrete or continuous. Examples are the binomial distribution or the Poisson distribution as a discrete distribution and the normal distribution as a continuous one.

There can be no doubt that economic theory, especially mathematical economics, is deterministic and fashioned after the example of classical physical models.

It is not our intention to criticize economic deterministic models, just because they are (somewhat feeble) imitations of classical deterministic physics. It is perhaps unavoidable that all other sciences are powerfully influenced by the most successful science and this was undoubtedly true of physics in the nineteenth century. Also, we might point with pride to the fact that in one memorable instance classical economics influenced the development of biology. It is well known that Darwin's famous theory of evolution was strongly influenced by the Malthusian population theory. Hence, the influence has not always been one-sided.

But if we contemplate contemporary rather than nineteenth century physics, we must observe a great change. True enough, relativity theory is deterministic and perhaps constitutes a powerful climax of classical physics. But since the rise of quantum theory modern physics has otherwise become stochastic, i.e. it uses the results of probability theory. This makes the results of classical physics not useless. The law of large numbers assures us that if the number of particles is large (and for macro-systems it is enormous), deviations from the mean values (mathematical expectations) will be small.

Probability considerations enter classical deterministic physics in connection with the theory of errors of observations. Also, in econometrics, stochastic elements are mostly considered in a somewhat primitive fashion. We distinguish errors in the variables and errors in the equations. Errors in the variables are similar to observational errors, and we generally assume all the convenient statistical properties: normality, independence, no autocorrelation. On the other hand, errors in equations are supposed to be the joint effect of many variables omitted from the equation question, whose single effect is small. Again, mostly the convenient assumptions mentioned above are made for the errors in the equation (Tintner 1966).

There are perhaps a number of other principal difficulties in our path.

Economic variables (e.g. amounts produced, prices) cannot become negative, and modern methods of linear programming (Dantzig 1963, Kantorovich 1963) take this into account. Hence conventional methods, which use the normal probability distribution or its generalization, the classical diffusion process, must be used with extreme caution. We propose to use instead the log-normal distribution (Aitcheson and Brown 1957). For some empirical applications see: Champernowne (1953), Cootner (1967), Granger and Morgenstern (1963), Tintner and Patel (1966). On the other hand, there is the possibility that Pareto distribution might be more appropriate (Mandelbrot 1960, Simon 1957, Steindl 1965). This would create a number of mathematical difficulties since these distributions have very thick tails and in general infinite variances (Feller 1966).

The proposal to introduce stochastic methods into economics can, however, be emphasized by contemplating the development of operations research. Operations research, in our opinion, is nothing else but the econometrics of the enterprise, both private and public enterprise. As a matter of fact, some of the most important contributions to operations research have come out of the nationalized French industries (Massé 1959, Lesourne 1960). The Russian contribution is also important (Tintner and Fels 1967, Zauberman 1967).

The book by Bharucha-Reid (1960) is remarkable by giving a very broad survey of the application of the theory of Markov processes in many fields. Economics is prominent here by its absence. But many interesting applications of stochastic processes to biology, physics, astronomy, astrophysics, and chemistry are given. The survey of the applications of stochastic processes in operations research deals with the theory of queues. Here Bharucha-Reid treats telephone traffic and servicing of machines. Similar methods are of course important for inventory theory (Arrow *et al.* 1962). Stochastic methods have also been utilized by Holt *et al.* (1969) for economic planning in the private enterprise: they deal with production, inventories, and the workforce.

For further attempts to use stochastic models in management science see: Arrow *et al.* (1962), Cootner (1967), Lesourne (1960), Massé (1959), Murphy (1965), Sengupta (1967), Weingartner (1967).

The powerful methods of modern information theory, related to the theory of stochastic processes, have been used in the analysis of economic problems in Theil (1967).

In a recent survey (Tintner 1969) the author has tried to point out the possibility of using the modern methods of mathematical control theory in our field. See also Bellman (1957, 1967), Whittle (1963).

Probabilistic considerations are not exactly foreign to modern economics. If we consider size distributions (Steindl 1965) we realize that these problems are really very old. They can be traced to the famous Pareto distribution of incomes and the voluminous literature concerned with these problems. Unfortunately, these ideas have never been well integrated into the main body of economic theory.

But the application of stochastic processes in economics faces still formidable difficulties. It is doubtful if the theory of evolutionary processes is well enough developed for it to be feasible to apply these methods to problems of economic development. Statistical methods applicable to the type of processes we are considering are virtually non-existent in the case of small samples and even large sample methods (which do not seem to be particularly applicable in economics, where we frequently have a few observations) are relatively scarce and almost entirely confined to stationary processes (Grenander and Rosenblatt 1957, Hannan 1960). In economic language, they might be applicable to seasonal fluctuations and perhaps the business cycle but leave us almost helpless to deal with problems of the trend (economic development). It will take a great deal of hard work and mathematical ingenuity to develop more adequate statistical methods in time series analysis.

There is moreover a fundamental challenge which has been put forward forcefully by Mandelbrot (1963). It is suggested on the basis of some empirical evidence connected with commodity prices that the distributions involved may belong to the family of stable divisible distributions (Feller 1966, p. 531). If this is the case, we are typically dealing with distributions, which have been widely used for approximating the income distribution, at least for relatively high incomes.

If Mandelbrot is right, this would indeed create a very difficult situation in economic statistics. Let us note that most biological and physical applications utilize the normal distribution and most applications in operations research utilize the Poisson distribution or some of its variants. All these distributions, and also the lognormal distribution, have of course finite variances. Hence, least squares methods and related methods have some desirable properties. The statistical problems connected with the Pareto and similar distributions are entirely different and new methods of dealing with problems of estimation, confidence, and fiducial limits, test of hypotheses, etc., seem to be called for. Perhaps we might have to utilize nonparametric methods in this field.

Most econometricians probably think that the use of normal distribution might be justified (in a fashion) by the appeal to a kind of central limit theorem. This is indeed true for a great variety of statistical problems and investigations have shown that traditional statistical methods are relatively robust. But this robustness and general adequacy of traditional statistical methods might ultimately prove an illusion. It is, e.g., easy to show that if we are sampling from a normal distribution the median is relatively inefficient compared with the arithmetic mean: if we have a random sample of 100 items, it would take a sample of 157 items in order to obtain the same accuracy with the sample median as with the sample mean, if we measure accuracy by the variance.

This is true enough as long as the population from which we sample is normal. But suppose we sample from the Cauchy distribution, then it is well known that the distribution of the sample mean is exactly the same as the distribution of each individual item in the sample. In this (we concede: extreme) case we gain nothing by computing the arithmetic mean of the sample. We might just as well have picked out one of the items in our sample at random.

If probabilistic considerations of the type discussed might make us sceptical about our statistical procedures, they are reinforced by the work of Basmann (1961). Econometric models are unfortunately not based upon large samples. It is extremely difficult to derive small sample distributions of econometric estimates. Basmann has succeeded in doing so and has discovered that, even if our errors or deviations have normal distributions, the distribution of econometric estimates is very complicated. But they are related to the Cauchy distribution and have infinite variances. Here Mandelbrot gets support from a statistician with extreme classical prejudices. The work of Basmann shows that even if we start with (in my opinion rather unrealistic) classical assumptions of normality, we might with our empirical econometric estimates end up with random variables with infinite variances. These variables belong again to the family studied by Mandelbrot.

Having presented the economic statistician and econometrician with some reflections about the way in which more useful ideas might be introduced into economic statistics, we now turn to the concern of the mathematical economist. In contradiction to many other social sciences, economics, especially mathematical economics, has reached a certain maturity (Tintner 1968). Our times have seen a certain decline of the neo-classical point of view (Fels and Tintner 1967) but this has been more than compensated by the rise of linear methods, e.g. linear programming, activity analysis, input-output analysis, and related methods. With game theory economics has for the first time achieved a model which was not derived by analogy with the natural sciences. Many beautiful theorems have been derived, especially in connection with competitive economic systems. The challenging problem of economic development has been boldly attacked and if the actual theoretical results are still meagre, they might be promising.

Just as nineteenth-century deterministic physics has not in practice been replaced by twentieth-century stochastic physics, but is still used as a valid approximation in the majority of physical problems (especially by engineers), so we might also provisionally retain the somewhat less impressive results of deterministic economic theory, especially mathematical economics. They only have to be reinterpreted as concerning perhaps certain mean values of the economic variables. Also, since it is much less certain that the law of large numbers applies in our field, we might be more cautious than the classical physicist about the validity of our results, even as crude approximations.

2. Stochastic processes applied to economic development

If we consider probability distributions not as unchanging, but possibly evolving in time, we obtain stochastic processes. Stochastic processes may be defined as families of random variables depending upon a parameter (Fisz 1963). A random variable is a (discrete or continuous) variable, which can assume certain given values with definite probabilities. The parameter upon which the families of random variables depend is frequently time. Hence, e.g., we may envisage a normal distribution which can be characterized by just two magnitudes, its population mean (mathematical expectation) and population variance which measures the dispersion about the mean. In elementary probability theory we assume that the probability distribution is fixed, e.g. we may sample from the same normal distribution with (unknown) population mean and variance. Think now of a family of normal distribution where the mean and variance are (e.g. linear) functions of time. We then have a stochastic process, in this particular case, a diffusion process. The statistical problems connected with such stochastic processes are much more difficult than traditional statistics, which concerns itself with fixed given (but unknown) probability distributions. Many problems connected with the statistical treatment of stochastic processes (Bartlett 1962, Fisz 1954) are known under the name of time series analysis (Tintner 1968, Davis 1941).

We propose to follow the example of modern physics and to consider economic phenomena frankly and fundamentally from a stochastic point of view, i.e. to treat economic variables as random variables. A random variable is a variable which can assume given values with definite probabilities. More specifically, we will try to use the theory of stochastic processes in this field. This may, among other things, meet the criticism of Hayek (1952) that with economic phenomena we cannot assume that we are sampling from a static probability distribution, which is fixed for all times. Econometric models also assume sampling from fixed probability distributions. Instead, we will make the assumption that we are dealing with families of probability distributions, which change their form in time. This, as indicated above, can be accomplished by using the theory of stochastic processes.

We might argue that stochastic processes might be used in economics, that we might imitate the physicists, or that a cultural lag of fifty years is long enough. However, we shall see that there are more compelling reasons for advocating the use of stochastic processes in the analysis of economic phenomena.

However, this is by no means an easy matter. Economic time series contain typically trends and irregular cycles. If we confine the use of stochastic processes to stationary processes (Hannan 1960), we start from extremely unrealistic assumptions. A stationary stochastic process is such that its character is not changed by translations in time. Moreover, we preclude ourselves from the analysis of economic phenomena which are connected with economic development. These phenomena were already in the forefront of the concern of the classical school of economics (e.g. Ricardo, Malthus, Marx) and recently economics has for obvious practical and theoretical reasons paid much attention to these phenomena. For an attempt to introduce stochastic factors into evolutionary economic theory, see Haavelmo (1954).

But the theory of evolutionary time series or stochastic processes is not yet very well developed. Especially, we frequently lack statistical methods which would enable us to deal with this type of phenomena (Tintner 1968). We should not overlook the great mathematical and statistical difficulties which make such an approach challenging but also very laborious.

Dynamic econometric systems appear typically as systems of difference equations. A difference equation is an equation which involves the variables (endogenous and predetermined variables) at different points in time. If also random variables enter into a difference equation, we have a stochastic difference equation.

Example 1

A simple stochastic difference equation has been fitted to British data on total industrial production, excluding building, 1700-1939 (Tintner and Thomas 1963, Tintner and Sengupta 1964). Using the idea of stages of economic development, we conclude on the basis of the methodology of Quandt (1958): if we distinguish two stages, the transition occurs in 1834; if we assume three stages, we have 1791 and 1869 as the years of transition; for four stages, the switching points are 1777, 1820, and 1869.

Example 1 may be considered as inspired by the theory of stages of economic growth. A complex set of stochastic difference equations is approximated by a simple stochastic difference equation, which holds however only in a given stage of economic development. These ideas may be of some limited help in studying the history of economic growth, but are evidently not useful for prediction.

A Poisson distribution is one of the simplest statistical distributions. If we are dealing with a Poisson distribution, we have a discrete random variable, which can assume all nonnegative integer values. The mean value (mathematical expectation) and the variance in this case have the same value.

A Poisson process is a stochastic process where the variable in question (x) is characterized by a mean value which is a linear function of time. It may be derived by the following assumption: consider the value of a random variable in a given (small) time interval. Neglecting possibilities which depend upon higher powers of the time interval, we have only two transitions with nonnegligible probabilities: the transition probability from a value x to $x + 1$, which is assumed to be proportional to the time interval in question; and the probability of no change, which is 1 minus this probability. By making the time interval as small as we like, we derive a Poisson process.

Whereas time in a Poisson process is a continuous variable, the state variable x (e.g. national income) takes discrete values. This constitutes an additional difficulty, since the scale of the random variable in question has to be estimated.

Example 2

A Poisson process (pure birth process) has been fitted to Indian data, 1948-62 (Tintner *et al.,* 1964). The mean value of the Poisson variable appears as $78.0385 + 41270 (t - 1947)$. This is also the variance of the process. It is a linear function of time.

Next we consider the possibility that not only time, but also the state variable (e.g. national income) might be continuous. The classical diffusion process assumes a normal distribution, where both the mean and the variance are linear functions of time. For reasons indicated above, this theory cannot be used in economics, because many economically significant magnitudes are intrinsically nonnegative (prices, quantities produced and consumed, national income, etc.). Hence it seems more appropriate to use the lognormal distribution (Aitcheson and Brown 1957). In this case it is not the variable itself, but its logarithm which is normally distributed.

The stochastic process, which corresponds to the diffusion process, is the lognormal diffusion process. In this case the logarithm of the variable in question (e.g. national income) is normally distributed and the logarithm has a mean value (mathematical expectation) and variance, which are linear functions of time.

Hence the variable itself has an exponential trend. Also, the variance of the variable in question is an exponential function of time.

Example 3

A lognormal diffusion process has been fitted to Chilean data (Tintner and Bello 1968) for 1940-64. Real national income in Chile then appears as lognormally distributed, i.e. its logarithms follows the normal distribution. Then the logarithm of real national income is a normal variable with mean 0.03648 $(t - 1939)$ and variance: 0.00170965 $(t - 1939)$. One should observe that both the mean and variance of the logarithm of national income are linear functions of time.

3. Stochastic programming in economic planning

The method of linear programming is now generally used in economics and operations research (Beckman 1968, Bellman 1957, Dantzig 1963, Fels and Tintner 1966, Kantorovich 1963, Kornai 1967, Nemchinov 1964, Wagner 1969, Zauberman 1967). It consists in maximizing (or minimizing) a linear function of the activities (the objective function) under conditions, which are linear inequalities.

This method appears to us unrealistic, if applied to a concrete economic problem. It assumes that all the data involved, i.e. the coefficients of the objective function and the constants involved in the inequalities, are known (sure) numbers. Whatever may be the case in other applications, this assumption is very unrealistic in economics and operations research. Our data are not such that errors of observations, etc., are absent.

Instead of treating the data in a linear programme as given, it seems more realistic to consider them as random variables, whose joint distribution is known or at least can be estimated. Then our problem becomes a stochastic linear programming problem. See: Dantzig 1963, Fels and

Tintner 1966, Faber 1970, Massé 1959, Lesourne 1960, Tintner and Sengupta 1964, 1972, Wagner 1969.

We can look at problems of stochastic programming from two different points of view: (1) the passive approach tries to estimate the distribution of the objective function. Even under the most convenient assumptions, this can only be done by numerical methods. In planning, this method would be useful if we compare two different plans, e.g. planning in India and Egypt. See also Bereanu 1967, Sengupta *et al.* 1963, Tintner and Sengupta 1972.

More relevant seems to be the second approach: (2) active stochastic linear programming. Here we take the fundamental planning situation as given and concentrate on the allocation of resources, which are the control variables, actually under the control of the planner. Again, except in the simplest situations, results can only be computed by using numerical approximations.

For alternative approaches to stochastic programming, see also: Dantzig 1963, Charnes and Cooper 1959, Wagner 1969.

Example 4

We consider data given by the UAR First Five-Year Plan, 1960-5 (Tintner and Ferghali 1967). Assuming the supply of capital and the total labour force as given, we consider the output-input coefficients in the agricultural sector and the industrial sector as independent normally distributed variables, whose means and variances are estimated on the basis of empirical data. We consider five different policies, i.e. allocation of labour and capital to industry and agriculture. Then it is possible to approximate the distribution of the objective function, i.e. the value of total output (agricultural output plus industrial output) in the last year of a five-year plan by a normal distribution. These normal distributions are approximated by numerical methods for each of the five different policies, i.e. allocations.

The mean, standard deviation, and lower 5 per cent probability level are given.

Following statistical practice, we assumed in Example 4 normal distributions. But for reasons indicated above, this seems not very realistic. Hence, in the following Example 5, we have used distributions where the variables in question cannot assume negative values.

Example 5

Consider a stochastic generalization of the two-sector Mahalanobis

(1955) planning model for a five-year plan in India. Assume further that the marginal output-investment coefficients for the consumption and investment industries are independent random variables with empirically determined gamma distributions (Tintner and Sengupta 1964). Making our decision variable L_i, the proportion of new investment devoted to the investment industry we derive the following characteristics for the distribution of the national income in the last year of a five-year plan in this dynamic model:

TABLE 1

| | L_i | | |
	1/3	1/2	2/3
Mathematical expectation	180.10	174.20	166.46
Lower 5% point	138.94	142.10	143.89
Mode	160.83	157.31	159.89

The distribution of the objective function may be approximated by a beta distribution. We see that the present policy of the Indian government ($L_i = 1/3$) is preferable from the point of view of the mathematical expectation and the mode. But if the criterion is the best which can be attained with 95 per cent probability, $L_i = 2/3$.

Example 6

Using the same data as in Example 5, Tintner and Raghavan (1970) considered the possibility of varying the allocation of new investment over the years of the five-year plan.

The highest mean value of the national income in the last year of a five-year plan is achieved, if $L_i(1) = 1/3, L_i(2) = 1/3, L_i(3) = 1/4, L_i(4) = 1/5$. $L_i(5) = 1/10$, where $L_i(x)$ is the allocation of new investment to the investment industry in year x of the five-year plan. This policy also maximizes the mode and the lower 5 per cent probability point. On the other hand, the coefficient of variation (standard deviation divided by the mean) is minimized by the following policy: $L_i(x) = 2/3, x = 1,2,3,4,5$.

We should note the limitations of this model. It is essentially the simplest possible version of the Mahalanobis (1955) planning model and distinguishes only two sectors. The estimation of the distribution of the marginal coefficient is based upon 16 observed values. The distributions in question are derived by numerical methods and can only be considered pretty crude approximations. Hence, from the point of view of economic policy, these results are only suggestive and should perhaps not be taken too seriously.

They show, however, that it is at least in principle possible to introduce stochastic elements into planning (Tintner 1960, 1971). Our example also shows what should be obvious: The best economic policy in planning depends upon the criterion adopted.

In both examples we get different results if we maximize the conventional measures of success, mean value and mode, or the lower 5 per cent point (Example 5) or minimize the coefficient of variability (Example 6).

4. Stochastic control theory applied to economic policy

Control theory has recently been used extensively for the treatment of dynamic economic problems (Bellman 1967, Intrilligator 1971). However, for reasons indicated above, deterministic control methods seem to be poorly adapted for dealing with concrete economic problems, which always seem to involve stochastic elements.

Hence we may tentatively utilize stochastic control theory. See Aoki 1967, Astrom 1970, Dreyfus 1968, Kushner 1971, Tintner 1969.

Up to now, we have only considered the possible representation of economic time series as stochastic processes. But for the purposes of economic policy it is important to introduce policy variables. Hence, we will give some examples of stochastic processes (families of random variables), which depend upon certain policy variables. These are then our control variables.

In the following Examples 7, 8, 9 we show how the idea of a lognormal diffusion process can be (tentatively) used for the solution of certain problems of economic policy, if control variables are introduced. We should, however, consider the limitations of these models: the lognormal diffusion process can at best be considered a pretty crude approximation of a much more complicated stochastic process which underlies the empirical economic data. Also, we have introduced the policy (control) variables in a very simple fashion into our models.

Example 7

Fitting a lognormal diffusion process to India data 1948-61 (Tintner and Patel 1965) we took also the influence of government expenditure into account. The mean value of the logarithm of Indian real national income appears as

$$0.01118(t - 1947) + 0.001623 \sum_{i = 1948}^{t} G_i,$$

where G_i is government expenditure in year i. This is our control variable. The variance of the logarithm of real Indian national income is then estimated as $0.005494 (t - 1947)$. This model enables us to estimate future real national income in India by making hypotheses about future government expenditure for the period 1965-71.

Example 8

A lognormal diffusion process has been fitted to Indian data (Tintner and Patel 1966). Using data for 1951-64, we obtain the following results: the mean value of the logarithm of real per capita agricultural production in India appears as a linear function of time and of our control variable, the sum of real per capita government expenditure on agriculture in India, lagged three years. The variance of the logarithm of real per capita agricultural production in India appears as a linear function of time. With the help of our estimates, we are able to predict real per capita agricultural production in India under various hypotheses about future real per capita government expenditure on agriculture.

Example 9

Indian data from the period 1951-64 are used in order to estimate lognormal diffusion processes for the following crops (Tintner and Patel 1969): wheat, rice, and sugar cane. The resulting exponential trends are extrapolated for the following years up to 1976. The yields per hectare for rice, wheat, and sugar cane are also considered as results of a stochastic process, which depends upon the proportion of the area irrigated under the crop to total area under the crop. This is our control variable. Again, the results are extrapolated under four different hypotheses about irrigation up to 1976. Finally, the yield per hectare of wheat is considered as a stochastic process which depends upon the proportion of area irrigated and also upon the change of the amount of nitrogeneous fertilizer used per hectare. Here we have two control variables. Again, the results are extrapolated under four different hypotheses about change of irrigation and use of fertilizer. The predictions cover the period 1964-76.

Example 10

Using Indian data from the period 1951-64 (Tintner 1969), we set up a stochastic model for the development of Indian agriculture (real per capita agricultural production). Using real per capita government expenditure on agriculture in India lagged four years as our control variable, we are able to determine the policy which is optimal in this sense: it minimizes government expenditure and at the same time maximizes real per capita agricultural production in India for a given year.

In this model we replace a stochastic difference equation derived empirically from the Indian data by corresponding stochastic differential equation. This involves again the control variable (real per capita government expenditure on Indian agriculture lagged by four years). The policy assumed implies that we minimize at the same time the integral of the square of the control variable over the planning period and maximize the state variable (real per capita agricultural production) for the terminal year of the planning period. Using the methods of dynamic programming. (Bellman 1957), it is possible to derive policies which are optimal in this sense. However, the results seem to be quite unrealistic, as far as the actual agricultural policy in India is concerned.

References

AITCHESON, J. / J. A. BROWN (1957). *The log-normal distribution.* Cambridge UP.
AOKI, M. (1967). *Optimization of stochastic systems.* New York, Academic Press.
ARROW, K. J. *et al.*, eds. (1962). *Studies in applied probability and management science.* Stanford UP.
ASTROM, K. J. (1970). *Introduction to stochastic control theory.* New York, Academic Press.
BARTLETT, M. S. (1955). *An introduction to stochastic processes.* Cambridge UP.
BASMANN, R. L. (1961). A note on the exact finite sample frequency functions of generalized classical linear estimators in two leading overidentified cases. *J. Amer. Statist. Soc.,* 56, pp. 619-36
BECKMANN, M. J. (1968). *Dynamic programming of economic decisions.* New York, Springer
BELLMAN, R. (1957). *Dynamic programming.* Princeton UP.
—— (1967). *Introduction to the mathematical theory of control processes.* New York, Academic Press.
BEREANU, B. (1967). On stochastic linear programming. *Zeitschr. für Wahrscheinlichkeitstheorie,* 8, pp. 148-52
BHARUCHA-REID, A. T. (1960). *Elements of Markov processes and applications.* New York, McGraw-Hill.
BORCH, K. H. (1968). *The economics of uncertainty.* Princeton UP.
BUCY, R. S. / P. D. JOSEPH (1968). *Filtering for stochastic processes with applications to guidance.* New York, Interscience.
CHAMPERNOWNE, G. D. (1953). A model of income distribution. *Econ. J.* 63, pp. 313-51

CHARNES, A. / W. W. COOPER (1959). Chance constrained programming. *Management Science*, 6, pp. 73-9

COOTNER, O. H., ed. (1967). *The random character of stock market prices.* Rev. ed. Cambridge, Mass. MIT Press.

DANTZIG, G. B. (1963). *Linear programming and extensions.* Princeton UP.

DAVIS, H. T. (1941). *The analysis of economic time series.* Bloomington, Indiana, Principia.

DREYFUS, S. E. (1968). Introduction to stochastic optimization and control, in H. F. Karreman, ed., *Stochastic optimization and control.* New York, Wiley, pp. 3-24.

FABER, M. M. (1970). *Stochastisches Programmieren.* Wuerzburg, Physica.

FELLER, W. (1968). *An introduction to probability theory and its applications.* 3rd ed. vol. I, New York, Wiley.

—— (1966). *An introduction to probability theory and its applications.* vol. II, New York, Wiley.

FELS, E. / G. TINTNER (1966). *Methodik der wirtschaftswissenschaftlichen Arbeitsmethoden.* Munich, Oldenbourg.

FISZ, M. (1963). *Probability theory and mathematical statistics.* 3rd ed. New York, Wiley.

GRANGER, C. W. / O. MORGENSTERN (1963). Spectral analysis of New York stock exchange prices. *Kyklos*, 16, pp. 1-27

GRENANDER, W. / M. ROSENBLATT (1957). *Statistical analysis of stationary time series.* New York, Wiley

HAAVELMO, T. (1954). *A study in the theory of economic evolution.* Amsterdam, North Holland.

HANNAN, E. J. (1960). *Time series analysis.* London, Methuen.

HAUPTMANN, H. (1970). Schaetz und Kontolltheorie. Berlin, Springer.

HAYEK, F. A. (1952). The counterrevolution of science. Glencoe, Ill., Free Press.

HOLT, C. C. *et al.* (1960). *Planning, production, inventories and work force.* Englewood Cliffs, NJ, Prentice Hall.

INTRILLIGATOR, M. D. (1971). *Mathematical optimization and economic theory.* Englewood Cliffs, NJ, Prentice Hall.

KANTOROVICH, L. V. (1963). *Calcul économique et utilisation des resources.* Paris, Dunod.

KOOPMANS, T. C. (1957). *Three essays on the state of economic science.* New York, McGraw-Hill.

KORNAI, J. (1967). *Mathematical planning of structural decisions.* Amsterdam, North Holland.

KUSHNER, H. (1971). *Introduction to stochastic control.* New York, Holt, Rinehart & Winston.

LESOURNE, J. (1960). *Techniques économiques et gestion industrielle.* Paris, Dunod.

MAHALANOBIS, P. C. (1955). The approach of operational research to planning. *Sankhya*, 16, pp. 3-130.

MANDELBROT, B. (1963). The variation of speculative prices. *J. of Business*, 36, pp. 394-419.

MASSÉ, P. (1959). *Le choix des investissements.* Paris, Dunod.

MOOD, A. M. / F. A. GRAYBILL (1950). *Introduction to the theory of statistics.* 2nd ed. New York, McGraw-Hill.

MUKERJEE, V., *et al.* (1965). A generalized Poisson process for the explanation of economic development with applications to Indian data. *Arthaniti*, 8, pp. 1-9.

MURPHY, R. E. (1965). Adaptive processes in economic systems. New York, Academic Press.

NEMCHINOV, V. S., ed. (1964). *The use of mathematics in economics.* Cambridge, Mass., MIT Press.

PRAIS, S. J. / H. S. HOUTHAKKER (1955). *The analysis of family budgets.* Cambridge UP.

QUANDT, R. E. (1958). The estimation of parameters of a linear regression system obeying two different regimes, *J. Amer. Statist. Ass.,* 53, pp. 873-80.

SENGUPTA, J. K. / G. TINTNER (1966). An approach to a stochastic theory of economic development and fluctuations, in *Problems of economic development and planning; essays in honor of Michael Kalecki.* Warsaw: PWN Polish Scientific Publishers, pp. 373-391.

—— *et al.* (1963). On some theorems of stochastic linear programming with applications. *Management Science,* 10, pp. 143-59.

SENGUPTA, S. S. (1967). *Operations research in sellers competition.* New York, Wiley.

SIMON, H. A. (1957). *Models of man.* New York, Wiley.

STEINDL, J. (1965). *Random processes and the growth of firms.* New York, Hafner.

THEIL, H. (1967). *Economics and information theory.* Amsterdam, North Holland.

TINTNER, G. (1960). The use of stochastic linear programming in planning. *Indian Econ. R.,* col. 5, pp. 159 ff

—— (1966). Some thoughts about the state of econometrics, in S. R. Krupp, ed., *The structure of economic science.* Englewood Cliffs, NJ, Prentice-Hall, pp. 114-28

—— (1968). Time series (general), in D. L. Sills, ed., *International encyclopedia of the social sciences.* New York, Macmillan, XVI, pp. 47-59

—— (1968). *Methodology of mathematical economics and econometrics.* Chicago UP.

—— (1969). What does control theory have to offer? *Amer. J. Agric. Economics.* 51, pp. 383-93

—— (1971). Systematic planning and decision models, in E. O. Heady, ed., *Economic models and quantitative methods for decisions and planning in agriculture.* Ames, Iowa State UP.

—— / I. BELLO (1968). Aplicación de un proceso de difusión logarítmico-normal al crecimiento económico de Chile. *Trabajos de estadística,* 19, pp. 83-97

—— / S. A. FERGHALI (1967). The application of stochastic programming to the UAR first five year plan. *Kyklos,* 20, pp. 749-58

—— / E. FELS (1967). Mathematical economics in the Soviet Union. *Communist Affairs,* 5/5, pp. 3-8

—— / R. NARAYANAN (1966). A multidimensional stochastic process for the explanation of economic development. *Metrika,* 11, pp. 85-90

—— / M. PATEL (1969). A lognormal diffusion process applied to the growth of yields of some agricultural crops in India. *J. Development Stud.,* 6, pp. 49-57

—— / R. C. PATEL (1965). A lognormal diffusion process applied to the economic development of India. *Indian Econ. J.,* 13, pp. 465-74

—— / R. C. PATEL (1966). Lognormal diffusion process applied to the development of Indian agriculture with some considerations on economic policy. *J. Indian Soc. Agric. Statist.,* 18, pp. 36-44

—— / N. S. RAGHAVAN (1970). Stochastic linear programming applied to a dynamic programming model for India. *Economia internazionale,* 23, pp. 3-15

TINTNER, G./J. K. SENGUPTA (1964). Stochastic linear programming and
        its application to economic planning, in *Political economy and econo-
        metrics; essays in Honor of Oskar Lange.* Warsaw, PWN, pp. 601–618.
—— / J. K. SENGUPTA (1972). *Stochastic economics.* New York, Academic
        Press.
—— / J. K. SENGUPTA / E. J. THOMAS (1966): Applications to the theory of
        stochastic processes to economic development, in I. Adelman / E.
        Thorbecke, eds., *The theory and design of economic development.*
        Baltimore, John Hopkins Press, pp. 99-110.
—— / E. J. THOMAS (1963). Un modèle stochastique de developement écono-
        mique avec application à l'industrie anglaise. *R. d'Econ. Politique,* 73,
        pp. 143-47
WAGNER, H. M. (1969). *Principles of operations research.* Englewood Cliffs, NJ,
        Prentice Hall.
WEINGARTNER, H. M. (1967). *Mathematical programming and the analysis of
        capital budgeting problems.* Chicago, Markham.
WHITTLE, P. (1963). *Prediction and regulation.* London, English UP.
ZAUBERMAN, A. (1967): *Aspects of planometrics.* New Haven, Yale UP.

II THE ASSIMILATION OF STOCHASTIC METHODOLOGY IN SOVIET THEORY

by Alfred Zauberman

(1)   On the acceptable broad definition, a system is stochastic if it is a
variable one, subject to random influence.[1] On this definition an economy,
even under the most intensive planning regime imaginable, constitutes a
stochastic system.

However, the emphasis on the immanently stochastic nature of planning is very new in Soviet and Soviet-influenced theory. For decades the
probabilistic approach was considered to conflict with the accepted deterministic philosophy. In his most recent writing on mathematical planning
Kornai is explicit on this conflict.[2] As he puts it, when following "fatalis-
tic views" the planner becomes a prisoner of his own techniques. For instance, he may detect a trend-line fitting his statistical data and therefrom
take it that this trend reflects a very rigid law that cannot be evaded for
the future. But –

the truth is that all historical laws, tendencies, and trends in the behaviour
of economic systems over time are *stochastic* regularities with greater or
smaller dispersions. The deviations from the mean are at least partly explained by the quality of decision-making: whether they are more or less
clever, or more or less intelligent.[3]

Thus Kornai ascribes the traditional anti-probabilistic stand of the planning theory to a misinterpretation of Marx's historical materialism. While accepting the argument on the logical trap into which Soviet traditional planning theory has got itself, we are inclined to surmise that the axiomatic determinism to some extent must have been, as it were, that theory's intellectual self-defence at a time when handling stochastic phenomena was still so very much underdeveloped.

Note

In Soviet literature the definitional framework for stochastic systems is extensively elaborated in Pugachev.[4] The system is stochastic — as is intuitively clear — when any signal $x \in X$ relates to a given distribution in the space of output signals Y. The behaviour of the stochastic system is determined, in Pugachev, by the transitional (conditional) probability $\mu(E \mid x)$ of the output signal belonging to the set $E \subset Y$ for a given input signal $x \in X$; this $\mu(.)$ is conceived as the system's "decision function". For each $x \in X$ the function represents normed measure, determined over some σ-algebra, $\mathscr{B}$, of sets of the Y space; and for every set $E \in \mathscr{B}$ it measures, with respect to some σ-algebra $\mathscr{A}$ of the X space, the function of the variable x. This definitional specification is extended to a join of stochastic systems which thus is itself stochastic.

A framework constructed in this fashion forms, in Pugachev, the basis of what is termed the "structural approach" to the investigation of complex systems. These are treated as components of a join. When each component's statistical properties are determined, those of the system as a whole become thereby determined too. (See also Note to sect. 7.)

(2) Stochastic modelling in general is a product of rather young vintage. It does not go back farther than Tinbergen's[5] celebrated work of the 1930s, paving the way to the shift from the deterministic to the stochastic mode in formalizing the dynamics in difference-equation terms. As Wold (whose own contribution to the field is so rich) notes, this transition means a shift towards explicitness of the residual discrepancy between the hypothetical model on the one hand and observation on the other: still in Wold's terms,[6] that means resorting to "*eo ipso* predictors" (conditional expectations subject to the residual disturbance). This forms the structural basis of his own contribution to the methodology of the build-up of the causal-chain system. Its core is the extrapolation device working by means of an iterative-substitution chain, from period to period and from variable to variable. We shall see how fundamentally engrained the method is in contemporary stochastic plan-modelling.

Two factors may be seen as strengthening the trend towards the probabilistic approach in Soviet planning theory. One is that the progressing formalization of this theory — and practice — leads to "self-revelation" of
assumptions: the stochastic element is naturally one of them. The second
one, logically interrelated, is that planning in an increasingly complex environment adds to risk and uncertainty. (The strategy precepts offered for
dynamic planning in Kantorovich-Makarov[7] are instructive from this angle.
These are that in technological choice-making, *ceteris paribus*, preference
should be accorded to mixed strategy; and that, as against more specialized
ones, "basic" branches and universal techniques should be given preference
— preference in the sense that for the latter, lower levels of precision would
be acceptable. The argument is that, as compared with the former, they are
to a lesser degree affected by risk and uncertainty. The easy objection that
these precepts, more likely than not, tend to be technologically regressive,
only underlines the dilemma confronted by the dynamic planner.)

(3)   When it comes to the optimization of the plan-construct, when the
theoretician of planning turns to the stochastic programming apparatus, he
finds himself in an area which is still largely under the pioneering impact of
the Tintner and Dantzig schools.

Very broadly, the main approaches in programming for situations affected by risk and uncertainty can be classified as those of stochastic programming in a strict sense, and of chance-constrained programming
(Dantzig-Madansky)[8].

In the accepted conception, the standard (linear) plan problem is considered to be stochastic in a strict sense if only probability distribution is
known with regard to the system of constraints or the objective function.

Write the standard statement of the plan programme:

$$\text{maximum } z = c'x \text{ subject to } Ax \leqslant b \text{ with } x \leqslant 0.$$

Under the by now classical stochastic, in the strict sense, approach — as
designed by Tintner and his associates[9] and developed by others — both
the matrix A and the vectors b and c will appear as some random variables
with a known probability distribution $P(A,b,c)$. Under the chance-constrained programming, as originated by Charnes and Cooper,[10] the con-
dition $Ax \leqslant b$ is replaced by $P(Ax \leqslant b) \geqslant \alpha$ where the last term — a
column vector with elements $0 \leqslant \alpha \leqslant 1$ — specifies the postulated set of
constraints which are probability measures of admissibility of constraint
violations. An important extension of the Charnes-Cooper type chance-

constrained system is owed to Kataoka's model[11] concerned with the distribution of the objective function and probabilistic constraints. (In the original construct the focus was on the problem of the fluctuating and uncertain values of coefficients, with less concern about the criterion functions.)

Of the two versions of the Tintner-Sengupta[12] type of stochastic linear programming, in one – the passive or "wait and see" version – the probability distribution of the objective function is derived explicitly or by numerical approximation, and the decision rules rest on some of its features. As against this in the other, the active or the "here and now" version, we have additional variables directly allocating resources to activities. In this approach – as formulated from the angle of the planning theory – we have a matrix of the planner's instrument variables

$$U = [u_{ij}]$$

$$\text{(where } 0 \leqslant u_{ji} \leqslant 1; \sum_{j} ij = 1\text{),}$$

the vector x describing the planner's targets forming the diagonal of a diagonal matrix M, and a diagonal matrix C with elements of $(c + y)$ in the diagonal. In otherwise familiar notation the plan programme then has the form

$$F = (a + \gamma) x \to \max$$

subject to $(B + b)X < C.U$. The feature of the "active" variant, then, is that the probability distribution of the F is derived and the u_{ij} are chosen so as to optimize the risk-preference functional which depends on the F and the U. (It has been argued that in so far as the characteristic of the active approach is the truncation of the passive-approach maximand, the chance-constrained programme may be looked upon as a special type of the former.)

The macro-planning theory will naturally find attractive the multi-stage type of stochastic programming: it does correspond to the realities of the planner's work in trying to formulate an optimal initial-stage decision plus optimal strategy rules for further stages and in resorting to some truncation when setting the plan horizon. Some chance-constrained construct would thus be particularly congenial to him. (Note that the stochastic linear programming problems are usually formulated as single-stage static problems: programming under uncertainty of the original kind is essentially a two-stage constraint: and under the chance-constrained approach one accepts sub-optimization resting on a subset of feasible decision-rules.) Thus the procedure outlined in Charnes-Dreze-Miller[13] well reflects the logic of the planner's procedures inasmuch as it handles the truncation of the many-stage or infinite-stage problem and replaces it by some more manageable "proximate" one; and it does so in its handling of the terminal conditions, whether by prescribing the terminal values of some of the variables and assigning some utilities to them, or by inferring properties of these conditions which could ensure consistence with the original problem's optimal solution. Specifically the Soviet planning theory finds itself facing a familiar issue in the Charnes-Dreze-Miller formulation of the rule for setting the horizon (at the time-point where information pertaining to it and going beyond it reveals itself irrelevant for the purpose of defining the optimal first-stage decisions). We have here in mind in particular the Kantorovich-Makarov[14] strategy recommendation for adopting a distant horizon, derived from Romanovskiy's analysis of the asymptotic behaviour of dynamic-programming processes.

(4)   To give an example of an iterative solution variant for a chance-constrained linear-programming type of problem we may quote — from Soviet literature — the Bulavskiy model[15] of the form:

Let $P(Ax > b > \beta)$ and describe the set of x satisfying this condition for all b and being non negative, as S_β with the tolerance level:

$$S_\beta = (x \mid x \geqslant 0, P(Ax \geqslant b) \geqslant \beta$$

the problem is then: min $c'x$ with $x \in S_\beta$.

Consider cases where components of b are independent, with normal distribution over some interval, that is

$$P\{b_i < x\} = \begin{cases} 0, \text{ if } x \leqslant -h_i \\[3mm] \int_{-h_i}^{x} \dfrac{dx}{2h_i} = \dfrac{x+h_i}{2h_i} \quad -h_i \leqslant x \leqslant h_i \\[3mm] 1, \text{ if } x > h_i . \end{cases}$$

From the independence of the vector components

$$P\{Ax \geqslant b\} = P\left\{b \leqslant Ax\right\} = \prod_{i=1}^{m} P\left\{b_i \leqslant (Ax)_i\right\}$$

Assume $Eb < 0)$ then

$$P\{b_i \leqslant (Ax)_i\} = \begin{cases} \dfrac{(Ax)_i + h_i}{2h_i}, & -h_i \leqslant (Ax)_i \leqslant h_i \\ 1, \text{ if } (Ax)_i > h_i \end{cases}$$

Denote

$$\frac{(Ax)_i + h_i}{2h_i} = y_i$$

and

$$\bar{y} = \begin{cases} y_i, 0 \leqslant y_i \leqslant 1, \\ 1, y_i > 1. \end{cases}$$

The problem then takes the form

$$\prod_{i=1}^{m} \bar{y}_i(x) \geqslant \beta,$$

$$x \geqslant 0,$$
$$\min c'x$$

— it is one of minimizing a linear function over a convex set. For its solution the following modification of the gradient method is adopted (assuming $\bar{b}_i = 0$). Let x^0 be a feasible vector,

$$\prod \begin{matrix} x^0 \geqslant 0, \\ \bar{y}_i(x^0) > \beta. \end{matrix}$$

Introduce two sets of indices,

$$I_1^0 = \{i : y_i(x^0) > 1 \quad \text{or} \quad y_i(x^0) = 1 \text{ with } (Ac')_i \leqslant 0\},$$

$$I_2^0 = \{i : y_i(x^0) < 1 \quad \text{or} \quad y_i(x^0) = 1 \text{ with } (Ac')_i > 0\}$$

and determine the movement along the gradient

$$x = x^0 - \mu c' ; \mu > 0.$$

When the boundary between the points x^0 and x^1 is crossed we find the root of the equation ($*$), over the interval $(0,\bar{\mu},)$

$$\prod_{i \in I_2^0} \frac{(Ax^0)_i + h_i - z_i(Ac')_i}{2h_i} = \beta_i{}^x$$

The boundary point $x = x^0 - zc'$ lies on the surface

$$\prod_{i \in I_2^0} y_i(x) = \beta,$$

and also the surface of the type

$$\prod_{i \in I_2^0 \, Uv} y_i(x) = \beta$$

where the v is an arbitrary subset of the set I

$$I = \left\{ i : y_i(x^0) = 1, (Ac')_i = 0 \right\}.$$

The boundary limit $x^{k+1} = x^k - zc'$ (where z is the root of the equation ($*$)) lies on the surface

$$F_1(x) = 0, F_2(x) = 0, \ldots F_k(x) = 0$$

determined by the equations above. Find the external normal to these surfaces

$$n_r = (- \delta F_r/\delta x_1 \ldots, - \delta F_r/\delta x_n)$$

and normalize them and the vector c'. The vector z is found from conditions

$$(n_r, z) \leqslant 0; \quad r = 1, 2, \ldots, R,$$

$$\| z \| \leqslant 1$$

$$\max (- c', z).$$

In Bulavskiy the equivalent problem is: From among vectors z satisfying $(-n_r, z) \geq 0, |r| = 1, 2, \ldots, R$, find that for which

$$\| z - (-c') \| = \min.$$

The set r and the vector $y = \{y^i\}_{i \epsilon \{r\}}$ will be said to form a base of the vector $-c'$ if

(1) $$y^i = 0 \text{ with } i \epsilon \{r\} - \{\bar{r}\} ;$$

(2) $$(-n^i, -c' + \sum_{r \epsilon \{r\}} y^r(-n^r)) = 0 \text{ with } i \epsilon \{r\} ;$$

(3) $$y^i > 0 \text{ with } i \epsilon \{\bar{r}\};$$

(4) the system of vectors n_i for $i \epsilon \{\bar{r}\}$ is linearly independent.

The Bulavskiy tenet is then that if the set r and the vector y form the base with respect to the vector $-c'$ and if the vector

$$z = -c' + \sum_{r \epsilon \{r\}} y^r(-n^r)$$

satisfies the constraint system of the problem last stated, the z solves the problem. (A procedure is also offered for moving from one base to another and finding the optimal z in a finite number of steps.)

Generally speaking, the decision rules admitted in more recent versions of the chance-constrained model are more acceptable to planning theory than those prevalent in the earlier ones; the zero-order and the linear rules. Of particular interest is the Charnes-Kirby[16] n-period P-model which has admissibility of the class of rules restricted only by the condition of the decision rule for the given period being a function of the random variables of the past periods, while an implicit dependence on future-period random variables results from the coupling nature of the constraints. (Typical is the triangular model wherein each of the n periods generates two new constraints one of the form $P(X_j \geq 0) \geq \beta_j$ and the other coupling the decision rule for the jth period X_j to those of the past.)

The point also accepted in Soviet literature of the subject is that very broadly that class of stochastic programming will commend itself to the planning theory in which the plan problem is not restricted by any aprioristically determined relationships with its conditions' parameters: in other words, models in which the functional dependencies are rather deter-

mined in the course of the solution itself. However, so far the chance-constrained models which satisfy their requirements must depend on particular rather than general algorithms.

Note

The problem of stochastic plan-programming with probabilistic constraints has been investigated *i.a.* by Abramov and Bochkareva[17] when
formulated as min $c^T x$, $P\{Ax \geq b\} \geq \alpha$, $x \geq 0$, where $A = (a_{ij})$ is an
$(m \times n)$ matrix; $c^T = (c_1, \ldots, c_n)$ and $x = (x_1, \ldots, x_n)$ vectors in R^n;
$b = (b_1, \ldots, b_m)$ an m-dimensional random vector with the nonlinear function $F(y) = F(y_1, \ldots, y_m)$; $0 < \alpha < 1$. The problem is equivalent to that of
nonlinear programming min $c^T x$; $Ax - y = 0$; $F(y) = F(y_1, \ldots, y_m) \geq a$;
$x \geq 0$, that is minimization of $c^T x$ over the region D of vectors $(x,y) =$
$(x_1, \ldots, x_n, y_1, \ldots, y_m) \epsilon R^{n+m}$ satisfying these constraints. The problem
investigated is then for what kind distribution functions $F(y)$ the set
$D_\alpha = \{y \in R^m | F(y) \geq \alpha\}$ is convex. (A sufficient condition for convexity
of the set D_α is convexity of $F(y)$: this condition, however, is not met for
most distributions of relevance in practice.) Note definitions: the function
$g(y)$ defined on the convex set $M \subset R^m$ is α-quasiconvex where the set
$S_\alpha = \{y \in M | g(y) \geq a\}$ is convex and A-quasiconvex when $g(y)$ is α-convex
for each $\alpha \in A$ (the α and A being, respectively, a real number and a set of
such numbers). The problem investigated — of convexity of the set D_α — is
tantamount to that of α-convexity of the distribution function $F(y)$ where
the components of the vector b are independent, that is when

$$F(y) = (F_1(y_1) . F_2(y_2) \ldots F_m(y_m)).$$

(5)   There are also some Soviet contributions to the methodology of
handling the "complete" problem (in Wets's[18] sense) which are possibly
applicable to economic problems. Here one might refer to Vereskov's work
(presented as appertaining to "cybernetics" — a pointer to its overlapping
with stochastics in the Soviet rather vague delimitation of the disciplines).[19]

The starting point is the usual formulation: find the nonnegative vector
x satisfying $Ax = d$ and the requirement that for an arbitrary vector b^t —
out of a given set of values of b — there exists a solution for the problem,

$$Ex + Cy^t = b^t \; ; y \geq 0 \; ; (f,y^t) \to y \text{ min.}$$

The vectors y^t are meant to compensate discrepancy between Bx and b^t, while (f,y^t) are meant to form the "penalty" for adjustment of y^t. Then the vector x is selected such as to minimize the expected cost,

$$(c,x) + \sum_{t=1}^{N} Pt\ [\min (f,y^t)] \to \min.$$

Matrices A, B, and C and vectors c, d, and f are known; also values of the random vector b^t and the corresponding probabilities p_t, with $t = 1, \ldots, N$.

The particular case of the complete problem treated (by the two-stage method) is one where the conditions have the form

$$Bt(x + u^t - v^t) = b^t,$$

with the bracketed term and u^t and v^t nonnegative. The problem is complete where each of the sets $\{z \mid B^t z = b^t, z \geqslant 0\}$, $t = 1, \ldots, N$ is nonempty; otherwise no plan is available.

An economic interpretation is given for a Kantorovich problem of investment patterning[20] and a relatively simple path of a solution is outlined.

(6) Of late formalization of the stochastic plan problem in functional spaces has become widely accepted. In this the Soviet student draws his inspiration form Kolmogorov's "fundamentalism". To recall it, the point of departure in his fundamental system was the Lebesgue theories of measure and integration: the analogies between the measure of a set and the probability of an event and between the integral of a function and the mathematical expectation of a random variable. Every situation containing random factors is, in the Kolmogorov system, associated with the probability space – the trio;[21] (1) the abstract space of elementary events; (2) a σ-algebra of its subsets – the sets of events ξ, (3) the measure ($p(E)$), the probability that is of the event E, defined for $E \in \xi$ and satisfying the condition of $p(\Omega)$ equal unity. For a perfect probability space (on the theorem as reworked by Kolmogorov and Gnedenko), it is such that for any real-valued ξ – a measurable function – and any linear set B for which $\{W:g(W)\}$, there is a Borel measurable set $D \in B$ such that $P\{W:g(W) \in D = P, W:g(W) \in B\}$.

Yudin[22] – a leading Soviet protagonist of the search in this direction – maintains that for many stochastic plan-programming problems, a statement in terms of Hilbertian space is more productive than in primary probabilistic ones: that the objective functions of stochastic problems reveal themselves very often as linear or convex functionals in H^n. Thus the mathematical expectation of a linear form appears as a linear functional in H^n

$$L = E(CX) = (C, X)/,$$

and the dispersion of a linear form appears as a convex (downwards) functional:

$$D(CX) = (C_0 X - \overline{CX}, CX - \overline{CX}).$$

An example of a convex programming in Hilbertian space will then be

$$E(C_0 X)^2 + E(CX) \to \min,$$

$$E(AX) - b \leqslant 0,$$

$$E(C_k X)^2 - d_k{}^2 \leqslant 0; k = 1, 2, \ldots, s,$$

where the C's are n-dimensional random vectors; A is an $m \times n$ dimensional matrix with random elements, b an n-dimensional deterministic vector, d_k a deterministic constant. To ensure the existence of the $E(C_k X)^2$, $k = 0$, $1, \ldots, s$ it is required that the components of the random vectors C_k be "almost certainly" some constrained magnitudes. An analogous formulation of the control problem under incomplete information is given the form of a quadratic stochastic programme

$$E(C_0 X)^2 + E(C^0 X) \to \min. \; ; E(C_k X)^2 + E(C^k X) \leqslant b_k; k = 1, \ldots, m.$$

For a numerical method of solution of such and similar problems Yudin recommends a generalization, by Zukhovitskiy-Polyak-Primak,[23] of Zoutendijk's feasible-directions method.[24]

To recollect, this is a gradient method whose features are the special requirements with respect to the fixing of the starting point, and the direction and the length of the step. Particular emphasis is laid on the step being large, as against say the Arrow-Hurwicz short-step gradient procedure. In the algorithm evolved, a finite-dimensional quadratic programming problem is solved for the choice of the feasible direction along which the functional $f_0(x)$ is improved and the step-length is chosen: and as in Zoutendijk, the anti-zigzagging parameter is applied.

We start by adopting the initial plan-vector X_0: we then choose some positive, sufficiently small δ_1 and determine a set of index numbers $i \in I =$

$I(X_0:\delta_1)$ of the functionals $f_i(X)$, which in the X_0 plan either turn into zero or differ from zero by δ_1 at the most

$$I = I(X_0;\delta_1) = \left\{ i \in I \mid -\delta_i \leqslant f_i(X_0) \leqslant 0 \right\}.$$

To improve the initial plan, we then descend from X_0 in some direction $z^{(1)} \in H^n$. Along it, for the continuous convex functions, we will have negative derivatives:

$$\frac{\mathrm{d}}{\mathrm{d}t} f_i(X_0 + tz^{(i)}) \mid t = 0 = (\bar{V}f_i(X_0), z^{(0)}),$$

$$i \in I'(X_0;\delta_i) = I(X_0;\delta_i) \cup \{0\}.$$

Of directions thus characterized we select the one on which the slowest speed of decrease of the functionals will be greatest, i.e. we maximize

$$\min_{i \in I'(X_0;\delta_i)} \mid (\nabla f_i(X_0), z^{(i)} \mid).$$

As a normalization of the usable directions with the view to limiting the area of the fixing of $z^{(1)}$, the $\| z \| \leqslant 1$ is adopted. Then for the choice of $z^{(1)}$ our problem is that of

$$\max_{i \in I'(X_0;\delta_i)} (\nabla f_i(X_0), z^{(i)}) = \min_{\| z \| \leqslant i} \max_{i \in I'(X_0\delta_1)} (\nabla f_i(X_0), z).$$

Of relevance in this is the projection of the vector z on the subspace "stretched" over the vectors $f_i(X_0)$. Hence along the

$$z = \sum_{i \in I'(X_0;\delta_i)} \xi_i \nabla g_i(X_0),$$

the choice of the feasible direction is faced as one choosing some ξ, a feasible finite-dimensional vector, such as to ensure the minimax

$$\min_{\| z \| \leqslant 1} \max_{i \in I'(X_0;\delta_i)} \sum_{j \in I'(X_0;\delta_i)} (\nabla f_i(X_0), \nabla f_j(X_0)) \xi_j.$$

As an auxiliary in fixing the direction of descent a quadratic programming problem is formulated. In the primal the ξ is the minimand subject to

$$\sum_{j \in I'(X_0 ; \delta_i)} h_{ij\,j} \leqslant \xi, \quad i \in I'(X_0 ; \delta_i),$$

$$\| z \| = \| \sum_{i \in I'(X_0 \delta_i)} \xi \, i\nabla f_i(X_0) \| \leqslant i,$$

h_{ij} stands for the scalar product $(f_i(X_0), f_j(X_0))$. The dual — with a quadratic "indicator of quality" and otherwise linear — is written

$$u = \| \sum_{i \in I'(X_0 ; \delta_i)} \zeta_j \, \nabla f_i(X_0) \|^2 = \sum_{ij \in I'(X_0 ; \delta_i)} h_{ij}\zeta_i\zeta_j \to \min,$$

$$\sum_{i \in I'(X_0 ; \delta_i)} \zeta_i = 1,$$

$$\zeta_i \geqslant 0, \quad i \in I'(X_0 ; \delta_i)$$

(the ζ_i denotes components of the optimal-plan problem).

Now the length of the step. Let min u, subject to the constraints of the dual, be some u_1 not greater than δ_1. Then step 1, the t_1, along the $z^{(1)}$ is computed as the least positive root of

$$(\nabla f_0(X_0 + tz^{(i)}), z^{(1)}) = 0,$$

$$f_i(X_0 + tz^{(1)}) = 0, \quad i = 1, \ldots, m.$$

(Where any of these equations has no positive roots, its least positive root is taken to be ∞.) As a new approximation we take

$$X_i = X_0 + t_i z^{(1)}.$$

Then starting from X_1 we posit $\delta_2 = \delta_1$; from this the direction of fastest descent $z^{(2)}$ and the step-length t_2 is determined, and so on, till we arrive at the point X_k with the corresponding value δ_{k+1} such that the dual problem outlined here yields some $U_{K+1} \leqslant \delta_{k+1}$: we posit $\delta'_{k=1} = \delta_{k+1}/2$ and repeat the $(k + 1)$th iteration for δ'_{k+1} and so on.

Note

Yudin is responsible for the idea of what is termed "optimization in the mean", which focuses on a class of a type of situations rather on a single one: it is with a "uni-type situation" that solution modelling is concerned. As a set of the latter, in other words, it defines the region over which the stochastic problem is being defined. Understandably, then, some criterion has to be adopted to give the "optimization in the mean" a sufficient degree of precision. (Yudin has in fact elaborated an applicational regime: it rests on either some a priori statistical principles or "learning processes".)

The methodology (adjusted to stochastic variants of linear and quadratic programming and some particular problems of convex and nonconvex programming) corresponds to the way the economic planner faces his problems — to repeat, as a class of situations, rather than a single situation. And it is with the view to the planners' problems that — in Yudin's rules — algorithmization has to be designed. This would apply in particular in projecting specialized systems of planning and controlling and building up systems operating in ex ante unknown but *statistically stable* conditions.

(7) Yudin[25] has also provided — in the Hilbert-space terms — some generalization of the stochastic programming dual, with one or two noteworthy hints for economic planning. The problem, stated in these terms (H^n), is written

$$\sum_{j=1}^{n} (c_j, x_j) \to \sup,$$

$$\sum_{j=1}^{n} (a_{ij}, x_j) \leqslant b_i; \quad i = 1, 2, \ldots, m,$$

$$\| x_j \| \leqslant d_j; \quad j = 1, 2, \ldots, n,$$

it is being postulated that the set determined by the two conditions contains an interior point and that the problem is "substantially stochastic", meaning that for any $\lambda_1 \geqslant 0, i = 1, \ldots, m$

$$\Delta_j = c_j - \sum_{i=1}^{m} \lambda_i a_{ij} \neq 0; \quad j = 1, 2, \ldots, n,$$

which implies that for each of the random values c_j and a_{ij} are not functionally dependent. For this the dual is proved to be of the simple deterministic convex-programming form:

$$\inf_{\lambda \geqslant 0} \left\{ \sum_{i=1}^{m} \lambda_i b_i + \sum_{j=1}^{n} d_j \left\| c_j - \sum_{i=1}^{m} \lambda_i a_{ij} \right\| \right\}$$

The explicit expressions for the components of the optimal plan of the initial problem obtained is then (with $\Lambda = (\lambda_1, \ldots, \lambda_m)$)

$$x_j^* = \frac{d_j \left(c_j - \sum_{i=1}^{m} \lambda_i{}^* a_{ij} \right)}{\left\| c_j - \sum_{i=1}^{m} \lambda_i{}^* a_{ij} \right\|} = \frac{d_j \Delta_j}{\| \Delta_{j*} \|}$$

where $\Lambda^* = (\lambda_1{}^*, \ldots, \lambda^*{}_m)$ is the optimal plan of the dual problem.

The stochastic programme corresponds to the deterministic linear one:

$$\sum_{j=1}^{n} c_j x_j \rightarrow \max,$$

$$\sum_{j=1}^{n} a_{ij} x_j \leqslant b_i; \quad i = 1, 2, \ldots, m,$$

$$-d_j \leqslant x_j \leqslant d_j; \quad j = 1, 2, \ldots, n,$$

whose solution is relatively more difficult than that of the simple convex programme.[26] Hence the apparent paradox: finding the extremum under the conditions of more limited information was easier than getting the optimal plan with full information on the parameters of both the objective function and constraints.

The common-sense moral is drawn: the approach to the solution of an optimal plan-programme should be the simpler the poorer the information at the planner's disposal. This links up with Yudin's theories of complexity and of approximations (A:T, 5, 1972).

(8)   The concept of "informativeness" (*informatsyonnost*) has been introduced to Soviet writing by Yu. B. Germeyer — i.e. the concept denoting the state of information on the parameters in the problem's conditions. It has been employed by Kaplinskiy and Propoy[27] — in a way resembling that of Kushner — in their inquiries into a stochastic approach to problems of nonlinear programming.

The point of departure is the problem: find the vector $x = \{x^1, \ldots, x^n\}$ which secures (with exactness up to ϵ) $\inf_x f_0(x,b_0)$, subject to $f_j(x,b_j) \leqslant 0$ $(j = 1, \ldots, m)$.

An interesting development is obtained by randomization. The point-of-departure problem turns into that of finding the distribution function $F(x,B)$ yielding

$$\inf_F \int F_0(x,b_0)\,dF(x,B) = \omega$$

$$\text{subject to} \int f_j(x,b_j)dF(x,B) \leqslant 0 \quad (j = 1, \ldots, m)$$

$$F(\infty,B) = F_1(B),$$

where $F_1(B)$ is a given distribution of the parameter B. The solution is the joint distribution function of probabilities $F(x,B)$. Since the distribution of $F_1(B)$ is given, the problem is reducible, on the Bayesian principle, to finding the conditional distribution $F(x|B)$.

The solution procedure is based on the introduction of the Lagrangian function

$$\Phi(x,\lambda,B) = f_0(x,b_0) + \sum_{j=i}^{m} \lambda_j f_j(x,b_j).$$

Where the $f_j(x,b_j)$ is convex the regular problem obviously reduces to finding the saddle-point Lagrangian function in the domain $x \in X$ with non-negative λ. In the case of its nonconvexity — assuming that some continuity conditions are met — the existence of the saddle-point is secured by randomizing the Lagrangian function in the form

$$\Phi(F,G) = \iint [f_0(x,b_0) + \sum_{j=i}^{m} \lambda_j f_j(x,b_j)]\ dF(x,B)dG(\lambda),$$

where $F(x,B)$ is a joint distribution of x and B, and $G(\lambda)$ is the distribution of the $\lambda = (\lambda, \ldots \lambda_m)$ vector. It is assumed that $F(\infty, B) = F_1(B)$, where

$F_1(B)$ is the given distribution of B; it is moreover assumed that $\mu = \int \lambda dG(\lambda) \geqslant 0$; with F and μ satisfying these two assumptions, ultimately we have the two problems

$$\inf_{F} \sup_{\mu} \overline{\Phi}(F,\mu) = \omega_I; \sup_{\mu} \inf_{F} \overline{\Phi}(F,\mu) = \omega_{II}.$$

As a generalization of the point-of-departure problem it is shown that $\omega_{II} = \tilde{\omega}_I$, where $\tilde{\omega}_I$ is the value of the functional of this problem (in the generalized solution above). While the duality relation is satisfied for the deterministic case under convexity only, in the stochastic case it is met without this requirement when randomized strategies are applied. The solution of the point-of-departure programme thus reduced to is the investigation of a pair of dual problems of infinite-dimensional programming. Further, Kaplinskiy and Propoy show the way the solution of a number of stochastic programming problems, in randomized strategies, reduces the infinite-dimensional to a finite-dimensional programme.[28]

Note

The problem of nonlinear transformation of stochastic processes comes up against particularly big obstacles. The general methodology of their investigation in Soviet literature has been treated in several contributions by Skorokhod.[29]

The "complete" information of a stochastic process is represented in Skorokhod in this fashion: by (1) specification of finite-dimensional distributions — in particular for Gauss's and Markov's processes (2) by specification of the characteristic functional $\phi(l) = \int \exp\{i(l,x)\} \mu(dx)$ (*notation:* μ is measure in the function space of the process, (l,x) is linear functional in this space), and (3) by means of reference to probability density related to some other measure which is assumed to be known: the μ corresponding to the stochastic process is $\mu(A) = \int_A \rho(x)\sqrt{}(dx)$ (*notation:* $\rho(x)$ and $\sqrt{}$ are respectively the given density and measure in the function space). The fundamental transformations investigated by Skorokhod are of the forms (1) inertia-free, $y(t) = f(x(t))$; (2) integral, $y(t) = \int \ldots \int K(t,s_1, \ldots, s_k, x(s_1), \ldots, x(s_k)) ds_1, \ldots, ds_k$; (3) differential, $y(t) = \Phi(t,x(t), \ldots, x^{(k)}(t))$; (4) inverse (2) or (3). Throughout $x(t)$ and $y(t)$ denote respectively input and output. In the last case $y(t)$ is the solution of $Ly(t) = x(t)$, the L standing for the integral or differential transformation. (Cf. in the context *Note* to sect. 1 on Pugachev's definitional framework.)

(9)   Some of Yudin's conceptions are reflected in the build-up of "evolutional-simulative" ("ES") planning, the basic idea in which is to combine the advantages of the simulative approach with those of stochastic programming; the evolutional algorithms of the ES are an application of random search in the solution of a stochastic problem (in fact a more effective — since more "natural" — employment of the latter than the prevalent one in handling the approximative solution of deterministic extremization). Likhtenshtein[30] seems to have taken the initiative in exploring the possibilities of bringing in the elements of risk and uncertainty into a simulator-type model: his ES algorithms (convergent and "generalized") are an application of the Monte Carlo method.

To restate, the deterministic problem of search for the extremum

$$\max_{a \in D} (\min) \phi(a)$$

would consist in finding within some region of admissible plans D, the plan, a, in which an objective function ϕ mapping D into some linearly ordered set R, reaches its overall maximum. The "simulator" gives D and ϕ implicitly: permits finding the plan a from D and the corresponding $\phi(a)$. Say, let M be a set of natural numbers; simulations being numbered $e \in M$: in other words the simulation e would yield the pair a^e, ϕ^e. The adopted regime would establish the rules for establishing the total number of necessary simulations, N, and for choosing some result $(\hat{a}, \phi(\hat{a}) \in \{(a^e, \phi^e) \mid e = 1, \ldots, N\}$ as the approximate solution of the plan problem.

In the stochastic version the objective function is a random magnitude. The region of its values is $\phi^0 = \{\phi(a) \mid a \in D\}$ and the existence of the law of distribution $P\phi$ of such values follows from the uniqueness of the mapping of the ϕ. In the adopted definition the set

$$\beta_{P_a^0} = \begin{cases} a' \in D \mid P_\phi(\phi(a) \geqslant \phi(a')\} \geqslant & P^0 & \phi(a) \to \min \\ a' \in D \mid P_\phi(\phi(a) \leqslant \phi(a')\} \geqslant & P^0 & \phi(a) \to \max \end{cases}$$

is the set of the sufficiently realistic plans, the set $\bar{\beta}_{P_a^0} = D \backslash \beta_{P_a^0}$ is that of insufficiently realistic plans.

From the definitions it follows that the probability of finding the plan from $\beta_{P_a^0}$ on one simulation is $1 - P^0$. When treating simulation as a statistical test with two possible results $a^e \in \beta_{P_a^0}$, $a^e \in \bar{\beta}_{P_a^0}$, we find that over N simulations at least one of the plans, with probability $P^* = 1 - (1 - P^0)^N$, will belong to $\beta_{P_a^0}$. Thence $N \cong \log(1 - P^*)/(\log 1 - P^0) + 0.5$. The evolutionary algorithm is to find with given P^0 the N, to carry out N simulations and to find (a^e, ϕ^e), to choose the plan $\hat{a}$ such that $\hat{\phi}(\hat{a}) = \max(\min)$ $\{e \mid e = 1, \ldots, N\}$. Then the plan $\hat{a}$ is termed "*pseudo-best*".

The generalized algorithm rests on the following procedure: (1) perform N simulations and find (a^e, ϕ^e), $e = 1, \ldots, N$; (2) renumber ϕ^e with the use of numbers $n = 1, \ldots, m$, following its rising order so that $\phi_{(n)} < \phi_{(n+1)}$ for all $n \in (1, \ldots, m)$; (3) find frequencies $P^{(n)}$ of the appearance of the plans which give to the objective function the value $\phi^e_{(n)}$; then $P^n = \{\text{card } [a^e \mid \phi^e = \phi^e_n]\}/N$; (4) choose some n', (5) find $\phi^e_{(n')} - \phi^e_{(n)}$; (6) compute the penalty function $F(\phi^e_{(n')} - \phi^e_{(n)})$;[31] (7) compute

$$\underline{P} = \sum_{n=1}^{n'-1} F(\phi^e_{(n')} - \phi^e_{(n)}) P^{(n)}$$

and

$$\bar{P} = \sum_{n=n+1}^{m} F(\phi^e_{(n')} - \phi^e_{(n)}) P^{(n)}.$$

(8) if $\underline{P} \simeq \bar{P}$ then accept a plan, or any of the plans, giving the value $\phi^e_{(n)}$ to the objective function as the pseudo-best. The generalized algorithms are converging: $\phi(\hat{a}) \rightarrow \phi(a)$ with $N \rightarrow \infty$ and permit to find simultaneously the value P^0. If $\phi(a) \rightarrow \max$ then $P^0 \cong \sum_{n=n}^{m} P^{(n)}$; if $\phi(a) \rightarrow \min$ then $P^0 = \sum_{n=1}^{n'} P^{(n)}$, n' being the number of the "pseudo-best" plan.

The ES appears to carry promise in the search for the "best direction" of a plan, circumventing the build-up of a formal regression method.

(10) Of patent importance from the planning point of view is the stability of solutions adopted, which indeed transcends the issue of stochastic programming only. It arises in a parametric as well as a stochastic approach and lends itself to the error-theoretic treatment.

In Western writing *i.a.* the contribution of the Tintner school is of relevance for the planner. (Note Sengupta's introduction of the element of a price of stability — in the sense of the cost for securing a higher degree of it in terms of the objective function's sub-optimality.) In Soviet literature a noteworthy contribution is to be credited in particular to Arbuzova and her associates, largely concerned with the stochastic mod ϵ-stability: understood as constancy of the optimal basis with probability $(1 - \epsilon)$; the problem is then stated as that of $\max\limits_{l=1,2} P(A(\xi), B(\xi), C(\xi)) \epsilon S^l \geqslant 1 - \epsilon)$, where the A, B, and C are random parameters. The object of the work is broadly to elucidate the sufficient conditions of the ϵ-stability in linear and quadratic programming and to outline the general theory of the stability of convex programmes.

In the realm of economics we may refer to Arbuzova's paper[32] on the mutual connection between the stochastic stability mod ϵ of the problems of a linear programme. We may draw attention in particular to the Arbuzova algorithm for testing the stochastic stability mod ϵ of a plan programme with random coefficients of the objective function. The problem is set in the form

$$\min [c_1(\xi)x_1 + \ldots \ldots + c_n(\xi)X_n] = C$$

$$a_{11}x_1 + \ldots \ldots + a_{1n}x_n \geqslant b_1$$

$$\ldots \ldots \ldots \ldots \ldots \ldots \ldots \ldots \ldots \ldots \ldots$$

$$a_{m1}x_1 + \ldots \ldots + a_{mn}x_n \geqslant b_m$$

with x positive. The variables and constraints are renumbered so as to leave free the latter with subscripts $1, \ldots k + 1 \ldots m$ for average values of c_j.

The matrix

$$\begin{pmatrix} a_{11} \ldots \ldots a_{1k} \\ \ldots \ldots \ldots \\ a_{k1} \ldots \ldots a_{kk} \end{pmatrix}$$

is denoted M and the co-factor of a_{ij} in the M is denoted Δ_{ij}. Then the hyperplanes are formed

$$\Delta c_j - \sum_{i=1}^{k} \sum_{\nu=1}^{k} (-1)^{i+\nu} a_{ji} \Delta_{i\nu} c_\nu = 0; \qquad j \leqslant n - m + k$$

$$\text{and} \quad \sum_{j=1}^{k} \Delta_{ij} c_j = 0, \qquad i > k.$$

Then Mc_j is substituted into the normalized equations of hyperplanes; the distances to the latter from the MC point will appear as $d_1, \ldots, d_n$, and the shortest of them $d = \min d_j$ (where $j = 1, \ldots, n$). The stability is taken as sufficiently established when the inequality

$$\sum_{j=1}^{n} Dc_j \leqslant \epsilon d^2$$

is satisfied (where D is the space of admissible plans); the testing inequality is obtained as a generalized Chebyshev inequality for mathematical expectation.

(11) At the time of writing fundamentals of the theory of indeterminacy and probability are being intensively re-thought — in the context of applicability in economic planning. There is a good deal of intellectual courage in the Yefimov-Spivak[33] tenet that in constructing an optimization model of planned economic systems the concept of mathematical probability — nonnegative, σ-additive, normed measure — can and should be employed in a much wider class of situation than that permitted by the *objective* probability concept (in "non-mass" collections the probability characteristics being possibly determined by expert evaluation or with reference to some inductive principles, such as those of maximum entropy or invariance). The key point in the argument is that the concept of *subjective* probability — as it develops within the frame of the Bayesian decision-making theory — does correspond to the logic of the man-machine dialogue, and thus it is in agreement with the line of advance of both the conceptual basis and technology of planning: the methodology of the Bayesian theory of statistical solution permits applying the optimality principle by means of sequential decision-making; note the nexus with control theory (cf. our Part II).

The established Soviet approach has been based on Kolmogorov's theory, immediately related as it is with the "objective" concept. But the Yermolov-Spivak contention is that contemporary methodology of probability evaluation, resting on Kolmogorov's classical axiomatics, does apply to all concepts of probability (it does, that is, to the subjective concept no less than to the objective; and as a matter of fact also to the concept of logical probability. Note that the concept of statistical probability is considered to be concerned with determinacy, i.e. statistical determinacy, rather than indeterminacy.)

By way of an execursus, we may note here Kolmogorov's recent revision and reformulation[34] of the logical foundations of the theories of information and of probability: as a matter of fact its roots can be found in his earlier attempts (and also in the independent attempts by Solomonoff,[35] in his writings on formal theory of inductive inference). It links up with subsequent formalizations by Martin-Loef.[36] The Kolmogorov new formalism rests on the concept of random sequences, in turn found to be analogous — for infinite sequences — to von Mises's concept of the "collective"; the substance is the random Bernoulli-type sequences. The entropy $H(x|y)$ is the length of the sequence of the 0's and the 1's in the programme P, which permits building up the object x, which has under control the object y, i.e. $H(x|y) = \min l(p)$, $A(P,y) = C.$

Kolmogorov's main conclusion is this. The basic information-theoretic concepts could and should be formulated without recourse to the probability theory; these concepts lend themselves to being employed as a basis of a new concept of "*the random*" — in agreement with contemporary ideas on randomness as meaning the absence of regularity (*zakonomernost*). (Kolmogorov's fundamental formula — in conventional symbolism

$$H(\xi h) = \sum_{x,p} p(\xi = x, \eta = y) \log_2 p(\xi = x|\eta = y)$$

— presupposes the "universal" programming method A,A' with the property $H_A(x|y) \leqslant H_{A'}(x|y) + C_A$. His caveat is that all the propositions of the algorithmic theory of information in their general statement are exact only up to the (0)1-type components, and that when turning to the probability-theoretic formulation, one has to content oneself with a far "*coarser*" regularization!)

(12) To end up, we may come back to the matter broached at the start. Randomness is no longer denied as the planner's inseparable companion. It is seen as such in both its "objective" and "subjective" forms (typically for the former is the technical progress — no less than physical environment; for the latter the human element wherever it enters the planning and running of the economy).[37] What remains then of the old determinism of Soviet planning theory is not much more than the tenet on basic stationarity in the development "law" of a complex system. But the meaningfulness of even this broad generality is not unquestioned: the "law" has its worrying "dialectics". We have seen how the difficulty is faced by the leading school in the Soviet theory of perspective planning (ch. 3). System-theoretic-oriented students[38] attribute the trouble to two factors; one is the slope angle of the plan-functional as it approaches to the point of optimum; the other is the inevitable error affecting the plan's initial information and consequently the plan throughout its path. The "zone of indeterminacy" — which is thus formed at its approaches to the extremum of the formal optimum, and the wider the greater the impact of the two contributing factors — is characterized by the implied set of development variants: for each of them the functional-optimand differs by less than the error in information sought. Three inferences follow: *firstly*, the proposition on the non-existence of a unique optimal solution for the problem of

optimal "perspective" development of complex systems; *secondly* the implied proposition that the dividing line between a plan and a forecast is hardly clear; *thirdly* the dependence of advances in plan-modelling on research in the informational aspect. As observed by Melentyev,

Without exploring the cumulative effect of error in initial information input one cannot have any certainty in recommending one kind of a model as against another for the purposes of optimizing complex development systems. The snag in this research is however that computational mathematics has not evolved as yet, any generalized methodology for solving this problem.[39, 40]

(Related aspects of informational plan-problems are discussed by me elsewhere.[41])

Notes

1. The next few pages form a bridge between the present subject and matters treated in Part II of this book. We shall present a Soviet-designed probabilistic plan model, owed to Dynkin[42] (or, to be more exact, one of the versions of such a model published by him).

Its foundations are formed by Gale's well-known deterministic construct. Its datum is: a state space Z with initial $z \in Z$ and mappings a_t: to each corresponds a non-empty subset $a_t(z)$. The plan is the sequence $z_1, \ldots, z_N \in Z$ if for each $t = 1, \ldots, N$ the $z_t \in a_t(z_{t-1})$; it is optimal for max $\Sigma u_t(z_t)$. Z is a matrix space, u_i and a_t are resp. upper semi-continuous and quasi-continuous — which guarantees the existence of the optimal plan; further Z is a closed convex set in Euclidean space, u_t and a_t are resp. convex functions and mappings. Translated into economic terms, z_t describes the "state of production"; a_t the state of technology: it is given as a set of all $z' \in \mathcal{T}_t$ for which $g_t(z_t') \leqslant h_{t-1}(z_{t-1})$ where g and h denote the vectors of input and output.

The probabilistic element in the system is some random parameter $s \in S$ — denoting, say, the state of technological knowledge or perhaps a phase in a business cycle — with known probability distribution; a_t and u_t are dependent on $s^t = (s_1, \ldots, s_t)$, measurable and upper-bounded. Now, for any s the plan is presented by a sequence of functions $\zeta(s^t) \in a_t(s_t, \zeta_{t-1}(s^{t-1}))$ $(t = 1, 2, \ldots, N)$. It is optimal when the mathematical expectation $U(\zeta) = E\Sigma u_t(s^t, \zeta_t)$.

Firstly the existence is proved of $\zeta_t(s^t) = F_t(s^t, \zeta_{t-1}(s^{t-1}))$ — the optimal plan; the $F_t(.)$ are found from the equations

$$v_t(s^t, z) = \psi_t(s^t, F_t),$$

where the v_t, ψ_t are given by the recurrent:

$$v_{N+1} = \psi_{N+1} = 0, \qquad v_t(s^t, z) = \sup_{z' \in a_t(s^t, z)} \psi_t(s^t, z'),$$

$$\psi_t(s^t, z) = u_t(s^t, z) + \int_S p_t(ds_{t+1} \mid s^t) v_{t+1}(s^{t+1}, z),$$

the $(p_t(ds_{t+1}|s^t)$ is conditional probability of s_{t+1} with known s'**; the max $U(\zeta) = Ev_1(s_1, z_0)$. Where $s_1, \ldots, s_N$ is a Markovian process the functions F_t can be chosen so as to depend on s_t, u, z but not on $s_1, \ldots, s_{t-1}$.

The next theorem is on optimal prices and starts from what has been established — for the deterministic case — by Gale: viz. that for their existence it is sufficient that a constant k could be found such that for any t, s^t and any $z, \hat{z} \in Z_t, w, \hat{w} \in W$

$$|h_t(z) - h_t(\hat{z})| \leqslant k\rho(z, \hat{z}), \qquad |u_t(z) - u_t(\hat{z})| \leqslant k\rho(z, \hat{z}),$$

$$\rho(\mathcal{T}_t^{\,w}, \mathcal{T}_t^{\,\hat{w}}) \leqslant k\|w - \hat{w}\|,$$

where $\mathcal{T}_t^{\,w} = \mathcal{T}_t \cap \{z : g_t(z) \leqslant w\}$, and the distance $\rho(A, B)$ between two sets A and B is defined as the larger of the two numbers, i.e.

$$\sup_{z \in A} \rho(z, B), \quad \sup_{z \in B} \rho(z, A).$$

By definition the prices are optimal, $\pi_t(s')$, if for any optimal plan, as defined, $E \sum [u_t(\zeta_t) + (\pi_t, h_{t-1}(\zeta_{t-1}) - g_t(\zeta_t))] \leqslant E \sum u_t(\bar{\zeta}_t)$. (!) (For the w note: W is an l-dimensional arithmetic space; W^* is its conjugate space. Denote $\gamma \in W_+^*, \gamma \in W^*, (\gamma, w) \geqslant 0$ with $w \geqslant 0$. Introduce in W the norm $\|w\|$, equalling the sum of the coordinates' absolute values; denote further ζ_t the set of all measurable $\zeta(s^t)$, functions satisfying $\zeta(s^t) \in \mathcal{T}_t(s^t)$.

Take in (!) $\zeta_t = \bar{\zeta}_t$; considering that $g_t(\bar{\zeta}_t) \leqslant h_{t-1}(\bar{\zeta}_{t-1})$, we have with probability 1, $(\pi_t, g_t(\zeta_t)) = (\pi_t, h_{t-1}(\zeta_{t-1}))$. (!!). It is then proved that subject to (!!), the inequalities (!) are equivalent to the requirement that for all $\zeta_t \in \zeta_t$:

$$E[u_t(\zeta_t) + (\pi_{t+1}, h_t(\zeta_t)) - (\pi_t, g_t(\zeta_t))]$$

$$\leqslant E[u_t(\bar{\zeta}_t) + (\pi_{t+1}, h_t(\bar{\zeta}_t)) - (\pi_t, g_t(\bar{\zeta}_t))]$$

wherefrom it follows that, if the u_t is a strictly concave function, we have the equations

$$u_t(\bar{\zeta}_t) + (\bar{\pi}_{t+1}, h_t(\bar{\zeta}_t)) - (\pi_t, g_t(\bar{\zeta}_t))$$

$$= \sup_{z \in \mathcal{T}_t} [u_t(z) + (\bar{\pi}_{t+1}, h_t(z)) - (\pi_t, g_t(z))]$$

with probability 1, where

$$\bar{\pi}_{t+1} = E(\pi_{t+1}|s^t).$$

This stochastic analogue of the Galean system has been further developed by Dynkin himself, and other Soviet students of the subject, in several directions. Dynkin evolved a model of a (concave) stochastic dynamic programme (the reader might have noticed that in the system presented here the sequence defined as the plan has a dynamic-programming type of organization; standard methods of dynamic programming have been used by Dynkin in proving his theorems). Others have extended the Dynkin model to the infinite time-dimension case and to systems with parameters changing, ensuring stationarity of the stochastic processes.

2. I have pointed in the context (Part II) to the intrinsic link between the control-theoretic construction and a stochastic treatment of its optimization (especially so with respect to dynamic programming). Here – as a sample of the problem formulation – I would summarize a simple model designed by Gorstko.[43]

We have as given the differential equation $dx/dt = ax + u + r$ with $x|_{t=t_0} = x_0$ (a is a constant; r is a random magnitude with a known probability density of $f(r)$; u is control (arbitrary number)); $t_i \epsilon [t_0, T]$. The problem is to choose $u(t_i) = u_i$ ($i = 0, 1, \ldots, N-1$) such as to minimize

$$R_N = \sum_{i=1}^{N} \int_{-\infty}^{\infty} \ldots \ldots \int_{-\infty}^{\infty} (x_i - y_i)^2. \qquad (!)$$

$$f(r_1)f(r_2)\ldots f(r_N)dr_1 \ldots dr_N + \lambda \sum_{i=0}^{N-1} u_i^2$$

where $(x_i - y_i)^2$ is thought of as a penalty for deviation of x_i from y_i and λ is the "price" (positive) of the control; the $(y_1, \ldots, y_N)$ are given N numbers. It is shown (by mathematical induction) that for an N-step solution process with a random error r, with probability density $f(r)$, mean $\bar{r}$, and dispersion σ^2, the initial optimal control has the form

$$\bar{u}_0 = \bar{r}A_{tN} + x_0 B_{tN} + \sum_{i=1}^{N} y_i C_{tN}^i$$

where the $A_{tN}, B_{tN}, C^1_{tN}, \ldots, C^N_{tN}$ (!!) are coefficients depending on $t_1, \ldots, t_N$. From (!) and (!!) the whole sequence is found $\widetilde{u}_0, \bar{u}_1, \ldots, \bar{u}_{N-1}$ (since $\widetilde{u}_1 = \widetilde{u}_0(M_1), \ldots, \widetilde{u}_{N-1} = \widetilde{u}_0(M_{n-1})$) the M's being sequential states.

Notes

1. cf. H. Cramer/M. R. Leadbetter, *Stationary and related stochastic processes*. (New York, 1967), p. 28.
2. "The place of mathematical planning in the control of the economic systems", *First seminar on mathematical methods and computer techniques* (Geneva, 1972), fasc. 2.
3. Ibid., p. 197.
4. "Stochastic systems and their connections", in *Problems of control and information theory* (Budapest) I/1 (1972); also the same in *Doklady*, 197/6 (1971).
5. *An econometric approach to business cycle problems* (Paris, 1937).
6. "Forecasting by the chain principle", in his *Econometric model building*, (Amsterdam, 1964).
7. In Nemchinov, *Primenenye matematiki* . . . , iii. 57. We may note in passing the very simple, typical stochastic dynamic plan problem sketched out in Kantorovich-Makarov:

    The problem is to determine the volume of output in m points where we know the production functions $F_i(X)$, $G_i(X)$, ($i = 1, 2, . . , m$)-current inputs and investment with output volume equal x. The datum includes also the volume of consumption and its forecast for some sequence of years as laws of distribution $P(x)$, that is requirements are $\leq x$. Determine the volume of investment in capacities such as to minimize the mathematical expectation of total discounted expenditure on output and transport and loss incurred by failure to satisfy requirements.
8. "On the solution of two-stage linear programs under uncertainty", *Proc. 4th Symp. on Math. Statistics and Probability* (Berkeley, 1961).
9. J. K. Sengupta, *et al.*, "On some theorems of stochastic linear programming with applications", *Management science*, Oct. 1963.
10. A. Charnes/W. C. Cooper, "Chance-constrained programming", ibid., Oct. 1959.
11. S. Kataoka, "A stochastic programming model", *Econometrica*, Jan. 1963.
12. G. Tintner/J. K. Sengupta, "Stochastic linear programming and its application to economic planning", in *On political economy and econometrics; essays in honour of Oskar Lange.* See also this source for earlier references.
13. Charnes *et al.*, *Econometrica*, Apr. 1966.
14. In Nemchinov, *Primenenye matematiki* . . . iii.
15. V. A. Bulavskiy, "Iterativnyi metod reshenya obsheney zadachi lineynogo programmirovanya" (Dissertation, Novosibirsk 1962) as referred to by V. Soldatov, in Kantorovich, *Matematicheskoye programmirovanye*.
16. A. Charnes/M. J. L. Kirby, "Some special P-models in chance-constrained programming", *Management Science*, Nov. 1967.
17. L. M. Abramov/I. I. Bochkareva, in *Opt. plan.*, 16 (1970).
18. cf. e.g. R. Wets, "Programming under uncertainty: the complete problem", in *Zeitschr fur Wahrscheinlichkeitstheorie und verwandte Gebiete*, 4 (1966).
19. cf. restatement in E. G. Golshtein/D. B. Yudin, *Novyie napravlenya v lineynom programmirovani* (Moscow, 1966).
20. For outline see p. 221
21. A. N. Kolmogorov, *Osnovnyie ponyatya teorii voroyatnosti* (Moscow, 1937) (Engl. trans. *Foundations of the Theory of Probability* by A. T. Bharucha-Reid, New York, 1956).
22. D. B. Yudin, in *EMM*, 6 (1968).
23. Zukhovitskiy/Polyak/Primak developed the algorithm in their writings related to the concept of a "normalized equilibrium point" of a concave n-persons

game. It generalizes the fastest-descent method. Its specific property consists in the choice of the direction of descent, characteristic of a simultaneous solution of the primal and dual problems of convex programming.

The determining of the length of the step and the smoothing out of the course, preventing a zigzag motion, is carried out by means of positive parameters λ_k which satisfy the conditions $\lambda_k \to 0$, $\Sigma_k = 1^\lambda k = \infty$ which characterize the methods of a generalized gradient descent. Cf. S. I. Zukhovitskiy *et al.*, in *Doklady*, 185/1 (1968) and the same ibid., 163/2 (1965).

24. cf. also *Methods of Feasible Directions*, 1960.

25. In *EMM*, 2 (1969); also the same, in *Doklady*, 177/6 (1967).

26. For an admirable discussion of the impact of a stochastic character of co-efficients of a linear programming problem on methods of decomposition the reader is directed to A. M. Irving, *Structured linear programmes with stochastic coefficients*, (Nat. Econ. Planning Unit, Univ. of Birmingham, Jan. 1969).

27. A. I. Kaplinskiy/A. I. Propoy, in *Avt. i tel.*, 3 (1970); and *ibid.*, 10 (1971).

28. In this the point-of-departure is this line of argument: Find distribution $F(x)$ for which
$$\int f_O(x)\, dF(x) \to \inf, \int f_j(x) dF(x) \leqslant 0, x \in X, \text{ where } X \text{ is a given set of n-}$$
dimensional Euclidean R^n. Now let $y_j = f_j(x)$ $(j = 0, 1, \ldots, m)$ and consider the image of the set $X \in R^n$ in R^{m+1}. Let further $\{Y = y \in R^{m+1} \; y = f(x), x \in X\}$. In the general case $\underline{Y}$ is a non-convex non-closed set. Construct coY — its convex envelope in R^{m+1}. The mathematical expectation of $f_j(j = 0, 1, \ldots m)$ corresponds to the construction of such an envelope: the point-of-departure problem is equivalent to finding inf Y_O for non-positive y_j with $y \, coY$. It has been proved that for building up of the envelope $Y \in R^{m+1}$ no more than $m + 2$ points. $Y \in Y^*$ are required in the general case. Thus

$$co\, Y = \left\{ \sum_{k=0}^{m+1} f_j(x_k)p_k, j = 0, \ldots, m| \; p_k \geqslant 0, \sum_{k=0} p_k = 1, x_k \in X \right\}, \text{ the point-of-}$$

departure problem is completely characterized by the $(m + 2)$ vectors $x_k \in X$ of numbers p_k $(k = 0, \ldots, m + 1)$ all non-negative,

$$\Sigma_{k=0}^{m+1}, p = 1. \text{ The state of the system is described by the vector}$$
$z = (x_o, \ldots, x_{m+1}, p_o, P_{m+1}$ in R.

29. A. V. Skorokhod, *Kibernetika*, 1 (1966); cf. also his paper in *Uspekhi matematicheskikh nauk*, 3 (1965).

30. V. E. Likhtenshtein, in *EMM*, 6 (1971).

31. The penalty function may be possibly made dependent on various parameters. It is "payable" for the deviation from the posited plan version. Take $\Phi(a^{posit}, a) = \text{sign } (\phi (a) - \phi(a^{posit})$. Then the mathematical expectation of loss from deviation would be of the form $\Phi_E(a^{posit}) = \pi \int_a F_\phi P^o \, a(\phi(a) - (a^{posit}) dP_D \, |$
$$-|\int_{a \in \bar{\beta}} P^o \, a F(\Phi(a) - \phi(a^{posit}) dP_D$$

where P is probability measure on D.

32. N. I. Arbuzova, in *EMM*, 4 (1966). For a definition of stability mode see her and V. Danilov's paper in *Doklady*, 162/1 (1965). The matter of stochastic ϵ-stability (stability mod ϵ) is further pursued in Arbuzova's paper in *EMM*, 1 (1968) for particular forms of linear programming. Cf. also for her earlier work in the field the article, jointly written with V. Danilov, in *Doklady*, 162/1 (1965).

33. V. M. Yefimov/V. A. Spivak, *EMM*, 5 (1972).

34. A. N. Kolmogorov, *Problemy peredachi informatsyi*, 5/3 (1969); cf. also his "New interpretation of the von Mises concept of random sequence", *Sankhya*, 1963, ser. A25, no. 4.

35. A. Solomonoff, "Formal theory of inductive inference" in *Information and Control*, 4 (1966).

36. P. Martin-Loef, "The definition of random sequences", ibid., 9 (1966).

37. What follows restates the reasoning in L. A. Melentyev, in *EMM*, 4 (1967), p. 503.

38. Ibid.

39. Ibid, p. 503. The problem is one of a probabilistic formulation of some elements of initial information. Further issues are those of the optimal volume of such information and of the adverse effect of an information "surplus" which is related to the question of the optimum size of mathematical models.
    A noteworthy point made concerns the treatment of the development processes as a continuum in time, which again influences the error in the information input.

40. cf. Federenko's points on indeterminacy of situations in perspective planning and difficulties in their quantification (in his report to the 1970 conference on methodologies of economic prognostication) discussed in Part I.

41. cf. my "Notes on systemic approach to large scale, decentralization and related matters", in *Jahrbuch der Wirtschaft Osteuropas*, 1973.

42. E. B. Dynkin, *Doklady*, 200/3 (1971).

43. A. B. Gorstko, in *Opt. pian.*, 2 (1964).

PART II

THE CONTROL-THEORETIC APPROACH TO PLANNING

6

THE CONTROL-THEORETIC PROBLEM

(1)   Three problems have been legitimately singled out as central in the theory of dynamic controlled systems. These are (1) controllability, (2) observability, (3) stability. Broadly, to follow Krassovskiy,[1] they lend themselves to be defined as concerned, respectively, with (1) the appraisal of the propelling forces, securing the transfer-motion of the object from the given into the desired state; (2) determining the latter's unknown coordinates from magnitudes observed; and (3) ensuring steady-state motion with given information. All of them have per se considerable analytical interest. Here they present themselves in connection with the problem of *optimality* in control. To begin with the last of three mentioned, the problem of stability is common to a number of disciplines; this alone may justify relegating it to a separate section of our discussion. Observability[2] relates directly to the theory of information.

In this section it will be treated jointly with controllability, which is focal. We may only broadly indicate now that the information which has to be fed into the controlling device will include in particular that on the state of the object, on the relevant operators, on disturbances, and on the aims of control.

Once the aims – the objective function – are introduced, optimality may be treated explicitly. And this is here *the* central theme, and I will give its formalization, following its admirably simple and clear statement in Feldbaum.[3]

Notes
   1. The concept of controllability was first introduced (in the theory of thermodynamics) by Carathéodory; cf. Lee/Markus, *Foundations of optimal control theory*.
   2. The concept of complete controllability has been developed by

279

Popov in the context of that of hyperstability. This concept has been extended by Halanay. If we take

$$\dot{x}(t) = Ax(t) + Bx(t - \tilde{t}) + b\eta(t);$$

this system (the columns of B being colinear with b) is defined as completely controllable if for positive T and for every continuous vector function ϕ defined over $[- \tilde{t}, 0]$ there exists a piecewise continuous control u such that the solution corresponding to the initial function ϕ and control u vanishes on $[T, T + \tilde{t}]$. Cf. V. M. Popov, *Hiperstabilitatea sistemelor automate* (Bucharest, 1966); A. Halanay, *Differential equations, stability, oscillations, time lags* (New York, 1967).

3. Problems of controllability and observability are investigated systematically in R. E. Kalman, "Contributions to the theory of optimal control", *Bol. soc. mat. mex.*, 5 (1960). This is a part of Kalman's pioneering work in modern algebraic "translation" of the system theory. The main theoretical tool at the present stage of development is the theory of modules over a principal-ideal domain.

Of late Kalman and his associates' stress in their theory of regulators (for linear "plants" = dynamic systems) is on two fundamental properties of the plant, i.e. complete (1) controllability (by suitable input every state is shiftable to zero), and (2) constructibility (the system's internal state is determinable from the history of extremal outputs and inputs). As the authors point out, it is a surprising discovery going back only to the end of the 1950s that the two properties are also sufficient for the task. The concept of observability is construed accordingly: controllability and observability are described by equations of the type $x = Ax + Bu$, $y = Cx + Du$, the state, input, and output denoted respectively as x, u, y. (cf. Kalman *et al.*, *Topics in mathematical system theory* (New York, 1969)).

4. Both concepts, controllability and observability, are extensively examined by Markus in a succession of papers. He investigated in particular the general nonlinear differential-equations system and consequently focused on processes locally observable and controllable (cf. L. Markus, "Controllability of nonlinear processes", *SIAM J.*, 3 (1965); and the same, "Controllability and observability", in Caianiello, ed., *Functional analysis and optimization* (New York, 1966)).

5. Fundamentals of controllability under optimum — in the special context of hierarchical devolution — have been given rigour in a perceptive inquiry by McFadden (in Kuhn/Szegö, *Mathematical systems theory and economics*). In a dynamic system $x = ASP(x - x^*)$ (1) whose states are described by the real N-dimensional vectors $x \in R^N$, a controlling agency

$k = 1, \ldots, K$ receives a signal $z_k \in R^N$ and operates the control $u \in R^{JK}$ with a linear strategy $u_k = S_k(z - z_k^*)$, the star denoting the target state; S_k is a $J_k \times N$ matrix, $S \subset \mathscr{S}$ of feasible strategies; there are two "transformers – the information transformer $z_x = P_k x$, the P_k being a diagonal matrix (diagonals 0, 1) and the state transformer, taken to be linear, $\Delta x = Au$, A being an $N \times J$ matrix, $J = \Sigma_{k=1}^{K} J_K$, $u = u_1, \ldots, u_k$). Under "full" decentralization (where by definition each agency receives information only on the state variable it controls) with $\Delta x = Au$, with linear control $u = L$ $(x - x^k)$, $L \equiv SP = \text{diag}(s_{11}, \ldots s_{NN})$ the sufficient existence condition for the u ensuring stability for any $x(0)$ is that A have a nested sequence of non-zero principal minors; a sequence of principal minors of order $1, \ldots, N$ is termed nested where the determinant of the $(n - 1)$ order is a principal minor of the determinant of order n in the sequence $n = (2, \ldots, N)$. Optimality of decentralized control is then treated with reference to cost entailed to the planner in deviation from the target – a quadratic loss function

$$c = \sum_{t=0}^{\infty} \delta^t (x(t) - x^*)' Q(x(t) - x^*)$$

(δ – discount rate; Q – real symmetric positive-definite matrix and $c \epsilon [0, \infty]$).

6. In anticipating a subject at which we shall arrive at some point, we may give here a definition of controllability of a stationary system, as formalized (for a linear case) by Gabasov, Kirillova, and Krakhotko.

Consider a control system (!)

$$D_\alpha(p)x(t) = Bx(t - h_1) + Cx(t - h_2) + \int_0^{h_2} R(s)x(t - s)ds + K_\beta(p)u(t).$$

Here the x and r are respectively n- and u-dimensional vectors, the n's positive numbers; further

$p \equiv d/dt$, $D_\alpha(p) = p^\alpha + A_1 p^{\alpha-1} + \ldots + A_{\alpha-1} p + A_\alpha$, $K_\beta(p) = K_0 p^\beta +$
$+ K_1 p^{\beta-1} + \ldots + K_{\beta-1} p + K_\beta$, $\beta < \alpha, A_1, A_2, \ldots, A_\alpha, B, C -$

are constant matrices $(n \times n)$, the K's constant matrices $(n \times r)$

$$R(s) = \sum_{i=1}^{l} \sum_{j=0}^{m_i} R_{ij} \frac{s^j}{j!} \exp(a_i s),$$

R_{ij} are constant matrices $(n \times n)$, $a_i, i = 1, \ldots, l$ constant numbers. The initial conditions (given) are

$$x_0(.) = \begin{cases} x(\theta) = \phi(\theta), & -\max\{h_i, i = 1, 2, 3\} = -h \leqslant \theta < 0, \\ x^{(i)}(0) = x_0^i, & i = 0, 1, \ldots, \alpha - 1, \end{cases} \tag{!!}$$

where $\phi(\theta)$ is a function, continuous with $\phi(\theta)$. To each $u(t)$ control of the class $C^{(\beta)}$ there corresponds a uniquely continuous solution $x(t)$, $t \geqslant 0$ for the (!) solution, satisfying (!!).

The state $x_o(.)$ is defined as controllable if for any n-vector c there exists the control $u(t)$, $t \geqslant 0$ and a number t_i, $> \infty$ such that the trajectory $x(t)$ corresponding to the state $x_0(.)$ and control $u(t)$ satisfies the condition $x(t_i) = c$. And the system (!) is defined as controllable if all its initial states are controllable (cf. R. Gabasov *et al.*, in *Doklady*, 203/3 (1972)).

7. Controllability of nonlinear systems has been explored in Soviet literature in particular by Roitenberg in a series of papers. Dynamic systems considered are of the type described by nonlinear differential equations (see e.g. *Vestnik Mosk. Univ.*, 1969)

$$x_j = \sum_{k}^{n} A_{jk}x_k + \psi_j(x_1,\ldots,x_n,u_1,\ldots,u_r,t) + \sum_{l=1}^{r} B_j u_i. \qquad (!)$$

It is shown that this nonlinear system has the property of controllability when the system of scalar equations

$$F_j(u_1,\ldots,u_r,v_1^*,\ldots,v_r^*,\xi_1^*,\ldots,\xi_n^*,t) \equiv \sum_{l=1}^{r} B_{jl}u_l - \qquad (!!)$$

$$- \sum_{t=1}^{r} B_{jl}v_l^*(t) + \psi_j(\xi_1^*(t),\ldots,\xi_n^*(t), \quad u_1,\ldots,u_r,t) = 0$$

is soluble with respect to the unknown u's: controls $u_1(t),\ldots,u_r(t)$, $0 \leqslant t \leqslant T$ bring the system (!) from the state $x(0)$ into the origin of co-ordinates by the time point $t = T$. The theorem is then proved that for the nonlinear system to be controllable it is sufficient that (1) the rank of the matrix $\|B\ AB\ A^2B\ldots A^{n-1}B\|$ be zero; (2) the matrix B possesses $s = n-r$ rows whose all elements equal zero, i.e. $B_{v_1 l} = 0$, $B_{v_2 l} = 0$, $\ldots$, $B_{v_s l} = 0$; (3) the rank of matrix B be zero; (4) equations in (!) for which $j = v_1,\ldots, j = v_s$ do not contain nonlinear forces, that is elements ψv_1, ψv_2, $\ldots \psi v_s$ of the vector ψ are all equal zero; (5) the Jacobian of the system of functions $F_{\sigma_1}, F_{\sigma_2},\ldots, F_{\sigma r}$, forming the left-hand sides of (!!), not equal identically zero, with respect to the control variables u does not equal zero for any value of $t\epsilon[0,T]$, viz.

$$\begin{Vmatrix} \dfrac{\partial \psi_{\sigma_1}}{\partial u_1} - B_{\sigma_1 l} & \ldots & \dfrac{\partial \psi_{\sigma_1}}{\partial u_r} - B_{\sigma_1 r} \\ \cdot & \ldots & \cdot \\ \dfrac{\partial \psi_{\sigma_r}}{\partial u_1} - B_{\sigma_r 1} & \ldots & \dfrac{\partial \psi_{\sigma_r}}{\partial u_r} - B_{\sigma_r r} \end{Vmatrix} \neq 0.$$

(2) It was Feldbaum[4] who first stated rigorously problems of finding the control which under given conditions secures the postulated quality of the system's motion. (One will also recall the simultaneous contribution by Lerner[5]). Let us describe as the "controlled magnitude" parameters which characterize the state of the object $x_1 \ldots, x_n$. These may be considered as the coordinates of the vector $\bar{x} = (x_1, \ldots, x_n.)$

This vector $\bar{x}$ is thought of as the system's "output".

The object is under the impact of operations by the controlling device, say $u_1, \ldots, u_r$, forming the vector u with co-ordinates $u_j (j = 1, \ldots, r)$, thus $\bar{u} = (u_1 \ldots, u_r)$. We further allow for the object's being under some disturbing impact $(z_1, \ldots, z_l)$, which brings about the deviation of the path of the object from some "ideal". This again we take as a vector $\bar{z} = (z_1, \ldots, z_l)$.

The vector z thus describes the "disturbance" (or "noise"). The $\bar{u}$ and $\bar{z}$, between them, are the, so far presented, elements of "input".

The process can now be described in terms of vectoral functions as $\bar{x} = \bar{F}(\bar{u}, \bar{z})$ where, to restate, the $\bar{x}$ is the state-variable function (or "output" function), the $\bar{u}$ is the control-variable function, and $\bar{z}$ is the disturbance function, the x describing the process "as such", the u and z the respective "impacts" of controls and disturbances. The "law" that organizes the process — its algorithm — is the operator F. Conceivably it may vary in its mathematical nature. Usually it is expressed as a differential-equations system

$$dx_1/dt = f_i(x_1, \ldots, x_n; u_1, \ldots, u_r; z_1, \ldots, z_l; t),$$

the scalar t being time. In compact vectoral form we may write

$$d\bar{x}/dt = f(\bar{x}, \bar{u}, \bar{z}, t),$$

the $\bar{f}$ being in the general case nonlinear. Where the initial conditions $\bar{x}_i^{(0)} = (x_i)_{t=0}$ are a datum and the $\bar{u}(t)$ and the disturbance $\bar{z}(t)$ are known, the vector $x(t)$ will be found. Realistically we may be given some constraints on controls under which the system has to work. Say, this has the form

$$\sum_{\nu=1}^{r} \lambda_\nu^2 u_\nu^2 \leqslant N,$$

the λ^2 and N being some given functions of time or constants. Or possibly there may be constraints on the co-ordinates x_i of the controlled object — constraints on their function or functional — say, of the form

$$H_u(x_1, \ldots, x_n) = H_u(\bar{x}) \leqslant 0 \quad (u = 1, \ldots, m).$$

To put all this in a different way, $\bar{u} \in \Omega(\bar{u})$ and $\bar{x} \in \Omega(\bar{x})$: here the Ω is an admissible region of, respectively, r and n dimensional vectors, u and x. In a very general case we may have some constrained functional

$$L_u \left[\bar{u}(t), \bar{x}(t) \bar{z}(t) \right] \in \Omega_u(L) \qquad (u = 1, \ldots, m)$$

with explicit constraint (including the constraining time), say of the form

$$L = \int_0^T \left[\sum_{\nu=1}^n \alpha_\nu x_\nu^2 + \beta u^2 \right] dt \leqslant N$$

where the T, α, β, N are positive constants.

Our next stage is the building into the system of the aim — its objective function: say, we may for sufficient generality see as our optimum the minimum value of

$$Q(\bar{x}, \bar{x}^*, \bar{u}, \bar{z}, t) \rightarrow \min,$$

where the x^* is a given impulse; in a particular case this might be

$$Q = \int_0^T [x(t) - x^*(t)]^2 \, dt.$$

In general, the system may be a stochastic one. In particular the objective function may be of the shape

$$Q = E\{Q_1\} = \int_{\Omega(\bar{z})} Q_1 (\bar{x}, \bar{x}^*, \bar{u}, \bar{z}) P(\bar{z}) d\Omega(\bar{z})$$

where $\bar{z}$ is some random magnitude with the probability density $P(\bar{z})$, the $\Omega(\bar{z})$ is the region of variation of the disturbance, $\bar{z}$; and $d\Omega(\bar{z})$ its infinitely small element. Where nothing can be said a priori about the probability distribution, one will usually resort to some minimax optimality.

A few more words about the meaning of the impulse variable x^*. It embraces all that forms the system's regime and is not determined beforehand by the formulation of its goal (except for the disturbance z). It can possibly mean a "behavioural instruction" — an "instruction" as to the output value of x; it can be formed as a collection of n magnitudes $x_1^*, \ldots, x_n^*$ forming the co-ordinates of the vector $\bar{x}^*$, i.e. $\bar{x}^* = (x_1^*, \ldots, x_n^*)$; it may be postulated that $\bar{x}_i$ be equal x_i^*, the latter being a function of time.

Obviously where x^* is a regular function, known ex ante, it can possibly be made implicit in the objective function. This is not the case where x^* is a random magnitude, say a function of time unknown ex ante; this would apply in particular where the problem is set as that of pursuit of

the goal whose motion is not known beforehand. In such a situation we
would postulate $[x^*(t) - x(t)] \to$ min. It is the role of the control device to
bring the $\bar{x}$ as close as possible to the $\bar{x}^*$.

(3)   Although we have talked here throughout of generality, in fact the
optimal-control theoretic problem can be variously set. In particular, it
may be posed as one determining the algorithm (the strategy) in such a
way as to satisfy the given Q when the operator, or in the stochastic case
its probabilistic characteristics, are given. Alternatively it may be set as
finding the algorithm of the controlling "device" when the datum is time.
A problem which has played a particularly important role in the development of the theory of optimal control is that of time-optimal processes. In
the usual formulation time becomes the minimand, and what is sought is
the algorithm for the control $u(t)$ such as to transfer the object from its
initial into the terminal state, both states being given — over the shortest
possible time period. We will also have an opportunity to discuss the case
where $T \to \infty$. Infiniteness of the horizon crucially affects the shape of our
problem. (The relevance for planning is obvious).
    For another aspect of generality, a few more remarks on the differences
in the nature of the operator. We have tacitly admitted nonlinearity of
functions but we have so far been reticent on the matter, which too has
had a great significance in the history of the discipline. As will be seen, the
property of discontinuity has been of relevance: from the applicational
point of view — as well as that of effective formalization-systems for which
the functions, specifically those of admissible controls, are *piecewise* continuous (to be more specific, arbitrarily piecewise continuous) have been
found to be of particular relevance (implying, that is, that when defined on
F, the F is divisible into a finite number of "pieces", so that it is continuous on the interior of every piece; and, moreover, it approaches some
finite limit as a point moves in the interior and approaches a boundary
point). We will have something to say in particular about the sliding
regimes where the number of discontinuities is infinite.
    Conventionally we classify control systems as open and closed. In the
former the controller does not receive direct information on the $\bar{x}$, actual
state of the controlled object; in the latter such information is supplied by
feedback (the system is described as a feedback system).
    Another observation on the informational aspect. It is customary to
distinguish among optimal systems those with the feasibly complete and
with incomplete information on the controllable object, and to subdivide
the latter into those with passive and with active collection of information.

(4) The first sub-class has by now a history of several decades of investigation, going back to the fundamental works of Wiener and Kolmogorov (specifically for linear systems). What is postulated here is the statistical characteristics of random input elements. At the point of departure the system, as a whole, is considered as a "filter" — a device straining and eliminating "impurities" (generally we define as a "filter" a procedure for isolating non-systematic components of a time series).[6] Our x enters some communication channels where it is being "mixed" with random disturbances or "noise": we have thus a signal-cum-noise "mixture". Thus the filter's task is to release the output value of x as close statistically as feasible to the "true" x^* or its known transformation. Then — at the next stage we try to decompose the "filter" into our controlled "object" and the algorithm, possibly linked by some feedback mechanism of the system (some adaptive mechanism). In trickier cases, especially those of nonlinear systems, we would require ex ante some data on the structure of the filter for which the algorithm is being sought.

The interest in the investigation of the active-collection sub-class is largely owed to the pioneering work of Feldbaum and his associates.[7] In this class the information is being collected independently of the algorithm, or the controller's strategy. Generally our operation is to watch the output values and on this basis to form hypotheses on the x^*. Several variants have been constructed — under this heading — with respect to the $x(t)$ function, according to the degree of availability of information on it. The most difficult case is where the $x(t)$ is a random function with characteristics which at best are only partially known. It is with such a type of system that Feldbaum's conception (we might as well say this now — a conception fruitful also in the sphere of economics), which has become known as that of "dual-control" theory, is concerned. What is meant by this term is this. We handle here systems in which our knowledge of the z (above p. 283) should and could be obtained by rational experiment rather than by passive observation only (hence the label "active"): the object is, as it were, tested by the tentative impacts of the u, and the results y are analysed by the controlling device. The control system is thus dual in the sense that it is "learning" as well as controlling. In this sense the system is of the adaptive kind: one will notice at once the trend towards self-teaching and self-steering. Because of the approach to the informational aspect, we have here the merging of the statistic (probabilistic) and the regular elements of the control problem — a feature of modern development in the discipline.

This development over the past two decades along the lines we have in-

dicated has led to something which can be treated as a general statement
of the optimal-control problem; also to a vigorous tracing of the way
whereby more particular problems stem from it. Thus we can trace the
linkage with the case of the optimal "regular" strategy (this we obtain
when postulating for one of the values of $u(t)$ probability one, and zero
for the rest). As we are well aware by now, great cognitive significance has
been found in the particular case: one where each state of the object is
taken to be independent of its history. Also the particular case where the
time element drops out of the general statement: this is the case of
stationarity.

(5)   We have had an opportunity to stress at several points that there is
nothing sacrosanct about any particular apparatus. It has also been evident
from our story that it is the calculus of variations that lends itself as the
"natural" way for handling our problems: the classical calculus — at least
as a conceptual point-of-departure. (Further on we shall point to the
"snags" which inhibit its employment in the treatment of optimal-control
problems and which have stimulated the search for "non-classical"
methods more suitable for the purpose.) This *is* a logical point of departure
since the problem's substance is dealing with the extremal values of definite integrals, with the integrand forming a known function of one or
more dependent variables and their derivatives of the first or higher orders:
determining such variables so that the integral reaches its extremum which
leads to the solution.[8]

For well over two centuries the established route in this has been that
of Euler. In the usual notation, consider the integral $\int_a^b f(x,y,y')dx$ where
$y' = dy/dx$. Then for $y(x)$, to minimize that integral, the necessary condition is that $y(x)$ satisfies the Euler differential equation

$$\partial f(x,y,y') / \partial y - d/dx. \ (\partial f(x,y,y') / \partial y') = 0.[9]$$

(Actually, the problem is likely to present itself in such a way that it requires the satisfaction of the Euler-Poisson differential equation and may
entail a potential function with Dirichlet properties.)[10]

As would usually be the case, we may have the *extremum* constrained —
say the problem of determining the curves minimizing

$$I = \int_{x_0}^{x_1} F(x;y_1,\ldots,y_n;y_1',\ldots y_n')dx$$

subject to the additional constraint

$$\phi_i(x; y_1 \ldots, y_n) = 0; i = 1, \ldots m; m < n.$$

The solution is then sought in the familiar fashion by resorting to the Lagrangean multipliers. We form the integral

$$I = \int_{x_0}^{x_1} [F + \sum_{i=1}^{m} \lambda_i(x)\phi_i] \, dx = \int_{x_0}^{x_1} F^* \, dx$$

with starred F standing for

$$F^* = F + \sum_{n}^{m} \lambda_i(x)\phi_i.$$

Then we proceed as if the extremum was unconstrained — i.e. solving the Euler equations which here appear as

$$F_{y_i}^* - d/dx \, . \, F_{y_i}^* = 0 \quad \text{with } j = 1, \ldots, n.$$

These n equations and the m equations of our additional constraint permit determining the unknown functions y and λ, while the limiting conditions $y_j(x_0) = y_{j0}, y_j(x_1) = y_{j1}$ allow us to determine the $2n$ constraints.

Further implications. First, as we have already hinted, the two points of the path may not be fixed. Rather they may be expected to lie on some curve or plane. Here we try to obtain help from the transversality condition. This condition generalizes the tenet on the shortest line segment joining a point to a curve. Take a curve G with parametric system of equations $x = X(s)$, $y = Y(s)$. Further let there be the integral

$$I = \int_{x_1}^{x_0} f(x,y,y')dx$$

with one point, say (x_1, y_1), which has been fixed while the other, (x_2, y_2), is required to lie on some curve G. Then for the function $y = y(x)$ to minimize this integral, the transversality condition which had to be satisfied at the (x_2, y_2) has the form

$$(f - y'f_{y'})X_s + f_{y'} \, Y_s = 0.^{11}$$

Note in the context that where our function space embraces functions

which at best are only piece-wise smooth (as is the case very often in applications), the "broken extremal" must satisfy at each "corner" the
Weierstrass-Erdmann (corner) condition.

(6)   A major source of difficulties stems from the initial-value problem,
which presents itself as the two-point boundary value problem — sometimes in fact as a multi-point problem of this kind in particular in the case
of interior-point or of a state-variable inequality constraint. The usual
methodological assumption is the knowledge of the *complete* set of boundary conditions with respect to either the initial or the terminal point; this
assumed solution is pursued starting from that point; as often as not this
assumption is not validated in application.[12]
     From the solutional point of view "initial" is any point belonging to
the optimal path leading from $(x(t_0), t_0)$ to the terminal hypersurface.
Where this property is not known — as would be often the case in application — one has to build up a family of optimal paths (a "field of extremals" in the classical calculus) such as to possess all the possible initial
points located at least sufficiently near the computed optimal paths.[13]
     Further on we shall see the important implications for the employment
of some methods of solution to optimal control of economic systems. At
this point we may only add Dreyfus's observation on the crucial importance — in the field of application — of the availability of methods for the
numerical solution of differential equations (a solution not often practicable before the electronic-computer era). In any case, as Dreyfus remarks
the numerical solutional procedures available are "rather impotent" where
we have at each of a set of points a less than complete specification of the
boundary conditions.[14] All this cautioning is well to remember when the
"inheritance" of the "two-point boundary value" problem from the classical calculus by the non-classical approaches is considered.

(7)   The scope of this study does not permit the pursuit of further
development in the classical formulation of conditions for the minimum
(in particular, the necessary conditions of Legendre, Jacobi, Weierstrass —
and the Weierstrass-Erdmann condition; note here Weierstrass's "discovery" of the sufficiency condition for the minimizing arc based on the
concept of the field of extremals passing through a fixed point); except
to hint at those which can be seen as of special significance for the non-
classical advance. Thus motivated, I shall mention the build-up of the
classical terminal-control formalism specifically as such, that is, for which

the criterion function is evaluated at a (given) terminal point rather than shaped as an integral in a way traditional in the classics.

This more modern formalism is typified by Mayer's terminal-control problem. In its simple statement it takes the form

$$I = \int_{x_2}^{x_1} f(x,y(x),y'(x))dx$$

with $y(x_0) = y_0$ and $y(x_1) = y_1$.

Two additional variables are being introduced: $y'(x) = u(x); v(x) = f(x,y,u(x))$. These form the constraints which, together with the boundary conditions stated, that is, $y(x_0) = y_0; y(x_1) = y_1$ and $v(x_0)$ being zero, constrain the Mayer problem min $I(y) = $ min $v(x_1)$.

A step further along this line is the formalism of the Bolza problem for it combines a terminal and integral components in the criterial function.[15,16]

$$I = h[x_1,y(x_1),x_2,y(x_2)] + \int_{x_1}^{x_2} f(x,y,y')dx$$

constrained by conditions

(1) $Z_j(x,y,y') = 0;$

(2) $h_k[x_1,y(x_1),x_2,y(x_2)] + \int_{x_1}^{x_2} f_k(x,y,y')dx = 0.$

The problem is set as one of determining an arc for which $I = $ min.[17]

The transformation of the Bolza problem into that of Mayer and these two into the Lagrange form has been explored for quite a time. Fundamentally all the three are equivalent. Bliss, who considers the problems of Lagrange, Mayer, and Bolza (with variable end-points) as the most general problem of the calculus of variations, involving only simple integrals, treats the last as the "most economical" — in particular, because it covers them by means of simple specializations (and because in each of them second variation presents itself as the Bolza problem).[18]

Note

Analytical construction of a quasi-terminal control system is suggested by Krassovskiy.[19] The guiding idea is to cope with certain inadequacies encountered usually in the synthesis of optimal terminal controls in feedback systems: partly-mathematical complication entailed in the integration of nonlinear controls in partial derivatives or systems — rather unwieldy — of ordinary nonlinear differential controls; and partly qualitative limitations, in particular the inexplicitness of transition processes leading to the terminal state. In the Krassovskiy method the syntheses of optimal controls is carried out by minimization of the functional — the sum of a given function of values of the phase co-ordinates of the object's terminal state and integral valuations of controls and control signals in the optimal system: the subintegral function of control signals for stable objects and full-order controllability is a positively determined function of phase co-ordinates: it is this function that serves the purpose of appraising the transition processes.

Hence the concepts and term of the "quasi-terminal" control. Its technical attraction is first and foremost in that the solution is secured by solving linear equations.

(8) The formulation of the two problems — those of Bolza and of Mayer — makes, as it were, a bridge linking the classical and the non-classical methodology. To anticipate what follows, the focus on the terminal makes this proposition true in particular, within the latter, of the Bellman system. (See Dreyfus's excellent study).

Finally, still within the classical framework, of crucial importance for the non-classical advance are the theories of Hamilton and Jacobi.[20] These have indicated the extremals as the "characteristic curves" of a first-order partial differential equation taking for a function $S(x,y)$ a canonical form (in terms of canonical variables):

$$S_x = F(x,y,z) - S_y z \; ; S_y = F_y{}'(x,y,z).$$

In the integrand of the classical problem, $F(.),z$ takes place of y' and is conceived as implied in (x,y). The solution function of the two equations is identifiable with the min $F(.)$ between the two points, fixed initial and variable (x,y).

This theory, demonstrating the use of a general solution of the partial differential equations has offered itself as a methodological "introduction" to that of dynamic programming. The latter is validly seen as a generalization of this theory — such as would embrace combinatorial and multi-stage handling of control problems.[21] Indeed, as we shall see, it has been resorted to of late by some students as a point of departure for broader generalizations of the theory of optimal control.

The fundamental role the Hamilton-Jacobi theories played in its application to classical mechanics and quantum theory is generally recognized. It is right to add the merits in formalization of contemporary planning theory.[22]

(9) Developments in methodology of solution of the optimal-control problem will be discussed in the next section. Before we proceed, however, we shall present the argument on the existence of the solution to this problem. In Soviet literature its general formulation is owed to Filippov's work. Its importance will appear in our discussion in several contexts (in particular in connection with the so-called sliding regimes).

The Filippov treatment of the existence problem for the optimal-control solution is very broadly as follows.[23]

We have a system of n equations

$$dx/dt = f(t, x, u) \qquad\qquad (!)$$

Here x and f are n-dimensional vectors and the $u = u(t)$, an r-dimensional vector, which for any values of t and x taken values from the given set $Q(t,x)$. The problem considered is to find such $u(t)$ — for given x^0 and x^* — that with $u = u(t)$ the solution $x(t)$ of the equation (!) (with the initial $x(0) = x^0$) reaches x^* in the shortest possible time while $u(t)\epsilon Q(t,x(t))$. It is assumed that the $f(t,x,u)$ is continuous with respect to the set of t,x,u, and continuously twice differentiable with respect to x, and that

$$x \cdot f(t,x,u) \leqslant C(|x|^2 + 1)$$

(the dot denoting scalar-vector multiplication; $|x|$ the length of the vector x) holds for all t,x and $u\epsilon Q(t,x(t))$. We postulate $Q(t,x)$ closed and finite and denote $R(t,x)$ the set that passes over $f(t,x,u)$ as u moves through $Q(t,x)$. By a further postulate for any t,x, and any positive ϵ, there exists a positive $\delta = \delta(\epsilon,t,x)$ such that for $|t' - t| < \delta, |x' - x| < \delta$, the set $Q(t',x')$ is contained in the neighbourhood ϵ of the $Q(t,x)$ set; then the set $R(t,x)$ as well as the set $Q(t',x')$ will be semi-continuous.

When these conditions hold and the $R(t,x)$ is convex for any t and x, the Filippov theorem states: Let there be at least one measurable function $\widetilde{u}(t)\epsilon Q(t,\widetilde{x}(t))$, such that with $u = \widetilde{u}(t)$ the solution $x(t)$ of the equation (!) (with the initial condition $x(0) = x^0$) reaches point x^* in some t^*, the solution being defined as the absolutely continuous vector-function which almost everywhere satisfies the equation (!) — under the assumptions (and the solution does exist by virtue of the Carathéodory theorem). Then there exists also an optimal control defined as a measurable function $u(t) \in Q(t,x(t))$ when the solution $x(t)$ of the equation (!) (with the initial condition $x(0) = x^0$) reaches the x^0 point in the shortest possible time. On different assumptions, the propositions close to this theorem were independently arrived at by Bellman, Glicksberg and Gross.[24]

At a next stage the possibility of non-existence of the solution for a non-convex set $R(t,x)$ is shown and the sliding regimes are defined. Take the problem

$$dx/dt = -y^2 + u^2; \quad dy/dt = u; |u(t)| \leqslant 1$$

$$x(0) = y(0) = 0; \quad x(T) = 1, y(T) = 0, T > 0; \quad T = \min \tag{!!}$$

Since dx/dt is not greater than 1, T at least equals 1; thus for any solution of (!!) T is greater than 1, and the sequence of solutions will be the minimizing one if $|u_n(t)| \leqslant 1$, $|y_n(t)| \leqslant 1/n$; this will be so because then $x_n(t_n) = 1$ for $1 < t_n < 1 + 1/(n^2 - 1)$. Any minimizing sequence converges to $x(t) = t$, $y(t) = 0$ which is not the solution of (!!) for any $u(t)$ and the optimal control does not exist. Such situations are defined as those of a sliding regime. In order to secure that the solution where the T would be as close as desired to $T = 1$, the $u(t)$ must move sufficiently frequently between values close to $+1$ and to -1. Let both ϵ_n and δ_n be tending to zero; also, for any time interval greater than δ_n, let the proportion of values for t for which $|u_n(t) - 1| < \epsilon_n$ differ from a half by less than ϵ_n, and let the same to hold for $|u_n(t) + 1| < \epsilon_n$: the sequence $u_n(t)$ is a minimizing one.

From the proof of the Filippov theorem which we omit, it follows that the sliding regimes appear where over some $\epsilon < t < 0$ the vector $dx(t)/dt$ does not belong to the set $R(t,x)$, and it then belongs to its complement up to a convex set. (We return to the problems of sliding regimes in the context of "pathology" of controlled systems[25,26].)

Note

The advance in the existence theory of optimal control for nonlinear systems over the decade following Filippov's pioneering theorems is well presented by Polyak.[27] Results analogous to Filippov were obtained in the early 1960s by Roxin and Warga[28] (special cases of integral functionals were treated by Cesari, Ivanova, and Ioffe)[29]. As a rule the contributions require meeting the Filippov conditions, i.e. that the set $Q(x,t) = \{Q(x,u,t), u \in M\}$ be convex in E^n for all x and t. The point is, however, that $Q(x,t)$ is r-dimensional in E^n; as a matter of fact, as a rule the dimension of control is smaller than that of phase co-ordinates; and convexity is compatible with smaller dimensionality only in the case of linearity. Neustadt[30] proved existence without the Filippov condition but required that $\varphi(x,u,t)$ and $F(x,u,t)$ be linear on x. Polyak, in the paper here referred to, drops in his existence theorem both the Filippov and the linearity-on-x conditions (for the nonlinear control problem, that is, with the integral functional, fixed time and free right end-point). The same paper also obtains new results for continuity and uniqueness, the convergence of minimizing sequences, the sufficiency of the Maximum Principle; it goes beyond the Bellman-Gliksberg-Gross results; also beyond the original result of Rozonoer[31] (where the sufficiency of the Maximum Principle is established by placing conditions on the Hamiltonian).

The line of reasoning, originated by Cesari's existence theorem seems to have reached in recent years some definitive conclusions in the writings of Brunovsky. He has proved that the Cesari condition is both necessary and sufficient for the lower-closure set of feasible trajectories.[32]

(10) It is not easy to try to systematize the proliferating and voluminous work on the methodology of the optimal-control solution. None of the known classifications can be ideal, but in the view of this writer, that by Litovchenko[33] approaches it. If we accept his ordering of the matter, we should distinguish four broad classes of methods:

(1)   The method of dynamic programming.

(2)   The method with a strictly variational approach leading to the solution of the extremal problem for a system of ordinary differential equations with the subsequent selection of the "true" extremum. Of its two sub-classes, one (*a*) directly handles the "non-classical" characteristics of the optimal-control process as usually faced, and (*b*), the other, tries to do this by eliminating them.

(3)   The method of the Bellman-Lyapunov functions.

(4)   The method of the functional analysis.

Of these, the penultimate one is placed, as it were, in the common territory of the theories of control and stability, and we shall deal with it in the context of the latter; the last one will be considered in due course in this chapter.

With regard to (2) we may recall some of the "non-classicisms" — elements of optimal control formulation — which would not lend themselves to accommodation by the "traditional" approaches of the calculus. The very appearance of the *explicit* control variable is one of the complications: so is the formulation of constraints to be obeyed by this variable —

as inequalities. Most serious are the complications on two counts: (1) the closedness of the control space, U: as often as not the vector of control would be placed on a boundary; (2) the discontinuities of the control, with their time-points possibly unknown, formalized as piecewise-continuous magnitudes.

The non-classical advance in the calculus has gone precisely in the direction of a *direct* treatment of such "complications" in control-theoretic formalism.[34] But, parallel to this line of development, notable attempts have been made to seek the solution via elimination of the "non-classicisms" encountered. In some this consisted in "opening" the U space — transforming it by means of some "artifex". Major attempts — in particular Soviet attempts — in this direction have been made by applying the Miele transformation and building into the system a "fictitious" control. As a rule this has been combined with re-stating the control problem as the classical Mayer-Bolza problem (though some have resorted, for the purpose, to the non-classical method listed here under (1) — dynamic programming). The pioneering work has been done by Lurye and Troitskiy[35] who formulated (at the beginning of the 1960s) the problem of control as that of Mayer-Bolza with its class of "free" functions extended as a piecewise continuous one and the open U defined by a finite-differentiable relationship of the shape

$$\phi = \phi(u,x,t) = 0; \phi = (\phi_1, \ldots, \phi_\rho); l < n + r.$$

In this way the problem has entered our class (2a) of the Maximum Principle.

While characterizing the main stream of inquiries the method indicated by no means presents the whole range of approaches. Thus, to give some further examples,[36] the classical procedure of variation was applied by Desoer in the optimal-time control system of the form

$$\{\dot{x} = Ax + u, \ |u| \leqslant a_i, \ \mathrm{Re}\lambda_i \leqslant 0, i = 1, \ldots, n\}$$

reduced to the isoperimetric problem of the classical calculus. Generally the classical method has been applied where the conditions of optimality — in respect of continuity — can be treated as those of the curve's behaviour "in the small". In some exercises the classical apparatus has been employed where the control function is subject to "breaks" on passing through a given plane; N. N. Krassovskiy has treated this kind of cases in a system — with a criterion $(t_2 - t_1)$ — taking the form

$$\{\dot{x} = \phi(x,t) + b(t)u; |u| \leqslant 1\}.$$

We shall meet again the names of the pioneers and related work in further contexts. It may be observed that some classes of problems discussed here fit the context of functional analysis on which something is said later.

It is on the two remaining families of methods — those of our classes (1) and (2a), which dominate the theoretical realm of our subject — that we shall concentrate presently.

(11) The fundamental idea — of great conceptual and cognitive power and simplicity — behind the Bellman dynamic programming is that optimal strategy can be designed in a sense without following up the system's behaviour, its history. This constitutes the substance of the Principle of Optimality which, in its author's formulation, says that an optimal policy has the property that whatever the initial state and initial decisions are, the remaining decisions must constitute an optimal policy with regard to the state resulting from the first decision. Or, to take the "reversed" version formulated by Dreyfus: the optimal sequence of decisions in a multi-stage decision-process problem has the property that whatever the final decision and state preceding the terminal one, the prior decisions must constitute an optimal sequence of decisions leading from the initial state to that state[37] preceding the terminal one.[38,39]

Once we find ourselves in the area of multi-stage decision-making, one may be usefully reminded of Dreyfus's forewarning that one cannot solve a multi-stage decision-process problem by sticking to the rule of making sequentially optimal single-stage decisions only. This is so since it is not only the arc value but the effect of different changes in state that must be considered: hence it is the value of the composite effects that has to be calculated and minimized at each application of the fundamental-recurrence relation rule.[40,41]

We may also at this point indicate the nexus with the Markovian approach: In Markov too, whatever the way the present state has been shaped, it, and only it, determines future development. The property is established by a combination of induction and proof by contradiction.

(12) Of fundamental importance for the handling of the optimal-control problem (indeed well beyond any specific solutional technique) is Bellman's functional equation.[42] With the optimality criterion

$$\int_{t_1}^{t_2} f_0(x,u,t)dt$$

it has the form

$$\sup_{u \in U} [\partial\omega/\partial t + \sum_{i=1}^{n} \partial\omega/\partial x_i \cdot f_i(x,u,t) - f_0(x,u,t)] = 0$$

where x^1 is not fixed, and the limiting condition for the "price function" are

$$\omega(t_2, x(t_2)) = 0.$$

This first-order nonlinear partial differential equation generalizes the Hamilton-Jacobi equation of the classical calculus (hence it is termed by some writers — the "Hamilton-Jacobi-Bellman equation"). Boltyanskiy and Krotov have proved its property of sufficiency, viz. the existence of the continuous differentiable function $\omega(t,x)$ is sufficient for the corresponding control $u(t,x)$ to be optimal.

Further on we shall refer to the restatement of the equation as the Bellman-Lyapunov equation. As it appears, it was originally N. N. Krassovskiy who first noticed the nexus between the functions and functionals of Bellman and Lyapunov (but, as it appears also, about the same and independently this was found by Kalman, Bertram and Lyetov). The substance of the nexus is that, for certain problems with special sign-determined criteria of optimality, the Bellman function satisfying the equation stated is, subject to some conditions, also the Lyapunov function. (Thus the methods of the Lyapunov theory of stability find application.) In this sense and to this extent the solution of the optimal control problem reduces to the determining of such "optimal" Lyapunov function.

The function stated above is the cornerstone of the various formulations of the dynamic-programming problem. Thus, to take that of the time-optimum ("fastest motion") problem, as it appears in this statement. Postulate:

(a) the existence of the optimal transition from point x to point x_1 of the phase space; if the transition time is T we denote $\omega(x) = -T(x)$ which is a function of n variables $\omega(x) = \omega(x^1, \ldots, x^n)$. (In this sense this function is continuous and differentiable with respect to each variable $x^1, \ldots, x^n$.)

(b) the property for the function $\omega(x)$ of having everywhere except at point x_1 continuous partial derivatives $\partial\omega/\partial x^1, \ldots, \partial\omega/\partial x^n$, then for a control process described by $\dot{x} = f(x,u), u \in U$ we have

$$\sum_{i=1}^{n} \partial\omega(x)/\partial x^i \cdot f^i(x,u) \quad \begin{cases} \leqslant 1 \text{ for all points } x \neq x_1 \text{ and } u \\[2mm] \equiv 1 \text{ for any optimal process} \\ (u(t), x(t));[43] \end{cases}$$

thus optimality is reached at the $l.u.b.$ value.

In this reasoning the Optimality Principle reveals itself as a sufficient as well as the necessary condition of optimality. It is sufficient as well as necessary, that is, when the two postulates (a) and (b) above — of existence and of continuous differentiability — are met. And in anticipating further discussion we may also note that the method stands out for its universality.

(13) The methodology of Bellman's functional-equation approach in discrete formalism[44] is presented in his fundamental work with brilliant simplicity. We have a function $f_N(x)$ defined as that of maximum return from an N-stage process starting from some initial nonnegative quantity x, so that $f_1(x) = \max [g(y) + h(x - y)]$. If we confine our problem at first to a two-stage process, the return at the next stage will amount to that from the first stage plus that of the second when what is left for allocation amounts to $ay + b(x - y)$ to be used optimally. Extending our reasoning to an N-stage process, we arrive at the "basic functional equation" of the Bellmanian system which, with $f_1(x)$ as before, becomes

$$f_N(x) = \max_{0 \leqslant y \leqslant x} [g(y) + h(x - y) + f_{N-1}(ay + b(x - y))].$$

The solution rests on the tabulation of the sequence of functions $\{y_k(x)\}$ and $\{f_k(x)\}, k = 1, 2. \ldots$. It has the form — given the sequence, N and x —

$$\bar{y} = y_N(x); \bar{y}_1 = y_{N-1}(a\bar{y} + b(x - y)); \ldots\ldots\ldots;$$

$$\bar{y}_{N-1} = y_1(a\bar{y}_{N-2} + b(x_{N-2} - \bar{y}_{N-2})$$

the $(\bar{y}, \ldots, \bar{y}_{N-1})$ being allocations maximizing total return. (There is in Bellman a computational hint: programming the digital computer to print out sequences of the y values, in addition to tabulating sequences f_k and y_k.)[45]

Highly illuminating for the powers of the Bellmanian method in its generalizing continuous formalism is the reasoning presented by Bellman and Dreyfus: the calculus of variations treats the extremal curve as a locus of points to be determined with a differential equation employed; the theory of dynamic programming treats the extremal as an envelope of tangents with the optimal direction to be determined at each of its points. Since a curve — in the Euclidean geometry's duality — is a locus of points *or* an envelope of tangents, the two approaches appear as mutually dual in this sense, and "reinforcing" each other.

The reasoning rests on formalizing the dynamic programming approach to variational problems along the lines which are in themselves of great analytical interest.[46]

We start from the conception of minimizing the integral of the familiar form

$$I(y) = \int_a^b F(x,y,y')dx$$

and we postulate in virtue of the additivity property

$$\int_a^b = \int_a^{a+\Delta} + \int_{a+\Delta}^b ;$$

the y is constrained by the requirement $y(a) = c$: the a and c constants measure respectively the system's initial state and the duration of the process. In this we move from the system where the a and c are parameters to where they are parameters with respective ranges of variation $-\infty < a < b$ and $-\infty < c < \infty$; and we now minimize the function $f(a,c) = \min I(y)$.

Following the logic of the Principle of Optimality we write for the new function

$$f(a,c) = \min_{y(a,a+\Delta)} \left[\int_a^{a+\Delta} F(x,y,y')dx + f(a + \Delta, c(y)) \right] ;$$

this minimization is performed over all y defined over $a \leqslant x \leqslant a + \Delta$ with $y(a) = c$, $c(y) = y(a + \Delta)$. The $f(a,c)$ is assumed to be continuous and to have first and second partial derivatives. Assuming continuity of $y'(x)$, for a sufficiently small Δ, the choice over $[a, a + \Delta]$ is equivalent to a choice of $y'(a)$.

Then we write

$$\int_a^{a+\Delta} F(x,y,y')dx = F(a,c,y'(a))\Delta + 0(\Delta)$$

with $c(y) = c + y'(a)\Delta + 0(\Delta)$ and putting $y'(a) \equiv v$, the fundamental equation is expressed as

$$f(a,c) = \min_v [F(a,c,v)\Delta + f(a + \Delta, c + v\Delta)] + 0(\Delta).$$

With $\Delta \to 0$ we have in the limit the nonlinear partial differential equation

$$- \partial f/\partial a = \min_v [F(a,c,v) + v \cdot \partial f/\partial c]$$

(a discrete version is also evolved by the authors).

Starting from this reformulation, Bellman and Dreyfus demonstrate how the basic results of the classical calculus are obtainable from the functional equation derived from the Bellmanian Optimality Principle and how this technique helps to evade some difficulties.

(14) A handy description of solutional procedures in dynamic programming (with an eye to economics) can be found in Soviet literature in Berkovich's survey.[47] The programming problem has there the form – in standard notation –

$$F(x(u)) = \sum_{t=0}^{T-1} \Theta_t(x(t); x(t+1)) \to \min \qquad (!)$$

subject to $x(t + 1) = f(x(t),u_t); x(t) \in X_t; x(0) = x_0; u_t \in U_t; t = 0, 1, \ldots,$ $T - 1$. Inasmuch as each admissible strategy is fully determined by the sequence of admissible controls $u = (u_0, \ldots, u_{T-1})$, the objective function is conceived here as a function of control; hence the problem is taken as finding the sequence $u^* = (u_1^*, \ldots, u_{T-1}^*)$ minimizing the $F(.)$.

Denote the minimum value of the functional $\sum_k^{T-1} \Theta_t$ for $\{x(t); u_t; t = k + 1, \ldots, T\}$ satisfying the (!) as $F_k(x(k))$. Then by applying sequentially the Optimality Principle to the functions $F_1, F_2 \ldots \ldots \ldots$, we have a system of functional equations (as its exact statement):

$$F_0(x(0)) = \min_{u_0} [\Theta_0(x(0), x(1) + F_1 x(1))]$$

$$\ldots \ldots \ldots \ldots \ldots \ldots \ldots \ldots \ldots \ldots \ldots \ldots$$

$$F_i(x(i)) = \min_{u_i} [\Theta_i(x(i), x(i+1)) + F_{i+1}(x(i+1))]$$

$$F_{T-1}(x(T-1)) = \min_{u_{T-1}} [\Theta_{T-1}(x(T-1), x(T))]$$

(the $F_i x(i)$ being the Bellman function). The solution proceeds "backwards" — starting from the end.

In diagrammatic interpretation, let $ABCD$ correspond to min.F. Then of
all broken lines linking point B with the vertical T, it is to the BCD that
the min $F_i = \sum_{i=1}^{T-1} \Theta_i$ will correspond and the sum is precisely the value
of the Bellman function $F_1(x(1)$ for $x(1) = B$: and this is so since the optimal path from B is independent of trajectory leading to D.

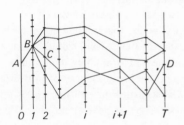

(15) The technical point to bear in mind is that in the multi-stage
dynamic-programming optimization the intermediate stages are not determined before the problem is solved in its entirety. This qualifies the employment of the functional equation. Hence the use of what is known as
the embedding procedure. It is formed of two steps which consist respectively (1) of tabulating — for every stage — the optima as related to the
criterion for every possible value of the state variable, and (2) utilizing the
tabulations for forming the optimal for the process as a whole: moving in
our tabulations from the last stage backwards to the initial stage; as the
latter we take, in every step, that stage for which tabulation is carried out.
Note that, insofar as the optimand's values will be computed for some
number of the state-variable values, interpolation has to be resorted for its
in-between values.[48]

What has been presented illustrates the role of dynamic programming,
well described as one permitting the substitution of the sequence of minimizations for the minimization of a complex function of many variables,
in each of the minimization processes the minimum being determined with
fewer functions of one of several variables.[49]

Note

The concept of dynamic programming tends to widen as a classificatory
concept well beyond what it defined in Bellman's original discovery. It is

illuminating to see its place in a Kantorovich-Romanovskiy recent appraisal of tendencies in mathematical programming as a general theory of extremization.[50]

With this approach dynamic programming as a class embraces problems with a large number of variables wherein the selection of the values of variables is carried out sequentially with the choices made influencing in a relatively simple way the possibilities of selecting the remaining variables. The technique rests, then, on formulating a "local" maximization problem for each variable or group of variables such that in its solution the "best" value is found from the global point of view.

Thus understood, dynamic programming presents itself as methodology employed in a wide range of fields. Here would belong the theory of linear economic models, nonlinear programming in particular with respect to separability problems, probabilistic theories of optimization, in particular the theory of sequential statistical procedures and of optimal control of Markovian processes (see also our Note on sequential statistical search methods below).

In problems of dynamic programming *sensu largo* thus understood, a link with linear programming is accentuated. In probing into its asymptotic properties the limiting stationary states of processes appear as computable by means of linear programming. One will recognize without difficulty that this is the approach in some modelling by the Kantorovich school, in particular in the Kantorovich-Makarov construct discussed further on.

It seems tenable that conceived in this way dynamic programming overlaps the areas of the theory of mathematical programming and of the optimal-control theory, by its nature being closer to the former.

(16) The essence of the Pontryagin method is the Maximum Principle,[51] which offers an effective approach for the solution of the optimal-control problem α for a wide class of dynamic nonlinear problems. (Originally formulated by Pontryagin and his associates in the early 1950s; in the second half of the decade he and Boltyanskiy and Gamkrelidze provided proof that it is a necessary characteristic of both the linear and nonlinear systems and also — with some not unduly restrictive exceptions[52] — sufficient for the former. Subsequently Rozonoer proved its validity for linear discrete (discrete-continuous) systems.)[53]

The substance of the Principle appears from the following reasoning. Let $u(t)$ be an arbitrary admissible piecewise-continuous control over $t_0 \leqslant t \leqslant t_1$ with a corresponding solution, $x = x(t)$, of the system $\dot{x}_i =$

$f_i(x_1, \ldots, x_n; u_1(t), \ldots, u_r(t))$, with the initial condition $x(t_0) = x_0$.
Consider further some auxiliary unknown functions $\Psi = (\Psi_1, \ldots, \Psi_n)$; if
we assumed that $x(t)$ and $u(t)$ are known, we could write down the auxiliary system of linear differential equations

$$\partial\Psi/\partial t = - \sum_{\alpha=1}^{n} \partial f^{\alpha}(x(t), u(t))/\partial x_i \cdot \Psi_{\alpha}.$$

For any initial condition $\Psi(t_0) = \Psi_0$ this has the unique solution
$\Psi = (\Psi_1(t), \ldots, \Psi_n(t))$.

We then consider the function

$$H(u,x,\Psi) = \sum_{\alpha=1}^{n} f_{\alpha}(x,u)\Psi_{\alpha}.$$

When the values of Ψ and x have been fixed, the H clearly becomes the
function of the u parameter. Denote its least upper bound,

$$\sup_{u \in U} H(u,x,\Psi) = M(x,\Psi).$$

The left-hand side is the maximum of the values of H if the latter reaches
the upper bound of U. Thence the Maximum Principle. Its theorems say:
If $u(t)$ is the optimal control and $x(t)$ the corresponding optimal trajectory,
then in the family of functions generated by them, $\{\Psi = \Psi(t)\}$, there exists
a vector function $\Psi = \Psi(t)$ such that $H(u(t), x(t), \Psi(t)) = M(\Psi(t), x(t))$;
further, for any $t_0 \leqslant t \leqslant t_1$ we then have $M(\Psi(t), x(t)) = M(\Psi(t_1), x(t_1))$,
which is non-negative.

Thus stated the Principle lends itself to restatement in analytical form
with the help of the Hamiltonian $dx_i/dt = \partial H/\partial\Psi_i$; $\partial\Psi_i/\partial t = - dH/dx_i$;
$H(u(t), x(t), \Psi(t)) = M(x(t), \Psi(t))$.

We have then a complete system of canonically conjugated equations;
for the optimal chains containing $(2n + r)$ unknowns we have the same
number of relations ($2n$ differential and r finite); this is so since the last
relation in our system may be written

$$\left.\frac{\partial H(u, x(t), \Psi(t))}{\partial u_j}\right|_{u - u(t)} = 0 \qquad j = 1, \ldots, r.$$

For our system of $2n$ differential equations the solution depends on
exactly the same number of parameters — initial conditions. This is so, for

while on the one hand, of these one drops out (since the functions Ψ_a are determined only up to the multiplier); on the other, we get an extra one by considering the time formulation, $(t_1 - t_0)$, as a parameter. We handle the $2n$ parameters so that $x(t_0) = x_0$ and $x(t_1) = x_1$ hold. Our system satisfies only one trajectory, and if we assume that the technical and mathematical argument establishes the existence of an optimal trajectory, this one must be optimal. But how legitimate is this assumption?

The validity has been established for the linear case of the form $\dot{x} = Ax + Bu$ (the A and B being linear operators transferring respectively X and B into X) with the postulate of the region of the u's variation being a convex polyhedron $(u_1, \ldots, u_r)$, where for any of its edges w the vectors $(Bw, ABw, A^2Bw, \ldots, A^nBw)$ are linearly independent in the space X. As a matter of fact, linearity of the system simplifies the Hamiltonian statement (above). We have then the function $H(u,\Psi,x) = (\Psi . Ax) + (\Psi . Bu)$ as that of the variable $u \in U$: it reaches its maximum simultaneously with (Ψ,Bu). The Maximum Principle is then stated

$$\dot{x} = Ax + Bu; \; \dot{\Psi} = -A^*\Psi; \; (\Psi(t), B(u(t)) = P(\Psi(t))$$

where the $P(\Psi) = \max_{u \in U} (\Psi,Bu)$.

The procedure is then this: For each of the $\Psi(t)$ we search for the optimal $u(t)$: it is uniquely determinable, piecewise-constant, its values being only the polyhedron's vertices of the U polyhedron; thence we obtain the optimal trajectory $x(t)$.

As the co-author of the system, Mishchenko, unequivocally puts it: what is not clear is the way the initial values of the functions $\Psi_1, \ldots, \Psi_n$ are to be found in solving the system $\dot{\Psi} = -A^*\Psi$ so as to satisfy $x(t_1) = x_1$. The difficulties in finding it rise with the complexity of the system, and we shall see further on how serious the difficulty is applicationally.

Note

In the synthesis for a class of systems, the L class, the conjugated variables p can be expressed as functions of the phase co-ordinates and some arbitrary constants c; thus the Hamiltonian would be of the form $H(x,u,c)$.[54] As against the procedure in the general situation here one can *sequentially* handle (1) the dynamics of the system in the build-up of the Hamiltonian, (2) the constraints on the control, when identifying on the $H(x,u,c)$ all the potential "candidate controls" for optimality, and (3) the problem's boundary conditions: a set of the c's corresponds to each optimal trajectory. The relief here, as against the general case, then consists in that there is no need to treat all these requirements simultaneously. Note that the class contains among others (linear) stationary systems.

(17) What has been said so far, then, is a very broad sketch of the development in the field during the past decade and a half or so. In perspective two lines are discernible in it. One direction — as pointed out by Westcott[55] is that resting on the impulse-transfer function, originated by Wiener; along it — at the next step — constraints have been taken into account, and further on there has been the generalization of the approach to systems with varying parameters. The other direction, we would say, originates in the work of Feldbaum and Lerner: it is that of nonlinear dynamic optimization. This rests on taking as the constraints the system's differential equations in the minimization of the control-performance criterion; and bringing into the mathematics of the approach the Lagrangean multipliers and the Hamiltonian; the culmination is in the Pontryagin Principle (Westcott). The development of the Bellman construct is parallel.

We may as well at this intermediate stage hint at certain arguments with respect to the structure of the calculus-of-variation approach to the control-theoretic problem, be it classical or non-classical. Thus it has been argued by Schapiro[56] — and the argument is strikingly presented — that the approach depends more on analytical ingenuity than direct perception and requires justification by hindsight: that Lagrange multipliers — in the calculus of variation — have no "physical meaning"; that it is a "topsy-turvy way" of treating the control system by bringing it in in the guise of side constraints; that similarly unnatural is the introduction of the adjoint variables "out of the hat". We would be inclined to see in the methodological (and technical) ingenuity an admirable virtue rather than a shortcoming: the "physical" non-existence of the Lagrangeans is not relevant since the question arises as to what is meant by the "physique" in question (one will think of Lagrangeans interpreted as prices — on this more below): and the same is true of the Pontryagin-type introduction of the conjugate variables. What would seem relevant would be whether the technical ingenuity helps to solve the "natural" problem rather than the "naturalness" or otherwise of technique itself.

(18) The publication of the Bellman and the Pontryagin principles, when they had crystallized, stimulated intensive research in control-theoretic problems in many directions. Work on alternative formulations of the principles, their mutual relationship and that with the classical calculus has

greatly contributed to the advance of the discipline. What follows is meant
to be no more than a rather arbitrary illustration of the development.

It would seem that it was Rozonoer who first established the link between the two Principles. About the same time its simple and elegant
demonstration, plus a procedure for obtaining the Pontryagin Principle
from that of Bellman, was published by Desoer.[57] He showed that the
Maximum Principle only expresses the regime of optimality in the choice,
at each point, of trajectory independently of particular conditions imposed, the assumption being that the control signal is restricted to a specific closed and bounded region. Incidentally there is also in Desoer an indication of the way certain relevant properties can be brought out in the
study of the Maximum Principle; this includes the so called bang-bang controls for nonlinear systems where, that is, the controls shift drastically from
one to another point of the boundary — within the admissible-control
region. (A lucid geometric interpretation of the connection between the
two Principles can also be found in Feldbaum; in substance it links up with
that of Desoer).[58,59]

(19) Among studies providing a more general look at the two Principles
and, through them, at the central control-theoretic problem, one may
single out those by Hestenes[60] and Berkovitz.[61]

Hestenes could in fact refer to his own formulation of an Extremum
Principle (as early as 1950) by the translation of the Bolza problem:
On this path it has been shown in what sense the Maximum Principle is
derivable from, and equivalent to, the Euler, the Lagrange and the
Weierstrass conditions. Further proceeding from the general theory of op-
timal control, as essentially the Hamilton-Jacobi theory, Hestenes has defined the generalized optimality embracing a Minimum Principle.[62]
Berkovitz's inquiry moves on very similar lines but focusing rather on
Mayer's formulation of the problem of extremum (see above). This is also
the point of departure of the more recent study, by Gumowski and Mira.[63]
It shows in particular the role of the Maximum Principle as applying essentially to a degenerate Mayer problem — one in which the derivative of the
minimizing function $y(x)$ does not appear directly. Speaking generally, the
Gumowski-Mira stand may be taken as symptomatic of a tendency to re-
affirm the potentialities of the classical constructs as against the modern
"artifices". In this the original, geometrically-oriented, theory of
Carathéodory[64] is rediscovered. The focus is on his treatment of the
boundary-value problem. To restate it briefly, the Carathéodory system
rests on his fundamental partial differential equations and the related

family of geodosically equidistant surfaces (in the geometric treatment of extremals the concept of the quickest-descent curve is resorted to; the condition — necessary and sufficient — for an arc to have the direction of such descent at intersection with surface is the latter's transversality to that arc); the connection with the Hamilton-Jacobi system is immediate.[65] It is attractively demonstrated that the relation between the "equidistants" and the extrema is identical with that of the Fermat principle and the optimal, shortest-time path of a ray — as related to the Bernoulli brachistochrone and the Huygens Principle.[66,67] It is contended that both the dynamic programming and the maximum-principle programming are particular cases of the Carathéodory formulation. Specifically, the particularity of the former lies in its rather involved method of stating the fundamental equation. As seen, the weakness of dynamic programming would consist in the lack of distinction between local minima and non-trivial local lower limits affecting the concepts of transversality and of admissible neighbourhoods. (The point is made that therein originates the usual misconception of the dynamic-programming versus classical-calculus issue — centring on the Euler equation and disregarding fundamental contributions by Carathéodory and for that matter also by Hilbert, Hadamard, and Wiener.) Of particular relevance for the realm of planning theory may be on a stress that the recurrence type of processes employed in programming brings about a gradual loss of continuity and on the risk entailed in discretization, either in the Euler method or dynamic programming. While the ingenuity of the Pontryagin Maximum Principle is conceded, it is maintained that the method offers less information about the extremal problem than the Carathéodory formulation: the canonical equations of the former form but a part of characteristic equations of Carathéodory.

Having restated the argument of Gumowski-Mira — itself a symptom of what may be described as the classical "reaction" — it is not unfair to say that the Gumowski-Mira reappraisals have contributed to the establishment of some balance in the issues of classics versus non-classics. What we would, however, stress — from our angle — is the decisive issue of tractability as well as heuristic merits: it is from this point of view that the "modern" artifacts have powerfully opened up a new era in the field. This is true in particular of the great discoveries of Bellman and Pontryagin.

Since this section was written its subject has been surveyed by Jacobson and Mayne. They strongly and convincingly present the opinion that dynamic programming offers applicationally more scope than is generally realized. They deal in particular with the point raised by some students that the classical approach and the reachable-set theory (see on this *passim* our references to Halkin, to whom the powerful concept is owed) would be preferable because they yield rigorous results without severe requirements of smoothness (which applies in particular to the bang-bang type of control). This is, in our view, a valid corrective of certain opinions with which we shall be concerned in the Part devoted to application.[68]

At this intermediate stage, however, it might perhaps be of some expositional help to recapitulate the basic elements of "vulnerability" — from the applicational angle — of the two Principles on which the literature of the subject has mainly concentrated.

(20) Some of the weaknesses of the Bellmanian method have been extensively elaborated upon by the Pontryagin school in their celebrated book. The main ones are these. It entails finding not only the optimal controls but also the $\omega(x)$ function. The Bellman equation is one in partial derivatives (complicated by the sign max.) First and foremost the difficulties arise from the two postulates (of existence and of continuous differentiability) for the function $\omega(x)$ — for a function, that is, of which nothing can be known a priori (in actual fact, even in the very simple linear cases it does not prove itself to be automatically everywhere differentiable; the writing down of the Bellman equation is as often as not very difficult: for one has to handle variables which do not lend themselves to embedding in the sequential system.[69] However, it is only fair to record the recognition of the method's universality — universality greater than that of the Maximum Principle — which we would say may be a source of strength as well as weaknesses. The point has been made that in fact it was evolved with an eye to optimal-control processes beyond what are describable by differential-equations systems; and that in some cases it may have heuristic virtues, even though it may lack in them a rigorous logical basis.

As to the Pontryagin Principle, its chief handicap (hinted at in the foregoing remarks) is the search for the appropriate initial conditions required for the solution of the conjugate system. There is no indication to guide us as to the way to determine them, as they are endogenous to the system. (On suggested ways of handling the problem see, for instance, our sect. 6, p. 289 above.)

To generalize the observation, in this family of control-theoretical systems there is the difficulty — practical as well as theoretical — of expressing the auxiliary Lagrangeans in terms of the phase co-ordinate x. They are not related to the substance of the problem itself.

A special category of difficulties arises with respect to sliding regimes where the optimal solution does not exist (owing to non-convexity). In Soviet literature the pioneering contribution to the study of such regimes, as the important case of the pathology of optimal-control systems (deviation from the general existence theorem), is owed to Filippov. His argument is presented later on. Further work in this field with implications for the control-theoretic formalization of the problems of planning is discussed separately.

Note

In the latter 1960s the Pontryagin school gave a good deal attention to the problem of the Bellman equation and the solution of the Bellmanian optimal-control problem based, as it is on the existence (as pointed out hardly ever realizable) of continuous differentiability of the equation.[70]

The work was initiated by Boltyanskiy,[71] who showed the way of weakening of the, seldom materializing, condition of continuous differentiability of $S(t,y)$ (see p. 292 for symbolism), devised that is a *quasi*-solution with breaks in the partial derivatives of $S(t,y)$ over some "good" set of points.

The Boltyanskiy attempts to weaken the difficulties entailed in the possible non-differentiability of the Bellman function have been pursued in Soviet literature — in particular by Kun and Pronozin[72] — in a different way, through an approximation procedure. The problem formulated is as usual: that of controlling the motion described by $z = f(z,u)$, $z \in R^n$, $u \in U \subset R^n$ where R^n is the n-dimensional Euclidean space, U_r the control region, f the locally Lipshitzean image from $R^n \times U$ to R^n. Moreover it is assumed that the image f satisfies the Filippov condition $< z, f(z,u) > \leqslant C(1 + \|z\|^2)$, with $(z,u) \in R^n \times U$, the $< z, f(z,u) >$ being a scalar product of the vectors z and $f(z,u)$, the $\| . \|$ — the Euclidean norm and C some positive number. (For stochastic case, see A:T, 1 (1973)).

While it is provable that for the examples in Pontryagin *et al.* there exists an ϵ-solution of the Bellman function, Kun and Pronozin establish the existence of such a solution for linear problems with non-degenerate control regions. Now, the *exact* synthesis (assuming its existence) in control problems is as a rule a discontinuous function; thus there is no certainty that such synthesis does ensure the uniqueness and a continuous dependence on initial conditions. While this is true of the exact synthesis, it is shown that there exists a smooth ϵ-synthesizing function in linear problems with a non-degenerate control region. The build-up of the smooth ϵ-solution and the ϵ-synthesizing function in linear problems with a non-degenerate controls rests here on "internal" approximation of the initial control region U by means of some canonical control region U.

(21) The last few years have witnessed a remarkable progress in the generalization of optimal control, welded at the turn of the decade into a consolidated discipline.

It is by now generally accepted that its origins should be related to the work of Dubovitskiy and Milyutin,[73] "rediscovered" of late by students in the West as well as in the Soviet Union. Intended by the authors to generalize the Lagrangean methods, it has yielded a generalization of the calculus of variations; then in generalizing the approach to constrained problems of the extremum, it has exemplified the methodology i.a. on the control-theoretic problem. The methodological approach to the Pontryagin Principle is characteristic for the basic idea: in presenting the proof, elements specific to the Maximum Principle are "isolated" from those immanent in the general system (the former related, that is, to formulation in terms of ordinary differential equations).

A crucial step on the way to generalizations in our field has been made by one of the co-authors of the Pontryagin fundamental study: by the mid-1960s Gamkrelidze had formulated[74] a general extremal problem in the theory of differential equations and obtained for such extremality the necessary conditions. Of the problems thus formulated both the classical variation-calculus problem and standard optimal-control problem reveal themselves as particular cases: and the Maximum Principle shows itself implied in the "necessary condition of extremality" derived.[75] Consider vector differential equation $\dot{x} = f(x,t)$ where f is a fixed element of F; also a differentiable manifold N in R^{2+2} with boundary M. Let the solution $z(t), t_1 \geq t > t_2$ be an F,N extremal, the F being a quasi-convex family of functions. There exists then an absolutely continuous vector-valued $\psi(t) \neq 0$ such that $z(t)$, $\psi(t)$, $t_1 \leq t \leq t_2$ satisfy for almost all t

$$\dot{z}(t) = \frac{\partial \bar{H}(\psi(t), z(t), t)}{\partial \psi} = \bar{f}(z(t), t), \quad \psi(t) = -\frac{\partial \bar{H}(\psi(t), z(t), t)}{\partial x} = -\psi(t)\bar{f}_x(z(t), t$$

and that

$$\int_{t_1}^{t_2} \bar{H}(\psi(t), z(t), t)dt \geq \int_{t_1}^{t_2} H(\psi(t), z(t), t)dt = \int_{t_1}^{t_2} \psi(t)f(z(t), t)dt$$

holds for every element $f(x,t)$. The transversality condition is that if $f(z(t),t)$ is continuous at the end points t_1, t_2, then the vector

$(\bar{H}(\psi(t_1),z(t_1),t_1), -\bar{H}(\psi(t_2),z(t_2),t_2), -\psi(t_1),\psi(t_2)$ is orthogonal to M at $q = (t,t,z(t))$. The formulation of the theorem and proof have been facilitated by a concept of quasi-convex sets.[76]

The basic conception of unity of the area had by that time guided the work of several students in addition to Gamkrelidze, in particular Ghouila-Houri, Warga,[77] *et al.*; the subject has been considered by some broadly as that of "relaxed controls"; and has had various ramifications.[78,79]

The Gamkrelidze generalization is at the same time a striking attempt at integration into a logical whole of various elements owed to the calculus of variations and contributions to the control theory proper. Thus, to start with, Gamkrelidze points out (as do Dubovitsky-Milyutin, independently), the classical Lagrange problem has revealed itself to be a special case of the optimal-control problem; further, necessary conditions for the Maximum Principle have showed themselves to contain all the classical first-order necessary conditions: we have then the link with the Euler-Lagrange equations, the Lagrange multiplier rule, Legendre's necessary conditions, and the Weierstrass inequality; also many new results are now seen as contained in Valentine's work (reference to Berkovitz and Hestenes).[80] Finally, Gamkrelidze acknowledges the link of his basic unification ideas with those of generalized curves, relaxed variational problems, and "chattering" controls respectively treated by Young,[81] Warga,[82] and Gamkrelidze himself. (The link between the basic theorems of mathematical programming and those of the Maximum Principle has been systematized in Soviet literature also by Pervozvanskiy.)[83]

(22) The work of Gamkrelidze (starting from the extension of the Maximum Principle to problems with constraints on the phase coordinates) and the generalization of the fundamental theorems of nonlinear programming, specifically the Kuhn-Tucker theorems, by Dubovitskiy-Milyutin, have been paralleled chronologically in the West by independent work of the greatest importance in the same direction — by Halkin and Neustadt[84] in the first place. They have systematically advanced the study of the "conversion" of optimal control into a mathematical programme: in most recent work they have treated optimal control as such a programme in infinite-dimensional spaces. They attacked the overall problem by first building up a very general mathematical-programming problem and formulating a necessary condition for it. They have then shown that the typical problem in optimal control can effectively be "rephrased" as such a problem. Then the study of dynamics of a control problem has led to the proof that the assumptions of the Halkin-Neustadt basic theorem of the "con-

version" do hold in the time dimension too. It has been shown in particular that this theorem gives rise to the Maximum Principle.

In Halkin's system[85] we have a set L of real-valued functions ψ_i defined
on it; the problem is that of finding an element $x \epsilon L$ which minimizes ψ_0
on the set of $x \epsilon L$ which satisfies the constraints $\psi_i(x)$. In this system,
where L is finite dimensional and the ψ linear, we have the linear programme; where L is still finite-dimensional but the latter nonlinear – we
have nonlinear not-necessarily-convex programming of various kinds
according to the properties of the ψ: and, taking one further step, we see
both the calculus of variations and the optimal-control theory as mathematical programming – in a very generalized system where the set L is an
infinite-dimensional set of functions.

As noted – within the same school of thought – by Polak,[86] the fundamental change over a few years consists in the fact that various constrained
minimization problems – specifically the classical-calculus, nonlinear programming, and optimal control problems – have all come to be viewed as
special cases of a canonical, basic optimization problem. To be more specific, the subject of the Polak inquiry is the consideration of the constrained
minimization problem in finite-dimensional spaces and the straightforward
generalizations needed to secure the extension of results to linear topological spaces: the Kuhn-Tucker conditions and the Maximum Principle are
the main applications dealt with. In fact it is on the Pontryagin-type control system that the inquiry centres. This is also true of Neustadt's work.
It formulates generalizations of the considered class of optimal-control
problems; reduces the class to one of the generalized mathematical-programming problem: starting from the general necessary conditions for the
latter, it arrives at particular necessary conditions for the optimal-control
problems.

To both Halkin and Neustadt (and associates) we owe very major inno-
vations – both conceptual and methodological.

A major area of convergence in the study of matters treated in this section is the topological framework. There again we see the tendency toward
generalization. Gamkrelidze in particular (in his recent work joint with
Karatishvili)[87] has been exploring extremality in topological spaces.

This has also been one of the focuses of Neustadt's study. Indeed, that
is the area of Neustadt's interesting experimenting[88] with the fundamental
framework. Thus rather than follow the accepted stand in regarding optimal control problems as mathematical programming problems in *abstract*
linear vector spaces, he had adopted a new "viewpoint" of the problems
by working with a Cartesian product of the space of the right-hand-side of

the system's differential equations with the initial conditions space R^n. It appears in the exercise as an imaginative and fruitful unorthodoxy. This has been followed by a Halkin-Neustadt examination of controlled systems as programming in general normed spaces.[89]

At his next step — no less imaginative, and original (on optimal control operators with operator restrictions[90]) — Neustadt adopts a linear vector space of continuous operators from C_n, the space of continuous functions from a compact interval in a Euclidean space, into itself. In this it differs from previous treatment by several students, including himself and Halkin, also — in Soviet literature — Dubovitskiy-Milyutin, Pshenichnyi, Gamkrelidze-Karatashvili (with all of whom this is the space either of phase trajectories, or a product of control space and phase trajectory space, or of rhs of differential equations).

We started this section with pointing to the pioneering role in the field of Dubovitskiy and Milyutin. We may finish by noting its acknowledgment by Halkin — and his revision of their optimization formalism and "detection" of its weaknesses in the treatment of equality and operator constraints. This he has strengthened with some results of the search for generalized necessary conditions in mathematical programming applicable to optimal control — the results of his own work and that of Polak and associates.[91]

(In a logical link-up we can mention also Dantzig's observations on the relation of generalized programming and control theory. They point in particular, as it were, to an aspect converse to that examined by those starting from the control-theoretic end. As Dantzig[92] argues, insofar as (given a control) the Maximum Principle is the provider of the optimality test, demonstrably the Pontryagin procedure is based on computing what can be formalized as the decomposition sub-problem and on testing whether the minimum of $u(t)$ is secured; thence it follows that in the particular case the Maximum Principle is yielded by the decomposition principle of mathematical programming (of the Dantzig-Wolfe type); moreover it offers a procedure for successive improvement of the policy vectors which in turn generate controls.)

(23) The impressive strides made during the last few years — largely thanks to Dubovitskiy, Milyutin, Neustadt, Halkin and their associates — by the inquiry into the common fundamentals of the hitherto compartmentized methodologies and approaches have not remained without certain reservations by some students. In fact one of these pioneers in this field[93] (Milyutin) does not conceal his view on limitations of the adventure: in

one of his latest contributions he points out that in his inquiries the general schema of necessary conditions in extremization of the optimal-control problems has proved to be different for virtually every one of these problems (specifically he found in formalizing sufficiency, with reference to stationarity conditions, that he is ultimately back at the Maximum Principle). At least he offers a hypothesis as to the cause (and suggests a line of investigation into observed theoretical phenomenon).

More controversial would seem reservations by a school of thought which would stress that the line of development towards generalization has taken the theory of optimal control, as such, off its proper paths such as traced out at the origins by conceptions of the maximum-speed problem (Gabasov and Kirillova; cf. above discussion of Polak's argument). It is not easy to see, in our submission, what has been lost to the knowledge of optimal controls by unravelling the theoretical roots of steered processes. Moreover, as will be seen from what follows, this inquiry — by its sheer logic — has induced a further important cognitive advance in the area of extremization; the advance is "dialectical".

(24) By way of a conclusion to the section we feel we should give at least a few lines to Pshenichnyi's book[94] (which appeared when the section was completed). Pshenichnyi, who had himself made noteworthy contributions to the body of literature on the subject, has now very successfully organized it as a discipline — the theory of necessary conditions of the extremum.

The unity of the systematized subject reveals itself among other aspects also in that we have in Pshenichnyi the presentation of its general mathematical apparatus and its application to the major groups of the "sub-subjects" traditionally compartmentized as mathematical programming, game theory, problems of momenta, the discrete Maximum Principle. (Technically the apparatus on which the theory of necessary conditions for extremization rests is functional analysis: in substance, in fact on a few basic concepts and theorems, such as those of weak convergence and of bi-compactness and the theorem of separability of convex sets.) Pshenichnyi works essentially with the deductive method — first, general results in the field are presented, and then their "concretization" in a specific problem is demonstrated.

It is a legitimate claim of Pshenichnyi that the discipline he has been instrumental in establishing has permitted the viewing of wide classes of problems from a unitary angle. (In particular, the study has made it possible to build up necessary conditions in problems embracing functions non-differentiable in the usual sense of this concept: what has proved sufficient to consider are the functions only differentiable directionally instead.)[95,96]

Note

In Pshenichnyi's formulation[97] the discrete version of the Maximum Principle has this substance: In a system $x - f(x, u) = 0$ where

$$x_{k+1} - x_k - \int_{t_k}^{t_{k+1}} f(x_k; u(t))dt = 0 \ (!); \ a_i(x_0) = 0 \ (!!); \ \phi(x_k) \leqslant 0 \ (!!!)$$

for $\bar{x}_k$ to be the optimal trajectory and $u(t)$ — the optimal control the necessary condition is the existence of numbers $\beta_0 \geqslant 0$, $\lambda_k \geqslant \alpha_i$, and vectors ψ_k some of which nonzero, such that

(1) $$\psi_0 + \left(\int_0^{t_1} \partial_x f(\bar{x}_0, \bar{u}(t)dt)\psi_0 = \sum_{i=1}^{p_0} \alpha_i \partial_{x_0} a_i(\bar{x}_0) + \lambda_0 \partial_{x_0} \phi(\bar{x}_0) \right);$$

(2) $$\psi_{k-1} - \psi_k - \int_{t_k}^{t_{k+1}} \partial_x f(\bar{x}_k, \bar{u}(t)dt)\psi_k + \lambda_k \partial_{x_k} \phi(\bar{x}_k) = 0 \ ;$$

(3) $$(\psi_k, f(\bar{x}_k, \bar{u}(t)) = \max_{u \in U} (\psi_k f(\bar{x}_k, u))$$

(4) $$\psi_{N-1} + \lambda_N \partial_{x_N} \phi_N(x_N) + \beta_0 \partial_{x_N} g_0(x_N) = 0$$

(5) $$\lambda_k \phi_k(\bar{x}_k) = 0; \ k = 0, 1, \ldots, N.$$

The convexity in the control system (!) is secured by the left-hand integral. The expression (3) is the Maximum Principle. Where $\Delta_k = \max | t_{k+1} - t_k | \rightarrow 0$ the result becomes an ordinary Maximum Principle.

(25) Ahead of later discussion we may indicate here some new methods of the finite control of concentrated, distributed, and discrete systems to which the contribution of Soviet students is very considerable. In following Feldbaum-Butkovskiy, we state the problem treated in this fashion:[98] find the control $u(t)$ such that x moving from $x(0) = x_0$ reaches x^* over the postulated time interval: $x(T) = x^*$, or without loss of generality we bring $x(t)$ into the origin (or taking in a new function, say $y = x - x^*$). The control $u(t)$ and the corresponding $x(t)$ and the impulse $F(t)$ are all zero for $t = T$. The solution of the finite-control system rests in the authors referred to on the application of the Fourrier transform, Wiener's theorems,

the theories of integer functions of a complex function, and those of inter-
polate functions of such a function.

Specifically when handling a Pontryagin-type problem one will find, by
some direct variational method, the *whole* set of admissible control
securing the system's motion from the initial into the terminal state; and
next one will choose the set of that control which extremizes the given
functional: we shall proceed this way rather than, as is usual, finding the
control for the set of extremals and then "sieving out" — by selecting the
initial conditions of the differential equations system — that extremal
which passes through the given origin and terminal points of the phase
space.

(26) This section is reserved for certain theoretical developments of what
one can describe as the pathology of the optimal-control systems. They
relate to some structural characteristics of the "established" control-
theoretic model which on the one hand affect their heuristic potential and
on the other constitute a handicap in their handling of reality. Hence the
importance — on both counts — of their "pathology" which, as we shall
see, is another domain of outstanding exploration in Soviet applied-
mathematical theory. A word about their place in the present attempt of
systematization. On the one hand this pathology is concerned with what
forms the subject-matter of the previous sub-chapter. But on the other
hand it directly relates to matters of stability: it is concerned with some
instabilities of the control-theoretic constructs and with the remedial ideas
proffered.

Our discussion here is confined to two problems of pathology for which
one can detect a common background. Historically it is formed by the revived interest (again originating in engineering but of obvious significance
in economic planning) in the celebrated Andronov-Pontryagin[99] theory of
"coarse systems" and small parasitic elements and the theory of oscillations, methodologically a starting-point for handling the "not-so-small"
structural perturbations. Their analysis brought out the need for sufficiently simplified "naïve" stability criteria.

The two problems which will be discussed here are those of the "incorrectly set", and of the sliding regimes — of optimal-control systems.

(27) We start with the problem of "irregular" systems. The most important contemporary development in this area is due to Tikhonov's "regulari-
zation" methodology[100] for control. What follows is an exposition — with

the symbolism preserved — of what we see as the essentials in his latest formulation of the "incorrectly set" control problem and the algorithm devised. The notion of incorrectness is akin to the classical Hadamard concept;[101] its special meaning in Tikhonov will appear from the exposition.[102]

For a Pontryagin or a Bellman world, the system of equations considered is

(1) $dx/dt = f(t,x,u), (x = x_1, \ldots, x_n), (u = u_1, \ldots, u_m), t_0 < t < T$

with the control functions $u(t)$ belonging to a complete functional class U with initial conditions $x(t_0) = u_0$, and a continuous non-negative functional $F[x]$ determined on the functions $x(t)$ over $t_0 < t < T$.

It is assumed that there exists within U an optimal control; there exists, that is, a function $\bar{u}^{(0)}(t)$ such that $x(t,\bar{u}^{(0)})$ realizes the minimum of the $F[x]$, the greatest lower bound

(2) $\inf_{u \in U} F[x(u)] = F_0$.

The approximation of the optimized control will usually be sought in a method of minimizing the functional F, whereby the sequence of functions $u_n(t)$ is computed such that

(3) $F_n = F[x(u_n)] \underset{n \to \infty}{\to} F_0$

and a function $u_n(t)$ for which the value of F_n is sufficiently close to F_0 to be accepted as the approximation to $\bar{u}^{(0)}(t)$.

It is further assumed that some constructional principle for the minimizing sequences considered is available, and that the U does not contain isolated elements. Whatever the accuracy adopted one will find a control $\bar{u}(t)$ such that

(4) $F[x(\bar{u})] \leqslant F_0 + \epsilon$

and that $(\bar{u}^{(0)}(t) - \bar{\bar{u}}(t))$ can take arbitrarily large values compatible with $\bar{\bar{u}}(t)$ belonging to the U. Then some $\bar{\bar{u}}(t)$ is chosen, coincident with $\bar{u}^{(0)}(t)$ everywhere except for a small interval $(t_1 - \eta, t_1 + \eta)$ near an arbitrary t_1 where the difference $(\bar{\bar{u}}(t) - \bar{u}^{(0)}(t)')$ is made to exceed some fixed number M_0 compatible with class U. For any accuracy δ the number η can be chosen such as to satisfy $|x(t) - \bar{x}^{(0)}(t)| \leqslant \delta$ and for a sufficiently small η, and therefore also δ, the inequality $F < F + \epsilon$ will hold.

Tikhonov's regularizing algorithm employed for finding the optimal control is constructed so as to make the minimized sequences converge to $\bar{u}^0(t)$. The smoothing functional has the form

(5) $$G^\alpha[u] = F[x(u) + \alpha\Omega[u]$$

where the regularizing functional is taken to have the form

$$\Omega u = \int_{t_0}^{T} \sum_{i=1}^{m} [k_1(t)\,(u_i')^2 + k_0(t)\,(u_i)^2]dt;\ k_1(t) > 0;\ k_0(t) > 0.$$

Then some decreasing sequence of numbers $\alpha_k \to 0$ and some controls $u^{\alpha\kappa}(t)$ are considered such that

(6) $$G^{\alpha k}[\hat{u}^{\alpha k}(t)] \leqslant G_0{}^{\alpha k} + \alpha_k c$$

where G_0 is the lower bound and c is a constant independent of α.

Two theorems which are proved provide an answer to the problem:
(A) If there exists a unique optimal control $u^{(0)}(t)$ of the problem (1) forming a smooth function, then the sequence of the functions $\hat{u}^{\alpha}k(t)$ satisfying

(7) $$G^{\alpha k}[\hat{u}^{\alpha k}] \leqslant G_0{}^k + \alpha_k c$$

uniformly converges to $\bar{u}^{(0)}(t)$

and

(B) If $\bar{U}$, being a set of elements U on which the $\Omega[u]$ is determined, is convex and complete, then there exists at least one function $u^\alpha(t) \in U$ which realizes the minimum of the functional

(8) $$G^\alpha[\bar{u}] = F[x(\bar{u})] + \alpha\Omega[u] \quad (\bar{u} \in U).$$

Note The proof for (B) starts with the proposition that the sequence of the minimizing functions uniformly converges to the function $\bar{u}(t) \in U$. It is shown that the $\bar{\bar{u}} \in U$ and that

$$\Omega[u_n{}^\alpha(t) - \bar{\bar{u}}(t)] \to 0, \quad (n \to \infty)$$

by proving that the sequence $u_n(t)$ is a Cauchy sequence:

$$\Omega[u_n{}^\alpha - u_m{}^\alpha] \to 0, \quad (n,m \to \infty).$$

(28) The other area of advance in pathology of control systems, neighbouring upon that discussed, to which we intend to call attention is — as
we said — that of the optimal sliding regimes. These are largely identified
with Krotov (who gave to the regime its name, which incidentally points
to inspiration from the automatic-control problem in mechanics), and
Gamkrelidze.

Here the concern is with the investigation — and the build-up — of an
algorithm for the situation where no solution exists for, and within, the
framework of the "established" optimal-control constructs, specifically
that of Pontryagin. The leading methodological conception borrowed from
the classical calculus is that of the limiting solution defined by a minimizing sequence.

First to formulate the problem and to attempt a method of solution
was Krotov,[103] by starting from the proposition that in the class of admissible pairs of the vector functions $y(t)$, $u(t)$ — class "D" — there may
not exist an absolute minimum $\bar{y}(t)$, $\bar{u}(t)$ of

$$(1) \qquad\qquad J = \int_0^{t_1} f^0(t,y,u)\,dt + F(y_0,y_1),$$

$$(2) \qquad\qquad \dot{y} = f(t,y,u),$$

but there will always exist the minimizing sequence $\{y_s(t), y_s(t)\} \in D$ such
that

$$(3) \qquad\qquad J(y_s,u_s) \to m, \quad m = \inf J(y,u) \quad y,u \in D.$$

Krotov also offered a method of solution for particular cases of non-
existence of the minimals $\bar{y}, \bar{u} \in D$. In this the functional $J(y,u)$ is determined for $y(t)u_i(t)$, so that say for the trio of the functions $y(t)$, $u_1(t)$,
$u_2(t)$ we have

$$(4) \qquad\qquad J(y,u_1,u_2) = \lim_{s \to \infty} I(y_s,u_s)$$

where $\{y_s,u_s\} \in D$ is the minimizing sequence of the adopted construction:
its property is that the sequence of trajectories in the phase space $y(t)$ converges to certain function $\bar{y}(t)$ — which is a function of zero nearness —
while the sequence of control $u_s(t)$ has no bounds but oscillates between
some fixed values of $u_i(t)$. (As given in the initial plane-problem $i = 1,2$;
also it is assumed that one of the functions $u_i(t)$ has the optimal value $\pm\infty$

if the region $Q(t)$ is unbounded and $u = \pm 1$ if $Q = [-1, +1]$). Where the $Q = [-1, +1]$, the functional is of the form

$$(5)\ J(y, u_1, u_2) = \int_0^{t_1} \left\{ f^0(t, y, u_1) + [f^0(u_2) - f^0(u_1)] \ \frac{\dot{y} - f(u_1)}{f(u_2) - f(u_1)} \right\} \ dt$$

or, to restate in other terms.

$$(6)\ J = \int_0^t \sum_{i=1}^{n+1} \alpha_i f^0(t, y, u_i) dt; \ \dot{y} = \sum_{i=1}^{n+1} \alpha_i f(t, y, u_i); \ \sum_{i=1}^{n+1} \alpha_i = 1; \ \alpha_i \geqslant 0$$

where $n = 1$, and under conditions adopted

$$(7) \qquad\qquad u_2 = \pm 1 = \text{sign} \ [\dot{y} - f(t, y, u_1)].$$

The Krotov conception has been generalized by Gamkrelidze,[104] starting from the Filippov's general theorem of existence for optimal processes:[105] this is extended by Gamkrelidze under the proposition that in practice there always exists a sequence of admissible controls such that the corresponding sequence of trajectories of the function $\dot{x} = f(x, u)$ (where f is continuous with respect to its terms and continuously differentiable with respect to x) converges to some limiting curve satisfying given boundary conditions while the values of the functional-minimand converge to its lower bound: this "limiting motion" of the phase-point along the limiting curve may be conceptually approximated as closely as required by that along the trajectory of the $f(x, u)$: then the sliding optimal regime is defined as that of the motion along the limiting curve which does *not* coincide with the trajectory of the f.

The gist of the argument is this. Assume that some points $a, b \in X_n$ can be connected by the trajectory of f. We can then choose a minimizing sequence of controls $u^{(k)}(t)$, $0 \leqslant t \leqslant t_k$, $k = 1, 2, \ldots$ transferring the phase point from a to b along the trajectories $x_{(k)}(t)$, $0 \leqslant t \leqslant t_k$ and minimizing the transfer time: $\lim t_{(k)} = T$. Assume that all trajectories $x_{(k)}(t)$ are limited modulo by the same constant which is valid in particular where $x \cdot f(x, u) \leqslant c |x|^2$ does hold. Thus some a priori valuations can be chosen for which the proposition is valid.

It is thus legitimate to postulate that the sequence of trajectories $x_{(k)}$, $0 \leqslant t \leqslant t_k$ uniformly converges to some limiting $x(t)$, $0 \leqslant t \leqslant T$. This curve is the optimal trajectory of f connecting a, b if the motion along it is realizable by some control; otherwise the motion along $x(t)$ is by definition the sliding optimal regime for the equation f. The problem is then one of finding the minimizing sequence of equations $u^{(k)}(t)$, $0 \leqslant t \leqslant t_k$.

Next for the f a controllable equation

$$\dot{x} = \sum_{\alpha=1}^{n} p_\alpha f(x, u_\alpha) = g(x, p, U)$$

is considered — an equation for which the control vector is $(p, U) = (p_1, \ldots, p_n, u_1, \ldots, u_n) \in T^n . \Omega^n$ where the point p belongs to the n-dimensional simplex $T^n = \{ p = (p_1, \ldots, p_n): p_1 + \ldots + p_n = 1, p_\alpha > 0, \alpha = 1 \}$ and point $U = (u_1, \ldots, u_n)$ to the n-th topological degree, Ω^n, of the set Ω. Thus the control for this equation is any measurable function with values in $T^n . \Omega^n$.

It is then shown — with reference to the Filippov existence theorem — that any random points $a, b \in X^n$ which can be connected by means of some trajectory of the equation (1) can also be connected by means of the optimal trajectory with the optimal transfer-time T. Generally, starting from a, b can always be reached by one of the two paths: either along the optimal trajectory of f or by a motion subject to the sliding optimal regime.

Moreover, it is shown that by means of an arbitrary control $U(t) = (p_1(t), \ldots p_n(t), u_1(t), \ldots u_n(t))$, $0 \leqslant t \leqslant t^*$, one can — for the equation transferring the phase point from a to b along $x(t)$ — construct a sequence of controls $u^{(k)}(t)$, $0 \leqslant t \leqslant t^*$, $k = 1, \ldots$ for the f, for which there correspond trajectories $x_{(k)}(t)$, $0 \leqslant t \leqslant t^*$, $x_{(k)}(0) = \alpha$ which converge uniformly to the trajectory $x(t)$ of the equation (1). The proof works with the tools of auxiliary — "base" and "weighting" — functions and "jumps". The time-segment $0 \leqslant t \leqslant t^*$ is subdivided into k sub-segments $I_i^{(k)}$, $i = 1, \ldots, k$, and in turn the sub-interval is broken up into n measurable non-intersecting sets, so that

$$I_i^{(k)} = \bigcup_{\alpha=1}^{n} \overset{(k)}{_{ia}}$$

satisfying

$$\overset{(k)}{\underset{i\alpha}{\mathscr{E}}} = \int p_\alpha(t) dt.$$

The base and weighting functions are then respectively $u_\alpha(t)$ and $p_\alpha(t)$. With the construction of the control $u^{(k)}$, $0 \leqslant t \leqslant t^*$, as defined, the point

$u^{(k)}(t)$ over $k \to \infty$ is thought of as "jumping with infinite frequency" from one base control to another and stopping at the base control $u_\alpha(t)$ for a segment of time whose density is given by the weighting function, and the motion of the phase-point $x_{(k)}(t)$ becomes a sliding one along the absolutely continuous trajectory $x(t)$. In this way the finding of the optimal sliding regime is reduced to the Maximum Principle and the Gamkrelidze solution follows its familiar lines.

While the Gamkrelidze approach would prima facie yield an answer to the problem, Krotov has subsequently demonstrated its serious difficulty.[106] It is that the Maximum Principle by itself does provide a solution — in his terms the minimum of the functional (5) — as a rule where we have the solution $\bar{y}(t)$, $\bar{u}(t) \in D$ of the initial problem of the minimum of (1), that is precisely where there is no need to resort to the auxiliary system: for as soon as the minimum of the (1) becomes a sliding one, the problem of the minimum of (5) degenerates — the Maximum Principle equations have then an infinite number of solutions.

An analysis of alternative methods of complete solution of the sliding-regime problems has led to Krotov's formulation of his Optimality Principle which reads:

Let the set $V(t)$ of admissible y,u be closed for all $t \in [0,t_1]$ and let there be a sequence $\{y(t),u(t)\} \in D$. For this to be the minimizing sequence it is necessary and sufficient that there exists a function $\phi(t,y)$ continuous on B and differentiable everywhere over B except for the set of values $t \in (0,t_1)$ of measure zero, such that for $s \to \infty$ the two conditions are met:

$$(Z) \quad R(t,y_s,u_s) \to \mu(t), t \in (0,t_1),$$

and

$$(\zeta) \quad \phi(\bar{\bar{y}}_{0s}, y_{1s}) \to \inf_{y_0 \in B(0), y_1 \in B(t_1)} \phi(y_0, y_1)$$

$$\mu(t) = \sup_{y,u \in V(t)} R(t,y,u),$$

$$\phi(y_0, y_1) = F(y_0, y_1) + \phi(t_1, y_1) - \phi(0, y_0),$$

$$R(t,y,u) = \phi_y f(t,y,u) - f^0(t,y,u) + \phi_t.$$

Where a minimum $\bar{y}(t)$, $\bar{u}(t) \in D$ exists the conditions (Z,ζ) take the form:

$$(Z') \quad R(t,y(t),\bar{u}(t)) = \mu(t), t \in (0,t_1)$$

and

$$(\zeta') \quad \phi(y_0,\bar{y}_1) = \inf_{y_0,y_1 \, \in B(0)XB(t_1)} \phi(y_0,y_1).$$

This principle is a working hypothesis: it is proved with respect to the conditions' sufficiency; their necessity is a conjecture. Krotov shows that all the known algorithms are contained in the principle.

The Krotov algorithm differs in its basic properties from those resting on either the Lagrange or the Hamilton-Jacobi method (it is conceived by its author as the "antipode" of the Hamilton-Jacobi-Bellman formalism). It has been designed as a method of solution of a degenerate problem and is essentially applicable only in cases of degeneracy as defined (see above). Certain properties of each of the alternative methods are indicated to commend it in the treatment of specific problems. Thus while the Hamilton-Jacobi-Bellman method displays small sensitivity to constraints on controls but a high one with respect to those on phase co-ordinates, in Krotov's method the constraints on the phase co-ordinates are of no importance.

In the cases of full degeneracy, that is with $k = n$, the solution $y(t)$ is obtained directly as a finite equation: compared with this the Lagrange formalism would require the solution of a limiting problem for a system of ordinary differential equations of the order $2n$, and — still more difficult — the Jacobi-Hamilton method would require a solution of an equation in partial derivatives. In a word, where applicable, the Krotov method has the virtue of solvability by elementary means. Hence one will be inclined to accept the claim that this may account for the fact that the method (in its original particular-case formulation — see above) was instrumental in the first discoveries of non-trivial regimes in a variational problem: and it has the record of effective application in practical problems of mechanics (specifically in aviation). Analogy in planning is tempting.

Notes

1. V. A. Kosmodieyanskiy has employed the Krotov procedure in establishing the sufficient conditions for the absolute extremum of Bolza-Mayer type variational problems (in "Dostatochnyie usloviya absolutnogo

ekstrema v odnoy variatsionnoy zadache tipa Boltsa-Meiera", *Prikladnaya matematika i mekhanika,* 1966). His system of equations has in addition to the control vector $u = u(t)$ a first-order instability vector $y = y(t)$.

2. The nature of connection between the functions of Bellman and of Krotov in dynamic-programming problems was investigated by I. V. Girsanov in *Vestnik moskovskogo universiteta* (Mathematics & Physics, no. 2, 1968). The general finding is that every Krotov function in a dynamic-programming problem is identical with Bellman's function in some other problem with identical conditions and a return function with a weaker optimum. Bellman's function appears then as, mathematically, an envelope of a Bellman-functions' set.

Girsanov's paper is interesting also for its rigorous analysis of the nature of the link between the stability of solution of the problem and the "correctness" of the problem-statement: the case of the equivalence of both is detected. (Girsanov essentially follows Krotov in defining the "correctness" of the statement of the problem: the definition is then that the problem of minimizing the functional $f_0(u)$ on the set Q is correctly stated if its solution exists, is unique and any minimizing sequence strongly converges to it.)

3. The generalization of the Bellman method by Krotov reveals itself from this reasoning. On Bellman's method optimal control is found from the equation (subject to boundary conditions of a particular problem):

$$\frac{\partial S(x,t)}{\partial t} + \sup_{u \in U} \frac{\partial S'(x,t)}{\partial x} f(x,u,t) = 0 \qquad (!)$$

In Krotov the *sufficient* conditions are found for the same problem from the equation

$$\frac{\partial \phi(x^0(t), t)}{\partial t} + \frac{\partial \phi'(x''(t), t)}{\partial x} f(x^0(t), u^0(t), t)$$

$$= \sup_{u \in U} \sup_{x \in X} \left\{ \frac{\partial \phi(x,t)}{\partial t} + \frac{\partial \phi(x,t)}{\partial x} f(x,u,t) \right\}. \qquad (!!)$$

As pointed out, in (!) we have one, and in (!!) two operations "sup", in (!) one *has* to solve, and in (!!) there is no need to solve the Bellman equation since the Bellman equation (!!) is obtained from the particular positum as to the function ϕ.

4. Since the Gamkrelidze-Krotov foundations had been laid more work has been done by several students on sliding-regime systems which add to the scope of application. From the latter angle of obvious interest are

achievements in the treatment of systems with variable structure. Thus —
in Soviet literature — Buyakas[107] has established that the motion in a system of this kind — to be more specific, a system with commutable
elements — is optimizable in the sense of a weighted integral error; in this
particular solutions of the Maximum Principle determine the plane of
stable sliding.

(In following the Maximum Principle, the optimal control, *if it exists*
should, at any time point maximize the *H* function, viz.

$$\max H = \max \left[\sum_{i=1}^{n-1} \psi_i x_{i+1} + \psi_n \sum_{i=1}^{n} a_i x_i + \psi_n \sum_{i=1}^{n-1} u_i x_i - 0 \cdot 5 \sum_{i=1}^{n} q_i x_i^2 \right] ;$$

where $u \epsilon [+b_i, - b_i]$; the solution for ψ being $\dot{\psi}_1 = - \partial H/\partial x_i$ (the a_i is the
object's parameter, b_i — constraint; a and b are vectors; Q is a positive
diagonal matrix with q_i along the diagonal).

In the system considered, the sliding regime materializes along $x(t)$ at
any time-point t. The control is $u(t)$ with its values in $G^* \backslash G$; the G^* is a
closed region of admissible values and G^* its convex envelope.

Postulate that there is a set of admissible values of control $u_i = \pm b_i$, a
convex closure of this set follows $\| u_i \| \leqslant b_i$. Here in the neighbourhood of
the plane $(c,x) = 0$, formed by particular solutions, it is necessary to switch
the control so as to make it obey the law $u_i = - \text{sign} \, (c,x) x_i$. When the
point gets into this plane, then further motion, under the sliding regime
for a system with variable structure that is, is optimal in the sense of the
minimum integral quadratic error if the motion in the $(c,x) = 0$ plane is
stable. By selecting various weight constants q_i in the optimized functional of the form $I = 0 \cdot 5(x, Qx)dt$ min the various planes are obtained.
But for the particular motion to be admissible the u^* must satisfy

$$- b_i \leqslant u_i^* = c_i a_{n-1} + c_i a_n - c_{i-1} - a_i \leqslant b_i \quad (!)$$

$$c_{n-1} + a_n = (c_{l-i} + a_l)/c_l \quad l = k+1, k+2, \dots, n-1.$$

If the coefficients a_i, $i = 1, \dots, n$ are variable but their variability does
not affect the inequality (!) the sliding regime is preserved.

(29) We have seen how difficulties encountered in the application of the
classical calculus have inspired the non-classicist approaches. In turn limitations in the latter have stimulated the search for some viable — and
sufficient for the empirical purposes — approximate solution method.[108]

In fact one line of advance has proved to be that of what is known as direct methods (direct in the sense of not entailing the solution of the Euler system of equations) evolved in the classical methodology. A well-established if only rough method is that of the Ritz functions. Its formalization has usually the shape

$$I_n(x) = \sum_{i=1}^{n} \alpha_i R_i(x).$$

Here the R is some, given, function; the α_i's, termed the Ritz coefficients, are constants. The integral becomes their function $I = I(\alpha_1, \ldots, \alpha_n)$: the α's are selected so as to minimize it, thereby solving a system of differential equations $\partial I/\partial \alpha_i = 0$. With a sufficiently large number of n we have an approximation — as desired; with $n \to \infty$ the theoretically exact solution is reached.

A prevalent procedure is that of successive approximation in the policy space or iteration, usually formed of correction steps successively made in gradient directions relative to an associated function which postulates its minimum accompanying the solution for x of the main problem. A combination of dynamic programming with the gradient method has proved itself in particular in cases of intricate criteria, especially so where we have to deal with nonlinearities.

In some cases the steepest descent method, forming a sequence of control functions up to the optimal control, proves adequate in coping with the difficulty of the two-point boundary-value problem. It helps in this way in the application of the Maximum Principle. From the practical point of view it is worth stressing the computer's ability to form the sequence of control functions or parameters determining optimal control.

In one of the latest fruitful explorations in the field, Gabasov and Kirillova[109] have addressed themselves to the problem of approximation of the Pontryagin vector ψ_0 (we recall this stumbling-block in the application of his Maximum Principle). In this the problem of minimizing the functional is reduced to that of determining the extremum of some convex function $\lambda(g)$ of a finite number of variables equal to the order of the system. In a geometrical interpretation of the $\lambda(g)$, a convergent path of successive approximations is obtained leading to the ψ_0.[110]

Some approaches designed in more recent years have shown more promise than the classical Cauchy-Hadamard method evolved for finite-dimensional spaces. One may mention in particular that offered by

Kantorovich[111] in his basic work on functional analysis in normed spaces. The problem of finding the solution of the system of functional equations is reduced to the search for the minimum of some nonlinear functions: for this purpose successive approximations are pursued such as to make the passage from one to the next one along the direction of the fastest decrease of the functional.

For a quadratic function with a positive quadratic form it was proved by Kantorovich that

$$\frac{f(\bar{x})}{f(x)} = \frac{(\Lambda - \bar{\lambda})^2}{(\Lambda - \lambda)^2}$$

taking f optimal at zero and the Λ to be the largest and λ the smallest eigenvalue of the quadratic form.

The method permits determining the rate of convergence at its possible worst.

Also certain refinements have proved useful in the Newton step-by-step approximation. Take the equation $f(x) = 0$ and γ_i an approximation to one of its roots; the next step leads to $\gamma_{i+1} = \gamma_i - f(\gamma)/f'(\gamma_i)$, the $f'(\gamma_i)$ being the derivative of $f(x)$ evalued at the point $x = \gamma_i$, and so on.

Kantorovich and, independently, Temple, are credited with pioneering the new variant of the gradient method (steepest descent) they evolved. (The basic idea behind it being that the fastest descent of the functional in the vicinity of some point is secured by the direction opposite to that of the functional gradient at this point.) Slow convergence has induced the search for other effective gradient methods connected with that of conjugate gradients, essentially of multi-step descent type.[112]

Successful experiments have apparently been recorded in control-theoretic work with the method of conjugate gradients. In this one starts from some estimated x_0 of the solution vector x; the corrective movement is in the directions which are mutually conjugate with respect to the co-efficient's matrix; they are selected successively so as to be in gradient directions with respect to a quadratic function becoming zero when the x of the original problem is solved.

Notes

1. At this stage computational algorithms for optimally controlled system still basically rely on the methods of gradient descent in the control space, the main theoretical effort being directed towards the acceleration of convergence in such procedures: this leads usually to making use of

second derivatives and to the Newton methods and its modifications. As pointed out, however, very few computers accept with sufficient ease algorithms employing second derivatives of the minimand function; hence the attempts to build up algorithms avoiding such derivatives; this is being achieved as a rule by expanding the respective space — largely by the method of conjugated gradients, thought of as an iterative gradient method "cum memory"; the latter means additional information as compared with the gradient at one point. In particular, in Soviet literature, Danilin and Pshenichnyi have produced in the 1970s algorithms for "accelerated convergence" where the second-derivative matrix is not being computed but instead the preceding computations of gradients are being made use of so that the respective expressions would tend toward this matrix.[113]

2. A method of conjugated gradients, claiming "competitiveness" with exact methods has been evolved by B. T. Polyak. To solve a system of linear equations / or minimization of a quadratic functional of the form $Ax - B^2$ we have:

$$x^{k+1} = x^k + \alpha_k p^k; \quad p^k = -r^k + \beta_k p^{k-1}; \quad r^k = A^*(A^k x - B);$$

$$\alpha_k = \|r^k\|^2 / \|Ap^k\|^2; \quad \beta_k = \|r^k\|^2 / \|r^{k-1}\|^2; \quad k \geqslant 1 \; \beta_0 = 0.$$

The x^k is an iterative sequence starting from arbitrary x^0, A^* being a transposed matrix. The method, formally iterative, is finite: x^n is the solution, n denotes dimensions. Cf. B. T. Polyak, "Method sopryazhennykh gradientov dlya reshenya zadach lineynogo programmirovanya", in *Sistemy programnogo obespechenya reshenya zadach optimalnogo planirovanya* (Moscow, 1970). See also his important survey of the gradient method for the minimization of functionals, in *Zhurnal vychislitelnoy matematiki i matematicheskoy fiziki*, 4 (1963).

Polyak has subsequently updated this survey and generalized theories of convergence in one-step iterative methods, of possible directions (Zoutendijk), in particular gradient projection, conditioned gradients, and others. New results were obtained in this, in particular with respect to gradient-projection methods for the case of perturbations, also modified Newton and Gauss-Newton methods subject to constraints. Cf. ibid, 4 (1971).

3. For a valuable contribution to the analysis of the effectiveness of the steepest-descent (gradient) method in the optimal-control solution (notoriously suffering from its slowness) the reader is directed to D. E.

Johansen's paper "Convergence properties of the method of gradients", in Leondes, op. cit., iv (1966). The basic feature is the direct relationship between the convergence rate of the method and the singularity of the second variation operator of the problem: fast asymptotic convergence rate where the operator has no small eigenvalues, and slow otherwise. We may also mention a technique evolved by the same author ("Optimal control of linear stochastic systems with complexity constraints", ibid.) for simplifying a control problem by putting constraints on the system's design without affecting criteria.

4. After this section was written I read in Falb ("Optimal control theory", in Kalman *et al., Topics in mathematical system theory*) a very useful classification of iterative procedures in the solution of most control problems. These are seen as broadly divided into direct and indirect ones. The former rest on reducing the control problem to that of a differential equation, specifically the Hamilton-Jacobi partial differential equation; the latter on a system of differential equations such as the canonical system of the Pontryagin principle.

In view of the latter, an extremal control and trajectory is bound to meet the canonical system of differential equations, the Hamiltonian minimization relationship and the boundary conditions (as determined by the initial point, the target set, and the transversality conditions). It is then demonstrated by the authors that the usual procedure is to start with trajectories, satisfying two of the three and to carry out changes till the remaining condition too is met: thus e.g. in the gradient techniques as adopted in Kantorovich-Akilov a start is made with the first and the third conditions met, and changes made till the second is satisfied too.

5. On the whole, as observed by Bryson and Ho, gradient methods tend to be successful in initial iterations but the convergence tends to deteriorate with the approaching solution; the converse is true of the second-order gradient methods (specifically also the Newton-Raphson method) using "curvature" as well as slope at the nominal point; while convergence is good at the approaches to optimal solution the methods may be troublesome at the start connected with the picking of a "convex" nominal solution. cf. Bryson and Ho, op. cit.; cf. also in the context Zangwill's *Nonlinear programming: a unified approach.*

(30) The work of Dubovitskiy and Milyutin, whose contribution to so many aspects of the theory of optimal control is now being discovered, have also a suggestion of an approximational solution technique for a prob-

lem covered by the Maximum Principle but "affected" by non-differentiability.

This is the substance of the method.[114] We have a functional

$$I(x,u) = \int_{t_0}^{t_1} \phi(x,u)\partial t$$

given over the solutions of the system $dx/dt = f(x,u)$; when $x(t_0) = x_0$;
$x(t_1) = x_1$; find $x(t)$, $u(t)$ minimizing I. Non-differentiable values of $u(t)$
belong to some set D in E^r.

We are concerned with the necessary conditions for the strong extremum and in this we resort to the neighbourhood concept. The sequence
$u_n(t)$ tends toward $u(t)$ if $| u_n^{(t)} |$ is uniformly bounded and converges to
$u(t)$ in measure.

We write an arbitrary function $u(t)$ in the form $u(\tau_\nu(t))$ where $u(\tau)$ is
some function and τ and t are related by $dt/d\tau = \nu(\tau)$ with a non-negative
ν. The $u(\tau)$ is evidently determined uniquely when $\nu(\tau) \neq 0$ and can be
arbitrarily postulated when $\nu(\tau) = 0$.

Then we consider $u(t,\delta) = u(\tau_{\nu+\epsilon\bar{\nu}}(t))$, $\nu + \epsilon\nu \geq 0$ for $\epsilon \leq \epsilon_0$. Then
where $\epsilon \to 0$, the $u(t,\epsilon) - u(t)$ will tend to zero. The point is that whereas
the $[u(t,\epsilon) \to u(t)]$ would be as a rule non-differentiable, the $\nu(\tau,\epsilon) =
\nu + \epsilon\bar{\nu} \to \nu(t)$ is differentiable with respect to ϵ. Hence to manipulate
variability we carry out variation of $\nu(\tau) \geq 0$.

(31) The term "dynamic programming" has been given in Soviet literature[115] to a construct which has little direct link with the Bellman model,
relying essentially as it does on the method of organized selection (first
suggested by Dubovitskiy and Milyutin)[116], but it is noteworthy as a procedure of some attraction in economic planning. This construct, owed to
Moiseyev, is characteristic in that it does *not* reduce the variational exercise — by means of the necessary conditions for the extremum — to a
limiting problem. Its problem is finding the minimum of the functional

$$I(u) = \int_0^T F(t,Lu)dt$$

(L is an operator, u is "control", a function of t, $u \in G$ the set of admissible
values of u). The u may be postulated such that if $t \in [0,t_1)$ or $t(t_2,t]$, then
the values of $u(t)$ must belong either to the shaded domain or its boundaries f_1 or f_2 (Fig. 1). The interval $[t_1,t_2]$ is "uncontrollable" in the sense

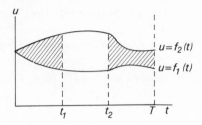

that the values of $u(t)$ are uniquely determined by its value $u(t_1)$. Then a set of points $\{u_{ij}\}$ is built up: the $(0, t_1)$ interval is broken up into N parts by points $t = h, 2h, \ldots$; on each of the straight lines within G the u_{ij} points are thus determined, i standing for the number of the vertical and j for the number of the point on it; the system of $\{u_{ij}\}$ is the "scale" of controls. In the polygonal approximation the operation which relates two points $u_{i+1,k}$ and u_{ij} with the function $u_{ij}^{i+1,k}(t)$ is a segment of a straight line

$$A(u_{ij}, u_{i+1,k}) \equiv u_{ij}^{i+1,k} = u_{ij} + \frac{-u_{ij} + u_{i+1,k}^0}{h}(t - ih).$$

Moreover we have defined a number

$$I_{ij}^{i+1,k} = \int_{ih}^{(i+1)h} F(t, Lu_{ij}^{i+1,k})dt.$$

The "step-by-step" — sequential — procedure is then this. Step one: fix point u_{ij} and with the use of the operator A connect it with all points u_{0s}, as in Figure 2; for each function obtained u_{0s}^{1j} calculate $I_{0's}^{1j}$. To the point u_{ij} take the corresponding number $I_0^{1j} = \min I_{0's}^{1j}$ and the control at which this minimum is reached; repeat for each point of the set u_{1j}. Step

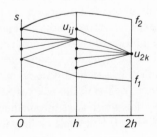

two: note point u_{2k} on the straight line $t = 2h$; again with the use of A construct the functions u_{ij}^{2k} and compute numbers I_{1j}^{2k}. Form $I_0{}^2{}^k{}_{1j} = I_0{}^{1j} + I_{1j}^{2k}$. This number is a function of the j. Le $I_0{}^{2k} = \min I_{0,1j}^{2k}$. Again to the point u_{2k} for an arbitrary k take the corresponding number $I_0{}^{2k}$ and control u where the minimum is arrived. Thus some collection of points u with the corresponding numbers $I_0{}^{N+1,r}$ − corresponding to each of them − is reached, the "control scale" is formed and the procedure repeated *ab initio*. The solution's exactness depends patently on the step h as well as the "scale".

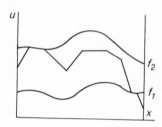

(Note that Moiseyev outlines also the way the Pontryagin-problem situations, with their limiting conditions, can be readjusted for a treatment with the "control scale".)

To repeat, the purpose of the method is to avoid some of the difficulties in the usual methods of organized selection, such as those of limiting descent, Newton method, and others: weaknesses arising from the need to solve the Cauchy problem inasmuch as that solution is, in the general case, unstable. In the Moiseyev procedure all the boundary conditions are met at each iteration step: thus the iteration process may be expected to converge independently of the first approximation.

(32) We have referred in quite a few contexts to the method of functional analysis. The present one seems appropriate for a few words in a generalizing fashion, since the class of these methods has proved its potentialities in providing a solution of the variational problem with a degree of exactness adequate in application; also because of its role played in integrating the investigation of constrained systems, both linear and nonlinear. It is owing to its nature as well as to this role that one will agree with Litovchenko's classification which gives this method an independent position in the discipline (see sect. 10). While evading the exact extremal solution, it has advanced the methodology of approximation for both piece-wise and smooth control problems. As a rule it reduces the problem of optimal control to the extremization of the convex function of a finite number of variables.

Chronologically the merit of originating the approach appears to be shared by R. E. Bellman, O. A. Gross, and I. L. Gliksberg[117] with Krassovskiy; further notable advances in this field in Soviet literature are due to other students, in particular to Gabasov and Kirillova. The original Krassovskiy[118] approach rests on certain propositions of functional analysis, specifically on the Hahn-Banach theorem for the L system in abstract functional spaces as adopted by Krein in his theory of moments.[119] Take L, a linear subset in B — the Banach space — and f defined on the L — a functional, real value, continuous and linear. It is proved that there exists a linear functional F defined on all B with the property that $f(x) = F(x)$ where the x is in L and the norm of f equals that of F.

Generally, the original treatment of the problems was posed in these terms. We have as a datum the initial and terminal states of the system, respectively $x = x_0$ and $x = a$, and the behaviour of the system observed is described by equations linear with respect to x_i and control functions u_j, the latter being subject to

$$\| u \| \equiv \max_t \ | u_j(t) | \leqslant 1$$

or

$$\| u \| \equiv \max_j \left(\int_{t_0}^{t} | u_j(\tau) |^p d\tau \right)^{1/p} < 1, p > 1.$$

Then in the early 1960s Neustadt,[120] in a study of the existence of optimal controls in the absence of convexity conditions, starting from a Lyapunov theorem, showed the applicability of a similar method in handling a system

$$\dot{x}_i(t) = \sum_{s=1} a_{is}(t) x_s + \phi_i(u,t),$$

where $\phi_i(u,t)$ are continuous functions and $u \in U$, the U being a given set.

Of recent work worthy of note is, in particular, the synthesizing study by Gabasov and Kirillova.[121] The focus is on the synthesis of the auxiliary linear system (the assumption being that with the adopted approach a stage-by-stage linearization does adequately permit linearization).

It follows from the lemma that for the synthesis-problem of the optimal system (as above) with

$$\phi_i(u,t) = \sum_{j=1}^{r} b_{ij}(t)u_j(t),$$

the solution is provided by

$$u(t) = \text{sign } B^*(t)\psi(t,\psi_0(x_0)),$$

where the ψ_0 is the initial condition for the system of equations conjugate with (ψ). Gabasov-Kirillova show the relations for which the $\psi_0(x_0)$ holds, and offer a computable procedure of its approximation. The optimality criteria here are some convex functionals or time (also adaptive systems are explored).

(33) The parametric aspect of the optimal-control has received a considerable amount of study from the beginning of the discipline. As early as 1959 Boltyanskiy[122] published his investigation of the sufficient conditions for the optimal processes with variable parameters: it has had an influence on the magnum opus by Pontryagin *et al.*, of which he is the co-author.

Related has been the problem termed that of the control quality. This, as it would appear, originated in the work of Rozonoer[123] in the late 1950s; this method is applied in a recent study — by Milyutkin[124] — of a system in first-order ordinary differential or linear equations whose motion is ruled by the Maximum Principle with variable lag-parameters.

We direct the reader to the proceedings of the Second IFAC symposium where sensitivity analysis was the central theme.[125] In particular to the report by Durato, Kokotović, and Kvakernaak and to: (1) the findings of Guardabassi, Locatelli, and Rinaldi to the effect that where the number of parameters becomes large enough, as related to that of state and control variables, the system becomes incontrollable structurally (proof offered for a linear time-invariant system); (2) the observations by Pervozvanskaya and Pervozvanskiy on the applicability of alternative apparatus for sensitivity analysis (in particular, the use of the sensitivity functions in control problems which lend themselves to the treatment by mathematical-programming apparatus; cf. also our discussion of their method above.

(3) Gumowski's and Mira's investigation of the problem of variable parameters from the angle of structural stability.

Among methodologies inspired by the idea of simplification of the formal apparatus for system description a noteworthy development can be claimed for the conception of approximating it as one with distributed parameters. This is yet another field in which the Lurye school has distinguished itself. The practical treatment of distributed-control systems is exceedingly complex: hence the endeavours to carry out the optimization by taking advantage of specific characteristics rather than relying on "ideal" controllers. On the whole the algorithmic apparatus evolved is oriented towards particular problems of practice (on this see a most valuable survey by Lurye, Butkovskiy, and Yegorov)[126] but certain general lines of approach have been elaborated, in particular by Lurye.[127] What follows is his formulation of the typical basic optimality problem.

Let S be a closed domain of a plane with piece-wise smooth boundaries Σ_1, Σ_2; and in it we have a system of equations in partial derivatives

$$\Xi \equiv z_x{}^i - X_i(z,\xi,u;x,y) = 0,$$

$$H_i \equiv z_y{}^i - Y_i(z,\xi,u;x,y) = 0, \qquad (!)$$

$$\partial X_i/\partial y - \partial Y_i/\partial x = 0, i = 1, \ldots, n.$$

The vector functions $z = (z^1, \ldots, z^n)$ and $\xi = (\xi^1, \ldots, \xi^\nu)$, which are the basic and parametric variables, respectively, describe the state of the system; the $u = (u^1, \ldots, u^p)$ describe the controls. Any partial-differential equation system is expressible in this form: we have here the particular case of the Pfaffian.

Next the constraints on the control functions. Of these the first r_1 and the remaining $(r - r_1)$, respectively, are given the form of finite equations and inequalities:

$$G_k(u;x,y) = 0, k = 1, \ldots, r_1, \text{ and } G_k(u;y,z) > 0, k = r_1 + 1, \ldots, r.$$

It is assumed that the boundary Σ_1 is known and the first n functions z^i are given, i.e. $z^i \mid_{\Sigma_1} = z_1{}^i(t), i = 1, \ldots, n_1$, the n_1 corresponding to the particular case; the outer boundary curve Σ_2 is not known except that we know the $n_2 < n$ of ordinary differential equations of the form

$$\Theta_{ik} \equiv \frac{dz^{ik}}{dt} - T_{ik}(z, v; t) = 0, \qquad i_k = i_1, \ldots, i_{n_2} \qquad (!!)$$

that hold along it. The boundary controls $v^x = v^x(t), x = 1, \ldots,$ are included into these equations. The values of the functions $z^{ik}(t = 0)$ are known. Finally the boundary controls are also connected by relationships of the form of equations and inequalities, respectively:

$$g_k(v;t) = 0, k = 1, \ldots, \rho_1, \qquad (!!!)$$

$$g_k(v;t) \geqslant 0, k = \rho_1 + 1, \ldots, \rho < \pi \qquad (!!!!)$$

In the Lurye treatment first the Bolza-Mayer problem is formulated, to determine, that is, the state variables and controls respectively z^i, ξ^j and u^k, v^x in such a way that — subject to (!) and the constraints — we have the functional

$$J = \iint_S F(z,\xi,u;x,y)dx\,dy + \oint_{\Sigma_1} f_1(z;t)dt + \oint_{\Sigma_2} f_2(z,v;t)dt = \min.$$

(the functions X, Y, T, F — all differentiable with respect to all the arguments). The necessary conditions of stationarity — the Euler, the boundary, and the Weierstrass-Erdmann conditions — are formed: in this, first, auxiliary controls $u_0 = (u_0^{r_1+1}, \ldots, u_0^r)$ and $v_0 = (v_0^{\rho_1+1}, \ldots, v_0^\rho)$ are being introduced and the inequalities in the problem-statement are replaced by equalities

$$G_k^0 \equiv G_k(u;x,y) - (u_0^k)^2 = 0, k = r_1 = 1, \ldots, r; \qquad (!!!!!)$$

$$g_k^0 \equiv g_k(v;t) - (v_0^k)^2 = 0, k = \rho_1 + 1, \ldots, r, \qquad (!!!!!!)$$

so that we have an open domain of control changes. (For the sake of simplicity it is assumed that there is only one point t_0 of discontinuity of $v^x(t)$; at point t_0 the variables $z^i(t)$ are continuous and for the Σ_2 this is the corner point.)

To build up the necessary conditions of stationarity we introduce the Lagrangeans — corresponding to the first pair of our equation system (!), $\zeta_i(x,y), \eta_i(x,y), i = 1, \ldots, n.$

For the constraints (!) and (!!!!!) the corresponding multipliers are

$$\Gamma_k(x,y), k = 1, \ldots, r_1; \ \Gamma_k^0(x,y), k = r_1 + 1, \ldots, r.$$

Analogously — for the equations (!!) and (!!!), (!!!!!!) respectively — the multipliers

$$\theta_{i_k}(t), i_k = i_1, \ldots, i_n; \ \gamma_k(t), k = 1, \ldots, \rho_1; \ \gamma^*(t), k = \gamma_1 + 1, \ldots.$$

With these multipliers brought in, the Hamiltonian is written

$$H(z, \xi, u, u_0) = \zeta X + \eta Y - F - \Gamma G - \Gamma^0 G^0,$$

$$n(z, v, v_0) = \theta T - f_2 - \gamma g - \gamma^0 g^0$$

and the Euler equations now have the form

$$\frac{\partial \zeta_i}{\partial x} + \frac{\partial \eta_i}{\partial y} = -\frac{\partial H}{\partial z^i}, \qquad i = 1, \ldots, n,$$

$$\frac{\partial H}{\partial \xi^j} = 0, \qquad j = 1, \ldots, v,$$

$$\frac{\partial H}{\partial u^k} = 0, \qquad k = 1, \ldots, p; \qquad \frac{\partial H}{\partial u^k} \equiv 2\Gamma_k^0 u_k^0 = 0, \qquad k = r_1 + 1, \ldots, r.$$

Eventually we have in Lurye the system of conditions:
(1) the "natural" boundary conditions along the boundary Σ_1

$$\frac{\partial f_1}{\partial z^i} + \zeta_i y_t - \eta_i x_t = 0, \qquad i = n+1, \ldots, n;$$

and along the unknown Σ_2 ($\delta_i = 0$ ($i \neq 1$); $\delta_i^j = 1$)

$$\delta_i^{ik} d\theta_{ik}/dt + \partial h/\partial z^i - \zeta^j y_t + \eta_i x_t = 0, i = 1, \ldots, n;$$

$$\frac{\partial h}{\partial v^x} = 0, \qquad x = 1, \ldots, \pi; \qquad \frac{\partial h}{\partial v^x} \equiv 2\gamma_x^0 v_0^x = 0, \qquad x = \rho_1 + 1, \ldots, \rho;$$

(2) the Weierstrass-Erdmann conditions along the Σ_0 – of discontinuity of controls

$$(\zeta_i y_t - \eta_i x_t)^{\pm} = 0, i = 1, \ldots, n; \quad (H)^{\pm} \equiv z_x^{-i}(\zeta_i)^{\pm} + z_y^{i-}(\eta_i)^{\pm};$$

and at point t_0 of discontinuity of the boundary controls on the boundary Σ_2

$$\theta_{ik}^-(t)_0 = \theta_{ik}^+(t_0); \theta_{ik}^-(t_0) \operatorname{grad} z^{ik-}(t_0) = \theta_{ik}^t(t_0) \operatorname{grad} z^{ik+}(t_0);$$

$$i_k = i_1, \ldots, i_{n_2}.$$

(3) the necessary Weierstrass conditions for the "strong relative mini-

mum" — supplementing the necessary stationarity conditions θ written in terms of inequalities for the Hamiltonian function

$$H(z,\Xi,U,U_0) \leqslant H(z,\xi,u,u_0),$$

$$h(z,V,V_0) \leqslant h(z,v,v_0);$$

(the lower-case and the capital letters, respectively, designating the optimal and the feasible solutions).

(34) We have indicated the intrinsic relationship of the optimal-control problem and the aspect of handling uncertainty.

The 1960s produced a rich crop in the domain of stochastic optimization, in general, too vast to treat it even cursorily here. From our special angle the reader will find in this study a discussion of Krassovskiy's work (see further p. 349). Also from this angle he may be directed to Fleming's investigation of Markovian optimization;[128] and particularly to Kushner's work on the applicability to stochastic control of dynamic equations of conditional probability density functions.[129]

The object of control is described by differential equations $\dot{x} = g(x,u,t) + \alpha$ with $\dot{y} = x + \beta$: the α and β are Gaussian white noises and the a priori probability density of the initial state of the system $P_0(x)$.[130]

Faced with the massive output of literature on stochastic optimization, in particular optimization of control, we shall confine ourselves largely to a glance at its potentialities with respect to the methodologies of our particular interest, those of Bellman and Pontryagin.

Note

A work of the early 1960s concerned with the two elements quite often jointly complicating a control system — randomness as well as nonlinearity — is that by Pervozvanskiy.[131] As Bellman rightly remarks in his preface to the English edition of the mid-1960s, while over the years many "catalogues" of solutional and approximational techniques have been accumulated for deterministic processes, nothing of the sort was available for problems and methods in the stochastic ones. The object of the Pervozvanskiy book is to fill up this lacuna, and it has succeeded in this to a considerable extent. It is essentially addressed to the engineer but the student of economic planning is likely to profit from it. His attention is drawn in particular to chapters 2 and 3 which deal with nonlinear transformations, both with and without feedback, the latter both stationary and nonstationary. Methods of statistical linearization are described. We would also draw attention to the section concerned with the application of the theory of Markov processes in the case of certain nonlinear systems (usefully supplemented by a discussion of fundamentals of these processes).

(35) The present writer is inclined to accept the claim for dynamic programming that within its framework both stochastic and deterministic processes can be treated by means of unified approach. The approach is dictated by the nature of the method. For if we consider the recurrence relation $x_{n+1} = g(x_n, y_n, r_n)$, the three bracketed terms denoting respectively the state, the control, and the "random" vectors (and assume additive utilities), the total measure of the N-stage process appears as

$$R_N = h(x_1, y_1, r_1) + \ldots + h(x_N, y_N, r_N).$$

Of the various possible ways of handling this stochastic quantity one would be to rely on the expected value of R_n over the random r_n as the criterion function. The Bellman versatile algorithmic factotum handles such a system in a natural way. It is legitimate to say that in a large sphere of problems the deterministic and stochastic processes are manageable within the same conceptual and analytic (and in fact also computational) framework.[132]

It is no less legitimate to maintain that in quite a few situations where insufficiency of information (as to the distribution of random variables, causal nexus, etc.) inhibits the "classical" techniques, the dynamic programming offers – at least conceptually – an effective approach, specifically in the case of what in Bellman's terminology makes an "adaptive" process.[133]

Note

In the context we shall note the methodological ramifications of dynamic programming and, at the same time, advances that tend to generalize it (which indeed corresponds to the trend in the various fields of the diverse theories of programming towards a general theory of extremization – see above). Among the latter we may draw attention to the family relationship of the dynamic-programming approach and that of the sequential statistical search methods to which noteworthy contribution has been made by some Soviet students. One could quote here in particular Mikhalevich's work:[134,135] he has presented a sequential Bayesian solution to various specific problems. This work is essentially algorithmically oriented: algorithms for numerical treatment of a variety of technical-economic problems are offered; but the method pursued is such as to give to the

Mikhalevich contribution also a generalizing theoretical significance.

The nexus of the approach with that of dynamic programming emphasizes itself in Mikhalevich's treatment of the link between the deterministic and probabilistic facets of sequential processes. Thus where the point of departure is the probabilistic facet of such a process the deterministic process will be one where after the individualization of objects $\Omega = \{\omega\}$ the result of the "experiment" is associated for each with probability zero or one.[136]

(36) What has been said about the relationship of a stochastic and dynamic-programming system applies with a particularly good reason to the connection between the latter and specifically the Markov model.[137] As early as a decade and half ago Bellman had formulated[138] what in substance forms the Optimality Principle for a Markovian decision process which shares the constructional philosophy with that of his programming design: that each position of the optimal trajectory in the process must be optimum with regard to the first transformation. The formalism in the treatment of the problem is to great extent due to Howard[139], resting as a rule on the summation of "rewards" for the step-to-step transformation; in this his focus is on dynamic programming. This formalism has by now received important elaboration in particular for the situations where the new vector in the transformation and/or the reward are random variables. The basic recursive relation is then in Howard — in his notation.[140]

$$\bar{v}(s|n) = \max_k \left\{ \bar{r}^k(s) + \sum_{s'} \bar{v}(s'|n-1)\mathscr{P}\left\{ s'|s, T^k \right\} \right\}$$

$$T_1 = T^k \quad \bar{r}_1(s) = \bar{r}^k(s),$$

(the s' stands for the new state; $\mathscr{P}\{\}$ for the probability of this becoming the new state where the original state and transformation applied are resp. s and T^k; the $\bar{r}(s)$ denotes expected reward in the application of transformation k). When additivity assumption is retained for the reward structure the dynamic programming appears still to be applicable in some problems where total reward does not make a simple sum (thus in multiplicative case logarithms of rewards are employed).

These matters have attracted the attention of Soviet students of control-theoretic approaches to planning, in particular important contributions have been made by Romanovskiy:[141] the starting point has been an inquiry into the asymptotic behaviour of the recurrence relations of dynamic programming in Markovian, or semi-Markovian, decision processes; and he arrived at an existence theorem for an optimal stationary policy, maximizing, that is, the reward (the results have been further elaborated by the author for a discrete deterministic dynamic programming treated as a particular case of a stochastic generalization). These and further investigations have been carried out in the context of his and the Kantorovich school's work on turnpike theory as applied in perspective planning; we discuss it at greater length in that context.

The formalism is broadly this. States x forming a given set X are related to a set of controls Q_x. For each $q_x \in Q_x$ we have probability distribution $p(q_x) = \{p_y(q_x)\}_{y\epsilon}$ and $c(q_x)$ the control "reward". A set $q = \{q_x\}$ – the "policy" – determines the transition probability matrix $P(q)$ of a Markov chain. This matrix determines the ergodic classes in X: for each such class S_α we have uniquely determined absolute stationary probabilities of states $\pi_\alpha(x)$. Then $\mu_q(\alpha) = \Sigma_{S_\alpha} c(q_x)\pi_\alpha(x)$ is the "characteristic" of S_α.

We postulate $\mu(x,q) = \Sigma_\epsilon \mu_q(\alpha)\pi_q(x,\alpha)$; we have for each x, $\mu(x,q) = \Sigma_y p_y(q_x)\mu(y,q)$ and define as the characterictic of the x state $E(x) = \max_q \mu(x,q)$. The theorem is proved to the effect that there exists a policy $\bar{q} = \{\bar{q}_x\}$ such that for all x, $E(x) = \mu(x,\bar{q})$.

·(37) The stochastic approach is not immanent in the Maximum Principle in the same way it is in the Optimality Principle: its fundamental statement has a deterministic frame. But important work has been done, in particular by Pontryagin jointly with Kolmogorov and Mishchenko, in introducing it into the treatment of the problem of pursuit. Pontryagin and his associates have demonstrated the applicability of their principle where the probability for the y's flight is known, its law has been postulated to be Markovian and described by the (Fokker-Planck-type) Kolmogorov parabolic differential equations (uniquely determining the system of transition probabilities for a Markov process).[142]

The probability of the phase point Q, being found at the time t at the position x, entering the required neighbourhood during $\sigma < t < \tau$ is taken as described by $\psi_0(\sigma,x,t)$. The control $u(t)$ and the corresponding trajectory $z(t)$ are shown to be optimal if they guarantee the extremum for the function of the form

$$I = \int_0^\alpha h(s)\partial/\partial d \, . \, [\phi_0(\sigma,x,s)]ds$$

the function is defined to be found within $0 < h(t) < 1$. The great difficulty is patently in the case where the pursuer knows at most the technical potentialities of the pursued and its position at a given time-point but not its controls beyond it. Of considerable interest are in general attempts to handle the problem of pursuit evasion by a game-theoretic approach.

(38) An important, systematic inquiry in Soviet theory into the possibilities of the Maximum Principle in statistical problems of optimal control has been conducted for a decade by Stratonovich.[143] The spectrum of this investigation has been gradually extended, starting from a system, in a discrete-time formulation, with co-ordinates postulated to be known exactly. From this case – the case of "complete observation" – it has moved to that of a disturbed one. On some of such cases the theory of the Maximum Principle statistical equation has proved itself to permit generalization; (cf. the results of Kushner and Sweppe).[144] It is the probing in such directions that has led Stratonovich to the supposition that the area of applicability of that principle is no less extendable than that of dynamic programming and Bellman's equation. It is, however, noticeable that here again the two-point boundary problem has shown itself to be the stumbling block for the Pontryagin system: the problem in which one has to fix for the co-ordinates the initial, and for the "impulses" the terminal, values; hence to make use of the latter one has to postulate the future values of the process observed, which, that is, have not been observed as yet but would be so in the future; then an averaging has to be carried out over such *possible* values. The specific equations with the average values resulting from this operation do not lend themselves to a sufficiently handy solution.

Clearly of particular interest is the case where the value of the process (y_t) observed enters the system sequentially, where, that is, at the time point t the known values are those of y_τ, $\tau \leqslant t$; and where the object is under the influence of chance disturbances as well as of the control signals.[145] This is the case to which Stratonovich turns in his last investigations[146] with the idea of proving that here too the generalized Maximum Principle is applicable, and if so of proving the superiority over the Bellman equation with regard to the familiar claim: that while the latter is an equation in partial derivatives, the Maximum Principle retains its advantage of being stated in terms of ordinary differential equations. Here, however, simply transferring to the complex statistical problem Stratonovich's earlier results would not do; indeed "the Pontryagin theory would need substantial additions and generalization applicable to problems with sequential information".[147] He has confined himself to one procedure based on the treatment of a specific random equation in *partial* derivatives: the Pontryagin equation is then of a stochastic type.

The solution of the problems considered last (i.e. to repeat, the ones where at t we know the value of $y_\tau, \tau < t$ and the system is under the double impact of control and chance) is the area in which generalized dynamic programme has been resorted to; and in which, in general, as against particular situations examined by Stratonovich, the preference would seem to me likely to continue.

As pointed out, Stratonovich works with a discrete-time system where the control $u_t^{t+\Delta}$ is determined from

$$\min E\left[-\int_t^{t+\Delta} \psi_{\mu\tau} d_\tau f_{\mu\tau}(x_\tau) + c_t^{t+\Delta} \,|x_t, u_t^{t+\Delta}\right].$$

The reasoning is expanded in the treatment of diffusion processes. The basic equation has the form

$$\frac{\partial \phi_t(x_t)}{\partial t} = -\frac{\partial \phi_t(x_t)}{\partial x_{\mu t}}\dot{x}_{\mu t} - E[C_t|y_{t_0}^{t_1}] = -\frac{\partial \phi_t(x_t)}{\partial x_{\mu t}}f_{\mu t}(x_t) - E[C_t|y_{t_0}^{t_1}].$$

Differentiating with respect to x_t we have

$$-\dot{\psi}_{\nu t} = -\left(\frac{\partial \psi_{\nu t}}{\partial t} + \frac{\partial \psi_{\nu t}}{\partial x_{\mu t}}\right)\dot{x}_{\mu t} = \psi_{\mu t}\frac{\partial \dot{f}_{\mu t}}{\partial x_{\nu t}} - \frac{\partial}{\partial x_{\nu t}}E[C_t|x_t, u_t]. \quad (!)$$

Postulating $\Delta \to 0$ (the functions $x_t, \varphi_t(x)$ being differentiable) we find ultimately that the optimal control is determined from the condition of maximum of

$$E[H_t|x_t, u_t], \quad H_t = -E[C_t|x_t, y_t^{t_1}] + \psi_{\mu t}\dot{f}_{\mu t}(x_{t_1}, u_t).$$

The generalized Pontryagin equations are obtainable from the function H_t as Hamilton equations, i.e.

$$\dot{x}_\mu = \frac{\partial H_t}{\partial \psi_\mu}; \quad \dot{\psi}_\mu = -\frac{\partial H_t}{\partial x^\mu}, \quad (\mu = 1, \ldots, n).$$

Thus in the generalized Maximum Principle for the optimality of the control u_t and trajectory x_t (where $t_0 \leqslant t \leqslant t_1$ and the initial $x_{t0} = x_0$), the necessary condition requires the existence of a non-zero continuous function $\psi_t = \psi_t(y_{t_0}^{t^1})$ satisfying the equation (!) such that the maximum of the conditional mathematical expectation $[H_t|x_t, u_t]$ holds at any t at the point $u_t = u \in U$.

One readily grants Stratonovich's suggestion that his inquiry provides a good deal of insight into the problem and indicates the direction of desirable further research. However, in our submission it is rather the strength of assumptions he had to adopt, and even more so the way he had to particularize the problem in order to reach the solution, that are illuminating of the scope the Maximum Principle offers to stochastic treatment.

(39) During the last few years important work has been done by Pontryagin and members of his school, in particular Mishchenko, Nikolskiy, and Gusyatnikov, in generalization of optimal control problems in terms of differential games of pursuit.

A good and up-to-date presentation of results can be found in Mishchenko's recent paper which consideres all the three alternatives with respect to the object pursued, i.e. where its motion is of deterministic, or random, or controlled species. The second (on the whole still inadequately explored) is in our submission of particular significance for a planner pursuing his objectives: it is examined by Mishchenko under some assumptions as to the nature of the randomness.[148] The motion of the object controlled (consider an economy) materializes in the more-than-two-dimensional Euclidean vectoral space and is described by the system of ordinary differential equations $\dot{z}^i = f^i(z^1, \ldots, z^n, u^1, \ldots, u^r)$ (z − phase coordinates, u − controls). The pursued random point Q, in its motion in R, obeys a Markovian law; if its situation at σ is known, the probability $P(\sigma, x, \tau, E)$ of its finding itself in the subspace $E \subset R$ at some $\tau > \sigma$ is uniquely determined. Suppose a "shadow" neighbourhood Σz of z moves jointly with it; suppose it is a sphere with an r radius. Since the initial positions of z and its "shadow" are known, the probability $\psi_u(\sigma, x, \tau)$ of a rendezvous over the time segment $\sigma \leqslant t \leqslant \tau$, of the neighbourhood $\Sigma_{z(t)}$ and point Q is uniquely determined. The value of $\psi_u(\sigma, x, \tau)$ is here the functional of $u(t)$ and the corresponding trajectory $z(t)$. In the solution the Maximum Principle is being applied. Where the radius r is small, the result appears as

$$\psi_u(\sigma, x, \tau) = r^{n-2} \int_\sigma^\tau p(\sigma, x, s, z(s)) \, \beta(s) ds + o(r^{n-2}).$$

For the pursuit-cum-evasion game noteworthy results appear to have been obtained only for the linear game. Thus we have presented in Mishchenko the game given by the differential equation $\dot{z} = Cz - u + v$ (z − vector of n-dimensional Euclidean space R^n, C − square matrix, u − pursuit control, v − evasion control, $u \in P$, $v \in Q$, both P and Q convex subsets in R^n; further: M, the set of completion of the game, is a linear vectoral subspace of R^n; L an orthogonal complement to M in R^n; and the π operator of the orthogonal projection from R^n to N).

Consideration is given to convex sets $\pi e^{rC} P$ and $\pi e^{rC} Q$ in the subspace L and their geometric difference, as defined, denoted $\hat{w}(r)$, which is assumed to be nonempty for nonnegative r. For that set, over the segment $[0,t]$ we define the integral

$$W(t) = \int_0^t \hat{w}(r)dr$$

such as to form a closed set continuously depending on nonnegative values of t.

We find in Mishchenko that with a *positive* value for t, with $\pi e^{tC} z_0 \in W(t)$, where z_0 denotes the initial state, at least something can be said about the termination of the game: i.e. that there exists some minimum $t = \tau(z_0)$ over which it can be concluded. Moreover, as it appears, this theorem can be proved to describe the whole set of points from which the game can be terminated — if some additional, defined, constraints are met with respect to the position in R^n of the sets P and Q, and some constraints on the C matrix.

A corollary are the Pontryagin-Mishchenko theorems on measuring distances and on securing evasion.[149,150]

Notes

1. Initiated by Rufus Isaacs[151] in the mid-1950s, the theory of differential games has given new apparatus to the analysis of the pursuit-evasion problems which for some has attracted the effort of Soviet mathematical-planning theory (indicated in our footnote).

The substance of the differential-game construct is the behaviour of agents each of whom tends to shape a dynamic system's states in following his objectives, when there is conflict of the objectives. As pointed out by Kuhn and Szegö[152] (in a preface to a beautiful volume they edited and published after the present book was written) the theory of such games absorbs those of both optimal control and of the "classical" theory of games. It generalizes and performs the role of both: the theory of optimal control appears then in fact as a particular case with the number of "players" reduced to one. It is promising as a framework for the treatment, from both angles, of competitive-co-operative situations in the dynamics of a planned system: its formalization of decomposition[153] provides a rigorous framework for the analysis of devolutional problems. Note the several formulations of the pursuit problem in dynamic-programming terms as well, both in Soviet and Western literature: some of the contributions admirably bring out the natural link between the discrete version of a differential game — the multi-stage game — and dynamic programming.[154]

2. Pontryagin's[155] fundamental formalization of the pursuit-game problem can be restated as follows:

Let R be Euclidean vector space of dimension n, M its subspace, and L its subspace — an orthogonal complement to M, of dimension ν: further let P and Q be manifolds homeomorphic to the sphere of dimension $\nu - 1$. Let a linear differential game — in R and terminating in M — be described as

$$dz/dt = Cz + U(u) - V(v)$$

where z is the vector of R; C a constant square matrix of dimension n; $u \in P$ and $v \in Q$ respectively the pursuer's and the evader's control parameters, U and V being their continuous functions. Two conditions are assumed to be satisfied, i.e. that

(1) the function $\pi e^{tC} U(u)$ gives a homeomorphic image of the manifold P into some convex hyperplane in L; the set thereby delimited in L is denoted $\hat{u}(t)$ and the boundary of $\hat{u}(\tau)$ belongs to the set. Analogous assumptions are made with respect to the function $\pi e^{tC} V(v)$;

(2) for an arbitrary $\tau > 0$ the convex set $\tilde{v}(t)$ can be translated into the interior of $\hat{u}(t)$. The convex set is a closed, bounded ν-dimensional subspace of L.

The theorem is then proved: Let z_0 be an arbitrary point of R not included in M and $\tau > 0$. Further, assume:

$$\eta(\tau) = \pi e^{\tau C} z_0 ; \quad \hat{w}(\tau) = \hat{u}(\tau) - \tilde{v}(\tau); \quad \hat{W}(t) = \int_0^t \hat{w}(r) dr.$$

For small values of τ, the point $-\eta(t)$ does not belong to $W(t)$. If for some value of τ an inclusion takes place, $-\eta(t) \in W(t)$ and τ_0 is the minimum value of τ for which it takes place, then commencing from the state z_0 the game of pursuit can be terminated over a time interval not greater than $T(z_0) = \tau_0$.

A signal feature of the problem as set is that what is pursued is not the evader as such but the place he occupied ϵ seconds ago (its knowledge is thus being implied). Hence in construing the control $u(t_1)$ at t_1, the value of $z(t_1)$ at the same time-point is used and the control $v(t)$ over the time-interval $t_1 < t < t + \epsilon$ where the ϵ is arbitrarily small and positive: for the solution the limiting $\epsilon \to 0$ is considered.

3. A very major contribution to the theory of differential games as a ramification of the theory of optimal control in Soviet literature has been made by N. N. Krassovskiy.

The latest of these contributions deals with the subject of "programming absorption" in such games. The frame of the analysis is as follows.[156] The game problem is one of approach-avoidance in the motion $x(t)$ described by $\dot{x} = f(t,x,u,v)$, $x[t_0] = x_0$ (!) the u and v being respectively the controls of the first and second player, constrained by $u \in P$, $v \in Q$ — both compact; their objectives are respectively to obtain and to prevent the meeting of the phase-point $x(t)$ with the closed set $\mathcal{M}$. Strategy $U - \mathcal{U}(t,x)$ is defined as a function $\{t,x\}$ which places the set $\mathcal{U}(t,x) \subset \mathcal{P}$ in correspondence with the position (t,x); the mixed strategy $\hat{U} - \mathcal{U}(u,x)$ is defined as the function $(t,x) \to \hat{\mathcal{U}}$ where $\hat{\mathcal{U}}(t,x)$ is the set $\{\mu(du)\}$ formed of measures $\mu(du)$ normed on $\mathcal{P}$. The strategies $V \div \mathcal{V}(t,x)$ and mixed strategies $V \div \tilde{\mathcal{V}}(t,x) = \{v(dv)\}$ are defined analogously. The motions $x[t,t_*,x_*,U)]$ or $[x,t,t_*,x_*,\tilde{U}]$ are determined as the boundaries of piecewise continuous $x_\Delta[t,t,x_*^\Delta]$ which satisfy the contingencies $\dot{x}_\Delta[t] \epsilon \mathcal{F}_Q(t,x_\Delta[t], u[\tau_k]\}$, $u[\tau_k] \epsilon \mathcal{U}(\tau_k, x_\Delta[\tau_k])$ or contingencies $\dot{x}_\Delta[t] \epsilon \mathcal{F}_Q(t,x_\Delta[t])$, $\mu(du)_{\tau_k})$, $\mu(du)_{\tau_k} \epsilon \mathcal{U}(t_k, x_\Delta[\tau_k])$ with $\tau_k \leqslant t \leqslant \tau_{k+1}$ where $\tau_0 = t_*$, $\tau_{k+1} \to t_k \leqslant \Delta$ $\Delta \to 0$, $x_*^\Delta \to x_*$, $F_Q = \tilde{co}\{f(t,x_*,u_*,v)\}$ or $F_Q = \tilde{co}\{\int f(t,x,u,v)\mu(du)\}$ with $v \in Q$. The motions $x[t,t,x,V]$ or $x[t,t_*,x_*,\tilde{V}]$ are determined analogously. The strategy U and $\tilde{U}$ brings about the encounter by the moment ϑ (or at ϑ) if any motion $x[t_0,t_0,x_0,U]$ or $x[t,t_0,x_0,\tilde{U}]$ hits $\mathcal{M}$ at least once in $t \in [t_0, \vartheta]$ ($t = \vartheta$). The strategy V, or $\mathcal{V}$, ensures avoidance up to the moment ϑ (at the moment ϑ) if no motion $x[t,t_0 x_0, V]$ or $x[t,t,x_0,\tilde{V}]$ hits M. Krassovskiy has evolved, for a Lipschitzean function f on x, an alternative of the saddle-point type — based on the concept of programming absorption of the sets by the process (!) in the mixed strategies class, and then analysed them in the three kinds of this "absorption" — minimax, maxmin, and mixed.

Take a linear system $\dot{x} = A(t)x + f(t,u,v)$ (!!) where the functions $A(t)$ and $f(t,u,v)$ are continuous. $\mathcal{M}$ is a convex bounded closed set. The (!!), from the position $[t_*,x_*]$ carries out at $\vartheta > t$ the programming absorption of $\mathcal{M}$ on maxmin if for any strategy $V \div v(t)$, $(\tilde{V} - \tilde{\mathcal{V}}(t))$ at least one move $x[(t_*,x,V) (x[t,t_*,x_*,\tilde{V}])$ hits $\mathcal{M}$ at $t = \vartheta$. From the position $[t_*,x_*]$ the (!!) is carrying out a programming absorption of $\mathcal{M}$ on minimax if for any function $\widetilde{V}(t,u)$ at least one move $x[t,t,x,V]$ which is determined by the equation in contingencies $\dot{x}[t] \in A(i)x[t] + F_{\mathscr{V}}(t)$ hits $\mathscr{M}$ at $t = \vartheta$.

(40) A domain related to stochastic processes is that of learning (self-teaching, self-tuning) systems. It has been an object of study almost from the very emergence of the theory of optimal control. Particular merits in this field should be ascribed to a branch of the probabilistic school eminently represented by Pugachev.[157]

As a matter of fact, the development of this field was stimulated by initial questioning of the very viability of control-theoretic methodology by those arguing that determining optimal systems presupposes the knowledge of the dispersion of signals and disturbances, while usually the probabilistic characteristics of the signals are unknown. The riposte has been based on two arguments. Firstly, that where dispersion of the materializations of signals corresponding to the system's work is large, as compared with that of disturbances, the characteristics of optimal systems only weakly depend on the probabilistic signals. The probabilistic characteristics of disturbances and noises, on the other hand, can as often as not be determined historically. Secondly, algorithms can be elaborated for empirical appraising the laws of distribution of signals from past cycles. This has in fact been the actual direction in the construction of algorithms for self-teaching systems.

The stage the theory of such systems has reached can be appraised in Soviet writing from Pugachev's latest inquiry into optimal learning in changing conditions. The results generalize its algorithmic development — for situations characterized by random changes of the input-signal characteristics, be it during or after completion of the process. One of the side-gains is the technique of dealing with the system's "informational amnesia".

The structure of the Pugachev system rests on the three functions $g(z)$; $k(w|z)$; $\delta_t(\widetilde{W}|z, w, \widetilde{w})$, depending on the two parameters, lambda and theta — the former a finite-dimensional vector, the latter a scalar one, so that we have $g(z) = G(z, \theta|\lambda)$; $k(w|z) = K(w, \theta|z, \lambda)$

$$\delta_t = (\widetilde{w}|z, w, \dot{w}) = \Delta_t(w, \theta|z, w, \widetilde{w}, \lambda).$$

In this notation Z stands for the input, and W the required output signals, respectively (the signs θ and λ designating the "true" and the "teaching" signals).

The meaning of the functions depends on whether we deal with a dis-

crete system or a continuous (analogue) system: i.e. where Z is respectively
a finite-dimensional or a random function, the analytical characteristic,
some function $g(z)$, is respectively the probability density of the input sig-
nal Z or some functional. The function $k(w|Z)$ defines the required output
signal W. Finally, the teacher's decision function $\delta_t(\tilde{w}|z,\hat{w})$ forms the pro-
bability density of the output signal $\tilde{w}$, i.e. for a discrete system — with
respect to $z,\hat{w}$, and for a continuous system — with respect to a functional
of $W,Z,\hat{W}$. The learning aims are, in brief notation, first to secure an
approximation of the decision function, a function of lambda, that is
$\delta(\hat{w}|z) = \Delta(\hat{w},\theta|z,\lambda)$, and then to reach optimum $\delta_{\text{opt}}(\hat{w}|z)$.[158]

(41) The stochastic element now has its established place in contemporary work on the synthesis. Krassovskiy's[159] latest generalization of the
problem of analytic construction of regulators with the given task of controls and controlling signals is here of particular interest. To recall, his
work in the field started with the treatment of an isoperimetric problem of
synthesis of control for a linear object, based on minimization of the quadratic functional with a particular form of an additional constraint. It subsequently moved to constraining the problem by some given values of the
integrals for given phases — for a nonlinear object. The generalization with
which we are now concerned consists in taking the object to be affected
by a white-noise type of disturbance with a given mathematical expectation of some integral valuations and functions of phase-co-ordinates. The
broad line of this generalization for the object

$$\dot{x} + F_j(x_1,x_2,\ldots,x_n,t) = u_i + \xi_i \quad (i = 1, 2, \ldots,),$$

(u_i is synthesized control, ξ_i are white noises, i.e. sequences of independent
random, δ impulses) is this. The full derivative of the function V

$$\dot{V} = \frac{\partial V}{\partial t} - \sum_{t=1}^{n} \frac{\partial V}{\partial x_i} F_i = -Q$$

is a datum.

Note that increments induced by the impulse $a_\nu\delta(t - t_\nu)$ — where a_ν is a
random magnitude — equal with the exactness up to $2 (F_i + u_i)\epsilon$

$$\Delta x_{i\nu} = \int^{t_\nu+\epsilon} [a_\nu\delta(t - t_\nu) - u_i - F_i]dt = a_\nu$$

— where ϵ is infinitely small. Each impulse brings about an instantaneous
"jumpy" change of phase-co-ordinates independent of the value of u_i.

The controls sought are those minimizing the functional

$$I = E \left[\int_{t_1}^{t_2} Q dt + V(x_1(t_2), \ldots, x_n(t_2), t_2) \right]$$

over the set of functions which meet the condition

$$E \left[\frac{1}{p} \sum_{i=1}^{n} \int_{t_1}^{t_2} \left| \frac{u_i}{k_i} \right|^p dt + \frac{1}{q} \sum_{i=1}^{n} \int_{t_1}^{t_2} \left| k_i \frac{\partial V}{\partial x_i} \right|^q \right] dt =$$

$$= C[x_i(t_1), x_2(t_1), x_3(t_1), \ldots, x_n(t_1), t_1],$$

(k_i being given coefficients, p, q positive numbers satisfying the Göldner relation $1/p + 1/q = 1$; $p \geqslant 1$; C dependent on initial conditions but same for all controls: E mathematical expectation).

The $\partial V/\partial x_i$ functions are the control signals of the optimal system.

In so far as less than full observability is postulated, the "whiteness" of the noise does not substantially circumscribe the generality. The noises would be taken in the form of white noises passed through some forming filters: the mathematical model as stated above would then include the equations for such filters.

In the case of full observability, we obtain — through some straight substitutions —

$$\dot{V} = - Q + \sum_{i=1}^{n} \frac{\partial V}{\partial x_i} (u_i + \xi_i)$$

and by integrating over time and taking the mathematical expectations

$$I = E \left[\int_{t_1}^{t_2} Q dt + V(x_1(t_2), \ldots, x_n(t_2), t_2) \right] =$$

$$= E[V(x_1(t_1), \ldots, x_n(t_1), t_1)] + E \left[\sum_{i=1}^{n} \int_{t_1}^{t_2} \frac{\partial V}{\partial x_i} u_i dt \right]$$

$$+ E \left[\sum_{i=1}^{n} \int_{t_1}^{t_2} \frac{\partial V}{\partial x_i} - \xi_i dt \right].$$

(42) In a sense a bridge between the two approaches — the deterministic and the stochastic — is formed by a class of adaptive optimal-control models: models, that is, handling the random elements with probabilistic

characteristics which determine themselves — with an increasing degree of precision — in the course of controlling the object. The pioneering in the field and the name "dual control" are owed to Feldbaum.[160] (We will, however, note Kalman's independent, important discovery of the duality principle in his study of the filter and the Wiener-Kolmogorov theories.)

In Feldbaum's "dual" system it is the controlling pulses that have a double nature. While carrying out the control they at the same time furnish information on the unknown parameters. The idea has been further elaborated by the Feldbaum school: it has been reworked in a noteworthy way by Medvedyev and Tarasyenko in their major *opus* on probabilistic methods in extremization.[161] The synthesis of automatic control has the following diagramatic form

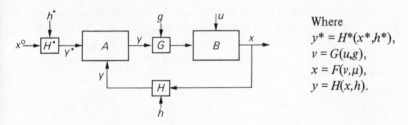

Where
$$y^* = H^*(x^*,h^*),$$
$$v = G(u,g),$$
$$x = F(v,\mu),$$
$$y = H(x,h).$$

(The A and B, respectively, are the controlling bloc and the controlled object, H^*, G, H are channels of communications, respectively — the "input", control and feedback channels, x is the "input" control signal, y is the "output" (the system's state); h is noise.)

Mathematically the H^*, G, and H are operators — some given functions which determine the interaction of noise and signal in the corresponding channel. In a general case the inter-bloc relations above would be multi-dimensional. Time is discrete: in the accepted notation x_t denotes the value at the time instant t, and x_i the totality of values $(x_0, x_1, \ldots, x_t)$, and similarly for other variables.

Bloc A generates the control impulses, u: as u obtains information on the feedback channel on the unknown parameters, it generates controls whose efficiency rises in the adaptive, self-steering process. The values of u_t can be determined on the basis of information available in A, i.e. $\{y^*_t, u_{t-1}, y_{t-1}\}$. The synthesis of A reduces to determining the functional U such that

$$u_t = U(y^*_t, u_{t-1}, y_{t-1}),$$

which should satisfy the requirements of optimality. In the general case
the functional will be stochastic in the sense that the relation between u_t
and the bracketed expression will be a random one; that is in the synthesis
of A, we can only determine the joint conditional probability density

$$P(u_t|y^*_{t}, y_{t-1}) = P(u_0) \prod_{s-1}^{t} P(u_s|y^*_s, u_{s-1}, y_{s-1}).$$

For methodological convenience the process of determining the controls is broken up into two phases: in the first it is assumed that the parameters μ_t are known, permitting the finding of the control u_i up to the
time instant n. In the second the problem posed is what to decide on the
μ_t on the basis of the information obtained up to time instant t: in this it
is assumed that the system will function up to the moment n — and should
do so at optimum. Thus the problem in the second phase is one of determining the specific values for μ securing the overall optimality.

It is shown that the optimal control can be reduced to the minimization
of expected risk

$$R = \sum_{t=0}^{n} R_t = \sum_{t=0}^{n} \int_{\Omega(\mu_t)} R_t(\mu_t) P(\mu_t) d\Omega$$

$$= \int_{\Omega(\mu_n)} P(\mu_n) \sum_{t=0}^{n} R_t(\mu_t) d\Omega,$$

where the Ωdt denotes the elements of the space on which the integration
is being carried out. Eventually the optimal control is determined from the
equation

$$\sum_{t=0}^{n} R_t(\mu_t) = \min_{P(u_t|y^*_{t}, y_{t-1}, \mu_t)}.$$

At the next stage the unknown valuation of the μ_t parameter is introduced
as some vector λ_t with elements λ_s where $0 < s < t$.

We then consider controls satisfying the equation

$$\gamma'_t(u_t, y^*_t, u_{t-1}, y_{t-1}, \mu_t) = \min_{u_t}, \quad t = 1, 2, \ldots, n,$$

where for all $t = 1, \ldots, n$ the γ'_t has a unique minimum with respect to any fixed value of other variables — controls parametrically dependent on μ_i. The optimal valuations of these parameters correspond to the solution of the functional equations

$$\int_{\Omega(\mu_t)} P(\mu_t)\gamma'_t(u^*_t(y^*_t, u_{t-1}, y_{t-1}, \lambda_t), y^*_t, u_{t-1}, y_{t-1}, \mu_t)\, d\Omega$$

$$= \min_{\lambda_t}, \, t = 1, 2, \ldots, n.$$

Ultimately the solution has the form

$$u_t^{**} = (u_t)\mathrm{opt} = u^*_t(y^*_t, u_{t-1}, y_{t-1}, \lambda_t^{**}), \, t = 1, 2, \ldots, n$$

where $\lambda_t^{**} = \{\lambda_0^*, \lambda_1^*, \ldots, \lambda_t^*\}$. We have now two systems of equations which, simultaneously solved, permit determining the structure of optimal control and the optimal values of the unknown parameters. Note that while, in principle, the information on the μ_t could be considered to be obtainable independently of the values of the sequence of y_t^*, the choice of u_t is dependent on y_t^* because of the requirement of optimum: hence the dependence of the value of λ_t on y_t^*.

The last two systems of equations reflect the substance of the dual control. To each of the two aspects of the control, the criterion and the informational aspects, there is a corresponding variational equation.

As Feldbaum puts it, already at the origins of the optimal control theory random factors were throwing their "shadow" on it — hence in fact the emergence of, and the growing realization of, the salient character of the problem of stability of motion and of the "coarseness" of the control system — a system which is implicitly assumed to be affected by unforeseen perturbations.

(43) Indeed, in Feldbaum's well-argued tenet, the problem of integrated randomization is bound to grow in its importance for the development of the optimal-control theory. The treatment of random factors and indeterminate situations becomes increasingly crucial with the increasing sophistication of systems with which the theory is concerned: the modern orientation towards feedback, and interest in adaptive and auto-didactic systems trace out the trend. It is readily admitted that the statistical approach is patently not the only one in handling indeterminate situation (as our

reader could see by now, other approaches — in particular the game-theoretic and the inductive-probabilistic — are conceivable alternatives.)

The Feldbaum method of synthesis finds a growing appreciation of students well beyond his school. It finds support — as pointed out in Wonham's recent article[162] — as far as the control-communication interplay goes in the Wienerian general cybernetical conception, and indeed in intuitive cognition. While on this point we may also note Wonham's incisive remarks on the general underdevelopment of the discipline — in particular the lack of common language of dynamics (differential equations and so on) and of information processing (logic, information theory). Few will disagree that the finding of integrating concepts and methods is a challenge for the future.

Notes

1. As noted, the beginnings of the theory of adaptive and learning systems go back to the 1950s when Feldbaum published the original version of his "dual" steering method.[163,164] (An independently arrived at Western pendant was the Bellman-Kalaba feedback system where, in the dynamic-programming procedure, the controller recognizes the system's statistical characteristics.[165])

(Crucial for the conceptual framework is the distinction between information a priori and "current" that is acquired in the course of the system's operation.[166] In Tsypkin's persuasive interpretation the two are interrelated as, respectively, the means of posing a plan problem, and of solving it. In dynamics, modelling the process would entail "dating" the control regime as the knowledge of functions and parameters, whether deterministic or stochastic, is being gained.

Another definitional distinction concerns the character of the learning-adaptive system in relation to the stochastic "nature" and its approximation. To begin with and recall, the articulation of stochastic approximation is owed to the celebrated Robbins-Monro[167] design of two decades ago — an iterative procedure for determining the radical of the regression equation (itself a stochastic variant of the von Mises-Pollaczek[168] iteration procedure). Of the massive work thus inaugurated one may refer to the two contributions sharing between them the status of the classics in the field: the Kiefer-Wolfowitz[169] procedure and Dvoretsky's[170] effective generalization in which the stochastic approximation is treated as an error-free deterministic successive approximation over which a random-noise component is superimposed.)

It is the belief of one school of thought in Soviet writing, as represented by Tsypkin,[171] that the initial phase in the development of the discipline – the stochastic "phase" – is by now left behind: a phase whose feature had been the pioneering in stochastic approximation and its ramifications. In that phase knowledge of at least the statistical characteristics was being assumed.

The growing awareness of the unrealism of such premises has led to the next – the "adaptive" – phase: for not only this knowledge but, as often as not, even the postulate of determining empirically the relevant elements has proved to be too far from reality. Thence the efforts to develop methods of control in situations with not merely incomplete information but where the very nature, deterministic or stochastic, of the problems would be unclear at the outset; or, what is of patent significance for economics, the securing of complete or near-complete a priori information would be too costly; this would then be the "sphere" of adaptive and learning methods, still inadequately defined as it is. The sphere would be essentially that of suboptimally or quasi-optimally controlled behaviour which, however, could possibly asymptotically converge to optimality.

Such periodization has given rise in Soviet writing to a controversy. This controversy is of interest not only to the historian of the discipline, for it throws light on the status and potentialities of the new theory; and indeed also on its substance.

What is specifically questioned in the periodization, by Stratonovich, is that the methodology of learning and adaptive processes lends itself to isolating from that of stochastic processes, which embrace mathematical statistics and the theories of filters, statistical solutions and dynamic programming; embrace them as against the apparatus of stochastic "search" based on stochastic approximation that is.[172] It is his contention, to put this in other words, that the indeterminacy of values – of signals and of impulses – does not differ in substance from that of a priori probabilities. In the a priori probability of mathematical statistics the conventional $p(x|a)$ is taken as indeterminate inasmuch as it is dependent on some indeterminate parameter, the a; but this by itself is no reason for setting the non-Bayesian mathematical statistics apart from the stochastic methodology; indeed by interpreting the a as a signal or disturbance (impulse) and giving it some distribution $p(a)$ the typical adaptivity problem, one with a priori probability $p(x|a)$, does become typically stochastic: by applying the standard methods of the stochastic "sphere" one obtains the optimal algorithm of stochastic approximation; in fact, if anything the absence of a priori data encourages, rather than discourages the Bayesian approach: the postulating of some a priori distribution (a multi-stage solution with different a priori distributions).[173]

In counter-arguing, Tsypkin is on the whole on the defensive (in fairness, though, it may be said that in his original work he did not insist on the strictness of this periodization; nor was he unprepared to grant that the distinction as between the a priori and current information is and can only be a matter of common sense and possibly of convention, if only because any modelling can absorb only some limited sources and volumes of information; moreover a priori information is immanently confined to a stock of information which requires some "renovation"). Once it is conceded that the search for an optimal algorithm is justified, the solution of the learning and adaptive problems is sought in probabilistic-iterative algorithms providing under some conditions the extremum to the mathematical expectation of the corresponding equations. (The critique questions their quality-measuring, optimality nature; and argues that they evade in particular the *Maximum Principle* approach even when extended to the stochastic case, see sect. 38 above). Tsypkin is no less on the defensive in his overall conclusion, which is that while some would try to build up an integrated theory based on a "unified" Bayesian theory of optimal control — by itself a well understandable inclination — we are still very far from a general theory of synthesis of optimal adaptive systems: the results obtained are connected with specific Bayesian type of optimality criteria and as a rule lead to strictly optimal algorithms only for quadratic functionals: as to the quasi-optimal algorithms, we naturally face the problems of convergence and of "distance" from the optimum.

(Fu[174] points out that from the "supervised" Bayesian type of learning some simple recursive learning algorithms are derivable with a suitable selection of the a priori distribution for the unknown parameter (the "unsupervised" one is likely to be computationally troublesome); on the other hand, the stochastic approximation — essentially a nonparametric parameter-estimation technique — does require information about noise statistics. For the purposes of estimating unknown functions — deterministic or probabilistic — the method of potential function is applicable.)

The sobering conclusions from the Soviet dialogue are well substantiated in Kulikowski's excellent treatise, oriented as it is to a considerable extent to application as well as theory.[175] As he points out, the generalizing of approximation procedures proves to have a rather limited scope; the common-sense rule is to rely as far as possible on a priori information, and on this one has, of necessity, to compromise. The simpler kinds of algorithms based on iterations, stochastic approximations, and gradient identification fail to secure, on the whole, a high degree of precision (while in fact convergence would call for the use of a complex apparatus of the decision functions). Whatever rules have been designed, they have been intended to serve the engineer; the economic planner (in this one will easily agree with Kulikowski) is on the whole in a more favourable position since he can content himself with a lesser degree of exactness. On the other hand he is at a disadvantage in that, unlike an engineer, he cannot follow the first principle: to adopt as the first iteration the optimal "output" corresponding to a model built up on fuller a priori information; he has to start from whatever the environment has to offer him.

In any case the plan modeller comes up against one considerable methodological difficulty. It is the conceptual − and still more operational − insulation of the learning from the controlling element in the system.[176]

2. In this note we follow Tsypkin in his formalizing the processes of learning. It is based on "penalizing" the system's unsatisfactory behaviour. Optimization is then treated as penalty minimizing, achieved either by re-structuring the automaton or changing the "teacher's" characteristics, respectively $f_\Gamma(\,.\,)$ and $\psi\,(\,.\,)$ (the Γ denoting "quantized" values). What is restated here is the second, the simpler case.

In the adopted notation: the system's state and the terminal values are respectively $a[\,.\,]$ and $x[\,.\,]$. Under its satisfactory and unsatisfactory behaviour we have respectively $u[n] = 0$ and $u[n] = 1$, the mathematical expectation of penalty $\rho\,.\,Q(x,c)$ is a functional of the vector $c = (c_1,\ldots,c_N)$ depending on the vector of random sequences $x = (x_1,\ldots,x_N)$ with density of distribution $p(X)$, the X being the space of vectors x; all these vectors are column matrices, T standing for transpose, thus we have a row matrix $c^T = [c_1,\ldots,c_N]$.

Tsypkin proceeds from the "environment" equation. Then a characteristic of $\psi_\Gamma(a)$ is sought such as to minimize ρ:

$$\psi_\Gamma(a) = \sum_{x=1}^{k} c_x \varphi_x(a) = c^T \varphi(a).$$

This will be possible if a system of linear independent functions is determined

$$\varphi_x(a) = \begin{cases} 1 \\ 0 \end{cases} \text{ where } \begin{cases} a = a^x, \\ a \neq a^x, \end{cases}$$

analytically

$$\varphi_x(a) = 1 - \text{sg}^2(a - a^x); \quad \text{sg } z = \begin{cases} 1 \\ 0 \\ -1 \end{cases} \text{ where } \begin{cases} z > 0, \\ z = 0, \\ z < 0. \end{cases}$$

The condition of the automaton's optimality appears as

$$\rho = \rho_{min} = \min_\varsigma E\{\theta_r(c^T\varphi(a), \xi)\},$$

and the algorithm of learning

$$\begin{aligned} c[n] &= c[n-1] - \tilde{\tilde{\nabla}}_c \pm \theta_s(c[n-1], 1), \\ c[n] &= c[n-1], \end{aligned} \quad \text{if } \begin{cases} c[n] \in A, \\ c[n] \bar{\in} A. \end{cases}$$

The penalty-nonpenalty concept underlies also Tsypkin's model of Markovian learning (a stochastic automaton corresponding to a Markovian chain when randomness covers also the initial system $a[0]$ and exit value $x[n]$ is identified with the state $a[n]$). The Markovian learning algorithm is given the form

$$\begin{aligned} a[n] &= a[n-1] - (y_0[n] - \text{sgn}(y_0[n] - a[n-1])) \\ a[n] &= a[n-1] \end{aligned} \quad \text{if } a[n] = \begin{cases} \in A \\ \bar{\in} A \end{cases}$$

Tsypkin ideas have been developed further by Varshavskiy, Vorontsova, and Tseytlin:[177] the graph below by them comes from his reproduction.

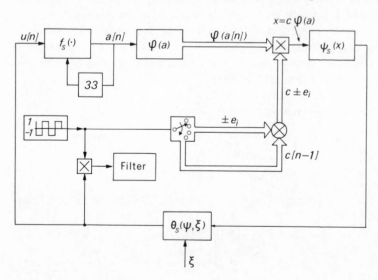

The learning is carried out under a constant characteristic of the transformer through a change of the random impulse ξ created by a special generator; in the process the transitional probabilities are being redistributed in such a way that the probability of transition from any state into a state entailing a penalty declines.

APPENDIX

A game-theoretic methodology in the treatment of control problems under conditions of incomplete information has been suggested by Zhelnin[178] — for a dynamic system described by

$$\dot{x} = f(x,u,\xi), \quad y(t) - \varphi(x,u,\xi,w) = 0,$$

$$I = \int_{t_0}^{T} f^0(x,u,\xi)dt + F[x(T)], \quad x(t_0) = x^0 \in X^0.$$

(*Notation:* x_i is a $(x_1, \ldots, x_n)$ vector of phase coordinates, $(u_1, \ldots, u_r)$ $u_i \in U$ control vector, $\xi_i (\xi_1, \ldots, \xi_q) \in \Xi$ vector of perturbations; I index of quality of control. Information on the current phase state is determined by the vector $y_i = (y_1, \ldots, y_p)$; $w_i = (w_1, \ldots, w_m) \in W$ — vector of error in measurement. The vectors $x^0 \in X^0$, $\xi \in \Xi$, $w \in W$ are taken as unknown, but the boundaries of the region of their values are taken as known; the x^0, Ξ, W, U are bounded closed regions of possible values of the respective vectors. It is assumed that the system of equations $y(t) - (x,u,\xi,w) = 0$ cannot be solved uniquely with respect to y,x,u,ξ,w, that is in terms of dimensionality $p < n + r + q + m$; hence the $y(t)$ represents "incomplete" information on the current phase state. The problem then consists in determining the optimal synthesis $u^*(y(t), t)$ that minimizes I. In the further argument it is assumed that over the interval (t_0, T) the $y(t)$ is known. The latter does not uniquely determine $x(t)$, $\xi(t)$, $w(t)$; there must exist therefore some *sets* of values of x^0 and the functions $\hat{\xi}(t)$, $\hat{w}(t)$: the observation yields the equations

$$\dot{\hat{x}} = f(\hat{x},u,\hat{\xi}), \quad y(t) - \varphi(\hat{x},u,\hat{\xi},\hat{w}) = 0;$$

$$\hat{I} = \int_{t_0}^{T} f^0(\hat{x},u,\hat{\xi})dt + F[\hat{x}(T)], \quad \hat{x}(t_0) = \hat{x}^0 \in X^0.$$

The choice is made for $\hat{I} = \hat{I}^*$ such as to ensure the minimum of the possible error in the estimate; the deviation of I from the I is measured by some

$\rho(I - \hat{I})$. The additional requirements conditioning a unique determination of the estimation vector $\hat{x}(t)$ are

$$\dot{x} = f(x,u,\xi), \quad y(t) - \varphi(x,u,\xi,w) = 0,$$
$$\dot{\hat{x}} = f(\hat{x},u,\hat{\xi}), \quad y(t) - \varphi(\hat{x},u,\hat{\xi},\hat{w}) = 0,$$

$$\rho^* = \min_{\hat{x}^0,\hat{\xi},\hat{w}} \max_{x^0,\xi,w} \rho(I - \hat{I}).$$

For what is then a differential game the necessary conditions of optimality — in pure strategies within the regularity region of the functional — are

$$\mathcal{H} = \max_{\{\xi \in \Xi,\ \hat{w} \in W,\ y - \hat{\varphi} = 0\}} \min_{\{\xi \in \Xi,\ w \in W,\ y - \varphi = 0\}} \psi \cdot f + \hat{\psi} \cdot \hat{f},$$

$$\dot{\psi} = -\frac{\partial \mathcal{H}}{\partial x} + \lambda \frac{\partial \varphi}{\partial x}, \qquad \psi(T) = -\frac{\partial \rho}{\partial x}, \qquad \dot{\hat{\psi}} = -\frac{\partial \mathcal{H}}{\partial \hat{x}} + \hat{\lambda} \frac{\partial \phi}{\partial \hat{x}},$$

$$\hat{\psi}(T) = -\frac{\partial \rho}{\partial \hat{x}}.$$

H is the system's Hamiltonian, the ψ and $\hat{\psi}$ vectors of the auxiliary variables, $\lambda(t)$ and $\hat{\lambda}(t)$ indeterminate multipliers (for the sake of simplicity it is assumed that $f^0 = 0$ and ρ is a scalar).

Notes

1. N. Krassovskiy, in A. I. Lurye/A. P. Proskuryakov, eds., *Analiticheskaya mekhanika, ustoichivost dvizhenya, nebesnaya ballistika* (Moscow, 1965).
2. A rigorous definition of observability will be found in J. C. Hsu/A. U. Meyer, *Modern control principles and application* (New York, 1968). The *completely* observable system (linear,, time-invariant) $x = Ax + Bu$, $y = Cx + Du$ is characterized by the property that the initial state x (0) can be derived whenever the matrices A and B and the output $y(t)$ — over a finite time interval — in response to the initial conditions $x(0)$ with $u(t) = 0$ are given.
3. A. A. Feldbaum, *Osnovy teorii optimalnykh avtomaticheskikh sistem*, 2nd ed. (Moscow, 1966).
4. A. A. Feldbaum, "K voprosu o sinteze optimalnykh sistem avtomaticheskogo regulirovanya", and A. Ya. Lerner, "Postroyenye bystrodeystvuyuschikh sistem avtomaticheskogo regulirovanya priogranichenii znacheniy koordinat reguliruyemogo obyekta"—both published in the vol. II of the second all-Union Conference (1953) on Automatic-Control Theory, Moscow, 1955.

    The antecedents of the discipline may be related directly to a paper of a quarter of a century ago by A. A. Feldbaum on the integral quality criteria of regulation in *Avt. i tel.*, 1 (1948).

5. A fascinating discourse by Lyetov on the philosophy of optimization is contained in his contribution to the *Third (1966 London) International Federation of Automatic Control Congress* (paper 12A, "Engineering/Philosophy in optimization in the problem of analytical design of optimal controllers"). It is written with an eye to problems of mechanics but the planning economist will find a good deal of interest in clear analogy.

6. A very simple presentation of the general theory of filters will be found in Hammer's contribution to P. C. Hammer, ed., *Advances in mathematical systems theory*, pp. 1 ff.

    A filter is considered adaptive if it measures, and adapts to changes in environment: adjusts, that is, its parameters to the changes in the characteristics of the signal—message cum noise—so as to keep the optimum estimate of the message, (cf. D. Q. Mayne, "Optimum non-stationary filters", in J. H. Westcott, ed., *Adaptive control* (1963).

    The readre will be referred to the Kolmogorov-Wiener filtering theory in the reformulation of Kalman and Bucy. Optimal filter is treated as producing for the dynamic system an optimal regulator—"dual" to the stochastic system in Kalman-Bucy sense. (R. E. Kalman/R. S. Bucy, "New results in linear prediction and filtering theory", *J. Basic Eng. Trans.*, 1961). For a recent reformulation of the Kalman-Bucy filter problem see Kalman et al, *Topics in mathematical system theory* (1969): the "best" linear filter, in an "expected-squared-error" sense is determined for a "signal" generated by a linear stochastic differential equation on a Hilbert space: thus a Wiener-Hopf type equation for the "optimal" filter is derived (technically crucial in the treatment is the use of Fubini's theorem involving interchange of stochastic and Lebesgue integration).

7. *Osnovy teorii* . . .

8. Ibid., p. 90.

9. Or in a more common notation for the functional $I = \int_{x_0}^{x_1} F(x, y, y') \, dx$ the necessary condition is the differential equation $\partial F/\partial y - d/dx. \, (\partial F/\partial y') = 0$.

10. Note, to anticipate further contexts, that (whatever the limitations in their application to a system's optimal control) the Euler equations have been employed, in substance, in some theoretical constructs which have subsequently become an important element in control-theoretic formulations of economic planning.

    Thus the famous contribution of Ramsey, formalizing the planning theory's concept of "millenium" (*Econ. J.*, 1928) is an important case of such an application.

11. When the transversality conditions to be met at "bounding" points are specified, the related constants can be determined in the solutions of the Euler equations.

12. Where we are confronted with only one-end variable, the necessary conditions lend themselves to formulation in terms of the manifold's "focal point": on this the initial end point would vary; see on this Bliss. A sufficiency theorem is formulated by him for a generalized problem of variable end-point with reference to Hahn's auxiliary theorem; cf. G. A. Bliss, *Lectures on the calculus of variations* (Chicago, 1946), p. 158; the source in Hahn is "Uber Variations probleme mit variablen Endpunkten", *Monatshefte für Mathematik und mat Physik*, 22(1911) see also reference to the Bolza problem with "separated end-conditions". ibid).

13. For a clear discussion of what is involved see A. E. Bryson/Y. C. Ho, *Applied optimal control* (Toronto, 1969).

14. S. E. Dreyfus, *Dynamic programming and the calculus of variations* (1965), p. 61.

15. cf. *Mathematische Annalen*, 1906.
16. Some remarkable advances in the "modernization" of the Bolza problem are owed to R. T. Rockafellar's building it into his theory of convex systems; cf. in particular his papers on the existence and duality theorems for convex problems of Bolza. Firstly, he has shown that when certain convexity assumptions and mild regularity assumptions—without requiring differentiability—are satisfied, the problem has, associated with it, a dual which is a "generalized problem of Bolza". Subsequently he has related the extremal value of problems of Bolza and given conditions under which optimal arcs exist; he has also established a class of problems for which the generalized Euler-Lagrange equation, or Hamiltonian equation, and transversality condition are necessary and sufficient for an arc to be optimal. cf. "Existence and duality theorems for convex problems of Bolza", *Amer. Math. Soc. Trans.*, 159 (1971).
17. Bolza, *Vorlesungen über Variationsrechnung* (1904).
18. Gilbert A. Bliss, *Calculus of variations* (Chicago, 1937), p. 187.
19. A. A. Krassovskiy, *Avt. i tel.*, 4 (1972). The subject is also treated by him in "New solution to the problem of a control system analytical design", *Automatica*, 1 (1971).
20. cf. Jacobi, *Vorlesungen ueber Dynamik*; W. Hamilton, "Second essay on a general method in dynamics", *Philosoph. Trans.*, Royal Soc. 1835; Bliss, op. cit.
21. E. Dreyfus, op. cit.
22. For an interesting discussion of the central role of the Hamilton-Jacobi theory in the calculus of variations, see Hanno Rund, *The Hamilton-Jacobi theory in the calculus of variations* (London, 1966).

  The reader is strongly advised to acquaint himself with the treatment of the Hamilton-Jacobi theory in Kalman, et al., *Topics in mathematical system theory* both with respect to the proofs and applicational indications. As to the former the sufficiency conditions are obtained by employing a Carathéodory lemma. As to the latter, of interest is in particular the case of a linear dynamic system with a quadratic cost functional (crucial in the solution is the introduction of the (operator) Riccati equation).
23. A. F. Filippov, *Vestnik moskovskogo universiteta*, serya Matematika, Mekhanika, Astronomya, 2 (1959).
24. R. Bellman et al., "*Some aspects of the mathematical theory of control processes*" (RAND Corp., Report R-313, Jan. 1958).
25. For methods of approximation to the continuous-control problem see a paper by Jane Cullum, "Discrete approximations to continuous optimal control problems", *SIAM J.* Feb. 1969. In this existence is proved of a direct method of determining the optimal solution whereby the system of linear equations is linear in the control and state variables with convex control and state variable constraints. The continuous problem as defined is shown to be replaceable by a sequence of finite-dimensional discrete optimization problems for which the approximation is offered.
26. We may refer in this, if only for lack of better context, to the work in Soviet literature on the convergence of the extremal problem to the solution of the continuous-optimum problem. This has been investigated in particular by B. Budak et al, in *Vestnik moskovskogo univeristeta* (scrya Matematika, Mekhanika) 2 (1968). Technically the question concerns cases where the differential statement is replaced by a difference statement. The authors link up with Tikhonov approach to incorrectly set control problems.
27. B. M. Polyak, ibid., 2 (1968).
28. E. Roxin, "The existence of optimal controls", *Michigan Math. J.*, 2 (1962);

J. Warga, "Relaxed variational problems", *J. Math. Anal. & Applications*, 1 (1962).

29. G. P. Ivanova, "O teoremakh sushchestvovanya v variatsyonnom vychislenii" *Doklady*, 170/2 (1966); I. D. Ioffe, "Preobrazovanya korrektno postavlyennykh variatsionnykh zadach", ibid. L. Cesari, "Un teorema di esistenza in problemi di controlli ottimi", Ann. Scuola Normale Pisa, 1 (1956).

30. L. W. Neustadt, "The existence of optimal controls in the absence of convexity conditions. *J. Math. Anal. Application*, 7 (1963).

31. L. I. Rozonoer's original paper, on the sufficiency conditions of optimality, in *Doklady*, 127/3 (1959); cf also his *O varyatsyonnykh metodakh issledovanya kachestva sistem avtomaticheskogo upravlenya* (Moscow, 1960).

32. P. Brunovsky, "On the necessity of certain convexity conditions for lower closure of control problems", *SIAM J.*, 6/2 (1968).

33. Litovchenko, "Teoria optimalnykh sistem", in R. V. Gamkrelidze, ed., *Matematicheskiy analiz; teoria vyeroyatnostej; regulirovanya* (Moscow, 1961).

34. cf. ibid.

35. A. Miele, "Some recent advances in the mechanics of celestial flight", *Jet Propulsion*, 9 (1958); V. A. Troitskiy, in *PMM*, 4 (1961).

36. see Litovchenko, in Gamkrelidze, *Matematicheskiy analiz*, pp. 164ff.

38. S. E. Dreyfus, op. cit.

39. A helpful description of the dynamic-programming programme is offered by McCann: to work from each end-point by small steps backwards in time; the procedure is repeated from the new family and so on, till the time interval is covered and one of the trajectories going through the starting point emerges as the best choice over time. Computationally the purpose is to escape from the solution of a two-point boundary-value problem: At the same time as McCann puts it a "complete record" of "what-to-do-next-whatever happens" may be of use in application. (Michael McCann, "Variational approaches to the optimal trajectory problem", in Westcott, ed., *Adaptive control*).

To put this in a different way, rather than considering the control function merely as a function, we regard it as that of the system's current states. (It is to this, the new approach, that Bellman basically ascribes the new formulation of multi-stage decision processes in the theory of dynamic programming).

R. Bellman, "New directions of research in the theory of differential equations", in J. P. LaSalle/S. Lefschetz, eds., *Nonlinear differential equations and nonlinear mechanism* (New York, 1963).

40. In yet another, didactically helpful, reinterpretation—by Arrow-Kurz— the Optimality Principle is the "observation" that if in the solution to the problem

$$\sum_{t=0}^{T} U[x(t), u(t), t + Sx(T)] \to \max, \text{ for a system } x_i(t+1) = T_i[x_1(t), \ldots,$$

$x_s(t), u(t), \ldots, u_n(t), t]$ with $x_i(o) = x_i$ the state at t_o is given by x, the optimal choice of control and state of variables is thereafter identical with that inherent in the "return function"

$$U(x, t_0) = \begin{cases} T \\ t = t_o \end{cases} U[\cdot] \to \max \text{ with respect to controls } u(t) \text{ and } x_i(t)_o = x_i$$

(Arrow/Kurz, *Public investment*, p. 28; standard notation.; S = scrap value).

41. Dreyfus, op. cit.

A point incisively made by Mesarovic and associates shows the kinship between the Bellmanian Optimality Principle and that of feedback control; under the latter the output of each stage is compared with the desired course and the error is being fed back—through a transformation so as to adjust the control. The strategy—the fixing of the initial-time control or of the feed-back-loop parameters—follows the adopted principle. (cf. Mesarovic et al., op. cit., p. 98).

42. We follow here in the main the source quoted in n. 52.

43. cf. Litovchenko, in Gamkrelidze. *Matematicheskiy analiz*, pp. 166, 168; reference to N. N. Krassovskiy, in *PMM*, 4 (1959); R. E. Kalman, in *Bol. Soc. mat. mex.*, 1 (1960); A. M. Lyetov, in *Avt. i tel.*, 4 (1961).

The equation as stated is usually referred to in Soviet literature of the subject as the Bellman-Lyapunov equation.

44. Bellman, *Dynamic programming*, (Princeton, 1957), pp. 7 ff. It is a point made by Bellman himself that one of the considerable advantages of beginning with the discrete case is that questions of existence of a solution are readily resolved (Another consideration is that simple modifications make possible the treatment of important classes of stochastic processes).

cf. his *Introduction to the mathematical theory of control processes*, ii (New York, 1971).

45. For a recent attempt to overcome some technical difficulties in the formulation of the cost function of a dynamic-programming system see C. Aumasson. "Quelques resultats généraux sur la programmation dynamique stochastique à temps discret", in A. V. Balakrishnan et al., *Symposium on optimization* (1970).

46. R. E. Bellman/S. E. Dreyfus, *Applied dynamic programming* (Princeton, 1962).

47. M. M. Berkovich, *EMM*, 1 (1968).

48. For a good presentation see L. T. Fan/C. S. Wang, *The discrete maximum principle* (New York, 1964), p. 132

49. A. A. Feldbaum/A. G. Butkovskiy, *Metody teorii avtomaticheskogo upravlenya* (Moscow, 1971).

50. cf. L. V. Kantorovich/I. V. Romanovskiy, "Matematicheskoye programmirovany, in *Matematika i kibernetika v ekonomike*, 1971.

51. The original work has appeared in Eng. trans: L. S. Pontryagin et al., *The mathematical theory of optimal processes* (London, 1962); our restatement follows that by E. F. Mishchenko, "Niekotoryte voprosy teorii optimalnogo upravlenya i presldedovanya", *Vtoraya Letniaya matematicheskaya shkola* (Kiev, 1965). By now several different presentations of the Pontryagin Principle have been published, both in the Soviet Union and in Western literature; of the latter we would mention in particular those by Dreyfus (Dreyfus, op. cit.) and H. Halkin, "On the necessary conditions for optimal control of nonlinear systems", *J. d'analyse mathématique*, 1964.

52. The exception is based on what has been termed by Boltyanskiy (who proved the sufficiency) the "condition of the generality of the situation". This in turn is related to the concept of subspace invariant with respect to trans-formation. cf. V. G. Boltyanskiy, *Matematicheskiye metody optimalnogo upravlenya*, 2nd ed. (Moscow, 1969).

53. L. I. Rozonoer, in *Avt. i tel.*, 1, 11 & 12 (1959). cf. also the same, in *Doklady*, 3 (1959).

54. G. Ya. Yakovenko, in *Avt. i tel.*, 6 (1972).

55. J. H. Westcott, summary of address in *Avt. i tel.*, 2 (1967), pp. 17ff.

56. S. Schapiro, "Lagrange and Mayer's problems in optimal control", *Automatica*, Jan. 1966. To be sure we do not question ingenuity: indeed in some of the

construct, it is brilliant. Very appositely Bellman adopts as one of his mottoes a quotation from Swift's *Gulliver's Travels* on the most ingenious architect who contrived a new method for building houses by beginning at the roof and working downwards to the foundations (R. E. Bellman, *Adaptive control processes, a guided tour* (Princeton, 1961), ch. 3).

57.   Charles Desoer, "Pontryagin's maximum principle and the principle of optimality", *J. Franklin Inst.*, Jan.–June 1961.

Here the optimal control steers the system from its initial state x_0 to a target in motion so that the cost of control along the optimal trajectory

$$\int_{t_0}^{t_1} f_0 \left[x^0(r), u^0(t), t \right] dt = \min.$$ The optimal control u^0 is shown to obey the

Maximum Principle at each point of trajectory: $\max < \tilde{g}(x), \tilde{f}(x, u) > = \tilde{g}(x)$, $f(x, x^0)$; denoting the minimal cost of motion $x_0 \to x$ as Γ, the $g(x)$ being related to $\nabla \Gamma$.

There is a controversial discussion of the various approaches in proving the Pontryagin Principle by Halkin ("Mathematical foundations of system optimization", in G. Leitmann, ed., *Topics in optimization* (1967)); it is Halkin's observation that the original proof by the Pontryagin team is "obscure" and "incomplete" (ibid., p. 199). The heuristic derivations of the Principle considered are those of Desoer, Dreyfus, Flugge-Lotz, Halkin, Kalman – all categorized as following the Caratheodory geodetic or the Bellman dynamic programming method. The point stressed is that the Pontryagin proof is based on the construction of special variants originated in McShane, which leads to the construction of some convex sets. (The same volume contains a proof by S. P. Diliberto: here the reasoning relates to the cone attached to each point of the trajectory–the measure of controllability in the Pontryagin system, and generated by the special perturbation in the control function. The results do not depend on the control set's convexity. A by-product of the exercise is the proof for the bang-bang principle for nonlinear systems.)

58.   The book by Intrilligator stands out for clear presentation of the relationship of the three basic approaches to the control problem, that of the classical calculus, of the Optimality Principle, and of the Maximum Principle. Thus it is well shown how, when specializing dynamic programming into the classical calculus of variations, we get the Bellman equation implying the necessary conditions of the classical calculus of variations, including the Euler equation and the Legendre, the Weierstrass, and the Weierstrass-Erdmann (corner) condition. So it is also shown how the Bellman equation and its boundary equation imply Maximum Principle, though not vice versa. (cf. Michael Intrilligator, *Mathematical optimization in economic theory*, (Englewood Cliffs, 1971).

The relation between the Maximum Principle and the Bellman function has been recently examined by N. P. Fedorenko. The problem considered is that of maximum velocity for the differential equation $dx/dt \in K(x), x(O) = x_0$. The Maximum Principle is obtained under some assumption with respect to the Bellman function $W(x)$ of this problem; some strong assumptions are also adopted for the function $Q(x, \psi) = \max(k, \psi)$. One of the assumptions

$$k \in K(x)$$

is in particular the existence of a hyperplane to the surface $W(x) = T$. In the context Fedorenko also examined the Cauchy problem for Bellman's dynamic programme equation. See N. P. Fedorenko, in *Zhurnal vychislitelnoy matematiki i matematicheskoy fiziki*, 2 (1969); the same, ibid., 6 (1970) and 4 (1971).

59.   Feldbaum, *Osnovy teorii* . . . , p. 123. An auxiliary continuous function of the point x in an $(n + 2)$ dimensional space $S = x_0 = S(x, \ldots, x_n, x_{n+2})$ is introduced and the geometrical locus—isoplanes—of points S = constant found. We have $\Psi = -S/x_i$ – the gradient of the scalar S in the space of x orthogonal to S = constant. Now the condition H = max coincides with that of minimizing the scalar product of the vector by the vector of velocity $f = dx/dt$. Since at the given point x is a datum, independent of u, that means maximizing the projection of the vector of velocity (f) on the direction of the normal to the isoplane at that point: the maximum equals zero.

60.   Magnus R. Hestenes, *Calculus of variations and optimal control theory*, (New York, 1967), p. 252ff.

61.   Leonard D. Berkovitz, "Variational methods in problems of control and programming", *J. Math. Anal. Application*, 3 (1961).

62.   In the Pontryagin formulation it is defined with the opposite sign; hence to minimize the performance index H has to be maximized.

63.   I. Gumowski/C. Mira, *Optimization in control theory and practice* (Cambridge, 1968), also the same, "Optimization by means of the Hamilton-Jacobi Theory", *Proc. 3rd IFAC Congress* (London, 1966) paper 7E.

64.   cf. Carathéodory, *Variationsrechnung und partielle Differential–gleichungen erster Ordnung*, 1935.

65.   Kalman developed sufficiency conditions for optimal control – the Hamilton-Jacobi theory – from Carthéodory's lemma ("The theory of optimal control and calculus of variations", in R. E. Bellman, ed., *Mathematical optimization techniques* 1960). (Santa Monica conference).

      Some years after this section was written I found in Samuelson's beautiful "Foreword" to Chakravarty's *Capital and development planning* a point on the revival of the classical variational theory at the time when it appeared to be a dead letter—in the context of optimal-control theory; and on how in this the classical methods of the great Carathéodory were "disinterred" (p. X) as well as those of Hamilton-Jacobi.

      The "re-discovery" of Carathéodory's work has played an important role in the development of modern convexity theory. See on this Rockafellar's *Convex analysis*. One will find there the formulation of a comprehensive version of Carathéodory's theorem covering the generation of convex cones and other unbounded convex sets and of ordinary convex hulls.

66.   The principle relating to the dependence domain: in an initial value problem for a partial-differential equation, at point i and time t, the value of the solution may be determined by the initial values of a portion of the whole range, which is called the dependence domain. The problem is said to be satisfying the Huygens principle where the dependence domain of every point is a manifold of no more than $(n - 1)$ dimensions—for an initial-value problem in an n-dimensional space.

      To the Huygens Principle we find related the "Hadamard conjecture" (that an equation differing substantially from the partial differential equation of the type termed "the wave equation" can meet this Principle).

      For an application of the Principle in economics see Samuelson's interesting paper "Efficient Paths in terms of the calculus of variations" in Arrow et al, eds., *Mathematical methods in the social sciences* (Stanford, 1960).

67. In the Gumowski-Mira restatement of the Carathéodory system for the extremal problem

$$I(x_0, x_i) = \min_{y \, \epsilon \, Y} I(y) = \min_{y \, \epsilon \, Y} \int_{x_0}^{x_1} F(x, y\,(x), \dot{y}\,(x)\,)dx$$

$$y(x_0) = y_0\,; \qquad y(x_i) = y_1$$

the solution leads through embedding $I(\bar{y}) = I(x_0, x_1, y_1, y_2)$ in a family

$$S(x, y) = S_1\,(x_0, y_0, x, y) \text{ or } S(x, y) = S_2\,(x, y, x_1, y_1)$$

combined with the singular transformation $\dot{y} = Y(x, y)$, which transforms every $y \, \epsilon \, Y$ into a unique function Y. Carathéodory's fundamental system is

$$F(x, y, Y) - (\partial S/\partial x + \partial S/\partial y \, . \, X) = 0; \quad \partial S/\partial y = \partial F/\partial Y.$$

The family of curves $S(x, y) =$ const. are his "geodesic equidistants". By replacing a set of Hamilton-Jacobi equations, Gumowski-Mira write, as equivalent to the fundamental system, what they term the Carathéodory partial-differential equation, the non-linear partial-differential equation

$$S(x, y, \partial S/\partial x, \partial S/\partial y) = 0.$$

(Gumowski/Mira, p. 121ff.) For the relevant Carathéodory apparatus—the method of geodesic equidistants as related to the Lagrangean system—cf. in particular Carathéodory's "Die Methode der geodaetischen Aequidistanten und der Problem von Lagrange", *Acta matematica*, 1926.

68. D. H. Jacobson/D. Q. Mayne, *Differential dynamic programming* (New York, 1970). As the title indicates, the work is concerned primarily with the differential statement of this construct.

For a presentation of time-lagged optimal-control synthesis with special consideration of suitability of dynamic programming see H. T. Banks, *et al.*, "The synthesis of optimal control for linear, time-optimal problems with retarded controls", *J. Optimization Theory and Applications*, Nov. 1971.

69. Pontryagin *et al.*, op. cit. cf. also Mishchenko, op. cit., pp. 100ff.

70. To recall, the Bellman equation is the nonlinear differential equation in partial derivatives with respect to some unknown $S(t, y)$, of the form

$$\min_{u(t) \, \epsilon \, U} [\partial S/\partial t + \sum_{i=1}^{n} \partial S/\partial y_i \cdot f_i(t, y(t), u(t)\,) + f_0\,(t, y\,(t), u\,(t)] = 0,$$

subject to

$$y' = f(t, y, u), y(0) = a, y\,(T) \, \epsilon \, g, y(t) \, \epsilon \, G, \; 0 \leqslant t \leqslant T,$$

the y being the trajectory with some space G containing the initial point and its region g at which the trajectory is aimed in the terminal time-point T.

The boundary condition for this equation is $S(T, y) = 0$.

71. cf. *Izvestya of the USSR Academy of Sciences*, Math. sect. 3, (1964); and, *Matematicheskiye metody optimalnogo upravlenya* (Moscow, 1966).

72. L. A. Kun/Yu. F. Pronozin, in *Doklady*, 200/6 (1971).

73. A. Ya. Dubovitskiy/A. A. Milyutin, *Zhurnal Vychislitelnoy Matematiki i Matematicheskoy Fiziki*, 3 (1965); 189/6 (1969); *Doklady*, 149/4 (1963); this work attempts a general statement of necessary conditions for an extremum in terms of conjugated cones.

The problem is that of determining the vector function $u(t)$ for a system:

$$F(x, t) = \int_O^T (x, u)dt$$ subject to the vector $f(x_1, \ldots x_n)$ satisfying the differential

equation $x' f(\dot{x}, u)$ and boundary conditions $x(0) = x_0$, $x(T) = x_T$.

74. R. V. Gamkrelidze, "On some extremal problems in the theory of differential equations with applications to the theory of optimal control", *SIAM J.*, ser. A, 3/1 (1965), pp. 106ff.

75. Ibid., p. 109.

76. Ibid., and restatement on p. 320; cf. also the same, in *Doklady*, 161/1 (1965). Note also his proof of the Pontryagin Principle for systems with constrained phase co-ordinates, ibid., 125/3 (1959).

77. Ghouila-Houri, *Problèmes d'existence de commande optimale; Séminaire d'automatique théorique* (Caen, Faculté des Sciences, 1965); J. Warga, "Relaxed variational problems", *J. Math. Anal. & Applications*, 4 (1962).

78. Among such ramifications we may mention some work in measure theory with application to control theory, as in Charles Castaing, "Some theorems in measure theory and generalized dynamical systems defined by contingent equations", in Kuhn/Szegö, *Math. systems theory*.

79. When on the subject of generalization of the optimal-control theory, it is only right to record an important step on this path, Kalman's presentation at the First IFAC Congress in Moscow in 1960 of his "pure" theory of control (with a new approach to the duality principle extended to problems of control and filtering). Cf. R. E. Kalman, "Ob obshchey teorii sistem upravlenya", in *Trudy i mezhdunarodnogo kongressa mezhdunarodnoy Federatsyi po Avtomaticheskomu Upravlehyu* (Eng. version "On the general theory of control systems", in *Proc.* 1st IFAC Congress, Moscow, 1960).

The paper contains also a most valuable survey of the state of the control-theoretic achievements at the beginning of the 1960s. Naturally further advances in the field (of which the reader is made conscious by the survey) have also helped the work on generalizations.

80. F. A. Valentine "The problem of Lagrange with differential inequalities as added side conditions", in Bliss, *Contributions to the Calculus of Variations* (Chicago, 1937) also L. D. Berkovitz, op. cit; M. R. Hestenes, op. cit.

81. L. C. Young, "Generalized curves and the existence of attained absolute minimum in the calculus of variations", *C. R. Soc. Sci. et Lettres*, Warsaw III/30 (1937), pp. 212 ff.

82. J. Warga, *J. Math. Analysis & Applications*, 4 (1964), pp. 111ff.

83. A. A. Pervozvanskiy, in *Tekh. kib.*, 2 (1967).

84. cf. H. Halkin/L. W. Neustadt, "General necessary conditions for optimization problems", in *Proc.* Nat. Acad. Sci. 56 (1966); and the same, "Control as programming in general normed linear spaces" in *Mathematical systems theory and economics*. For an overall critical survey of the field see L. W. Neustadt, "A survey of certain aspects of control theory", in Dantzig/Veinott, op. cit.

85. H. Halkin, in Balakrishnan/Neustdat, op. cit. One of fundamental, generalizing elements in the Halkinian methodology is his simple yet fascinating "Principle of Optimal Evolution". In its terms, if V is an

optimal control function, then for every $t \in [0, 1]$ the state x $(t; V)$
belongs to the boundary of the set $W(t)$, where $W(t)$ is the set of all states which
are reachable at the time.; in words—every event of an optimal process belongs to
the boundary of the set of possible events. cf. his paper on the necessary conditions for optimal control of nonlinear systems in *J. Anal. Math.*, 12 (1964).

86. E. Polak, "Necessary conditions for optimality in control programming", in
    Dantzig/Veinott, op. cit. pt. 2.

87. R. V. Gamkrelidze/G. L. Karatishvili, "Extremal problems in topological
    spaces", *Mathematical systems theory*, 1 (1967), pp. 229ff.

88. L. W. Neustadt. "Optimal control problems in mathematical programming in
    an unorthodox function space", in A. V. Balakrishnan, ed., *Control theory
    and the calculus of variations*, (New York, 1969).

89. Halkin/Neustadt, in Kuhn/Szegö, *Math. systems theory*, i. Here the authors
    define a "very general" mathematical problem and then in a theorem state a
    necessary condition for that problem.

90. Neustadt, "Optimal control problems with operator equation restrictions" in
    Balakrishnan *et al.*, eds, *Symposium on optimization*, (Berlin, 1970).

91. Halkin, "A satisfactory treatment of equality and operator constraints in
    Dubovitskiy-Milyutin optimization formalizm", *IOTA*, 6/2 (1970); also M.
    Canon *et al.*, "Constrained minimization problems in finite dimensional spaces",
    SIAM J., 4 (1966).

92. G. B. Dantzig, "Application of generalized linear programming to control
    theory" in J. Abadie, op. cit. We may draw attention also to Dantzig's paper
    which examines how a mathematical programming—specifically decomposition
    in the form of the generalized linear programme—is applicable to linear control
    processes as defined: the generalized linear programme as formulated differs
    from the standard one in that the vector of coefficients need not be constant.
    cf. "Linear control processes and mathematical programming", in Dantzig/
    Veinott, op. cit. pt. 2.

93. A. A. Milyutin, *Uspekhi matematicheskikh nauk*, Sept-Oct. 1970; R. Gabasov/
    F. M. Kirillova, in *Avt. i tel.*, 9 (1972).

94. B. N. Pshenichnyi, *Nyeobkhodimyie usloviya ekstremuma* (Moscow, 1969).

95. Pshenichnyi has coined the term "quasi-differentiable functional" (ibid.). The
    class of functionals thus labelled has been the subject of several papers cited
    here in different contexts.

96. We would like to draw the reader's attention to a survey by Gabasov and
    associates which orders the sphere of dynamic control from the angle of
    necessary conditions of optimality (the authors justify the adoption of this
    angle by the fact that these conditions are both an important unifying
    property and are relatively the most advanced in the exploration of the theory
    of control). See R. Gabasov et al., in *Avt. i tel.*, 5 & 6 (1971).
    The novum in the handling of the matter is also the treatment of
    optimality conditions of higher order as a rule connected with singularity
    problems. The generalized Newton-Raphson algorithm (for the solution of the
    two-point boundary-value problems) related with the Euler-Lagrange equations
    is also discussed.
    The survey by Gabasov and associates make a useful supplement to C. D.
    Johnson's "Singular solutions in problems of optimal control", in C. T.
    Leondes, ed., *Advances in control systems*, ii (1965). The second part i.a.
    restates Kelley's proof on the second-order conditions and obtains higher-
    order conditions by the Kopp-Mayer procedure for transformation of control
    variations: this is generalized for multidimensional singular controls (Goh's
    system); it also restates transformation of space-states method (its substance is

a change of phase co-ordinates and a shift to a new problem of smaller dimensions within which, as a rule, the original control problem is investigated by classical methods of variation calculus).

The reader will find it useful to consult in this context also H. J. Kelley et al., "Successive approximation techniques for trajectory optimization", *Proc.* Vehicle System Optimization Symposium, Garden City, New York, 1961.

97. B. N. Pshenichnyi, op. cit. para. 5, sect. 9.

98. Feldbaum/Butkovskiy, op. cit., ch. 16.

99. cf. A. A. Andronov/L. S. Pontryagin in *Doklady*, 14 (1937), and discussion in A. A. Andronov *Teoriya kolebaniy*, 2nd ed. (Moscow, 1959).

100. A. I. Tikhonov, in *Doklady*, 162/4 (1965).

101. J. S. Hadamard, *Leçons sur le calcul des variations* (Paris, 1910) and his *Lectures on Cauchy's problem* (Yale, 1923).

102. Recently Tikhonov has indicated the applicability of his method to stability problems—in the identification of the control objects: the difficulties encountered in the latter could be reduced to the mathematically "incorrect" problem.

cf. also in the context the paper on the application of the approach in problems of difference approximations for control problems by Budak et. al., cited n. 26 above.

103. V. Krotov, *Avt i tel.*, 12 (1962).

104. *Doklady*, 6, 143; 6, 1962.

105. cf. A. F. Filippov, op. cit.

106. V. F. Krotov, *Avt. i tel.*, 5 (1963).

107. V. I. Buyakas, "Osobyie reshenia Printsipa maksimuma v zadache optimal nogo upravlenya s peremennoy strukturoy" in A. M. Lyetov ed., *Optimalnyie sistemy avtomaticheskogo upravlenya*, (Moscow, 1967).

108. The search for an effective computational algorithm in three directions:
    (1) utilizing the Maximum Principle—finding the initial values of the adjoint systems
    (2) utilizing the methods of steepest descent in the control space
    (3) methods based on the theory of movements is indicated by B. N. Pshenichnyi, in "Linear optimal control problems", *SIAM J.*, 4 (1966). This article has also a good survey of developments in the first direction.

For an up-to-date survey of existing trajectory optimization algorithms and report on the authors' experience with them see E. Kopp/H. Gardiner Moyer, "Trajectory optimization techniques", in Leondes, op. cit., iv (1966).

A most useful survey of numerical solution of optimal programming and control problems is contained in ch. 7 of Bryson/Ho, op. cit. Three approaches in iterative procedures (with successive linearization) at present in use are ordered in three classes—of the neighbouring, the gradient, and the quasi-linearization methods. Under the first the nominal solution satisfies the system equations, the influence equations, and optimality conditions; under the second it satisfies the system and the influence equations, under the last the optimality conditions and possibly the boundary conditions. See in the context ch. 4, on direct methods of the calculus of variations, in Naum I. Akhiezer, *The calculus of variations*, Engl. trans. (New York, 1962).

109. P. Gabasov/F. M. Kirillova, *Avt. i tel.*, 2 (1966).

110. See in the context P. Varaiya, "Conditions of optimality", in Zadeh/Polak, op. cit. We draw attention in particular to the lemma resting on the concept of *approximation* as an abstract representation of the idea of perturbation. This is resorted to secure the Maximum Principle for discrete as well as continuous optimal control problems.

111. L. V. Kantorovich/P. Akilov, *Functional analysis in normed spaces*, Engl. trans. (Oxford, 1964).

112. cf. Faddeev/Faddeeva, op. cit., pp. 406ff.

113. Yu. M. Danilin/B. N. Pshenichnyi, in *Zhurnal vychislitelnoy matematiki i matematicheskoy fiziki*, 10/6 (1970).

114. Dubovitskiy/Milyutin, *Doklady*, 149/4 (1963).

115. N. N. Moiseyev, *Zhurnal vychislitelnoy matematiki i matematicheskov fiziki*, 3 (1964).

116. *Doklady*, 149/4 (1963).

117. *Some aspects of the mathematical theory of control processes* (Santa Monica, RAND Corp., R-313, 1958).

   The reader will also find of help ch. 9 on functional analysis in Bellman's *Introduction to the mathematical theory of control.* (1967).

118. N. N. Krassovskiy, *PMM*, 5 (1957) and *Avt. i tel.*, ii (1957); F. M. Kirillova, *Izvestya vysshikh uchebnykh zavedeniy, Matematika*, 2 (1961); cf. references.

   It appears that the first inquiry into the connection between the theory of moments and problems of optimal linear control is owed to Krassovskiy, who was also the first to establish, in his 1959 paper, for a class of piecewise constant controls–the existence of a feasible and optimal gravitation of the point $x = 0$: the domain would coincide with the space X in the case of an asymptotic stability of a non-controlled object; the assumption being made of certain conditions in the equation system of first approximation at $x = 0$. The implications from the angle of Lyapunov's theory are immediate.

119. Fundamental work on the theory of moments by M. G. Krein is contained in his joint work with N. Akhiezer, *O nektorykh voprosakh teorii momentov* (Kharkov, 1938). After a third of a century this is still a major work in the field (see also references in my *Aspects of planometrics*). The indirect relevance of Krein's work for our subject relates to his establishing the dual link between the problem of moments and that of the Cheybyshevian approximations.

120. L. W. Neustadt, "The existence of optimal controls in absence of convexity conditions", *J. Math. Anal. & Application,* 7 (1963).

121. R. Gabasov/F. M. Kirillova, "K probleme sinteza optimalnykh sistem", in V. Trapeznikov, ed., *Vsesoyuznoye sovyeshchanye po avtomatichsekomu upravlenyu.*

122. V. G. Boltyanskiy, in Uzbek *Doklady*, 10 (1959).

123. L. I. Rozonoer, in *Izvestya* of USSR Acad. of Sciences, 4 (1959).

124. V. P. Milyutin, *Avt. i tel.*, 6 (1968).

125. In *Automatica*, 5 (1964), pp. 251ff.

126. A. G. Butkovskiy *et al.*, "Optimal control of distributed systems", *SIAM J.* 6/3 (1968).

127. K. A. Lurye, "Optimalnyie zadachi dlya raspredelyennykh sistem", in Trapeznikov, *Vsesoyuznoye sovyeshchanye . . .*

128. W. H. Fleming, "Some Markovian optimization problems", *J. Maths. & Mechanics*, 1 (1963).

129. H. Kushner, "On the dynamic equations of conditional probability density functions with applications to optimal stochastic control", *J. Math. Anal. & Application*, 2 (1964).

   An important analysis of the mathematical apparatus of stochastic-control systems–specifically differential equations of such systems–is offered by Moshe Zakai, "On the relation between ordinary and stochastic differential equations and applications to stochastic problem of control theory" in *Proc.* 3rd IFAC Congress, London, 1966, paper 3B.

130. Since these lines were written I have been able to acquaint myself with important contributions—indicating the line of advance in the field—contained in the proceedings of the Mathematical Research Center at US Army University (H. F. Karreman, ed., *Stochastic optimization and control*, New York, 1968). For lack of space I have to confine myself to mentioning at least the papers by:

(a)   H. J. Kushner ("The concept of invariant set of stochastic dynamical systems and application to dynamic stochastic stability"). It links up with his results on stochastic Lyapunov functions and their uses in determining stability properties of Markov processes. The paper carries an extension of the notion of invariant set akin to the analogous deterministic construct by LaSalle (cf his *Introduction to stochastic control*, 1971).

(b)   W. H. Fleming ("Some problems of optimal stochastic control"). It offers among other things necessary conditions for a minimum akin to the Pontryagin principle in the non-stochastic control case; cf on this also Kushner's *Optimal control of partially observable diffusions* (Brown University, 1967).

(c)   A. V. Balakrishnan ("Stochastic systems indentication techniques"). It is concerned with cases of application of optimal-control theory where the necessary description of a system's dynamics and response to control imputs is unavailable or incomplete: the problem facing them is that of "identification" of the system. The approach in taking input and output measurements as ergodic processes is discussed. (The author notes the particular importance of the matter in the new and "esoteric" areas of application such as economics).

(d)   E. Dreyfus ("Introduction to stochastic optimization and control"). It links up with, develops and generalizes, and illustrates, his previous work on open-loop and feedback optimal control of a dynamic system indicating the effect of shifting the scheme into a stochastic environment. It provides new forms of necessary conditions for optimal open-loop control (discrete case) and analogous for Brownian motion processes.

131.   cf. A. A. Pervozvanskiy, *Sluchainyie protesessy v nelineynykh avtomaticheskikh sistemakh* (Moscow, 1962) (Eng. trans: *Random processes in nonlinear control systems,* New York, 1965). A more recent Soviet work dealing briefly with the subject is V. V. Solodovnikov, *Dynamics of linear automatic control systems* (Princeton, 1965).

132.   R. Bellman, "Dynamic programming and mathematical economics" in Andras Prekopa, ed., *Colloquium on application of mathematics in economics* (Budapest, 1965).

133.   Ibid.

134.   V. S. Mikhalevich, in *Kibernetika*, 1 & 2 (1965); see also appendix.

135.   We may also draw attention to the work of Shirayev, in particular his contribution to the proceedings of the third conference on information theory, Prague 1964, dealing with the theory of decision functions and control of observations with incomplete data.

136.   It is interesting to note the way Mikhalevich formulates his risk function:

(1)   We have the problem with the elements:

$$\Omega = \omega; \quad \mathscr{U} = \{a\}; \quad \Gamma; \quad P_\omega(dx_{a_k}/x_{a_1}, \ldots, x_{a_{k-1}});$$
$$C_\omega(x_{a_1}, \ldots, x_{a_k}, z); \quad \xi(d\omega); Z,$$

which are respectively, the set of "objects"; the set of "experiments" the set of sequential constraints; probability measure on the experiments results; cost schedule; a priori probability measure; set of decisions;

(2)   Our datum is further that for each ω and each Γ-admissible chain $x_{a_1}, \ldots, x_{a_{k-1}}$, the $P_\omega(x_{a_k}/x_{a_1}, \ldots, x_{a_{k-1}})$ is zero or one for every

$a \in \mathscr{U}_k(x_{a_1}, \ldots, x_{a_{k-1}})$; consequently the probability $P_\omega(x_{a_1}, \ldots, x_{a_k})$ will

have the same values.

We further symbolize as $\Omega_{x_{a_1}}, \ldots, x_{a_k}$ the subset formed of all the

elements with same $P_\omega(x_{a_1}, \ldots, x_{a_k})$. The assumption is that for every Γ-admissible chain $x_{a_1}, \ldots, x_{a_k}$ there is $\Omega_{x_{a_1}}, \ldots, x_{a_k} \subset \mathscr{B}\Omega$ with $B \in \mathscr{B}\Omega$

It is shown that $\qquad \xi_{x_{a_1}}, \ldots, x_{a_k}(B) = \dfrac{\xi(B \cap \Omega_{x_{a_1}}, \ldots, x_{a_k})}{\xi(\Omega_{x_{a_1}}, \ldots, x_{a_k})}$

for $x_{a_{k+1}} \in \mathscr{U}_{k+1}(x_{a_1}, \ldots, x_{a_k})$ and $A \in \mathscr{B}_{a_{k+1}}$

$$P\xi_{x_{a_1}}, \ldots, x_{a_k}(A) = \frac{\xi(x_{a_{k+1}} \overset{\cup}{\in} A \ \Omega_{x_{a_1}}, \ldots, x_{a_{k+1}})}{\xi(\Omega_{x_{a_1}}, \ldots, x_{a_k})}$$

where $\qquad X_{a_{k+1}} = \left\{ x_{a_{k+1}} \right\}$

$$P\xi_{a_{x_1}}, \ldots, x_{a_k}(x_{a_{k+1}}) = \frac{\xi(\Omega_{x_{a_1}}, \ldots, x_{a_{k+1}})}{\xi(\Omega_{x_{a_1}}, \ldots, x_{a_k})}$$

On Bayesian sequential rules it is demonstrated that the structural form of the sets $\Omega_{x_{a_1}}, \ldots, x_{a_k}$ exerts strong influence on the sequential regime of experiments (Mikhalevich, *Kibernetika*, 2 (1965), pp. 85ff).

137.   Bellman, *Introduction to the mathematical theory of control.*
138.   "A Markovian decision process', *J. Maths. & Mechanics*, 1957.
139.   R. A. Howard, *Dynamic probabilistic systems* (New York, 1971). (Note also the important contribution to the development of these ideas by D. Blackwell, espec. in "On the functional equations of dynamic programming", *J. Math. Anal. & Application*, 2 (1961).
140.   Howard, ii. 95.
141.   I. V. Romanovskiy, *Teorya veroyatnostey i yeye primenenya*, 1 (1965).
142.   cf. in Pontryagin et al., op cit., p. 323.
143.   See R. L. Stratonovich, *Avt. i tel.*, 7 (1962); the same, *Uslovnyie Markovskiye protsessy v zadachakh matematihcheskoy statistiki, dinamicheskogo programmirovanya i teorii igr*, paper presented at 4th All-Union Mathematical Congress, Leningrad, 1961; and the same, *Uslovnyie Markovskiye protsessy i ikh primenenye k teorii optimalnogo upravlenya* (Moscow, 1966).
       A formalization considered by Stratonovich in the paper discussed is also that in terms of the "Berge convexity" cf. C. Berge, "Sur une convexité regulière non-linéaire et ses applications a la théorie des jeux", *Bull. Soc. Math. de France*, 1954).
144.   H. J. Kushner/Sweppe, "A maximum principle for stochastic control systems", *J. Math. Anal. & Application*, 4 (1964).

145. Generally, in the treatment of statistical problems with incomplete observation an important element is the introduction of the concept of the space of sufficient co-ordinates in which the generalized Bellman equation is written; this applies to Stratonovich's writings hitherto quoted; cf. also Pontryagin et al., op. cit.
Stratonovich's publications of 1964 and 1966 cited above work with the apparatus based on the theory of conditional Markovian processes.

146. cf. R. L. Stratonovich, "Printsip Maksimuma i statisticheskiye zadachi optimalnogo upravlenya", in A. M. Lyetov, ed., *Optimalnyie sistemy avtomaticheskogo regulirovanya*, (Moscow, 1970). We have drawn largely on the chapter in our presentation of Stratonovich's work.

147. Ibid., p. 114.

148. E. F. Mishchenko, *Avt. i tel.*, 9 (1972).

149. cf. L. S. Pontryagin/E. F. Mishchenko, *Doklady*, 189/4 (1969), and the same, "Le problème d'un mobile controlable poursuivi par un autre", in A. V. Balakrishnan et al., eds, *Symposium on optimization*.

150. The distance $z(t)$ to the subspace M has been derived as $\xi(t) \geqslant Y(\eta(t))$ $\xi^k(0)$ with $\xi(0) \leqslant \epsilon$. Here ϵ is a positive number, γ – a nonincreasing function of its argument depending only on the game's regime; independent in particular, that is, on either the initial point or the course of the game; and η (t) is the distance of $z(t)$ tothe subspace L.

151. R. Isaacs, *Differential games* (London, 1965) (developing a construct originally presented in a series of RAND memoranda of 1954). The reader will find an excellent introduction to the subject of this note in L. D. Berkovitz, "A survey of differential games", in Balakrishnan/Neustadt, *Mathematical theory of control*. A related problem is discussed in V. Grenander, *A tactical study of evasive manoeuvres* (Stockholm, 1963, FOA, Report 126, Research Inst. of Nat. Defence).

152. Kuhn/Szegö, *Differential games.*

153. Ibid., papers by Berkowitz ("Lectures on differential games") and by A. Blaquière ("An introduction to differential games").

154. Thus Blaquière, ibid.; also his (joint with K. E. Wiese and F. Gérard) "Construction d'un couple stratégique optimal et calcul de la valeur du jeu dans un jeu multiétage quantitatif par application de la programmation dynamique", *CR Acad. des sciences*, 220A (1970).
Problems of imperfect information in game-theoretic situations have been investigated by a few authors. Michael Giletti has analysed situations with informational lag. In a recent paper he obtained open-loop Nash equilibrium strategies, computed Nash payoffs, and related the solution to that of an open-loop game with information time-lags (M. D. Ciletti, "Open-loop Nash equilibrium strategies for an N-person non-zero-sum differential game with information time-lag", in Kuhn/Szegö, *Differential games.*

155. In *Doklady*, 176/6 (1967).

156. N. N. Krassovskiy, (*Doklady*, 201/2 (1971)).
As early as the beginning of the 1960s D. L. Kelendzheridze (in a paper published in *Doklady* 138/3, 1961) formulated the necessary optimality conditions for a pair of controls in terms of a Minimax Principle; for the linear case, proof was given by means of the Maximum Principle, and for the general case, by means of dynamic programming (assuming the Bellman function to be twice differentiable).
More recently the pursuit-evasion has been examined as a minimum time problem in terms of a game-theoretic "rendez-vous" and the best strategy of capture established by Krassovskiy in *Doklady*, 181 (1968). Cf. also his

structure analysis of differential games for the minimax of time up to the encounter, in a paper joint with A. I. Subbotin, ibid. 190/3 (1970). (See also in the context his examination of sufficient conditions for the approximation of the extremal strategy to insure the pursuer's approaching the pursued at, or not later than, the given time point, ibid., 191/2, 1970).

The existence of the game-of-pursuit value of the forms

I. $F(x(t), y(t)) = \|x(T) - y(T)\|$

II. $F(x(t), y(t)) = \min \| x(t) - y(t) \|$
     $t \lfloor o, T \rfloor$

III. $F(x(t), y(t)) = \min t$ (where Δ = the set of all t for which
     $t \in \Delta$

$\| x(t) - y(t) \| = \varphi$, the radius of encounter known to players) – is investigated in N. N. Petrov, ibid., 190/6 (1970).

For an expanded presentation of the subject see Krassovskiy's recent book on game problems encounters in motion (*Igrovyie zadachi o vstreche dvizheniy*, Moscow 1970).

To be sure there are only a few problems in general form–in particular for differential equations of a high order–for which the extreme optimal control is obtainable in explicit form. These problems have been treated in V. Ya. Yakubovich's recent paper on the synthesis of optimal control in a linear differential game over a finite time interval (*Doklady*, 200/3 (1971)).

157. cf. V. S. Pugachev, *Teoriya sluchaynykh funktsiy* (Moscow, 1960), p. 596.
158. V. S. Pugachev, *Avt. i tel.*, 10 (1967). cf. also the same "A Bayes approach to the theory of learning systems", in *Proc.* 3rd IFAC (London 1966) Congress, paper 14A.
159. *Avt. i tel.*, 7 (1969).
160. *Osnovy teorii . . .*
161. G. A. Medvedyev/V. P. Tarasenko, *Veroyatnostnyie metody issledovanya ekstremalnykh zadach* (Moscow, 1967). pp. 73ff.
162. W. M. Wonham, "Optimal stochastic control", *Automatica*, Jan. 1969.
163. For definitional framework see L. A. Zadeh, "On the definition of adaptivity", *Proc.* IRE, 3 (1963).
164. On Feldbaum see p. 286.
165. R. Bellman/R. Kalaba, "Dynamic programming and feedback control", *Proc.* 1st IFAC Congress, Moscow, 1960.
166. On a priori current information see A. A. Krassovskiy, *Dinamika nepreryvnykh samonastraivayushchikhsya sistem* (Moscow, 1963).
167. H. Robbins/S. Monro, "A stochastic approximation method", *Ann. Math. Stat.* 1 (1951).
168. R. von Mises/H. Pollaczek-Gieringer, "Praktische Verfahren der Gleichungsauf-loesung", *Zeitsch. für angewandte Math. und Mech.* 9 (1929).
169. E. Kiefer/J. Wolfowitz, "Stochastic estimation of the maximum of a regression function", *Ann. Math. Stat.* 3 (1952).
170. A. Dvoretzky, "On stochastic approximation", *Proc.* 3rd Berkeley Symposium on Math. Stat. & Probability, 1 (1956).
171. See in particular Ya. Z. Tsypkin, *Adaptatsya i obuchenye v avtomaticheskikh sistemakh*, Glavnoye upravlenye fiziko-matemat. literatury (Moscow, 1968); also the same, in *Avt. i tel.*, 1 (1966). There is a recent presentation of the subject by Tsypkin, "Learning Systems", in J. T. Tou, ed., *Advances in information systems science* (New York, 1969), vol. i.
172. Tsypkin, *Avt. i tel.*, 1 (1968); R. L. Stratonovich, ibid.
173. Of the massive output of Soviet writing on the subject we rather arbitrarily refer in particular on stochastic search methods to D. G. Yudin/E. M. Khazen,

Avt. i vychislitelnaya tekh., 13 (1966); S. M. Movshovich, *Tekh. kib.*, 6 (1966); L. S. Gurin, ibid., 3 (1966). A collection of algorithms for random search will be found in L. A. Rastrigin's *Algoritmy i programmy sluchainogo poiska* (Riga, 1969). It contains an attempt at classification of methods by the editor, himself a pioneer in the field.

On methodology of stochastic approximation in general, see Ye. G. Gladyshev, *Teoriya vyeroyatnosti i yeye primenenye*, 2 (1957).

174.   K. S. Fu, "Learning control systems", in Tou, *Advances in information systems sciences*, i.

175.   Roman Kulikowski, *Processy optymalne i adaptacyjme w ukladach regulacji automatycznej*, (Warsaw, 1965), pp. 246ff.

176.   The point is made strongly in A. W. Phillips, "Models for control of economic fluctuations", in *Mathematical model building in economics and industry* (1968).

177.   V. I. Varshavskiy et al., "Obuchenye stokhasticheskikh avtomatov", *Biologicheskiye aspekty kibernetiki* (Moscow, 1962).

178.   Yu. N. Zhelnin, in *Doklady*, 199/1 (1971).

THE IMPACT ON SOVIET ECONOMICS AND PLANNING THEORY

(1)   Having sketched out Russian/Soviet contributions to the fundamentals of the theory of optimal controls and stability of systems, it is high time to address ourselves to our subject proper — its potentialities in economic planning, specifically in macro-economic planning.

We have had here more than one opportunity to indicate the close tie — virtually from birth — between the disciplines of optimal control and stability with the worlds of physics and engineering. Gradually the relevance of certain approaches, methods, and achievements in the former for the treatment of economic problems has revealed itself to the economist. Those related to the investigation of the system's motion over time and their connection with economic dynamics are one of the cases in point. The crystallization of formalized theory of economic planning emphasized this kinship: by definition of its subject, it is concerned with controls and their optimization of the economic system.

Interest in this discipline has been stimulated by the search for new theoretical and applicational equipment. The decades of the 1950s and 1960s were the period of assimilation of the basic tools for ensuring consistency and choice-making. As time passed the planning theoretician has become conscious not only of the great powers of these tools but also of their limitations. Economic planning deals by its very nature with the system's advance over time, and mathematical programming in its classical design has not offered an effective way of dealing with the dynamics of the system. This alone would account for the attraction of the control-theoretic approach and apparatus.

Note
    1. The assimilation of the optimal-control apparatus in economics has led in a natural way to the conception of a general theory of motion in the economic system. In fact that has some history by now: the idea of a kin-

ship between economics and physics goes back at least to Jevons's writing
of a century ago; soon afterwards Edgeworth had indicated the logic of
building up a general economic theory of motion on a universal principle
(and indeed the hope that one day social mechanics would parallel celestial
ones). But it was only in the 1960s that Amoroso[1] formulated mathematically the invariants of the economic system's automotion in exact correspondence with those in mechanics: this analogy is drawn for the states of
both inertia and of accelerated motion — statics and dynamics; and also
for the law of transformation and conservation of energy; the latter would
have its correspondence in pricing. But for a well-developed theory we
commend to the reader the very recent contribution by Magill,[2] for whom
the acknowledged inspiration is Hamilton's theory[3] of analytical mechanics, to which modern theory of control, specifically as developed by
Bellman and Pontryagin, has given a new significance;[4] to summarize,
Hamilton's characteristic equation can be identified with the function that
satisfies Bellman's equation; and his canonical equation of motion is the
one to which the Pontryagin approach will lead. The very elegantly
developed Magill theory gives a new rigour to, expands, and deepens — by
the analogy in physics — the duality implications which have been detected
for the Maximum Principle by a few economists in the last decade. As in
Amoroso, the energy function characterizing the motion in mechanics has
as its counterpart in economics the value (objective) function. The basic
principle in Magill is that of the "stationary basic value".[5] He fascinatingly
points to the difference in the working of the duality principle in this two
domains: in the one, in physics, it depends on the past; in the other, in
economics, essentially on the future. (Let us make the point that to be
exact, while economic processes and phenomena are irreversible and uni-
directional, direction in time is symmetric ("forwards" and "backwards"):
thence the inclination to draw analogies rather with thermodynamics,
whose processes are characterized by asymmetry.)[6] In Magill the difference
reveals itself as embedded in the two fundamental functions, respectively,
that is, in the action function and the present value function. It has its
consequences in the Legendre transformation in the two respective
spheres: in analytical mechanics it yields the desired positive conjugate
momenta and the Hamiltonian, and in economics the desired positive imputed values and the dual objective function.

2. Several Soviet writers have attempted to draw, and pursue in depth,
the analogy between thermodynamics and controlled economic processes.
Plyukhin[7] has applied the theory of chain reaction to his analysis of the
socialist economic mechanism We have already indicated Mikhalevskiy's

use of the concept of negentropy. In a paper on the R. and D. progress rate, Trapeznikov[8] argues that the rise in the rate of accumulated information as related to the volume of controlling information "spent" in the struggle with "disorder" (entropy) would be characteristic of economic advance (as in Schrödinger, every living organism "feeds" on negentropy). It would seem that it is Giuseppe Palomba's writing[9] that has found a strong echo in contemporary Soviet mathematical economics. (One finds extensive references to his reasoning, in particular in Vishnyev.[10]) Briefly, Palomba, in a statical interpretation, draws such an analogy between the thermodynamic function of entropy S and the economic system whose increment $dS_3 = dP/M$ (the P and M standing respectively for social product and volume of profit) whence $S_3 = \int dP/M$, identically as in thermodynamics. In a statistical interpretation Palomba tries to establish a parallel to the familiar Boltzman formula relating entropy to thermodynamic probability $S = k \log D_T$ (where D_T is the probability and k is some constant). For this purpose his introduces economic syntropy (negative entropy), which he connects with the quantity of information. (In Palomba, owing to the properties of their information mechanisms, perfect competition is anentropic; strictly individualist systems tend in general to stabilize entropy, and planning tends to reverse the sign of entropy.) In fairness it may be noted that Vishnyev is sceptical as to whether the thermodynamic concept of syntropy can by itself characterize the complex motion of an economic system.

(2)   In Part I we have introduced the writing of Razumikhin as among those who are representative of the "interdisciplinary" trend specifically for reception — in the theory of economic planning — of a close analogy with and borrowing apparatus from, mechanics and thermodynamics (see p. 72). His "mechanical" model for resource allocation[11] exemplifies his control-theoretically-oriented design. Technically it rests on the minimization of mean-square deviations of functions, representing resources, from some constants. As stated, the problem is that of finding $u_{ij}(t)$ — which is nonnegative over some interval $(t_i - t_j)$ and otherwise zero — such that with respect to the functions y and the auxiliary ones, ψ_ξ,

$$y_\xi = \lambda_\xi y_\xi + \sum_{i=1}^{n} c_{\xi i} \left[\sum_{r=1}^{k} b_{ir} u_r \right],$$

$$\psi_0 = 0$$

$$\psi_\xi = -\lambda_\xi \psi_\xi - \psi_0 \sum_{\eta=1}^{n} (\gamma_{\xi\eta} + \gamma_{\eta\xi})y_\eta, \quad \xi = 1, \ldots, n,$$

subject to the limiting

$$\vec{y(0)} = \{y_1{}^0, \ldots, y_n{}^0\}, \quad \vec{y(t)} = \{0, \ldots, 0\}, \quad \vec{\psi(0)} = \{\psi_1{}^0, \ldots, \psi_n{}^0\},$$

obtainable from linear transformation of y_ξ above.

The solution procedure is formulated so that the optimal control u_r implements the regular synthesis: the uniqueness of the optimal trajectory yielding extremum for the J functional is proved.

In the economic interpretation, the quadratic criterion is taken as a social-welfare function with variable marginal preferences: the linear case would be that of constancy of marginal preferences with respect to conflicting and non-commensurable goals. The constraints would be formed by the dynamic input-output statement, with investment in the capital-goods-producing sector being the controlling variables:

$$\int_{t_0}^{t_n} (u_t{}^{(s)} - L_s)^2 \, dt \rightarrow \min$$

where the L_s is taken to equal

$$1/(t_n - t_0) \int_{t_0}^{t_n} u^{(s)}(t)dt = \sum_{q_{ij} \in P_s} Q_{ij}{}^{(s)}/(t_n - t_0).$$

The $u_{ij}(t)$ characterizes the quantity q_{ij} of resources at t; it is associated with a Q_{ij} being the resource/hours required for performance: the Razumikhin resource-distribution function takes the form

$$\int_{t_i}^{t_j} u_{ij}^{(s)}dt = Q_{ij}^{(s)}, \, q_{ij} \in P_s.$$

Notes

1. The idea of borrowing from engineering the "regulator" for the formulation of economic policy and indicative planning problems has been suggested — in the West — in the well-known writings of R. G. D. Allen and W. Phillips.[12] Stone[13] perceptively indicated the potentialities it offers for keeping oscillation of the economy to a tolerable amplitude. In his

sketch of the control mechanism the economy is characterized by the system of equations

$$q_d = h + x - m \qquad h = \alpha + \beta q_s + \gamma D q_s ,$$

$$q_s = \frac{\theta}{D + \theta} q_d, \qquad m = q_s ,$$

$$x = \text{const.}$$

Here q_s stand for demand of output, h for home demand, x for exports, m for imports; the q_s for the supply of output; d/dt for the differential operator D, and $1/\theta$ some time constant of adjustment. Further, α is a constant and β and γ are proportionality coefficients for demand components; also μ is a proportionality coefficient (for imports).

The oscillatory stability is ensured by a control function meaning the injection (withdrawal) to (from) the system of purchasing power in proportion to some arbitrarily set level of reserves, i.e.

$$g = \sigma \frac{(x - m)}{D} .$$

The differential equation for q_s has then the form

$$D^2 + \frac{\theta(1 + \beta + \mu)}{1 - \theta\gamma} D + \frac{\theta\mu\sigma}{1 - \theta\gamma} q_s = \frac{\theta\sigma x}{1 - \theta\gamma} .$$

2. The genealogy of this approach leads us back to Tustin's[14] classical study of the early 1950s synthesizing statistical conceptions with those of system control, for the purpose of quantified economic decision-making. These have branched out into several important lines of development — both methodologically and in respect of techniques: an important influence on the latter has been that of Newton's[15] procedure.

We shall mention here in particular studies adopting the method of least-square regulation, as evolved by Whittle,[16] with the use of the Wiener-Hopf technique; it works with linear rules, quadratic performance criteria, stationary processes; and it has an attractive simplicity. (We shall see a reflex in some Soviet-designed economic control "mechanical" models based on the mean-square deviation criterion — cf. ch. 5). Also that developed by Holt[17] and associates — with some affinities with dynamic programming: it depends methodologically on resetting variables over time (rather than feedback and similar devices); it works with the matrix apparatus and its distinctive element is the reliance — with respect to decision and environmental variables — on the certainty-equivalence, (originated by Simon with an eye to dynamic programming, and generalized by Theil)[18].

The Holt methodology is essentially micro-oriented. But it has influenced various macro-economic control designs. Among the latest examples we may mention the Chow[19] model for ascertaining the dynamic behaviour of the economy under alternative control rules: a solution is obtained for the optimum-control problem under the assumptions of a stationary system and a quadratic objective function.

A class in itself is formed by constructs rather vaguely conceived in the literature of socialist countries as "cybernetical" instruments. We would mention here in the first place the outline — in Soviet literature — by Shreider, on dynamic planning and "automata"[20]; quite possibly one of the most elaborate is Oskar Lange's "cybernetical" modelling: translated into Russian it has exercised a noteworthy influence on Soviet thinking. On this we shall say something in the next section.

(3)   The tendency towards generalization has led some Soviet students to classify the control-theoretic constructs within a broad conception of "regulated" systems: a class which, while comprising extremization models at its "sophisticated" end — including self-teaching and self-organizing ones — would be wide enough to embrace at its basis models of a stimulus-reaction type (see in particular Mikhalevskiy's conception).[21]

Lange's model[22] — designed as a part of his "economic cybernetics" — is acknowledged in Soviet literature as the most exact statement of the theory of "regulation", specifically regulation of a "homeostatic" system (open, with constant structure), however institutionalized.

The system's "transmittance" is $S = y/x$ (the y,x being respectively the output and input functions); assuming proportionality, the adjustment which the system's "governor" introduces to the state of input is $\Delta x = Ry$. Thus the basic formula of the theory of regulation becomes $y = S/(1 - SR) \cdot x$, where the factor $(1 - SR)^{-1}$ expresses the feedback operation: the constructional resemblance of this feedback multiplier to the Keynesian multiplier is acknowledged.

The system's "response" (difference-differential) equation, in an operator form, appears as

$$\left(\sum_{r=0}^{k+1} \sum_{s=0}^{m} a_{rs} D^r E^{\Theta s} \right) y(t) = x(t)$$

where a_{rs} is a proportionality coefficient, D and E respectively are a differential and a lead operator[23] (it is assumed that the $y(t)$ can be differentiated and integrated the required number of times).

Then its general solution appears as

$$y(t) = \sum q_j(t)e^{\lambda jt} + S \cdot (1 - SR)^{-1} \cdot x(t)$$

where the system's behaviour is formalized as a sum of the two components: the second component, the particular solution of a non-homogeneous equation $\hat{y}(t) = S/(1 - SR) \cdot x(t)$, depends on the pattern of "feeding" the system; the first — the solution of the corresponding homogeneous equation — is independent of inputs: it depends exclusively on structural properties of the system: its characteristics are expressed by the characteristic roots, λ_j, of the equation. (Hence in Lange terminology they are called respectively the input and the structural component.)

Some comments by the present writer will be found in the introduction to the English version of Lange's work devoted to the subject.[24] Here we will confine ourselves to this comment. Lange has claimed for his construct a certain affinity with Bellman's dynamic programming construct: this may be tenable, especially with respect to the latter's discrete sequential form. The point to stress, however, is that — as against models of optimal control in the proper sense, and more generally models of extremization — the Lange-type regulation model has essentially only descriptive-analytic meaning, indicating the working of the propulsive forces of the economy's motion rather than offering a tool for explicit choice-making.

(4) It is proposed now to demonstrate the modelling of planning processes within the general control-theoretic framework.

We start with a system designed by Polterovich[25] (it will be seen to complement his theory of decomposition of a large-scale system, with which we here acquainted the reader in Part I, pp. 123ff). It is conceived as an "abstract" model of the functioning of a "hierarchic" system: to be more exact, of the functioning of its "cells" (one of the feature distinguishing the construct in Soviet writing is its strong focus on the micro-level). A, B are systems of cells and processes.

The micro-unit, the "cell", is characterized by a control-operator, control algorithm, L: jointly with a function χ, it determines the values of the vector x describing the "entry" of the production process: at work here is the operator of this process H. On the choice of the vector x depend the results of the process, y the input-output vector. The criterion at this level

– the cell's maximand – X is taken to depend on the "stimulation" (incentive) vector z (the value of this function is treated as a scalar). The mechanism of the feedback contains the incentive operator, R, as well as the external optimality criterion ϕ: this operator shapes the "stimulation" vector z according to the values of the extremal criterion, c – which would normally be profit – and a vector e chosen by the local control system.

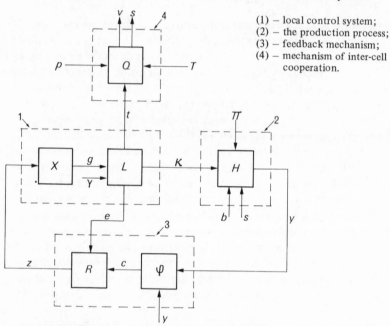

(1) – local control system;
(2) – the production process;
(3) – feedback mechanism;
(4) – mechanism of inter-cell cooperation.

L – control operator
H – operator of production processes
Φ – exogenous optimality criterion
R – stimulation operator
X – own optimality criterion
Q – interaction operator
κ – production process control
π – noise
y – input-output vector
b – constraints imposed by controlling agency
s – corrections of "b" (following controller-cells interaction)

t, T, p – impact on interaction mechanism of resp. a cell, other cells, controlling agency
v – correction of exogenous criterion (following interaction)
z – stimulation vector
c – exogeneous-criterion value
g – own-criterion value
γ – information on a cell's states and external interactions
e – effect on stimulation mechanism chosen by cell

A fourth operator Q takes care of the inter-cell operations: it maps the set of vectors $[t,T,p]$ into the set of vectors $[v,s]$; the terms in the first braces denote signals influencing the mechanism of inter-cell operations that come respectively from the cell concerned, from the remaining cells and the controlling centre. The inter-cell operations determine the values of terms in the second braces of the parameters of the external criterion v and the vector of external constraints on resources s. Depending on the nature of the inter-cell cooperation shaped by Q, t may, in particular, describe a cell's demand-supply relations, in which case v, with a corresponding sign, will stand for the price of resources s, bought and sold. Internal ("local") processes may be influenced by the controlling agency through the varying of the vectors p, that is prices, and h, that is the centralized allocation of resources and tasks.

As a cell's parameters become "crystallized" so does also its regime:

$$g = \chi(z), \qquad c = \phi(y,v),$$
$$z = R(c,e), \qquad y = H(x,h,s,\pi),$$
$$\{v,s\} = Q(t,T,p) = \{Q'(t,T,p), Q''(t,T,p)\}.$$

Inasmuch as the vector of information will usually be incomplete, the cell's control vector $\lambda = \{x,t,e\}$ will not be as a rule a single-valued function of g and γ: and depending on the vector of conditions $\omega = \{\pi,T,h,p\}$ (where the π denotes disturbances in the system), various values of γ may correspond to one and the same value of g; $g = \eta(\omega)$ where η is the superposition of χ, R, ϕ, H, Q' and Q''. The sets of controls $\Lambda = (\lambda)$ and $\Omega = (\omega)$ are taken as a datum: and so is $N = (\eta)$. The architecture of the system is completed by the proposition that the L is such as to make the values of λ — for any fixed $\eta \in N$ and $\omega \in \Omega$ — satisfy the condition

$$\eta(\lambda,\omega) = \max_{\lambda' \in \Lambda} \eta(\lambda',\omega).$$

The system of "stimulation" (incentives) rests on a lemma which is proved: if the function

$$v(c) = \max_{e \in E} \chi(R(c,e))$$

is increasing strictly monotonically, then for any fixed ω the vector δ satisfies

$$\mu(\delta,\omega) = \max_{\delta' \in \Delta} \mu(\delta',\omega)$$

where $\Lambda = \Delta \times E$; $\Lambda = (\delta)$, $E = (e)$, $c = \mu(\delta, \omega)$.

Assume that the value of the "external" criterion $\phi_k(y'_k)$ of the k-th cell is ∞. Then (from the lemma), the condition will be satisfied

$$y_k = \xi_k(x_k), x_k \in \Lambda_k, A_k(x_k) \leqslant h_k + s_k.$$

Let the overall criterion be given as

$$\sum_{k=1}^{m} \psi_k(y_k),$$

and the overall constraints have the form

$$\sum_{k=1}^{m} A_k(x_k) \leqslant d: \quad d = \sum_{k=1}^{m} (h_k + s_k)$$

the centre's problem is that of the programme

$$\sum_{k=1}^{m} u_k(x_k) \rightarrow \max, \quad \sum_{k=1}^{m} A_k(x_k) \leqslant d \text{ with } u_k(x_k) = \psi_k(\xi_k(x_k)).$$

$$x_k \in \Lambda_k,$$

Where the operators are known exactly, the centre, taking $h_k = A_k(x_k^0)$ can give to the cells the "external" criterion say of the form

$$\phi_k(y) = \begin{vmatrix} c_k^0, & y_k = y_k^0, \\ -\infty, & y_k \neq y_k^0, \end{vmatrix}$$

where $y_k^0 = \xi(x_k^0)$, c_k is some number.

Realistically, however, and in the light of experience, a situation is taken as more probable where the centre's state of information is far more precarious. Hence the accent on the tenet that it can steer the system without any knowledge of L_k, H_k and χ_k; then in virtue of the lemma above

$$c_k(h_k) = \max_{x_k \in \Gamma_k} \psi_k(y_k) = \max_{x_k \in \Gamma_k} \psi(\xi_k(x_k)) = \max_{x_k \in \Gamma_k} u_k(x_k)$$

$$\Gamma_k = (x_k : x_k \in \Delta_k, A_k(x_k) \leqslant h_k).$$

The centre is now expected to vary his h_k subject to $\Sigma h_k \leqslant d$, while receiving information on c_k and making use of the values $c_k(h_k)$. The search for the optimal h_k could be carried out by some analogy to a gradient method — an analogy restricted inasmuch as the gradients of the function-

optimand are estimated rather than computed (since the function itself is
not known exactly).

The final conclusions concern the workability of a regime resting on expanded inter-cell co-operation. The external optimality criterion of the
k-th cell is then $\phi_k(y_k, v_k) = \psi_k(y_k) + v_k$. The operator Q is determined by
the functions $v_k = v_k(\theta, p)$ and $s_k = s_k(\theta, p)$ where $\theta = \{t_1, \ldots, t_m\}$: the
t_k is the vector of co-operation adopted by the k-th cell, p is as before the
vector of the centre's influencing the mechanism of co-operation: the v_k
and s_k are either independent of p or chosen under fixed p. From the
lemma above and the relations stated, the value of the cell's external criterion is

$$c_k(\theta) = \max_{x_k \Gamma_k} u_k(x_k) + v_k(\theta),$$

$$\Gamma_k = (x_k : x_k \in \Lambda_k, A_k(x_k) \leqslant h_k + s_k(\theta))$$

and the x, corresponding to the regime now established, is sought from

$$u_k(x_k) \to \max$$

$$A_k(x_k) \leqslant h_k + s_k(\theta) \quad k = 1, 2, \ldots, m.$$

$$x_k \in \Lambda_k$$

In this the postulated behaviour principle is built up as one of a Pareto
optimum — a regime acceptable to Soviet planning literature.
(The vector $\theta \in 0$ is defined as Pareto-optimal for the system of functions
$c_k(\theta)$ on θ whenever the equalities $c_k(\theta) = c_k(\theta^0)$ hold for any $\theta \in 0$ such
that $c_k(\theta) > c_k(\theta^0)$.)

Under the Paretian equilibrium — so it is argued — two alternatives are
open to the builder of the system. In one, prices are formed by the cells
themselves independently in each transaction: the optimum is reached
without the intervention from the centre, which confines itself to devising
a synthesis of the two mechanisms — those of stimulation and co-operation
— and to setting the cells' external criterion. In the second alternative
prices are fixed by the centre and it is shown that the prices alone will take
the system to the optimum while leaving the resource allocation to the
cells themselves. The formal proofs will be omitted here — technically they
are not of particular significance; nor are the arguments adduced for and
against each of the alternatives with the balance hinted to be assessable
only empirically: the substance of the issue lies outside the scope of this

part of the study. It may, however, be interesting to remark that the theory of control has also provided a formal opening and exploration of the issue in Soviet planning theory (See chapters 1, 2).

(5)   Another noteworthy type of control-theoretic modelling of economic plans with a focus on problems of hierarchic organization and devolution, to which we shall turn, is owed to Kulikowski. (The version we shall deal with has been published by him in Soviet literature.)[26] It adds to our interest in the construct in that it illustrates an effective application of Feldbaum's resolving multiplier method; it well represents the functional-analytic approach in optimal-control methodology.

Kulikowski's own claim to the originality of the model presented here is based on that, while the known methods of decomposition are essentially of an analytic kind, his own is of a synthetic type: a valid claim (though we would point to a certain affinity with the Pugachev approach, see above). Optimization is thought of in Kulikowski as carried out by means of some nonlinear operator A, which brings about the $y(t) = A[x(t)]$; the x,y are conceivably elements of some Banach spaces. Given are two nonnegative functionals $F(x)$, $\Phi_0[x, A(x)] = \Phi(x)$, respectively measure of control and of output. It is assumed that for some nonnegative number λ there exists a unique control $x = \bar{x}$ for which, subject to $\Phi(x) = \phi$, the $F(x) = \min$. The solution is sought from $\psi(x) = F(x) + \lambda(x)$ where — in the right-hand term — λ is the Lagrange multiplier: and assuming that both functionals are strongly differentiable, the necessary condition of the minimum is written $\operatorname{grad} F(x) + \lambda \operatorname{grad}(x) = 0$. When the solution $\bar{x}(\lambda)$ is substituted in the functionals, we have $f = F[\bar{x}(\lambda)]$, $\phi = [\bar{x}(\lambda)]$. This is taken as the parametric expression of the XOY — central in Kulikowski's methodology and termed the "characteristic" of the optimal control: it is obtained as $f(\phi)$ or $\phi(f)$ when, that is, λ is eliminated.

Very broadly, in this methodology the synthesis and optimization rest on compression of the "characteristics" of subsystems. Take for generality that XOY has the parametric form. Then for each subsystem

$$df_i/d\phi_i = dF_i[\bar{x}(\lambda_j)]/d\Phi_i[\bar{x}(\lambda_i)] = \lambda_i$$

the economic interpretation of the Lagrangean being that its inverse, λ^{-1}, equals the output increment owed — under optimum — to the additional input unit. The problem becomes one of finding $\lambda_i's$ when

$$f = \sum_{i=1}^{n} F_i[\bar{x}(\lambda_i)],$$

subject to

$$\sum_{i=1}^{n} \Phi_i[\bar{x}(\lambda_i)] = \phi,$$

which is a given number. From the Lagrange function the necessary optimality condition is $df_i/d\phi_i = dF_i[\bar{x}(\lambda_i)]/d\lambda_i \cdot d\lambda_i/d\Phi_i[x(\lambda_i)] = \mu = $ const.

The $\lambda_i's$ are postulated to be equal for all subsystems: then the overall value for λ is obtained from

$$\sum_{i=1}^{n} \Phi_i(\lambda) = \phi.$$

On such an equation for each subsystem minimizing its local cost (resource expenditure) rests the devolution, where the centre determines the λ, meaning price. In an alternative interpretation, the λ is related to "intensification" in the feedback chain – in the linear dynamic process with feedback relationship and quadratic quality criterion.

In the Kulikowski static, deterministic, multi-level schema the XOY's are known and taken to have the form $A_i^{\alpha} B_i^{\beta} \dots, Z_i^{\omega} = k_i^q$, and accordingly the overall optimand

$$Z = \sum_{i=1}^{n} [k_i^q A_i^{\alpha} B_i^{-\beta} \dots]^{1/\omega}.$$

It is for the adaptive or evolutionary system variant – where the parameters XOY change over time – that the Feldbaum method of resolving multipliers and "dual control" is applied, the maximand being the mathematical expectation $E\{Z_t\}$. Suppose the y distributes the resources $A, B, \dots$ over $t = 1, \dots, n$. The quantity $Z_{i,t}$ being ascertained (ex post) over t, the corresponding $k_{i,t} = [A^{\alpha}_{i,t} B^{\beta}_{i,t} \dots, Z^{\omega}_{i,t}]$ are being found and employed in estimating $k_{i,t+1}$ from $k_{i,t}, k_{i,t-1}, \dots, k_{i,t-N}$ possibly in Bayes's procedure.

(6)   Our consideration in selecting the next example of control-theoretic modelling is the adoption of an approach from the "pathology" of the theory of optimal control.[27]

Effective use of the Krotov formalism has been made in Soviet mathematical-economic literature by Belaga and Kromer — for their two-sector plan model.[28] The sectors are those producing consumer and capital goods with capital stocks respectively X_1 and X_2; the production functions are Cobb-Douglas with exponential technical progress

$$X_3 = A(X_1^{\alpha_1} L_1^{\beta_1} R_1^{\gamma_1})e^{\pi t}, \; X_4 = B(X_1^{\alpha_2} L_2^{\beta_1} R_2^{\gamma_2})e^{\pi t}$$

(where L and R denote respectively labour and land); constraints equalities describe time-lags, the capital assets' wear-and-tear, and "exogenous load" consumption.

Denote μ_1, μ_2 the two sectoral amortization rates and μ_3, and μ_4 the two sectoral input-output time-lags; we have then respectively

$$X_1 = (X_3 - C) - \mu_1 X_1,$$

$$X_2 = (X_2 - C) - \mu_2 X_2$$

and

$$X_3 + \mu_3 X_3 = A(X_1^{\alpha_1} L_1^{\beta_1} R_1^{\gamma_1})e^{\pi t},$$

$$X_4 + \mu_4 X_4 = B(X_2^{\alpha_2} L_2^{\beta_2} R_2^{\gamma_2})e^{\pi t}.$$

The consumption "load" is assumed to take a constant share in both sectors' gross outputs $C = c(X_3 + X_4)$, it being postulated that

$$X_3 > \frac{c}{1-c} X_4.$$

(We shall not probe here into the economic rationale of this not uncontroversial postulate.) The plan problem is seen as that of finding the control which, given the initial values t_0, x^0 and the terminal value t_1, optimizes the functional $F = \xi(x_1 + x_2)$. The planner's strategy is thought of in terms of setting the proportions $X_1/X = V_1; L_1/L = V_2; R_1 R = V_3$. Introduce additional variables $x_5 = V_1; x_6 = V_2; x_7 = V_3$ and new control parameters $u_1 = V_1; u_2 = V_2; u_3 = V_3$.

In the co-ordinate system as described — for a non-inertial control case — the plan is eventually written

$$\dot{x}_1 = -\mu_1 x_1 + x_5[(1-c)x_3 - cx_4], \qquad\qquad \dot{x}_5 = u_1,$$

$$\dot{x}_2 = -\mu_2 x_2 + (1-x_5)[(1-c)x_3 - cx_4], \qquad \dot{x}_6 = u_2,$$

$$\dot{x}_3 = -\mu_3 x_3 + ax_1{}^{\alpha_1} x_6{}^{\beta_1} x_7{}^{\gamma_1} e^{\delta_1 t}, \qquad\qquad \dot{x}_7 = u_3;$$

$$\dot{x}_4 = -\mu_4 x_4 + bx_2{}^{\alpha_2}(1-x_6)^{\beta_2}(1-x_7)^{\gamma_2} e^{\delta_2 t},$$

$$x_i \geqslant \bar{x}_i > 0, \qquad x_3 > \frac{c}{1-c} x_4, \qquad i = 1, 2, 3, 4;$$

$$0 < \bar{x}_j \leqslant x_j < x_j^= < 1, \ j = 1, 2, 3, 4;$$

$$|u_k| < k^*, \ k = 1, 2, 3;$$

$$F(x) = \xi(x_1 + x_2).$$

On the Krotov Optimality Principle the problem reduces itself to finding a piecewise smooth function satisfying

(1) $$F(x) + \phi(x_1 t_1) \equiv \xi(x_1 + x_2) + \phi(x_1 t_1) \text{ const},$$

(2) $$\sup R(t,x,u; \phi(x,t)) \equiv c(t), u \in G,$$

where $c(t)$ is an arbitrary piecewise continuous function and

(3) $$R(t,x,u; \phi(x,t)) \equiv \sum_{i=1}^{7} \phi_{x_i} f_i(t,x,u) + \phi(t).$$

In the model a nonlinear equation is obtained in partial derivatives with respect to $\phi(x,t)$

(4) $$\sum_{i=1}^{4} \frac{\partial \phi}{\partial x_i} f_i(t, x) + \sum_{j=1}^{7} k^* \left| \frac{\partial \phi}{\partial x_j}(t, x) \right| + \frac{\partial \phi}{\partial t}(x, t) = c(t).$$

The procedure consists in the following:
   1. the function $\tilde{\phi}(x,t)$ — the approximate solution of the equation — is

found as a polynomial of variables $x_1, x_2, \ldots$ with coefficients depending on t: in the case treated

(5)
$$\widetilde{\phi}(x,t) = \sum_{s=1}^{7} w_s(t) x_\delta;$$

2. the function $\widetilde{\phi}(x,t)$ satisfies (1) in the case treated

$$\widetilde{\phi}(x_1 t_1) = \sum_{s=1}^{7} W_\delta(t_1) x = \xi(x_1 + x_2) + \text{const};$$

3. Over the region considered $N + 1$ curves are chosen $x = {}^r x(t)$, $r = 1, 2, \ldots N + 1, t_0 \leqslant t \leqslant t_1$, where N is the number of the terms of the polynomial $\phi(x,t)$ (here $N = 7$) for which the (4) is to be met. Thence a system of N ordinary differential equations is obtained with respect to the coefficients of the polynomial $\phi(x,t)$.

The Krotov synthesis permits confining the search of the optimal control to a limited number of curves — a clear benefit in tackling the economic planner's problems. In the Belaga-Krotov exercise the maximand is capital stock $X_1 + X_2$. Hence Krotov's functional has to be taken with $\xi < 0$: in turn this entails changing the sign for the w. Like Pontryagin's parameters ψ — the vectors of conjugated states — the w's of the Krotov-type system too lend themselves to the interpretative analogy with the Lagrangean multiplier as prices, and the respective equations they satisfy as describing price dynamics.

(7)   The potentialities of Tikhonov's model for the theory of economic planning have recently been demonstrated by himself in a published paper.[29]

The reasoning is presented on the example of a linear-programming problem, incorrect in the sense of Hadamard, with a determinant close to zero and satisfying — within the given range — the compatibility condition. The method suggested rests on adding a constraint requiring the solution to be that of a norm-wise minimum ("normed solution"). The norm is $\|X\| = [Q(X - X^0)]^{\frac{1}{2}}$ where X^0 is some fixed point and

$$Q(X) = \sum_{i,j} p_{ij} x_i x_j$$

a positively determined form; the optimal plan is normal if $||\bar{X}|| \leqslant ||X||$ for any optimal plan of the problem X, and a clear economic interpretation of the model can well relate to the selection of the new plan — with the new data. The preference is then for a plan which *ceteris paribus* calls for minimum deviation from the original one. The measure of deviation is the weighted-square expression. In other words, the norm gives us the cost of changing the adopted version of the plan into another one.

An algorithm is designed for an approximate solution with the use of two parameters α and λ, such that for some postulated positive ϵ, the $||\bar{z}^\alpha - \bar{z}^{(0)}|| < \epsilon$ only if these parameters are co-ordinated with ϵ and δ, the exactness of the entry-data, and the δ is sufficiently small.

The model indicates the error-theoretic path along which the stability problem can be attacked in planning dynamics.

Note

1. The linear plan-programming problem is considered by Tikhonov:[30] find $z = \{z_j\}, j = 1, \ldots, n$ of n dimensional R^n satisfying

$$C(z) = \sum_{j=1}^{n} c_j z_j \rightarrow \max; \text{ with } Az = \bar{u}, A = \{a_{ij}\},$$

$$\bar{u} = \{\bar{u}_i\} (i = 1, \ldots, m, \ j = 1, \ldots, n)$$

c_j and z_j being nonnegative. Only approximate input data are given, respectively A, u and C, and δ is the order of error.

Where the problem is incorrectly set in Hadamard's sense, however accurately data are specified, there can be disparity in solution as desired.

The algorithm presented for the approximate solution rests on parameters $z_\lambda^\alpha = R(\tilde{A}, \tilde{u}, \tilde{C}, \alpha, \lambda)$. Again $||\tilde{z}_\lambda^\alpha - \bar{z}^{(0)}||$ is smaller than some positive ϵ with which the α and λ are compatible. The z_λ^α is defined as minimizing the quadratic function

$$M_\lambda^\alpha[\tilde{z}, A, \bar{u}, C] = ||A\tilde{z} - \tilde{u}||^2 + \alpha(\bar{C}^2(z) + \lambda\Omega[z]); \Omega[z] = ||z - z^{(0)}||^2$$

$z^{(0)}$ is the point in $R^{(n)}$ with respect to which the "normal" solution is sought (the solution is termed "normal" when it is the closest to the coordinate origin or a pre-assigned $z^{(0)}$).

Virtually at every stage of our study indications have revealed themselves of possibilities for economic planning. Be it the aspect of complexity of relations (their nonlinearities), or instability or uncertainty, or the size of the problem (with implications for computation) — new avenues appear worthy of theoretical and applicational exploration. This, we submit, is true in particular of methodologies and instrumentations which go beyond, or expand, assimilated programming approaches. Translating his plan from the programming into the control-stability-theoretic "language" is likely to be increasingly rewarding to the theoretician (and ultimately — also the practitioner) of planning.

2. The translation of programming into optimal-control problems has its own and expanding methodology. To give one effective illustration, the Moiseyev formulation:[31]

We have a general linear-programme problem: minimize the linear form

$$I = \sum_{k=1}^{N} g_k u_k \qquad \text{(I)}$$

subject to $u_k \geqslant 0$ (which is control) and

$$\sum_{k=1}^{N} a_{kj} u_k = b_j \qquad \text{(II)}$$

where $j = 1, \ldots, M; k = 1, \ldots, N$.

To turn this into an optimal-control problem new variables x_j are brought in — functions of the index $s = 1, \ldots, N$, which meet the difference equations $x_j(s) = a_{sj} u_s$ (III). When reformulated, the problem is: determine the vector $u(s)$ minimizing the form (I), and the phase trajectory $x(s)$ satisfying the conditions $x_j(0) = 0, x_j(N) = b_j$. The k index will now denote the time-factor.

To obtain a continuous version of the system we posit

$$N = 1/\Delta t; \quad a_{ij} = a_j(t_i)\Delta t; \quad g_i = c(t_i)\Delta t.$$

When this is posited the (I) and (III) take the form

$$I = \int_0^t c(t)u(t)dt; \quad dx_j/dt = a_j u.$$

Thus a degenerate problem of the calculus of variations is arrived at, the (I, III) being a discrete analogue.

3. A very instructive experiment in Western literature in testing control-

theoretic methodology for numerical solution of plan problems has been carried out by Kendrick and Taylor.[32] It is instructive from both angles — of computation as well as modelling (as to the latter, it is an originally conceived merger of the neoclassical nonlinear designing of the asymptotic optimal growth in the Samuelson-Solow-Koopmans fashion with the finite-horizon linear-programming build-up of the plan): thus a multi-sectoral model with nonlinear performance indices and constraints has been evolved and, in its solution, the two techniques, of conjugate gradient and of neighbouring extremal, have come to be tried out. As to the latter, the test confirms the strong handicap from guessing the controlled system's initial costate variables; this is due to the very high sensitivity of the terminal values of state variables to changes in guesses of the initial costate.[33] The main handicap of the gradient algorithm (i.e. successive adjustment of the control-variable history following the indications of the Hamiltonian's gradient), which is essentially more helpful in handling large-scale economic plans, is found to be the slow-down of convergence as optimum is approached (the remedy attempted is the use, close to the optimum, of either the neighbouring extremal or the second-order gradient to take account of the Hamiltonian curvature).

4. The assimilation of control-theoretic formalism in economic theory has reopened the search for a rigorous answer to the question of existence with respect to optimal economic strategy — the question posed a decade ago by Tinbergen and Chakravarty[34] with respect to saving with infinite horizon. In the generalized case the substance is the optimum path in shifting the economy over the plan horizon, from the initial to a postulated terminal state. It has been reformulated as an optimal-control theoretic problem by several authors, notably in an aptly generalized form by Kumar[35] — as one of planning with a finite horizon (linking up with contributions by Karlin[36] and Yaari[37]). In the Kumar formulation we have a system with state variables forming a vector y and control variables, vector z. The economic problem is that of maximizing the welfare function of the form

$$W(z) = \int_0^T g_0(y,z,t)dt$$

subject to the dynamic structural equations $dy_i/dt = g_i(y,z,t)$, to stated initial and terminal conditions and to local and global constraints. With the use of Helly's selection principle the existence theorem is proved for such a system under the assumptions that the set of feasible policies for it is non-empty; that the components of the $z(t)$ are uniformly bounded and meet the Lipschitz condition $|z_i(t_k) - z_i(t_{k-1})| < K|t_k - t_{k-1}|$ (where K is the same constant throughout); that the responses y^z are uniformly bounded too; and that the g_i's and their partials and the $g_0(y,z,t)$ are continuous.[38]

Technically the existence of optimum is connected with the compactness of the feasible-policy set and the continuity of the welfare function.

For the linear system the problem has been demonstrated to be tantamount to a continuous, or infinite, programming problem – as stated by Bellman[39] (also by Koopmans): in that case the existence of optimal policy is reduced to the duality problem for the programme.

Essentially – as will appear from our further discussion – specific problems entailed can be treated and have been treated by means of either of the two non-classical variational instruments, the Optimality and the Maximum Principle. But as Kumar validly points out, specifically the latter does not (we would qualify – does not in the general case) establish the sufficiency condition for optimality; and one has to know in advance the answer to the issue of the existence, and uniqueness, of optimal policies: in the case of established non-existence the exercise could be helpful in identifying the causes in either the substance or in the statement of the strategy (posing its problem).

(8)   While, as we have said, the control theory in general as such had no initial working connection with economics, this is not true of Bellman's theory. In actual fact he and his school have formalized in their terms the economist's – and indeed the planner's – central problem: that of the allocation of resources.

The reader cannot do better than acquaint himself with the Bellman-Dreyfus chapter devoted to this matter.[40] At least the conceptual attraction of the model for the planner is patent: to mention only a few of its crucial elements, we have here the formalization of the planner's basic problem in terms of recurrence relations, the reduction of dimensions, the inherent unified mode of treatment of the deterministic and the stochastic approaches, each of them reducing some of the crucial difficulties of the programming apparatus with obvious consequences for computation. (Dreyfus in particular has designed a theory of numerical solution for the optimization problem resting on successive approximation in policy spaces – a gradient method based on concepts and techniques of dynamic programming.) Central in the assimilation of theory for planning is Bellman's showing that when his $F(x_1 \ldots, x_n)$ is interpreted as "return" owed to "allocation" $(x_1, \ldots, x_n)$, and the $G(x_1 \ldots, x_n)$ as the cost of this "allocation", the Lagrangean multiplier obtains the meaning of the price quite analogously to what we are well used in our interpretation of mathematical programming in the strict sense. It is further shown that the synthesis of the functional-equation techniques of dynamic programming with the Lagrange multiplier also yields the method of decomposition of complex processes.

(9) To restate Bellman's[41] own basic formulation of the resource allocation problem, assuming known utility functions, i.e.

$$R_N = \sum_{i=1}^{N} g_i(x_{i1}, x_{i2}, \ldots, x_{iM}), \quad \sum_{i=1}^{N} x_{ij} \leqslant c_j$$

is transformed into

$$f_N(c_1, c_2, \ldots, c_M) = \max_{R} \; [g_N(x_{N1}, x_{N2}, \ldots, x_{NM}) +$$

$$+ f_{N-1}(c_1 - x_{N1}, \ldots, c_M - x_{NM})]$$

with x_{Nj} nonnegative, not exceeding c_j $(j = 1, \ldots, M)$. Then bringing in the Lagrangean multiplier and replacing the M by imposed K constraints, we get as our criterion

$$R_N(\lambda) = \sum_{i=1}^{N} g_i - \sum_{j=K+1}^{M} \lambda_j \left(\sum_{i=1}^{N} x_j \right).$$

The — "natural" to dynamic programming — multi-stage functional equation (note: common to both deterministic and stochastic approach) is then

$$f_N(p) = \max_{q} \; [g(p,q) + \sum_{i} w_i f_{N-1}(T_i(p,q))].$$

In the light of the critique of the Optimality Principle Bellman's emphasis on the computability aspect is by itself noteworthy. In the case of multidimensionality at least, monotinicity if not convergence to the absolute extremum is demonstrated by Bellman as obtainable in successive approximation or polynomial approximation. Thus in the case sketched out above difficulties are likely in coping with the storage of the $f_N(\alpha_1, \ldots, c_M)$ values at lattice points in the c-space; but, as he argues, relief can be secured by exchanging time possessed for space: storing, that is, the functional values with the use of the polynomial approximation (i.e. $g_j(c)$ polynomials).

$$f_N \cong \sum_{j=1}^{N} \alpha_j{}^{(N)} g_j(c)$$

— assuming the $g_j(c)$ determined, the storage of the f_N entails storing only the coefficients $a_j{}^{(N)}$.[42]

Note in the applicational study of the Bellmanian school the indication of relief the stage-by-stage procedure can be expected to bring in coping with dimensionality. Specialized models designed for reduction of macro-processes to a sequence of one-dimensional problems (vide the Bellman-Dreyfus model of multi-stage production processes utilizing complexes of industries[43]) are of natural interest to Soviet planning theory, concerned as it is with computational fitness of theoretical constructs.

But at the same time note the congeniality of fundamental underlying theoretical thinking. The "bottleneck" approach implicit in the modelling — an approach in which a system's behaviour is ruled by resources and capacities in shortest supply — has been fundamental in Soviet strategy ever since the formative years of that strategy. Note also the nexus of sequential methods — borne out in the Bellman-Dreyfus reasoning — with the steady-state strategy as programmed à la von Neumann; also the significance accorded to Markov-type processes where decisions are made at each stage; these points are broached by us in their respective contexts.

Note

In his inquiry into numerical methods in the theory of optimal systems N. N. Moiseyev (*Chislennyie metody v teorii optimalnykh sistem*, Moscow, 1971) gives thought to the employment — in economic planning — of a "resource", distributing it between the "programming" and the "correcting" controls so as to secure sufficient stability. As the discrete analogue of the problems of synthesis, the dynamic system, whose motion is described by the vectoral equation $\dot{z} = Az + w + F(t)$, is considered. (A is a matrix with coefficients which are some given functions of time depending programmed motion, the $F(t)$ is a random vector function of time whose mathematical expectation $F(t) = 0$; the initial values of components of the z are un-fixed since they are considered to be random values with zero mathematical expectation; we are assumed to possess the control of a vector w, employable for adjusting the z. The equation above is changed into a difference equation $z_{k+1} = \Phi_k z_k + v_k + f_k$; $k = 0, \ldots, N-1$ where N is the number of the break-up segments $[0,T]$. Using a simplest difference form of the first order of exactness we have $\Phi_k = I + A(t_k)\tau$; $v_k = w(t_k)\tau$, $f_k = F(t_k)\tau$, where $t = T/N$ is the step in time, I — identity matrix. Assuming that the fundamental solutional system of $\dot{z} = Az$ is known, the formalism would not present particular difficulties with v_k and f_k being some functions of discrete moments of time uniquely determinable from values entering the original equation.

Our functional is likely to prove non-representable in analytical form. In handling the problem the computational difficulties and the memory volume involved will grow so fast that numerical solution may be found intractable even where the number of steps, N, is relatively small. Where a direct employment of dynamic programming in problems of synthesis with constrained controls proves ineffective, Moiseyev's advice is to try the method of a penalty function.

(10) To return to the subject treated in Part I in the context of the new Soviet theory of growth, the Soviet application of the theory of optimal control to economic planning — specifically — very-long-run ("perspective planning") rests largely on the "marriage" of dynamic programming with turnpike theories; the assimilation of the latter for the purpose — to recall what was said in that context — had started in the early 1960s once some of the "unrealism" of the original Neumannian system was mitigated by Kemeny-Morgenstern-Thompson *et al.*; and the Dorfman-Samuelson-Solow turnpike conjecture validated by Radner, Morishima, McKenzie, Nikaido *et al.* (I have treated this matter at greater length in a contribution to the Vienna 1970 Seminar on advances in the von Neumann theory; the reader may be referred at the present stage again to that paper.)[44]

In this theoretical "marriage" the work of the Kantorovich school has been path-breaking. The fundamentals were elaborated around the mid-1960s by two of its members, Romanovskiy and Makarov. In Romanovskiy's[45] system we have admissible processes $(x,y) \in Z$ with a vector c of value of products at the terminal stage T. The states of the (homogeneous) process are normalized by some vector $\xi \geqslant 0$, $\Sigma_{\xi i} = 1$; for every admissible $(x,y) \in \widetilde{Z}$ we take some number $K(x,y)$ such that $K = \log \Sigma y_i / \Sigma x_i$; we consider further some $K(\xi,\eta) = \text{logmax } \Sigma_i y_i$; $\eta = y/\Sigma y_i$. The maximand — the logarithm of the maximum value of output at the terminal point — appears then as

$$f_T(\vec{\xi}) = \max \; [K(\vec{\xi},\vec{\eta}) + f_{T-1}(\vec{\eta})] \; ; f_0(\vec{\xi}) = \log \Sigma_i c_i \xi_i,$$

a Bellman-type (dynamic programme) recurrence relation. The Romanovskiy findings are then these for the plan problem with a horizon tending to infinity (and goals made depending on the terminal state).

The maximum growth in the von Neumann problem materializes in a one-step cycle; hence there exists a state in which a maximum stationary growth is secured; under optimal control in a dynamic problem of planning production with an objective function depending only on the terminal state, the structure of the process at the intermediate "steps" of the process — with $T \to \infty$ — approaches the best structure of the von Neumann problem. In this there exists a constant K, independent of T, such that the sum of deviations from this optimal structure does not exceed that magnitude K; the average growth-rate in this dynamic system asymptotically does not depend on the vector c and approaches the maximum growth-rate of the von Neumann system. (These tenets are valid for a closed system; the asymptotic process is more complicated for an open system since it entails the "switch-over" of structures similar to those characteristic of optimal control in the continuous case.)

The asymptotics of a linear dynamic model of an economy have been further explored by Makarov,[46] establishing the nexus between the Bellman and the von Neumann systems. For a closed system Makarov works with a sequence of convex closed cones z_t in Euclidean space. The (x,y) which belongs to it $(x_1 \ldots, x_{n(t)}, y_1 \ldots, y_{n(t+1)})$ is a process (x and y inputs and outputs) with some vector $f(t)$ forming its exogenous component. Where z_t are polyhedral cones generated by a finite number of basic processes, the $(Z_k, f(t))$ is of the von Neumann family. In the adopted notation

$$R_{x_0,t} = \left\{ Y' | (X,Y) \in Z_t, \; X \in R_{x_0,t-1}, Y' = Y + f(t) \right\}$$

with $R_{x,t}(i_1, \ldots, i_k)$ being the projection of $R_{X,t}$ on to the sub-space of products i.

The Bellman-type problem (denoted D) is then

$$\sum_s a_0^{(s)} h^{(s)} \max, s = 1, \ldots, S, \quad \sum_s a_i^{(s)} h^{(s)} \geq b_i, i = 1, \ldots, n;$$

with the dynamic programme the sets $R_t(D)$ are related as follows

$$R_t(D) = \left\{ X | x_{i_{t+1}} = \sum_{s_t} a_{i_{t+1}}^{(s_t)} h^{(s_t)} - b_{i_t}; \; \sum_{s} a_i^{(s)} h^{(s)} \geqslant b_i \right\}$$

The proved existence theorem is that the von-Neumann type system as defined above can be built up for any D so that, for every time interval, the $R_t(D)$ and the $R_{X_0,}{}^1{}_t$ coincide).

Then in the familiar fashion the dual is formulated: the equilibrium state of the $M(Z)$ model is characterized by the process $(X, Y) \in Z$ and the price vector $P = (p_1, \ldots, p_n)$, $P \geqslant 0$, $\Sigma_i p_i \geqslant 0$ and a positive number a such that $a\bar{X} \leqslant Y$; $(\bar{Y},P) - (\bar{X},ap) = 0$; $(Y,P) - (X,aP) \leqslant 0$; $(\bar{Y},P) > 0$.

(11) Some further contributions too of the Kantorovich school to the turnpike theory are discussed in our Part I. These encompass various control-theoretic aspects. For the sake of continuity we recall here studies concerned with comparative characteristics in the behaviour of different types of systems – discrete versus continuous.

From an elaboration of the asymptotic behaviour of discrete optimal trajectories of control-led linear systems Makarov[47] has moved to the examination of continuity. In this[48] generalized theorems (more general, that is, than those owed to Bellman and Tyndall)[49] on existence, duality and also on the number of "switch-overs" have been established. Here the basic framework is that of continuous convex programming; the problem turns into that of continuous linear if (in conventional notation) each cone Z_t, $t \in [0,T]$ becomes multihedral; then it is being proved that for any plan $\bar{u}$ of such a problem with a constant Z an admissible plan u with a finite number of switch-overs $\bar{u}(T)A = u(T)A$ will be found.

Next[50] (in his survey and generalization of models of an economy's optimal growth of 1969) Makarov formulates his concept of a strongly u-optimal system – a counterpart to the known theorems of the weakly u-optimal [In the conventional notation a trajectory $\bar{x}(t), \bar{\gamma}(t) \}_{t=0}^{t=\infty}$ of the $M(Z)\lambda$, $\lambda \geqslant 1$, model, technologically admissible with (x_0, y_0) is *strongly* u-optimal if for any trajectory $\{x(t), \gamma(t)\}_{t=0}^{t=T}$ a time-instant t_0 can be found from which onwards $\bar{\gamma}(t) \geqslant y(t)$ and if there is for any $\epsilon > 0$ – a time-instant t_ϵ such that $\bar{\gamma}(t) + \epsilon e^{(\lambda-1)t} \geqslant \gamma(t)$ for all $t \geqslant t_\epsilon$; the previous inquiry did establish the duality and the existence theorems for the problem of finding the trajectory $\{\bar{x}(t), \bar{\gamma}(t)\}_{t=0}^{t=T}$ where the value of $\bar{\gamma}(T)$ is the greatest of all the $x(T)$ yielded by the technologically admissible trajectories $\{x(t), \gamma(t)\}_{t=0}^{t=T}$]. Now it has been indicated – though without rigorous proof — that this, as indeed most of the results obtained for system with noncontinuous time, can be transferred to the theory of continuous systems without any change.

A particular issue examined further on by Makarov is that of time discount in a turnpike system.[51] The problem, posed by him somewhat differently than by Koopmans[52]) leads to the existence theorem when the "coefficient of reduction" — in substance the rate of interest — is applied. [The formulation is this: the model's (Ω, u) trajectory sequence $(x_t, c_t)_{t=0}^{t=\infty}$ is such that x_t and $c \subset R_+^n$, $(x_t, x_{t+1} + c_t) \in \Omega$ for all t (where x_t is output at t, c_t — a vector of "products directed to final use" over t). The trajectory $(x_t, c_t)_{t=0}^{t=\infty}$ is optimal if

$$\sum_{t=0}^{\infty} u(\bar{c}_t)\mu^{-t} \geqslant \sum_{t=0}^{\infty} u(c_t)\mu^{-t}$$

where μ is the "reduction coefficient"; the optimal trajectory then is turnpike of $(\bar{x}_t, \bar{c}_t) = (x, c)$ for all t. Then let $C = \{c \subset R_+^n \mid C = y - x; (x, y) \in \Omega\}$ and let also $\lambda_0 = \max \lambda$ where maximum is determined on the set $\{\lambda \mid \lambda x \leqslant y_0; (x, y) \in \Omega\}$. The theorem is that the turnpike exists where the model (Ω, u, μ) possesses the properties: (1) the set C is bounded, (2) $\mu < \lambda_0$; (3) $u(c) = 0$ if $c^i = 0$ at least for one i.]

(12) Makarov's investigations are generalized, developed, and supplemented by several writers, in particular Rubinov, Shapiyev, and Zhafyarov.[53] All the three have worked on turnpike theorems — in a stronger form in strict-equilibrium systems. Inquiries into variable technology take a considerable part in this writing.

Rubinov is concerned with technologically variable production in some classes of trajectories — their primal and dual characteristics. Specifically in a finite-dimensional, dynamic production system forming a family of $\{E, (X_t)_{t+\epsilon}, (K_t)_{t\in E}, (A_{\tau,t})_{\tau, t\in E}\} = M$, where $X_t (t \in E)$ is a finite-dimensional vectoral space, $K_t (t \in E)$ is a convex, closed, "reproduction" cone in the K_t space; $A_{\tau,t}$ a convex, positive, homogeneous closed Gale-type image such that the cone $A_{\tau,t}(K_t)$ contains the interior point of the cone K_t. Further a sub-model, M^x, of this model is considered: a sub-model that is generated by the point x, viz., $\{E, (L_t^x)_{t\in E}, (\Gamma_t^x)_{t\in E}, (A^x_{t\in E})_{(\tau, t)\in E}\}$ (here Γ denotes the facet of the cone; $L_t^x \equiv \Gamma_\tau^x - \Gamma_t^x$). This is the framework within which the trajectories' optimality and "effectiveness" are defined. The trajectory $\chi = (x_t)_{t\in E}$ of M is "effective" if it is an optimal trajectory of

M^x: every effective trajectory of M is its optimal trajectory, but not necessarily vice versa; but if x is an interior point of K then the sets of all optimal and all effective trajectories coincide.[54]

Of immediate significance for the Kantorovich-Makarov system is Zhafyarov's inquiry[55] into the uniqueness of equilibrium prices in a Neumannian system defined by a $Z(A,B)$ cone – a generalization of the Leontievian dynamic model.

(13) A further and large step in the adventure of mathematical generalizations, one that touches on several areas of economic-mathematical theories (in particular on the theory of convex functions, discussed above, theory of Neumann-oriented growth, sect, 17, below) is a major joint contribution by Makarov and Rubinov.[56] It is their theory of modelling economic dynamics; its general construct is a dynamic system determined by a family of superlinear mappings defined on cones in some, not necessarily finite-dimensional, spaces. It is within this formal framework that the issues of a developing economy's optimal trajectories are revisited. (The study of superlinear point-to-set mappings is one of the "novelties" in mathematical economics; it is now believed to offer a logical generalization of operators (linear, positive). Its importance is now recognized as comparable to that of the topological theory of point-to-set mappings as stimulated, in its time, by the requirements of the theory of games.)

In the present context we must content ourselves with the presentation of only one of the point-of-departure fundamentals, i.e. the theorem on the dual "characteristic" of the optimal trajectory (which – this is worth pointing out – is convincingly seen as a *pendant*, within the adopted framework, to the Kuhn-Tucker theorem in convex programming *and to Maximum Principle* in the theory of optimal control).

The general model of economic dynamics is here given the form

$$M = \left\{ E, (X_t)_{t \in E}, (K_t)_{t \in E}, (a_{\tau,t})_{\tau, t \in E, \tau < t} \right\}$$

where E is a set of time moments; $E \subset R_+^1$ with $0 \in E$ and sup $E > 0$; X_t is a finite-dimensional arithmetic space; K_t – "reproducing" cone in the X_t space; $a_{\tau,t}(K_\tau, K_t)$ with $a_{\tau,t}(K_t) \cap (\text{int } K_t) \neq \emptyset$; moreover it is assumed that the co-ordination condition $a_{t,t''} = a_{t',t''} a_{t,t'} (t, t', t'' \in E; t < t' < t'')$ is satisfied; for simplicity's sake K_t is taken to be a cone with nonnegative components only.

The economy's trajectory, the $\chi = x_{t \in E}$ of the model, is defined as optimal (respectively weakly optimal) if there exists a functional $f \in K^*_T$ such that $f = \emptyset$ and $f(X_T) = \max f(y) > 0$, respectively

$$f(X_T) = \max_{y \in a_0 \cdot T(x^0)} f(y).$$

The fundamental theorem enunciates that for the trajectory $\bar{\chi}$ to be (weakly) f_T-optimal, it is necessary and sufficient that for any positive ϵ a family $\phi = (f_t{}^\epsilon)_{t \in E}(f_t{}^\epsilon \in K_t^*; t \in E)$ be found such that firstly, for any trajectory $\chi_\epsilon = (x_t)_{t \in E}$ of M the function $h_\chi: h_\chi(t) = f_t{}^\epsilon(x_t)(t \in E)$ be a decreasing function; secondly, $h_{\bar{\chi}}(0) - h_{\bar{\chi}}(T) < \epsilon$ and thirdly, $f \neq 0 (t \in E)$, $f_T{}^\epsilon = f_T$. (The postulates being here that $x_0 \in K_0$, $f_T \in K_T^* (x_0 \neq 0, f_T \neq 0)$ and $\bar{\chi} = (x)_{t \in E}$ is the M model's trajectory starting from x_0.)

(14) The work of Romanovskiy[57] we have in mind here is an extension of the Makarov inquiries in several important directions, in the first place by additionally considering the relationship of the properties of the deterministic versus stochastic system. (In a sense the idea is to synthesize some findings on the Markovian system i.a. of Howard, Bellman-Dreyfus, Blackwell, and his own, and economic systems forming processes with continuous sets of states — i.a. by Radner, Nikaido, Koopmans, Morishima.)

In the first place, from the results obtained (see sect. 9) Romanovskiy[58] turns to the asymptotic behaviour of the recurrence relations in the dynamic programming for Markovian and semi-Markovian decision processes; and offers a proof for the existence of a stationarity-ensuring, maximizing policy (see above). This is treated, as, theoretically, the *generalizing* situation: a special case, that is, of an optimizing stationary control of a discrete deterministic process of dynamic programming; and the asymptotic course of such a process with a continuous set of states is traced. As a by-product of the inquiry the behaviour of the maximand (income) for an extending horizon is observed.

Of considerable theoretical interest is — in one alternative — the handling of stationarity of a controlled system, specifically in cases of infinite growth of the function f_n in recurrence relations of dynamic programming. Here the problem considered is

$$f_0{}^\alpha(x) = \mathcal{H}(x); \quad f_n{}^\alpha(x) = \max_y [k(x,y) + \alpha f_{n-1}{}^\alpha(x)],$$

the $f_n{}^\alpha(x)$ converging to a limit (denote it $f^\alpha(x)$) satisfying

$$f^\alpha(x) = \max_y \; [k(x,y) + \alpha f^\alpha(x)]$$

generating some optimal control $y^a(x)$, to which — with control suitably selected and subject to some conditions — there is a corresponding measure μ^a; from the measures μ^α, when $\alpha \to 1$, a sub-sequence converging to some measure can be chosen such as to form the optimum solution — an approach found with respect to Markovian processes in Blackwell.[59] (As Romanovskiy appositely notes, the method is related to the basic one (as above) broadly in the same way as is Abel's method to Cesàro's summation formula for divergent series.)

Romanovskiy is representative of the view that the direct-analysis approach to asymptotic behaviour of optimal control is more fruitful than that resting on a comparison as between the processes' infinite trajectories — "*efficiency*" of programmes: the approach ascribed to Makarov, Koopmans, and Gale[60] [the definition rests on this statement: the "programme" is a sequence $X = \{X_n\}$ assuming feasibility of motion $X_n \to X_{n+1}$ for any n. Let the sequence $\Phi = \Phi(x) = \{\phi_n\}$ be determined by $\phi_0 = 0$; $\phi_n = \phi_{n-1} + k(x_{n-1}, x_n)$, the ϕ_n being "income" from the n-th step in following X. Suppose X is better than X^0 if, from some n onwards, we have $\phi_n > \phi'_n$. X is "efficient" if there is no "better" programme in this sense]. Romanovskiy's preference for the approach rests on the fact that the analysis of efficiency is much more complicated and, on the other hand, wherever the programme is "efficient" as defined — specifically in the case of the turnpike — it is placed almost entirely within the neighbourhood of the optimal stationary state.

The formalism is broadly this. The economic system's states are described by the nonnegative vector $(x_1, \ldots, x_t)$; the x_0, initial state, and number of steps T are given, and so is $u(x)$ — a nonnegative function of first order appraising the terminal state x_T. What is sought is the control such that for the collection $(x_1, x_2, \ldots, x_T)$; $(x_{i-1}, x_i) \in Z$; $i = 1, \ldots, T$ the $u(x_T) = \max$. The system is assumed to be homogeneous (the cone Z and function u are homogeneous): hence its states can be normalized; thus the state of the system at every time-point is described by a probability vector $\xi = (\xi_1, \ldots, \xi_T)$; $\Sigma \xi_i = 1$ while "memorizing" the scale; the simplex of the normalized states denote Ξ. Then for any two states $\xi, \eta \in \Xi$ we posit $k(\xi, \eta) = \log \, (\max\{\lambda | (\xi, \lambda \eta) \in Z\})$. Denote $\mathcal{H}(x) = \log u(x)$. Since $u(x)$ is homogeneous, first order, we write $\mathcal{H}(\alpha \eta) = \mathcal{H}(\eta) + \log \alpha$. If $f_T(\xi)$ denotes the logarithm of the maximum valuation of the terminal state of the

T-step trajectory, starting from ξ, then this function will satisfy the re-currence relation

$$f_0(\xi) = \mathcal{H}(\xi); \; f_T(\xi) = \max_\eta \, [k(\xi,\eta) + f_{T-1}(\eta)] \, .$$

The model appears quite close to that of the discrete dynamic-program-ming system: the difference is only that in that model — a deterministic construct — sets of states are fixed from which the optimal "zones" can be reached, all the rest forming a sub-model without connection with them.

An interesting point is made, in the context, with regard to Makarov's idea of the asymptotic properties of a trajectory — its turning into a stationary state over a finite number of steps. As Romanovskiy argues, in particular, where technological processes employed in equilibrium form a Leontief model with a diagonal output matrix, the trajectory — under Radner's assumptions — does turn into an optimal stationary state over a finite number of steps.

(15) The explorations then on the "marriage" of the Bellmanian and Neumannian systems have formed the basis of the fundamental Kantorovich-Makarov[61] construct for optimal control.

Its core forms a Neumannian block of pairs of matrices[62] $A = \|a_i^s\|$ and $B = \|b_i^s\|$; each technology (s) is described by the pair of equidimensional vectors $a^s = (a_1{}^s, \ldots, a_n{}^s)$ and $b^s = (b_1{}^s, \ldots, b_n{}^s)$; the latter — the output vector with all components nonnegative — relates to the former, which is the input vector, with all components non-positive, for the preceding plan-interval. Technologies and ingredients related to one plan-interval are con-stant over the whole of the plan period; where a technology is employed starting from $t \geqslant 1$, this technology and the corresponding constraints are zero for all $t < 1$. All multi-interval fixed-capacity (capacity-stock) forming technologies resolve themselves in this fashion into series of "current" ("flow") technologies, each embracing only a pair of immediately adjoin-ing plan intervals; a capacity which gestates over a longer time segment appears in an ingredient series reflecting the consecutive degrees of its maturity. The Kantorovich-Makarov, formally a finite-horizon, plan has then this formalism based on the sequential pairing of the matrices:

(1) Denote the state of the system[63] at t by $X(t)$ and the vector of quanti-ties of "ingredients" available at the start of the period t;

(2) let $Y = (Y(1), \ldots, Y(T), Y(T+1))$ be the vector of constraints for the model's matrix (as above), the $Y(t)$ being the vector of ingredient quantities coming into, or being taken out, at the beginning of period t.

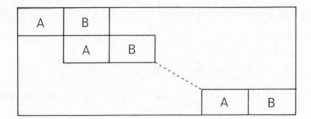

Thus $Y(1) = X(1)$. The $Y(t)$ is termed the exegoneous vector (in Soviet terminology the "load" vector);

(3) the "plan" of the system for the period t is then defined as $H(t) = [h^1(t), \ldots, h^r(t)]$; in other words this is the vector of the levels — intensities — in the use of technologies;

(4) the nexus between $H(t)$ and the $X(t + 1)$ is expressed as $X(t + 1) = BH(t) + Y(t + 1)$;

(5) the perspective plan reveals itself as feasible if $AH(t) \leqslant X(t)$;

(6) the perspective plan is optimal, $\bar{H} = (\bar{H}(1), \ldots, \bar{H}(T))$, if it is the solution of the linear programming problem with the matrices as above, with constraints Y and some collection of products — of postulated structure — to be the maximand over T;

(7) the vector of "objectively conditioned valuations" — shadow prices in Kantorovich's terminology, corresponding to the dual solution of the optimal plan-problem — is then $\pi = (\pi(1), \ldots, \pi(T + 1))$. In terms of this vector two growth-rates of the economy are defined under optimum:

$$\alpha(t) = (X(t + 1), \pi(t))/(X(t), \pi(t))$$

and

$$\beta(t) = (X(t + 1), \pi(t))/X(t + 1), \pi(t + 1))$$

respectively, the technological or "natural" and the economic growth rates. The nature of the $\alpha(t)$ and the $\beta(t)$; the adjustments of their form in an "open system"; the intrinsic properties of the dual which they reflect, the nexus between them and the rates of return from investment (of "investment efficiency") and of profit (discussed in the related contexts of Part I) have patently a Neumannian character.

[It is shown that if

$$(Y(t + 1), \pi(t + 1)) > 0 \ (=, <),$$

$$\alpha(t) > \beta(t) \ (=, <).$$

Further denote $Y(t) = Y(t) + Y'(t)$ where $Y'(t)$ is the vector of resources and final consumption, and $Y''(t)$ is the vector of the foreign trade balance. Then the "proper" and the "internal" technological growth-rates are respectively

$$\alpha'(t) = \frac{((X(t + 1) - Y(t + 1)), \pi(t))}{(X(t), \pi(t))}, \qquad \alpha''(t) = \frac{((X(t + 1) - Y''(t + 1)), \pi(t))}{(X(t), \pi(t))} .$$

It is then shown that *ceteris paribus*, depending on the "load"-vector value, the growth-rates will differ as follows:

$$(Y(t + 1), \pi(t)) > 0 \ (= 0; < 0)$$

entails

$$\alpha(t) > \alpha'(t) \ (=; <).$$

$$(Y''(t + 1), \pi(t)) > 0 \ (=; <)$$

entails

$$\alpha(t) > \alpha''(t) \ (= ; <).]$$

From the Romanovskiy inquiry two conclusions, decisive for this system, have been drawn (conclusions with respect to the von Neumann model's relevance for the issue of the asymptotic behaviour of the dynamic (linear) "plan-programme" and its optimality). These are: *firstly* the existence of the limiting plan under some assumptions with respect to the system's "load" – exogenous vector $Y(t)$ – is proved, specifically so for a mathematically closed model (with $Y(t) = 0$, $t = 2, 3, \ldots$) under some additional conditions imposed on the two matrices A,B; *secondly*, with $t \to \infty$ the limiting plan $H(t)$ tends towards the optimum of the corresponding von Neumann system (in other words the directing cosines of the vectors $\bar{H}(t)$ have as their limit the directing cosines of the Neumannian $\bar{H}(t)$ with matrices A,B – see below).

From this, law-of-motion consequences for the plan construction are deduced. The one which would seem to follow directly is that it is the criterion for the terminal plan – in the sense indicated – that should be adopted by the planner. However, on practical grounds the precept is this: because the matter of the finding of the terminal plan is not sufficiently explored, as yet, theoretically (and in any case is computationally difficult), the planner would be advised to handle the plan-problem with the linear programming techniques for a sufficiently distant horizon with the idea that the plan thus obtained would be abandoned at some point of the Neumannian path.

This policy precept has given rise in Soviet planning theory to a controversy, as yet unresolved, as to the right time-instant at which the abandoning should take place. This is discussed in chapter 3.

Note

Subsequently Kantorovich-Makarov expanded their ideas[64] on the objective function for the system whose production potential is described by a collection of technological coefficients

$$\{a_{ij}^s, \ w_i^s, \ f_i^s, \ b_{ij}^s, \ q_i^s\}; \ i,j = 1, \ldots, n; \ s = 1, \ldots, N$$

(symbols in braces denote: input coefficients; labour coefficients with given capital stock; capital-output coefficients; capital-input coefficients, i.e. input per unit of a unit of depreciation of stocks). The initial state of the system is described by F_0^s that is stocks (s stands for kind of stocks) and W_1 standing for manpower. The "consumption sphere" is π — the set of admissible vectors $(c_1^1, \ldots, c_n^1, c_1^2, \ldots, c_n^2, \ldots c_1^T, \ldots, c_n^T)$ — convex and polyhedral (in order to keep the programme linear). The structure of consumption is determined for each time-interval; the π is formed of a variety of vectors of the form $(\lambda_1 c^1, \ldots, \lambda_T c^T)$ where the $\lambda_1, \ldots, \lambda_T$ are arbitrary, nonnegative numbers; possibly c is broken up into $c' + c''$, respectively exogenously fixed vector of consumption, e.g. defence and social services, and household consumption making up a convex set. The vector of possible variation of consumption $c = (c_1^1, \ldots, c_1^T)$ makes the "closing" constraint (the four others are those on uses of output, on labour, allowance made for the working versus leisure-time policy; on capital; and on the terminal stocks, allowance made for additions and depreciation over the plan[65] period). Thus all constraints are written down for the system with the unknown variables sought $\{x_t^s, k_t^s, c^t\}$, $t = 1, \ldots, T$ (x and k are output and capital-formation levels). Thus the optimality criterion is expressed by some function $\Phi(c, F_T)$ depending on $c = (c^1, \ldots, c^T)$ and the vector of capital stocks for beyond-the-plan period $F_T = (F_T^1, F_T^2, \ldots, F_T^N)$ where $F_T^s = f^s q^s x_T^s + k_T^s$.

When final consumption is fixed for each plan year (the set π is formed of one point) and a suitable constraint is put on the working week, terminal capacity stock — the "bequest" in capital — becomes the maximand. A difficult matter is admittedly the pricing of the terminal stock: the favoured alternative considered for planning practice is extrapolation: possibly — of technology, labour resources, and final consumption, rather than prices — for the whole plan period. A variant of the criterion is one with the "beyond-T" development planned, for $T + 1, T + 2, \ldots$, that is tending to infinity with the assumption that the set of technologies remains constant and labour resources grow monotonically so that output per capita remains constant. There is only a broad hint at handling this case of the ∞-optimal plan, as in Makarov.[66,67]

Of other variants indicated two are of particular interest. *First*: with the π formed of the vectors $(\lambda_1 c^1, \ldots, \lambda_T c^T)$ as above, the problem being to find the plan maximizing

$$\sum_{t=1}^{t \in T} \lambda_t \rho^{-t}$$

subject to the condition that terminal capacities be secured not smaller than some posited value; the λ is the "time-reduction coefficient" — time-discount for consumption; a technical difficulty lies here in measuring terminal capacities: dealing with "absolute" magnitudes rather than prices. (Possibly some growth factor could be postulated; both this and the discount rate would be arbitrary.) *Second*: an infinity version; the plan-problem here is to find the plan determined over the whole time-semiaxis so as to maximize

$$\sum_{t=0}^{\infty} \lambda_t \rho^{-t}$$

(in these cases λ must not exceed the growth-rate of labour otherwise the existence of the optimal plan would not be established).

(16) The problem of continuous programming — convex and linear — as formulated by Bellman as the "bottleneck" problem has attracted attention of Soviet students because of its relevance in economic planning, specifically — pricing under optimum. The characteristic features of the

dual solution have been examined in particular by Makarov[68] (who also investigated the problem of the optimal plan's "switches" involved); in this he has moved beyond Tyndal's propositions (in proving the duality for the Bellman construct[69]).

As stated by Makarov, the convex problem has this content: let there be an n-dimensional nonnegative vector x_0, of the initial state — a positive T — the plan period, a family of closed convex cones $\{Z\}$, $t \in [0,T]$ in the $2n$-dimensional Euclidean space describing technology, and, describing the valuation, an n-dimensional vector c. The optimand sought is $\bar{z} = cx(T) =$ max subject to

$$(1) \qquad x(t) = x_0 + \int_0^t z(\tau)d\tau \text{ for all } t \in [0,T];$$

$$(2) \qquad z(\tau) = y(\tau) - x(\tau), (x(\tau), y(\tau)) \in Z_\tau \text{ for all } \tau \in [0,T].$$

(the x,y,z interpretable respectively as input, output, net result). A feasible control transfers $x(t_1)$ into $x(t_2)$ wherever

$$x(t_2) = x(t_1) + \int_{t_1}^{t_2} z(t)dt \text{ and } z(t) = y(t) - x(t),$$

$(x(t), y(t)) \in Z_t$ for all $t \in [t_1, t_2]$ where $x(t) = x(t_1) + \int_{t_1}^t z(\tau)d\tau$.

In characterizing the optimal control two additional constraints are introduced with respect to the technology: *firstly*, the existence of some positive constant K such that

$$\max_{t \in [0,T]} \max_{(x,y) \in Z_t} \sum_i y_i / \sum_i x_i \leqslant K$$

and *secondly* that for any time-point we have $(e_i, y) \in Z_t$ where e_i is a unit vector corresponding to the i-th co-ordinate. Then for the feasible control to be optimal it is necessary and sufficient that there exists an n-dimensional vector function π possessed of the three properties, viz. (1) $\pi(T) = c$, (2) $x(t)\pi(t) \geqslant x(T)c$ for any $t \in [0,T]$, and state $x(t)$ and any control $\bar{z}$ feasible for $x(t)$ and transferring $x(t)$ into $x(T)$, and (3) for the trajectory $\bar{x}$ corresponding to the control $\bar{z}, \bar{x}(t)\pi(t) = \bar{x}(T)$.

A theorem is established — for any optimal plan u of the continuous linear problem with a constant cone Z — to the effect that a plan u will be found with a finite number of "switches" with $(\bar{u}(T)A) = u(T)A$. For this syst with the technology matrices A,B the duality problem is formulated: to find the n-dimensional vector-function minimizing $\pi(0)x_0$ subject to

$$\pi(T) = c; \ A\pi(t) \geqslant Ac + \int_t^T (B - A)\pi(\tau)d\tau \text{ for all } t \in [0,T])$$

(17) While the Kantorovich school concentrates on stratégic distant-horizon plan modelling — "marrying" in this Kantorovich's concepts (of optimization and heuristic architecture of the plan) with those of Neumannian type of growth and Bellman's procedural approaches — outside this school a large crop of constructs is being designed to employ straightforward Bellmanian programming methods in the treatment of some specific aspects of dynamic planning. In this we shall draw attention to the work of Krivenkov and Arzamastsev.

The focus in Krivenkov's[70] series of investigations is on optimization of "production processes" understood in fact as the working of the basic micro-unit ("enterprise"). In this the basic framework of analysis is a version of the Bellman-type, discrete-time, "bottleneck-problem" model. It has the form

$$x_1(k\Delta + \Delta) - x_1(k\Delta) = \beta u_1^k - u_2^k - u_3^k.$$

$$x_2(k\Delta + \Delta) - x_2(k\Delta) = \alpha u_2^k$$

and inequalities

$$u_i^k > 0 \quad (i = 1, 2),$$

$$u_1^k + u_2^k + u_3^k < x_1(k\Delta)$$

(constraint on circulating capital — for short — "resources")

$$\beta u_1^k < \mu x_2(k\Delta)$$

(constraint on capacities). The diagrammatic description is presented on the facing page and the notation is as follows. The β and α are respectively coefficients of "reproduction" and capacity expansion, Δ the time period of discreteness, μ maximum output/capacity/period. The state of the system is determined by $x(t)_1$ — stock of output, and by $x_2(t)$ the productivity over period Δ (redistribution of resources is carried out only at the

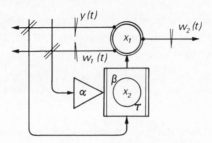

time-points $t = k\Delta$ ($k = 1, 2 \dots$)). The $u_i{}^k$ designates output going into expansion of x_i ($i = 1, 2 \dots$) and $u_3{}^k$ that taken out of production "without equivalent" respectively.

It is, however, the continuous variant that is Krivenkov's principal concern. It is arrived at by postulating that $\Delta \to 0$. We have now the system of differential equations

$$\frac{dx_1}{dt} = (\beta - 1)u_1(t) - u_2(t) - u_3(t), \quad \frac{dx_2}{dt} = \alpha u_2(t);$$

and inequalities

$$u_i(t) \geqslant 0 \ (i = 1, 2), 0 \leqslant x_1(t), \beta u_1(t) \leqslant \mu x_2(t) .$$

Here the $u_i(t)$ and μ denote respectively

$$\lim_{\Delta \to 0} \frac{u_i^k}{\Delta}$$

and

$$\lim_{\Delta \to 0} \frac{\mu}{\Delta}$$

– with the values of "intensity" defined as velocity of ingredients' motion – and output per time unit.

The implications of this system are examined by restating the problem of optimization as

$$x_1(T) = \int_0^T [(\beta - 1)u_1(t) - u_2(t)] \, dt = \max.,$$

subject to

$$u_3(t) \equiv 0, x_1(0) = C_1, x_2(0) = C_2, \mu = 1$$

for an operational unit ("enterprise"). This problem is being solved here by applying Pontryagin's Maximum Principle; the Hamiltonian $H(\psi, x, u)$ takes the form $H = \phi_1 u_1 + \phi_2 u_2$ where

$$\phi_1(t) = \beta - 1; \quad \phi_2(t) = -\frac{(\beta - 1)}{\beta} a \cdot (t - T) - 1;$$

the system being linear the Principle is the sufficient as well as necessary condition of optimality.

Without restating the line of further reasoning we may indicate the basic result which is this. The system reveals itself as deprived of an important parameter of the enterprise's dynamics, i.e. the length of the full cycle of production. As the marginal values of concern are arrived at, the parameter reaches the zero value. The operational handicap is then that the production unit appears to be working with zero "resources" (as defined, that is circulating capital). The analysis of inequalities determining the pace of "reproduction" processes shows that constraints with respect to capacities have retained their meaning while those with respect to the "resources" — have disappeared. To put this in other words, the system as modelled has no concept of circulating capital; its pace of work is determined solely by its installed capacities. The corollary is that planning the enterprise's work by means of a continuous variant of the bottleneck programme carries a bias in performance indices; it does so since in expanding production nothing is allowed for an entailed expansion of circulating capital resources.

In a series of contributions Krivenkov has tried to adjust the "machinery" of the system (again with the optimality test based on Pontryagin's Maximum Principle). Krivenkov's functional-analytic design rests on the common sense proposition that the regime of expansion of (circulating-capital) resources is indispensable while the regime of expansion of the capacity stock is rational if and only if there is a sufficient surplus of these resources to support it.[71]

However, the ultimate conclusion of this series (including his recent book carrying an admirable comparison of ten alternatives in modelling production) is that it is Bellman's discrete "bottleneck"-problem construct that shows itself heuristically to provide the most convenient, qualitative and quantitative, description of planned production processes: most convenient both from the point of view of the supporting, analytical and, numerically oriented, mathematical apparatus, and of the degree of economic exactness.[72]

(18) Our chapter 4 has shown the difficulties of comparing efficiency of investment projects over time. The tempting idea would be to base the selection of projects on a stage-by-stage optimization of return. This is the idea made use of by Arzamastsev in his "qualitative" analysis of conditions for the "comparative efficiency" of capital investment.[73] The problem is given this form: taking the totality of capital resources available for allocation to investment $K_{\tau-1}$, as between the projects which, at the step τ, form some function Q_τ, determine the optimal-control functions $\phi_\tau{}^0$ at all steps such as to secure to the totality of projects installed maximum return D_Σ over T. Rewritten in terms of the Optimality Principle the problem has the form

$$R_{\tau,N}^y(K_{\tau-1}) = \max_{\phi_\tau} \left\{ a_\tau D_\tau(K_{\tau-1,\phi_\tau}) + R_{\tau+1,N}^y(K_\tau) \right\}$$

where $R_{\tau,N}^y(K_{\tau-1})$ is the posited maximum total of income at all steps starting from t and ending at the step N with some given value of $K_{\tau-1}$. It is shown that

$$K_n = \frac{\gamma_n t_n}{\gamma_{n-1} t_{n-1}} \beta K_{n-1} + \gamma_n t_n D_{\tau=n}$$

where γ stands for the economy's rate of investment and β for its growth of national income (taken to be constant over time). Suppose that

$$r_\tau = (\gamma_\tau t_\tau / \gamma_{\tau-1} t_{\tau-1})\beta; \quad s_\tau = \gamma_\tau t_\tau,$$

then

$$K_\tau = r_\tau K_{\tau-1} + s_\tau D_\tau,$$

where r_τ and s_τ are some fixed coefficients.

For the last step N we have

$$R_{N,N}(K_{N-1}, \varphi_N) = a_N D_N(K_{N-1}, \varphi_N)$$

The problem of finding the $D_\Sigma \to$ maximum for the whole plan period T is reduced to that of finding the $\phi_\tau{}^0$ which secures maximum D_τ at each step with a given value of $K_{\tau-1}$. Here again the advantage of the formulation is that at each stage the link with the past is only via the $K_{\tau-1}$ whatever its "pre"-history.

(19) Methodological properties of the dynamic programming construct which seem to have a particular appeal to the planning-oriented theorist are those which have been incisively singled out by Westcott.[74] These are: that the solution is formed progressively rather than, in anticipation, as a whole, by means of mathematical manipulation; this appeals also to one who is thinking in terms of an adaptive system operated in multi-stage decision processes. Further, that the decision-making procedure is carried out backwards over the whole period, one step at a time — as a rule starting from adopted targets. Also that the optimum trajectories must terminate in states that are optimum from the point of view of any future envisaged path — again a normal consideration for the planner, requiring certain beyond-the-horizon developments.

(20) Difficulties resulting from a system's complexity when superimposed on its dynamics have stimulated the modellers' search for sufficient ways of approximate optimizing. One workable attempt is by Pervozvanskiy.[75] Its principle is borrowed from what is traditional in engineering projects where the law of control combines the programming part with a correcting one which makes use of current information on the system's deviations — assumed to be small — from the programmed path. In Pervozvanskiy the system's basic motion is described by the recurrent relations of the dynamic programme

$$B_t(S) = \min \, E\{R(t) + B_{t+1} [S + P - Q]\} \quad (t = 0, 1, \ldots, T - 1), \quad (!)$$

$$B_\tau(S) = \sum_k \rho_k [T, S],$$

the Bellman function $B_t(S)$ describes here the optimal value of the system's mean risk entailed in a process initiated at point t from the state S. (The vector S describes the levels of intermediate products' stocks; P and Q, respectively, mutual deliveries and uses of products.) Technologies ensuring the minimum risk rest on a set of functions phi's and zeta's, the former known and the latter being some random sequences with known probability characteristics; thus for inputs and outputs

$$x_{ki} = \varphi'_{ki}(t,u_i) + \zeta'_{ki}(t), \quad k \in K_i(i) \cap K_\Pi,$$

$$y_{ik} = \varphi''_{ik}(t,u_i) + \zeta''_{ik}(t), \quad k \in K_2(i) \cap K_B;$$

$$\varphi'_{ki}(u_i,t) = n_{ki}, \quad k \notin K_\Pi, \quad \varphi''_{ik}(u_i,t) = m_{ik}, \quad k \notin K_B = F_{t,i}(m_{ig},n_{ki}).$$

This allowed for, the (!) is rewritten

$$R_t(S) = \sum_k \rho_k(t, S_k) + \min\left[\sum_{i \in I} F_{t,i}(m_{i,k}, n_{ki}) + EB_{t+1}(S + P - Q)\right] \quad (!!)$$

The idea of the transformation is formally to separate the two optimizations — of production and of mutual deliveries as is usual in decentralization. The "proper" approximation of control starts from a quasi-static approach, assuming constancy of inventories and disregarding random factors. Then we turn to "local" approximation with additive corrective processes postulated to be in a small neighbourhood of the programmed values taking $m_{ik} = y_{ik} + \mu_{ik}$, $n_{ki} = \bar{x}_{ki} + v_{ki}$, (bar denotes optimum) $F_{t,i} \approx \hat{F}_{t,i} = F_{t,i}(\bar{y}_{ik}, \bar{x}_{ki}) + \Delta F_{t,i}(\mu_{ik}, v_{ki})$. (Implementation of the approximation thus localized is in Pervozvanskiy only broadly hinted at as possibly carried out by least-square methods, or, where tractable, by taking the dual of a linear programme.) When their local approximations are substituted for the functions in (!!), we have

$$\hat{B}_t(S) = \beta_0 + \beta(S) + \min_{S - A \leqslant V \leqslant S} [F(\mu, v) + E\hat{B}_{t+1}(S - V + Z)]. \quad (!!!)$$

The F, to restate, reflects the system's efficiency changes resulting from *small* deviations of mutual inter-component supplies. The multidimensional problem (!!!) is broken up into a set of unidimensional problems whose number agrees with that of "inventory elements" which are the intermediate products: the (!!!) has the solution

$$B_t(S) = (T - t)\beta_0 + \sum_k \hat{B}_{t,k}(s_k),$$

where the last term is determined by the unidimensional recurrent relations

$$\hat{B}_{t,k}(s_k) = \rho_k(t, s_k) + \min_{s_k - A_k \leqslant v_k \leqslant s_k} [F_k + EB_{t+1}(s_k - v_k + \zeta_k)].$$

A feature which enhances the student's interest in the Pervozvanskiy model is the focus on the state of inventories, an index of a multi-component system's efficiency which has of late attracted a good deal of attention. In the Pervozvanskiy exercise efficiency is explicitly dependent on intermediate products' "reserves" through the mutual deliveries' fluctuations (thence, technically, the scope for non-equilibria of deliveries and inputs, explainable by changes in stocks). The price for tractability achieved is the turning of the overall problem into a set of control problems "*in the small*"; and the accepting of a static framework for appraising the oscillations in mutual deliveries. The overall problem of the optimum in dynamics — the optimal capacity formation problem — is not explicitly treated.

The model may prove more effective as a scheme for computation in a complex large-scale system than for devolution in decision making. As we have suggested, that corresponds to the predominant interest of Soviet theorizing.

On the whole in what was meant to be a dynamic "analogue" of his celebrated exercise (joint with Pervozvanskaya, see ch. 2, and Appendix 3), Pervozvanskiy appears to be by now pessimistic as to the feasibility of a rigorous, generalized, "decentralistic" (or, we would say, devolutional) solution for an overall problem with mutual heterogeneous deliveries. Indeed, it is his view that only the "architecture" of his model, viz. confining his exercise in approximate optimization to a "localized" approach, has permitted to shift what may be an insoluble problem to a set of independent problems of control, "in the small", of inventories in "individualized" products; and the solution of the static problems for a system as a whole is to give an "objective" estimate of fluctuations in mutual deliveries. The per se feasible conclusion reached then stresses the dependence of the system's efficiency on the level of intermediate-product stocks through such deliveries: this is seen as providing scope for allowing the basic plan-programme for a supplies-inputs imbalance as possibly feeding the inventories[76] (this is formalized by means of the Charnes-Cooper and Kataoka techniques).

(21) The 1960s saw the assimilation of the Pontryagin system into economic dynamics. This is the theme of the present section.

As we have indicated, the work of Pontryagin and his associates was not addressed to the economist. Yet an intuitive interpretation of the Maximum Principle into the latter's "language" offers itself immediately. This suggests itself when we look upon the Principle as the system's optimizing "law of motion" in the general sense; and, taking it from the general to the particular, as embodying also such a law for an economic system optimally steered towards his goals by a policy-maker, however institutionalized.[77] To restate the law, let us once again turn to the formalization of the minimum-time problem (a problem which is both one of · the areas of most effective application of the Principle, and is of patent relevance for economics as often as not facing the issue of "fastest speed"). In the conventional notation it is describable in differential equations

$$dx_i/dt = f_i(x_1, \ldots, x_n, u_1, \ldots, u_r) \qquad (!)$$

The solution will be found under the assumption that initial conditions — the state x^0 at the initial time instant t^0 — are known: the solution meaning the values of the function $x_1(t_1), \ldots, x_n(t)$. The substance of the maximum-velocity is to find such value of feasible controls $u(t)$ as would transfer the system from the initial state x^0 into some postulated state x_1^* over the shortest time period with $t_0 \leqslant t \leqslant t_1$. As is often done in handling optimization of an economic system here too we bring in the auxiliary functions $\psi_1(t), \ldots, \psi_n(t)$ for which we have a system of differential equations

$$d\psi_i/dt = - \partial H(\psi,x,u)/\partial x_i \qquad (!!)$$

with

$$H(\psi,x,u) = \sum_{i=1}^{n} \psi_i f_i(x,u) = \psi_1 f_1(x,u) + \ldots + \psi_n f_n(x,u).$$

To restate then the Principle, it announces that where the control $u(t)$ and the trajectory $x(t)$ are optimal, there exists a non-trivial solution of (!!), $\psi_1(t), \ldots, \psi_n(t)$ such that for any time-point $t_0 \leqslant t \leqslant t_1$ the conditions

$$H(\psi(t), x(t), u(t)) = \max_{\bar{u} \in u} H(\psi(t), x(t), u))$$

and

$$H(\psi(t), x(t), u(t)) \geqslant 0$$

are satisfied.

"Intuitively" the economic content of the terms of the system in "fastest motion" lends itself plausibly to this interpretation: the economy's phase co-ordinates, x_i the capacity (capital) stocks; the control parameter u the net investment rate as *the* adopted strategy tool; the Hamiltonian, H, net national product; the Hamiltonian multiplier $\psi(t)$ the time-weighting coefficient — the instantaneous valuation of $\dot{x}$, the capacity (capital) increment (as it were the valuation of the system's energy generation).[78]

To follow up the Pontryagin formalism, the Maximum Principle could here also intelligibly be supplemented by making explicit the non-trivial transversality condition $\psi(t) [x(t) - x_{t_1}] = 0$ with $\psi(t)$ nonnegative: again "naturally" that "reinterprets" itself as pinpointing the postulated beyond-the-horizon endowment.

This is then the point of "transliteration" into economics — a notional scaffolding. Its elaboration has by now a vast literature and — for didactic reasons and rather eclectically — we may refer ourselves here to what for short we may call the French school. Thus we may refer ourselves to Armand's well systematized reasoning on the meaning of the Pontryagin "auxiliaries" when transplanted into economics, the reasoning which with patent logic starts from the link between the Maximum Principle and the Kuhn-Tucker theorem which (as we would put this) dynamizes this price. The important role of the theorem consists not merely in establishing the existence of the price equilibria but, as Armand validly remarks, in forming the basis for the schemes of devolution in decision-making (cf. Gale).[79] Armand's incisive observation is that in this respect the potential role of the Pontryagin principle is similar:[80] it is so since — for a particular class of programmes — it is a generalization of the Kuhn-Tucker conditions to the continuous dynamic case. As an analogy to the decomposition *in space* we would have decomposition *in time*. Here too it is the dual price that is decomposer — a price obtained by ascending the optimal trajectory. As Armand argues, since the state of the system is taken to be generated by the initial condition of the system and past decisions, and the decision-making is instantaneous, "the future can be brought in only through the bias of prices";[81] this "bias" is shaped by the objective function. (The argument is also noteworthy for its presentation of the logic of the Pontryagin algorithm.)[82]

The double role of the Pontryagin function can be thus given further precision — as has been done in the extension of the Armand reasoning by Albouy. Once one is concerned with the trade-off "arbitrage", over time, one has to observe the variables of state as well as those of control. In this the conjugated functions of Pontryagin associated with the system's evolution both provide "authentic" dual variables and ensure the intertemporal coherence of the instantaneous regulation with the dynamic one: the dynamic optimization is broken up into a sequence of independent static optimizations through the build-up of a new function of instantaneous evaluation, that is the Hamiltonian. The argument leads eventually to Albuoy's[83] well tenable characterization of the nature of the price derived from the Pontryagin system: it is that in substance the $\psi(t)$'s reveal the price of the use of the variables of states; we have thus a rent-type price, a "rental" paid for the employment of stocks. In this way the theory of dual-programming price is generalized to embrace that of the price of stocks as well as the price of flows. Also in extending the Armand idea, Albuoy shows that the Maximum Principle should be viewed as a generalization — for a particular class of programmes — of the continuous case of the Kuhn-Tucker conditions.

We are thus once again on the track of a seminal integration of theoretical thought. We have a clear link with the recent formulation by Pallu de la Barrière[84] of the general methodology of the treatment of the influence of constraint-parameters of an optimized dynamic system: in other words, of the cost of constraint stated in Pontryagin's terms, limiting the evolution of the system with a possible allowance for the discontinuities of the capital formation under the influence of investment as well as those of velocity — under the influence of impulses in the "mechanical" or economic system.

Note

Attention may be drawn here to a significant reformulation of the Maximum Principle in terms of the convex-function theory — with immediate implications for optimal pricing — by Rockafellar.[85] We have noted in Part I his reinterpretation of Lagrangean-type optimal price as the equilibrium price — equilibrium recognizable in that the incentive for perturbation is being "neutralized". The line of ideas is extended to dynamics — the Hamiltonian formulation à la Pontryagin: now the classical theory is expanded by resorting to Fenchel's conjugacy correspondence rather than the Legendre transformation: convexity rather than differentiability is postulated; convexity is assumed for the Lagrangean function: its extremals corresponding to the minima would not necessarily be finite throughout. In the event the Principle takes the form of the generalized Hamiltonian equations entailing subgradients rather than gradients. The reader is advised to acquaint himself with the illuminating exemplification of the formalism — in Rockafellar — for an economy equipped with a perfect optimizer-"controller" operating with the dual "convex dynamic system" (formed — to restate it — of dynamic semi-groups, built up of bifunctions, as defined, rather than linear transformations).[86] The Rockafellar reformulations extend the area of application of the Maximum Principle in planning theory.

(22) Chronologically the credit for employing the Maximum Principle in the theory of growth should be shared by Uzawa, Sengupta, and Kurz. (We revert to Kurz's contribution in a somewhat specific context.) Uzawa's basic theme[87] was optimum technical change in an aggregate model of economic growth; this, however, had been placed within a broader problem of engaging scarce resources in some positive quantities and in analysing the pattern of the allocation of scarce resources resulting in an optimum growth. The focus in the inquiry is then on the primary-factor ratio securing a blaanced growth under optimum (and "switches" that have to be carried out when the initial capital-labour ratio deviates, upwards and downwards, from the "balanced" ratio); and as we shall see, this direction anticipates a further development of particular interest to us.

The output in Western literature on the Pontryaginian principle in economic dynamics has been too prolific to be dealt with adequately here. (A list of applications of the Maximum Principle to the theory of optimal economic growth more or less complete up to the end of the 1960s will be found in Shell.)[88] We shall broach the subject of the major contributions in due course.

Note

A ramification of the use of the Pontryagin principle in economic dynamics is a control-theoretic formalization of the theory of capital. An interesting attempt has been made by Dorfman[89] — it makes in a sense an extension of Solow's[90] outline of the "technocratic" theory of capital (see our Part I). It is in substance a theory of the capital's value maximized by optimal employment in growth generation. Technically the reasoning centres on the Hamiltonian $H = u(K,x,t) + \lambda(t)f(K,x,t)$ (k — stock of capital; notation otherwise conventional) and the partial derivative with respect to K equated to $\dot{\lambda}$; the "modified" Hamiltonian appears then as $H^* = u(k,x,t) + d/dt.\lambda k = u(k,x,t) + \lambda k + \dot{\lambda} k$.

For some time-interval Δt, the $H^*\Delta t$ would mean the sum of profits realized over the Δ and the increase in the value of capital stock: would mean, that is, the value of total contribution of activities to profits, current and future. Maximization of H^* with respect to x and k results in $\partial u/\partial x + \lambda \partial f/\partial x = 0$; $\partial u/\partial k + \lambda \partial f/\partial k + \dot{\lambda} = 0$.

The implied "plan" is to trace out the time-path of x and λ so as to secure the yields and capital increment maximum for any short time-interval. This is synthesized in $\partial H/\partial \lambda = \dot{k}$; $\partial H/\partial x = 0$; $\partial H/\partial k = -\dot{\lambda}$ with the logical reciprocity of the k and $-\lambda$.

In the context we may note the comment Dorfman's paper has evoked in Soviet literature. Kantorovich[91] has recently referred to this

construction of a theory of capital by means of the Pontryagin principle as
an example of a persuasive and useful "economic interpretation of
mathematical facts". We have here then one of the cases where the language of mathematics proves of help in overcoming the chasm — in some
of the most controversial areas — traditionally dividing the Soviet and
Western economic thinking.

(23) The Arrow-Kurz theory of investment and rate of return[92] can also
be considered a "capital theory" (in Dorfman's sense) developed with the
aid of the Pontryagin principle. Among its most important findings (we
may note at least in passing here) is that on the nature of the, deceptively
"banal", relationship between the rate of interest and marginal productivity
of capital. For the system in long-run steady growth they are equal and
shown to be determined by "subjective" rate of discount, the elasticity of
marginal utility of consumption and the rate of the labour-augmenting
technological progress. The equality is demonstrated to be disturbed where
the system gets out of balanced growth. Now the discrepancy between the
(historically shaped) marginal productivity of capital and the rate of interest tends — by patterning investment and consumption — to move the
latter rate to its asymptoptic level. These observations presuppose adjustment mechanism under an "automatic" regime; they make, however, an
interesting comment on the Kantorovich-Makarov "quadruplet" of rates
under the optimally planned system with hints on the planner's job (see
sect. 17).

(24) It was only very recently that Soviet planning theory discovered the
Maximum Principle, though the Principle had been recognized, in the
accepted classification, as the foundation of the mathematical theory of
optimal processes in general, in turn directly related to problems of the
theory of "automatic regulation". At the end of the 1960s an application
in strategic economic planning was initiated in the TsEMI: the result,
Smirnov's model, was presented at the Geneva international conference on
input-output techniques[93] (a version published subsequently in the USSR,
while employing the Hamiltonian apparatus, refrains from explicitly invoking the Pontryagin principle).[94] At the time of our writing the apparatus is
being employed only selectively in the treatment of specific economic
problems.
  However, by the early 1970s Western uses of the Maximum Principle
have evoked a considerable and increasing interest in Soviet literature.

True the emphasis has remained on the Principle's being only a *necessary* condition of optimality. Yet it is recognized now that by isolating those classes satisfying at least the necessary conditions, the Principle is helpful in narrowing down the class of controls and trajectories among which the optimal ones have to be sought (and in cases of a unique solution, it does naturally offer the sufficient solution as well). More, the other merit has found recognition too: i.e. that, as against the theorems of classical calculus of variations, the Maximum Principle does hold for any region of admissible values, including the *closed* set $u(t)$ which is of particular significance in applied economic problems.[95]

We now turn to Smirnov's model of all-economy planning – as it has been restated by him in Soviet literature. The version retains its original Ramseyan-type optimand which is minimized:

$$\delta(x,y) = \int_{t_0}^{\mu[\lambda]} \lambda(t)[\hat{\pi}(t) - \pi(t,x,y)]\,dt \text{ min,}$$

subject to

$$x(t) = A(t)x(t) + K(t)\frac{dx}{dt} + y(t);$$

$$x(t_0) = x_0;$$

$$0 < \bar{y}(t) \leqslant y(t) \leqslant x(t).$$

The $A(t)$ and $K(t)$ are matrices respectively of input-output and incremental capital coefficients; the $x(t)$ and $y(t)$ are vectors of gross and net (final) product respectively. The π is social-welfare function, $\lambda = \lambda(t)$ is some adopted welfare weighting over time; with $t \to \infty$ we have lim $\lambda(t) = 0$; $\bar{y}$ is postulated minimum levels of consumption.

Restated in Lagrangean terms the optimality criterion is

$$L = \int_{t_0}^{\mu[\lambda(t)]} F(t,x,y,p)dt$$

where

$$F = F(t,x,y,p) = \lambda(t)[\hat{\pi}(t) - \pi(t,x,y)] +$$

$$+ (p(t), \frac{dx}{dt} - f(x,y)).$$

When the Hamiltonian is resorted to we have

$$H(t,x,y,p) = \left[p(t), \frac{dx}{dt} \right] + \lambda(t)[\hat{\pi}(t) - \pi(t,x,y)].$$

The link between the Hamiltonian and the $F(t,x,y,p)$ is expressed by the equality $F = H - (p,f)$, where $f = f(x,y,t) = K^{-1}[(t)(I - A(t)]x^0(t) - K^{-1}(t)y(t)$. Thence

$$\frac{\partial F}{\partial \dot{x}'} = p; -\frac{\partial F}{\partial x} = \frac{\partial H}{\partial x}; \frac{\partial F}{\partial y} = \frac{\partial H}{\partial y};$$

$$\frac{\partial F}{\partial \dot{y}'} = \frac{\partial F}{\partial \dot{p}} = 0; \frac{\partial F}{\partial p} = -\left[\frac{dx}{dt} - f(t,x,y)\right].$$

By substitution we obtain the necessary optimality conditions

$$\frac{d}{dt}p(t) = -\frac{\partial H}{\partial x'}; \frac{dx^0}{dt} = K^{-1}(t)\left[(I - A(t)]x^0(t) - K^{-1}(t)y(t); \frac{\partial H}{\partial y} = 0,$$

which, jointly with boundary conditions, enable us to solve the extremal problem for the economy. The necessary conditions can be rewritten in symmetric form:

$$\frac{dx}{dt} = \frac{\partial H^0}{\partial p} \quad \text{and} \quad \frac{dp}{dt} = -\frac{\partial H^0}{\partial x}.$$

Here

$$H^0(t,x,p) = \text{opt } H(t,x,y,p) \text{ and } y^0 = y^0(t)$$

is the optimal solution, satisfying the vectoral equation

$$\frac{\partial H}{\partial y} = 0.^{96}$$

Of the two canonical conjugate systems, the first describes the technological constraints of the economy, the second the value aspect of the growth processes, i.e. in terms of the vector function of Lagrangean multipliers $p(t) = (p_1(t), \ldots, p_n(t))$. Over the plan-perspective the criterion is minimization of the "deficit" of growth processes; the $y_{opt}(t) = y^0(t)$ obtains the minimum value and depends on the state of the system $x(t)$, that is

$$Q = \min \delta(x,y,t) = Q(x,t) \ (y \in Y).$$

The gradient of the $Q(x,t)$, taken with the minus sign, is determined by the equation

$$p(t) = -\frac{\partial}{\partial x} Q(x,t) = -\frac{\partial}{\partial x} \int_t^{\mu[\lambda]} \lambda(\tau)[\hat{\pi}(\tau) - \pi(\tau,x,y)]\, d\tau$$

which reveals itself as the vector-function of the integral optimal valuation of resources; the ith co-ordinate $\partial Q/\partial x_i$ of the gradient $\partial Q/\partial x$ shows the integral change of the criterion over $[t,T]$, caused by an infinitesimal change in the ith resource, whose trajectory is described by the function $x_i(t)$. It is the evaluation of consequences of additional use of resources over the whole perspective, from t to some foreseeable time point $T = [\mu(\lambda)]$, that is the specific property of economic interpretation of a variational problem.

Notes

1. This model gains from being placed by Smirnov (in his book which appeared after the completion of this chapter, i.e. *Modelirovanye i prognozirovanye sotsyalisticheskogo vosproizvodstva*, 1970) in his simple, but pedagogically admirable, theory of modelling planned growth. It starts from a Leontievian process (in standard notation)

$$\bar{x}_t = A_t\bar{x}_t + K_t\Delta\bar{x}_t + \bar{y}_t; \bar{x}_{t_0} = \bar{x}_0$$

where (assuming constancy of coefficients and existence of the matrix $K^{-1}(I - A)$ for our non-homogeneous system of difference equations) the solution would be the vector

$$\bar{x}_t = [I + K^{-1}(I - A)]^t x_0 + \sum_{n=0}^{t-1} [(I + S)^n K^{-1}]\bar{y}_{t-n-1}.$$

Then optimization is pursued for the trajectory described by a continuous "analogue"

$$dx_i/dt = \sum_{k=1}^n \tilde{a}_{ik}x_k(t) - \sum_{k=1}^n n_{ik}y_k(t); \quad i = 1, \dots, n;$$

$$\tilde{a}_{ik} = k_{im}^{-1}(\delta_{mk} - a_{mk}); n_{ik} = k_{ik}^{-1},$$

the δ being a Kronecker delta. Assuming a multicriterial system — a system with conflicting criteria, $z_j(t)$ — the feedback and co-ordination would be characterized by

$$P_1(z)dz_1 + P_2(z)dz_2 + \ldots + P_r(z)dz = 0$$

the P's interpretable as priority-parameters of objectives. Assuming the existence of the overall criterion functional

$$\int_{t_0}^{\infty} G[z(\tau)]dt \to \min,$$

the G being a Ramseyan-type objective, we link with the model presented above.

   Finally, a procedure of devolution is sketched out where the objective function would be a functional depending on local objectives of sub-systems $F[z_1(\widetilde{x}_1), \ldots, z_r(\widetilde{x}_r)]$, with $\widetilde{x}_i$ being a set of variables determining the state of the ith subsystem. If the controlling organ promulgates or ad-justs local parameters, optimization of the whole on some set $R(x,y)$ would be reduced to $g_i = \text{opt } [z_i(\widetilde{x}_i)]$; $(\widetilde{x}_i, \widetilde{z}_i) \in R_i \subset R$ for each subsystem. Following Sengupta-Ackoff, two methods of breaking up the objective into sub-objectives are hinted at: changing — by the centre — the para-meters of the local objectives, or changing the solution region R_i for the subsystems.

2. Smirnov's definitive version acknowledges, as a broad frame of the model, the general system theory with special reference to the Sengupta-Ackoff conceptions.[97] These conceptions appear to exercise a notable in-fluence on the present-day Soviet mathematical theory of planning.[98] (As a matter of fact they influence also socialist planning theory outside the Soviet Union; thus their inspiration is recognized by the Kornai school, in its present "anti-equilibrium" attitudes, cf. Part I. It seems that the attraction of Sengupta-Ackoff for Soviet theorists is enhanced by a numerical-algorithmic orientation which distinguishes them in general-system-theoretic literature.)

   On the Sengupta-Ackoff definition, the system is a set of activities (functions) that are connected in space and time by a set of decision-making and behaviour-evaluation practices; overall control is defined for this system as one of the constraints — along with availability of informa-tion and environmental conditions — on the decision-making of subsys-tems; it is essentially construed as a decompositional system. A premiss is multiplicity of objectives: the simultaneous pursuit of several types of outcomes is validly believed to be one of the most important and complex problems of normative analysis. (There again one detects the reflex in the present-day turn of Soviet planning theory to the problems of multi-criterial systems; cf. discussion in Pt. I.) Particular consideration in Sengupta-Ackoff is given to this multiplicity of aims as generated by de-centralization in the economy, understood as a reservation for sub-functional decision-makers the pursuance of their own aims. In Sengupta-Ackoff this is identified with what they term "goal decomposition": on this principle decentralization is thought of as organized by suitably ad-justed parameters appearing in the local objective functions; the latter in turn are conceived as "natural" — meaning appropriate to the activity con-cerned of the subsystem. It is in this that the basic difference is seen as against decentralization based on shadow prices — it is so since the possibi-lity of securing the "true optimum" is questioned for a system thus based (although the existence of shadow prices under optimum is not questioned). It would seem that the fundamental structure of the system does not differ in substance from that postulated by the theory of optimal control: the system in its general form is represented by the differential equations $dx_i/dt = f_i(x_1, \ldots, x_n, z_1 \ldots, z_m, t)$, the x's and the z' denoting respectively the state and decision variables. It is then hard to see how or in what sense "true optimum" can be secured by relying on some solution of the primal rather than the dual of the control problem, only.

In any case one cannot see the significance of the matter for Smirnov since he organizes his system by means of dynamic shadow prices obtained along the Pontryagin way.

(25) A few features of the Smirnov model — most of them related to the main focus (i.e. the focus on application in mandatory planning) deserve in our view to be re-emphasized:

Firstly, the dynamic consistency is sought by building into the system a Leontief-type dynamic input-output check; growth is thus endogenously fed by the capital-formation component, $K(t) \cdot dx/dt$; the controlling final-output component, $y(t)$, is reduced to consumption over time. The Leon-tievian consistency-preserving mechanism is "married" explicitly with that of Pontryagin.

Moreover this "marriage" could be thought to ensure steady growth. To recall, Leontief was pointing out that with assumed existence of one and only one real and positive root of the characteristic matrix of the system, it will be also the dominant root; starting with any combination of positive outputs the system would sooner or later approach the state of steady growth: all outputs would be then expanding at the equilibrium rate — the exponential rate equalling that root — while relative magnitudes of sectoral outputs would asymptotically approach those of the corresponding elements of the dominant characteristic vector . (The point was a subject of controversy in which Sargan contended that under realistic conditions a large explosive characteristic would tend to be formed; at a stage of the controversy he conceded however the workability of the Leontievian dynamic model as "a strictly planned system".)[99]

Secondly, the minimand — the "deficit" relates to the concept of social utility axiomatically taken as representing the *planner's* attitude with respect to the time-dimension in pursuance of his aim: the attitude is in fact taken as empirically established; such being the a prioristic stand, the issue started in Western literature by Arrow's famous "impossibility" theorem does not arise; nor does the Pigovian issue of the ethical basis of the time-discount. In Smirnov it is taken as "necessary" to postulate the convergence of the integral-minimand and to assume the existence of boundary condition in order to secure the minimum for the $\delta(x,y)$; this is then the justification for adopting the weight function $\lambda = \lambda(t)$ subject to $0 \leqslant \lambda(t) \leqslant 1$; $\lim_{t\to\infty} \lambda(t) = 0$ monotonically with respect to t. Characteristically for the a prioristic stand is the proposition that "naturally" the weighting must apply to ideal measurement of social needs as well as their satisfaction — as dependent on the expansion of the production potential over time.[100]

Thirdly, the plan-horizon (in strategic, very-long-run planning) is taken to be flexible — depending on the $\lambda(t)$; $T = \mu[\lambda(t)]$; thus this equality determines the horizon when $\lambda(T) = 0$ or $\lambda(T) \leqslant \epsilon$, the ϵ being as small as postulated: *a new concept of sliding horizons.*

Fourthly, the build-up of the plan programme is thought of as resting on "*feedback*" in several senses. The fixing of the plan-horizon is one. Further:

1. The optimal value and structure of the final bill of goods — the "load" in Soviet terminology — is thought as determinable in a feedback process, i.e. as a function of the economy's state, the system of integral valuation and time, that is $y^0 = y^0(x,p,t)$.

2. The valuation process is conceived of as one of a feedback type in relating the physical-term and price-term duality over time: the $x^0(t)$ determines the gross output in physical terms, its volume and composition, at optimum; on the other hand, determining the optimal control $y^0(t)$ entails determination of the vector function $p^0(t)$: this is required to fix the optimal control values $y^0(t)$. (Conceptually we would follow in

Smirnov the vector of the conjugated state, i.e. $\dot{p}(t) = \partial/\partial x \cdot Q(x,t)$; technically we are helped by the Pontryaginian physical-term and value-term duality over time $dp^0/dt = - \partial H^0/\partial x; dx/dt = \partial H^0/\partial p$.)

3. The planning procedure is thought of as informational feedback — essentially a vertical co-ordination of a centralist multi-level, hierarchically organized system. The processes of aggregation and disaggregation of variables are carried out in this procedural feedback. The Leontievian formalism of the dynamic-balance constraint provides for this the algorithmic basis.

4. It is in this feedback procedure that the peripheral and overall objective functions would be harmonized. The reasoning is partly borrowed from Pugachev:[101] suppose that some "improvement" in the system yielded an incremental dx for the input-output vector x: its significance is appraised from the point of view all subsequent results by means of the optimal prices p. Then the measurable value of the increment — measurable up to the constant multipliers determined by the system's dynamics — is pdx. The peripheral objective function is thus the functional

$$W = \int_{-\infty}^{t} pdx,$$

the t being the "current" moment. In fact what is in the feedback process focal is the stage-to-stage increment, say

$$W_2 - W_1 = \int_{t_1}^{t_2} pdx$$

taken to be effectively modelling the "local" criterion conceptualized as the p-expressed "profit" increment.

5. The parametrization of the system is treated (in the original version of the Smirnov paper) as a feedback adjustment.

[At least by way of an excursus we should note in the present context the importance — for planning purposes — of devices built into the plan-programming apparatus for ready testing of sensitivity, specifically sensitivity of the optimand, to variations in parameters.[102] Hence the vested interest of planning theory in the progress in parametric programming. In the original constructions it was designed to provide a solution to a linear problem as a function of a parameter which is introduced linearly into such problem. The natural way of sharpening the tool has been to establish conditions for securing the continuity of the set of the optimal plans — in both the primal and dual facets — and to relax the restrictive requirement of linearity. A considerable amount of work has been done in Soviet as well as Western research in the field; here too the interlinking of the two directions has revealed itself to the student (thus see as an example the Golshtein-Movshovich inquiry[103] into the continuous dependence of the set of solutions of a minimax problem on the parametric system, generalizing Mills's results[104] — for convex and semi-convex systems). By its very logic and structure the control-theoretic construct lends itself to immediate parametrization, which is yet another of its potential merits as an instrument for plan construction as validly argued by Smirnov.][105]

(26) Our story has made it evident that the Soviet mathematical theory of economic planning is a late-comer in the field of application of the Pontryagin apparatus; moreover that the process of that reception (confined as it is to our knowledge to but one major exercise [discussed above]) — is still strikingly hesitant. To be sure, in this, we have had in mind essentially what has become its principal area in Western writing — that of grand strategic planning. But since the closing years of the 1960s tentative attempts — even if very few only — have been made in Soviet literature to test its employability for the solution of suitably circumscribed particular problems. For the sake of balance in our picture we will introduce three models of this kind dealing with a specifically circumscribed problem of allocation of resources. (One more — that by Krivenkov — was already presented in a previous context).

In one of these two cases the Maximum Principle has been suggested — by Zimin and Ivanov[106] — for the treatment of allocation of resources in carrying out some prescribed "task" (within the system of network planning). The state of implementation of this task, j, at each time-point is assigned a "grade" $z^j(t)$; the task is considered completed when $z^j(t) = 1$. Thus the state of the system's performance is described by the vector $z = \{z^1, \ldots, z^N\}$; and the intensity of this performance is described by $dz^j/dt = u^j$, possibly constrained as $0 \leqslant u^j(t) \leqslant u^j$ max. Formulated as one of minimization over fixed time, the problem is stated as

$$I = \frac{1}{1+\mu} \sum \lambda_j (1 - z^j(T))^{1+\mu} \theta_-(1 - z^j(T)), \qquad (!)$$

where μ is some nonnegative number, λ_j an arbitrary number, $\theta(\xi)$ a function equal 0 or 1 for, respectively, negative and positive values of its argument; and the "−", "+" index determines this function's values at zero. (The θ is helpful in preventing overfulfilments of the task, considering the discrete character of the computer-type computation; the overfulfilment when permitted ($z^j(t) \leqslant 1$) could result in "cycling" the programme.)

Then in varying the control $u \to u + \epsilon\Delta u$, and thereby varying the phase variables and impulses $z \to z + \epsilon\Delta z$, $p \to p + \epsilon\Delta p$, we arrive at the inequality

$$\Delta I \geqslant \epsilon \sum_{j=1}^{N} p_j(T)\Delta z^j(T) - \epsilon \sum_{j=1}^{N} p_j(0)\Delta z^j(0) + \qquad (!!)$$

$$+ \epsilon \sum_{j=1}^{N} \int_0^T \left[-p_j - \sum_{i \in p_j^+} p_i u^i \prod_{\substack{t \in \Gamma_j^- \\ l \neq j}} \theta_-(z^l - 1)\delta(z^j - 1) \times \right.$$

$$\left. \times\ \theta_+(1 - z^i) \right]\Delta z^j dt + \epsilon \sum_{j=1}^{N} \int_0^T \Delta p_j[z^j -$$

$$- u^j \prod_{t \in \Gamma_j^-} \theta_-(z^l - 1)\, \theta_+(1 - z^j)]dt +$$

$$+ \epsilon \sum_{j=1}^{N} \lambda_j(1 - z^j(T))^\mu \theta_-(1 - z^j(T))\Delta z^j(T) -$$

$$- \epsilon \sum_{j=1}^{N} \int_0^T p_j \prod_{l \in \Gamma_j^-} \theta_-(z^l - 1)\theta_+(1 - z^j)\Delta u^j dt.$$

Let the impulses p_j satisfy the system of equations

$$p_j(t) = - \sum_{i \in \Gamma_j^+} p_i u^i \prod_{\substack{l \in \Gamma_i^- \\ l \neq j}} \theta_-(z^l - 1)\delta(z^j - 1)\, \theta_+(1 - z^i), \quad (!!!)$$

(where $\delta(.)$ is a Dirac delta function) and the boundary conditions

$$p_j(T) = \lambda_j(1 - z^j(T))^\mu \theta_-(1 - z_j(T)). \qquad (!!!!)$$

Since $\Delta z^j = 0$ and because of the last two conditions, the inequality above (!!) turns into the inequality

$$\Delta I > - \epsilon \sum_{j=1}^{N} \int_0^T p_j \prod_{l \in \Gamma_j^-} \theta_-(z^l - 1)\, \theta_+(1 - z^j)\Delta u^j. \qquad (!!!!!)$$

We then let the control $u(t)$ yield over the trajectory, determined by this equation, the maximum of the Pontryagin function

$$H = \sum_{j=1}^{N} p_j(t)u^j(t) \prod_{l \in \Gamma_j^-} \theta_-(z^l - 1)\, \theta_+(1 - z^j) \qquad (!!!!!!)$$

on all feasible constraints. Then the variation of the Pontryagin function on control coincides with the left-hand side of (!!!!!) and it is negative for the control value maximizing the function. It then follows from (!!!!!) that the indicated control is optimal. This establishes the sufficiency of the maximum principle for our problem.

Our next example deals with the use of the Pontryaginian principle for "testing optimality" of a plan; as we shall see its essence is the employment of the Hamiltonian multiplier as a check in the procedure of plan construction, designed by Dubovskiy et al.[107] This general procedure itself is of considerable interest in our context: it starts from a Leontievian dynamic intersectoral balance turned, by stages, into a time-optimal (terminal "targeting") development steering with capacity increment as the principal policy tool. Its form is:

$$T \to \min, \ \dot{V} = u; \ V(t) = Mu(t) + w(t) + V_0(t); \ V(0) = V_0; \ V(T) = V_1 + w_1$$

$$u(t) \geqslant 0; w(t) \geqslant 0; w_1 \geqslant 0. \qquad (!)$$

$V = u; (I - A)^{-1}B = M; (I - A)^{-1}P_0(t) = V_0(t); (I - A)^{-1}P_1 = V_1; V_1 = w_1).$
(A, B technology matrices; V, V_1, w, w_1 capacity installed, desired, surplus over desired, unused; P_0 guaranteed final uses.)

It is shown that a set of functions $u^i(t)$, $w^i(t)$ is at optimum if there exist functions $p_i(t)$ with the properties:

$$(\dot{\mathbf{p}}M + \mathbf{p})_i = 0, \text{ if } u^i > 0; \ (\dot{\mathbf{p}}M + \mathbf{p})_i \leqslant 0, \text{ if } u^i = 0;$$

$$\dot{p}_i = 0, \text{ if } w^i > 0; p_i \leqslant 0, \text{ if } w^i = 0; \qquad (!!)$$

and that the set of parameters w_1^i is at optimum if terminal values of $p_i(T)$ satisfy

$$p_i(T) = 0, \text{ if } w_1^i > 0, p_i(T) \geqslant 0, \text{ if } w_1^i = 0 \quad (i = 2, \ldots, n). \quad (!!!)$$

Then comes the application of the Maximum Principle. The Hamiltonian, constraints and equations for the impulses p of the problem (!) have the form

$$H = \mathbf{p}\mathbf{u}, M\mathbf{u} + \mathbf{w} = \mathbf{V} - \mathbf{V}_0(t), \dot{\mathbf{p}} = -\frac{\partial}{\partial \mathbf{V}} (\max_{\mathbf{u},\mathbf{w} \geqslant 0} H). \quad (!!!!)$$

Optimal u, w are found from

$$\max_{\mathbf{u},\mathbf{w} \geqslant 0} H = \max_{\mathbf{u},\mathbf{w} \geqslant 0} (\mathbf{p}\mathbf{u} + 0 . \mathbf{w}); M\mathbf{u} + \mathbf{w} = \mathbf{V} - \mathbf{V}_0(t). \quad (!!!!!)$$

The (!!!!!) belongs to a class of linear programmes whose conditions of optimality are

$$(\omega M + \mathbf{p})_i = 0, \text{ if } u^i > 0, \quad (\omega M + \mathbf{p})_i \leqslant 0, \text{ if } u^i = 0,$$

$$\omega_i = 0, \text{ if } w^i > 0, \quad \omega_i \leqslant 0, \text{ if } w^i = 0 \quad (!!!!!!)$$

The vector $\omega = (\omega_1, \ldots, \omega_n)$ in (!!!!!!) is that of a dual to (!!!!!). At the maximum point of H, determined by (!!!!!!), the value of H is

$$\max H = -\omega[\mathbf{V} - \mathbf{V}_0(t)].$$

When using (!!!!) for the derivative of the impulse vector we arrive at

$$\dot{\mathbf{p}} = -\frac{\partial}{\partial \mathbf{V}} (\max_{\mathbf{u},\mathbf{w} \geqslant 0} H) = \omega. \quad (!!!!!!!)$$

Thus the Maximum Principle conditions (!!!!!!) and (!!!!!!!) are identical with the required test of the plan's optimality.

The last of the three designs we present is by Eluashvili.[108] (We take it from an example given by him in a wider theoretical exploration: a methodology evolved by him for computation of multidimensional singular control, (evolved, as it appears, with an eye to application in economic planning).[109]

It is intended to deal with sliding regimes and generally with degenerate solutions (non-regular systems of optimal control in the sense that in their case there is no uniqueness of the optimal trajectory passing through each point of the space of states). As Eluashvili argues, algorithmically the treatment of many degenerate solutions boils down to that of regimes of singular control whose trajectories do not fill up the whole space of states. (Technically the method rests on the employment of the Poisson distribution. It employs the Hamilton apparatus, without invoking the Pontryagin principle.)

For us here of interest is the application by Eluashvili of the method to a plan problem of optimal resource allocation as formulated in Dobell and Ho:[110] allocation of output between consumption and investment leading to capacities of postulated structure: the optimal "budget" issues are being thus reduced to optimizing expenditure on capital accumulation and labour training: this is seen as ultimately determining the path of output, consumption, and employment.

The variables of the model are: $x_1(t)$ and $x_2(t)$ — resp. ratios of investment in productive assets and of population employed in production to the employable total; u_1 and u_2 — control of investment resp. into productive capital assets and training; t_i — plan horizon. The parameters-constants are $n, \delta, \mu, d, \gamma$ characterizing: the employable population's growth; personnel under training as required to sustain existing levels of output; training cost per capita; rate of discount. In these terms the problem is stated as

$$\dot{x}_1 = -(n + \delta)x_1 + x_2 f\left(\frac{x_1}{x_2}\right) u_1, \; x_1(0) = x_{10},$$

$$\dot{x}_2 = -(n + \mu)x_2 + \frac{1}{d} x_2 f\left(\frac{x_1}{x_2}\right) u_2, \; x_2(0) = x_{20},$$

$$I(u_1, u_2) = -\int_0^{t_1} (1 - u_1 - u_2)x_2 f\left(\frac{x_1}{x_2}\right) \exp(-\gamma t)dt \to \min,$$

$$U = \{(u_1, u_2): u_1 \geq 0, u_2 \geq 0, u_1 + u_2 \leq 1\},$$

$$f\left(\frac{x_1}{x_2}\right) > 0, \; f'\left(\frac{x_1}{x_2}\right) > 0, \; f''\left(\frac{x_1}{x_2}\right) < 0.$$

This problem of optimal control is then reduced to a Mayer-type functional

$$\dot{x}_0 = -(1 - u_1 - u_2)x_2 f\left(\frac{x_1}{x_2}\right) \exp(-\gamma x_2), x_0(0) = 0,$$

$$\dot{x}_1 = -(n + \delta)x_1 + x_2 f\left(\frac{x_1}{x_2}\right) u_1, \ x_1(0) = x_{10},$$

$$\dot{x}_2 = -(n + \mu)x_2 + \frac{1}{d} x_2 f\left(\frac{x_1}{x_2}\right) u_2, \ x_2(0) = x_{20},$$

$$\dot{x}_3 = 1, \ x_3(0) = t_0,$$

$$I(u_1, u_2) = x_0(t_1) \to \min.$$

For this the Hamiltonian and conjugated equations are of the form

$$H(x_0, x_1, x_2, x_3, \psi_0, \psi_1, \psi_2, \psi_3, u_1, u_2) = -\psi_0 x_2 f \exp(-\gamma x_3) -$$

$$- \psi_1(n + \delta)x_1 - \psi_2(n + \mu)x_2 + \psi_3 + x_2 f[\psi_0 \exp(-\gamma x_3) +$$

$$+ \psi_1]u_1 + x_2 f\left[\psi_0 \exp(-\gamma x_3) + \frac{1}{d} \psi_2\right]u_2,$$

$$\dot{\psi}_0 = 0,$$

$$\dot{\psi}_1 = + \psi_0 f' \exp(-\gamma x_3) + \psi_1(n + \delta) - f'[\psi_0 \exp(-\gamma x_3) + \psi_1]u_1 -$$

$$- f'\left[\psi_0 \exp(-\gamma x_3) + \frac{1}{d} \psi_2\right]u_2,$$

$$\dot{\psi}_2 = + \psi_0\left(f - f' \frac{x_1}{x_2}\right) \exp(-\gamma x_3) + \psi_2(n + \mu) -$$

$$- \left(f - f' \frac{x_1}{x_2}\right)[\psi_0 \exp(-\gamma x_3) + \psi_1]u_1 -$$

$$- \left(f - f' \frac{x_1}{x_2}\right)[\psi_0 \exp(-\gamma x_3) + \frac{1}{d} \psi_2]u_2,$$

$$\dot{\psi}_3 = -\gamma x_2 f(1 - u_1 - u_2) \exp(-\gamma x_3)\psi_0,$$

$$\psi_0(t_1) = -1, \ \psi_1(t_1) = \psi_2(t_1) = \psi_3(t_1) = 0.$$

When singular controls are computed we find the facet V_i to have the corresponding singular control

$$u_1 = (\delta - \mu)x_1/x_2 f, \ u_2 = 0,$$

determined on the set

$$\{(x,\psi): \psi_0 = -1, \psi_1 = \exp(-\gamma x_3),$$

$$\psi_3 = \exp(-\gamma x_3)[-x_2 f + (n+\delta)x_1] + \psi_2(n+\mu)x_2, n + \delta + \gamma - f' = 0,$$

$$\psi_2 < d \exp(-\gamma x_3), 0 \leqslant (\delta - \mu)x_1/x_2 f \leqslant 1\}].$$

(27) This section is concerned with the choice made as between the two rival principles of the post-classical optimal control[111] instruments in both the Western and the Soviet theories of strategic economic planning resting on turnpike-type constructs. We have seen how in Soviet literature the dominant school has evolved its Neumann-related quasi-turnpike model with the Bellman-type dynamic-programming control apparatus. A noteworthy development in Western growth theory — normative theory in substance policy-making, that is planning theory — is the parallel acceptance of the Pontryagin apparatus.

In sect. 21 we have noted in Uzawa's pioneering introduction around the mid-1960s of the Pontryagin apparatus[112] into the theory of economic growth, the focus on *the* "balanced" capital intensity such as to ensure the optimal path of advance. In the contemporary work of Kurz[113] this is given an explicit Neumannian framework. The issue of optimal investment is seen as the "fastest speed" development problem: there is then the familiar turnpike problem of reaching in minimum time the von Neumann path; and of maintaining the optimal investment policy for ever (the attaining of the Neumannian path is thought of as a maturation problem).

Very soon after the appearance of the Kurz paper the employment of the Maximum Principle in turnpike strategy received a fundamental formulation — from David Cass.[114] Here we have a generalized Dorfman-Samuelson-Solow "pure" production Neumann-derived system — generalized in the sense that intrinsic consumption value is allowed explicitly to move beyond the (logically minimized) "input" to sustain production. The basic framework is borrowed from Solow's neo-classical model, resting on three relations: an aggregate production function relating output-capital intensity (a function postulated to be under the regime of constant returns, positive marginal productivity of primary factors, diminishing marginal rate of substitution as between them); the allocation of output as between consumption and gross investment; the expansion of capital from some initial capital-labour ratio, with capital depreciating and labour expanding at some given positive rates; the strategic magnitudes — capital, output, consumption — all taken per capita. These relations provide the constraints for the plan programme's optimand, the

$$\int_0^T U(c)\, e^{-\delta t} dt$$

in the conventional notation, with the additional one requiring the value of capital — positive at the initial point — to reach at least a prescribed magnitude at the horizon point, $k(T) \geqslant k^T$.[115] It is for "characterizing" the optimum growth path in carrying out this plan-programme that the Maximum Principle is now invoked. At some point of our story we indicated what we considered to be the "intuitive" translation of the Pontryagin mathematics into planning economics. This scaffolding is here duly expanded (in particular to allow for the "depreciative" impact of time) on some of the strategic categories. To put it concisely, our control parameter becomes the gross investment ratio, nonnegative $s = z/f(k)$; the Hamiltonian multiplier, our imputed price of investment unit, is $q = q(t)$; and our Hamiltonian is formed now of two expressions: the imputed value of NNP $((\psi - q\lambda k)e^{-\delta t})$, with the imputed value of GNP, the $\psi = U(c) + qz$, the positive parameter lambda making the sum of the two rates, n and μ, growth of labour and depreciation of stocks (again the respective magnitudes taken per capita). Such are then the concepts which in Cass[116] are inserted into the Pontryaginian test — the necessary condition for the optimum path; and which indeed have become, taking it broadly, the elements of the Pontryaginian formulation, in Western writing, of the growth-control problem superimposed on the conceptual framework of the Neumann-cum-Phelps-Koopmans strategy of stationary advance. This is true also broadly of Shell's treatment, where it has found its, quite possibly definitive, crystallization, with the analysis deepened and expanded in some important directions.[117] Among the most important is the showing that the dynamic system implied by the Pontryagin conditions is *not* reducible to one of differential equations; rather we have here a system with an upper semi-continuous correspondence of the saving rate in price multiplier (s and q respectively — see the "translation" of terms in the footnote);[118] thence the system appears as one with a flow without uniqueness in Yorke's sense[119] — something Soviet applications have failed to note.

One will note in Shell the rigorous elaboration of what we describe here as the standard concepts. Thus in particular the concept of the Pontryaginian dual ($\dot{q} = (\delta + \lambda)q - \gamma f'(k)$) is elaborated to mean that the demand price of capital has to offer the putative "rentier" (under socialism, we would say, the capital owning society) a reward for waiting minus "rentals" obtained. Such interpretation can well be rationalized by the proposition that under a devolutional regime − an indirect variant of mandatory planning − the promulgated dual price has to be such as to generate "real" capital gain or its accountancy equivalent, a success indicator sufficient to induce the lower-echelon decision-makers (possibly unaware of the real-term primal in the centre's plan programme) to hold the stock of assets: the right stock in volume and composition; specifically the terminal stock induced by terminal price. The ideas have some further expansion in other variants of Western growth-theoretic employment of the Pontryaginian apparatus; in particular in the perceptive Burmeister-Dobel procedural interpretation: there it is, as it were, an encounter in a sort of planning-counter-planning, the price relations evolving in time dimension backwards, from the terminal valuation, while the quantity-term system advances from the initial endowment forward; a procedural analogue can be seen in Smirnov's reasoning within the framework of a "feedback" planning (above, sect. 27).[120]

In this fashion the Pontryagin apparatus performs in Cass-Shell the role of pinpointing the Golden-Rule capital intensity on the Neumannian ray. Or, to be more exact, the "Modified" Golden Rule, the modification consisting in that rather than being non-discriminatory as between generations it is subject to a generation's "impatience", securing the best balanced growth when allowance is made for social discount rate. Then the grand strategy instruction for the central policy-maker is promulgated to the effect that in following Pontryagin he should adhere to this Rule throughout − except for some finite period: and he is also told that the phases over which the factor-ratio would deviate from that implied in the Rule would shrink down to nil as the plan period is extended.[121] He is also instructed that when he thinks in terms of an infinite horizon − as may be thought, more "natural" to mandatory planning − he should proceed straight to the Turnpike and continue along it for ever after; patently a transversality condition in that case would not lend itself to economic interpretation as the beyond-the-horizon endowment; the technical trick would be to express the value of capital stock discounted as an improper integral with some extra-term, as in Radner when handling efficient infinite programmes (see on this the discussion in Shell;[122] see also the Arrow-Kurz[123] pointer to a "paradox" entailed in the Pontryaginian system with infinite horizon).

(28) To refer again to elementary issues the Pontryaginian control problem *is* determined, provided one knows "how to start it".[126] It is uniquely solvable if the initial conditions $(x^1(t_0), \ldots, x^n(t_0), \psi_1(t_0), \ldots, \psi_n(t_0))$ are known. To demonstrate *ad oculos* where we stand on this, it may be expositionally convenient to follow a four-step solutional procedure suggested by one of the co-authors of the Maximum Principle, Boltyanskiy. It is this: (1) find the solution $\psi(t)$ for an *arbitrary* value $\psi(t_0) = \psi_0$; emphasis here is on arbitrariness; clearly this is tractable with reference to the classical theorems on linear differential equations with constant coefficients where the roots of the characteristic equation are known; then (2) with some non-trivial solution $\psi(t)$ of the system known, find the $u(t)$ value satisfying the maximum condition: this is uniquely determinable from the maximum condition; then (3) with $u(t)$ known find the trajectory $x(t)$ starting from the given x_0: this boils down to the solution of the problem which, with $u(t)$ found forms a non-homogeneous linear system of ordinary differential equations with constant coefficients; and finally (4) find the ψ_0 for which the trajectory $x(t)$ passes through the origin.

Generally speaking the solution of the two-points boundary problem for the canonical system — in determining the values of the extremals (through the initial point) must be carried out numerically. The choice and application of the technique most suitable for the specific "situation" must to a considerable extent rely on intuitive judgment. The iterative techniques usually hinted at for the purpose are those of the steepest descent or gradient method, the Newton or Newton-Raphson (as discussed in Kantorovich-Akilov),[127] the convexity methods.

In any case a good deal of ingenuity is required to handle the questions of convergence, of error estimation and of the computer effects (truncation errors and "noises" of the computation procedure).

In particular, where the form of sequential improvement (specifically in handling a time optimal problem) does point to a reasonably fast convergence the elegant procedures (convexity methods) devised by Eaton and Neustadt,[128] may prove effective.

Boltyanskiy himself suggests another approximation procedure: resorting to a synthesizing function in which the optimal control would be sought in the form $u = v(x)$ rather than $u = u(t)$, this understood to mean that at each instant of time the solution would depend only on the space point in which the phase-point is located, and not on the motion's history; the build-up of the v would be carried out by a method roughly speaking converse to that of "shooting into the system's origin"; the idea is then of a sufficiently sensitive, nonlinear, "device" appraising the phase states, plus a re-switching "adjuster" sequentially implementing our equality

$u = v(x)$. But then in this fashion the trouble with the $u(t)$ is still there — only switched for the $\dot{x} = f(x,v(t))$ to the $v(t)$. Whether approximating the solution by "shooting" into the origin or its converse is adequate, is a question which probably cannot be answered in a general way on theoretical grounds. (As against the applicational areas of physics and engineering, to my knowledge, none of the members of the Pontryagin school has ever committed himself with respect to economics.)

Here lies the crux of the matter. The exact solution of the last step, critical problem has not been found as yet. Indeed the question arises: is it soluble at all? Appositely[129] Lyetov, when discussing the difficulties encountered in expressing the auxiliary multipliers in terms of the phase coordinates, x, remarks that the famous two-point boundary-value "stands in our way as a fortress attacked many times but as yet unconquered".

Notes

1. The experience in computation with the two principles has influenced developments in the theory in a noteworthy way. On the one hand the sequential discrete-form algorithmization agrees better with the computer's requirements: this gives an advantage to the basic discrete-term dynamic programme, evading as it does the difficulties of analytical formalism. The snag is in the recursive procedure: in general the number of points to be evaluated rises very fast with the numbers of state variables and levels (if they are respectively a and b, the number of points in state space considered would be b^a) — rapidly exceeding the computer's storage capacities. (A parallel would be the bringing in of the auxiliary variables in solving a problem under the Maximum Principle; one has to "guess" the values of the state variables and auxiliary multipliers (x^n, ψ^n) in advance; but as against the exponentially rising storage requirement entailed in growing dimensionality of the dynamic programme, here we have only a linear increase in the time of computation.)

Relief has been sought along various paths. One direction has been formulating the dynamic-programming statement of the decision-model as a Markovian or semi-Markovian process with rewards (as originated by Howard).[130]

A general direction has been to employ instruments from the theory of necessary conditions of optimality. In turn also to employ the Maximum Principle, discretized and weakened in various fashions.

[Attempts at discretizing the Maximum Principle started very soon after its enunciation by the Pontryagin school; they had been related to Rozonoer's establishing the common theoretical basis of that principle and

the Optimality Principle (see above). Algorithms for a simple nonlinear process in discrete-form of the Maximum Principle were presented at the beginning of the 1960s by Chang and Katz;[131] this has been subsequently elaborated by themselves and others. A major elaboration of the problems involved (also with an eye to application in technology) has come from Wang
and Fan),[132] and important theoretical contributions are owed to the
writings of Halkin[133] and also of Pshenichnyi.[134]]

To put this in a very broad way, as does Pshenichnyi,[135] for the class of
processes for which the control is described (in the conventional notation)
by equations of the type $\{x_{k+1} - f_k(x_k,u_k) = 0\}$, only in the systems in
which the set $f_k(x_k,u_k)$ is convex will the Maximum Principle hold (in a
form analogous to that of the principle for a system describable in ordinary
differential equations). Where the convexity is not a property of the set,
only a local Maximum Principle is obtainable.[136]

The test involved would be a "hypothesis" as formulated by Gabasov
and Kirillova.[137] It is that for a problem of optimal control of a continuous system to have a solution in the class of measured constrained controls it is necessary and sufficient that, with sufficiently small interval of
quantization (ξt), the optimal control of a discrete system approximating
a continuous system satisfies the Maximum Principle; such a generalization
has not been established.

The matter has its own kind of dialectics.[138] The common limitation of
the new weakened forms, such as that of the "local" principle, appears to
be that they do not turn into the Maximum Principle when — with the reduction of the "step" or the period of discretization — a discrete system
tends towards continuum. Thence the Gabasov-Kirillova attempt to formulate their Quasi-maximum Principle as a necessary condition of optimality
in discrete systems.

It would then be still tenable that in spite of its trouble with the computer's memory, it is the Optimality Principle that is the most universal
tool for the treatment of discrete processes.

A balanced assessment of the limitations and strength of both methods
from the computational point of view will be found in Fan and Wang.[139]
Though by now theoretically elaborated, the employment of the
Maximum Principle in processes with bounded variables is handicapped:
the formulations are very complicated when applied in numerical optimization problems; on the other hand the treatment of such processes by
means of dynamic programming is essentially handy since the optimal
decisions are determined for the allowable domain of state variables: the
constraints on the latter are then met automatically.

[The mathematical statement of the Gabasov-Kirillova Quasi-maximum Principle follows this line: In the treatment of the continuous

$$\frac{dy}{ds} = g(y,v,s), s_0 \leqslant s \leqslant s_1,$$

on a computer the *LHS* operator dy/ds is replaced by the difference $y(s + h) - y(s)/h$ where h is the quantization step in time (the smaller it is the more exact the approximation). Assume $t = s/h$, $x(t) = y(th)$, $u(t) = v(th)$, $f(x,u,t) = g(y,v,th)$, we arrive at the discrete system $x(t + 1) = x(t) + hf(x,u,t)$, which depends on the parameter h; in the general case our discrete system will have the form $x(t + 1) = f(x,u,t,h)$. (!).

We take as optimal control $u(t,h)$, $t \in T_h$; the trajectory of (!) $x(t,h)$, $t - 1 \in T_h$ is

$$\psi(t-1, h) = \frac{\partial f'(x,u,t,h)}{\partial x} \; \psi(t,h), \; \psi(t_1 - 1, h) =$$

$$= - \; \mathrm{grad} \; \varphi(x(t_1,h)),$$

$$H(x,\psi,u,t,h) = \psi' f(x,u,t,h),$$

$$\Delta_{\theta,u^*} x(t,h) = 0, \; t = t_0, \ldots, \theta,$$

$$\Delta_{\theta,u^*} x(\theta + 1, h) = \Delta_{u^*} f(x,u,\theta,h),$$

$$\Delta_{\theta,u^*} x(t + 1, h) = f(x + \Delta_{\theta,u^*} x,u,t,h) - f(x,u,t,h),$$

$$\theta + 1 \leqslant t \leqslant t_1 - 1,$$

$$\Delta_{\theta,u^*} J_h(u) = - \; \psi'(\theta,h) \; \Delta_{u^*} f(x,u,\theta,h) -$$

$$- \sum_{t=\theta+1}^{t_1-1} 0(\|\Delta_{\theta,u^*} x(t,h)\|) + 0_1 (\|\Delta_{\theta,u^*} x(t_1,h)\|),$$

$$0(\|\Delta x\|) \leqslant k \|\Delta x\|^2, 0_1 (\|\Delta x\|) \leqslant k_1 \|\Delta x\|^2.$$

Let $\epsilon, \epsilon > 0$ be some number, and introduce the set

$$U_\epsilon(\theta,h) = \left\{ u^*: 0_1 (\|\Delta_{\theta,u^*} x(t_1)\|) - \right.$$

$$- \sum_{t=\theta+1}^{t_1-1} 0(\|\Delta_{\theta,u^*} x(t)\|) \leqslant \epsilon, \; u^* \in U(\theta) \left. \right\}.$$

Then by the Gabasov-Kirillova theorem the optimal control satisfies for all $u^* \in U_\epsilon(t,h)$, $\epsilon > 0$, $t \in T_h$ the Quasi-maximum condition

$$H(x(t,h),\ \psi(t,h), u(t,h), t, h) \geqslant H(x(t,h),\ \psi(t,h), u^*, t, h) - \epsilon.]$$

2. As to technical aspects of computation for systems employing one of the two rival optimality principles, there is some Soviet literature empirically based. Thus the observations by Gnoyevskiy, Kamenskiy, and Elgolts[141] can be loosely summarized as follows.

To start with the Maximum Principle. Applying this principle leads to a boundary problem for a system of differential equations (see above); and the optimal trajectory, if it exists, will be its solution: there is, however, no general precept: each particular case calls for individual treatment and solutions have been found for a certain number of practical problems. A relatively well explored problem of considerable applicational importance is that of minimum time "optimal speed" transferring the system over shortest time period from some initial state $y(t_0) = a$ to the terminal state $y(T) = b$: in terms of linear differential equations, in conventional notation this has the form $dy/dt = A(t)y + c(t)u$, the optimal control $\bar{u}(t)$ satisfying $\bar{u}(t)$ sign $(\psi(t), c(t))$. Even here the solution meets with considerable difficulties. Notable help is offered by the Neustadt iterative procedure resting on $u(t,\gamma) = \text{sign}(\psi(t,\gamma), c(t))$ where the $\psi(t,\gamma)$ is the solution of the auxiliary system with initial value at $t = 0$. When the vector is found, then determining $\psi(t,\bar{\gamma})$ is based on the solution of the Cauchy problem for the system $\psi' = - A^*(t)\psi$, (* denotes transposed matrix), The stipulated properties of $F(\gamma)$ facilitate the procedure: at any point where grad $F(\gamma) = 0$, the $F(\gamma)$ reaches the maximum of its T equal to the shortest possible transfer time from a into the origin of the co-ordinate axis; the γ vector is of dimension n; hence the problem reduces itself to finding the extremal value of the function of n variables $F(\gamma)$.

Next the Optimality Principle. In its application, demands on the computer's memory and speed rise extremely fast with the size of the problem. In the conventional notation at the kth step the machine has to memorize the function $S(T - k\Delta t, y)$, depending that is on the n variables $(y_1,\ldots,y_n)$ and determined on a set (G_k). Usually the explicit analytical expression for the function $S(T - k\Delta t, y)$, depending that is on the n variables $(y_1, \ldots, y_n)$ store a table for $S(T - k\Delta t, y)$ values at a sufficient number of points of the G_k so as to approximate adequately the function — sufficiently exactly and smoothly. In a word it has to memorize some piecewise-continuous

r-dimensional vectoral function $u(\tau, T - k\Delta t, y)$ which depends on para-meters $(y_1, \ldots y_n)$ and is computed for k values of the argument τ: $T - \Delta t, \ldots, T - k\Delta t$.

As noted by Gabasov-Kirillova,[142] most of the modifications of the dynamic-programming method over the past decade or so have been de-signed with an eye to the easing of computation (taking advantage of structural properties, Lagrangean multipliers, extrapolation as in Bellman-Dreyfus); each of these methods "of struggling with 'the curse of dimen-sions' " offers an approximation to numerical solution and in a sense mitigates the requirements to the memory of the machine.

The overall conclusion is rather relativistic. Both Principles are mathematically and in economic application equivalent but the employ-ment of one of them rather than another must depend on specific charac-teristics of the problem. We fully share Beckmann's view that where the kit contains alternative tools it is the matter of the user's "art" to select the one most suitable for the purpose.[143]

(29) In summarizing our remarks it is legitimate to say that the theory of optimal control with its ramifications, young as it is, is by now one of the main pivots of Soviet formalized planning thought; this is true in particular of the *"Problematik"* of the large-scale system on which it increasingly centres. In a sense it epitomizes the mathematical revolution — the theme of our discussion.

As stock-taking is attempted certain lines of progress appear particularly impressive. The advance in what becomes termed "programmed control" was given special emphasis when the state and prespectives of the art were reported, by Lyetov, at the grand Soviet 1971 Symposium.[144] But at the same time the lags in certain directions came to the fore; thus the theory of feedback laws, specifically of their synthesis (as against the analysis) was argued to be an underdeveloped area in spite of its crucial relevance for the practice (see, however, n. 101 to this chapter). Seen from this angle the synthesis is a matter of equal "topicality" with that of programmed control, system analysis being the supplier of concepts and tools for the investigation of large-scale complex systems. From the same angle, the angle of the "man-machine dialogue" — mathematical simulation of a large-scale system is seen as a domain where intensive exploratory work is most acutely required, and — as quite a few optimists insist — is also prom-ising. (The imitation rests on multi-block models, some of the blocks being allocated to machines, others to humans; the latter would include in particular blocks concerned with logic and control). The approach is heuristic par excellence. Indeed the present day vogue in Soviet formalized planning thought is heuristics, concerned as it is with the investigation of processes of creative human thought and the search for ways of effective modelling of such thought with the computer's help.[145] (Parenthetically, its development as a fully-fledged discipline is dependent on evolving a new language of formalization (see Note), such as would permit the system of automated control to build up models of situations through exchange of information between the environment and the system, to analyse such models and to determine sequences of actions, corresponding to the environment and the system's structure and leading to a solution of the problem.)[146]

One will detect a fundamentally similar motivation in ideas on the need for advance in the theory of algorithmization as a fully fledged discipline of "optimization of the optimizing":[147] organizing with scientific rigour what hitherto has had to be fed largely by inventiveness relying on experience, common sense, and intuition. As it has been put by one of the distinguished Soviet pioneers in the field:[148] ". . . the soil is by now fully mature . . . for the mathematical treatment of essential tasks of control evolved by life itself". The empirical bias is not surprising in a country where the progress in the field is felt to be of relevance for the efficient working of the economic mechanism.

Note

In a retrospective look over the past decade and a half or so, the question arises as to why in an era of "computational explosion" the pace of advance in the man-machine dialogue (mentioned in our last paragraph) has been more modest than it would seem legitimate to expect. From the "camp" of the machine we hear about the underdevelopment of the mathematical support. *Audiatur et altera pars*; from the other "camp" we have now Kantorovich's most recent diagnosis − specifically of the principal causes of difficulties encountered in the large-scale control problems of optimal planning. His emphasis is on the *universality* of machines and computer languages: universality, as often as not, thought of as a self-evident virtue yet, in his appraisal, a characteristic which severely complicates the algorithmic descriptions and programmes, reduces their flexibility and adjustability for the necessary variations, combinatorial operations, diversified uses of information. Hence the therapeutical recommendation: to *particularize* both machines and languages so as to suit the large-scale economic problems at hand. Specifically the characteristics of the problems which should be allowed for in the first place are: (a) the presence of information "blocks", organized in a particular fashion and, as a rule, employed in some particular way, and (b) the fact that the mathematical algorithms in these problems consist largely in the application to these "blocks" of some group operations.[149]

Notes

1. Luigi Amoroso, *Le leggi dell'economia politica* (Turin, 1961).
2. M. J. P. Magill, *On a general economic theory of motion* (New York, 1970).
3. W. R. Hamilton, "On a general method in dynamics" and "Second essay on a general method in dynamics" in Royal Soc., *Phylos. Trans.*, respectively of 1834 and 1835 (reprinted in the *Mathematical papers of Sir William Rowan Hamilton*, ii (Cambridge, 1940).
4. Magill validly credits Samuelson and Solow with the first reference in economic writing to the Hamilton theory of analytical mechanics: although the context was essentially computational, the possibility of lending to the Hamiltonian momenta a price interpretation was alluded. Cf. R. M. Solow/ P. A. Samuelson, "A complete capital model Involving heterogeneous capital goods", *Q. J. Econ.*, 1956.
5. In the familiar notation the principle says that the motion's trajectory $x(t)$ of the economic system with an objective function $U(t, x, \dot{x})$ over $[o, T]$ is such that the present value of the system $P(x) = \int U(x, x, t)dt$ attains a stationary value; then the equation of motion is the Euler-type (Magill, equation $U_{x_i} - d/dt \, U_{\dot{x}_i} = 0$, op. cit., p. 34).
6. However, I find in Einstein the point that the sending of a signal *is*, in the sense of theormodynamics, an irreversible process—one connected with the growth of entropy; this is set against the tenet that, according to our present knowledge, all elementary processes are reversible (Albert Einstein, "Remarks on the essays appearing in the collective volume", in P. A. Schlipp, *Albert Einstein—Philosopher scientist*, Evanston, III, 1949).
7. B. I. Plyukhin, "K tsepnoy modeli rasshirennogo vosproizvodstva", in *Matematicheskiy analiz rasshirennogo vosproizvodstva* (Moscow, 1962).
8. V. A. Trapeznikov, *Avt. i tel.*, 4 (1971).
9. Giuseppe Palomba, "Entropie, information et sintropie des systèmes économiques", *Metroeconomica*, Apr. 1960.
10. S. M. Vishnyev, *Ekonomicheskiye parametry.*
11. B. S. Razumikhin, "Mechanical model and method of solution of the resources distribution problem", in *Proc. 3rd IFAC Congress*, (London, 1966) paper 7D.
12. Cf. in particular R. G. D. Allen, *Mathematical economics* (London, 1956).
    Sir Roy Allen in fact foresaw as early as the mid-1950s that the economist will increasingly have to follow the engineer's methods and experience: that he will have to do so as economic models must become increasingly complex and contain a growing empirical content: that this will correspond to the growing need for moving from the general to the particular.
    In *perspective* this appears as a remarkably correct prediction; as we see this at present, there is a growingly intensified *parallel* direction of analysis, in particular in the theory of economic planning: from the general to the particular and from the particular to the general; the latter is observable in the assimilation of the systems theory.
    A recent simple, elegant and illuminating recasting from the engineering

control-language of a dynamic model of an open-loop controlled macro-economic system—specifically a Keynesian-type economy and self-regulatory economy—will be found in Lawrence Markus's "Dynamic Keynesian economic system", in *Mathematical systems theories and economics*, i.

13. R. Stone, *Our unstable economy: can planning succeed?* (London, 1966), pp. 5, 7.

14. A. Tustin, *The mechanism of economic systems* (London, 1953).

15. G. C. Newton, "Compensation of feedback control system subject to saturation", *J. Franklin Inst.*, 1952.

16. P. Whittle, *Prediction and regulation by linear least-square methods* (London, 1963), esp. ch. 10.

17. C. Holt et al., *Planning, production inventories and work-force* (1960).

18. H. A. Simon, "Dynamic programming under uncertainty with a quadratic criterion function", *Econometrica*, 1956; H. Theil, *Economic forecasts and policy* (Amsterdam, 1958), esp. ch. 8.

19. G. C. Chow, *On the optimal control of linear economic systems*, IBM Research, Febr. 1969, presented at Eur. Econometric Conf., Brussels, 1969.

    To this broad class belongs Livesey's interesting exercise in applying a control-optimization routine to a nonlinear model fitted to the data of the British economy. The architecture of the model is designed so that it would yield control strategies and that it would explain the behaviour of variables-candidates for the role of controls, in particular balance of trade, price inflation, unemployment, consumption per cap. (cf. D. Livesey, *The modelling and control of the UK economy*, submitted to the 2nd World Econometric Congress, 1970).

20. Yu. Shreider, "Zadacha dinamicheskogo planirovanya i avtomaty", in *Problemy kibernetiki*, (Moscow, 1961), vol. v.

21. B. N. Mikhalevskiy, "Modeli ekonomichskogo regulirovanya" in Fedorenko, *Matematika i kibernetika v ekonomike.*

22. Oskar Lange, *Wstep do cybernetyki ekonomicznej* (Warsaw, 1965); (Engl. trans. *Introduction to economic cybernetics* (London, 1970).

23. D^r indicates r-fold differentiation or integration when n resp. $r > 0$ and $r < 0$; the $E^{\theta s}$ indicates a shift by θ_S—forward or backward when respectively $\theta_S > 0$ and $\theta_S < 0$; k, l, m denote the numbers of integrations, differentiations and leads.

24. Zauberman, "Preface" to *Introduction to economic cybernetics*

25. V. A. Polterovich, *EMM*, 2 (1968).

26. R. Kulikowski, *EMM*, 1 (1968); cf. also the same in *Archiwum aut. i tel.*, 3 (1966) & 4 (1967)

27. For some recent developments in the field of "incorrectly set" problems and their empirical applicability see the work by Latté and Lion, in Engl. trans. ed. by R. Bellman (*The method of quasi-reversibility—application to partial differential equations,* 1963). Although the work is addressed to an engineer, it is of technical interest, from the point of view of control-theoretic method, to the economic planner as well.

28. E. G. Belaga/V. F. Kromer, *EMM*, 3 (1968).

29. A. N. Tikhovov, *Zhurnal vychislitelnoy mat. i matematicheskoy fiziki,* 6/1 (1966). For a hint at the economic interpretation see also N. I Arbuzova et al., *EMM*, 3 (1969).

30. A. N. Tikhonov, op. cit.

31. cf. *Kibernetika*, 2/2 (1966).

32. D. Kendrick/L. Taylor, "Numerical solution of nonlinear planning models", *Econometrica*, May 1970.

33. The sensitivity problem has been traced as due the adjointness of the state differential equations (linearized about the optimal path) and the costate differential equations.

34. J. Tinbergen, "Maximization of utility over time", *Econometrica*, Apr. 1960; S. Chakravarty, "The existence of an optimum savings program", ibid., Oct. 1962.

35. T. Krishna Kumar, "The Existence of an optimal economic policy", ibid., OCt. 1969.

36. S. Karlin, op. cit., ii. 210.

37. E. M. Yaari, "On the existence of an optimal plan in a continuous time allocation process", *Econometrica*, Oct. 1964.

38. cf. also for related theorem E. E. Lee/L. Markus, "Optimal control for non-linear processes", *Archive for Rational Mechanics & Analysis*, 1 (1961) and reference in Kumar, op. cit., p. 605–2.

39. R. E. Bellman/R. S. Lehman, *Studies in bottleneck problems in production processes* (RAND Corp. paper 492, 1954); Bellman, *Dynamic programming* (Princeton, 1957).

40. Bellman/Dreyfus, op. cit. See also S. Dreyfus, "Dynamic programming and the calculus of variations" in *J. of Math. Anal. Applications*, 1960.

41. R. Bellman, "Dynamic programming and mathematical economics", in A. Prekopa, op. cit.; and discussion on pp. 241ff. For fundamental background see Bellman's *Dynamic programming*; Bellman/Dreyfus op. cit.; Bellman, *Adaptive control processes*, and his "On the reduction of dimensionality for classes of dynamic programming", *J. Maths Anal. & Applied.* 1961.

42. A rich study of the potentialities of dynamic programming in economic decision-making, in particular—as an alternative to both methods—is M. Beckmann's *Dynamic programming of economic decisions* (Berlin, 1968). A very imaginative application of the Bellmanian principle to maximization of consumption utility with reference to '*wealth*' will be found in Beckmann's recent paper. There utility is conditional on the present wealth, y, and the decision horizon n. If consumption is chosen at x, the next year's wealth is $(1 + i) (y - x)$. The Principle of Optimality has then the form:

$$v_n(y) = \max_{oxy} [u(x) + \rho v_{n-1}((1 + i) (y - x))]$$

(*i* and ρ are, respectively, rate of interest and of discount) *Optimal consumption plan; a dynamic programming approach*; presented at the Univ. of Namur, 1971; referred to with author's kind permission).

43. cf. ch. 7 in Bellman/Dreyfus, op. cit. We have there as the optimand-output function $f_N(c_1, c_2) = $ maximum $\{ z_a + f_{N-1} (a_2 z_s, c_2 + a_3 z_m)\}$ for $N = 2, \ldots$; the region of materials and capacities $z_a + z_s + z_m \geqslant c_1$, $z_a \leqslant a_1 c_1$, $z_s \leqslant$ (the c_1, c_2 are, respectively, initial stocks of materials and capacities) cf. also in the context Bellman, "Bottleneck problems, functional equations and dynamic programming", *Econometrica*, 4 (1954).

44. cf. Zauberman, "Soviet work related to the von Neumann model and turnpike theories and some ramifications—a critical review", in G. Bruckmann/W. Weber, eds., *Contributions to the von Neumann growth Model* (1971) (presented at the von Neumann Seminar in the Inst. for Advanced Studies). cf. also Zauber-mann's joint with G. Morton- "Von Neumann's model and Soviet long-term (perspective) planning", *Kyklos*, 1 (1969).

45. cf. I. V. Romanovskiy *Doklady*, 159/6 (1964). As it appears, some of the results have been achieved independently of those of Koopman's inquiry on related matters in *Q. J. Econ.* 3 (1964).
46. *Doklady*, 165/4 (1965).
47. V. L. Makarov, *Sibirskiy Mat. Zhurnal*, 4 (1966).
48. The same, *Doklady*, 176/5 (1967).
49. W. F. Tyndal's discussion in *J. Industr. & Applied Maths.* 3 (1965).
50. V. L. Makarov, *EMM*, 4 (1969).
51. *Optimizatsya*, 2/19 (1971).
52. Contribution to *Proc.* Symposium on national modelling, Novosibirsk, 1970.
53. A. M. Rubinov/K. Sh. Shapiyev, *Opt. plan.* 10 (1968); A. Zh. Zhafyarov, ibid., 19 (1971).
54. A. M. Rubinov, ibid., 14 (1969). The author relies largely on the properties of superlinear functionals and point-set mappings defined on a cone.
55. A. Zh. Zhafyarov, *Optimizatsya*, 2/19 (1971).
56. V. L. Makarov/A. M. Rubinov, *Uspekhi matematicheskikh nauk*, 25/5 (1970).
57. Romanovskiy, *Teorya veroyatnostey i yeye primenenye*, 1 (1965).
58. *Kibernetika*, 3 (1967); the same, *Opt. plan.*, 8 (1967).
59. D. Blackwell, "Discrete dynamic programming", *Ann. Maths. & Statist.* 33/2 (1962).
60. References to Makarov, *Sibirskiy Mat. Zhurnal*, 1962; T. C. Koopmans, "On the concept of optimal growth", Cowles Foundation Discussion Paper 163, and D. Gale, "Optimal programs for multisector economy with infinite time horizon", Brown Univ. *Technical Report*, no. 1 (1965).
61. L. V. Kantorovich/V. L. Makarov "Optimalnyie modeli perspektivnogo planirovanya" in Nemchinov *Primenenye matematiki . . .*, iii.
62. On attempts to solve the matrix-system problem (A, B matrices of input and output) see in particular the generalizing formulation by G. L. Thompson/R. L. Weil, "Von Neumann model solutions are generalized eigenvalues of matrix game kernels" *Econometrica*, July 1971. For experimenting in planning see i.a. M. J. Hamburger et al., "Computing results from the generalized von Neumann model and using them for planning", *Jahrbuch der Wirtschaft Osteuropas*, 1970.
63. Kantorovich/Makarov, in Nemchinov, op. cit., Kantorovich/Romanovskiy, "Matematicheskoye programmirovanye", in Fedorenko *Matematika i kibernetika v ekonomike.*
64. L. V. Kantorovich/V. L. Makarov, *Opt. plan.* 8 (1968).
65. These constraints are

1. $$S = \sum_{\gamma = 1}^{\gamma = i} n\gamma$$

$$\sum_{\gamma = j - 1} x_t^s \geqslant \sum_{S = 1}^{S = N} a_{ij}^s \, x_t^s + \sum_{S = N+1}^{S = 2N} k_t^s \, c_{ij}^s + c_j^t$$

$$p = \sum_{\gamma = 1} n_\gamma + 1 \quad i, j = 1, \ldots, n:$$

2. $$\sum_{s = 1}^{N} w^s x_t^s \leqslant W_t;$$

3. $f^s x^s_t \leqslant \mathscr{F}^s_{t-1}$;

4. $\mathscr{F}^s_t = f^s q^s x^s_t + k^s_t$

66. See above p. 400.
67. Numerical exercises have been made by V. D. Marshak (*Opt. plan.* 8 (1968)), with objective function formed of stocks at some time-reduced valuation plus ccnsumption with posited structure discounted on some principle. An algorithm for numerical treatment of the Kantorovich-Makarov system has been designed by V. F. Fefelov (*Optimizatsya*, 6 (1972)). It works with "aggregates" describing the functioning of initially existing capacities, completion of capacities in the process of gestation, the build-up of new capacities, consumption within the system.
68. *Doklady*, 176/5 (1967).
69. W. F. Tyndall, "A duality theorem for a class of continuous linear programming problems. (Before methodology of the problem was discussed also by hypotheses Tyndall has proved an analogue of the fundamental duality theorem of linear programming for "bottleneck" (continuous linear programming) problems. (Before methodology of the problem was discussed also by Wolfe, Lehman, and Koopmans.) Moreover in Tyndall the duality theorem, as proved, has been applied to a Leontief dynamic model of rpoduction. Cf. also n. 39 p. above.
70. Yu. P. Krivenkov, *Differentsyalnyie uravnenya*, 4/5 (1968); see also his "Matematicheskaya model proizvodstva dlya dinamicheskogo programmirovanya", in *Doklady I Vsesouyznoy konferentsyi po ekonomicheskoy kibernetike* (Moscow, 1966).
71. Krivenkov's "approximate" differential model is of the form

$$\frac{dx_1}{dt} = (\beta - 1) u_1 - u_2 - u_3, \qquad \frac{dx_2}{dt} = au_2,$$

$$A(\beta) ii_1 + \tau B^0(\beta)u_2 + \tau B^0(\beta) u_3 \leqslant x_1(l),$$

$$\tau\beta u_1 + \tau \frac{a}{2} u_2 \leqslant x_2,$$

where $A(\beta) = (\beta - 1)/\log \beta$ and the operator $B^0(\beta) = (\beta\log - \beta + 1)/(\beta - 1) \log \beta$.
72. Yu. P. Krivenkov, *Asimptoticheskiye i vychislitelnyie voprosy lineynogo dinamicheskogo programmirovanya* (Moscow, 1969).
73. D. A. Arzamastsev, *EMM*, 6 (1969).
74. J. H. Westcott, "An introduction to adaptive control", in Westcott, op. cit.
75. cf. A. A. Pervozvanskiy, in *Avt. i tel.*, 8 (1971); the basic idea of the approximated optimization for a system, described in dynamic-programming terms, was contained in a paper submitted by him at the Warsaw 1969 IFAC Congress.
76. The reliance on the regulative role of inventories would call for the application of some "insuring" device such as based on the classical Modigliani-Hahn approach (or a generalization such as has been formulated by G. D. Eppen/F. J. Gould, "A Lagrangian application to production models", *Operations Research*, 16/4 (1968). Their algorithm serve to discover production policy

minimizing the sum of production, holding, and penalty costs subject to capacity constraints and nonnegativity of inventories).

77. cf. G. P. Ivanova, "Matematicheskaya teoriya optimalnykh protsessov", in Fedorenko, *Matematika i kibernetika v ekonomike.*

78. As observed by R. T. Rockafellar ("Convex functions and duality in optimization problems and dynamics" in Kuhn/Szegö, *Mathematical systems theory*) in Hamilton's famous system the vector variable *p* is directly related to duality, for in the Hamiltonian equation of the planetary motion *H* is total energy and the *x* and *p* are respectively the position and the momentum.

79. D. Gale, "Nonlinear duality and qualitative properties of optimal growth", NATO Summer School 1969.

80. R. Armand, "Interpretation économique du principe du maximum de Pontriagin", *Metra*, 3 (1968).

81. Price, taken, *sensu largo* of scarce resources including time. An interesting exercise (in the search of optimal investment policy) by Dobell and Ho is a good demonstration of how the Lagrangian multiplier in its varying "roles" reveals itself as the implicit unit price—in terms of consumption good at time zero—for the consumption good, the physical capital asset and the trained labourer, all "delivered" at a given time point. (A. R. Dobell/Y. C. Ho, "Optimal investment policy" in Kuhn/Szegö, *Mathematical systems theory*.)

82. For the analogy in the treatment of the aggregation problem see the paper V. M. Polterovich, *EMM*, 6 (1969).

83. M. Albouy, *Interpretation économique du principe du maximum*, presented at the Eur. Econometric Conf., Brussels, 1969.

84. R. Pallu de la Barrière, "On the cost of constraints in dynamic optimization", in Balakrishnan/Neustadt, *Mathematical theory of control.* Of interest in the French writing is also the use of the Pontryagin apparatus for the "arbitrage" between time of work and leisure—in national planning (measuring marginal utilities of work in terms of consumption and leisure).cf. D. Lacaze/ D. Badellon, *Un modèle de croissance à deux variables de commande: arbirage entre loisir et consommation*, presented to the 2nd World Econometric Conf. 1970.

The Lacaze-Badellon approach is close to that of Elizabeth S. Chase ("Leisure and consumption", in Shell, *Essays on theory of optimal economic growth*.) Hers is a Ramseyan-type system with a modified "golden" regime; the essay has a discussion of differences between the dynamic and static determination of the labour supply. The utility index adopted depends on leisure, or fraction of population outside labour force, as well as per capita consumption.

85. In Kuhn/Szegö, *Math. systems theory*, i.

86. Ibid., pp 134ff.

87. H. Uzawa, in *Int. Econ. R.*, Jan. 1965; Sengupta, *Economica*, 1964.

88. In Kuhn/Szegö, *Math. systems theory*, p. 269.

89. R. Dorfman, "An economic interpretation of optimal control theory", *Amer. Econ. R.*, Dec. 1969.

90. R. M. Solow, op. cit.

91. In *Uspekhi mat. nauk*, 25/5 (1970).

92. Arrow/Kurz, op. cit., p. 73.

93. A. D. Smirnov, "Problems of constructing an optimal interbranch model of socialist reproduction", in A. P. Carter/A. Brody, *Contributions to input-output analysis*, 1 (Amsterdam, 1970) Proc. of Geneva 1968 Conf.)

94. The same, "Teoreticheskiye voprosy postroyenya sistemy optimalnogo funktsyonirovanya narodnogo khoziaystava", ch. 13 Fedorenko, ed., *Ekonomiko-matematicheskiye modeli* (Moscow, 1969).

95. G. P Ivanova, "Matematicheskaya teorya optimalnykh protesessov",
     in Fedorenko, *Matematika i kibernetika v ekonomike.*
96. In his attempt to relate the Pontryagin system and Leontief dynamic analysis
     Brody formulates the "steering" of his system by introducing a piece-wise
     smooth, bounded non-positive slack vector, y. His problem is then how to
     determine the time-path of this vector subject to equality of the form $B\dot{x} =$
     $(1 - A)x + y$. The dual-price vector then has the form $\dot{p}B = p(1 - A)$. The
     Hamiltonian is then formed in a way similar to that of Smirnov and
     eventually the problem appears as that of finding the time path of y such
     as to minimize

     $$\int_0^T F(p, x, y) - pB\dot{x} \, dt.$$

     cf. A. Brody, "Optimal and time optimal path of the economy", in Carter/
     Brody, op. cit. Cf. also references to Brody's reasoning in Part I.
97. S. Sengupta/R. L. Ackoff, "Systems theory from an operations research point
     of view", in *General systems*, 10 (1965).
98. In turn this work seems to be strongly influenced by Simonian ideas, in
     particular H. Simon's "On the application of servomechanism theory in the
     study of production processes", *Econometrica*, 1952.
99. cf. W. Leontief, "Lags and stability of dynamic systems" *Econometrica*,
     Oct. 1961 and "Rejoinder", ibid.; J. D. Sargan, "The instability of the
     Leontief dynamic model, ibid., July 1958 and "Rejoinder", Oct. 1961; and
     discussion in Zauberman, "Soviet attempts to dynamize interindustry analysis",
     Economia internazionale, May 1968.
100. Characteristically Volkonskiy sees in optimality criterion or objective function—
     in the theory of optimal economic planning—the reflection of the society's
     comparative preference with respect to the plan's alternative variants: the
     concept of "society" is not defined in the context. (V. A. Volkonskiy, "Polez-
     nost", in Fedorenko, *Matematika i kibernetika.*)
101. See his *Optimizatsya planirovanya.*
     In passing we may note here that most recent Soviet writing in the field of
     optimal control shows a certain "reaction" against exaggerated hopes staked on
     feedback constructs. Some writers have argued that feedback controls have
     proved difficult to model, and still more so in implementing; and above all
     that hopes put on mathematical properties of controls of the feedback type,
     especially with regard to random and not accounted for disturbances have
     proved unwarranted (cf. e.g. Gabasov/Kirillova, *Avt. i tel.*, 2 (1966), p. 51).
102. The concept of a system's sensitivity in this respect has been introduced into
     literature, as it appears, first by P. Dorato, ("On sensitivity in optimal control
     systems", *IEE Trans. Automat. Control.* 3 (1963)). His sensitivity vector
     measures the difference of the system's quality as against the computationally
     optimal, I, resulting from small variations in the parameter x; i.e.
     $\Delta I = I(u_0, x_0) - I(u_0, x)$, or a scalar product $\Delta I \, xdl \approx (\partial I/\partial x, x - x_0)$. (The
     x_0 is computationally optimal; the $\partial I/\partial x$ with its elements $\partial I/\partial x_i$ is the vector
     of sensitivity; $(x - x_0)$ is a column vector with components $\delta \, x_i = x_i - x_0$; u_0
     is optimal control with x_0.
     A similar line is followed in Soviet literature by K. B. Norkin/Yu. E.
     Sagalov *Avt. i tel.*, 4 (1971) in measuring the exactness of parameter determin-
     ation.
     $I(u, x) - I(u_i, x_i) = (\partial I \mid \partial x \mid u_0 x_0, x - x_i)$ and they adopt for the sensitivity
     measure of the optimal system the matrix of second derivatives of the adopted
     criterion.

        Cf. in the context also T. L. Saaty, "Coefficient perturbation of a constrained extremum", *Operations Research*, 7 (1959) where the parameter is introduced nonlinearly; R. L. Graves, "Parametric linear programming", in Graves/Wolfe, *Recent advances in mathematical programming.*

103.   cf. E. G. Golshtein/S. M. Movshovich, *EMM*, 6 (1968).

104.   H. D. Mills, "Marginal values of matrix games and linear programs", in H. W. Kuhn/A. W. Tucker, op. cit.

105.   Smirnov, op. cit.

106.   I. N. Zimin/Yu. I. Ivanov, *Zhurnal vychislitelnoy mat. i matematicheskoy fiziki*, May-June 1967.

107.   A. V. Dubovskiy et. al., *Avt. i. tel.*, 8 (1972).

108.   M. G. Eluashvili, *Avt. i. tel.*, 1 & 4 (1972).

109.   The concept of singular control originated in Rozenoer's writings of the turn of the 1950s. It refers to controls along which the Maximum Principle would not make it possible uniquely to eliminate, from the problem's formulation, the control parameters and thus to handle the task of extremization of a closed system of differential equations with respect to its variables.

110.   A. R. Dobell/Y. C. Ho, "Optimal investment policy: an example of a control problem in economic theory", *IEEE Trans. Automatic Control*, AC-12/1 (1967).

111.   The relative merits of the two nonclassical Principles for the purpose are discussed in Zauberman, "A Choice of Control for Turnpike" to appear in the Transactions of the *1972 Warsaw Symposium on Mathematical Methods in Economics.*

112.   H. Uzawa, *Int. Econ. R.* May 1964.

113.   M. Kurz, "Optimal paths of capital accumulation under minimum time objective", *Econometrica*, Jan. 1965.

114.   D. Cass, "Optimum growth in an aggregative model of capital accumulation" *R. Econ. Stud.*, July 1965; and the same, "Optimum growth in an aggregative model of capital accumulation: a turnpike theorem", *Econometrica*, Oct. 1966.

115.   R. M. Solow, "A contribution to the theory of economic growth", *Q. J. Econ.* 1965, in particular its section "Model of long-run growth".

116.   *Econometrica*, Oct. 1966, pp. 834ff.

117.   K. Shell, "Applications of Pontryagin's maximum principle to economics" in Kuhn/Szego, *Mathematical systems theory* (cf. also his "Optimal programs of captial accumulation for an economy in which there is exogenous technical change", in Shell, *Essays in the theory of optimal economic growth.*

118.   In applying the Pontryagin procedure we have in Shell:

the Hamiltonian —

$$He^{\delta t} \equiv (1 - s) f(k) + q[sf(k) - \lambda k]$$

the Hamiltonian multiplier — $q(t)e^{-\partial t}$; the optimality condition for plan-programme $(k(t), s(t)$); the existence of a continuous $q(t)$ such that

$$\dot{k} = sf(k) - \lambda k.$$

$$\dot{q} = (\delta + \lambda)q - [1 - s + qs]f^1(k).$$

s maximizing $[1 - s + qs]$ subject to $s \epsilon [0, 1]$;

Translation into the Pontryagin terms:

Pontryagin's	Shell's
x	k
u	s
t	t
t_0	o
t_1	T
U	$[0, 1]$
$f^0(x, u, t)$	$(1 - s)f(k)c^{-\delta t}$
$f(x, u, t)$	$sf(k) - \lambda k$
ψ_0	1
$\psi(t)$	$q(t)e^{-\delta t}$

Instantaneous maximization of H
with respect to $s \in [0, 1]$ –

$$s \in \begin{array}{c} \max \\ [0, 1] \end{array} [1 - s + qs] = \max$$

$$(1, q) \equiv \gamma(q);$$

transversality condition:

$$q(T)e^{-\delta T}[k(T) - k_T] = 0,$$

$$q(T)e^{-\delta T} > 0.$$

Notation:

$f(k(t), P(t)) = y$ – production function, twice continuously differentiable;
k – capital stock;
P – labour;
s – fraction of output saved – the planner's measurable control;
– all the above are values per worker;
$0 < T < \sim$ planning interval, overtime – t;
δ – the planner's discount rate ("subjective")
$\lambda = n + \mu$ – growth rate of the labour force + the "decay rate" of capital stock;
$\delta, \lambda, K_0, K_T$ – given, positive, scalar.

119. cf. James Yorke, "Spaces of solution" in Kuhn/Szegö, *Math. systems theory,* esp. pp. 390ff.

120. The Burmeister-Dobell formulation is didactically interesting i.a. because it starts from the formulation of the planned optimal growth problem in canonical variational form from which it is being restated à la Pontryagin. Thus (in the conventional symbolism) first the Euler-Lagrange equation and then the Legendre transformation is set out. In the exercise as it were an H inserts itself, the optimal policy assuming the form

$$\overline{H} = U[F(K) - \dot{K}(t, K, q) - \delta K] \exp(-\gamma t) + q\dot{K}(t, K, q)$$

$$\dot{K} = \frac{\partial \overline{H}}{\partial q}$$

$$\dot{q} = -\frac{\partial \overline{H}}{\partial K} = -U'[F(K) - \dot{K} - \delta K] \exp(-\gamma t)[F'(K) - \delta] \text{ the gamma denoting}$$

the discount factor.

Then the logic of the "jump" into the Pontryagin control system is effectively demonstrated.

(Incidentally it is the tenet of the authors that the Pontryagin school has enunciated a new and more powerful principle of an "invisible hand". The proposition is discussed in our Part I.)

Burmeister/Dobell, *Mathematical theories of economic growth,* ch. 11.

121. Sheil, in Kuhn/Szegö, *Math. systems theory,* Lecture III.

122. Ibid., p. 251.

123. Arrow/Kurz (op. cit., pp. 70ff.) argue that the Pontryagin solution is optimal where an optimal solution exists which is not guaranteed, and that the

problem is in substance the same as that known as the "paradox of growth stocks", a paradox relating to a distant future, thus to the way magnitudes behave as the horizon tends toward infinity (hence the relevance of observing, in the motion, the relation of the two asymptotic rates – of interest and of growth).

126. Ibid., p. 107.
127. V. G. Boltyanskiy, *Matematicheskiye metody . . .* , Kantorovich/Akilov, op. cit., cf. Kalman *et al.*, *Topics in math. system theory.*
128. J. H. Eaton, "An iterative solution to time-optimal control", *J. Math. Analysis & Application*, 1962 pp. 329ff; L. W. Neustadt, "Synthesizing time-optimal control systems", ibid, 1960.
129. Lurye/Proskuryakov, op. cit., p. 407.
130. See on this in particular R. A. Howard, op. cit., pp. 959ff.
131. S. L. Chang, "Digitized maximum principle", *Proc.* IRE, Dec. 1960; S. Katz, "A Discrete version of Pontryagin's maximum principle", *J. Electronics & Control*, 1962.
132. L. T. Fan/C. S. Wang, *The discrete maximum principle;* see in particular ch. 3 on the discrete Maximum Principle for simple feedback processes and ch. 7 on the generalized discrete Maximum Principle; see also the same, "A discrete version of Pontryagin's maximum principle "*Operations Research*, 15/1 (1967); the paper introduces the so-called weak form of the basic algorithm; it also presents its simplified derivation.
133. H. Halkin, "A maximum principle of the Pontryagin type for the system described by nonlinear difference equations", *SIAM J.* 4/1 (1966); cf. also his joint paper with I. Holtzman, "Directional convexity and the maximum principle for discrete systems", ibid. 4/2 (1966).
134. B. N. Pshenichnyi, *Nyeobkhodimyie usloviya ekstremuma.*
135. Ibid.
136. cf. in particular for derivation of the local Maximum Principle. B. W. Jordan/ E. Polak, "Theory of a class of discrete optimal control systems", *J. Electronics & Control*, 17/6 (1964) and in Soviet literature A. I. Propoy, *Avt. i tel.*, 7 (1965).
137. *Kachestvennyi metod optimalnykh protsessov* (Moscow, 1971).
138. Ibid., p. 486, N. Moiseyev, op. cit., observes that, along the optimal trajectory, the Hamiltonian may differ the more from its maximum value the larger the step of discretization. If the discrete system is not connected with a finite-dimensional approximation of continuous processes, then, generally, there may be no ground for assuming validity of the Maximum Principle p. 74.
139. Fan/Wang, op. cit., pp. 124ff.
140. *Kachestvennyi metod . . .*, p. 447ff.
141. L. S. Gnoyevskiy et al., *Matematicheskiye osnovy teorii upravlyavemykh sistem* (Moscow, 1969), p. 436.
     Among the quite a few Western sources the reader may be directed to Michael Intriligator, op. cit., pp. 330ff., 353ff.
142. *Avt. i tel.*, 9 (1972), p. 42.
143. Beckmann, *Dynamic programming of economic decisions*, p. 134.
144. A. M. Lyetov, *Avt. i tel.*, 9 (1972).
145. V. A. Bulinskiy, *EMM*, 6 (1972).
146. D. A. Pospelov et al., in *Problemy evristiki* (Moscow, 1969).
147. R. Gabasov/F. M. Kirilova, "Sovremennoye sostoyanye teorii optimalnykh protsessov", ibid.
148. loc. cit.
149. Kantorovich, *Optimizatsya*, 6 (23), 1972, p. 6.

ADDENDUM

The few pages which follow contain miscellanea — supplementary observations, allusions, references — on points which it was too late to bring into the main body of the book.

A. *To Part I*

(1) An incisive analysis of the role of the production function in optimal planning theory and practice is given by the distinguished Soviet mathematical economist, A. A. Konyus (the name was formerly spelt Konüs in the West) in *Problemy planirovanya i prognozirovanya*, ed. N. Fedorenko (1974). His overall conclusion is that, although it rests on a set of hypothetical premises, the function does help to discern the directions which, in one way or another, have to be borne in mind in optimal planning. (More controversial may prove the tenet that the implications help to "remove the contradiction which is sometimes pointed out as arising between the Marxian and the mathematical approaches in the analysis of fundamentals of political economy; and in revealing proportionality conditions for prices and values"—p. 105).

(2) Since Appendix 4 was written, the authors of the model discussed there have evolved (jointly with Granberg) their version of the "OMMM" — the grand intersectoral, interregional model of the Leontievian gravitational type.[1] The basic construct is given the form: $z^{rs} - k \cdot x^r u^s / 1_{rs}^{\beta}$. ($z^{rs}, x^r, u^s$ are volumes respectively of deliveries of output from region r to s, of output in r, use of output in s; 1_{rs} = distance or transportation cost from r to s; β k = constants.) The OMMM is adjusted by the authors so as to link up with the Soviet *two*-region (i.e. the region to the east and that to the west of the Urals) design conceived as an instrument for co-ordinating central and local planning, and numerically experimented with over the past half-decade.

B. *To Part II*

(1) The team which designed the Dubovskiy *et al.* model (discussed in sect. 26 p. 433) has devoted some effort also to an investigation of the asymptotic properties of an optimal trajectory in economic dynamics.[2] They offer the proof that, under certain conditions, independently of the shape of the functional and boundary constraints, the optimal trajectory is found within a small angular neighbourhood of a turnpike directionally coinciding with von Neumann's ray. The result is obtained in a continuous-time, linear dynamic-programming problem of Bellman's "bottleneck-process" type. Rather than resorting to the classical Radner procedure, the authors resort to an approach akin to that applied in the familiar proof for stability of solutions for differential equations by means of the Lyapunov function. It is thus of considerable interest for the "marriage" of a stability and optimality testing apparatus. The economic system considered, and notation, are those mentioned in our discussion of the Dubovskiy *et al.* model. Here for the system described we have an inde-composable matrix M endowed with two properties: (1) the eigenvalues of M, non-zero and non-unity, are not placed on the circle $\mathrm{Re}(1/\lambda) = 1$, (2) Jordan cells of order one correspond to the zero eigenvalues of M. It is proved then that for any $\mu > 0$ and $\sigma > 0$ there exists a $T(\mu, \sigma)$ such that for all $T \geqslant T(\mu, \sigma)$ we can find an interval $[t', t'']$ at every point of which the following relations hold (1) $\|Ve^{-t} - \gamma\| \leqslant \sigma$, $\|pe^{t-\mathrm{T}} - s\| \leqslant \sigma$, (2) $w(t) = 0, \psi(t) = 0$, (3) $(t'' - t')/T \geqslant 1 - \mu$. The γ and s are the right and the left-hand eigenvectors of the M matrix: i.e. $M\gamma = \gamma$, $sM = s$, $s\gamma = 1$. It is with reference to the function $L(t) = p(t)\bar{M}V(t)/p(t)V(t)$, $(\bar{M} = \gamma s)$ — all of them analogous to those of the Lyapunov function — that the smallness of the normed vectors $\|w\|e^{-t}$, $\|\psi\|e^{t-T}$ for a time interval of any length is established where the full time-period of the problem is sufficiently long.

(2) (*a*) Conditions for the existence of a continuous and continuously differentiable optimal Lyapunov function, providing an exact evaluation for the asymptotic-stability region, are rigorously established in G. A. Stepanyan–B. M. Shamrikov.[3]

(*b*) The "Comparison principle" — comparison with the vector-valued Lyapunov evokes considerable interest in Soviet control-theoretic writing. This is a field with a sizeable Soviet contribution; thus V. M. Matrosov, in a series of papers published in the late 1960s, established this principle in a general form for nonlinear differential equations in a Banach space with an unlimited partitionable operator;[4] cf. also his valuable survey of advances in methodology of Bellmanian vector-Lyapunov functions in the analysis of complex systems with distributed parameters.[5] On the last-named aspect one may note T. K. Sirazetdinov's monograph on the stability of systems with distributed parameters.[6]

(c) The very particular problem of stability of equilibrium to be reached by an economic system starting with arbitrarily given prices is treated in a brilliant (but somehow not widely noticed) paper by Kantorovich and Makarov on differential and functional equations arising in models of economic dynamics.[7]

(d) On the other hand, one is rather surprised to see little resonance of Western discussion on relative merits of alternative approaches to optimality and stability in the stochastic and deterministic build-up of an economic plan. (I have in mind in particular the excellent paper by G. C. Chow trying to quantify gains from *optimal* deterministic control policy over *sub*-optimal policy and the gains from *optimal stochastic* control over *optimal deterministic* control; also the alternatives presented in R. S. Pindyck's paper on optimal stabilization via deterministic control – both in a special issue on control theory of *Annals of Economic and Social Measurement*, Oct. 1972.)

(3) Questions of "irregularity" in optimal controls have increasingly occupied students both in the East and in the West in recent years. I have tried to do somewhat more justice to the theme in my paper "Beyond the Pontryagin Principle", to appear in the Munich *Jahrbuch*, vol. 6. Here I wish at least to indicate the crucial contribution by R. Gabasov and F. M. Kirillova, not only to the body of the discipline (and, as related, to the methodology of functional analysis in linear systems) but also to its systematization and organization; from that angle surveys published by them[8] are of signal relevance. In this conceptual "organization" sliding regimes appear as part of the theory of singular controls; and in turn optimality conditions of singular controls appear as part of those of high order (the latter has hardly been treated in its generality). To recall, it is strongly emphasized in Gabasov–Kirillova that the Maximum Principle is but a necessary *first*-order optimality condition (sufficiency condition, with certain reservations, for linear systems). The breakdown of the Maximum Principle test is a "signal" of "irregularity" – a term somewhat misleading, considering the frequency of occurrence.

(4) The modelling of the economy's steered advance, formalized as a post-classical variational problem, has been interestingly synthesized by Mikhal-evskiy. He deals, that is, with models solvable by means of the Maximum or

the Optimality Principle (or one of their generalizations), yielding (1) the valuation of endogenous variables, and (2) the choice of control policies. The focus is on models where the policy elements are the distribution of gross investment and determination of its shadow prices, ψ, which enter the Hamiltonian – in familiar notation $H = u(C^n - \psi I^n)$ – such as to secure growth along the optimal trajectory possibly under a "golden" regime of capital accumulation.

Mikhalevskiy's study is noteworthy also for investigating the limitations of the broad family of known models, in particular limitations with respect to "operativeness". However, on this count the merits are acknowledged of the designs by R. Sato–E. Davis,[9] F. Shupp,[10] A. Goldman,[11] also by S. Gomulka,[12] the last in recognition of the care taken in handling technological progress.[13]

(5) The treatment of the Pontryagin optimal trajectory for the case of exogenous technical progress is notoriously tricky.[14] For the endogenous scientific-technical progress a sketch by B. S. Mityagin[15] has this content: Output is $Y = AF(K. L) = C + I + S$, where C, I, S stand for consumption, investment and innovation respectively. For capital increment we postulate $K = I - \mu K$, and A is considered to be determined by $\dot{A} = \tau S - \sigma A$, the parameters, τ and σ, are resp. coefficients of "efficiency" of science and expenditure on "organization and control". Endogenous (as assumed) changes in manpower resources are supposed to be $\dot{L} = \gamma C + \nu L, (\gamma,\nu) > 0$, the coefficients reflecting resp. "natural" growth and impact of living standards. The economy's criterion is $\int_0^T c(t)e^{-\delta t}dt, c = C/L$. The system is linear and not lagged. The planner's task is to allocate optimally output Y to consumption, investment, promotion of science, i.e. to choose measurable functions $s_i(t) \geq 0, (i = 0, 1, 2), 0 \leq t \leq T, s_0(t) + s_1(t) + s_2(t) = 1$, such that we reach maximum for the criterial functional, subject to constraints indicated and $C = s_0 Y, I = s_1 Y, S = s_2 Y, K(T)/L(T) = k_1$. The existence of the optimal plan – where at least one admissible exists – is derived from general principles of convex analysis[16] considering concavity of the production function. The shadow prices derived from Pontryagin's Maximum Principle evaluate expenditure on science (ψ_2) as well as on investment (ψ_1). Mityagin's overall conjecture, which agrees with common sense, would be this: Where $\tau < \tau^*$, (τ^* derived from remaining parameters) and $T \to \sim$, when for optimal control $s_2(t) > 0$, tends towards zero; the reverse is true when τ is large; in words – where science is

"inefficient" there is no point in spending resources on its promotion; where it is highly efficient, investment should be carried over relatively short intervals: over the rest of time, the residuum of product, when consumption is provided for, would be channelled to science. (Note: the concept of "science" appears to be taken *sensu largissimo*, not merely covering "natural" sciences.)

(6) Problems of mutlicriterial systems are discussed in my *Differential games and other game-theoretic topics in Soviet literature* (New York, 1975). Here I would like to draw attention to M. S. Salukvadze's important generalization in his study of optimization of control systems under vector-valued performance criteria, in particular to his paper presented at the IFAC Paris 1972 Congress. Technically of considerable interest is the ingenious formulation of the variational problem in terms of Mayer, which in turn is solved on the basis of the Maximum Principle.

(7) Discovery of applicational limitations of the Maximum Principle encourages a search for remedies. Thus Shmidt[17] has lately investigated ways of handling situations with phase-constraints in problems with an infinite as well as finite horizon (notably the impact on the former of von Weizsäcker, on the latter of Arrow/Kurz).[18] Discussion of models of this family is also a subject of the study by S. V. Dubovskiy, A. P. Uzdimir, and Yu. V. Shalayev, *Matematicheskiye modeli ekonomicheskikh protsessov*, 1974.

The crop of applications for the Pontryaginian Principle in Soviet modelling of economic plans is expanding still at a rather slow pace as compared with the West. Here we draw attention to a paper by Fedoseyev on optimal control in a three-sectors model for an under-developed economy.[19]

(8) In class by itself are inquiries — such as that by V. I. Arkin and V. Levin,[20] into variational problems with operator-valued constraints (integral inequalities) where controls are measurable n-variables functions. Here a postulated *continuum* of participants leads to abandoning the convexity assumption. For the purpose A. Lyapunov's apparatus is generalized and the Maximum Principle is reformulated. A supposition that in the framework a strict price-decentralization is tractable, whatever individual properties (utility functions, local constraints), awaits validation.

C. *Some generalizations*

By the time this volume appears, among themes which preoccupy the Soviet theorist, problems of general equilibrium, if anything, have gained in status: in particular those with *continua* of participants (one notes inspiration from Aumann's, from Vind's, but especially from Hildenbrand's ideas)[21]: a symposium of studies discussed at TsEMI's seminars in the first half of the 1970s witnesses the trend (see Mityagin's foreword)[22].

Understandably it is not only the issue of the existence of "good prices" but also the questions as to how to pin-point the corresponding equilibrium locus and as to how an economy behaves outside it that nag Soviet students (cf. Polterovich's recent extension of his tenets discussed in the present volume)[23].

Theories of duality are still tempting in the search for a more and more general formalization. Under this heading further elaborations of the illuminating conceptions of Makarov-Rubinov deserve to be hinted at; thus, in particular, the one by A. M. Vershik and M. M. Rubinov[24] on the "strong general theory of duality" (fixing primal to be followed by "selection" of a "suitable" dual where existence of duality is established).

In the context we draw attention to a study of *local* minima in a problem with constraints: an analysis by E. S. Levitin, A. A. Milyutin, and N. P. Osmolovskiy of the link-up between the necessary and the sufficient conditions for a local minimum of various[25] orders; the "ideal" adopted in the examination of such a link-up and generalization is here the second order (with constraints on state coordinates). In spite of qualifications recorded in our study, probings in the direction of a "general theory of extremization" appear to proceed unabated.

Notes

1 A. G. Aganbegyan/K. A. Bagrinovskiy/A. G. Granberg, *Sistema modeley narodnokhozyaistvennogo planirovanya* (1972), pp. 283 ff.

2 Cf. A. N. Dyukalov/A. Ye. Ilyutovich, *Avt. i Tel.*, 3 (1973).

3 *Doklady*, 213/5 (1973).

4 *Differential Equations*, 8, 10 (1968) & 5, 7, 12 (1969).

5 *Avt. i Tel.*, 1 (1973).

6 Cf. in particular his *Ustoichivost sistem s raspredelennymi parametrami* (Kazan, 1971).

7 *Uspekhi matematicheskikh nauk*, 5 (1970).

8 *Avt. i Tel.*, 5 & 6 (1971) and – on functional analysis – *J. Opt. Theory & Appl.*, 2 (1971).

9 *Econometrica*, 5 (1968).

10 Ibid.

11 Ibid.

12 *Ekonomista*, 4 (1966).
13 See in particular B. N. Mikhalevskiy's *Sistema modeley srednesrochnogo narodno-khozyaistvennogo planirovanya* (Moscow, 1972).
14 See K. Shell's handling of it in Shell, ed., *Essays on the theory of optimal economic growth* (1967).
15 *Uspekhi matematicheskikh nauk*, 3 (1972).
16 'On optimization of control systems according to vector-valued performance criteria'.
17 A. G. Shmidt, in V. S. Mityagin, ed., *Matematicheskaya ekonomika i funktsyonalnyi analiz* (1974).
18 Arrow/Kurz, *Public investment* . . . ; C. von Weizsäcker, *Rev. Ec. Stud.*, 1965
19 A. V. Fedoseyev, *Zhurn. Vych. Mat i Mat. Fiz*, 4(1972).
20 In Mityagin, *Matematicheskaya ekonomika* . . . , pp. 7ff.
21 R. J. Aumann, *Econometrica*, 1966; K. Vind, *Intern.Ec.Rev.,* 1964; W. Hildenbrand, *Core and equilibria in a large economy* (1974).
22 Mityagin, *Matematicheskaya ekonomika* . . . , pp. 3ff.
23 Ibid., pp. 203ff.
24 Ibid., pp. 35ff.
25 Ibid., pp. 139ff.